HUMAN DIGNITY IN ASIA

Using interdisciplinary methods, this book is a pioneering exploration of Asian understandings of human dignity and human rights. It encompasses rigorous scrutiny of dignity jurisprudence in major Asian apex courts, detailed philosophical analysis of dignity in religious traditions, and contextualized socio-political analysis of religious dignity discourse in several Asian societies. This is an innovative systematic survey of how human dignity is understood in Asia, demonstrating how those understandings converge and diverge with other parts of the world. Synthesising legal, philosophical, and sociological expertise, this volume furthers the dialogue between Asia and the West, and advances debates on whether human rights are universal or particular to any one region. As many of the world's liberal democracies are challenged by polarization and populism, this comparative study of human dignity broadens our horizons and offers a potential alternative to a rigidified social imagination.

Jimmy Chia-Shin Hsu is Associate Research Professor of Law, Academia Sinica, Taiwan. He was the ASLI Visiting Fellow at National University of Singapore in 2016 and Visiting Scholar of Harvard-Yenching Institute for 2016–2017. He serves on the board of Taiwan Association for Philosophy of Law and as co-chair of the Freedom of Expression Research Group of the International Association of Constitutional Law.

Human Dignity in Asia

DIALOGUE BETWEEN LAW AND CULTURE

Edited by
JIMMY CHIA-SHIN HSU
Academia Sinica

Shaftesbury Road, Cambridge CB2 8EA, United Kingdom

One Liberty Plaza, 20th Floor, New York, NY 10006, USA

477 Williamstown Road, Port Melbourne, VIC 3207, Australia

314–321, 3rd Floor, Plot 3, Splendor Forum, Jasola District Centre, New Delhi – 110025, India

103 Penang Road, #05–06/07, Visioncrest Commercial, Singapore 238467

Cambridge University Press is part of Cambridge University Press & Assessment, a department of the University of Cambridge.

We share the University's mission to contribute to society through the pursuit of education, learning and research at the highest international levels of excellence.

www.cambridge.org
Information on this title: www.cambridge.org/9781108814331

DOI: 10.1017/9781108886598

© Cambridge University Press & Assessment 2022

This publication is in copyright. Subject to statutory exception and to the provisions of relevant collective licensing agreements, no reproduction of any part may take place without the written permission of Cambridge University Press & Assessment.

First published 2022
First paperback edition 2023

A catalogue record for this publication is available from the British Library

ISBN 978-1-108-83574-9 Hardback
ISBN 978-1-108-81433-1 Paperback

Cambridge University Press & Assessment has no responsibility for the persistence or accuracy of URLs for external or third-party internet websites referred to in this publication and does not guarantee that any content on such websites is, or will remain, accurate or appropriate.

I dedicate this book to **Yun-Ying Liu**, *my beloved mother, and to all the courageous women in Asia, who made great sacrifice for love in the face of life's trials and cultural constraints, and who lived out a life of dignity, grace, and beauty.*

Jimmy Chia-Shin Hsu

Contents

Notes on Editor and Contributors		page ix
Preface		xv
List of Abbreviations		xvii

	Introduction: Human Dignity, Human Rights, and Cultural Change in Asia Jimmy Chia-Shin Hsu	1
1	Human Dignity in Indian Constitutional Adjudication Pritam Baruah	21
2	The Development of Individual Dignity in Japan: Overcoming Constraints in Law, Family, and Society Keigo Obayashi	40
3	Constitutional Discourse on Human Dignity in South Korea: A Critical Appraisal Chaihark Hahm	62
4	Human Dignity in the Jurisprudence of the Taiwan Constitutional Court Jimmy Chia-Shin Hsu	87
5	The Human Dignity Factor: Interpreting the Philippine Constitution J. R. Robert Real	110
6	Human Dignity in the Jurisprudence of the Indonesian Constitutional Court Nadirsyah Hosen	139

7	Dignity as a Constitutional Value in Hong Kong: Toward a Contextual Approach? Kelley Loper	160
8	Human Dignity and Relational Constitutionalism in Singapore Li-ann Thio	187
9	Personal Dignity under Chinese Constitutional Law Xiaobo Zhai	220
10	Virtue, Dignity, and Constitutional Democracy: A Confucian Perspective Sungmoon Kim	243
11	Buddhist Philosophical Approaches to Human Dignity Anton Sevilla-Liu	269
12	Dignity and Status in Ancient and Medieval India Timothy Lubin	285
13	Human Dignity, *Pancasila*, and Islam: Contexts and Contestations in Indonesia Etin Anwar	308
14	Catholicism and Human Dignity in the Philippines Jonathan T. Chow	332
15	Protestantism and Human Dignity in South Korea JinHyok Kim	356

Index 379

Editor and Contributors

Editor

Jimmy Chia-Shin Hsu is Associate Research Professor of Institutum Iurisprudentiae, Academia Sinica, Taiwan. He received his LLB from National Taiwan University, LLM from National Chengchi University, and LLM and JSD from the University of Chicago Law School. His research interests include legal philosophy, constitutional theory, comparative constitutional law, and philosophy of punishment. He received the ASLI Visiting Fellowship from the National University of Singapore Law Faculty in early 2016 and the Visiting Scholarship of Harvard Yenching Institute 2016–17. He serves on the board of the Taiwan Association for Philosophy of Law and as co-chair of the Freedom of Expression Research Group of International Association of Constitutional Law. His recent works include "The Ultimate Test of Fidelity: Judicial Responses to Civil Disobedience in Hong Kong and Taiwan" (coauthored with Anne S. Y. Cheung, in *Democracy and Rule of Law in China's Shadow*, edited by Brian Christopher Jones, Hart Publishing, 2021); "Right to Life and Capital Punishment in Transnational Judicial Dialogue" (the *Asian Journal of Comparative Law*, first-view December 2021).

Contributors

Pritam Baruah, PhD (UCL), BCL (Oxon), BA LLB (NALSAR), is Professor and Dean of the School of Law at BML Munjal University, India. He is a legal philosopher working on the intersections of legal theory, moral philosophy, and cognitive science. He has written on theoretical and doctrinal uses of dignity and privacy by courts and the nature of interpretive concepts. His current work examines how constitutional courts employ moral values in decision-making; and the epistemological underpinnings of theories of adjudication. Previously Pritam taught at OP Jindal University and the National University of Juridical Sciences, Kolkata, and has held visiting professorships at the University of Ottawa, the Chinese University of

Political Science and Law (Beijing), NLSIU (Bangalore), and Humboldt University.

Keigo Obayashi is Professor of Law at Keio University in Japan. He teaches constitutional law. He studied governmental systems, comparing Japan with the United States, and received his Bachelor of Laws, Master of Laws, and Doctorate of Laws from Keio University. His doctoral thesis was published as *The U.S. Constitution and the Executive Privilege* (2008, in Japanese). He later published another book, *The Constitution and the Risk* (2015, in Japanese). He is coeditor of *The Minority Opinion of the Supreme Court* (2016, in Japanese) and editor of *The Constitution Under the COVID-19 Crisis* (2021, in Japanese). Recently, Obayashi is interested in individual dignity and freedom of speech from the viewpoint of comparing foreign law. His article "Free Speech Jurisprudence in Japan: The Influence of Comparative Constitutional Law," which is collected in *Hate Speech in Japan: The Possibility of a Non-regulatory Approach* (Cambridge University Press, 2021, pp. 341–362), is one such example.

Chaihark Hahm is Professor of Law at Yonsei University School of Law in Seoul, Korea. He teaches and writes on constitutional theory, comparative constitutional law, Confucian political theory, Korean legal culture and history, citizenship education, and human rights. His works in English have appeared in the *Journal of Democracy*, the *American Journal of Comparative Law*, and *I•CON: International Journal of Constitutional Law*, among others. He is coauthor of *Making We the People: Democratic Constitutional Founding in Postwar Japan and South Korea* (Cambridge University Press, 2015) and an editorial board member of I•CON. He holds law degrees from Seoul National University (LLB), Yale University (LLM), Columbia University (JD), and Harvard University (SJD).

J. R. Robert Real is a professional lecturer at the De La Salle University College of Law and at the Far Eastern University Institute of Law in the Philippines teaching constitutional law, public international law, and privacy law. He previously worked as a senior court attorney at the Office of the Chief Justice of the Philippines where he had handled more than 200 cases involving mostly constitutional rights issues. He was also a research associate at the National University of Singapore Centre for International Law, during which time he presented papers on international human rights law and ASEAN law at various international conferences. He obtained his LLM from the University of Michigan–Ann Arbor (Grotius Fellow), his MBA–JD from the De La Salle University–Far Eastern University Consortium (Best Thesis), and his BSc–Commerce from the De La Salle University. He is coauthor of the Teaching and Reaching International Law in Asia (TRILA) Project Report 2020.

Nadirsyah Hosen has been working as a senior lecturer at the Faculty of Law, Monash University, since 2015. Prior to this role, Nadir was an associate professor at the School of Law, University of Wollongong. He is internationally known for his expertise on Shari'a and Indonesian law.

Kelley Loper is an associate professor, director of the LLM in Human Rights Programme, and co-editor-in-chief of the *Asia-Pacific Journal on Human Rights and the Law* in the Faculty of Law at the University of Hong Kong. She has published extensively on the rights of refugees in Asia, the rights of persons with disabilities, and discrimination against sexual and gender diverse people. Her scholarship focuses on issues related to the implementation of international human rights law in domestic contexts. She teaches courses on international human rights law, comparative equality, and non-discrimination law and serves on the board of the Hong Kong Dignity Institute.

Li-ann Thio, BA (Hons) (Oxford), LLM (Harvard), PhD (Cambridge), is Provost Chair Professor at the National University of Singapore where she teaches and researches international human rights law, constitutional and administrative law, and comparative public law, with a focus on law and religion. She is a barrister (Gray's Inn, UK) and was a Nominated Member of the Singapore Parliament (2007–9). She was formerly chief editor of the *Singapore Journal of Legal Studies* and of the *Singapore Journal of International & Comparative Law* and is a former general editor of the *Asian Yearbook of International Law*. A prolific scholar, she has published more than 100 law review articles and book chapters, as well as several books.

Xiaobo Zhai is an associate professor at the University of Macau. He holds an LLB from Zhengzhou University, an LLM from Peking University, and doctorates from the Chinese Academy of Social Sciences and from University College London. His research interests include legal philosophy, constitutional theory, and Bentham studies. His publications in English have appeared in *Law and Philosophy*, the *Journal of Legal History*, the *International Journal of Constitutional Law*, and *Law, Culture and the Humanities*. His edited volume *Bentham's Theory of Law and Public Opinion* was published by Cambridge University Press in 2014.

Sungmoon Kim is Professor of Political Theory at the City University of Hong Kong, where he is also the director of the Center for East Asian and Comparative Philosophy. Kim's research has appeared in journals such as the *American Political Science Review*, the *Journal of Politics*, the *British Journal of Political Science*, *History of Political Thought*, the *European Journal of Political Theory*, the *Review of Politics*, *Contemporary Political Theory*, and *Philosophy East and West*, among others. As 2016/2017 Berggruen Fellow at Harvard University's Edmond J. Safra Center for Ethics, Kim is the author of *Confucian Democracy in East Asia: Theory and Practice* (Cambridge University Press, 2014), *Public Reason Confucianism: Democratic Perfectionism and Constitutionalism in East Asia* (Cambridge University Press, 2016), *Democracy after Virtue: Toward Pragmatic*

Confucian Democracy (Oxford University Press, 2018), and *Theorizing Confucian Virtue Politics: The Political Philosophy of Mencius and Xunzi* (Cambridge University Press, 2020).

Anton Sevilla-Liu originally taught at Ateneo de Manila University, Philippines. He studied for his PhD under Buddhist philosopher Sueki Fumihiko at the Graduate University for Advanced Studies, Japan. He is now Associate Professor for Philosophy of Education at Kyushu University. Research themes include Japanese philosophy, education for awakening, and clinical pedagogy. He is author of the book *Watsuji Tetsurô's Global Ethics of Emptiness* (2018) and translator of Sueki's *Buddhism and Ethics at Odds: A Buddhist Counter-Position* (2016).

Timothy Lubin is Jessie Ball duPont Professor of Religion and Adjunct Professor of Law at Washington and Lee University, USA. After earning degrees at Columbia University (BA, PhD) and Harvard University (MTS), he taught as lecturer at Harvard University and the University of Virginia. He examines the formation and spread of Brahmanical norms and legal institutions in the ancient and early medieval periods in South and Southeast Asia, based on the study of texts and epigraphy. He has also written on colonial-era reception of Hindu law and legal pluralism in the modern world. He coedited *Hinduism and Law: An Introduction* (Cambridge University Press, 2010) and coauthored *A Śaiva Utopia: The Śivadharma's Revision of Brahmanical* Varṇāśramadharma (UniorPress, 2021). His recent articles include "The Theory and Practice of Property in Premodern South Asia," "Towards a South Asian Diplomatics," "Customary Practice in the Vedic Ritual Codes as an Emergent Legal Principle," "Writing and the Recognition of Customary Law in Premodern India and Java," and "Legal Diglossia: Modeling Discursive Practices in Premodern Indic Law."

Etin Anwar is Professor at Hobart and William Smith Colleges, Geneva, New York. She teaches classes on Islam, environmental apocalypse, and comparative ethics. She is the author of *A Genealogy of Islamic Feminism: Pattern and Change in Indonesia* (Routledge, 2018) and *Gender and Self in Islam* (Routledge, 2006). She has published several articles on Ibn Sina, Meister Eckhart, Ibn Arabi, anti-Americanism, and women's movements in Indonesia in various journals including *Islamic Studies, Islam and Christian-Muslim Relations*, and *Hawwa*.

Jonathan T. Chow is Assistant Professor of Political Science at Wheaton College, Massachusetts, USA. His research focuses on the relationship between religion and transnational norms, the international politics of "pariah states," and regional politics in Southeast Asia. He has held visiting fellowships at Georgetown University's Berkley Center for Religion, Peace and World Affairs; the Ateneo Center for Asian Studies at Ateneo de Manila University (Philippines); and the Asan Institute for Policy Studies (South Korea). Dr. Chow received his BA from Williams College and an MA and PhD in Political Science from the University of California, Berkeley.

JinHyok Kim is Associate Professor of Systematic Theology at Torch Trinity Graduate University in Seoul, South Korea. He teaches and researches theology, philosophy, and ethics with special focus on nineteenth- and twentieth-century European Christian thought. He received his BA and ThM from Yonsei University (South Korea), his MDiv from Harvard Divinity School (United States), and his DPhil from the University of Oxford (United Kingdom). He worked as a visiting doctoral researcher at the University of Heidelberg (Germany) and as a postdoctoral research fellow at Heythrop College, University of London (United Kingdom). He has published *The Spirit of God and the Christian Life* (Fortress Press, 2014) and articles on modern Christian thought, political theology, theological aesthetics, and the relationship between religion and literature.

Preface

In the past decade, there has been a booming literature on comparative dignity jurisprudence and philosophy. While it has probed widely across regions, it has left a visible gap on Asia. This book is meant to fill this gap. It grows out of my research project funded by my institute, Institutum Iurisprudentiae, Academia Sinica, Taiwan. I invited scholars of multiple disciplines who specialize in Asian public law and major religious and philosophical traditions in Asian contexts. The book investigates how human dignity as a legal concept features in judicial and political discourse in major Asian jurisdictions, which include India, Japan, South Korea, Taiwan, the Philippines, Indonesia, Hong Kong, Singapore, and China. It also examines dignity in three religious or philosophical traditions heavily concentrated in Asia, including Confucianism, Buddhism, and Hinduism. Further, it investigates the idea of human dignity as expressed by representative voices of major religions in particular societies, including Islam in Indonesia, Protestantism in South Korea, and Catholicism in the Philippines.

This project was first conceived when I was a Visiting Scholar at Harvard Yenching Institute in 2016. I thank Michael Rosen, who was my mentor during my stay at Harvard, for his precious friendship and his extraordinary book on the history of the idea of dignity, which inspired my interest in this fascinating concept. I thank Tom Ginsburg, Albert Chen, and Kevin Y. L. Tan for their advice at the early stage of this project on what jurisdictions to be included. I am immensely grateful for all the contributors to this book, including Pritam Baruah, Keigo Obayashi, Chaihark Hahm, Robert Real, Nadir Hosen, Kelley Loper, Li-ann Thio, Xiaobo Zhai, Sungmoon Kim, Anton Sevilla-Liu, Timothy Lubin, Etin Anwar, Jonathan Chow, and JinHyok Kim. This book owes what it is to their excellent scholarship. I thank all the participants at the conference on "Human Dignity in Asia," which was held in Taipei in July 2018. My special thanks go to Michael Rosen and Christopher McCrudden for giving keynote speeches and to Mary Anne Case for her very helpful participation at the conference. I am grateful to the former director Dr. Tzu-Yi Lin and the current director Dr. Chien-Liang Lee of Institutum

Iurisprudentiae, Academia Sinica, Taiwan, for their continued support for this project. My sincere thanks go to Joe Ng at Cambridge University Press for his guidance along the way and Gemma Smith for her editorial assistance. I would also like to thank my assistants Naifei Wu, Chiawen Huang, Huei-Ya Chen, Yun-Chung Lin, Fang-Sin Cao, and Cheng-Ching Lin for their great job of indexing this book. Lastly, I express sincere gratitude to my wife, Yoshing, and children, Jerome and Celina, for standing by me through good times and bad.

Abbreviations

AA	Additional Articles of the Constitution
AIDS	Acquired Immunodeficiency Syndrome
AMS	Algemene Middelbare scholen
Asabri	Asuransi Sosial Angkatan Bersenjata Republik Indonesia (Indonesian Armed Forces Insurance)
ASEAN	Association of South East Asian Nations
Askes	Asuransi Kesehatan Indonesia (Indonesian Health Insurance)
BOR	Bill of Rights Ordinance
BPJS	Badan Penyelenggara Jaminan Sosial (Social Security Providers) BPUKI Badan Penyelidik Usaha-Usaha Kemerdekaan Indonesia (Dokuritsu Junbi Chosa-kai)
CBCP	Catholic Bishops' Conference of the Philippines
CEDAW	Convention on the Elimination of all Forms of Discrimination Against Women
CFA	Court of Final Appeal (Hong Kong)
CR	Cultural Revolution
CSHRS	China Society for Human Rights Studies
DAAD	Deutscher Akademischer Austauschdienst (German Academic Exchange Service)
DPR	Dewan Perwakilan Rakyat (People's Representative Assembly)
ESC	economic, social, and cultural (rights)
FDWs	female domestic workers
GBHN	Garis-Garis Besar Haluan Negara (Broad Guidelines of State Policy)
GDP	gross domestic product
GHQ	General Headquarters
GPCL	General Principles of the Civil Law
GNI	gross national income
HBS	Hoogere burgerschool
ICCPR	International Covenant on Civil and Political Rights

ICESCR	International Covenant on Economic, Social and Cultural Rights
ISDV	Indies Social Democratic Association
ISSA	International Social Security Association
ITE	Information and Electronic Transactions
Jamkesmas	Jaminan Kesehatan Masyarakat (Community Health Insurance)
Jamsostek	Jaminan Sosial Tenaga Kerja (Workforce Social Security)
JIBDA	Jong Islamieten Bond Dames Afdeeling (Young Muslim League Women's Section)
KMT	Kuomintang
KNPB	Korean National Prayer Breakfast
LGBT	lesbian, gay, bisexual, and transgender
LGBTQ+	lesbian, gay, bisexual, transgender, and queer or questioning
MCA	Mental Capacity Act
MK	Mahkamah Konstitusi (Constitutional Court)
MPs	Members of Parliament
MPR	Majelis Permusyawaratan Rakyat (People's Consultative Assembly)
MULO	Meer uitgebreid lager onderwijs
NCCK	National Council of Churches of Korea
NCCS	National Council of Churches in Singapore
NGOs	nongovernmental organizations
NPC	National People's Congress
OFWs	overseas Filipino workers
P4	Pedoman Penghayatan dan Pengamalan Pancasila (Guideline for Instilling and Implementing Pancasila into Practice)
PAP	People's Action Party
PCRH	Presidential Council for Religious Harmony
PERPU	Peraturan Pemerintah Pengganti Undang-Undang (Government Regulation in Lieu of Law)
PIL	Public Interest Litigation
PKI	Partai Komunis Indonesia (Communist Party of Indonesia)
PM	Prime Minister
PNI	Perserikatan Nasional Indonesia (Indonesian Nationalist Association)
POHA	Protection from Harassment Act
PRC	People's Republic of China
ROC	Republic of China
SAR	special administrative region
SJSN	Sistem Jaminan Sosial Nasional (National Social Security System)
SPC	Supreme People's Court
STOVIA	School tot Opleiding van Inlandsche Artsen (School for the Training of Native Doctors)

Taspen	Dana Tabungan dan Asuransi Pegawai Negeri (Civil Servants Pension Fund)
TCC	Taiwan Constitutional Court
UDHR	Universal Declaration of Human Rights
UN	United Nations
US, USA	United States of America
UUD	Undang-Undang Dasar (the Constitution)
WAD	women and development
WCC	World Council of Churches
WID	women in development
WWII	World War II

Introduction

Human Dignity, Human Rights, and Cultural Change in Asia

Jimmy Chia-Shin Hsu[*]

1 CONSENSUS AND DIVERGENCE OF HUMAN DIGNITY IN THE POSTWAR ERA

The concept of human dignity, as one commentator observes, is "here, there, and everywhere"[1] in contemporary human rights discourse. Its prominence, however, has generated ever more controversies in recent years. The contemporary debate is driven by the paradoxical prominence and elusiveness of this concept in judicial interpretation. Its meaning is notoriously hard to pin down, as manifested in the easy appropriation by both sides of such controversies as abortion, euthanasia, same-sex marriage, and other heated issues in bioethics. Some have argued that the elusiveness of the concept of human dignity should raise no more concern than other seriously contested normative concepts such as liberty, justice, and equality.[2] Others have considered it especially troubling.[3]

It is generally agreed that, when this concept was adopted in the United Nations Charter and the Universal Declaration of Human Rights, it served as a placeholder to allow countries of widely divergent cultures to agree on the underpinnings of the universal human rights. In the immediate postwar era, dignity jurisprudence first developed in particular jurisdictions such as West Germany and the United States. It then underwent a significant growth driven by the development of international human rights regimes since the 1970s and then by the spread of constitutionalism and judicial review during the third-wave democratization in the 1980s and 1990s. The growth of dignity jurisprudence and its spread around the globe ensures that it

---

[*] I thank Margaret Lewis, Chien-Chih Lin, Yu-Jie Chen, Ya-Wen Yang, Cheng-Yi Huang, Rung-Guang Lin, and Yang-Sheng Chen for their very helpful comments on the draft of this chapter.
[1] Luís R. Barroso, "Here, There, and Everywhere: Human Dignity in Contemporary Law and in the Transnational Discourse," *Boston College International & Comparative Law Review* 35, no. 2 (2012): p. 331.
[2] Jeremy Waldron is reported to hold this view. Christopher McCrudden, "In Pursuit of Human Dignity: An Introduction to Current Debates," in *Understanding Human Dignity* (Oxford: Oxford University Press, 2013), p. 13.
[3] Neomi Rao, "Three Concepts of Dignity in Constitutional Law," *Notre Dame Law Review* 183, no. 86 (2011): 190.

can no longer serve merely as a placeholder in international human rights instruments or a directive value in domestic constitutions. Rather, it is expected to guide judicial decisions on controversial legal and political issues on all levels of tribunals. Further, human dignity as a legal concept has come under increasing stress, as the *ius commune* of transnational human rights law emerges.[4] As courts around the world look to each other for guidance and inspirations, the diversity of construal and contexts poses a challenge for principled adjudication that takes comparative legal sources seriously.

The diversity, however, should not obscure the common ground that emerged after World War II. It is now generally acknowledged that the career of human dignity as a legal concept began mainly after the war. Its immediate origin may be traceable to the interwar period, when the Catholic Church and intellectuals employed it to revive the natural law tradition, with an aim to resist the collectivistic excess of fascism and communism.[5] Nevertheless, human dignity's postwar prominence in such foundational documents as the United Nations Charter, the Universal Declaration of Human Rights, and German Basic Law was a solemn response to the Holocaust and other state atrocities that the great Enlightenment ideas of liberty and equality alone seemed unable to deflect. As "life, liberty, and the pursuit of happiness" and "liberté, égalité, fraternité" symbolize the spirit of human rights at the dawn of modernity in the late eighteenth century, the image of man emancipated from the ancien régime came to be encompassed in corporate ideologies, such as nationalism, fascism, and communism in the nineteenth and early twentieth centuries.[6] As Hannah Arendt aptly remarked, "As mankind, since the French Revolution, was conceived in the image of a family of nations, it gradually became self-evident that the people, and not the individual, was the image of man."[7] Postwar human rights discourse responded to this tragic development, and human dignity is employed to convey the emotional gravity and the axiological significance attached to the personal or the individual against its dissolution in corporate identities.

The postwar human rights leitmotif shaped what Christopher McCrudden calls the "minimum core" of the content of human dignity.[8] This conceptual core has three elements. The first is the "ontological claim": every human being possesses an intrinsic worth, merely by being human. The second is the "relational claim": this intrinsic worth should be recognized and respected by others. The third claim is the "limited state claim": the intrinsic worth of the individual requires that the state

---

[4] Paolo G. Carozza, "'My Friend Is a Stranger': The Death Penalty and the Global Ius Commune of Human Rights," *Texas Law Review* 81, no. 1031 (2003): 1036–1042.
[5] Samuel Moyn, *Christian Human Rights* (Philadelphia: University of Pennsylvania Press, 2015), 25–64.
[6] Michael Freeman, *Human Rights: An Interdisciplinary Approach* (Malden, MA: Polity Press, 2011), 32–36.
[7] Hannah Arendt, "The Perplexities of the Rights of Man," in *The Portable Hannah Arendt*, ed. Peter Baehr (New York: Penguin Books, 2000), 32.
[8] Christopher McCrudden, "Human Dignity and Judicial Interpretation of Human Rights" *European Journal of International Law* 19, no. 4 (2008): 655, 679.

should be seen to exist for the sake of the individual and not vice versa. Similarly, James R. May and Erin Daly identified four elements in the overlapping consensus of the definition of human dignity: 1) dignity is inherent in the human person; 2) everyone has equal dignity; 3) dignity means human worth; 4) dignity is universal.[9] These formulations demonstrate that the concept of human dignity bears strong connections with liberty and equality. In other words, human dignity crystalizes and enhances these foundational political values, while adding its own weight to the postwar understanding of legitimate international and domestic political order. Jeremy Waldron's idea of dignity captures the intricate dynamics well: as he says, "The modern notion of human dignity involves an upward equalization of rank, so that we now try to accord to every human being something of the dignity, rank, and expectation of respect that was formerly accorded to nobility."[10] Waldron's conception of human dignity as elevated rank, however, does not give sufficient weight to the alternative conception of human dignity as worth, the precious value inhering equally in every person. The two conceptions, namely elevated rank and worth, together entail another important conception, namely dignity as anti-humiliation.[11] All these conceptions contribute to theorization of the core content of human dignity. The core areas of application cover cases involving cruel, inhuman, and degrading treatment or punishment, as well as constitutional protection of human life and physical and mental integrity.[12] Further, it is uncontroverted when it is used to condemn colonialism, slavery, human trafficking, and racial discrimination.

Beyond the core, however, the meaning of human dignity diverges, and the need to conceptualize the complex meanings of human dignity grows. While conceptualization is needed to identify common grounds, it is needed even more to understand divergence and facilitate constructive engagement across jurisdictions. For example, commentators have noted the difference between the heavily liberty-and-rights-oriented American constitutionalism and the comparatively communitarian and value-oriented European dignity jurisprudence.[13] Further, since the 1960s and 1970s, arguably reflective of social changes in the West toward so-called "expressive individualism,"[14] dignity has increasingly been associated with privacy, autonomy, self-fulfillment, and self-realization. This particular conception of human dignity has played a significant role in undermining legal moralism by lifting bans and restrictions on abortion,

---

[9] James R. May and Erin Daly, *Advanced Introduction to Human Dignity and Law* (Cheltenham, UK: Edward Elgar, 2020), pp. 42–43.
[10] Jeremy Waldron, *Dignity, Rank & Rights* (Oxford: Oxford University Press, 2012), p. 33.
[11] See Avishai Margalit, *The Decent Society* (Cambridge, MA: Harvard University Press, 1998).
[12] Paolo Carozza, "Human Dignity in Constitutional Adjudication," in *Comparative Constitutional Law*, edited by Tom Ginsburg and Rosalind Dixon (Cheltenham, UK: Edward Elgar, 2011), pp. 462–463.
[13] Neomi Rao, "On the Use and Abuse of Dignity in Constitutional Law," *Columbia Journal of European Law* 14, no. 2 (2008): 201–256; Edward J. Eberle, *Dignity and Liberty: Constitutional Visions in Germany and the United States* (London: Praeger, 2002).
[14] See Robert N. Bellah et al., *Habits of the Heart: Individualism and Commitment in American Life* (Berkeley: University of California Press, 2008).

contraceptives, sodomy, and pornography and enhancing equal protection and anti-discrimination of formerly marginalized groups such as the gay, lesbian, and transgendered. The relatively new development of dignity as autonomy and privacy has global influence, but it has progressed the farthest in the West compared to other parts of the world. Still another development that has wide and yet uneven influence conceives of dignity as a judiciable right to dignified living, a right to subsistence, or a right to life with dignity. This socioeconomic strand of dignity has been applied in various jurisdictions to basic needs of life such as employment, housing, health, food, water, and healthy environment.[15]

To facilitate dialogue across the divergent strands of dignity jurisprudence, it is necessary to investigate what this concept means and does in various jurisdictions. The current international literature has already probed widely across regions, but the development in Asia is rarely reported and analyzed.[16] This book aims to fill this gap. It first investigates how human dignity as a legal and constitutional concept features in judicial and political discourse in Asian jurisdictions, which include India, Japan, South Korea, Taiwan, the Philippines, Indonesia, and Hong Kong. These jurisdictions are selected for the following reasons. First, all of them are Asian constitutional democracies or, in the case of Hong Kong, an autonomous region with an established tradition of rule of law, though the latter is a tradition that has eroded during the course of writing this book. They have functional judiciaries exercising meaningful degree of judicial review in protection of constitutional rights. Second, all the courts in these jurisdictions have adopted human dignity in their constitutional jurisprudence. In most jurisdictions, human dignity is based on constitutional texts, as in South Korea, Japan, the Philippines, Indonesia, and India. Hong Kong channeled this concept into its jurisprudence through the linkage in its Basic Law to ICCPR. Taiwan adopted it through judicial interpretation. Next, this book includes two additional jurisdictions – Singapore and China – that are surveyed not because of the judicial usage of human dignity but because of its roles in statutes, executive order, policy papers, or official and public discourse. Singapore is the banner country of the Asian values debate of the 1990s. How human dignity is positioned in its political culture is of great significance in how we understand this concept in Asia. Even though human dignity as a legal concept is rarely used by the Singaporean courts, the Singaporean political leadership has deliberately employed this idea in their formation of the political culture as a multiethnic secular state to balance individual well-being and common good. In the case of China, its 1982 Constitution encompasses, for the first time in history, the concept of dignity. Article 38 of the Chinese Constitution reads: "The personal dignity of citizens of the People's Republic of China is inviolable. Insult, libel, false charge or frame-up directed against citizens by any means is prohibited." It is

---

[15] May and Daly, *Dignity and Law*, 104–111.
[16] For a rare and valuable work, see Man Yee Karen Lee, "Universal Human Dignity: Some Reflections in the Asian Context," *Asian Journal of Comparative Law* 3, no. 1 (2008), Article 10.

generally acknowledged among Chinese scholars that this Article is meant to address the atrocities during the Great Proletariat Cultural Revolution of 1966 to 1976.[17] As will be demonstrated in this book, the idea of "personal dignity" has exerted influence on legislative deliberation and public discourse.

This book goes beyond human dignity as a legal concept by engaging cultural and religious traditions of this region. In addition to those chapters dealing with human dignity as a constitutional or political concept, there are six chapters addressing human dignity in the contexts of Asian cultural and philosophical traditions. There will be three chapters addressing how human dignity can be understood in three religious or philosophical traditions heavily concentrated in Asia: Confucianism, Buddhism, and Hinduism. Further, Christianity and Islam have significant presence in Asia. In view of the already abundant literature on human dignity in the doctrinal or philosophical systems of these religions, alternatively we investigate the meaning of human dignity via representative voices of these religions in particular societies. They include Islam in Indonesia, Protestantism in South Korea, and Catholicism in the Philippines. This part of the book does not aim to give a comprehensive picture of the tremendously diverse religious and cultural landscape in this region. Rather, it aims to showcase representative patterns of thinking regarding the idea of human dignity in Asian cultures.

2 HUMAN DIGNITY AND HUMAN RIGHTS SINCE THE ASIAN VALUES DEBATE

It is a significant fact that human dignity as a legal concept has not only made its way into the constitutional jurisprudence of multiple Asian jurisdictions but also begun to play effective roles in them. It reminds us of how far we have come from the "Asian values" debate of the 1990s. In that debate, Southeast Asian national leaders such as Lee Kuan Yew of Singapore and Mahathir Mohammed of Malaysia, echoed by the Chinese government, challenged the universalism of human rights and championed cultural relativism, which was epitomized in the 1993 Bangkok declaration. When the Bangkok declaration was issued, the third-wave democratization was making its way into East Asia. It is precisely in the ensuing era that human dignity as a constitutional concept entered most of the jurisdictions surveyed in this book, with the exceptions of Japan and India, whose new constitutions acquired the concept not long after WWII. The People Power Revolution in the Philippines in 1986 set democratization in motion, and human dignity was written into the 1987 Constitution. South Korea and Taiwan began democratization in the late 1980s. In South Korea, human dignity was written into the 1962 Constitution but was given a new life in the 1987 Constitution, as the Korean Constitution Court was

---

[17] 戴耀廷 (Benny Y. T. Tai) and 李敏儀 (Man Yee Karen Lee), "中華人民共和國憲法中關於「人的尊嚴」的論述 [The Discourse on 'Human Dignity' in the Constitution of the People's Republic of China]," 香港社會科學學報 [Hong Kong Journal of Social Sciences] no. 38 (2010): 59, 65.

established and human dignity became a judiciable right. In Taiwan, the concept of human dignity was adopted into constitutional jurisprudence in 1995 through judicial interpretation. Hong Kong Basic Law went into effect in 1997, adopting the concept of human dignity through its connection with ICCPR. The 1997 Asian financial crisis struck hard in Northeast and Southeast Asia, which undermined the self-confidence boosting the Asian values claim. In 1998, Indonesian President Suharto resigned and democratization began in earnest. Human dignity was incorporated into the bill of rights of the Indonesian constitutional amendments in 2000. Moreover, by the second decade of the twenty-first century, Taiwan and South Korea became widely considered to be consolidated liberal democracies. In 2009, the primary regional organization of Southeast Asia, the Association of South East Asian Nations (ASEAN), established the ASEAN Intergovernmental Commission on Human Rights, and in 2012 it adopted the ASEAN Human Rights Declaration, which, in its first general principle states: "All persons are born free and equal in dignity and rights."

2.1 *Populism and Authoritarian Threat of Democracy*

Despite notable progress, this region has not been immune from the recent rise of populism, democratic recession, and the threat of authoritarianism. Notably, the election of Rodrigo Duterte in 2016 to the Philippines presidency led to unaccountable extrajudicial killings in his war on drugs. His pursuit of "independent foreign policy" encompasses a fiercely anticolonial bent directed at the United States.[18] Moreover, he has considered human rights advocacy groups as impediments to his war on drugs and anti-terrorism measures.[19] Despite all this, he continues to enjoy consistently high approval ratings. Similarly, under the highly popular Prime Minister Narendra Modi, India regressed from "free" to "partly free" under the Freedom House rating in 2020, for the first time since the late 1990s. Modi consolidated a "Hindu-majoritarian brand of politics, concentrated power excessively in the hands of the executive, and clamped down on political dissent and on the media."[20] In Indonesia, President Joko Widodo faced the challenge of rising Islamist politics by "fighting illiberalism with illiberalism," in order to preserve religious pluralism as upheld in the 1945 Constitution.[21] As Herlambang P. Wiratraman remarks, this "authoritarian turn" has been "characterized by state-led attacks on freedom of

---

[18] Julio C. Teehankee, "Duterte's Resurgent Nationalism in the Philippines: A Discursive Institutionalist Analysis," *Journal of Current Southeast Asian Affairs* 35, no. 3 (2016): 70, 78.

[19] "Philippines: Duterte Threatens Human Rights Community Call for Police to Shoot Activists 'Reprehensible,'" Human Rights Watch, News Release, August 17, 2017, www.hrw.org/news/2017/08/18/philippines-duterte-threatens-human-rights-community (accessed April 3, 2021).

[20] Milan Vaishnav, "The Decay of Indian Democracy: Why India No Longer Ranks Among the Lands of the Free," *Foreign Affairs*, March 18, 2021.

[21] Edward Aspinall and Marcus Mietzner, "Nondemocratic Pluralism in Indonesia," *Journal of Democracy* 30, no. 4 (2019): 104–118.

expression, criminalization, and the shirking space for civil liberties. In addition, the ever-expanding state surveillance, extra-judicial killings in Papua and alleged cases of human rights abuses by those linked to the state's circle of power are all manifestations of growing impunity in Indonesian politics and governance."[22]

In addition, the sharp power of China has cast a long shadow in this region. The collapsing of the "one country, two systems" framework in Hong Kong is Beijing's blunt response to the loud clamor of the people of Hong Kong for genuine democracy. It resulted in rapidly shrinking spaces for freedom of speech, the press, assembly, and association, as well as rising threats to the personal security of political dissidents under strained judicial independence. China's ambition toward Taiwan has not only posed future military threat; it has already initiated aggressive misinformation warfare to meddle with Taiwan's electoral integrity and domestic policy formation.[23] The threat has also led to further polarization of Taiwan democratic politics. China's rise has provided the background against which the serious controversy on Article 9 of the Japanese Constitution occurred. In 2014, Prime Minister Shinzo Abe's government offered a constitutional reinterpretation to allow its Self-Defense Forces to defend other allies in case of war being declared on them. The geopolitical challenge in an increasingly multipolar world further consolidated the dominance of the ruling Liberal Democratic Party, which, under the Abe administration, may have eroded informal rules guarding its liberal democracy.[24] Moreover, the dominance of institutional power in Japan has undermined vertical accountability on human rights issues involving gender gaps, same-sex marriage, the LGBTQ, anti-discrimination legislation, national human rights institution, migrant workers, environmental rights, and more.[25]

2.2 Human Dignity and Cultural Continuity and Change in Asia

The actual protection of human dignity and human rights may wax and wane under the vicissitude of geopolitics and domestic sociopolitical dynamics. Ideally, however, the core understanding of human dignity as embodied in government measures and judicial interpretation should serve as an anchor of government actions, especially in times of uncertainty. Yet what is the core content of human dignity as

---

[22] Herlambang P. Wiratraman, "Political Cartels and the Judicialization of Authoritarian Politics in Indonesia," *International Journal of Constitutional Law Blog*, February 21, 2021, www.iconnectblog.com/2021/02/symposium-constitutional-struggles-in-asia-part-ii-political-cartels-and-the-judicialization-of-authoritarian-politics-in-indonesia/.

[23] Rush Doshi, "China Steps Up Its Information War in Taiwan: Taiwan's Election Is a Test Run for Beijing's Worldwide Propaganda Strategy," *Foreign Affairs*, January 9, 2020, www.foreignaffairs.com/articles/china/2020-01-09/china-steps-its-information-war-taiwan (accessed April 3, 2021).

[24] Maiko Ichihara, "Japanese Democracy after Shinzo Abe," *Journal of Democracy* 32 no. 1 (January 2021): 83–84.

[25] Akiko Ejima, "Thin but Resilient Constitutionalism in Japan?", *International Journal of Constitutional Law Blog*, February 22, 2021, www.iconnectblog.com/2021/02/symposium-constitutional-struggles-in-asia–part-iii–thin-but-resilient-constitutionalism-in-japan/.

understood in these jurisdictions? Will it withstand the test of time? To what extent does it converge and diverge with those in other parts of the world? These are the background questions of this book. Here I offer my preliminary thoughts to consider these issues.

To begin with, it is important to understand the times as the past has shaped them. In the immediate postwar era, when a large part of the non-Western world was striving for decolonization, human dignity as enshrined in the UDHR was not understood to mean constraining state authority alone. To those societies still colonized by Western powers or threatened by them, it primarily meant national self-determination aspiring for a competent statehood to be treated on equal terms. Further, as most of these nations were underdeveloped, human dignity also meant national development and elevation of socioeconomic well-being. Both goals required nation-building and state-building, which mandated establishment and strengthening of a nation state aspiring for modernization. To the extent that the idea of human dignity was received into these societies through constitution-making after WWII, as Albert H. Y. Chen remarked, human dignity was initially embedded in constitutions aiming to limit and control the state, while, paradoxically, legitimizing and enabling it to withstand domestic and external challenges.[26] The situation is similar in other parts of non-Western world. Yet in much of sub-Saharan Africa, tribalism and kinship loyalties were never replaced by modernized nonpatrimonial political authority.[27] In Latin American and the Middle East, European-style state structures always had limited reach over indigenous societies.[28] By contrast, Northeast Asian and Southeast Asian societies pursued modern states on the basis of a tradition of a strong state, capable of governing through a centralized bureaucracy over tribes, kinship groups, ethnicities, and other social groups. As Francis Fukuyama forcefully argued, China developed the world's earliest modern state, one millennium earlier than Europe. Neighboring countries such as Korea, Japan, and Vietnam borrowed heavily from Chinese ideas of statecraft.[29] In Southeast Asia, the legacy of the Western colonial government, complemented by that of indigenous proto-states such as the Malayan Malacca Sultanate and the Javanese Mataram Sultanate, has continued to shape contemporary political practice and imagination of legitimate political authority over the individual and a tremendous diversity of ethnicities and religions.[30]

As mentioned, human dignity entered most of the Asian jurisdictions, except India and Japan, during the third-wave democratization of the late 1980s and 1990s.

---

[26] Albert H. Y. Chen, "The Achievement of Constitutionalism in Asia: Moving beyond 'Constitutions without Constitutionalism,'" in *Constitutionalism in Asia in the Early Twenty-First Century*, ed. Albert H. Y. Chen (Cambridge: Cambridge University Press, 2014), 6.
[27] Francis Fukuyama, *Political Order and Political Decay* (New York: Farrar, Straus and Giroux, 2014), 285–298.
[28] Bruce Gilley, *The Nature of Asian Politics* (Cambridge: Cambridge University Press, 2014), 34.
[29] Francis Fukuyama, *The Origins of Political Order* (London: Profile Books, 2011), p. 128.
[30] Gilley, *Asian Politics*, 7.

It was also a time when human dignity as individual autonomy and self-realization ascended upon other layers of meanings of dignity in the West, and its influence has gradually spread to Asia in the following decades. The question then arises as to whether this new conception was an unavoidable logical extension of other conceptions and whether its prominence would prove normatively desirable for Asian societies. This question parallels the recent controversy in revisionist human rights history that also prompts us to consider whether a qualitative break in the concept of human rights occurred in the last quarter of twentieth century. For example, Samuel Moyn argued that there was indeed such a break in the idea of human rights in the 1970s. He argued that the idea of human rights as solely borne by the individual unembedded from the state was formed at that time.[31] Daniel J. Elazar remarked that the 1970s marked the rise of a "postmodern conception of rights."[32] Seth D. Kaplan considers the UDHR to be more accommodative of both "thin and thick" societies, while the idea of rights in the West has evolved after the 1970s toward one that is more acceptable by thin Western societies than by thick non-Western counterparts.[33] This book does not engage the debate directly. Yet the debate poses interesting questions useful for framing our investigation of Asian understanding of human dignity and human rights. Since human dignity is the conceptual hallmark of the contemporary idea of human rights, competing understandings of human rights would be embodied in competing conceptions of human dignity.

2.3 Cultural Development or Cultural Conflict?

This inquiry is further related to contemporary reflections on the idea of human rights in an age of polarization and populism. As Ronald Inglehart and Pippa Norris argue, the rise of populism and polarization within the Western countries may be attributable not only to economic disruption and inequality caused by globalization but also to what they call populist "cultural backlash" against the cultural transformation since the 1970s.[34] Their argument implicates a developmental view of Western culture toward individualistic liberal values. Similarly, Edward Rubin argues that the West is moving from a "morality of higher purposes" to a "morality of self-fulfillment," and the transformation seems irreversible.[35] However, what if the

---

[31] Samuel Moyn, *The Last Utopia: Human Rights in History* (Cambridge, MA: Harvard University Press, 2010).
[32] Daniel J. Elazar, "How Present Conceptions of Human Rights Shape the Protection of Rights in the United States," in *Old Rights and New*, ed. by Robert A. Licht (Washington, DC: AEI Press, 1993), p. 46.
[33] Seth D. Kaplan, *Human Rights in Thick and Thin Societies: Universality without Uniformity* (Cambridge: Cambridge University Press, 2018), pp. 6–7.
[34] Pippa Norris and Ronald Inglehart, *Cultural Backlash: Trump, Brexit, and Authoritarian Populism* (Cambridge: Cambridge University Press, 2019).
[35] Edward L. Rubin, *Soul, Self, and Society: The New Morality and the Modern State* (Oxford: Oxford University Press, 2015).

backlash is rooted in a deeper cultural conflict that is irresolvable, and the best a society can hope for is an ideology that is broad and flexible enough to accommodate the conflicting visions? This alternative interpretation of the cultural conflict is implicated in Jonathan Haidt's finding that the political division in the United States is deeply rooted in moral psychology.[36] Thomas Sowell explains political conflicts with two conflicting visions stemming from two different understandings of human nature, one he calls "constrained vision" and the other "unconstrained vision."[37] These are but examples of two competing cultural interpretations of the crisis of Western democracies. One is the developmental view and the other the conflictive view. Which view offers a better explanation of the challenges in Western democracies will have significant impact on how we understand the future of dignity and rights in general – and how the Asian societies that embrace human rights should chart their course.

From the perspective of Asian societies, the earnest reception of human dignity as a legal concept during the third-wave democratization means reception of the new conception as well as the old ones. It is hence worthy of investigation how this new conception of human dignity interacts with other conceptions of dignity in Asian societies on concrete issues. The conceptual evolution of human dignity in these Asian jurisdictions would involve complex dynamics of legal transplant. As Alan Watson indicated, legal transplantation does not require congruence of the received norms with local culture and tradition. For it to happen and even endure, all it takes is a reasonable degree of congruence between the cultures of legal or governing elites of both the exporting and importing societies.[38] In other words, it is not uncommon that there is a "divergence of law and society" when legal transplants occur.[39] There may hence be a gap between the legal elite culture and the culture surrounding the legal system.

This claim, however, should not be overstated. Democratization brought about not just political transformation but also profound social transformation. Despite variations in practice, the wide acceptance of the ideas of democracy and human rights protection, along with genuine improvement in certain countries, greatly transformed the political landscape upon which the claim of Asian values relied. To varying degrees, the political systems in this region have become more sensitive to popular perceptions of legitimacy and social movements. The legal and political elite as local agents may "localize" or "translate" these norms through local "language and sets of meanings rooted in their own particular cultural and

---

[36] Jonathan Haidt, *The Righteous Mind: Why Good People Are Divided by Politics and Religion* (New York: Penguin Books, 2013).
[37] Thomas Sowell, *A Conflict of Visions: Ideological Origins of Political Struggles* (New York: Basic Books, 2007).
[38] Alan Watson, "Legal Transplant and Law Reform," *Law Quarterly Review* 92, no. 79 (1976).
[39] Alan Watson, "Legal Change: Sources of Law and Legal Culture," *University of Pennsylvania Law Review* 131, no. 5 (1982–1983): 1121–1151, 1135.

normative milieu."⁴⁰ Political and social transformation in major Asian countries undermined the view that culture is a unitary, stable "set of values, psychological dispositions, and behaviors (both individual and social) that gave a group of people a common identity and way of life," a view presumed in the claim of Asian values. Instead, it gave credibility to the alternative view that culture is "a congeries of ways of thinking, believing, and acting that are constantly in the state of being produced; it is contingent and always unstable."⁴¹

Nonetheless, even as we recognize culture as an unstable field of constant contestation, we do not have to take culture and tradition as always being fluid in its entirety. Culture and tradition constitute the epistemic backdrop against which all agents acquire their interpretive horizon.⁴² Even when particular practices or beliefs of a culture are contested, it does not mean that the underlying layers of symbols, meaning, and values are not at work in framing and guiding the contestation. The "first round" of Asian values debate may have waned and its static view of culture undermined. Yet this does not mean that there remains nothing distinct about Asia, even considering the diversity within. The global diffusion of human rights brings not only convergence but also consciousness of difference. Economic development and modernization have brought significant social changes to many of the East and Southeast Asian societies. The developmental success not only gave some East and Southeast Asian societies the self-confidence to assert their own cultural distinctness against the West; it also unleashed social forces moving these societies toward a higher degree of gender equality, the rise of expressive individualism, changes of family structure and power relationships, and higher protection of individual rights. However, cultural legacies such as stronger family ties, a paternalistic model of governance, patrimonial patterns of social networks, and greater emphasis on social harmony may continue to shape a modernized, yet not necessarily Westernized, Asia. As Ronald Inglehart and Christian Welzel argue, socioeconomic development tends to bring substantial changes in people's worldviews toward self-expression values, and yet such changes are path-dependent. Cultural traditions continue to influence the trajectory of cultural changes.⁴³ Investigation of Asian understanding of human dignity must be conducted against this more nuanced idea of modernization and cultural change, transcending the rather blunt "universalism versus particularism" framework. The questions are: to what extent does human dignity serve as a conceptual arena in which human rights

---

⁴⁰ Gregoria Bettiza and Filippo Dionigi, "How Do Religious Norms Diffuse? Institutional Translation and International Change in a Post-Secular World Society," *European Journal of International Relations* 21, no. 3 (2015): 621–646, 623.

⁴¹ Lynda S. Bell, Andrew J. Nathan, and Ilan Peleg, "Introduction: Culture and Human Rights," in *Negotiating Culture and Human Rights*, ed. Lynda S. Bell, Andrew J. Nathan, and Ilan Peleg (New York: Columbia University Press, 2001), p. 11.

⁴² Hans Georg Gadamer, *Truth and Method* (New York: Continuum, 1989, 2nd rev. ed.), p. 397.

⁴³ Ronald Inglehart and Christian Welzel, *Modernization, Cultural Change, and Democracy: The Human Development Sequence* (Cambridge: Cambridge University Press, 2005), p. 4.

negotiate with cultural changes? To what extent does human dignity feature universal values and Asian distinctness? This book does not claim to resolve these questions. But it takes important steps to address these questions.

3 OVERVIEW OF THE BOOK

Instead of introducing the chapters in the order they appear, I present them here in an order that weaves the overarching themes throughout the book and highlights the dialogical elements in it. For this purpose, I begin with Chapter 8, "Human Dignity and Relational Constitutionalism in Singapore," written by Li-ann Thio. Thio's contribution bridges the legal part of the book with the cultural part, by representing human dignity in the context of a philosophy of governance consciously held by the Singapore government, as evidenced in laws regulating political defamation and the treatment of migrant workers. She contrasts two primary conceptions of human dignity: one is liberal, individualistic, and egalitarian, most prominently embraced in the West; and the other communitarian, relational, and elitist. The Singapore government, dominated by the People's Action Party since the nation's founding, has been able to articulate and practice a communitarian conception of human dignity. This conception prizes mutuality and reciprocity among the state, the society and the individual – hence "relational constitutionalism" – instead of one that solidifies individual rights as the sole anchor in such relationships, even though recent development shows signs of the elitist culture abating.

Such a level of coherence in governing philosophical and practice, however, can hardly be seen in larger, more competitive and pluralistic democracies in this region. A more common pattern is conflict and incoherence in the idea of human dignity as manifested in judicial decisions. In Pritam Baruah's Chapter 1, "Human Dignity in Indian Constitutional Adjudication," he meticulously documents and analyzes the idea of human dignity as employed by the Indian Supreme Court. He indicates that, in the Preamble of the Indian Constitution, human dignity is closely related with fraternity. Human dignity could be interpreted as "rights generating," to be balanced by the "duty-apt" fraternity. Notably, while dignity is found in the Preamble, the Directive Principles, and the Fundamental Duties, it is not textually based in the chapter on Fundamental Rights. This may suggest an understanding of dignity similar to the Singaporean conception. However, the Indian Supreme Court has given the concept a life that goes far beyond the limited textual base, first through association with the right to life in Article 21 as "a right to life with dignity" and then to be unleashed as a core value underpinning all fundamental rights. The flourishing of unanchored dignity jurisprudence, however, has raised concerns about arbitrariness and incoherence in the Court's uninhibited interpretation that masks value conflicts, for example between individualistic and communitarian conceptions, that went seriously under-reasoned.

The concern of conceptual vagueness and interpretive inconsistency can be seen in other jurisdictions too. In Chapter 3, "Constitutional Discourse on Human

Dignity in South Korea: A Critical Appraisal," Chaihark Hahm points out that the "human dignity and worth" clause in Article 10 of the 1987 Constitution has been subject to abuse and overuse by claimants and that it has generated interpretive difficulties such as the relationship between dignity and worth, as well as whether it is a goal or value whose justiciability has to be mediated through other rights. Interpretive issues notwithstanding, the Korean Constitutional Court has produced a significant body of dignity jurisprudence that embodies liberal democratic values and reflects social change in family structure and sexual relations. In effecting social change, dignity as individual autonomy and self-determination has played a significant role. For example, it has facilitated the Court's decisions to recognize the terminally ill patient's right to refuse life-sustaining treatment, decriminalize adultery, liberalize marriage between persons of same surname and ancestral origin, and decriminalize a man's seducing a woman into sexual relations through a false promise of marriage. It should be noted that comparative dignity jurisprudence, especially that of Germany, has been influential in the Korean Court and legal academia. Still, foreign influence has to be negotiated with a strong Confucian tradition in the Court's management of social change. Arguably influenced by the Confucian conservative tradition, for example, the Court has upheld criminalization of prostitution, enhanced punishment of physical crimes committed against "lineal ascendants," and, most controversially, capital punishment *per se*, despite extended executive moratorium.

The theme of negotiating between individual autonomy, social change, and social conservatism is also prominent in Keigo Obayashi's contribution in Chapter 2, "The Development of Individual Dignity in Japan: Overcoming Constraints in Law, Family, and Society." The postwar Japanese Constitution was drafted by the Supreme Commander for the Allied Powers with an aim to free the individual from the statist system of *Kokutai*, which, under the divine authority of the emperor, forged all subjects into one national family with individuality dissolved. The *Kokutai* system is underpinned by *Iye*, the patriarchal family system that grants authority over family affairs to the head of the household. To reform the Japanese political system and society, it was necessary to tackle both. To that end, the postwar Constitution enshrines individual dignity in Article 13 and prescribes gender equality and individual autonomy on marriage and family affairs in Article 24. Obayashi indicates that the Japanese dignity jurisprudence promotes individual privacy, such as the right not to have one's photo taken without permission, the right not to be fingerprinted without reasonable cause, and the right not to have one's private life exposed in a novel. It also deals with constraints on individual autonomy on marriage and family matters. The Court sometimes liberates individuals from social restraints, such as equalizing the status of legitimate and illegitimate children on inheritance and invalidating penal enhancement of parricide. At other times the Court preserves long-standing social customs, such as upholding the requirement that a married couple adopt one surname for the family. Obayashi argues that the Court has been deferential to the mainstream public opinion, unless it is sure that a social change is taking place in a certain direction.

A similar pattern of social change can also be witnessed in Taiwan. In my own Chapter 4, "Human Dignity in the Jurisprudence of Taiwan Constitutional Court," I observe that preservation of individual autonomy emerged as a constitutional value in the jurisprudence of Taiwan Constitutional Court (TCC), and it has been associated with human dignity increasingly after 2003, when a new group of Grand Justices are appointed. The increasing juxtaposition of human dignity and individual autonomy by TCC was mainly devised for the purpose of generating new unenumerated rights, such as the right to privacy, right to reputation, right to personality, and the right to same-sex marriage. In this chapter, I narrate the trajectory of the concept of human dignity in TCC's jurisprudence during Taiwan's democratic transition. Unlike South Korea's new 1987 Constitution, which guided its democratic transition, Taiwan waded into transition through incremental constitutional amendments to its original 1947 Constitution, which never incorporated human dignity in its text. The TCC deftly introduced the concept in its interpretation and gradually expanded its institutional use. It was first used to reinforce fundamental rights and dismantle authoritarian remnants. Then it has been used to expand the scope of fundamental rights and to negotiate and effectuate social change, including legalization of same-sex marriage.

In Chapter 5, "The Human Dignity Factor: Interpreting the Philippine Constitution," J. R. Robert Real traces the evolution of the Philippine Supreme Court's dignity jurisprudence to its founding in 1901, when Spain was ousted by the United States as the new colonizer after the Spanish-American War. Real identifies important historical, cultural, and international factors that shaped how human dignity has been developed by the Court. He first indicates that the Philippine dignity jurisprudence has been shaped by three traumatic historical events: namely, more than three centuries of Spanish colonial oppression, the Japanese wartime atrocities, and the authoritarian rule of President Ferdinand Marcos. Before WWII, the Court already began to employ dignity language to alleviate the social and economic conditions of the poor and the marginalized, as well as to promote women's suffrage. After the Philippines gained independence in 1945, the Court applied the egalitarian and humanitarian senses of human dignity to ensure that Japanese war criminals were treated with respect. In the 1973 Constitution, human dignity was first given its textual base in the *Declaration of Principles and State Policies*. Human dignity has been given the most prominent place in the 1987 Constitution, which marked a new democratic era in the wake of the People Power Revolution that ended Marcos' dictatorship. Real then analyzes four areas of issues, including national security, criminal punishment, informational and decisional privacy, group identity and culture, and satisfaction of essential needs. On these issues, the Court developed its dignity jurisprudence under the multifarious influences of the Catholic Church, US constitutional law, and a society increasingly prizing individual dignity and autonomy.

In Chapter 6, "Human Dignity in the Jurisprudence of Indonesian Constitutional Court," Nadirsyah Hosen offers a narrative quite distinct from that of the Philippines. Instead of being marked by breaks of constitutional identity, the Indonesian Constitution maintains surprising continuity with its 1945 Constitution despite significant constitutional amendments, the most consequential of which took place in 1999 to 2002 when the country transitioned to democracy. The continuous constitutional identity places the new bill of rights under the weight of the founding ideology of Pancasila, which includes: belief in one God, humanitarianism, national unity, representative democracy, and social justice. Hosen analyzes the Indonesian Constitutional Court's dignity jurisprudence, which is marked by the tension between Article 28 I and Article 28 J. The former gives unlimitable protection to the right to life, the right to be free of torture, and several other rights, while the latter subjects rights in general to limitations determined by law. The (un)limitability of the right to life with regard to the death penalty has given rise to a series of cases in which the Court upheld the death penalty *per se*. This highlights a distinct aspect of Asian dignity jurisprudence. Except the Philippines – under heavy Catholic influence and Hong Kong under British colonial rule – all jurisdictions surveyed in this collection retain the death penalty in law or in practice, irrespective of regime types, level of liberalness, or stages of development. In addition, Hosen analyzes how the Court limited those "unlimitable" rights in face of challenges posed by anti-terrorism and domestic political strife, as well as how the Court continued to promote social, economic and cultural rights, all in dynamic interaction with the concept of human dignity.

In Chapter 7, "Dignity as a Constitutional Value in Hong Kong: Toward a Contextual Approach?", Kelley Loper introduces how the dignity jurisprudence has developed under the Hong Kong Basic Law, a mini-constitution under the People's Republic of China's "one country two systems" framework, and the Bill of Rights Ordinance, which incorporates the ICCPR into the Hong Kong legal system. Loper observes that dignity jurisprudence in Hong Kong is still at its nascent stage of development. The courts have invoked dignity in a small number of cases and involved limited types of rights, which may lead to an impression that dignity is relevant only when serious breaches of fundamental rights are involved. The courts have referred to dignity in cases involving, for example, the right to be free from cruel punishment in non-refoulement claims, the right to equality and nondiscrimination in social welfare distribution, and the right to be treated with dignity in prison. Still, Loper aptly argues that dignity jurisprudence in Hong Kong could expand if the courts take a more holistic approach by wedding dignity as a universal value to contextual conditions, thus enabling a more "spacious" view of dignity that cuts across civil, political, economic, social, and cultural rights. Hopefully, such development may establish a bulwark to preserve liberty and dignity in Hong Kong.

China is a rising regional hegemon of Asia. The development of dignity in China has far-reaching implications, not only for Hong Kong but for the whole region and beyond. In Chapter 9, "Personal Dignity under Chinese Constitutional Law," Xiaobo Zhai offers an in-depth analysis of the dignity clause in the Chinese Constitution. Article 38 of the 1982 Chinese Constitution reads: "The personal dignity of citizens of the People's Republic of China is inviolable. Insult, libel, false charge or frame-up directed against citizens by any means is prohibited." Zhai indicates that it is widely agreed that this provision is a direct response to the Great Proletarian Cultural Revolution (1966–76), in which Mao Zedong mobilized tens of millions of Chinese people to engage in an orgy of violence and destroyed public institutions and social trust. Zhai argues that this Article should not be regarded as a narrow social right but as a fundamental constitutional value and principle undergirding the 1982 Constitution. Even though it is not a justiciable right under the Chinese legal system, notable progress has been made in legal protections of dignity and improvement of the socioeconomic well-being of the people. Zhai also documents wide usage of personal dignity in legislation and public policy papers. Despite such progress, Zhai cautions that the major problem with personal dignity in China lies in its implementation, and there is still a long way to go to achieving fuller protection of this fundamental right.

From the next chapter on, we enter the philosophical and cultural part of the collection. In Chapter 10, "Virtue, Dignity, and Constitutional Democracy: A Confucian Perspective," Sungmoon Kim provides an intricate analysis of contemporary Confucianist scholarship's exploration of the idea of human dignity in classical texts. Kim identifies two contending accounts of human dignity, namely meritocratic dignity versus egalitarian dignity. The former understands human dignity as a moral achievement, attainable only through a long process of moral self-cultivation, while the latter, inspired by Mencius who believes that human nature is good, is based on universal, heaven-endowed moral potential. Kim recovers the moral potential aspect of Xunzi, who traditionally has been regarded as holding a meritocratic conception of dignity. By this move, Kim reinforces the egalitarian conception of dignity, which supports constitutional democracy and a strong judiciary protecting universal human rights. Kim's argument is an admirable attempt to recover the egalitarian potential of Confucian human dignity. Nevertheless, his engagement in the debate also reveals how strong a tradition there is in Confucianism to view dignity meritocratically, since at the center of its virtue ethics is the ideal of moral self-cultivation, which necessarily prizes the result of self-cultivation and uses it to measure individual moral attainment.

Confucianism is an important part of the cultural traditions in the several jurisdictions surveyed in this book, including Japan, South Korea, Taiwan, Hong Kong, China, and Singapore. Singapore's pattern of governance under the PAP self-professedly echoes the Confucian meritocratic tradition. The variety of regime types and liberalness may undermine the relevance of "culture" in understanding conditions conducive to democratization and liberal democracy of Asian countries. Yet this is the case only if one holds a rigid and static idea of culture. As aforementioned, we do not have to marginalize the relevance of culture even if we hold a dynamic and contestable idea of it. Even in liberal democracies such as Japan, South Korea, and Taiwan, we can identify distinct aspects of human rights development – such as retention of the death penalty, permissiveness of abortion, state support of familial relations, and acceptance of a strong state responsible for the socioeconomic well-being of the people – that may be explainable at least in part by cultural factors properly understood. Although this book has yet to engage specific rights more closely with the cultures in which they are embedded, the dialogical attempts in this book reveal important questions not clearly raised before.

In Chapter 11, "Buddhist Philosophical Approaches to Human Dignity," Anton Sevilla-Liu discusses human dignity in early Buddhism and schools of Mahayana Buddhism, which has tremendous influence in East Asia. On early Buddhism and human dignity, Sevilla-Liu engages with contemporary Buddhist thinkers and points out that the Buddhist noble truths on human potentiality to liberate oneself from suffering could lead to inner dignity but not necessarily to inherent dignity, since for such potential to be realized it requires a lifetime of practice that is not necessarily attainable by everyone. Further, it is not clear why one person's potential for liberation from suffering imposes duty of respect on others. Note that this line of inquiry echoes Sungmoon Kim's discussion of Confucian meritocratic conception of dignity, which together contrasts with the inherent dignity grounded on *imago dei* in Christianity. Sevilla-Liu believes that the questions legitimately posed for early Buddhism could only be addressed by Mahayana Buddhism. He then explores schools of Mahayana Buddhism in Japan. In Nishitani Keiji's Zen philosophy, dignity can be grounded on an ability to free everyone from suffering that is ontologically shared by everyone; in Tanabe Hajime's view of Pure Land Buddhism, dignity can be found in the way of repentance and serving as the mediator of salvation; in Watsuji Tetsuro's Confucian Buddhism, dignity rests with the potential to free oneself from egotism for the sake of one's community. Toward the end, Sevilla-Liu remarked that these schools of Buddhism, despite their variance, are all a long way from the modern understanding of dignity, which means freedom of a rational subject to maximize utility. Instead, they all point to the moral freedom from egoistic desire. This remark resonates with Oliver Sensen's distinction between the traditional and contemporary paradigms of human dignity in the West, as dignity in Buddhism echoes the Western traditional dignity paradigm, which primarily entailed duty on dignity-bearers to live up to a certain moral standard.[44] This aspect of dignity may be relevant to contemporary discussion on the right-constraining function of dignity.

---

[44] See Oliver Sensen, "Human Dignity in Historical Perspective: The Contemporary and Traditional Paradigms," *European Journal of Political Theory* 10, no. 1 (2011): 71–91.

In Chapter 12, "Dignity and Status in Ancient and Medieval India," Timothy Lubin explores ancient and medieval Hindu sources to see whether a concept of human dignity can operate within an inegalitarian social order. Lubin draws on Jeremy Waldron's idea of human dignity as a status claim that levels up people of low social status to enjoy treatment once reserved for the privileged. Lubin found that while the Brahmanical Sanskrit sources generally affirmed the special dignity and privileges (and duties) of Brahmin status, ascetic movements and medieval devotional bhakti literature provides countervailing resources for an egalitarian view of spiritual enhancement. Note that it is precisely from the ascetic movements that Mahatma Gandhi drew inspirations to advocate social reform in India. Also, Sanskrit texts on good governance and legal process formulate universal standards of justice and equity that could cut across ranks. As all these divergent views of human worth and status could coexist and even be cited side by side, Lubin observes that, in practice, social customs and legal order find ways to compartmentalize the universalistic human traits and sort people into hierarchical social ranks. The dire consequences and tenacity of the caste system constitute the social background against which to understand Pritam Baruah's analysis of the Indian Supreme Court's dignity jurisprudence. Lubin's observation also offers precious lessons to recent philosophical analysis of human dignity, in that it is not enough just to point out common traits in humanity, be it rationality, autonomy, and so on. Rather, human dignity demands inclusive and egalitarian practice grounded on social imagination that obligates people to value commonality higher than difference or tribal hostility.

From the next chapter on, we enter the last section of the book that introduces the idea of human dignity and its relations with a religious tradition in the sociopolitical contexts of a particular society. Etin Anwar's Chapter 13, "Human Dignity, Pancasila, and Islam: Contexts and Contestations in Indonesia," could well be read alongside Nadirsyah Hosen's contribution in Chapter 6. Anwar takes a genealogical approach to narrate the shaping and contesting of human dignity through modern Indonesian history. The narration centered on the complex relations between Pancasila, the founding principle of the Indonesian state, and Islam, Indonesia's largest religion. During the colonial era of over three-and-a-half centuries before Independence, the Dutch colonizer adopted race-based governance policies. For indigenous social and political activists, human dignity primarily means national autonomy and the aspiration to be treated as equals to the Western powers on the basis of a united and equal humanity. Human dignity in the public discourse at this stage also involved an agenda for social justice to address the poverty and injustice caused by exploitive colonial policy. The ideas that inspired the national independence movements crystallized in the Pancasila. After Independence, the (re)interpretation of Pancasila became the primary political discursive arena to interpret human dignity. Through the Old Order and Suharto's New Order, development was the state's primary concern, and the cultural and social changes needed for development solidified the state's power. The New

Order under Suharto used Pancasila to homogenize diverse ethnicities and marginalize political-oriented Islamists. The tension between Pancasila as a secular political ideology and Islamism continues to this day. Anwar argues that while Islamist political agenda and the authoritarian tendency of Indonesian state elites are the sources of social and political tension, Islam as an ethical framework and Pancasila are actually mutually reinforcing, and together they could provide robust foundations for understanding and furthering human dignity in Indonesia.

Jonathan T. Chow's contribution in Chapter 14, "Catholicism and Human Dignity in the Philippines," provides an excellent companion to Robert Real's Chapter 5 on the Philippine Supreme Court. Chow reviews Catholic teachings regarding human dignity and how the Catholic Bishops' Conference of the Philippines (CBCP), the official representative of the Catholic Church, has interpreted dignity on issue areas such as electoral politics, labor and poverty, contraception, and capital punishment. Chow introduced how the Catholic Church came to acquire a deeply embedded societal role in the Philippines through the Spanish and American colonial era all the way to the democratic era. The Catholic Church has employed dignity language in its social teaching and public discourse to address poverty, economic inequality, and political corruption, against the political background of economic inequality, underdevelopment, and concentration of power and wealth in oligarchic landowning dynasties. The Church's political influence reached its peak during the 1986 People Power Revolution but has diminished ever since. This is evidenced by the Church's recent loss of political and popular support for its condemnation of legislation mandating universal access to reproductive health services, for which the Church invoked human dignity to implement the Vatican's teaching against contraception and to oppose abortion. The Catholic Church's dwindling political influence, Chow argues, has enfeebled its criticism of and opposition to the war on drugs of President Rodrigo Duterte, who has consistently enjoyed high popular support.

In Chapter 15, "Protestantism and Human Dignity in South Korea," JinHyok Kim examines the relationship between human dignity and Protestantism, one of the largest religions in South Korea, through the country's modern history. Kim divides the history into three periods. The first is from early Protestant missions in the late nineteenth century through the end of Japanese colonization in 1945. In this period, Protestant missionaries from the West introduced the idea of human dignity through their missionary practice of medical aide, education, and famine relief, to dignify and enhance the lives of the miserable and the oppressed in a highly hierarchical premodern society. The second period is from postwar independence to the end of Korean War (1945–53). This was a time of civil strife and war between the North and the South. The brutal persecution of Christians by the communist North resulted in serious fear of communist invasion and conquest in the South. This caused the Protestant churches, joined by a large number of Christian refugees from the North, to offer firm support for President Rhee Syngman to fiercely oppress and purge suspected communists, sometimes resulting in tragic bloodshed, such as in the Jeju 4.3 incident. The third period is national reconstruction to the eve of democratization (1953–87). In this period, politically attentive Protestant churches were roughly divided into those who supported the authoritarian governments for economic development and fear of communism, and those dissident churches who opposed authoritarianism and advocated for human rights and human dignity. Kim's chapter is a useful companion to Chaihark Hahm's Chapter 3 on the post-democratization Korean Constitutional Court. Further, the tragedies leading up to the Korean War and the authoritarianism during the Cold War remind us how fragile human dignity can become when people are driven by insecurity, fear, and hate.

1

Human Dignity in Indian Constitutional Adjudication

Pritam Baruah[*]

1 INTRODUCTION

The Supreme Court of India has accorded an exceptionally high status to human dignity as a constitutional value. Human dignity has been held to be 'the founding faith of the Constitution' and the 'core of Fundamental Rights'. According such high status to dignity in the Indian context is intriguing as the constitutional text lists dignity as one of many values such as equality, liberty, fraternity, and justice. Dignity is not articulated as a supreme value or as a source of rights. In fact, it does not find any mention in the chapter on Fundamental Rights.[1] How then has the Court explained the special significance of dignity, and what implications does that have for constitutional adjudication?

Towards answering these questions, this chapter conducts a bottom-up exercise in mapping the application of human dignity by the Supreme Court of India (hereafter 'the Court'). Section 2 describes the place of dignity in the constitutional text. Section 3 examines how dignity has figured as a source of unenumerated Fundamental Rights and points out inconsistencies in judicial reasoning about dignity in this context. Section 4 first describes how dignity has been employed as a foundational value both for the Fundamental Rights and for the Constitution itself. By examining landmark cases on non-discrimination, the right to die, and privacy, I point out how dignity figures as a right, a value justifying rights, and a reason for limiting rights. Section 5 examines the status of dignity as an absolute value or a limited right.

I draw the following conclusions from this mapping exercise. First, the Court's articulation of the content of dignity is perilously thin even if it leans towards a Kantian intrinsic-worth account. Second, the Court has transitioned from

---

[*] I thank Akruti Ramchandran, Prarthana Bhatija, and Raja Venkata Krishna Dandamudi for research assistance. The chapter has benefitted from comments by participants in workshops at the Human Dignity in Asia Conference, Academia Sinica Taipei, the IVR Annual Conference 2019, and the Faculty Research Seminar Series at Jindal Global Law School.
[1] Part III of the Constitution of India is on Fundamental Rights. They act as standards for judicial review for legislative and executive action.

unanchored speculation on the content of dignity to uninhibitedly relying on academic literature across disciplines on dignity. This transition has not lent more clarity to the content of dignity; rather, it raises questions about the use of extralegal materials in judicial decisions. And finally, the Indian experience, akin to several other jurisdictions, raises concerns that arise when legal actors employ moral and political values as justifications for decisions.

The primary evaluative lens that I employ for these conclusions is that of the content of dignity. I prioritize content over the institutional role that dignity can play (e.g. as an agreement-gathering tool that generates a sort of overlapping consensus on moral and political disagreement). In the burgeoning literature on dignity in philosophy, law, and bioethics, the questions of content and of institutional roles have emerged as central concerns about dignity.[2] The standard view on content, particularly in law, is that the content of dignity is indeterminate. Consequently, dignity has been characterized as an essentially contested concept, an interpretive concept, and a placeholder.[3] Debates in law have particularly invited fresh philosophical reflection on dignity along these lines.[4] Indeterminacy allows sustaining arguments about dignity being culture-relative, on the one hand, and universal and foundational on the other.[5] Despite such debates on content, Kantian intrinsic-worth accounts and rank-and-status-based accounts have emerged as substantive theories of the content of dignity.[6] I argue here that, in Indian constitutional adjudication, it is the intrinsic-worth account articulated by individual autonomy and self-worth that has been firmly established by judicial decisions.

Questions about the institutional role of dignity are necessarily dependent on the question of content. If a concept must play a justificatory role in adjudication (i.e. as a source of reasons for decisions), then determination of its content is necessary. Content assumes special significance if one is committed to a reason-giving account of constitutional adjudication, which distinguishes adjudication from a notable

---

[2] Christopher McCrudden (ed.), *Understanding Human Dignity: Proceedings of the British Academy* (Oxford: Oxford University Press, 2013) (for the legal and philosophical academic interest in dignity).
[3] Christopher McCrudden, 'Human Dignity and Judicial Interpretation of Human Rights', *European Journal of International Law* 19, no. 4 (2008): 655.
[4] Michael Rosen, *Dignity: Its History and Meaning* (Cambridge, MA: Harvard University Press, 2012); Jürgen Habermas, 'The Concept of Human Dignity and the Realistic Utopia of Human Rights', *Metaphilosophy* 41, no. 4 (2010): 464–80.
[5] Paul Carozza, 'Human Dignity and the Judicial Interpretation of Human Rights: A Reply', *European Journal of International Law* 19, no. 5 (2008): 931; Stephen Riley, *Human Dignity and Law: Legal and Philosophical Investigations* (Abingdon, UK: Routledge, 2018); Christopher McCrudden (ed.), *Understanding Human Dignity: Proceedings of the British Academy* (Oxford: Oxford University Press, 2013) (for the legal and philosophical academic interest in dignity).
[6] Immanuel Kant, *Groundwork of the Metaphysics of Morals*, tr. Mary Gregor (Cambridge: Cambridge University Press, 1998) (for the intrinsic worth account). For status-based accounts, see Jeremy Waldron and Meir Dan-Cohen, *Dignity, Rank, and Rights* (New York: Oxford University Press, 2012); and Laura Valentini, 'Dignity and Human Rights: A Reconceptualization', *Oxford Journal of Legal Studies* 37 (2017): 862.

aspect of constitution-making.⁷ Ideas such as Rawls' 'overlapping consensus', Cass Sunstein's 'incompletely theorized agreements', or Christopher McCrudden's dignity as a 'placeholder' have gained considerable traction in legal theory.⁸ Such views highlight the agreement-generating role that dignity and other vague values can assume when faced with moral and political disagreement. To be sure, agreement-generating views might explain the role of values in constitution-making as they are suited to bringing people together without having to determine specific rights. Content may not have a significant role in such contexts. Adjudication, however, is a different enterprise, both in terms of purposes and expectations. While in constitution-making we lay out a future project of a political community based on values and other considerations, in adjudication we expect justifications for the determination of rights when faced with disagreement on narrow and focused issues.⁹ Employing concepts in adjudication thus warrants reliance on the content of concepts that litigants employ. Such constraints of justification may be beneficially absent in constitution-making.¹⁰

An additional reason why adjudication is a reason-giving exercise is related to how we view the authority of courts. If courts are authoritative bodies that bind people, then the exercise of legitimate authority requires that courts consider the reasons relevant to the dispute being adjudicated in a transparent manner. Legitimacy, in part, requires that courts provide transparent justifications for their decisions. If courts employ concepts such as dignity as sources of reasons, then transparency cannot begin without what dignity means (i.e. what its content is). For these reasons, I will employ content as a benchmark to assess how the Court has employed the concept of dignity.

2 DIGNITY IN THE CONSTITUTIONAL TEXT

Dignity finds textual space in the Preamble, the Directive Principles of State Policy, and the Fundamental Duties.¹¹ Dignity finds no mention in the chapter on

---

7   Pritam Baruah, 'Human Dignity in Adjudication: The Limits of Placeholding and Essential Contestability Accounts', *Canadian Journal of Law and Jurisprudence*, no. 27 (2014): 329.
8   See generally Samuel Freeman, 'Public Reason and Political Justification', *Fordham Law Review*, no. 72 (2004): 2021 (for a comparison of Rawls' and Sunstein's views).
9   For reason-giving views of adjudication, see Ronald Dworkin, chap. 4 in *Taking Rights Seriously* (London: Duckworth, 1977); Ronald Dworkin, chap. 3 and 7 in *Laws Empire* (Oxford: Hart Publishing, 1998); Neil McCormick, chap. 5 in *Legal Reasoning and Legal Theory* (Oxford: Oxford University Press, 1978); Mattias Kumm, 'Institutionalising Socratic Contestation: The Rationalist Human Rights Paradigm, Legitimate Authority and the Point of Judicial Review', *European Journal of Legal Studies* 1, no. 2 (2007): 1; Mattias Kumm, 'The Idea of Socratic Contestation and the Right to Justification: The Point of Rights-Based Proportionality Review', *Law and Ethics of Human Rights* (2010) 4, no. 2: 142.
10 Cass Sunstein, chap. 2 in *Legal Reasoning and Political Conflict* (Oxford: Oxford University Press, 1996).
11 In the Preamble: 'and to promote among them all FRATERNITY assuring the dignity of the individual and the [unity and integrity of the Nation]'; Fundamental Duties: 'Art. 51A. It shall be the duty of every citizen of India – . . . (e) to promote harmony and the spirit of common brotherhood

Fundamental Rights. Despite limited textual mention, the extensive application of dignity in Fundamental Rights adjudication was made possible by creative interpretive techniques. Initially, courts did not consider the Preamble to be a part of the Constitution.[12] This was later overruled by the view that it was an integral part of the Constitution,[13] containing its ideals and aspirations.[14] The values in the Preamble have since assumed an important interpretive role.

In the Preamble, dignity is to be assured by fraternity. The textual proximity of the two values might be indicative of their mutual content. Until recently, fraternity had not figured as prominently as dignity in judicial decisions.[15] Scholars have, however, pointed out that the relationship between the two values points towards an empowering idea of dignity.[16] Upendra Baxi suggests that dignity and fraternity have distinct roles: dignity being rights-apt and fraternity being duty-apt, where dignity has a rights-generating role. To play that role, however, a question of content must be settled first as it is the content of dignity that would justifiably determine what kinds of rights it supports.

In the Directive Principles of State Policy, dignity figures in the context of the state's responsibility towards the healthy development of children.[17] The Directive Principles themselves are non-justiciable.[18] However, courts employ them to interpret Fundamental Rights by taking Directive Principles and Fundamental Rights to be complementing and supplementing each other.[19] The balance and harmony between the two is held to be a basic feature of the Constitution.[20]

In the Fundamental Duties, Art. 51A invokes dignity in the context of derogatory practices related to women within a sub-clause about brotherhood amongst the people of India. Dignity's connection with fraternity therefore resonates in this provision. The role of dignity in the Fundamental Duties has not yet witnessed adjudicative action.

amongst all the people of India transcending religious, linguistic and regional or sectional diversities; to renounce practices derogatory to the dignity of women'. For the Directive Principles, see n 17.

[12] *Berubari Union and Exchange of Enclaves*, Re, 3 SCR 250 (1960).
[13] *Kesavananda Bharti v. State of Kerala*, 4 SCC 225 (1973).
[14] Subbarao J in *Golak Nath v. State of Punjab*, 2 SCR 762 (1967).
[15] Smaran Shetty and Tanya Sanyal, 'Fraternity and the Constitution: A Promising Beginning in Nandini Sundar v. State of Chhattisgarh', *NUJS Law Review* no. 4 (2011): 439 (for how fraternity has been applied). Recently fraternity has received more attention in the concurring opinion of Justice S. Ravindra Bhat in *Prathvi Raj Chauhan v. Union of India and Others*, Writ Petition [C] No. 1015 (2018).
[16] Upendra Baxi, 'The Place of Dignity in the Indian Constitution', in Marcus Düwell, Jens Braarvig, Roger Brownsword, and Dietmar Mieth (eds.), *The Cambridge Handbook of Human Dignity* (Cambridge: Cambridge University Press, 2014), pp. 429–30.
[17] 'Art. 39 (f) that children are given opportunities and facilities to develop in a healthy manner and in conditions of freedom and dignity and that childhood and youth are protected against exploitation and against moral and material abandonment'.
[18] 'Art. 37. The provisions contained in this Part shall not be enforceable by any court, but the principles therein laid down are nevertheless fundamental in the governance of the country and it shall be the duty of the State to apply these principles in making laws.'
[19] 3 SCC 84 (1969).
[20] *Minerva Mills Ltd. v. Union of India*, 2 SCC 591 (1980).

The limited textual significance of dignity stands starkly in contrast with the singularly high status accorded to dignity in judicial decisions. In what follows I map how the Court has applied dignity; categorize its application through the lens of content; and bring out inconsistencies that future decisions might have to iron out. I employ the term 'inconsistency' as opposed to 'incoherence', as the facts of different cases may warrant a distinctive application of the concept that may not immediately cohere or make sense, considering earlier decisions. Such incoherent decisions can still be justified in the context of a specific case. Inconsistencies on the other hand suggest contradictions and, in that sense, share a tenuous relationship with other decisions.

3 UNANCHORED REASONING: DIGNITY AS A SOURCE OF RIGHTS

Human dignity has been central to the Court's reading of unenumerated rights into the Constitution. Article 21 of the Constitution, which declares a right to life and personal liberty, has been the preferred source for pronouncing unenumerated rights.[21] Dignity has figured prominently in expanding the scope of this right, as the Court has read the right to life as meaning a right to life with dignity. Though this interpretation was made famous by the decision in *Francis Coralie Mullin*, a case concerning the right of persons in detention,[22] its application was extended not only to other civil political rights but also to socio-economic rights. In employing dignity to expand the right to life by pronouncing unenumerated rights, the Court at times takes a minimum-requirements view: that dignity guarantees the bare minimum necessities of life. At other occasions it takes a maximalist view: that dignity guarantees human flourishing. The roots of the minimum-requirements view are found in *Francis Coralie Mullin*, the first case in which dignity was specifically invoked as a justification. The Court held that the right to life with dignity must include the right to basic necessities and 'the right to carry on such functions and activities as constitute the bare minimum expression of the human self'.[23] This indicated that the burden that dignity put on the state was of securing the basic necessities of life. However, subsequent cases, especially involving socio-economic rights, suggest a maximalist view of dignity.

In the context of the right to food, the Court invoked both maximal and minimal standards of dignity in articulating the justification for the right. The Court acknowledged the minimal standard in *Francis Coralie Mullin* in that the right to life and personal liberty implied something 'more than mere survival or animal existence'. However, it went on to hold that the right included aspects of life that would 'make

---

[21] Anup Surendranath, 'Life and Personal Liberty', in Madhav Khosla, Pratap Bhanu Mehta and Sujit Choudhury (eds.), *Oxford Handbook of Indian Constitutional Law* (Oxford: Oxford University Press, 2016), pp. 746–61.
[22] *Francis Coralie Mullin v. Administrator, Union Territory of Delhi*, 1 SCC 608 (1981).
[23] *Francis Coralie Mullin v. Administrator, Union Territory of Delhi*.

a man's life complete and worth living'. This included 'enjoyment of life and its attainment – social, cultural and intellectual – without which life cannot be meaningful'.[24]

A maximalist interpretation of what dignity requires is affirmed by other cases such as those on the right to residence, where the Court articulates the objective of the right to dignity as developing a person into a 'cultured being'.[25] A maximalist interpretation of dignity might also be supported by decisions that hold that dignity, along with equality, is the basis of all Fundamental Rights as well as other parts of the Constitution such as the Preamble and the Directive Principles.[26] Drawing such a connection entails that dignity is not limited to interpreting the right to life alone. Rather it is germane to understanding the values in the Preamble that include social and economic justice, liberty, equality, and fraternity.

This expansive interpretation gets further vindicated when dignity is related to the Directive Principles, which aim at promoting social welfare and the common good. These principles articulate a range of state obligations including protection of women and children, prevention of concentration of wealth, the right to work, workers' rights, compulsory education, public health, and a uniform civil code. It is no coincidence that the Court often employs the Directive Principles when it imposes positive obligations on the state to protect Fundamental Rights. A good example is the landmark case on the prohibition of bonded labour, where the Court held that the link between the Directive Principles and the right to life with dignity is fundamental to an understanding of the right to life under Article 21.[27] The uniqueness of this view merits extracting this long passage:

> 14. It is the fundamental right of everyone in this country, assured under the interpretation given to Article 21 by this Court in Francis Mullen's case, to live with human dignity, free from exploitation. This right to live with human dignity enshrined in Article 21 derives its life breath from the Directive Principles ... and at the least, therefore, it must include protection of the health and strength of workers men and women, and of the tender age of children against abuse, opportunities and facilities for children to develop in a healthy manner and in conditions of freedom and dignity, educational facilities, just and humane conditions of work and maternity relief.

This is a peculiar excerpt since here dignity itself is derived from different specific requirements that are posited in the Directive Principles. It appears that the Court thinks that components of a dignified life are articulated in the Directive Principles; however, in doing so it seems to have made freedom and dignity a part of the components of a dignified life articulated exclusively through socio-economic

---

[24] *PUCL v. Union of India*, I.A. Nos. 94 and 96 in W.P. (C) No. 196 (2001) and I.A. No. 82/2008 in W.P. (C) No. 196 (2001). Decided on: 23 January 2012.
[25] *Chamelli Singh v. State of U.P.*, 2 SCC 549, para. 8 (1996).
[26] *Masilamani Mudaliar v. Idol of Sri Swaminathaswami Thirukoil*, 8 SCC 525 (1996).
[27] *Bandhua Mukti Morcha v. Union of India*, 9 SCC 322 (2000).

rights. Perhaps the Court intends that the Directive Principles provide an indication of what a dignified life should be, but then dignity would only be aimed towards securing socio-economic rights. This conclusion is not implied by the present case alone. In *Re: Noise Pollution*,[28] dealing with implementation of laws restricting use of loudspeakers and high-volume sound systems, the Court held:

> 9. Article 21 of the Constitution guarantees life and personal liberty to all persons. It is well settled by repeated pronouncements of this Court ... [that] the right to life guarantees a right of person to life with human dignity. Therein are included, all the aspects of life which go to make a person's life meaningful, complete and worth living.

Such an extensive view of the right to life with dignity suggests that the right included all socio-economic rights within its fold. In contrast, in other cases, the Court again leans towards a minimal-requirements interpretation of the right. For example, in cases on the right to food itself, the Court employs dignity along with the idea of self-reliance to indicate that the state's role was to provide conditions where individuals could feed themselves. The Court contrasts the right with notions of 'command economics of big government' and the unsuitability of the state in being a 'super-entrepreneur'.[29] Such ideas that the Court finds unfavourable could otherwise well justify extensive state obligations to provide for a socially, culturally, and intellectually meaningful life, which the Court had earlier held to be entailed by the right to life with dignity.

There are numerous other cases where dignity has been employed as a source right.[30] The number and variety of cases do indicate that the Court favours an expansive meaning of dignity. However, one implication of such interpretation is that it takes focus away from other values that might better justify specific rights. Another undesirable development has been that the content of dignity gets short-changed to an extent that belies commonly held intuitions about human dignity. Both these trends are noticeable in the right to education cases.

The right to education was inserted as a fundamental right under Article 21 A in 2002 by the 86th Amendment to the Constitution of India. The amendment was preceded by a judicial decision that had already pronounced the right to be a fundamental right by reading the Right to Life along with the Directive Principles of State Policy. Education was pronounced to be essential for a dignified life by the Court:

> The dignity of man is inviolable. It is the duty of the State to respect and protect the same. It is primarily the education which brings forth the dignity of a man .... An

---

[28] AIR 2005 SC 3136.
[29] *Kapila Hingorani v. State of Bihar*, 6 SCC 1, para. 50 (2003).
[30] *State of M.P. v. Kedia Leather and Liquor Ltd.*, 7 SCC 389 (2003); *Virender Gaur v. State of Haryana*, 2 SCC 577 (1995); *Subramanian Swamy v. Union of India*, 13 SCC 356 (2015); *Prem Shankar Shukla v. Delhi Admn*, 3 SCC 526 (1980); *Devidas Ramachandra Tuljapur v. State of Maharashtra*, 6 SCC 1 (2015); *Vikram Deo Singh Tomar v. State of Bihar*, Supp. SCC 734 (1988).

individual cannot be assured of human dignity unless his personality is developed and the only way to do that is to educate him.[31]

Watchers of the Court would vouch for the staple nature of the language employed by the Court. A charitable reading of the passage might suggest that the Court only intends to say that a life with dignity requires that every individual must have an equal opportunity to be educated, and that burden falls on the state. However, it is difficult to ignore that the Court does not invoke equality but rather inviolability of dignity. It simultaneously indicates dignity to be a latent value that is capable of being 'brought forth' and 'developed' through education. It is difficult to ignore the counter-intuitive implications that the words chosen by the Court have for the content of dignity. The Court seems to indicate that dignity is assured only if an individual is educated and if that dignity is increasingly realized through education. Such a view can perhaps be supported on a novel interpretation of performance-based dignity, where dignity is a virtue realized through human actions, as opposed to existing just by virtue of being human.[32] On what view of a life with dignity does such an interpretation become plausible, since the Court holds that the right to education flows from the right to life with dignity?[33]

My ascribing a plausible performance-based view to the decision is not as far-fetched as it might seem, as in the same case the Court notes that 'the Fundamental Rights . . . cannot be appreciated and fully enjoyed unless a citizen is educated and is conscious of his individualistic dignity'.[34] Observations of this nature surely indicate that the Court views dignity as a virtue to be realized. As much as this might seem absurd according to the enlightenment-based Kantian view of dignity, it is not unknown to other views on the nature of virtues. In that sense, the Court's observations do bring in alternative ways of looking at dignity in Indian constitutional jurisprudence, even though this stands in tension with the Court's view in other cases, discussed in the following section, where it unambiguously embraces the Kantian view.

Another question that arises in the right to education case is regarding the relationship between education and dignity. The Court does not explain why dignity is the best-candidate justification in relating education to the right to life. An intrinsic relationship between the two can be justified by other values that might provide more specificity to the relationship. Arguably obligations to provide education can be justified by the constitutional mandate to achieve social and economic justice, to ensure equality of opportunity, or to facilitate the liberty of thought and expression. These values find mention not only in the Preamble and Directive Principles but also in the Fundamental Rights, where freedom of thought and expression as well as equality find express mention. Significantly, there is also

[31] *Mohini Jain v. State of Karnataka*, 3 SCC 666, para. 8 (1992).
[32] See Sungmoon Kim's Chapter 10 in this volume, on Confucian tradition.
[33] *Mohini Jain* (n 31), para. 12.
[34] *Mohini Jain* (n 31), para. 13.

more legal material (e.g. on equality of opportunity, freedom of speech and expression, and socio-economic rights) that can be employed to articulate the relationship between the right to life and education. By recourse to dignity, to the exclusion of other values, perhaps an opportunity was lost to anchor socio-economic rights such as education to multiple constitutional values in a deeper manner.

The cases discussed in this section surely accorded dignity a high status, but they did so in an unanchored manner. In employing dignity in its reasoning, the Court rarely referred to literature on dignity as reasons for its conclusions. Even the Constituent Assembly Debates were not invoked to support the significant weight accorded to dignity. In this sense, its reasoning was not anchored to sources about the content of dignity or its role. The Court employed dignity with confidence, without anticipating any objections that might arise to its application. This is perhaps explained by the wide powers the Court assumed during the development of its Public Interest Litigation (PIL) jurisdiction, where it assumed wide powers to relax rules of standing in fundamental rights cases. Socio-economic rights cases discussed in this section were landmark decisions in the exercise of the Court's PIL jurisdiction. The Court's PIL jurisprudence has, however, drawn severe criticism in terms of excessive exercise of judicial power and in being populist.[35] In its application of dignity, at least, the first line of criticism would be vindicated in that there has been an unanchored exercise of wide judicial powers.

4 UNINHIBITED REASONING: DIGNITY AS THE FOUNDATION OF FUNDAMENTAL RIGHTS

A set of landmark decisions in 2017 and 2018 reaffirmed the Court's view that the role of dignity in constitutional adjudication was not limited to the right to life. Dignity captured something that related to all the Fundamental Rights, whether as a value that was the 'core' of all Fundamental Rights or one that tied all Fundamental Rights together. There was also a marked shift in the manner that dignity was employed in judicial reasoning. Unlike in the cases discussed in Section 3, the Court expressly and extensively relied on academic literature on dignity. The most noted of these decisions was the Court's decision on the right to privacy in *KS Puttaswamy v. Union of India* (hereafter 'the privacy decision').[36] A nine-judge bench of the Court declared the existence of a fundamental right to privacy by overruling previous decisions. The decision of the nine-judge bench arose out of a reference made to it by a five-judge bench of the Court that was hearing challenges against the AADHAAR (Targeted Delivery of Financial and Other Subsidies, Benefits and Services Act, 2016). The Act promised targeted delivery of governmental services

---

[35] See Anuj Bhuwania, chap. 4 in *Courting the People: Public Interest Emergency in Post-Emergency India* (Cambridge: Cambridge University Press, 2016), (for a contemporary critical appraisal of public interest litigation in India).
[36] *KS Puttaswamy v. Union of India*, 10 SCC 1 (2017).

through a mandatory unique identity number assigned to each citizen based on personal data including biometric information. Violation of the right to privacy was one of the chief challenges to the Act. The nine-judge bench answered the reference by declaring that the right to life and personal liberty included a fundamental right to privacy.

In doing so, the Court articulated a fundamental relationship between dignity and privacy, mediated through the ideas of liberty, personhood, and autonomy.[37] This view was first articulated in the Indian context by the Delhi High Court in the Naz Foundation decision.[38] The High Court grounded its view of the right to privacy in the concept of personhood rooted in personal autonomy, which in turn was explained in terms of human dignity.[39] The High Court, however, did not elucidate the content of dignity and how it was related to autonomy, personhood, and privacy. In the privacy decision, the Court filled this gap by devoting an entire section to the concept of dignity to articulate its relationship with liberty and individual autonomy. In doing so, it prizes dignity over other values when it holds that 'dignity is the core which unites the Fundamental Rights because the Fundamental Rights seek to achieve for each individual the dignity of existence'.[40] Privacy is accorded an even higher status as it is held to be 'the constitutional core of human dignity'.[41] In fact, the Court holds:

> Dignity cannot exist without privacy. Both reside within the inalienable values of life, liberty and freedom which the Constitution has recognized. ... (Privacy) ... straddles across the spectrum of Fundamental Right and protects for the individual a zone of choice and self-determination.[42]

These statements mystify the relationship between dignity and privacy. To state that privacy is the core of dignity is an intriguing proposition. Surely, dignity can perhaps exist even without privacy as undignified acts can be of a public nature. For example, caste- and gender-based unfair discrimination is often aimed at public humiliation, and opposition to them is also public in nature.[43] Recent objections to Dalit (lower caste) grooms riding horses is a case in point. These objections are attempts at

---

[37] Mariyam Kamil, 'Puttaswamy: Jury Still out on Some Privacy Concerns?', *Indian Law Review*, no. 1 (2017): 190, 193–4.
[38] *Naz Foundationv v. NCT of Delhi*, 160 Delhi Law Times 277 (2009).
[39] Pritam Baruah, 'Logic and Coherence in Naz Foundation: The Arguments of Non-Discrimination, Privacy and Dignity', *National University of Juridical Sciences Law Review*, no. 3 (2009): 505–24.
[40] Chandrachud J, in KS Puttaswamy (n 36) Para. 107 (for the view that the Court relates privacy to liberty, dignity, and autonomy).
[41] Chandrachud J, in KS Puttaswamy, Para. 3(E) [Conclusion]. Such a link between dignity and privacy was proposed in some of the earliest scholarly debates on privacy. See Edward J. Bloustein, 'Privacy as an Aspect of Human Dignity: An Answer to Dean Prosser', *New York University Law Review* 39 (1964): 962.
[42] Chandrachud J, in KS Puttaswamy Para. 169.
[43] Pritam Baruah and Zaid Deva, 'Justifying Privacy: The Indian Court's Comparative Analysis', in *The Indian Yearbook of Comparative Law 2018* (Singapore: Springer, 2019).

humiliating members of the Dalit community by publicly denying their equality as human beings.[44] The attempted humiliation and its contestation are public in nature and involve questions of dignity without raising privacy issues. It might therefore be the case that the Court's statement means that every violation of privacy led to subjecting an individual to indignity, rather than the other way around.

The relationship between dignity and privacy becomes further complicated when the Court states that 'the right to privacy is an element of human dignity' and that 'the sanctity of privacy lies in its functional relationship with dignity'.[45] If one were to read this statement along with the previous ones quoted earlier, privacy appears to be the core element of human dignity, and the relationship between the core of dignity and its other elements is a functional one where 'privacy ensures that a human being can lead a life of dignity by securing the inner recesses of the human personality from unwanted intrusion'.[46] What, however, begs examination is precisely what these 'inner recesses' are and why they are related to dignity.

One way of understanding the relationship is perhaps that privacy enables a person to lead a dignified life by preventing certain indignities brought about by unwanted intrusions.[47] Dignity is the core value that deserves protection, and privacy is instrumental in doing so. Given the possibility of dignity being violated in ways that do not involve questions of privacy, privacy in those cases cannot share a functional relationship with dignity, and neither can it therefore be the core of dignity, conceptually, without further explanation of the content of both concepts.

4.1 Individualistic and Communitarian Dignity

It might be alleged that expecting such exacting explanations from courts is neither pragmatic nor desirable. However, in the Indian experience with dignity in the right-to-privacy case, lack of more specific reasons has been counterproductive. Soon after the privacy decision, the Court pronounced its decision in the challenges to the AADHAAR Act that had made the reference about the right to privacy. In the AADHAAR case, a five-judge bench of the Court upheld the validity of most of the provisions of the Act.[48] Justice Sikri authored the majority opinion, which relied extensively on dignity again but proposed a novel proposition that sits oddly with the privacy decision.

The privacy decision relied on dignity and individual autonomy to articulate privacy as a private inviolable zone for the individual immunized from interferences by the state and society. This individual-centric view was echoed in several other

---

[44] 'Upper Caste Men Attack Dalit Groom for Riding Horse in Rajasthan," *The Wire*, 30 April 2018, https://thewire.in/caste/upper-caste-men-attack-dalit-groom-for-riding-horse-in-rajasthan.
[45] Chandrachud J, in KS Puttaswamy (n 36) Para. 113.
[46] Chandrachud J, in KS Puttaswamy Para. 113.
[47] Baruah and Deva, 'Justifying Privacy'.
[48] *KS Puttaswamy v. Union of India*, Writ Petition (Civil) No. 494 of 2012 (2020). Hereafter 'KS Puttaswamy (5-judge)'.

decisions including the concurring opinions by Justice Sikri in cases recognizing the rights of transgender persons and legalizing passive euthanasia.[49] In these decisions, Justice Sikri had articulated the three elements of the fundamental right to dignity as personal autonomy, self-expression, and the right to determine.[50] In the AADHAAR decision, however, Justice Sikri's opinion added a further element that militates against this very view. He held that there was a communitarian aspect to dignity: 'Dignity as a community value ... emphasizes the role of the state and community in establishing collective goals and restrictions on individual freedoms and rights on behalf of a certain idea of the good life.'[51] The fundamental elements of dignity were now therefore 'intrinsic value, autonomy and community value'.[52] Justice Sikri added that individualistic and communitarian values of dignity were to be balanced by the test of proportionality.

The decision in the AADHAAR case adds a novel element to the understanding of dignity in Indian constitutional law. Earlier decisions on dignity as a source of rights clearly spoke of dignity as a value that justified individual rights. Similarly, a string of decisions in 2018 (discussed in the following section) also speak of individual dignity as the foundation of Fundamental Rights as well as the very basis of the Constitution itself. The idea of community dignity therefore stands out as tangential in Indian constitutional law.

4.2 Dignity, Anti-Exclusion, and the Transformative Project

In 2018, the Court made extensive use of dignity as a foundational constitutional value in cases on decriminalization of homosexuality, legalization of passive euthanasia, and gender-based discrimination. These cases continued in the same vein as the right to privacy decision in terms of identifying equality, liberty, and dignity as building the 'edifice of the constitution'.[53]

In *Navtej Singh Johar*, the Court, in a decision running over 300 pages, read down section 377 of the Indian Penal Code to decriminalize consensual sexual acts between adults of the same gender.[54] It held that, for LGBT communities, sexual orientation was 'intrinsic to their dignity, inseparable from their autonomy and at the heart of their privacy'.[55] Chief Justice Deepak Misra's opinion stated that gender identity was inalienable, and this was guaranteed by the right to life and liberty with dignity.[56] The Court not only held dignity to be one of the founding promises of the

---

[49] *Common Cause* v. *Union of India*, 5 SCC 1 (Supreme Court of India 2018); *National Legal Services Authority* v. *Union of India*, 5 SCC 438 (Supreme Court of India 2014).
[50] Sikri J in *National Legal Services Authority* v. *Union of India* (n 49) para. 206.
[51] Sikri J in *KS Puttaswamy* v. *Union of India*, Writ Petition (Civil) No. 494 of 2012, para. 116 (2020).
[52] Sikri J in KS Puttaswamy (n 51) para. 116.
[53] *Navtej Singh Johar and Ors* v. *Union of India*, 10 SCC 1, para. 416 (2018).
[54] *Navtej Singh Johar and Ors* (n 53) para. 416.
[55] Chandrachud J, in *Navtej Singh Johar and Ors* (n 53), para. 610.
[56] *Navtej Singh Johar and Ors* (n 53), para. 10.

Constitution but also related it to the importance of human dignity in the UDHR, implying that the concept of dignity had a similar foundational role in the Indian Constitution.[57] Across its opinions, the Court lay emphasis on how dignity was an anathema to social exclusion of identities including sexual orientation.

In the same year, in *Common Cause* v. *Union of India*, the Court legalized passive euthanasia in cases of terminally ill persons. Dignity figured prominently in the decision of the Court, sometimes as a constitutional value and sometimes in mysterious metaphors:

> Human dignity is beyond definition ... To some, it may seem to be in the world of abstraction and some may even perversely treat it as an attribute of egotism or accentuated eccentricity.... Dignity ... is a combination of thought and feeling ... and, as stated earlier, it deserves respect even when the person is dead and described as a 'body'.[58]

Notwithstanding the metaphors, the Court was consistent about dignity being a fundamental value that was a part of the right to life and that recognized all human rights that a person enjoyed.

This line of thinking about dignity was again affirmed in the temple-entry decision.[59] The decision stands out in its application of dignity as it employs the concept to deny claims based on the right to freedom of religion. In this case the Court was faced with the constitutionality of a practice that prohibited menstruating women from entering a Hindu temple. It held that the practice was not protected by the right to religion as it violated the dignity and equality of women. Individual dignity was given primacy over social customs and the Court held that 'the rights guaranteed under Part III of the Constitution have the common thread of individual dignity running through them'.[60] Customs and usages could not escape constitutional scrutiny, as that would 'deny the constitutional vision of ensuring the primacy of the individual'.[61] In a particularly metaphorical phrase, the Court states that 'the primacy of individual dignity is the wind in the sails of the boat chartered on the constitutional course of a just and egalitarian social order'.[62] Given the emphasis on individual dignity, the decision in this case is difficult to square with the decision in the AADHAAR decision where community dignity was a basis for curtailing individual rights. In fact, in the temple-entry decision, the Court unequivocally stated that, where there was a conflict between community beliefs such as religious ones and individual dignity, the latter has preference as the purpose of the Constitution 'is

---

[57] Navtej Singh Johar and Ors (n 53), para. 139.
[58] Dipak Misra (CJI) in *Common Cause* v. *Union of India*, 5 SCC 1, para. 156 (2018).
[59] *Indian Young Lawyers Association and Others* v. *State of Kerala & Ors* Writ Petition (Civil) No. 373 of 2006 (2018).
[60] Indian Young Lawyers Association (n 59), para. 95.
[61] Indian Young Lawyers Association (n 59), para. 101.
[62] Indian Young Lawyers Association (n 59), para. 102.

to ensure a wider acceptance of human dignity and liberty as the ultimate founding faith of the fundamental text of our governance'.[63]

These lines of cases, culminating in the temple-entry case in 2018, unequivocally prioritize dignity as a constitutional value, despite holding that dignity, liberty, and equality 'constitute the trinity which defines the faith of the Constitution'.[64] For instance in the same case the Court holds:

> The founding faith upon which the Constitution is based is the belief that it is in the dignity of each individual that the pursuit of happiness is founded. Individual dignity can be achieved only in a regime which recognizes liberty as inhering in each individual as a natural right.[65]

Dignity is held to be the 'unwavering promise of the Fundamental Rights'[66] that enables the exercise of liberty.[67]

The extensive use of dignity in these decisions has also sharpened its application in constitutional adjudication. Apart from acting as a justification, it has led the Court to articulate principles that have a practical edge. In *Navtej Singh Johar* and the temple-entry case, the Court has employed dignity to articulate an 'anti-exclusion principle' that makes any form of social exclusion of identities constitutionally suspect.[68]

The Court also takes dignity to be central to the transformative project of the Indian Constitution: 'The fundamental freedoms which Part III confers are central to the constitutional purpose of overseeing a transformation of a society based on dignity, liberty and equality.'[69] This implies that dignity will be invoked in Fundamental Rights cases that challenge existing social exclusions and stereotypes and that involve appeals to liberty and equality.

What, however, brings all this into question is that the temple-entry decision is currently under review by a nine-judge bench of the Court. The decision is likely to have implications for how dignity is understood. The precise reason for review is that the Court will re-examine whether collective ideals of the good life in the form of religious beliefs are defeated by interests based on human dignity, liberty, and equality. Which side the Court leans will determine the status of dignity in Indian constitutional law, a question that has hitherto gone unnoticed.

5 THE STATUS OF DIGNITY: ABSOLUTE OR LIMITED

In articulating the relationship between dignity, equality, and liberty, the Court, especially in the privacy case and the cases in 2018, employed terms such as

---

[63] Indian Young Lawyers Association (n 59), para. 12.
[64] Indian Young Lawyers Association (n 59), para. 49.
[65] Indian Young Lawyers Association (n 59), para. 12.
[66] Indian Young Lawyers Association (n 59), para. 15.
[67] Indian Young Lawyers Association (n 59), para. 15.
[68] Indian Young Lawyers Association (n 59), para. 8.
[69] Indian Young Lawyers Association (n 59), para. 11.

'inalienable', 'the core of Fundamental Rights', 'natural rights', and the 'founding faith of the Constitution' to describe the nature of dignity. This suggests that dignity is understood as an absolute value. In contrast, the Court's consistent view has also been that dignity is a part of the right to life and personal liberty under Article 21. This poses a textual dilemma. If dignity is a part of the right to life, then the restrictions on the right would apply to dignity. At least in *Francis Coralie Mullin*,[70] the Court unequivocally stated that any deprivation of human dignity would constitute a violation of the right to life and that such deprivation would have to be in accordance with reasonable, fair, and just procedure established by law. Dignity in Article 21 was therefore not absolute. It could be limited by the due process of law, as several landmark decisions held that the words 'procedure established by law' in Article 21 mean 'due process of law'. Due process of law meant that the law must be just, fair, and reasonable. The limitable nature of dignity was also implied when the Court stated that 'the magnitude and content of the right [to life with human dignity] depends on the extent of economic development of the country'[71] but must include the right to basic necessities and 'the right to carry on such functions and activities as constitute the bare minimum expression of the human self'.[72] The Court also stated that the right to live with human dignity is a part of personal liberty.[73]

In the cases after *Francis Coralie Mullin*, both views in a sense have been abandoned. Dignity is no longer understood as limited to questions of personal liberty. It has been extensively employed in socio-economic rights cases and in cases of non-discrimination that involve questions of socio-economic justice and equality. Dignity is also no longer seen as a specific right to a dignified life within the confines of Article 21. As the discussion in Section 4 demonstrates, dignity is employed both as a part of Article 21 as well as a value that unites all Fundamental Rights and articulates the 'founding faith' of the Constitution.

Despite the clarity about the foundational role of dignity, the dilemma posed by the *Mullin* case does not disappear. In fact the idea of a right to life with dignity as a limited right finds support in the decision of the Court upholding the constitutionality of the death penalty.[74] In that case, the Court recognized the limited nature of the right to life under Article 21, and dignity was conspicuously absent from the reasoning of the Court. Recognizing dignity simultaneously as a limited right under Article 21 and as an absolute value that justifies the entire Constitution will violate the principle of non-contradiction, unless Article 21 is read as an absolute right or dignity is clearly understood to have two constitutional locations with different

---

[70] *Francis Coralie Mullin v. Administrator, Union Territory of Delhi*, 1 SCC 608 (1981).
[71] *Francis Coralie Mullin* (n 70), para. 8.
[72] *Francis Coralie Mullin* (n 70), para. 8.
[73] *Francis Coralie Mullin* (n 70), para. 11.
[74] Anup Surendranath, 'Life and Personal Liberty' (n 21), p. 764 (for a discussion of death penalty cases in India).

status: the right being limited by due process of law; and the value being absolute in it being the very foundation of the Constitution. In terms of how the law has developed after *Mullin*, dignity has mostly figured as an absolute value, even though sometimes articulated as a right.

For example, in *M. Nagaraj v. Union of India*,[75] the Court held that dignity was akin to principles such as reasonableness, fairness, and social justice that inform and connect various Fundamental Rights, particularly Articles 14, 19, and 21, which were beyond the reach of the state. Similarly, in *Mehmood Nayyar Azam v. State of Chhattisgarh*[76] it was held that the right to life with dignity includes within itself the right against torture, especially by public authorities, and, though other Fundamental Rights could be restricted, this right could never be stripped away. In *In Re Inhuman Conditions In 1382 Prisons*,[77] the Court held that prisoners cannot be denied their Fundamental Rights under Art. 21 despite being detained in prison. Though there may be certain restrictions on one's movement and behaviour, their basic human dignity guaranteed under Art. 21 could not be taken away.

These cases concerning the rights of persons in police custody unambiguously hold dignity to be a value that is absolute. Perhaps this is so given the severity of the grievances brought before courts, which highlight the importance of the protection of citizens from the abuse of the coercive powers of the state. In protecting basic civil and political rights of individuals in such cases, the Court relies on the content of dignity as the intrinsic worth of all individuals by an appeal to inalienable natural rights that form the basis of rights guaranteed by the Constitution. Interestingly, a similar trend is noticed in cases that involve egregious violations of socio-economic rights not only by the state but also by other individuals.

In *People's Union for Democratic Rights v. Union of India*,[78] the Court was seized with the matter of multiple violations of labour laws that occurred during the Asian Games. The Court held that certain rights such as those protected by Art. 17, 23, and 24 protect the individual against the world in general and essentially help in protecting the individual's right to life with human dignity.[79] Human dignity, according to the Court, could not be violated under any form, even under the garb of a voluntarily entered contract.

These cases indicate that, in the case of the violation of both civil-political and socio-economic rights, it is the concept of dignity as the intrinsic worth of the individual that has found favour with the Court. The intrinsic worth of the

---

[75] *M. Nagaraj & Others v. Union of India & Others*, 8 SCC 212 (2006).
[76] *Mehmood Nayyar Azam v. State of Chhattisgarh*, 8 SCC 1 (2012).
[77] *In Re Inhuman Conditions in 1382 Prisons*, 3 SCC 700 (2016).
[78] *People's Union for Democratic Rights v. Union of India*, 3 SCC 235 (1982).
[79] Article 17 abolishes the practice of 'untouchability' that was a part of the caste system whereby certain castes were treated as untouchable, and proximity and bodily contact with them was considered impure. Article 23 deals with prohibition of traffic in human beings and forced labour. Article 24 prohibits employment of children in factories and other hazardous activities.

individual has also been held to be absolute and non-derogable in nature, as it cannot be violated under any condition.

6 CONCLUSION

The extensive application of dignity by the Court throws up critical issues about its content, status, and role in constitutional adjudication. Close attention to content was absent in the numerous decisions prior to 2017. The Court employed dignity in an unanchored manner, without either citing literature on dignity or carefully working out its application to facts. Dignity was almost axiomatic for any discussion on the right to life. Since 2017, the Court has referred to dignity in an uninhibited manner, citing a wide range of academic literature on dignity that has emerged in law and philosophy. In the decisions on the right to privacy, the AADHAAR Act, and the temple-entry case, the Court has devoted entire sections to reviewing literature on dignity. Philosophers including Immanuel Kant, Ronald Dworkin, Jeremy Waldron, and Michael Rosen figure in the Court's literature review, in addition to the voluminous legal scholarship on dignity that has emerged in the past two decades. How that literature has been employed, however, is controversial, especially because of the tension between individual and community dignity that was pointed out in Section 4. The trend of uninhibited application of dignity also raises questions of method. How does the Court choose which philosophical and academic materials to invoke? Does the Court sufficiently analyse the views it invokes in a structured manner (e.g. by addressing objections to them)? Can the Court be accused of cherry-picking literature that suits predetermined conclusions?

These questions regarding method legitimately arise as the Court settles on views without enough attention to opposing views. For example, in Justice Sikri's opinions in the passive euthanasia and AADAHR cases, Ronald Dworkin's views are easily accepted, and so is the view that dignity has a communitarian aspect. In political and moral philosophy, the two views would be considered incompatible unless there has been a resolution of the perennial debate between individualism and communitarianism. In the AADHAAR case, the Court employs both traditions in a single breath and controversially states that the doctrine of proportionality must be employed to adjudicate between these two philosophical views.

In the right to privacy, decriminalization of homosexuality, and temple-entry cases, the Court states that dignity, liberty, and equality are intrinsically connected. Its articulation of this trinity of values has surely favoured individual rights over claims by the community and the state. However, its assertion of the connectedness of the three values reveals little about the individual content of dignity. What comes forth is that the three values are connected, not how so. For instance, the Court does not articulate the Kantian object formula to demonstrate how in any of these cases individuals are treated as mere means to an end; nor does it identify how unequal treatment in terms of intrinsic worth is distinct from other unequal treatment, if there is such a distinction. It is arguable that the Court's view of dignity militates precisely against any such distinction. On the Court's view, every violation of liberty, equality, or dignity perhaps involves all three. This view runs a risk of rendering the three values incomprehensible in that their distinct contribution to questions of rights is unascertainable. Indeed, constitutional scholars have pointed out how indiscriminate recourse to dignity might result in losing grip over it.[80]

This risk of losing grip over dignity is real in India due to the inconsistencies in judicial reasoning about dignity pointed out in this chapter. It is therefore worth asking why such inconsistencies have arisen in the first place. One set of answers emerges from institutional reasons. Arguably, heavy workload reduces the time available for individual decisions that would otherwise have allowed for a careful development of dignity doctrine. Another set of answers stemming from the nature of values is already popular: that values are necessarily vague in being essentially contested, interpretive, or evaluative concepts, and thus determinacy of content is impossible. Despite being popular, this view does not go deep enough to provide a compelling argument for why values are necessarily vague.[81] Indeed, there are accounts that articulate the content of values including dignity, just as there are others that articulate the content of justice or autonomy.[82] In any event, characterizing values as necessarily vague does not aid judges in employing them in reasoning with values. Though it may be debated whether the vagueness of values like dignity is beneficial for judicial reasoning, at least in the Indian context, lack of determinate content has led to problematic inconsistencies about what decisions dignity requires.

A final set of answers that may explain the inconsistencies pointed out in this chapter arise from expertise-based concerns. Judges in India can claim expertise over legal knowledge as they are appointed based on their training and experience in law. The procedure for appointment of judges to the higher judiciary in India is exclusively through elevating counsel before high courts and the Supreme Court and through promotion of judges from the lower judiciary. Their claim to expertise over law is thus legitimate in that the law as a discipline has dense and rich legal materials that justifiably constitute a distinct body of knowledge over which cognitive expertise may be claimed. When adjudication is faced with extralegal areas of knowledge, courts either consult authoritative texts in those disciplines or constitute expert committees. When it comes to constitutional values, however, the question of

---

[80] Horst Drier, 'Human Dignity in German Law', in *The Cambridge Handbook of Human Dignity*, edited by Marcus Düwell, Jens Braarvig, Roger Brownsword, Dietmar Mieth (Cambridge: Cambridge University Press 2014), 375.

[81] For criticisms of ascribing a generally vague character to values, see Pritam Baruah, 'Are There Any Interpretative Concepts', in *Dignity in the Legal and Political Philosophy of Ronald Dworkin*, edited by S. Khurshid, L. Malik and V. Rodriguez-Blanco (Oxford: Oxford University Press 2018), pp. 130–60; Pritam Baruah, 'Human Dignity in Adjudication: The Limits of Placeholding and Essential Contestability Accounts', *Canadian Journal of Law and Philosophy*, no. 27 (2014): 329.

[82] For example, John Rawls on Justice, Joseph Raz on autonomy or Immanuel Kant on human dignity.

expertise does not arise in the absence of a critical mass of legal materials that may ground a claim to expertise.

In the case of dignity, there is limited legal material that lawyers can claim cognitive expertise over. Literature on dignity is found in disciplines outside law, such as philosophy, and bioethics. Even if some legal philosophers argue that law is the proper starting point for discussions on dignity, such practice-based views need strong justification given the historically significant philosophical materials on dignity.[83] In this sense, recent decisions in dignity are a welcome start to acknowledging literature in other disciplines. However, the future challenge remains in providing structure in invoking such materials in judicial decision-making. At the least, this involves lawyer-turned judges being acquainted with literature on constitutional values such as dignity, and further thinking on how judicial reasoning should function in non-autonomous legal contexts (i.e. in contexts where legal materials do not support a claim to legal expertise).

---

[83] Jeremy Waldron, 'Dignity and Rank', *European Journal of Sociology* 48, no. 2 (2007), doi:10.1017/s0003975607000343.

2

The Development of Individual Dignity in Japan

Overcoming Constraints in Law, Family, and Society

Keigo Obayashi[*]

1 INTRODUCTION

After World War II, "human dignity" came to be seen as a fundamental value that underlies constitutional democracy. As Rex Glensy said: "Human dignity is a concept that has captured the attention of philosophers, scholars, and jurists alike."[1] George Fletcher also pointed out that "no one would question whether the protection of human dignity was a primary task of contemporary legal culture, especially in Europe and North America."[2] However, the concept of "human dignity" varies significantly by country.[3] Some constitutions expressly include "human dignity" in their texts, such as in Germany,[4] while other constitutions use the terms like "individual dignity," such as in Japan.[5] The Japanese Constitution intends to develop individualism, which requires the government to respect all citizens as individuals by providing them with individual dignity. Professor Ashibe, a leading scholar in Japanese constitutional law, asserted that individualism is derived from the principle of human dignity.[6]

According to the Supreme Court Justice Jiro Tanaka, individual dignity is a framework of the Japanese Constitution. He affirmed:

> The reason why all the constitutions of the modernized nations demand respect of individuals and guarantee equality under law is to break down the authority and

---

[*] I give special thanks to Mark Nevitt for his helpful review.
[1] Rex D. Glensy, "The Right to Dignity," *Columbia Human Rights Law Review* 43 (2011): 65.
[2] G. P. Fletcher, "Human Dignity as a Constitutional Value," *University of Western Ontario Law Review* 22, no. 2 (1984): 171.
[3] Neomi Rao, "Three Concepts of Dignity in Constitutional Law," *Notre Dame Law Review* 86 (2011): 183, 269. Rao points out that dignity is a "slippery concept" and suggests that there are actually three kinds of dignity: "the dignity of the individual associated with autonomy and negative freedom; the positive dignity of maintaining a particular type of life; and the dignity of recognition of individual and group differences."
[4] German Basic Law states that "human dignity shall be inviolable." See Grundgesetz für die Bundesrepublik Deutschland [Grundgesetz] [GG] [Basic Law], May 23, 1949, BGBl. I at Art. 1 (Ger.).
[5] Article 13 stipulates that a person "shall be respected as [an] individual," and Article 24 refers to "individual dignity"; see Articles 13 and 24 of the Constitution of Japan in 1946.
[6] Nobuyoshi Ashibe, *Constitutional Law*, 7th ed. (Tokyo: Iwanami Shoten, 2019), 82.

subordination relationship under feudalism, to recover human dignity and equality, and to establish a peaceful society and nation through cooperation of every individual in an equal position for the realization of individual dignity. The spirit of the Japanese Constitution should be deemed to rest upon this point.[7]

That is, individual dignity is the core of the Constitution. Indeed, the Supreme Court of Japan has enforced individual dignity, inter alia, by protecting privacy. Although systematic constraints on individual dignity remain in the family system, the Supreme Court has induced changes incrementally.

This article introduces the development of individual dignity in constitutional cases in Japan. First, I examine the original meaning of individual dignity through the enactment process of the Constitution. Next, I clarify the relationship between society and individual dignity. Then I scrutinize two factors of individual dignity in light of the hybrid approach in academic discussion. Finally, I shed light on individual dignity in Japan by reviewing constitutional case law, with a focus on recent developments.

2 THE DAWN OF INDIVIDUAL DIGNITY IN JAPAN

The Japanese Constitution provides for *individual dignity* rather than *human dignity*. This is due to a variety of reasons that predate WWII and Japan's enactment of its Constitution.

2.1 *The Original Meaning of Individual Dignity*

2.1.1 Individuality: Lost in the Meiji Era

The emperor's position was a key feature of government system in the Meiji Constitution.[8] In Japanese myth, emperors were regarded as descendants of gods, the creators of Japan. This myth became apparent around the seventh and eighth centuries and became prevalent in Japanese society. As a result, emperors reigned as living gods. The Meiji Constitution prescribed that Japan be governed by the emperor forever and that the emperors be deemed a sacred sovereign.[9]

Under the Meiji Constitution, all people owed their obedience to the emperor.[10] The people shall serve the emperor as one national family. In this unique

---

[7] Parricide penalty-enhancement case, 27 Keishu 265, at 277 (Sup. Ct. G.B. April 4, 1973) (Tanaka, J., concurring in the judgement) (Sonzokusatsu case).
[8] The formal name of the "Meiji Constitution" is "the Constitution of the Empire of Japan, 1889."
[9] The relative provisions are: "The Empire of Japan shall be reigned over and governed by a line of Emperors unbroken for ages eternal" (Art. 1), "The Emperor is sacred and inviolable" (Art. 3); and "The Emperor is the head of the Empire, combining in Himself the rights of sovereignty, and exercises them, according to the provisions of the present Constitution." This translation relies on Project Gutenberg's "The Constitution of the Empire of Japan, 1889."
[10] Chapter II of the Constitution lays forth the "Rights and Duties of Subjects."

government system, known as *Kokutai*, each person was denied individuality because *Kokutai* required one national family under the emperor in order to maintain Japan's national integrity.[11] Each person had to give up his or her own individual personality for the whole society. This promoted a group-oriented society in Japan. The *Iye* system that granted the head of the household control of the family also supports *Kokutai* in the sense of people being a unified family group. It was seen as unnecessary for a person to have his or her own personality or even privacy at home.

2.1.2 The Liberation of the Individual and the Enactment Process of the Current Constitution

During the occupation following the end of WWII, the Supreme Commander for the Allied Powers (General Headquarters: GHQ) from the United States believed that Japan needed a constitutional amendment to allow for individual rights and a democratic government. General Douglas MacArthur, head of the GHQ, instructed the Japanese government to submit proposals for a constitutional amendment. However, the proposal mirrored the content of the Meiji Constitution. MacArthur refused it and suggested that a draft be developed by the GHQ, which sought a free and democratic society by changing sovereignty from the emperor to the people and emancipating them from traditionally binding social systems.

Individual freedom is crucial to a free and democratic society. The GHQ draft stated that "the feudal system of Japan shall cease. All Japanese, by virtue of their humanity, shall be respected as individuals."[12] The GHQ wanted to end the landlord system and the traditional family structure. However, the Japanese government deleted the reference to the feudal system because Japan, in fact, lacked a feudal system.[13] Although the GHQ opposed the removal because the existent landlord–tenant system was functionally similar to a feudal system, this aspect remained deleted. As for the outcome of the current version, in the draft of March 6 the wording was changed to "All of the people shall be respected as individuals."[14]

The enactment process revealed the GHQ's original intention to establish individualism by abolishing the feudal system. Although the text regarding the feudal system was removed, the core concept, individualism, was left in the text. The issue

---

[11] Carl F. Goodman, "Contemplated Amendments to Japan's 1947 Constitution: A Return to *Iye*, *Kokutai* and the Meiji State," *Pacific Rim Law and Policy Journal* 26 (2017): 17, 32.

[12] "The Article 12 of the GHQ Draft, Alfred Hussey Papers; Constitution File No. 1, Doc. No. 12," in *Constitution of Japan*, 12 February 1946 (National Diet Library): 4.

[13] "Irie Toshio Doc. No. 15 (in the Draft for the Amendment of the Constitution of Japan published on March 6th), the details of the discussion in the GHQ on March 4th, and 5th" (National Diet Library): 6–7.

[14] "Article 12 of the Draft for the Amendment of the Constitution of Japan, Alfred Hussey Papers; Constitution File No. 1, Doc. No. 26," in *Constitution of Japan*, 12 February 1946 (National Diet Library): 3.

of emancipation from socially binding constraints, particularly the family system grounded in a group-oriented society, was shifted to Article 24 of the current Constitution, which provides for equality of both sexes and the right to marriage. Article 24 also concerns individual dignity. The GHQ draft stipulated:

> The family is the basis of human society and its traditions for good or evil permeate the nation. Marriage shall rest upon the indisputable legal and social equality of both sexes, founded upon mutual consent instead of parental coercion, and maintained through cooperation instead of male domination. Laws contrary to these principles shall be abolished, and replaced by others viewing choice of spouse, property rights, inheritance, choice of domicile, divorce and other matters pertaining to marriage and the family from standpoint of individual dignity and the essential equality of the sexes.[15]

This suggests the equality of both sexes and the right to marriage based on individual dignity. While debating matters with the GHQ, the Japanese government argued that the sentence "The family is the basis of human society and its traditions for good or evil permeate the nation" should be deleted because it was incompatible with Japan's legal system.[16] As the GHQ agreed with this, the draft of the March 6 version became:

> Marriage shall be based only on the mutual consent of both sexes and it shall be maintained through mutual cooperation, with the equal rights of husband and wife as a basis. Laws shall be enacted considering choice of spouse, property rights, inheritance, choice of domicile, divorce and other matters pertaining to marriage and the family from the standpoint of individual dignity and the essential equality of the sexes.[17]

Considering this enactment process, the GHQ intended for the government to eliminate the notion of existing laws binding individuals in the family system and to pass new laws based on individual dignity. Instead of abolishing the feudal system in Article 12 (present-day Article 13), the Special Law was enacted to put an end to the traditional *Iye* system.[18]

2.1.3 Individual Dignity in the Constitution of 1946

Article 13 and 24 are concerned with individual dignity in the current Constitution. Article 13 stipulates: "All of the people shall be respected as

---

[15] "Article 23 of the GHQ Draft, Alfred Hussey Papers; Constitution File No. 1, Doc. No. 12," in *Constitution of Japan*, 12 February 1946 (National Diet Library): 6.
[16] "Irie Toshio Doc No. 15 (in the Draft for the Amendment of the Constitution of Japan, published on March 6th), the detail of the discussion in the GHQ on the March 4, 5" (National Diet Library): 9.
[17] "Article 22 of the Draft for the Amendment of the Constitution of Japan, Alfred Hussey Papers; Constitution File No. 1, Doc. No. 26," in *Constitution of Japan*, 12 February 1946 (National Diet Library): 5.
[18] Act on Emergency Measures of Civil Code with Implementation of the Constitution of 1946 (Act of 1947 No. 74). Article 3 claims that the provision of the household, family and *Iye* shall not apply.

individuals."[19] To be respected as an individual, each person must have his/her own personality and be able to make decisions about his/her own life. It is also necessary for individuals to be able to preserve their personal identity and privacy. In short, Article 13 recognizes individual dignity. Article 24-2 states: "With regard to choice of spouse, property rights, inheritance, choice of domicile, divorce and other matters pertaining to marriage and the family, laws shall be enacted from the standpoint of individual dignity and the essential equality of the sexes."[20] This requires that marriage and the family system be consistent with individual dignity and equality of the sexes. Given that Article 24-1 approves of the right to marriage, the system that constrains marriage contravenes Article 24-2, because such regulations degrade individual dignity. For instance, the law that imposes betrothals on men only as a requirement of marriage goes against Article 24-2. In another example, the law requiring that both members of an engaged couple take the husband's surname also violates Article 24-2. The family system must respect individual dignity. Article 24-2's original intent indicates that individuals should not be unreasonably constrained by family. The law shall not impair individual decision-making about family formation and place a heavy burden on family matter since the individual is guaranteed the right to form his/her own family based on his/her own dignity.

Complying with Articles 13 and 24 of the Constitution of 1946, the revised Civil Code of 1947 provided the Code's principle of interpretation. Article 2 prescribes: "This Code must be construed in accordance with honoring the dignity of individuals and the essential equality of both sexes."[21] In short, other provisions in the Civil Code shall be interpreted in light of individual dignity.

2.2 Family Solidarity Remaining in Law and Culture

However, some constraints on individual autonomy persist. Although the Diet abolished the existing household system in the Civil Code,[22] the Civil Code contains some elements of the *Iye* system.

The inheritance rights of children born out of wedlock is a typical example. In the revision of Civil Code in 1947, the system of traditional family inheritance was eliminated, and a new inheritance system was introduced.[23] However, Article 900-(4) of the revised Civil Code mentions the factor of traditional family inheritance. Article 900-(4) provides that "the share in inheritance of a child out of wedlock shall be one half of the share in inheritance of a child in wedlock."[24] This provision's

---

[19] Article 13 of the Constitution of Japan, 1946.
[20] Article 24 of the Constitution of Japan, 1946.
[21] Article 2 of the Civil Code of Japan.
[22] The Civil Code of Japan, Act No. 89 of 1896.
[23] The Law on the Partial Amendment of the Civil Code, Act No. 222 of 1947.
[24] Article 900-(4) of the Civil Code of Japan.

purpose is to protect the family based on marriage by distinguishing legitimate children from illegitimate ones.

However, the distinction leads to an illegitimate child having an inferior legal status, although his/her inferior legal status is not his/her fault. In doing so, the law arguably degrades the dignity of illegitimate children. In short, Article 900-(4) protects the family system at the expense of individual dignity. The legislature's preservation of family solidarity creates conflict between the family system and individual dignity. Although family solidarity in itself is not wrong, it is necessary to consider its relationship to individual dignity.

The family naming system also raises a constitutional problem in that it constrains a woman's choice of surname and leads to de facto discrimination against her. The current family naming system requires both members of a couple to take the surname of either the husband or the wife. Superficially, it seems like the system treating the husband and the wife fairly because they can choose as they like. However, since the traditional *Iye* system mandates the choice in favor of the husband's surname, Japanese women face huge pressure to change their family names after getting married, even though some women do so willingly to demonstrate their love for their husbands. As a result, most couples choose the husband's surname; this has become common in Japan.

However, some women feel this is de facto compulsion. They believe that there is a strong connection between the surname requirement and the outdated *Iye* system, because since the Meiji Era the surname has been required to represent one's family or the extended family. In particular, working women do not want to change their family names because it negatively affects her work.

2.3 *Connections with the Old System Remaining in Society*

Some laws have an adverse effect on individual dignity, although other laws seem to respect it. The Family Register Act established in the Meiji Era required registration of family surname under the *Iye* system. In that system, one's surname represents one's extended family. The Diet revised the Family Register Act in 1948 and narrowed the requirement for one surname only to cover the married couple and their children. This is one example compromising individual dignity.

However, some laws contain elements both respecting individual dignity and constraining it. Protecting honor by laws is one typical example. In general, protecting honor is viewed as respecting individual dignity, but this does not necessarily lead to such an outcome. Honor is reflected in one's social reputation. Historically, family reputation has been especially important since the Edo Era (1603–1867). At the time, an individual had to do everything for his/her family reputation. This relationship between honor and society continues. As long as society controls honor, protecting it does not mean respecting individual dignity.

Furthermore, protecting honor sometimes takes priority over individual rights. One example is freedom of expression in defamation cases. Article 21 of the Constitution grants freedom of speech. Before revising the Penal Code of 1947, the provision on defamation did not permit exemptions. Following the request of Article 21 of the Constitution, the Diet established exemptions from defamation in criminal law. The Penal Code of Article 230–2(1) provides:

> When an act [defamation] prescribed under paragraph (1) of the preceding Article is found to relate to matters of public interest and to have been conducted solely for the benefit of the public, the truth or falsity of the alleged facts shall be examined, and punishment shall not be imposed if they are proven to be true.[25]

This is an important revision to accommodate freedom of expression and defamation. However, even if Article 230–2(1) establishes exemptions, whether it maintains proper balance depends on practice. Although the punishment for defamation is linked to the protection of dignity, applying it strictly constrains freedom of expression. The Supreme Court has made convictions in defamation cases every year. Although defendants claim exemptions to their own cases, exemptions are rarely approved. Even if defamation occurs through the Internet, the Court tends to apply the same standard regarding whether an exemption is allowed.[26] The Court also applies the same standard to civil defamation cases on the Internet.[27]

When courts judge defamation cases, the issue arises as to whether the defendant's expression has degraded the victim's social reputation. On this point, protecting honor related to social relationships constrains individual rights. Although this is for individual dignity, it constrains other individual rights.

3 THE HYBRID APPROACH

3.1 *Hybrid Approach as Academic Theory*

3.1.1 Individualism Approach and Human Dignity Approach

When it comes to "individual dignity," there are two approaches in Japan. Considering the meaning of respecting an individual in Article 13 of the Constitution, Professor Oshikubo separates the concepts of individualism and human dignity.[28] According to him, the former focuses on respecting individual separately from the community; it treats individuals as different from others. On the other hand, the latter emphasizes one's personality as a human being; it presumes the ideal of a person based on the community.

---

[25] The Penal Code of Article 230–2(1), Act No. 45 of 1907.
[26] 64 Keishu 1 (Sup. Ct. 1st. P.B., March 15, 2010). [Ramenkagetsu case].
[27] 240 Minshu 149 (Sup. Ct. 2d. P.B. March 23, 2012).
[28] Michio Oshikubo, "Article 13," in *Constitutional Law: New Commentary on Basic Law* (2011): 100–2.

This distinction is reflected in the model referred to by the framers in the constitutional enactment of 1889 and the constitutional revision of 1946. The Meiji Constitution was devised based on the constitutions of the Kingdom of Prussia. The post-war Japanese Constitution was influenced by the United States. The current Constitution drastically changed the content of the former. However, some Japanese constitutional scholars who studied the Prussian Constitution have continued to study the German Constitution focusing on German Basic Law. As a result, there has been debate about the nature of individual dignity.

The phrase of "human dignity" is absent from the US Constitution. However, the Supreme Court began to use it in the 1940s. The mention of dignity began in separate opinions. In *Skinner v. Oklahoma*, in a concurring opinion, Justice Jackson stated that there was a limitation on the criminal sterilization act at the expense of dignity.[29] After that, Justice Murphy referred to this term in his dissenting opinion in *In re Yamashita*.[30] Murphy said: "While peoples in other lands may not share our beliefs as to due process and the dignity of the individual, we are not free to give effect to our emotions in reckless disregard of the rights of others."[31] That is, he argued that individual dignity should be protected universally.

Although the Court explicitly mentioned the phrase, it stressed autonomy and personal choice as factors of human dignity. In an abortion case, the Court referenced human dignity. For example, in *Casey*, the Court held that "the most intimate and personal choices a person may make in a lifetime, choices central to personal dignity and autonomy, are central to the liberty protected."[32]

In recent cases, the Court has tended to refer to it in the context of same-sex issues. In *Lawrence v. Texas*, the issue was whether the criminal law punishing sexual activity by a same-sex couple at home was constitutional. The Court said that "adults may choose to enter upon this relationship in the confines of their homes and their own private lives and still retain their dignity as free persons."[33] The Court held that the statute was unconstitutional as it imposed a stigma on same-sex couples. In 2015, *Obergefell v. Hodges*,[34] regarding same-sex marriage, mentioned that homosexuals did not have dignity in terms of their own distinct identity.[35] However, "liberties extend to certain personal choices central to individual dignity and autonomy, including intimate choices that define personal identity and beliefs."[36]

These American approaches regard dignity as the core of liberty based on individualism. The fact that the Court generally says "individual dignity" and not "human dignity" also illustrates jurisprudence focused on individualism. Although

---

[29] *Skinner v. Oklahoma*, 316 U.S. 535, 546 (1942) (Jackson, J., concurring).
[30] *In re Yamashita*, 327 U.S. 1, 26 (1946) (Murphy, J., dissenting).
[31] Ibid., p. 41.
[32] *Planned Parenthood of Southeastern Pennsylvania v. Casey*, 505 U.S. 833, 851 (1992).
[33] *Lawrence v. Texas*, 539 U.S. 558, 567 (2003).
[34] *Obergefell v. Hodges*, 135 S. Ct. 2584, 2597 (2015).
[35] Ibid., p. 2596.
[36] Ibid., p. 2597.

dignity itself is not a fundamental right, it is necessary to protect liberty through personal choice, privacy, and identity against government intervention and compulsion. It is remarkable that dignity requires not to impose stigma. If a law imposes stigma on a person, an imposed-upon person is not treated as a citizen. In other words, stigma deprives people of civil liberty, because an imposed-upon person is seen as having civil rights. This requirement is derived from equal protection. Therefore, individual dignity in the United States is grounded in liberty and equal respect, which are negative or based on defensive rights.

The German Basic Law explicitly provides for human dignity. Article 1 states: "Human dignity shall be inviolable. To respect and protect it shall be the duty of all state authority."[37] This indicates the governmental duty to protect human dignity as well as not to violate it.[38] Human dignity sometimes places constraints on liberty because the protection of dignity entails an objective order of values. The drafters of the Constitution were heavily influenced by the ideas of Immanuel Kant, who argued that one should never treat humans as objects of manipulation but always as ends. The Constitutional Court of Germany took a Kantian approach to interpreting human dignity. For example, in the Life Imprisonment case,[39] the Court mentioned that it is contrary to human dignity to make the individual a mere tool of the state because each person must always be an end in himself/herself.

In the Abortion I case,[40] the German Constitutional Court struck down the Abortion Reform Act, which granted pregnant women the right to secure an abortion in the first twelve weeks of pregnancy. The Court held that the law did not adequately protect the life of the fetus and did not clearly condemn the act of abortion with reference to human dignity, which is at the top of constitutional value. As the state has a duty to protect life under human dignity, the legislature needs to revise the statute with clear condemnation.

In addition to the duty to protect life, the Kantian approach emphasizes the concept of personhood with rationality and self-determination.[41] The Court extended this notion to the interior human personality in the Microcensus case.[42] The Court held that the Micro-census was inconsistent with human dignity, as the state was forcing people to register and catalogue their entire personalities, even if it was done anonymously through a statistical survey, thereby treating people as objects. In this result, human dignity includes personality and human autonomy.

[37] Article 1 of the German Basic Law.
[38] Marc Chase McAllister, "Human Dignity and Individual Liberty in Germany and the United States as Examined through Each Country's Leading Abortion Cases," *Tulsa Journal of Comparative and International Law* 11 (2004): 491, 495–500.
[39] Life Imprisonment Case, 45 BVerfGE 187 (1977).
[40] Abortion I, 39 BVerfGE 1, 36–37 (1975).
[41] Edward J. Eberle, "Human Dignity, Privacy, and Personality in German and American Constitutional Law," *Utah Law Review* 1997 (1997): 963.
[42] Microcensus, 27 BVerfGE 1 (1969).

The American and German approaches differ in certain ways. The first is the underlying nature of the right to human dignity. The American approach is defensive or subjective and does not carry a sense of responsibility. On the other hand, the German approach views human dignity not only as subjective but also as an objective right, including the duty to protect life as an end. The American approach can be called the liberty model, as it functions by prioritizing individual liberty against government. Meanwhile, the German approach perceives the duty as an objective; this is called the objective model. According to the objective model, human dignity functions as a constraint of another right and the interior limits of personal choice.

There is another difference in terms of personal choice and privacy. The American approach referring to the cases of abortion and same-sex couples is based on privacy and self-determination. It only concerns individual freedom and does not necessarily involve questions of how human society should be organized. Although this approach demands equal respect, it is unbounded by a strong sense of moral order because it focuses on freedom to pursue one's own vision of liberty or happiness. In contrast, the German approach is grounded in the philosophy of human capacity and dignity. It emphasizes one's personality as the unity of the psyche and the body. Personality is constructed through self-discovery and self-understanding, along with moral values. In short, the American approach consists of individualism, while the German approach is based on moral objectivism.

3.1.2 The Theory of Hybrid Approach

Considering the enactment process of the Japanese Constitution of 1946 that was affected by the US notion, for the people to be "respected as individual" means to demolish totalitarianism in wartime.[43] This implies that each person shall be respected as a moral agent with personal autonomy.[44] This concept connects with individualism. Article 13 highlights the right to self-determination in choosing the purpose of one's own life and values.[45] It recognizes that each person has a personality with dignity and should be respected for the purpose of free development of character.[46] Individualism requires the government to respect individual intentions, thoughts, and privacy, as each person has one's own raison d'etre. Therefore, individualism is concerned with the core of the relationship between government and persons.[47]

---

[43] Toshiyoshi Miyazawa, *Constitutional LawII* (Tokyo: Yuhikaku, 1959): 213.
[44] Koji Sato, *The Theory of Japanese Constitution*, 2nd ed. (Tokyo: Seibundo, 2020): 194–5.
[45] Yasuo Hasebe, *Constitutional Law*, 7th ed. (Tokyo: Shinseisha, 2018): 97.
[46] Masakazu Doi, "Article 13," in *Commentary on Constitutional Law* (2017): 69.
[47] Tsunemasa Arikawa, *Dignity and Status: Constitutional Thinking and Issue of "Japan"* (Tokyo: Iwanami Shoten, 2016): 3–56. Arikawa examines individual dignity concerning constitutionalism in view of individualism and status.

Article 24 is also important. It established a marriage system based on mutual consent and protection of equal rights of husband and wife. Section 2 of this Article refers to dignity and declares that marriage and family laws shall be enacted from the standpoint of individual dignity and the essential equality of the sexes. This clause was drafted by Beate Sirota Gordon, a member of the drafting team of the GHQ. She insisted that the family and marriage system should be based on the consent of both men and women, and the law should be enacted based on equality between them. The phrase of individual dignity is adopted here. It indicates not only individualism but also the right to equal concern and respect.

Considering both articles, the framer intended individualism, which goes against the totalitarian government and emphasizes freedom from collectivistic social structure. It is motivated by individualism and autonomy rather than human status in collectivities.

There are controversies over the relationship between individual dignity, as in the US approach, and human dignity, as in the German approach.[48] As Article 13 refers "respected as individuals" and 24–2 refers to "individual dignity" instructed by the GHQ, it is understood as individual dignity based on individualism as in the United States. However, some scholars who have studied German Basic Law suggest that the purpose of individual dignity in the Japanese Constitution is almost the same as human dignity because human dignity in German Basic Law has universal value.

Although these two approaches are similar in that respecting an individual is grounded in human rights, some maintain that these ideas are the same concept because they are based on personality, while others claim that they are different notions because individual dignity stresses individual rather than personality-based dignity.[49] José Llompart, a Spanish scholar in Japan, distinguished individual dignity from human dignity.[50] According to Llompart, individual dignity means individualism against totalitarianism. On the other hand, human dignity means that one has a personality, requiring the government not only to avoid violating it but also to protect it as well. He contended that the Japanese approach took the former route, because the enactment process of the current Constitution and the text indicated individualism.

Japanese individual dignity is familiar with the individualism approach. Nevertheless, even if individual dignity is based on individualism, there is room to accommodate the human dignity approach. Professor Koizumi pointed out that the dominant theory regards both approaches as compatible.[51] It suggests that human dignity does not deny individual autonomy, while individual dignity agrees with prohibition of genocide from the viewpoint of humanity. In fact, the Japanese

---

[48] Koichi Aoyagi, *Human Dignity in the Constitution* (Tokyo: Shogakusha, 2009): 4–44; its chap. 1 deals with individual dignity versus human dignity in Japan.
[49] Yuki Tamamushi, *The Doctrine of Protecting Human Dignity* (Tokyo: Shogakusha, 2013): 7–19.
[50] José Llompart, "'Individual Dignity' and 'Human Dignity' as a Matter of Japanese Constitutional Interpretation: The Unconstitutional Case of the Parricide," *Hanrei Times* 377 (1979): 8.
[51] Yoshiyuki Koizumi, Article 13," in *The Outline: Constitutional Commentary* (2018): 85.

Supreme Court has indicated a hybrid understanding of individual dignity based on individualism.

3.2 *The Establishment of Autonomy*

3.2.1 Privacy

Japanese courts have developed individual dignity in different situations in numerous contexts. The Supreme Court elaborated on autonomy grounded in individual dignity. The Court has mentioned "individual dignity" in the theft case[52] for the first time. In this case, the defendant argued that the court should not issue prison sentences for misdemeanors such as theft because this disproportional prison sentence violates Article 13. Although the Court refused the argument, it outlined the meaning of Article 13, stating that Article 13 means "individual dignity and respect of personality." It did not clarify whether this indicates individualism or moral personhood. After that, the Court sometimes referred to "individual dignity and respect of personality" in a criminal case.[53] The Court simply mentioned the issue in dicta and did not find a violation.

This approach is similar to that of the United States, in that it is a criminal case. To ensure individual dignity, it is critical to express one's concerns to the government. Moreover, the Court uses "individual dignity" instead of "human dignity." Given these points, the Japanese Court seems to think that Article 13 is similar to the US case law. However, the argument of individual dignity was not well-received, since lawyers found it difficult to use individual dignity as it was still seriously underdeveloped. From this perspective, it is difficult to argue that prison sentences go against individual dignity at that time.

About twenty years after the Japanese Constitution was enacted, individual dignity began to be used to protect private life. The *Utagenoato* case,[54] named for the title of the novel it concerns, is a landmark case in private life, although it is a lower court decision. The plaintiff claimed that the novel violated his privacy, because it publicized information about his private life, particularly his romantic relationships. The Tokyo district court held that the publication of others' private lives without reasonable grounds must not be allowed because the idea of individual dignity based on constitutional law was ensured by respecting each person's personality and shielding one from undue intervention. Thus, the court deduced privacy from constitutional principle without referring to Article 13.

Five years later, the Supreme Court approved of the freedom of individual private life in a case called *Kyotofugakuren*.[55] This case concerned the right not to have

---

[52] 1 Shukei 535 (Sup. Ct, G.B., March 24, 1948). [Setto case].
[53] See, for instance, the theft probation case, 2 Keishu 1377 (Sup. Ct. 1st P. B., October 21, 1948); the robbery probation case, 12 Shukei 551 (Sup. Ct. 1st. P.B., July 14, 1949).
[54] 15 Kakyu Minshu 1317 (Tokyo Dist. C., Sep. 28, 1964).
[55] 23 Keishu 1625 (Sup. Ct. G.B., December 24, 1969).

one's photo taken without permission. If protesters want to walk on a public road, city ordinances require them to apply for the demonstration. The local government gave conditional approval, stating that they must walk along the edge of the road. The police took the photos of demonstrations as evidence the protesters were walking contrary to the conditions of the demonstration. The Court held that all people have the freedom not to have their photo taken without permission as part of the freedom of individual private life protected by Article 13. The Court also approved an exception whereby a crime was just committed, the preservation of evidence is necessary and urgent, and the photo was taken through reasonable means. As for the outcome, this case was constitutional as it met that requirement.

In the Fingerprint case,[56] the Court approved of the freedom not to be fingerprinted in 1995. Foreigners who stayed for a long time were required to register their fingerprints with the Japanese government. Some foreigners thought that the system was unconstitutional and filed a lawsuit. The Court recognized that all persons have the freedom not to be fingerprinted due to individual private life protection mentioned in Article 13. Notwithstanding, the Court held that this system was constitutional because its purpose was rational and the means reasonable.

It was vital for individual private life to be affirmed under Article 13 in these cases. Although the relationship between privacy and individual dignity remained ambiguous, for the Court did not refer to "individual dignity" in these privacy cases, the Court deduced privacy through Article 13, which provided "respect as individual." Therefore, privacy and individual dignity seem to be on common ground.

3.2.2 Right to Self-Determination

Self-determination is one of many factors affecting individual dignity. If a person cannot determine his/her own affairs, that person is not respected as an individual. Intervening in private matters denies personality, which is derived from individual dignity. Therefore, maintaining individual dignity requires self-determination.

The Japanese Supreme Court has not held that self-determination is a right under Article 13 of the Constitution. However, the Court has sometimes referred to freedom as an individual's private life. For example, in the Prisoner Smoking case, the Court held that even if the freedom to smoke is included as a fundamental right based on Article 13, it may be constrained in such circumstances.[57] The Court merely mentioned the possibility of such a right but did not approve of it in this case.

In the case of Jehovah's Witness, the Court granted a patient the right to decide whether to receive an operation.[58] A Jehovah's Witness patient refused to receive blood transfusions in any scenario because of her religious beliefs. She came to the hospital hoping to have an operation without receiving a blood transfusion. The doctors

---

[56] 49 Keishu 842 (Sup. Ct. 3rd. P.B., December 15, 1995).
[57] 24 Minshu 1410 (Sup. Ct. G.B. September 16, 1970). [Hishuyosha Kitsuen case].
[58] 54 Minshu 582 (Sup. Ct. 3rd. P.B. February 29, 2000).

performed the operation without explaining to her that the hospital had a policy of providing a blood transfusion in the event that there was no alternative means of saving the patient's life, and in the course of the operation they actually gave the patient a blood transfusion. The Court held that the doctors shall be liable for damages, as they had deprived the patient of her right to choose whether or not to undergo the operation. The Court held that

> when a patient has an expressed intention of refusing to receive any medical treatment involving a blood transfusion on the ground that receiving a blood transfusion contradicts his/her religious beliefs, the right to make such a decision must be respected as part of the patient's personal rights.[59]

Although the Court did not mention the right to self-determination based on Article 13, its affirmation of the right to refuse blood transfusion, which derived from the right to personality, was similar to the right to self-determination.

In the lower court, there is another case that approved of self-determination. The Yokohama district court in the Death with Dignity in Tokai University case held that a patient could decide to stop his or her own treatment if some requirements were satisfied.[60]

There are matters of self-determination. In the Wearing a Seatbelt case, a driver filed a lawsuit seeking the freedom not to wear a seatbelt in the car. The Supreme Court held that the requirement was reasonable and did not violate Article 13.

Therefore, on matters that involve important aspects of a person's way of life, the court tends to respect personal decisions. In contrast, matters of personal preference are not entitled to the same amount of respect. Although these are similar matters, the differences seem to relate to individual dignity. One's way of life concerns individual dignity because, if we cannot determine our own way of life, our personality – which is equivalent to dignity – is degraded. Although personal preferences also relate to individual dignity, they are not as close to individual dignity as one's way of life. Moreover, we should take public interest into account. Any harm to society, such as not using a seatbelt on public roads, will cause damage to society, in that not wearing a seatbelt has a negative influence on safety and smooth-flowing traffic.

3.3 Constraint on Other Rights

3.3.1 Honor as a Personal Right

These issues are concerned with defensive rights against the government. This is the classical approach of individual rights in Japan. On the other hand, when personal rights collide with other constitutional rights, the Supreme Court has used personal rights to constrain other constitutional rights, such as seen in Germany. Although

---

[59] Ibid. p. 586.
[60] 877 Hanrei Times 148 (Yokohama Dist., March 28, 1995).

there are some differences between German and Japan, such as the term "human dignity" in Germany and "individual dignity" in Japan, as well as the absoluteness of the right in Germany and the relativeness of the right in Japan, their legal systems are similar in that dignity constrains other rights.

The Hoppo Journal case[61] is one such example. The issue involved the prior restraint of publication. The Court mentioned that Article 13 protected individual honor as a personal right and considered the balance of personal right and freedom of expression. According to the Court, prior restraint would be accepted when a publication involved the public interest, the content was true, and publication caused irreparable harm.

The Supreme Court referred to "the protection of individual reputation as the personal right (Article 13, Constitution)";[62] the right to honor is derived from a personal right based on Article 13. Generally, the right to honor means the interest not to be degraded in social evaluation and public reputation. In that sense, the right to honor entails both an individual right and objective protection. In the Hoppo Journal case, Justice Atsushi Nagashima stated: "In the case of civil defamation it has been made clear that the question of whether objective reputation has been illegally damaged is important."[63] This indicates that honor is protected from an objective angle. The objective approach is similar to that of Germany.

3.3.2 Author's Personal Rights in Copyright Law

The Japanese court gives priority to an author's personal rights/moral rights of authors in copyright law when it conflicts with freedom of expression. Article 59 of the copyright law states: "An author's moral rights are exclusive to that author, and are inalienable." It gives authors the right to "make a work public," the "right of attribution," and the "right to integrity."

In a copyright case, a defendant may argue that parody violates copyright. This would lead to a confrontation between freedom of expression and an author's personal rights. In such cases, the Japanese court has tended to prioritize author's personal rights.[64] This right differs from a constitutional personal right because it is based on copyright law. However, "personal rights" in the broadest sense may include moral rights. Statutes sometimes shape various personal rights, such as defamation law and copyright law. Therefore, courts have used personal rights to constrain constitutional rights in copyright cases. This tendency is similar to that of Germany, because copyright law provides author's personal rights. By contrast, the US copyright law does not give such right.

---

[61] 40 Minshu 872 (Sup. Ct. G.B., June 11, 1986).
[62] Ibid., p. 877.
[63] Ibid., p. 897. (Nagashima, J., concurring).
[64] See, for example, Montage case, 34 Minshu 244 (Sup. Ct. 3rd. P.B., March 28, 1980).

Human dignity in Japan lies in a middle position between those of the United States and Germany. The Japanese court recognizes individual dignity as a defensive right, like in the United States. However, the court sometimes uses personal right to constrain other rights, like in Germany. Therefore, the Japanese view of human dignity is a hybrid of the perspective of the two other nations. The phrase "individual dignity," used by Japanese courts, shows this hybrid character.

In view of the constitutional cases, however, we can see individual dignity as originally emerging from within Japan, rather than having a hybrid aspect. The Japanese Supreme Court has made rulings following Article 13 and 24–2 of the current Constitution, which suggests that individual dignity in Japan requires freedom from obsolete legal systems as well as from government intervention.

4 TOWARD INDIVIDUALISM BY THE JUDICIARY

In light of the enactment process in the Constitution of 1946, Article 13 protects private matters from government intervention, and Article 24 promotes liberty from family and social constraints in the family system. The Supreme Court has enforced the former in early times. The Court could directly review the constitutionality of a government action because Article 13 does not require any particular legal system. In contrast, Article 24–2 requires the legislature to enact the family provisions that uphold individual dignity and the essential equality of the sexes. The Supreme Court has deferred to the legislative judgments about the family system because the Court thought that the Article 24–2 delegated the content of the legal system to the legislature. However, the Court could review the reasonableness of the system as the time goes by. As a result, the Court has tended to change its stance in the twenty-first century.

4.1 *Against Government*

Since the *Kyotofugakuren* case, privacy has often been protected by the Supreme Court. The Supreme Court sometimes strictly reviews government wrongdoing regarding privacy. The Zenka-shokai case[65] concerned the responsibility of the local government, corresponding to a criminal record inquiry by lawyers. The Attorney Act[66] granted the Bar Association the authority to make inquiry into public organizations necessary for a case. The local department handled a request and disclosed a relative's criminal record. Although the local government responded

---

[65] 35 Minshu 620 (Sup. Ct. 3rd. P.B. April 14, 1981).
[66] Act No. 205 of June 10, 1949. Article 23–2: (1) An attorney may request the bar association to which he/she belongs to make inquiries to public offices or public or private organizations for information necessary for a case to which he/she has been retained. The bar association may refuse the request if it finds such request to be inappropriate. (2) A bar association may, pursuant to the request set forth in the preceding paragraph, request public offices or public or private organizations to provide necessary information.

based on the law, the Supreme Court held that the action was illegal because the public institution disclosed the information without paying attention to how to manage it.

4.2 Family versus Individual

On the other hand, the approach of constitutional judgments regarding Article 24 differs from that of Article 13. The Diet revised the Civil Code following the passage of Article 24-2 in 1947. It appeared that the traditional *Iye* system was abolished. However, the provision of family solidarity remains that may compromise individual dignity. Nonetheless, the Supreme Court upheld the constitutionality of the law, thus deferring to legislative discretion. However, Article 24-2 provides that laws shall be enacted from the standpoint of individual dignity and essential equality of the sexes. Even if the Court defers to legislative discretion, it is necessary to carefully determine whether the law follows the request. The Supreme Court now tends to consider this point more carefully than before.

4.2.1 The Parricide Penalty-Enhancement Case

In one criminal case, the Supreme Court reveals how it perceives individualism and equality relative to the solidarity of the family. Article 200 of the Penal Code stipulated that whoever was guilty of murdering a lineal ascendant should be punished by death or life imprisonment. Compared to regular murder under Article 199, for which the minimum imprisonment was three years, the difference of sentencing range between Article 199 and Article 200 is big. In the Parricide Penalty-Enhancement case,[67] the defendant argued that Article 200 was unreasonable discrimination in comparison to the punishments of outlined in Article 199 for ordinary murder. The Supreme Court held that Article 200 was unconstitutional, because it contradicted Article 14. According to the Supreme Court, the legislative purpose of Article 200 was admissible, as it seemed that killing an ascendant deserved social and moral denunciation and was to be strictly prohibited by punishing the perpetrator more severely than in an ordinary homicide. However, restricting the sentencing range to death or life imprisonment goes far beyond the legislative purpose and unreasonably discriminates against a perpetrator compared to the punishments of Article 199 for ordinary murder.

The ruling indicates that there is a limit to protecting the ascendant while maintaining protection of the ascendant based on social and moral perspectives. However, a social and moral controversy continued. The Court's ruling in 1973 caused controversy in political branches. As a result, Article 200 remained until 1995.[68]

---

[67] *Sonzokusatsu*, 27 Keishu 265.
[68] However, the prosecutors did not apply Article 200 at all between 1973 and 1995.

4.2.2 The Inheritance of Illegitimate Children

There are some constitutional issues involving the family in the Civil Code. Article 900-(4) prescribes the inheritance of illegitimate children. As described earlier, the distinction in inheritance degrades their dignity. Despite its dubious constitutionality, the Supreme Court has approved of Article 900-(4)'s constitutionality until recently. In 1995, the Court held that "a contemporary system of inheritance is closely related to the idea of family in a given country, and the system cannot be established without considering the rules of marriage and family in that country. It should be concluded that the way the inheritance system is established is left to the reasonable discretion of the legislature by taking all these into consideration."[69] On institutions of the family system, the Court chose deference to the legislature.

Nevertheless, the judgment has been criticized, and the 1995 case was decided by a narrow margin. Superficially, it was a 10–5 case. Five justices in the majority wrote concurring opinions or agreed with it. Four justices in concurring opinions agreed with constitutionality at the time except for possible future revisions.

In the twenty-first century, it is time to change.[70] The Supreme Court made a decision of unconstitutionality about Article 900-(4) in a 2013 case.[71] The Court said that it was necessary to review "in light of the Constitution that provides for individual dignity and equality under the law."[72] Given social change, such as the actual number of children born out of wedlock and the percentage of such children in Japan, the Court indicated:

> Even if the legal marriage system itself is entrenched in Japan, it is now impermissible, as a result of such change in the recognition, to cause prejudice to children by reason of the fact that their mother and father were not in a legal marriage when they were born – a matter that the children themselves had no choice [in] or chance to correct. Rather, it can be said that a notion that all children must be given respect as individuals and that their rights must be protected has been established.[73]

As a result, the Court held that Article 900-(4) was unconstitutional because the distinction in the inheritance between children born in wedlock and children born out of wedlock had lost reasonable grounds by the time that the plaintiff's inheritance commenced. Looking at Article 900-(4) based on individual dignity and equality, the reasonableness of legislative fact, which needed the distinction to

---

[69] 49 Minshu 1789, at 1794 (Sup. Ct. G.B. July 5, 1995). [Hichakushutsushi Sozokubun of 1995 case].
[70] Keigo Obayashi, "The Turning Point of Constitutional Lawsuits and the Indication of Judicial Activism: A Forbidden Remarriage Term Case and Family Name Case as the Trigger," *Horitsujiho* 1100 (2016): 66. It is pointed out that the Supreme Court has gradually tended to deal with judicial activism in the twenty-first century, particularly after the Zaigaihojin case concerning the voting rights of Japanese citizens residing abroad. See 59 Minshu 2087 (Sip. Ct. G.B. September 14, 2005. [Zaigaihojin case].
[71] 67 Minshu 1320 (Sup.Ct. G.B. September 4, 2013). [Saikonkinsikikan case].
[72] Ibid, p. 1324.
[73] Ibid, p. 1330–1.

maintain legal marriage, was lost due to social change. In short, this distinction violated equal protection under Article 14 of the Constitution.

Twenty-two days after the judgment, the Supreme Court ruled in another case concerning the illegitimate children regarding the notification of birth on the family register: the Illegitimate Children on Family Register case.[74] The Family Register Act[75] requires that a statement as to whether a child was born in or out of wedlock be made in a written notification, to be submitted upon filing a notification of birth. The plaintiff argued that this violated equal protection under the Constitution. The Court held that the requirement was constitutional because the notification did not generate any legal effect and was necessary for the distinction between the Legitimate Children and the Illegitimate Children on the official record. In contrast to the inheritance of illegitimate children, there is a difference in that the law in this case does not affect legal status. If the registration of "illegitimate" were to cause any damage, the law would violate individual dignity and equal protection.

4.2.3 The Same Family Name

Article 750 of the Civil Code stipulates that a husband and wife shall adopt the surname of the husband or wife in accordance with that which is decided at the time of marriage. Although legally a husband and wife are able to choose their own surname as they like, some women think that this is unconstitutional because it in effect compels women to choose their husband's surname. Indeed, 96 percent of married couples in Japan choose to take the husband's surname.[76] Some women consider it de facto compulsion. Changing one's surname causes some disadvantages in social life, such as interrupting one's former career. They also think that this system continues the patriarchal family structure dating back to before WWII.[77]

In the 2015 ruling delivered by the Supreme Court, the plaintiffs claimed via the State Redress Act that Article 750 violates Articles 13, 14, and 24.[78] Regarding Article 24, the Supreme Court mentioned that it leaves the establishment of specific systems primarily to the Diet's reasonable legislative discretion. However, it further indicates that laws should be enacted from the standpoint of individual dignity and the essential equality of the sexes. Therefore, the Court stated that whether the provision in question was reasonable would be judged in light of the requirement of individual dignity and the essential equality of the sexes and be beyond the scope of the Diet's

---

[74] 67 Minshu 1384 (Sup. Ct. 1st. P.B. September 26, 2013).
[75] Act No. 224 of 1947. The Article 49, paragraph (2), item (i) provides that "Article 49 (1) A notification of birth shall be submitted within 14 days thereof (if the birth took place abroad, within three months). (2) The following matters shall be entered in the written notification: (i) the gender of the child, and whether the child is born in or out of wedlock."
[76] "The Report of 'Status of Marriage' in 2016" (Ministry of Health, Labor and Welfare, 2016): 10.
[77] The same surname system was introduced as a legal system in Japan in 1898, when the Former Civil Code (Act No. 9 of 1898 prior to the amendment by through Act No. 222 of 1947) was enacted.
[78] 69 Minshu 2586 (Sup. Ct. G.B. December 16, 2015).

legislative discretion. The Court claimed that the provision did not involve gender inequality and that it was left up to the couple getting married to decide which surname they adopt. Moreover, the Court asserted that the effect of the disadvantages caused by one of them changing the surname could be alleviated to some degree by using a common name. Consequently, the Court held that this system was not unreasonable in light of the requirement of individual dignity and the essential equality of the sexes.

It is important for the Supreme Court to carefully consider whether the law upholds individual dignity and the essential equality of the sexes, depending on the social situation. Justice Kiyoko Okabe, a female Justice, wrote an opinion joined by other two female justices. In her concurring opinion in the judgment, she said that a surname represents individuals' backgrounds, attributes, blood relationships or family, ethnicity, origin, and other factors. According to her, "In view of the fact that, in reality, more than 96 percent of married couples choose the husband's surname upon marriage, it can be said that the legal interference with a surname's identification imposes the burden of feeling a loss of identity on women." Considering the functions of a surname, she stated that "only women, in most cases, would experience a reduction in the surname's identification function, which supports the basis for individual dignity, and only women would have to feel a loss of identity. Such a system cannot be regarded as a system established from the standpoint of individual dignity and the essential equality of the sexes."[79] Therefore, she concluded:

> The Provision has gradually become less reasonable along with the changes in society after the amendment was made to the Civil Code in 1947, and at least by now, it has become unreasonable in light of the requirement of individual dignity and the essential equality of the sexes and gone beyond the scope of the Diet's legislative discretion, and hence it should inevitably be judged to be in violation of Article 24 of the Constitution.[80]

As described, both the majority opinion and Okabe's opinion upheld the provision constitutional given individual dignity and the essential equality of the sexes. The difference in the evaluation of the legislative fact regarding a surname's function and dramatic progress in women's advancement in social change has resulted in different conclusions. The majority opinion mentioned that "how this type of system should be designed, including the circumstances concerning these matters, is a matter that needs to be discussed and determined by the Diet."[81] Considering

---

[79] Ibid, p. 2603–4.
[80] Ibid., p. 2605. This is not a dissenting opinion but a concurring opinion because she dismisses the petition of plaintiffs, even though she judges the law unconstitutional. The plaintiffs brought a suit based on the State Redress Act in this case. If the Diet intentionally violates the Constitution and recklessly leaves it unaddressed, the law results in illegality. However, she does not think that the law is illegal, because it is not clear that the Diet intentionally violates the Constitution.
[81] Ibid., p. 2596.

both opinions, the reasonableness of this system depends on the social situation, and it might become unreasonable in the future.

4.3 *The Social Change Doctrine*

The Supreme Court has gradually enforced individualism in the family system. In particular, examining the congruence between individual dignity and social change as a factor of constitutional judgment indicates that individual dignity receives more emphasis.

This Social Change Doctrine is an approach to judging the constitutionality of a law by considering social change. This is remarkable in that society has functioned as a factor in respecting the individual. Prior cases have deferred to legislative discretion, taking family solidarity and its relationship to society into account. Namely, society was regarded as a constraint on individuals. The new conception of society regards society as supporting individualism because it requires the legal system to match individual dignity in relation to social situation. This change exemplifies the ascending individualism. Now, society plays the role of a catalyst toward progress in individual dignity rather than placing a constraint on it.

There is still a problem for individual dignity in this approach. The Social Change Doctrine stresses the social situation that reflects the majority opinion or custom. When plaintiffs who argue that their dignity must be protected have the same opinion as most people in the society, problems do not arise. Yet if those plaintiffs' belief contradicts those of society, their dignity will not be protected because they are in the minority. From the perspective of modern constitutionalism that requires minority protection, it is necessary to consider not only social change endorsed by the majority but also social change by the minority.

5 CONCLUSION

This chapter reveals how individual dignity functions in constitutional cases. The original meaning of individual dignity in Japan involves not only autonomy from the government in Article 13 but also liberty from the traditional constraints of society and family solidarity in Article 24.

Academic theory first borrowed the foreign idea of individual dignity in the Japanese Constitution. It is thought that individual dignity entails both factors. This understanding supports privacy based on autonomy and balancing conflict between personality and other rights.

However, the issue in Article 24 needs an original response because it concerns the context of Japan. Recently, the Supreme Court took steps to integrate the concept of individual dignity into the family system in response to social change. Judicial review relying on social change is one method to overcome the problem of "counter-majoritarian difficulty."[82] That is how judicial review overrides political decisions based on majority, because it grounds the majority's will or public voice. This approach is legitimized in part by the national review system,[83] through which the people review the appointment of the Supreme Court justices in certain general elections. Under the system, the justices can exercise judicial review more actively, as they cannot be recalled by the will of the people. On the grounds of this system, the Supreme Court can protect individual dignity standing on the side of the public.[84]

Furthermore, the Supreme Court has used the Social Change Doctrine in equal protection, such as in the case of Illegitimate Children. One former Supreme Court justice, Katsumi Chiba, looks back at the Illegitimate Children case in his book and points out that the Court has stressed individual dignity in light of recent worldwide developments in order to change the existing law.[85]

Japanese society has been transformed to support individual dignity and to free it from constraints. The approach connecting individual dignity with social change in case law endorses this transformation. As the Supreme Court takes up the Social Change Doctrine, it is necessary to pay attention not only to future cases but also to social change.

---

[82] Alexander Bickel, *The Least Dangerous Branch: The Supreme Court at the Bar of Politics* (Bobbs-Merrill, 1962): 6.
[83] Article 79–2 of the Constitution provides, "The appointment of the judges of the Supreme Court shall be reviewed by the people at the first general election of members of the House of Representatives following their appointment, and shall be reviewed again at the first general election of members of the House of Representatives after a lapse of ten (10) years, and in the same manner thereafter."
[84] In fact, no one Justice has been dismissed so far under national review.
[85] Katsumi Chiba, *The Constitutional Case Law and the Viewpoint of the Justice* (Tokyo: Yuhikaku, 2019), p. 244.

3

Constitutional Discourse on Human Dignity in South Korea

A Critical Appraisal

Chaihark Hahm

1 INTRODUCTION

The Constitution of the Republic of Korea provides, in Article 10, that "all citizens possess the dignity and worth as human beings, and have the right to pursue happiness. It shall be the duty of the State to confirm and guarantee the inviolable fundamental human rights of individuals." This is the opening article of Chapter II of the Constitution, entitled "Rights and Duties of Citizens," and is thus commonly regarded as a proclamation of the highest principle governing the protection of basic rights. Some even claim that it is an expression of the deepest commitment of the sovereign people of Korea[1] and is the very grounds for the existence of the constitution.

Historically, though, Korea's constitutional text did not always include a reference to human dignity. The first constitution of 1948, adopted after regaining independence, contained no article on "human dignity and worth"; this clause only entered the constitution via the fifth revision in 1962.[2] This was the result of General Park Chung-hee's coup d'état the previous year. While documents are lacking which might explain why the military government chose to include a provision on human dignity, commentators generally believe that it was related to the regime's attempt to shore up its legitimacy. Also, given that many Korean constitutional scholars received their legal education in Germany, it is not hard to imagine that a desire to emulate the German Basic Law may have played a part in the entry of human dignity into Korea's constitution.[3]

---

[1] Throughout this chapter, "Korea" refers to the Republic of Korea, aka South Korea.
[2] The Korean Constitution has gone through nine revisions. Some were partial amendments, while others involved total rewritings. Despite such differences, the general practice among scholars and practitioners has been to refer to all of them serially as the "nth revision." For a brief of the history of constitutional revision in Korea, see Dae-Kyu Yoon, *Law and Political Authority in South Korea* (Boulder, CO: Westview Press, 1990).
[3] Bang Seung-Ju, "Hŏnpŏp Che 10 Cho," in *Hŏnpŏp Chusŏksŏ (Commentaries on the Constitution)*, edited by Hanguk Hŏnpŏp Hakhoe (Seoul: Pagyŏngsa, 2013), 286. As is well known, the German

The next stage in the textual transformation was the inclusion of the "right to pursue happiness" through the eighth constitutional revision in 1980. This was the result of the coup d'état by General Chun Doo-hwan, who seized power after Park's assassination in 1979. Perhaps the same considerations relating to regime legitimacy were at play, although this time the reference evidently was the United States (or the postwar constitution of Japan, adopted under American occupation).[4] One document from the period suggests that the inclusion of the right to pursue happiness was in part an attempt to respond to the complaint that the provision on human dignity by itself was too vague and abstract.[5] The revision of 1980 also included two more articles that mention the term "dignity." One is the current Article 32(3): "Standards of working conditions shall be determined by law in such a way as to guarantee human dignity"; the other is Article 36(1): "Marriage and family life shall be entered into and sustained on the basis of individual dignity and equality of the sexes." These provisions were retained (although the articles were renumbered) when the current constitution was adopted through the ninth revision in 1987.

Despite its relatively late textual incorporation, "dignity and worth as a human being" is universally regarded by scholars and practitioners as the most fundamental value of Korea's constitutional order. They agree that it should guide the overall implementation of the constitution. It is the ultimate goal that every basic rights provision in the constitution is designed to realize. As such, it provides guidelines for determining the level of acceptable limitations on basic rights. Indeed, not only the interpretation of individual rights provisions but also the operation of the entire state apparatus must conform to the dictates of this highest principle. Some commentators even claim that, because it lies at the very core of the constitutional commitment of the sovereign people, it cannot be altered even via the amendment procedure.[6] At the level of constitutional value, in other words, there is little disagreement among commentators and the courts about the role of human dignity. Indeed, statements by Korean scholars and courts are almost indistinguishable from celebrations of human dignity found in other jurisdictions. For example, the following words from Aharon

---

Grundgesetz begins with the proclamation in Article 1(1): "Human dignity shall be inviolable. To respect and protect it shall be the duty of all state authority."

[4] For example, Virginia Bill of Rights, June 12, 1776, Sec. 3; United States Declaration of Independence, July 4, 1776, Para. 2; Constitution of Japan, May 3, 1947, Art. 13.

[5] A report was prepared in 1980 by a "Study Group" within the Ministry of Government Legislation for the purpose of providing assistance and reference materials for the constitutional revision process. It includes a summary of arguments both for and against the inclusion of certain new rights such as the right to pursue happiness. See Bang, "Che 10 Cho," 339–340.

[6] On this view, human dignity constitutes an important limit to constitutional change. This of course is a reflection of the influence of German constitutional jurisprudence. Even though Korea's Constitution does not contain any "eternity clause," such as Article 79(3) of the *Grundgesetz*, many German-educated Korean scholars claim that such limitation must be inferred from the purpose and structure of the Constitution. E.g., Huh Young, *Hanguk Hŏnpŏpnon* [Korean Constitutional Law] (Seoul: Pagyŏngsa, 2016), 339.

Barak on the functions of human dignity as a constitutional value could have just as easily been spoken by Korean jurists:

> It provides the theoretical foundation for human rights; it assists in the interpretation of human rights at the sub-constitutional level; it is one of the values that every constitutional right is intended to realize; it plays a role in the limitations to constitutional rights and in determining the limits to such limitations; it plays a primary interpretative role in those cases where the constitution does recognize a constitutional right to human dignity.[7]

Yet, the devil is always in the details. Such apparent "overlapping consensus" at the international level notwithstanding, it is also well known that there are significant variations in the way that each country gives meaning to the value of human dignity.[8] To the extent that there is a distinctly Korean conception of or approach to implementing human dignity, it must be sought by examining not only the text of the Korean constitution but also the vibrant system of constitutional adjudication that has developed over the past three decades. The political history and cultural traditions of the nation are also important factors that shape the Korean understanding of human dignity. At the same time, it should be noted that Korea's politics and culture are being reshaped and redefined via the constitutional process, which includes fleshing out the meaning of human dignity.

2 POVERTY AMIDST PLENTY: LACK OF CLARITY DESPITE MANY DECISIONS

Despite the high-sounding proclamations by Korean jurists about the status of human dignity as the highest constitutional value, its concrete meaning and contours are far from settled. The Korean Constitutional Court's engagement with the clause on human dignity and worth tend to raise more questions than answers. In part, this may be because the Court is a relatively young institution that only started hearing cases in 1988. This does not, however, mean that the Court has had few occasions to interpret Article 10, which contains the clause. If anything, there has been an excess of cases where the parties invoked "human dignity and worth" (and the right to pursue happiness) to justify their claims. For many observers, Article 10 is being overused and abused, which in turn is contributing to the lack of clarity and precision in its meaning. It is indeed common practice for anyone claiming infringement of one's basic rights by public authorities to include reference to "human dignity and worth" as additional grounds for their complaints. Just in case the argument based on specific rights provisions does not stick, in other words,

---

[7] Aharon Barak, "Human Dignity: The Constitutional Value and the Constitutional Right," in *Understanding Human Dignity (Proceedings of the British Academy)*, ed. Christopher McCrudden (Oxford: Oxford University Press, 2013), 362–63.

[8] Christopher McCrudden, "Human Dignity and Judicial Interpretation of Human Rights," *European Journal of International Law* 19, no. 4 (2008): 697–712.

claimants are wont to assert that their human dignity and worth have been violated as a result of some government action or inaction.

Rather than addressing these claims individually, however, the Constitutional Court has tended to show a rather dismissive attitude toward such invocations of Article 10. In many cases, it does not even bother addressing the claim based on human dignity, apparently content to find that other provisions on more specific rights have not been violated. The following is not atypical:

> Petitioners claim violation of human dignity and worth ... yet do not provide any concrete basis for [a finding of] unconstitutionality. Moreover, given that this basic right in principle has a more supplemental nature to other concrete basic rights, and since there is in this case a more directly applicable right ... whose violation will be assessed, we shall not consider this matter separately.[9]

Often, the court will merely state that the issue at hand is "obviously" not related to the principle of human dignity and refuse even to discuss why Article 10 is not applicable. In one case, it stated: "There is no room to think that the petitioners' dignity and worth as human beings ... have been violated by [the statutory provision at issue], and so their claim has no merit."[10]

The Court's attitude is understandable given that the human dignity and worth clause is being used as a fallback, a catch-all provision by almost everyone claiming violation of his or her constitutional rights. Given that the Court has no discretion about which cases to decide, it is inundated each year with hundreds of cases filed by citizens utilizing the system of constitutional complaint. In so many of these, the argument based on human dignity and worth is at best a long shot. The Court may thus be forgiven for being dismissive of, and even irritated by, such frivolous invocations of Article 10.[11] This perhaps explains so many of the Court's decisions in which it does not even bother to state why the clause on human dignity and worth is not relevant. As a result, we have a situation of "poverty amidst plenty" where, despite the repeated and routine invocations of the clause, its meaning remains deeply underarticulated in the Court's jurisprudence. In stark contrast to the high number of cases where the clause is mentioned, few cases have attempted to formulate a generally applicable standard for its application. This is evidently problematic since human dignity and worth supposedly embody the highest principle of Korea's constitutional order. Even when the Court is not so dismissive,

---

[9] Const. Ct. 99 Hun-Ma 112 (consolidated) (December 14, 2000).
[10] Const. Ct. 93 Hun-Ba 5 (January 25, 1996).
[11] Although not directed at the clause on human dignity and worth, at least one justice of the Constitutional Court has warned against the abuse of Article 10 in constitutional adjudication: "Citizens must first invoke the ordinary specific basic rights [provisions] whose substance are more concrete, and if this is unsuccessful then invoke the right to pursue happiness as the supplemental basic right of last resort. This is a natural corollary of the need to avoid the excessive invocation of the right to pursue happiness and to prevent frivolous lawsuits and the devaluation of regular specific rights provisions." Const. Ct. 94 Hun-Ma 136 (July 21, 1995) (Justice Cho Sŭng-hyŏng).

however, its interpretation of the human dignity and worth clause, as will be shown, has been less than analytically rigorous.

To be sure, it may be unfair to criticize the Court for not being more systematic in its approach. The first sentence of Article 10, which contains the human dignity and worth clause, is itself a veritable interpretive landmine: for commentators it is the source of endless disagreements. To begin with, the precise nature of the relationship between "human dignity and worth" and the "right to pursue happiness," both of which appear in the same sentence, is unclear. As mentioned, the right to pursue happiness may have been inserted into the same Article so as to make the clause on human dignity and worth more concrete. In fact, however, the introduction of this "right" has only created confusion and controversy. Some scholars go so far as to say that it is a mere ethical proclamation and deny that it has any legal significance.[12] Others use this as the basis for reading into the Constitution the expansive, German-inspired, concept of "general freedom of action."[13] As for the Court, it sometimes views it as a separate basic right. Yet, it also frequently refers to "human dignity and worth" and the "right to pursue happiness" in the same breath, as if to suggest the two clauses comprise one value from which to derive new rights not specified in the Constitution's text.[14] In such cases, the implication seems to be that there is no need to distinguish the two concepts.

The next textual issue is the relationship between human "dignity" (in Korean *chonŏm* 尊嚴) and "worth" (*kach'i* 價值) – are they two different concepts, or does the phrase "dignity and worth as human beings" constitute one concept? Interestingly, the Charter of the United Nations (1945) and the Universal Declaration of Human Rights (1948) both refer to the "dignity and worth of the human person." While it is unclear if they influenced the Korean Constitution, such genealogy, even if established, would be of little help because these two documents are notorious for deliberately leaving important terms undefined and undertheorized.[15] The view of most commentators in Korea is that the clause refers to one concept and that there is no need to make a distinction between the two terms.[16] Since the German term *Würde* is etymologically related to *Wert*, which means "worth," the drafters of the Korean Constitution may have felt the need to make explicit this aspect by using two terms to translate the concept.[17] Predictably,

---

[12] Huh, *Hanguk Hŏnpŏpnon*, 344.
[13] Soo-Woong Han, *Hŏnpŏphak* [*Constitutional Law*], 6th ed. (Paju: Bobmunsa, 2016), 543–552.
[14] For example, Const. Ct. 95 Hun-Ka 6 (July 16, 1997) (consolidated) (using the two concepts as basis for deriving a right to determine one's own destiny).
[15] Paweł Łuków, "A Difficult Legacy: Human Dignity as the Founding Value of Human Rights," *Human Rights Review* 19, no. 3 (2018): 318–319.
[16] Bang, "Che 10 Cho," 292–293. One scholar flatly states that the Korean phrase is a translation of "human dignity" in English. Jong-Sup Chong, *Hŏnpŏphak Wŏllon* [*Principles of Constitutional Law*] (Seoul: Pagyŏngsa, 2016), 408.
[17] Jeremy Waldron argues that, despite established practice, the English word "dignity" is an inapt translation of *Würde* as the term is used by Kant, which is "much closer to 'worth.'" Jeremy Waldron, *Dignity, Rank, and Rights* (Oxford: Oxford University Press, 2012), 24. Drafters of the Korean

though, the Constitutional Court has shown scant interest in this issue and appears to assume that "human dignity and worth" is one concept.

In practical terms, the more important issue is what legal effect the clause on human dignity and worth might have. On this too, however, there is no consensus among scholars, while the Court has not been consistent. A few Korean constitutional scholars prefer to read the clause as a general statement of an objective principle of constitutional law. On this view, the proclamation that everyone possesses human dignity and worth cannot be grounds for a subjective right that could be invoked by individual citizens in concrete cases.[18] It is rather a statement of the supreme goal that all the other basic rights specified in the constitution must strive to achieve. In some of its decisions, the Korean Constitutional Court seems to agree with this position. It has often referred to the human dignity and worth clause in Article 10 as "the highest constitutional value."[19] In relation to other rights provisions, it has stated that human dignity and worth is "the ultimate goal and basic principle of all basic rights protection."[20] At least one justice has written that the clause represents "the highest constitutional principle that is binding on other provisions of the constitution."[21] Yet, despite such pronouncements, according to the vast majority of the Court's decisions, human dignity and worth is not just a guiding principle but also a specific ground for challenging state law and government action.

3 INTERPRETIVE CONFUSION: FROM ABSTRACT PRINCIPLE TO CONCRETE RIGHT

In numerous decisions, after affirming human dignity and worth as "the core of the constitution's philosophy" and referring to Article 10 as a statement of the "basic principle of the constitution," the Constitutional Court has indicated that the state must protect not only the specifics rights provided for in the Constitution but also the freedom and rights not enumerated in the text. While protection of rights should be sought initially through the specific constitutional provisions on basic rights, "if [government] restrictions on basic rights encroach upon human dignity and worth, or if measures aimed at implementation of basic rights fail to provide for even the basic minimum level of protection and thereby harm the dignity and worth of human beings," this would merit a finding that the Constitution has been violated.[22] The unmistakable implication of this language, which has been repeated almost verbatim in later decisions, is that the clause on human dignity and worth by

---

Constitution may have inadvertently covered both the modern Kantian connotation related to "worth" or "value" and what Waldron calls the more ancient connotation of dignity as rank and status.

[18] Huh, *Hanguk Hŏnpŏpnon*, 339–342; Chong, *Hŏnpŏphak Wŏllon*, 412.
[19] For example, Const. Ct. 2013 Hun-Ba 322 (May 31, 2018) (consolidated); Const. Ct. 2015 Hun-Ka 28 (June 28, 2018) (consolidated).
[20] Const. Ct. 2000 Hun-Ma 327 (July 18, 2002).
[21] Const. Ct. 91 Hun-Ma 31 (October 1, 1992) (Justice Han Byeong-Chae, dissenting).
[22] Const. Ct. 98 Hun-Ma 216 (June 1, 2000).

itself could become the basis for holding unconstitutional some legislation or executive action. It is clear that the Court wishes to give a more expansive reading to "human dignity and worth." The clause is not merely a statement of value. What is not clear, however, is the process by which the clause – which does not specify a "right" – is understood to provide the basis for specific rights that may be invoked by individuals.

3.1 One-Step or Two-Step Process of Derivation?

In some of its decisions, the Court seems to say that human dignity and worth may act as the textual basis for recognizing rights that are not enumerated in the Constitution, especially in situations where the specific rights provisions are unable to provide proper remedy for an aggrieved individual. On this reading, the clause is the source of "supplemental" rights and as such may act as justification for the Court's articulation and protection of unenumerated rights.[23] In this regard, Article 10 seems to be read as a basis for implementing the general principle, enunciated in Article 37(1), that rights "shall not be neglected on the grounds that they are not enumerated in the Constitution."

Interestingly, the Court often goes through a two-step process when deriving unenumerated rights from the human dignity and worth clause. It first posits a "general right to personality [*ilbanjŏk inkyŏkkwŏn* 一般的人格權]" that may be derived from this clause and then uses this general right as the basis for recognizing more specific rights.[24] The influence of German constitutional jurisprudence should be obvious.[25] The Court invoked such a general right to personality as the basis for recognizing the "right of reply" of individuals whose dignity (and privacy) had been harmed by the mass media.[26] It has relied on similar reasoning to recognize the right of self-determination regarding the use of personal information.[27] The Court has also held that the parents' right to access information regarding the sex of their unborn child[28] as well as the right of the provider of sperm or ovum to decide

---

[23] The Court is more explicit on this in relation to the right to pursue happiness, which it has described on many occasions as "a basic right supplemental to other basic rights." For example, Const. Ct. 99 Hun-Ma 112 (December 14, 2000); Const. Ct. 2003 Hun-Ma 173 (November 24, 2005).

[24] In other cases, the Constitutional Court has referred to both "human dignity and worth" and the "right to pursue happiness" as grounds for the general right to personality. For example, Const. Ct. 2003 Hun-Ma 282 (July 21, 2005).

[25] Edward J. Eberle, "Observations on the Development of Human Dignity and Personality in German Constitutional Law: An Overview," *Liverpool Law Review* 33 (2012): 201–233. See also Donald P. Kommers and Russell A. Miller, *The Constitutional Jurisprudence of the Federal Republic of Germany*, 3rd ed. (Durham, NC: Duke University Press, 2012), 399–400. Unlike in Taiwan, however, few justices of the Constitutional Court are constitutional scholars who received their higher education in Germany. This may explain the relatively less overt German influence on the Korean Court's judgments. See also Chapter 4 in this volume by Jimmy Chia-Shin Hsu.

[26] Const. Ct. 89 Hun-Ma 165 (September 16, 1991).

[27] Const. Ct. 2003 Hun-Ma 282 (July 21, 2005) (consolidated).

[28] Const. Ct. 2004 Hun-Ma 1010 (July 31, 2008) (consolidated).

how to dispose of the embryo[29] are specific instances of the "general right to personality" that flows from human dignity and worth. Other examples of specific rights that arise from the general right to personality include the right not to be photographed without consent[30] and an individual's right to protect one's reputation (or honor).[31]

At other times, however, the Court seems to derive a more concrete "right to personality" from the clause on human dignity and worth, which is held up as sufficient basis for finding a state action unconstitutional. In these cases, in other words, rather than going through the above-mentioned two-step process to articulate a right that arises from the general right to personality, it just invokes the "right to personality that flows from human dignity and worth," which is declared to be directly violated by some government measures. These cases almost always involve inhumane or degrading treatment of individuals involved with the criminal justice system. They include being forced, inter alia, to use unsanitary toilets in detention cells that provide almost no privacy,[32] to endure excessive and humiliating bodily searches,[33] and to wear prison uniforms in detention centers prior to a final guilty verdict.[34] These cases make clear that even inmates of prison and detention centers are entitled to a certain level of respect that cannot be dispensed with. By foregoing the two-step inference, the Court is perhaps implying that such degrading treatments are a more direct form of affront to human dignity and worth. It may be too hasty to conclude that the Court regards the core of human dignity as a demand for what the political philosopher Michael Rosen has called "respectfulness."[35] The Court, however, does seem more eager to find a direct violation of the human dignity and worth clause when the harm involved is one of humiliation and degradation.

3.2 No Derivation Needed?

In another set of cases, the Constitutional Court appears to regard the clause on human dignity and worth as a concrete "right" in itself rather than a source from which unenumerated rights may be derived. For example, after reciting the words of Article 10, the Court has often stated that this provision shows that the Constitution is dedicated to guaranteeing the "individual's right to personality" (*kaein ŭi inkyŏkkwŏn* 個人의 人格權) and the right to pursue happiness. It is, in other words, using the term "individual's right to personality" as a synonym for "human dignity and worth."

[29] Const. Ct. 2005 Hun-Ma 346 (May 27, 2010).
[30] Const. Ct. 2012 Hun-Ma 652 (March 27, 2014).
[31] Const. Ct. 2002 Hun-Ma 425 (October 27, 2005).
[32] Const. Ct. 2000 Hun-Ma 546 (July 19, 2001).
[33] Const. Ct. 2000 Hun-Ma 327 (July 18, 2002).
[34] Const. Ct. 97 Hun-Ma 137 (May 27, 1999) (consolidated).
[35] Michael Rosen, *Dignity: Its History and Meaning* (Cambridge, MA: Harvard University Press, 2012), 61–62.

The phrase "the individual's right to personality and the right to pursue happiness as provided by Article 10" has become formulaic and is repeatedly employed by the Court. To be sure, the Court sometimes proceeds to infer a more specific right from this individual's right to personality and to that extent a process of derivation may still be necessary. For example, it has held that presumed in this "individual's right to personality" is a right of self-determination of one's own fate, which in turn includes the right to decide on whether, and with whom, to engage in sexual relations,[36] the right to choose one's marriage partner,[37] and the right to decide on matters regarding pregnancy and childbirth.[38] It may thus be of little practical importance to focus on how the Court reads the human dignity clause, since it is being used as the basis from which to infer other specific rights. Nevertheless, when the Court reads Article 10 as guaranteeing "the individual's right to personality and the right to pursue happiness," it is no longer using this provision as a source from which a new and unenumerated right might be derived. Rather, Article 10 itself is being interpreted as a provision that guarantees a specific right called the "individual's right to personality." This means that, to be analytically precise, Article 37(1) on the state's duty to respect unenumerated rights need not be invoked when Article 10 is at issue. It is not clear, however, if the Court is aware of this interpretive innovation.

Lastly, in a handful of cases, the Constitutional Court actually invoked the clause on human dignity and worth as a basis for finding a state action unconstitutional – without even bothering to elucidate whether it is a right or not. These also involved degrading treatments within the criminal justice system. In one case, it held that being forced to wear excessive restraining devices for long periods was a violation of human dignity and worth.[39] The use of double steel manacles and a leather one during the better part of the inmate's confinement in prison made it difficult even to "maintain the minimum level of dignity as a human being."[40] In addition to violating the constitutional provision on freedom of the person (Art. 12), such degrading treatment was a direct violation of clause on human dignity and worth. In a more recent case, the Court found that being forced to share an excessively small prison cell with four to five other inmates was a violation of human dignity and worth.[41] If the area allotted to each inmate is so small as to make it difficult for a person of average height to lie down flat without touching other cellmates, then

---

[36] Const. Ct. 89 Hun-Ma 82 (September 10, 1990); Const. Ct. 2000 Hun-Ba 60 (October 25, 2001); Const. Ct. 2008 Hun-Ba 58 (November 26 2009) (consolidated).
[37] Const. Ct. 95 Hun-Ka 6 (July 16, 1997) (consolidated).
[38] Const. Ct. 2010 Hun-Ba 402 (August 23, 2012).
[39] Const. Ct. 2001 Hun-Ma 163 (December 18, 2003).
[40] The Korean word for "dignity" in this passage is *p'umwi*, which is different from the term used in the human dignity and worth clause of Article 10. The significance of this will be discussed later in this chapter.
[41] Const. Ct. 2013 Hun-Ma 142 (December 29, 2016).

that by itself was an abuse of the state's punishment power and a violation of the inmate's human dignity and worth.

This last case is particularly noteworthy in that the Court refused even to consider possible violations of other basic rights. The function of human dignity and worth clause is apparently no longer supplemental. The Court stated:

> While the complainant raises claims that the said incarceration violated his right to pursue happiness, right to personality, and the right to live a life worthy of a human being, we shall not consider those separately because they can all be subsumed under the complainant's argument based on violation of the dignity and worth as a human being.

The Court evidently reversed the order of analysis employed in other cases. Rather than considering the possible violations of specific rights first and then looking to the human dignity and worth clause to fill any gaps in rights protection, it chose to go straight to human dignity without bothering to determine whether other specific rights were insufficient to provide adequate remedy. Even though the Court did not characterize human dignity and worth as an independent right, its invocation of the clause as the only basis for finding the incarceration unconstitutional strongly suggests that it is regarding the clause as a statement of a concrete right. If this reading is correct, then "human dignity and worth" can function like any other basic rights provisions and may be invoked as the most apposite provision without considering the applicability of other basic rights provisions.

Using the human dignity and worth clause of Article 10 this way will have several implications. First, this may give more "muscle" to the ideal of human dignity by making it a concrete right that may be invoked and implemented through constitutional adjudication. This was probably the motivation behind the Court's decision in that case. It apparently wished to make clear that human dignity and worth should yield some immediate, tangible benefits rather than remain a vague, abstract ideal. Secondly, as noted, in terms of interpretive approach, there will be no need to invoke Article 37(1) on unenumerated rights because the human dignity and worth clause is an expression of a specifically enumerated right. Third, and more seriously, now that human dignity is a concrete basic right just like any other rights, it may be subject to lawful limitations and restrictions. According to Article 37(2), basic rights may be restricted "when necessary for national security, maintenance of order, or public welfare." The same Article also provides that, even when permitted, such restrictions may not violate the core, or "essential content," of the affected right. This means that from now on the Court will have to engage in the task of discerning what constitutes the "essential content" of human dignity and worth and what sort of restrictions may or may not be imposed. This further raises the question whether the Court is equipped with the necessary competence to engage in such a philosophically complex (and politically charged) undertaking as distinguishing the core of human dignity from its periphery. Moreover, if some restrictions on human dignity and worth are permitted while other are not, it may become harder to maintain the view that human dignity and worth is the highest ideal and supreme value of Korea's constitutional order. It will also be less clear how the right to dignity, which is just another basic right, could be described as the ultimate goal to be realized by all the other basic rights guaranteed in the Constitution.

4 HUMAN DIGNITY IN KOREA'S CULTURAL AND POLITICAL CONTEXT

According to Christopher McCrudden, judiciaries around the world have invoked human dignity to protect at least four different values: 1) individual autonomy; 2) freedom from humiliation; 3) protection from discrimination; and 4) satisfaction of basic human needs.[42] Similarly, Michael Rosen finds that dignity in the modern West is an amalgam of several strands of meaning deriving from different philosophical, religious, and rhetorical traditions, all of which pull in different directions.[43] Some scholars even question why such different values should be subsumed under one rubric.[44] Thus, it may not be surprising that judicial interpretations of dignity would yield inconsistent results, not only across national boundaries but also within the same jurisdiction. Perhaps the task of a comparativist is to highlight the tensions within a country's approach to human dignity and to show the unique ways in which that concept is deployed and contested. In the following, a number of issues will be discussed that tend to bring out the distinctive hue of the Korean debate on human dignity.

4.1 *Autonomous Individual and Traditional Culture*

One striking aspect of the Korean Constitutional Court's jurisprudence on human dignity is the apparent centrality of individual autonomy, or the right to self-determination. As mentioned, this was the basis for protecting the individual's right to control personal information. It was also invoked to protect a person from being photographed without consent. In a similar vein, the Constitutional Court has emphasized the right to self-determination in a series of cases which held that media companies may not be ordered by the government to make a public apology for unfair and biased reporting.[45] This right to autonomous decision-making also

---

[42] McCrudden, "Human Dignity and Judicial Interpretation," 685–694.
[43] Rosen notes four different strands: 1) dignity as status; 2) dignity as intrinsic value; 3) dignity as dignified behavior; and 4) dignity as demand for respectfulness. Rosen, *Dignity*, 10–61. For him, even the German *Grundgesetz* is a not-entirely-successful attempt to amalgamate two quite different ways of understanding dignity – the Kantian and the Catholic. Ibid., 76–119.
[44] Conor O'Mahony, "There Is No Such Thing as a Right to Dignity," *International Journal of Constitutional Law* 10, no. 2 (2012): 551–574.
[45] Const. Ct. 2009 Hun-Ka 27 (August 23, 2012); Const. Ct. 2013 Hun-Ka 6 (July 30, 2015). Dignity of a corporation, that is a nonhuman entity, will be discussed later in this chapter.

featured prominently in a case concerning the right to refuse life support. The Court reasoned that a right to cease life-sustaining treatment should be recognized for patients with terminal illness for whom such treatment is no longer aimed at a cure but has become merely a bodily intrusion.[46] Letting nature take its course by ending such artificial intrusion, it stated, would better cohere with the value of human dignity.

Particularly noteworthy is the fact that, in a number of cases, the Court has highlighted the individual's "right to sexual self-determination" (sŏngchŏk chagigyŏlchŏngkwŏn 性的 自己決定權) as grounds for striking down legislations. In 2009, it held unconstitutional Korea's seduction law – namely, a provision in the Criminal Code which punished a man for luring a woman into sexual relations "through a false promise of marriage."[47] It pointed out that underlying this provision was a "patriarchic and moralistic sex ideology" that extolled the purity and chastity of women only and as a result failed to respect them as autonomous subjects with the right to self-determination.

Similarly, in 2015, the Court said that criminalization of adultery was unconstitutional.[48] After noting that preservation of married life should be left to the free will of the couple rather than being enforced through state penal laws, the five-justice majority pointed out that the Criminal Code article on adultery imposed excessive restraint on individuals' right to sexual self-determination (as well as the right to privacy). A sixth justice agreed for a slightly different reason – punishing even the unmarried partner with whom a married person committed adultery was excessive and an undue restraint on the right to sexual self-determination.[49] With this case, the Court reversed its earlier decisions of 1990, 1993, 2001, and 2008, all of which had rejected constitutional challenges to the same provision.[50]

Given Korea's conservative Confucian cultural background, which supposedly prioritizes the family over the individual and espouses very strict sexual ethics, the Court's emphasis on the right to make autonomous, personal decisions regarding sexual matters seems rather surprising. As if to provide an explanation, the Court in the adultery decision stressed that the public's attitude toward adulterous acts had changed over time and pointed to the criminal law's ineffectiveness as a means for

---

[46] Const. Ct. 2008 Hun-Ma 385 (November 26, 2009). The Court, however, ruled that this right, which can only be exercised by the patient, did not generate an obligation on the part of the state to enact legislation that specified the precise conditions and procedures for exercising that right. The constitutional complaint was thus rejected, in which family members of a terminally ill patent alleged that the legislature's failure to enact the necessary laws was unconstitutional.

[47] Const. Ct. 2008 Hun-Ba 58 (November 27, 2009) (reversing a previous decision in 2002).

[48] Const. Ct. 2009 Hun-Ba 17 (February 26, 2015) (consolidated).

[49] A seventh justice had no problem with punishing adultery but joined the majority in striking down the provision because he thought it was unconstitutional to prescribe only imprisonment with hard labor for all adulterous acts without regard to the different circumstances and varying degrees of culpability.

[50] It bears noting that, in the 2008 decision, five out of nine justices were of the opinion that the article was not in conformity with the Constitution. It was upheld nonetheless because, according to the Constitution, six votes are required to invalidate a statute.

preserving the sanctity of marriage life. It may be that Korean society is now more defined by a liberal individualistic outlook and no longer so influenced by traditional Confucian mores. If this is so, it should at least be noted that the Court is not exactly a neutral observer of this alleged decline of the Confucian influence in Korea. It has been an active player in the ongoing societal discussion over the continuing relevance of Confucianism, and it has invoked human dignity and worth as grounds for de-emphasizing the relevance of tradition.

In 1997, for example, the Constitutional Court held unconstitutional a provision in the Civil Code that prohibited marriage between persons sharing the same surname and the same ancestral origin. Widely seen as the bedrock of the Confucian family structure based on exogamy, this prohibition was pronounced as an undue restriction on, inter alia, the individual's right to sexual self-determination.[51] It is at least arguable that through decisions such as this the Court reduced the place and power of the Confucian tradition in Korea and reoriented Korean society in more a liberal and individualistic direction.[52]

It would be a mistake, however, to conclude that the liberal individualistic notion of autonomy and free will exhausts the Constitutional Court's understanding of human dignity. In relation to the criminalization of prostitution, for example, the Court rejected the argument based on autonomous individuals' right to make personal decisions.[53] Although it acknowledged that punishing the sale of sex affects the right of sexual self-determination of both the seller and the buyer, the Court nevertheless concluded that it was constitutional to ban prostitution through criminal law. It reasoned that the use of state penal authority was legitimate when it is aimed at preventing the commodification of sex so as to safeguard the constitutional value of human dignity and worth. It even warned that such disregard for human dignity will have a wider social effect by encouraging the development of the sex industry, which will obstruct the normal flow of capital and labor and thereby distort the economic structure. By invoking the human dignity and worth clause as justification for restricting the right to make autonomous decisions by sellers and buyers of sex, it actually pitted the value of human dignity against the individual's right to self-determination.

Whether or not this is a reflection of the staying power of Confucian social mores is difficult to verify. It does show, however, that the Court does not understand human dignity and worth solely in terms of individual choice. Its view, at least in this case, seems to be that human dignity not only is distinct from, but also takes precedence over, the individual's right to make autonomous choices.[54]

---

[51] Const. Ct. 95 Hun-Ka 6 (July 16, 1997) (consolidated).
[52] For more, see Chaihark Hahm, "Law, Culture, and the Politics of Confucianism," *Columbia Journal of Asian Law* 16, no. 2 (2003).
[53] Const. Ct. 2013 Hun-Ka 2 (March 31, 2016).
[54] For a critical analysis of the tension between decisions that use human dignity as grounds for strengthening basis rights and those that use human dignity as grounds for limiting basic rights, see

Apparently, human dignity is a society-wide (perhaps a species-wide) ideal that cannot be determined or disposed of by a few individuals.[55]

4.2 Human Dignity, Family, and Filial Piety

In another set of cases that revealed the tension between human dignity and the Confucian tradition, the Court held unconstitutional certain provisions of the Civil Code related to family structure. Here, however, the reason was not so much because those laws violated the individual's right to make autonomous decisions but more because they treated citizens as mere objects of state law. A provision that mandated that the surname of a child be the same as its biological father's without exception was held unconstitutional.[56] Given that a family may consist of children who are not biologically related to their father (e.g. through adoption or remarriage of the mother), the Court held that it was a violation of the individual's right to personality for the law not to allow for ways of changing the child's surname. By coercing the universal use of the biological father's surname and failing to respect the diverse needs of individuals and families, the state had regarded the citizens as mere objects of legal regulation.

The Constitutional Court was more explicit in its criticism in the case on the "head of the household" system.[57] For the law to require that each "family" be constituted under the authority of a household head (*hoju* 戶主) was held to be unconstitutional because it failed to respect the family members as individuals with equal dignity and worth. The Court first stated that allowing only sons to become heads of the household, with daughters being allowed only under exceptional conditions, was a violation of the principle of equality. The Court then pointed out that this hierarchical "household" sanctioned by the law only contributed to the maintenance of a patriarchic family structure and thus treated each individual not as a person with dignity but as a mere tool for the preservation of a particular type of family system prescribed by the state. It thus violated not only Article 10 but also

---

Lee Sang Soo, "Hŏnpŏp Chaep'anso Kyŏlchŏngmun ŭl t'onghaesŏ bon In'gan Chonŏm ŭi Ŭimi: Chonŏm Kaenyŏm ŭi Kwayong kwa Namyong [Meaning of Human Dignity as Seen Through the Constitutional Court's Decisions: Overuse and Abuse of Human Dignity Concept]," *Sŏgang Pŏmnyul Nonch'ong* [*Sŏgang Law Review*] 8, no. 1 (2019): 111–156.

[55] For similar reasoning employed by courts of other jurisdictions on cases involving peep-shows, dwarf-throwing, and pornography, see McCrudden, "Human Dignity and Judicial Interpretation," 705–706. Elsewhere, McCrudden frames this as the "self-regarding duty" entailed by the idea of human dignity. *Litigating Religions: An Essay on Human Rights, Courts, and Beliefs* (Oxford: Oxford University Press, 2018), 112–113.

[56] Const. Ct. 2003 Hun-Ka 5 (December 22, 2005) (consolidated).

[57] Const. Ct. 2001 Hun-Ka 9 (February 3, 2005) (consolidated). For a sophisticated discussion of this case as an instance of a constitutional debate taking place within a constitutional order that is simultaneously committed to liberal democratic ideals and Confucian values and mores, see Sungmoon Kim, *Public Reason Confucianism: Democratic Perfectionism and Constitutionalism in East Asia* (Cambridge: Cambridge University Press, 2016), 107–137.

Article 36(1), which requires that "marriage and family life ... be entered into and sustained on the basis of individual dignity and equality of the sexes." The patrilineal family structure, widely regarded as a Confucian institution rooted in Korean history, could no longer be enforced by the state.[58]

When it comes, however, to enforcing the Confucian virtue of "filial piety" (*hyo* 孝), there is apparently a limit to the applicability of this demand for treating each member of the family as an individual with dignity. The Constitutional Court, for example, has upheld provisions in the Criminal Code that provided for heavier punishment for physical crimes committed against the perpetrator's "lineal ascendants." Pointing to the extreme moral depravity involved in causing bodily injury to one's parents and grandparents, thereby bringing about their death, the Court indicated that such provisions are justified due to the act's "heightened degree of social blameworthiness" (高度의 社會的 非難可能性).[59] It stated that promotion of filial piety has historically been a part of Korean legal culture and that this virtue is still an essential component of Korea's contemporary social ethics. It basically repeated the same reasoning in a later case that challenged mandatory heavier punishment for murder of one's lineal ascendants.[60] Similarly, in a case involving a provision of the Criminal Procedure Code that barred the filing of a criminal complaint against one's own or one's spouse's lineal ascendants, the Court stated that the article serves a legitimate purpose of promoting peace and harmony within the family.[61]

Although these laws were challenged mainly on grounds of equality, it is worth noting that arguments based on human dignity were also made by petitioners. Both arguments, however, were rejected by the Court, only to be heeded by the dissenting justices. In the case on murder of lineal ascendants, the dissent pointed out that Article 36(1) of the Constitution states that "family life shall be ... sustained on the basis of individual dignity" and that this mandates a "democratic family relationship" where all family members are respected equally as individuals with dignity. In the case on the ban on criminal complaints, five dissenting justices maintained that family in modern society is "not an authoritarian organization composed of a one-person family head and other members subordinate to him" but rather a democratic relationship wherein all members of the family are each respected as individual persons.

Such dissenting opinions may be an indication that the Court might change its views in the future. The 2002 case on aggravated punishment for death resulting from bodily injury was decidedly unanimously. Eleven years later, in the 2013 case on heavier punishment for murder, at least two justices were willing to question the

---

[58] Japan during the prewar period also had a similar family system enforced by the state, which was abolished after the war under the United States' occupation. See Chapter 2 in this volume by Keigo Obayashi.
[59] Const. Ct. 2000 Hun-Ba 53 (March 28, 2002).
[60] Const. Ct. 2011 Hun-Ba 267 (July 25, 2013). For a similar case in Japan that reached the opposite conclusion, see Chapter 2 in this volume by Keigo Obayashi.
[61] Const. Ct. 2008 Hun-Ba 56 (February 24, 2011).

need to prioritize the goal of preserving harmonious family relationships over treating children as individuals with equal dignity. In the 2011 decision on prohibition of criminal complaints against lineal ascendants, a majority of five justices dissented. Here, the views of four justices became the controlling opinion, because only five were in favor of striking down the provision, one vote short of the constitutionally required minimum of six votes. These may or may not suggest a trend toward emphasizing human dignity regardless of one's position within the family and away from the Confucian, hierarchical notions of family. For now, affirming the traditional virtue of filial piety apparently does not violate the injunction against treating children as mere objects in the service of traditional family system.

4.3 *Right to Life*

Although the Korean Constitution includes no provision on the right to life, most commentators agree that it is a basic right that may be derived from the clause on human dignity and worth. Interestingly, however, the Constitutional Court has stated that the right to life is a "transcendental [*sŏnhŏmjŏk* 先驗的] and natural-law right [自然法的 權利] based on the survival instinct and raison d'etre of human beings" and as such must be protected even though it is not specifically mentioned in the Constitution.[62] As a "natural right," the right to life apparently need not be derived from any particular text. The Court even declared that this natural right also belongs to a fetus which is "life in the making." Such expansive pronouncements notwithstanding, the Court's jurisprudence allows for various forms of restriction on the right to life.

First of all, the Court has held in numerous cases that capital punishment is not inconsistent with the right to life. In fact, the holding of the 1996 decision that characterized it as a natural right was that the death sentence is not unconstitutional. In reaching this conclusion, however, the issue of human dignity was never addressed. The Court merely went through a proportionality analysis to find that the imposition of capital punishment may be justified in exceptional circumstances where it is unavoidable and necessary to protect other lives or other public goods with value comparable to that of the criminal's life. Nevertheless, the decision may have been indirectly influenced by debates on human dignity. The Court started out by stating that there is no textual basis in the Korean Constitution for recognizing absolute basic rights that could never be restricted. The unstated reference is clearly the German *Grundgesetz*, where the provision on human dignity is understood to be absolute and unamendable.[63] The Court's implicit reasoning appears to be that,

---

[62] Const. Ct. 95 Hun-Ba 1 (November 28, 1996). The term for "transcendental" may also be rendered "a priori." The implication seems to be that it precedes and does not require the state's recognition or validation – hence, perhaps, the invocation of natural law.

[63] Dieter Grimm, "Dignity in a Legal Context: Dignity as an Absolute Right," in *Understanding Human Dignity (Proceedings of the British Academy)*, edited by Christopher McCrudden (Oxford: Oxford University Press, 2013).

since the right to life in Korea is not based on human dignity, which furthermore is not an absolute right, there is no textual obstacle to concluding that the right to life can be restricted just like any other rights.

The non-absolute nature of the right to life was also evident in the Court's 2019 decision which held that criminalization of abortion is "not in conformity with the constitution."[64] It reversed an earlier decision,[65] rendered seven years previously, which had stated that, just as a person's physical condition and developmental state is irrelevant to the person's right to life, so the level of growth of a fetus should not affect its status as a holder of the right to life. It had specifically rejected the view that the level of protection accorded a fetus might vary depending on how many weeks had elapsed since conception or on its "stage of biological differentiation."

The new decision, by contrast, began by highlighting women's right to self-determination, derived from the individual's general right to personality, which is protected under the clause on human dignity and worth. It then proceeded to review whether the provision that made abortion a crime unduly restricted the right to self-determination, specifically the pregnant woman's right to decide whether to maintain pregnancy and to give birth. To be sure, it also reaffirmed that the fetus is a subject of the constitutional right to life and that the state has a constitutional duty to protect fetal life. The Court declared, however, that it is permissible for the law to distinguish life according to its developmental stages and to provide different levels of protection for each. It also reasoned that, in order for the pregnant woman's right to self-determination to be meaningful, she must be given sufficient time in which to can make an informed decision, based on all relevant factors,[66] as to whether to carry her pregnancy to full term. The Court concluded that, during such decision-making time, it should be permissible for the state to provide different levels and means of protecting fetal life.

Instead of specifying how long that decision-making time should be, however, the plurality opinion merely noted that it could be up to twenty-two weeks when the fetus is generally thought to become viable outside the womb (under the current state of technology). It thus gave the legislature until the end of 2020 to formulate a suitable system for regulating the practice of abortion, including the proper length of the decision-making time. The minority opinion, by contrast, would have preferred to stipulate that during the first trimester a woman should have an unfettered right to decide whether to terminate her pregnancy. Both opinions, however, agreed that the criminal code's blanket prohibition on abortion failed to meet the

[64] Const. Ct. 2017 Hun-Ma 127 (April 11, 2019). It chose not to render a judgment of "simple unconstitutionality" because that would have eliminated all grounds for punishing abortions, including ones that should be banned – for example, those done after the fetus becomes independently viable.
[65] Const. Ct. 2010 Hun-Ba 402 (August 23, 2012).
[66] The Court mentioned such factors as: her own physical, psychological, social, and financial conditions; the possibility of receiving state assistance during pregnancy, childbirth and child-rearing; advice and counselling from associates; and available options in case she decides to terminate her pregnancy.

proportionality test because the ban was not particularly conducive to the public good of protecting fetal life, and neither was the restraint on the woman's right to self-determination the least restrictive means for achieving that goal. The justices stressed that providing a better social and institutional environment that could prevent unwanted pregnancies and reduce the demand for abortion would be more conducive to protecting fetal life and that criminalizing abortion has had limited deterrent effect. Evidently, in this case, the right to life, albeit a natural right, had to yield to the right to self-determination, derived from human dignity.

4.4 Dignity of Nonhumans?

One curious feature of the Korean Court's jurisprudence is its affirmation of the dignity of nonhumans or, more precisely, legal persons. In a case arising from a defamation suit, the Court considered whether a magazine publisher may constitutionally be ordered by a court to publish an apology (in lieu of or in addition to paying monetary damages) as a form of civil remedy.[67] It reasoned that such coerced apology necessarily forces someone to say something that the person does not believe in and that the person is compelled to adopt an ethical stance at variance with one's own. As such, it was a violation of the person's constitutional right to conscience. More importantly, the Court also stated that court-ordered apology thwarts the free and unobstructed development of the person's right to personality, protected under the clause on human dignity and worth. The Court took it for granted that the "right to personality" should be guaranteed to all "persons," be they natural or legal. Not surprisingly, the dissenting opinion pointed out that the Court's reasoning raises such bizarre issues as whether a publishing company can have a conscience and what it would mean for it to "freely develop its personality."

In later cases, the Court has continued to affirm the position that media companies cannot be ordered by the government to publish an apology. One case involved whether a broadcasting company may be compelled by a government commission to make an "apology to viewers" for having broadcast a program that failed to observe the standards of "fairness and objectivity."[68] Another case involved a determination by a different commission that a news outlet should apologize to its readers for running an article, during election period, which was inflammatory and unfair to a particular candidate.[69] In these cases, the Court avoided relying on the right to

---

[67] Const. Ct. 89 Hun-Ma 160 (April 1, 1991). For more on this case, see Chaihark Hahm, "Negotiating Confucian Civility through Constitutional Discourse," in *The Politics of Affective Relations: East Asia and Beyond*, edited by Chaihark Hahm and Daniel A. Bell (New York: Lexington Books, 2004). For a similar case in Taiwan, see Chapter 4 in this volume by Jimmy Chia-Shin Hsu.

[68] Const. Ct. 2009 Hun-Ka 27 (August 23, 2012). The order was issued by Korea Communications Commission upon a determination by Korea Communications Standards Commission.

[69] Const. Ct. 2013 Hun-Ka 6 (July 30, 2015). During election periods, the Press Arbitration Commission sets up a Deliberative Commission on News Reports on Elections that monitors the quality of news regarding candidates and election campaigns.

conscience but continued to cite the right to free development of personality as grounds for holding such government-ordered apologies unconstitutional.[70]

It is certainly odd that the right to personality, which is usually deployed as the individual's shield against unscrupulous reporters and media companies, should be invoked in these cases to protect the media. This is particularly so given that the media companies were not contesting that they had engaged in inappropriate behaviors (i.e. defamation, unfair and biased programming, and inflammatory and partial reporting). They were merely objecting to being forced to make an apology.

More fundamentally, though, these decisions are difficult to reconcile with the historical background that caused human dignity to become such a central term in contemporary constitutional and human rights discourse. It is well known that the Universal Declaration of Human Rights (1948), the International Covenant on Civil and Political Rights (1966), and the International Covenant on Economic, Social and Cultural Rights (1966) all refer in their preambles to "the inherent dignity ... of all members of the human family." As expounded by Germany's *Bundesverfassungsgericht*, the respect and protection of human dignity "is based on the idea of man as a spiritual-moral being endowed with the freedom to determine and develop himself."[71] According to one commentator, the famous Article 1 of the German *Grundgesetz*, which declares the inviolability of human dignity, was formulated with a view to protecting and safeguarding the "inner freedom" of human persons, which had proven so vulnerable during the Nazi era.[72] It seems beyond doubt, therefore, that the global emphasis on human dignity, in the post–World War II era, had little to do with protecting the rights of legal persons.

It is uncertain if the Korean Court was consciously attempting to break new grounds and go beyond its putative model to extend the applicability of the human dignity provision to legal persons. It is more likely that it was engaging in a rather sloppy, if formalistic, reading of constitutional text. The Korean words for "human" (*ingan*) and "person" (*inkyŏk*) both share the syllable *in* ("man"), which may have blurred the analytic distinction between the two concepts.[73] Plus, the word for person (*inkyŏk*) is also part of the Korean term for "right to personality" (*inkyŏkkwŏn*), thus making it easy to think that any person can be the holder of the right to freely develop one's personality. If we are to take these decisions seriously, we might have to conclude that the protection offered under the rubric of human dignity is not

---

[70] In both cases, the dissent pointed out the absurdity in supposing that a corporation should be allowed to freely develop their personalities.

[71] 45 BVerfGE 187, 227 (1977) (quoted in Eberle, "Human Dignity and Personality in German Constitutional Law," 207).

[72] Christoph Goos, "Würde des Menschen: Restoring Human Dignity in Post-Nazi Germany," in *Understanding Human Dignity (Proceedings of the British Academy)*, edited by Christopher McCrudden (Oxford: Oxford University Press, 2013), 86–92.

[73] I am grateful to Mary Anne Case for pointing out that in Western languages "human" is clearly different from "person" such that there is very little likelihood of confusing the two.

necessarily for something inherent in human beings but for an incident of legal capacity that is granted by the state to artificial "persons."

4.5 Human Dignity and Japanese Colonial Occupation

Korea regained independence in 1945 after thirty-five years of Japanese colonial occupation, but the memory of that era still haunts Korean society and sometimes generates notable judicial pronouncements. One of the delicate issues that continue to plague the postwar relationship between the two countries is Japan's acknowledgment of its responsibility for the occupation and its numerous harms. Countless Korean who had been victimized in various ways by the Japanese imperial government sought legal redress in Japan, only to be met with unsympathetic response. The Japanese courts would invariably cite one of the agreements signed by the two governments upon normalization of diplomatic relations in 1965.[74] Their reasoning was that Korea had agreed to forego all claims of its individual citizens against Japan in return for a "contribution" by Japan of $300,000,000 in goods and services as well as hundreds of millions of dollars in low-interest loans. Some of these victims then started turning to the Korean government claiming that they had never authorized the state to give up their individual claims and that none of the monetary contribution or assistance made by Japan were conveyed to them.

In a pair of decisions rendered in 2011, which put the government in a tight diplomatic spot, the Korean Constitutional Court sided with these individuals.[75] In one case, the claimants were former "comfort women" who had been forced to work in wartime brothels operated by the Japanese imperial army; in the other, they were former conscripts stationed in Hiroshima and Nagasaki, who sustained injuries and lifelong misery when atomic bombs were dropped in those cities. The Court pointed out that, according to the Korean government's own position, such individuals' claims for compensation were never even mentioned during the negotiations leading up to the 1965 claims agreements and thus cannot be deemed to have been extinguished by that treaty.[76] This meant that there is a disagreement between Korea and Japan over the proper interpretation of that agreement, which also provides for actions that may be sought (i.e. diplomatic negotiation or arbitration) by either party in case of an interpretive dispute. The Court then reasoned that in this case the

---

[74] The full name of the treaty is Agreement on the Settlement of Problems Concerning Property and Claims and on Economic Cooperation between the Republic of Korea and Japan.

[75] Const. Ct. 2006 Hun-Ma 788 (August 30, 2011); Const. Ct. 2008 Hun-Ma 648 (August 30, 2011).

[76] This position, articulated by the Korean government in 2005, was in fact a relatively new development. Until then, the implicit Korean position was closer to the view that all individual claims had been extinguished by the 1965 Agreement. Under a more populist and nationalistic regime, however, Korea started to take a stance more protective of its own citizens and more assertive toward Japan. For Japan's position on the issue, see Shin Hae Bong, "Compensation for Victims of Wartime Atrocities: Recent Developments in Japan's Case Law," *Journal of International Criminal Justice* 3, no. 1 (2005): 187–206.

government's failure to take any action to resolve the disagreement constituted a violation of its constitutional duty to protect and realize the human dignity of all citizens. Due to the government's inaction, the validity of claims of the former comfort women and the survivors of atomic blasts against the Japanese government were in a limbo, as it were.

These decisions are noteworthy because the Court stressed in both cases that human dignity not only acts as a "limit on state power" (by shielding the individual from infringement by the state) but also represents a "mission of state power" by imposing a duty on the state to protect the individual's dignity when it is threatened by others. In contrast to other decisions discussed here, the Court used human dignity and worth as an affirmative goal to be pursued by the government rather than as a defensive measure against the government. It also emphasized the fact that these claimants have had to endure a lifetime of intolerable harm to their dignity and worth as human beings. It was the state's duty urgently to bring an end to such neglect.[77]

Another aspect of the colonial experience that still affects Korean society is the issue of individuals who collaborated with the Japanese colonial authorities. In the tribunal of public opinion, they probably deserve the least respect and protection from the state. Many think they should be punished and humiliated for having enjoyed wealth and status at the expense of their compatriots. Recently, the Constitutional Court had occasion to consider the degree to which the human dignity and worth clause protects such "traitors to the nation." A couple of statutes were enacted in 2005 for the purpose of rectifying past wrongs committed during the colonial period. One authorized the investigation of individuals who had allegedly collaborated with the colonial authorities. Upon determination that the person had engaged in "pro-Japanese anti-national activity" (親日反民族行爲) as defined by the statute, another law authorized the confiscation of their properties acquired by such persons as reward for their collaboration.

A number of individuals claimed that an official determination that their ancestors had engaged in pro-Japanese anti-national activity caused their reputation and that of the deceased ancestors to suffer and therefore that the law that specified the nature of such activities was unconstitutional. The Court ultimately rejected these claims.[78] In one case, it basically stated that the claimants did not have standing because all those activities were done by their ancestors.[79] In others, the Court applied the proportionality test and concluded that the harm to the reputation was

---

[77] Related to these cases, the Korean Supreme Court affirmed in October 2018 that a Japanese firm had a duty to compensate for forced labor and unpaid wages of Korean conscripts during the colonial period. A diplomatic row ensued when the firm's assets in Korea were seized to enforce the judgment.
[78] Also rejected were arguments that the determination essentially constituted an imposition of punishment with any opportunity of defense and that it violated the equality principle by invidiously singling out these individuals to effectively create a "caste." A different set of cases challenged the law on confiscation of "pro-Japanese properties" but were also unsuccessful.
[79] Const. Ct. 2006 Hun-Ma 1298 (September 24, 2009).

not excessive and that the public interest served by setting the historical record straight significantly outweighed the restrictions on the right to personality.[80] What is noteworthy, however, is that, in all of these cases, the Court recognized that the deceased could be the subject of the right to social reputation and esteem, which is included in the general right to personality that derives from Article 10. The decisions, although unsatisfactory to the claimants, were all reasoned on the premise that dead persons also deserve to be protected from serious distortions in the evaluation of their personality.[81] It may thus be inferred that the application of the idea of human dignity is not limited to living human beings.[82] To be sure, none of these decisions explicitly referred to the concept of human dignity. As seen, however, the Court has routinely derived the general right to personality from the clause on human dignity and worth. It may thus have inadvertently expanded the scope of subjects that are entitled to dignity to include deceased persons (in addition to legal persons).

4.6 Dignity outside Article 10?

One complicating factor in understanding the Korean discourse on human dignity stems from the fact that in the Korean language the law sometimes employs a term different from those found in Article 10 but which also means "dignity." Rather than *chonŏm* (dignity) and *kach'i* (worth), the term *p'umwi* (品位) is used and sometimes becomes the subject of constitutional discussions. It is often used in relation to a legal duty to maintain the dignity of certain positions or offices, such as that of a public official or an attorney-at-law. The relevant statutes specifying the rights and duties of these professions include articles to the effect that no member of the profession should engage in behavior that harms one's own dignity (*p'umwi*).[83] These laws even provide for disciplinary actions in case a person has failed to maintain his or her dignity.[84] In this context, "dignity" clearly means maintaining "dignified behavior." Further, it is specific to a particular status or profession (e.g. dignity of a public official).[85] The obvious premise is that not everyone has this kind of dignity and that even the same person may fail to comport oneself in the requisite dignified manner. It is certainly not something that everyone is endowed with. It is more a standard that requires

---

[80] Const. Ct. 2008 Hun-Ba 111 (March 31, 2011); Const. Ct. 2012 Hun-Ba 19 (May 20, 2013).
[81] This may be another instance of the German influence. On the famous *Mephisto* case of 1971, which held that tarnishing the memory of the dead was inconsistent with human dignity, see Eberle, "Human Dignity and Personality in German Constitutional Law," 227–228.
[82] For a fascinating reflection on the possible philosophical grounds for respecting the dignity of dead persons, see Rosen, *Dignity*, 129–160.
[83] State Public Officials Act, art. 63; Attorney-at-Law Act, art. 24(1). In fact, similar provisions can be found in laws on patent attorneys, certified judicial scriveners, certified tax accountants, and certified public accountants.
[84] State Public Officials Act, Art. 78(1)(iii); Attorney-at-Law Act, Art. 91(2).
[85] Cf., Rosen, *Dignity*, 6, 13, 31–38.

continuous work to maintain. Rather than acting as the individual's protection against encroachment by the state, it functions as a burden on members of those professions.

In fact, one public official challenged this "duty to maintain dignity" in the Constitutional Court, arguing that the law failed to provide a clear definition and that the disciplinary actions mandated by it were excessive. The Court, however, disagreed and held that an average public official was perfectly able to foresee what constitutes behavior that harms the dignity of the profession and that the law provides for individualized process for determining the particular form of disciplinary action so as to prevent excessive sanctions.[86]

What is interesting is that neither the claimant nor the Court in this case invoked the human dignity and worth clause of Article 10. In all likelihood, this is because the law on public officials did not employ the terms used in that clause (*chonŏm* or *kach'i*) but only referred to *p'umwi*.[87] So, in the Korean context, this case falls outside the usual discussion on human dignity. It is thus tempting to conclude that, in Korea, dignity inherent in all human beings (protected by Art. 10) is clearly distinguishable from "dignity" (*p'umwi*) associated with rank or position. Yet that may be too rash, because the term *p'umwi* is also used, on occasion, in connection with Article 10. It was invoked by the Court in the case on degrading treatment of prison inmates. As mentioned, being forced into overcrowded facilities or to wear excessive restraining devices made it difficult to maintain even the minimum level of dignity (*p'umwi*) and thus constituted a violation of Article 10. Here, the Court clearly used *p'umwi* to mean an attribute of all human beings. Even a convicted prisoner must be afforded the possibility of comporting him- or herself in a "dignified" manner befitting members of the human species.[88] The Court, however, has yet to clarify the nature of the relationship between duty to maintain *p'umwi* and "human dignity and worth."

5 CONCLUSION

This chapter has attempted to give an account of the Korean constitutional discourse on human dignity and to highlight certain themes and features that seem to bring out the local "flavor" of that discourse. At a general level, Korean scholars and the Constitutional Court make pronouncements regarding human dignity that closely resemble statements by commentators and courts from other jurisdictions. This, of course, is not an accident, given that most Korean jurists, both academics and practitioners, are fairly well informed about major decisions

---

[86] Const. Ct. 2013 Hun-Ba 435 (February 25, 2016).
[87] The provision on disciplinary action also mentioned conduct that harms one's *ch'emyŏn* (體面), which literally means "face" as in "losing one's face," and *wishin* (威信), which connotes "authority and trustworthiness."
[88] On the idea of "dignity as nobility for the common man" or that "human dignity involves an upwards equalization of rank," see Waldron, *Dignity, Rank and Rights*, 22, 33–36.

and theories of other countries, particularly Germany. For example, many commentators start the discussion on human dignity by referring to the German scholar Günter Dürig's famous "object formula."[89] Once we delve into the detailed discussions, however, it is clear that in Korea human dignity is sometimes invoked in rather unexpected contexts and interpreted in ways that may appear somewhat surprising to foreign observers.

As mentioned, the Korean Constitutional Court's jurisprudence on human dignity is less than systematic or consistent. It often declares that the human dignity and worth clause in Article 10 is the "source" from which other unenumerated rights may be derived. At other times, it seems to read the clause as a specific rights provision that may be used to find a government action unconstitutional. This may be due to the inherent ambiguity of the constitutional provisions on human dignity. It may also reflect the inconsistent enthusiasm of justices, some of whom are more eager to provide protection to individuals when specific rights provisions do not offer adequate solutions.

The discourse on human dignity becomes even more confused because of another provision, which deals with the state's duty to provide social welfare and social security (Art. 34). Its first section guarantees "a life worthy of human beings" to all citizens. Scholars explain that this idea comes from the German term *ein menschenwürdiges Leben*, which is commonly rendered in English as "a life of dignity." Yet the Korean term, which might also be translated as "a life befitting human beings," contains no reference to dignity. Commentators and the Court nevertheless routinely interpret this provision by relating it to the concept of human dignity and worth. This of course raises not only the practical question of how much welfare benefits and assistance is needed to ensure a life of dignity but also the conceptual issue whether the goal of dignity in this context means the same thing as dignity that supposedly inheres in all humans from birth (or conception).[90] Not surprisingly, debates regarding the proper interpretation of this provision tends to replicate the same discussion, seen in this chapter in relation to Article 10, as to whether this is a statement of a general principle of social welfare or a concrete judicially enforceable right.

In sum, numerous factors contribute to the confused state of the discourse on human dignity in Korea, and not all of them can be attributed to the Court. Yet the apparent trend in its decisions toward reading the human dignity and worth clause in Article 10 as a provision on a specific justiciable right tends to prevent the formulation of a manageable criterion for applying that clause with a modicum of rigor and consistency. In many cases, the Court's decisions are rich in factual detail as to how a statute or government action resulted in an intolerably inhumane situation but analytically very thin in terms of presenting a generally applicable

---

[89] For example, Bang, "Che 10 Cho," 296–299.
[90] For a discussion of problems raised by such confusing usage of human dignity in the Indian context, see Chapter 1 in this volume by Pritam Baruah.

test. As a result, each case seems to be decided on an ad hoc, case-by-case basis. Such decisions tend to offer little guidance for the future. It is probably unrealistic to hope for a deeper philosophical engagement with the concept of human dignity. It should, however, be realistic and legitimate to demand that the Court be aware of the diverse and potentially conflicting ways in which it is employing the concept of human dignity.

4

Human Dignity in the Jurisprudence of the Taiwan Constitutional Court

Jimmy Chia-Shin Hsu[*]

1 THE ENTRY OF HUMAN DIGNITY INTO TAIWAN'S CONSTITUTIONAL DISCOURSE

The absence of the concept of "human dignity" in the text of the Constitution of the Republic of China (ROC) makes it an exception in East Asia, in contrast to the Japanese Constitution and the South Korean Constitution. However, the language of human dignity may not have been foreign to the framers of the ROC Constitution when it was first passed in 1946. The Republic of China was a founding signatory state to the United Nations Charter (1945), which enshrines "the dignity and worth of the human person" in its Preamble. Moreover, the Republic of China's delegate to the UN and vice-chairman of the Human Rights Commission, Dr. Chang Peng-Chun (張彭春), played a pivotal role in the drafting of Universal Declaration of Human Rights.[1] Despite the absence of the specific wording of human dignity, the 1947 ROC Constitution was by no means short of fundamental rights protection. Compared to more recent constitutions, the Second Chapter of the ROC Constitution is very concise in terms of the rights enumerated[2] and the articulation of their nature and boundary.[3] Further, it includes a generic clause, Article 22, that protects unenumerated rights. Alongside the several

---

[*] I thank Chaihark Hahm, Pritam Baruah, Michael Rosen, Christopher McCrudden, Kelley Loper, Sungmoon Kim, Wenchen Chang, Mary Anne Case, Yentu Su, Hsiao-Wei Kuan, and participants at the panels of the 7th Asian Constitutional Law Forum at Thammasat University, Bangkok, in 2017, and the symposium of Human Dignity in Asia: Dialogue between Law and Culture at Academia Sinica, Taiwan, in 2018. The research for this chapter is funded by the Ministry of Science and Technology, Taiwan (MOST 107–2410–H–001–058–MY2).

[1] Sumner Twiss, "Confucian Ethics, Concept-Clusters, and Human Rights," in *Polishing the Chinese Mirror: Essays in Honor of Henry Rosemont Jr.*, edited by Marthe Chandler and Ronnie Littlejohn (New York: Global Scholarly Publications, 2008), pp. 60–61.

[2] These include equal protection, right of personal security and liberty, right to civil trial, right of residence and migration, freedom of speech and press, freedom of secret correspondence, freedom of religion, freedom of assembly and association, right to subsistence, right to work, right to property, right of petition and litigation, right of election, recall, initiative and referendum, and right to public offices through examination.

[3] For the English translation of ROC Constitution, see the Laws & Regulations Database of Republic of China: http://law.moj.gov.tw/Eng/LawClass/LawAll.aspx?PCode=A0000001 (last visited June 23, 2017).

rights, the general limitations clause in Article 23 permits restrictions of the fundamental rights by law only insofar as "may be necessary to prevent infringement upon the freedoms of other persons, to avert an imminent crisis, to maintain social order or to advance public welfare." Most significantly, judicial review was stipulated in Article 171 such that "laws that are in conflict with the Constitution shall be null and void" and "if doubts arise as to whether a law is in conflict with the Constitution, interpretation thereon shall be made by the Judicial Yuan." This task of the Judicial Yuan is assigned to the grand justices in Article 79, laying the foundation of one of the oldest constitutional courts in Asia.

As is well known, the Civil War between Chiang Kai-shek's Nationalist government and the Chinese Communist Party broke out soon after the Constitution was enacted. The emergency regime of "Temporary Provisions Effective during the Period of National Mobilization for Suppression of the Communist Rebellion" (The Temporary Provisions) overrode the Constitution. As the Nationalist government was defeated in the Civil War and relocated to Taiwan in 1949, the territory bound by the Constitution was dramatically reduced to the island of Taiwan and a few adjacent islets. The ROC Constitution, the fundamental rights chapter in particular, continued in a state of limbo shackled by the Temporary Provisions and the Martial Law under Chiang Kai-shek and his son Chiang Ching-Kuo's authoritarian regime until democratization began in 1987.[4] In over a decade of democratic transition, the Constitution was amended seven times in the form of Additional Articles of the Constitution (AA). All of the Additional Articles concern governmental structures. None adds to or changes People's Rights and Duties. The sea change of heightened fundamental rights protection during democratization has been effectuated through legislative actions as well as innovative constitutional constructions by the Council of Grand Justices, later called the Constitutional Court (hereinafter the Taiwan Constitutional Court/TCC).

The word "dignity" (zun yan 尊嚴)[5] could already be found in the jurisprudence of the TCC during its early years under the authoritarian regime.[6] However, rather

---

[4] For a historical account of Taiwan's Constitution, see Jiunnn-rong Yeh, *The Constitution of Taiwan: A Contextual Analysis* (Oxford: Hart Publishing, 2016), chap. 2; Tom Ginsburg, *Judicial Review in New Democracies: Constitutional Courts in Asian Cases* (Cambridge: Cambridge University Press, 2003), chap. 5.

[5] "Dignity" is translated into the Chinese language as "尊嚴/zun yan." While it requires further etymological study to ascertain the earliest of such translation, it is undisputable in contemporary Chinese speaking world that "尊嚴/zun yan" is the most accurate translation of "dignity." The phrase of "尊嚴/zun yan" is composed of two characters. The original meaning of the first character "尊" (zun) dates back to the ancient Shang dynasty (roughly 1600–1046 BCE) and referred to the wine container used in royal religious rituals. This character was then used to mean the noble and elevated status of a class of natural or human beings as well as the attitude appropriate to address such a class of beings, namely "respect." The second character "嚴" (yan) means respect as well, and it can also mean solemn and dignified manners. The combination of "尊" and "嚴" as "尊嚴" (zun yan) to mean noble status and dignified manners deserving of respect can be found in classical literature as early as the writing of early Confucian philosopher Xunzi (316–237 BCE).

[6] 江玉林 (Yu-Lin Chiang), "人性尊嚴與人格尊嚴 (Human Dignity and Dignity of the Person)," *Taiwan Jurist* 20 (June 2004): 117.

than being applied to humanity in general, the concept of dignity was applied to corporate entities, institutions or offices, such as civil servants,[7] the courts,[8] the judiciary as a whole,[9] and even general concepts such as "the law."[10] "Dignity" was inserted into the constitutional text for the first time during the 1992 constitutional amendments in Article 18, Paragraph 4, of the Additional Articles.[11] The provision was not intended as an addition to the Second Chapter of People's Rights and Duties. All provisions in Article 18 were stipulated as so-called Fundamental National Policy, which are directives rather than norms. Neither was the word "dignity" applied to all human persons. Rather, it referred to the dignity of women. It reads: "The State shall protect the dignity of women, safeguard their personal safety, eliminate sexual discrimination, and further substantive gender equality."[12] To this day, this clause remains the only place where the word "dignity" appears in Taiwan's constitutional text. However, in the following years, through the Interpretations of Taiwan Constitutional Court, human dignity made its way deep into the Court's jurisprudence and has been widely accepted as a supreme constitutional value.

How did human dignity enter deep into Taiwan's constitutional jurisprudence, despite its precarious textual base? The concept of "human dignity" debuted in JY Interpretation No. 372 (1995).[13] It was delivered by a new term, the sixth term, of grand justices, who were sworn into office only the year before.[14] It was the first term of justices that were nominated by President Lee Teng Hui, a reformist, after the

[7] *JY Interpretation No. 71* (1957).
[8] *JY Interpretation No. 159* (1979), the dissenting opinion of Justice Chen Shih-Ron.
[9] *JY Interpretation No. 253* (1990), the dissenting opinion of Justice Chang Teh-Sheng; *JY Interpretation No. 329* (1993), the dissenting opinion of Justice Chang Teh-Sheng; *JY Interpretation No. 342* (1994), the concurring opinion of Herbert Han-Pao Ma.
[10] *JY Interpretation No. 144* (1975), the dissenting opinion of Justice Wang Ji-Jong.
[11] Through subsequent amendments, the same paragraph is currently in Article 10, Paragraph 6.
[12] After a series of constitutional revision, this provision is now in Article 10, Paragraph 6, of the current Additional Articles to the Constitution. The women's dignity clause can be seen as the culmination of three decades of the "women's movement" in Taiwan. It is meant to supplement the formal and general equal protection guaranteed in Article 7, which reads, "All citizens of the Republic of China, irrespective of sex, religion, race, class, or party affiliation, shall be equal before the law" by positively directing state efforts to promote women's status in a deeply patriarchal ethnically Chinese society. For an excellent account of the constitutional history of this provision, see 陳昭如 (Chao-ju Chen), "改寫男人的憲法:從平等條款、婦女憲章到釋憲運動的婦運憲法動員 [Rewriting a Male Constitution: Constitutional Mobilization by the Women's Movement from the Gender Equality Clause and Women's Charter to the Constitutional Litigation Movement]," *Taiwan Journal of Political Science* 52 (June 2012): 43–88.
[13] Because Article 171 of the Constitution commissions the task of constitutional interpretation to the Judicial Yuan, the official title of the Court's decision is Judicial Yuan Interpretation. And the Interpretations are numerically designated. In this chapter, it will be referred to as, for instance, *JY Interpretation No. 372* (1995).
[14] Since the inception of the Court in 1948, the length of one term of grand justices is nine years, according to the Organic Act of the Judicial Yuan. The justices were nominated by the president and confirmed by the Control Yuan. It means legally the president could renew the whole composition of the Court every nine years, even though in practice some justices got renominated for consecutive

democratic transition was initiated in 1987. The new term of justices proved significant. They expanded judicial power to facilitate liberalization and transition into full democracy.[15] Among the seventeen justices, eight were former academics who had acquired their doctoral degrees in Germany, the United States, or Austria.[16] In this Interpretation, the TCC addressed the constitutionality of a Supreme Court (a court separate from the Constitutional Court) precedent about what level of domestic strife constitutes a legitimate cause for divorce in the Civil Code. This case presented a great opportunity for the Court to invoke the newly enacted dignity of women clause. And the Court went further. On top of it, the Court invoked the Universal Declaration of Human Rights. The Court opined: "The protection of human dignity and personal security are promulgated in the Universal Declaration of Human Rights, and these values underpin the protection of the people's rights and freedoms in this Constitution. Article 9, Paragraph 5 of the Additional Articles ... are framed in consonance with these values."[17] Skillfully, the Court broke free from the immediate frame of gender equality and used the women's dignity clause as a gateway to the idea of human dignity enshrined in the UDHR. Besides international human rights documents, the influence of comparative constitutional jurisprudence was also evident. In his concurring opinion, Justice Su Jyun-Hsiung (蘇俊雄), formerly a professor of criminal law at National Taiwan University with a doctoral degree from the University of Freiburg in Germany, elaborated that human dignity is the foundational constitutional value. He invoked not only the UDHR but also Article 1 of the German Basic Law as well as Article 13 of the Japanese Constitution. Justice Su's extensive elaboration demonstrated the deep influence of German constitutional discourse in Taiwan. He followed the German Basic Law by upholding human dignity to be "inviolable," a "fundamental right that the state shall accord absolute protection," for which he explicitly invoked the German concept in parentheses: "unter dem absoluten Schutz des Grundrechtes."[18]

JY Interpretation No. 372 paved the way for human dignity to play further roles in the ensuing years. And Justice Su Jyun-Hsiung's German approach would prove to

---

terms. In the constitutional amendment in 1997, the term was shortened to eight years after the sixth term, and the term of eight justices of the seventh term was limited to four years so that in the future the president can only nominate part of Court at a given time. See Article 5 of the Additional Articles of the Constitution.

[15] Tom Ginsburg, *Judicial Review in New Democracies: Constitutional Courts in Asian Cases* (Cambridge: Cambridge University Press, 2003), chap. 5.

[16] They were Weng Yueh-Sheng (the chief justice), Liu Tieh-cheng, Chung-Mo Cheng, Vincent Wen-sheng Sze, Wu Geng, Wang Tze-chien, Tai Tung-hsiung, and Su Jyun-hsiung. Among them Chief Justice Weng Yueh-Sheng, Justice Liu Tieh-cheng, and Justice Wu Geng were renominated from the previous term. All others were new members. For lists of former Justices of the TCC, see www.judicial.gov.tw/constitutionalcourt/en/p01_04.asp.

[17] *JY Interpretation No. 372* (1995), Reasoning, Para. 1.

[18] There is no official translation of separate opinions of individual justices. The translation is my own. The whole text is available online in the TCC website in Chinese. For Justice Su's opinion in *JY Interpretation No. 372*, please see www.judicial.gov.tw/constitutionalcourt/P03_01_detail.asp?expno=372&showtype=%B7N%A8%A3%AE%D1 (last visited June 23, 2017).

be more influential than international human rights law or any other apex courts. Even though the UDHR was critical in setting up the stage for human dignity, the influence of international human rights law in furthering the use of human dignity was quite limited in the first two decades of Taiwan's democratic transition. This is partly due to Taiwan's isolation from the development of international human rights law, ever since Taiwan lost its UN membership in 1971. Taiwan had no access to international human rights regimes, and it did not ratify such foundational documents as the International Covenant on Civil and Political Rights (ICCPR) and the International Covenant on Economic, Social and Cultural Rights (ICESCR) until 2009.[19] By the early 1990s, the diffusion of knowledge of international human rights law was limited to a small segment of the legal academia. It means that when the TCC was ready to play an active role in Taiwan's democratic transition, for Taiwan's legal profession international human rights law was not a ready and accessible body of intellectual resource.

Even though the TCC has been reluctant to make explicit references to foreign law and judicial precedents in its main holding and reasoning, reference to foreign sources is widely seen in separate opinions. According to David Law and Wen-Chen Chang, referencing or "considering" foreign law at the TCC is simply not controversial at all.[20] Like its counterparts in other new democracies, the TCC did not have many domestic resources to rely on in the face of challenges presented by democratic transition. Foreign constitutional jurisprudence, particularly those jurisdictions of established liberal democracies, offered invaluable discursive resource to buttress the Court's legitimacy. In contrast to the American debate in which use of foreign law is depicted as a dangerous practice of unconstrained judicial discretion, for a court without a thick layer of constitutional traditions to draw on laws of influential foreign jurisdictions can be perceived to constrain judicial discretion.[21]

Of all the established liberal democracies, the United States has been geopolitically the most influential on Taiwan after World War II. The ruling Kuomintang (KMT/Nationalist Party) relied heavily on US financial aid and development programs after the breakout of the Korean War, for which the United States reversed its earlier policy of abandoning the defeated KMT and decided to incorporate Taiwan into its Far Eastern front against communist aggression.[22] American law, through direct or indirect involvement of US government personnel in the development programs, exerted the most influence on regulations regarding economic development. In the following decades, such influence gradually expanded to all

---

[19] For a detailed historical account, please see Yu-Jie Chen, "Isolated but Not Oblivious: Taiwan's Acceptance of the Two Major Human Rights Covenants," in *Taiwan and International Human Rights: A Story of Transformation*, edited by Jerome A. Cohen, William P. Alford, and Changfa Lo (New York: Springer, 2019), pp. 207–226.

[20] David S. Law and Wen-Chen Chang, "The Limits of Global Judicial Dialogue," *Washington Law Review* 86 (2011): 560.

[21] Id. at 570–571.

[22] Denny Roy, *Taiwan: A Political History* (Ithaca, NY: Cornell University Press, 2002), 111–113.

areas of law, as Taiwan's rapid economic development enabled a better-off generation of legal professionals to pursue legal studies in the United States.[23] Japanese law has long had deep influence on the legal regimes of the Republic of China, because it was mainly with the help of Japanese legal experts that late imperial and early republican China began to develop its modern civil and criminal codes.[24] Germany likewise entered the picture, because the historical lineage of the ROC legal system is traceable to Prussia through Japan's reception of European continental legal systems during the Meiji reform.[25] Moreover, in the late 1950s and 1960s, the postwar economic and democratic development of West Germany attracted a new generation of young legal researchers, whose overseas study was made possible by the comparatively low tuition cost and scholarships offered by the German Academic Exchange Service (DAAD).[26] The generation of German trained legal scholars has come to constitute the backbone of law faculties in major universities since the 1970s. By the early 1990s, this generation had come of age and occupied posts of distinction, including in the TCC. In her separate opinion of JY Interpretation No. 588 (2005), Justice Peng Feng-chi, trained in the University of Munich, could characterize the dominant German influence on the introduction of human dignity into Taiwan's legal discourse rather candidly:

> The meaning of "human dignity" differs according to historical, cultural, and religious factors. When the scholars of this country introduced this constitutional concept, most of them looked to Article 1, Paragraph 1, and Article 79, Paragraph 3 of the German Basic Law. They described its normative status and effects as the supreme constitutional value. The State shall respect and protect it, and shall by no means violate it. It constitutes the core of the constitution that is not subject to change through constitutional amendments.[27]

German influence on the introduction of human dignity into Taiwan's constitutional discourse is indeed remarkable. However, despite the enthusiasm of German-trained legal scholars or TCC justices, the transplantation is carried out on a very different soil. The life of human dignity in Taiwan's constitutional discourse commenced from a constitutional milieu that is quite different from that in Germany.

First, human dignity is enshrined in Article 1, Paragraph 1, and Article 79, Paragraph 3, of the German Basic Law, while it entered into TCC discourse through judicial construction on a very narrow textual base of "women's dignity." The absence of a clear textual base may have led the TCC to be more measured in its

---

[23] 王泰升 (Tay-sheng Wang), 台灣法律現代化歷程 [The Process of Legal Modernization in Taiwan] (Taipei: National Taiwan University Press, 2015), pp. 178–186.
[24] Id. at 195–205.
[25] Hiroshi Oda, The Japanese Law, 3rd ed. (Oxford: Oxford University Press, 2011), 15.
[26] Wang, Legal Modernization in Taiwan, 205–209.
[27] Justice Peng Feng-Chi, partly concurring, partly dissenting opinion, JY Interpretation No. 588, p. 23. The pagination here is derived from the officially released document that combines the Interpretation and separate opinions available on the TCC website:
www.judicial.gov.tw/constitutionalcourt/p03_01.asp?expno=588 (last visited June 12, 2017).

use of human dignity than it otherwise would have been. It also means that the TCC's use of this concept may be more selective, since avoidance of this concept does not necessarily trigger objections based on the constitutional text.

Further, the German Basic Law has a list of fundamental rights more extensive than that in Taiwan's Constitution. While the first difference may lead to TCC's caution in the use of human dignity, this difference has mixed implications. On the one hand, given the precariousness of textual base of human dignity, the Court may be willing to use human dignity only in conjunction with a particular enumerated right. Since the list of fundamental rights is short, the Court does not have many solid fundamental rights along with which to use human dignity, hence limiting the frequency of its use. On the other hand, precisely because the list of enumerated rights is short and the need to create unenumerated rights is great during democratization, the Court feels the need to enlist human dignity to generate new rights.

Third, German Basic Law was enacted in the aftermath of WWII, marking a clear break from the past of the Third Reich. By contrast, even though human dignity was brought into TCC jurisprudence during Taiwan's transition away from authoritarianism, the formal identity of the ROC Constitution remained intact from 1947, only to experience a sea change of substance through incremental constitutional revisions and rapid political and social transformations starting in the late 1980s. There is hence more ambiguity in the new democratic constitutional jurisprudence and its relationship with the past. It means that, in some areas, the Court may not be at total liberty to depart from the extant order.

These are but a few of the most salient differences that mark the constitutional milieu into which human dignity is planted in Taiwan, and they are by no means exhaustive. But they are useful for showing that the constitutional text, structure, and history would jointly complicate the trajectory of human dignity jurisprudence in Taiwan. Still more important than the institutional setting is the constitutional culture with which it comes to interact, as well as the particular value orientation that shapes judicial interpretations of this constitutional concept. In this chapter, I frame my analysis of TCC jurisprudence in terms of the "institutional uses" of the concept of human dignity.[28] Meanwhile, I seek to identify value orientations manifested in these cases. The institutional uses of human dignity in Taiwan's constitutional jurisprudence include the following dimensions: first, human dignity as it gives purpose to enumerated rights; second, human dignity as it sets limits to constitutional duty; third, human dignity as it constitutes the absolute boundary of state action; fourth, human dignity as it gives rise to unenumerated fundamental rights. My narrative will proceed not only according to these uses but also roughly in the chronological order by which these roles were taken.

---

[28] Christopher McCrudden, "Human Dignity and Judicial Interpretation of Human Rights," *European Journal of International Law* 19, no. 4 (2008): 712.

2 GIVING PURPOSE TO ENUMERATED RIGHTS

Before democratization, a remarkable feature of the TCC was that there were only a few Interpretations involving fundamental rights.[29] When fundamental rights were involved, the Council rarely labored to articulate the purpose of their protection. The reasoning usually began with the purpose of the statute in question, followed by minimal reasoning as to its legitimacy, and then was typically concluded with an oracle-like decision, at times even without clearly identifying the rights involved. One typical example with grave consequences is *JY Interpretation No. 194* (1985). It dealt with the constitutionality of mandatory death penalty for drug trafficking in Article 5, Paragraph 1, of the Drug Control Act during the Period for Suppression of the Communist Rebellion. On such a grave issue, the Court laid out its reasoning in one single paragraph. It began with admitting that "it is indeed a stringent rule." Then it laid out the purpose of the statue: "However, had drug trafficking not been outlawed during the period for suppression of the communist rebellion, public health, national security and social order would have been endangered." The conclusion immediately ensued: "This provision is therefore not contrary to Article 23 of the Constitution. Furthermore, the application of Article 5, Paragraph 1 of the Act does not discriminate by gender, religion, race, class or political party. Thus, this provision is not contrary to Article 7 of the Constitution."[30]

At the dawn of democracy in Taiwan, the TCC had very few resources to draw on from among its four decades of precedents when interpreting fundamental rights and liberties. The four decades between the enactment of the ROC Constitution and its democratic revival alienated the new democracy and its constitutional framing. This temporal gap and other features of ROC constitutional history together shaped the interpretative methodology of the TCC in the democratic era.

First, the ROC Constitution was enacted by the representatives of the whole Chinese population in 1947, instead of the people of Taiwan. Although the original constitutional convention included representatives of Taiwan, the drastic change of identity of "we the people" nevertheless created a serious sense of discontinuity. Second, the discontinuity was worsened by the early years of the KMT's gross misrule followed by decades of white terror. The iron fist fomented the growth of a new Taiwanese national identity seeking to break away from the Chinese national identity embodied by the ROC Constitution. Third, the Chinese national identity embodied by the ROC Constitution was used as a pretext to prolong the Martial Law regime, which tarnished the ROC Constitution in the eyes of the increasingly disaffected Taiwanese democrats. Fourth, the incremental constitutional revisions in the following decade preserved the content of the Preamble, the First Chapter of

---

[29] As of the end of 1987, there were 220 Interpretations. Of these, twenty involved fundamental rights: *JY Interpretations Nos.* 37, 130, 153, 154, 156, 160, 166, 170, 179, 187, 191, 192, 194, 200, 203, 205, 211, 213, 217, and 220.

[30] *JY Interpretation No. 194* (1985).

the basic form of the Republic, and the Second Chapter of the People's Rights and Duties. The new democratic constitutional ethos regarding the fundamental rights found few expressions in the constitutional text. All these factors together alienated the framers' intentions and the original public understanding of the constitutional text on issues of fundamental rights for the TCC in the democratic era. Intentionalism and originalism have been largely sidelined for fundamental rights interpretation since the dawn of democracy.

It is against this background that human dignity made its way into the TCC's constitutional discourse. In 1994, the sixth term of grand justices were sworn into office. It was by this term of grand justices that human dignity was introduced. The aforementioned *JY Interpretation No. 372* was delivered within the first six months of the sixth term of justices' office. The grand justices of this term were the first term nominated by the reformist President Lee Teng-Hui, and they proved to be highly influential in facilitating democratic transition. They actively invalidated one statute/administrative order after another enacted in the previous authoritarian era. It turned out, however, to be a tricky undertaking. The identity of the Constitution was nominally the same, and People's Rights and Duties remained undisturbed. What was dismantled on the constitutional level was the Provisional Provisions and the sub-constitutional martial law. Nonetheless, not all the statutes or administrative orders that came into question involved the dismantled regime. In other words, the Court had to grapple with the fact that these statutes or administrative orders co-existed with the Second Chapter of the Constitution for decades. It was hence not enough for the Court to invoke the fundamental rights in the Constitution. The Court was in urgent need of a whole new discursive framework within which to elevate the significance of fundamental rights to check expediencies pursued by the state. Neither the constitutional text nor the alienated history of constitution-framing provided such discursive resource. Given the German-trained background of many of the sixth-term grand justices, the wealth of postwar human-dignity-centered German constitutional jurisprudence became the most readily accessible discursive resource.

From the very start, it seemed that the German-trained Justices in the Court intended to introduce the German understanding of human dignity with full force. The first substantial articulation of human dignity appeared in Justice Su Jyun-Hsiung's concurring opinion in *JY Interpretation No. 372*. He advocated: "Human dignity is inviolable. It existed prior to the state as an inherent doctrine of natural law, which is widely recognized in constitutions of modern civilized nations";[31] and added: "Human dignity as a right is inviolable, and requires the state's protection and respect. Human dignity is the core of a person's sphere of private life, and is an indispensable right to preserve one's life and to freely develop one's personality. It is

---

[31] Justice Su Jyun-Hsiung concurring opinion of *JY Interpretation No. 372*, para. 2. www.judicial.gov.tw/constitutionalcourt/P03_01_detail.asp?expno=372&showtype=%B7N%A8%A3%AE%D1 .

a fundamental right that requires absolute protection of the state in accordance with the law."[32] In this significant opinion, Justice Su conceived of human dignity as 1) existent prior to the state as part of natural law, and hence by implication unamenable; 2) inviolable; 3) requiring absolute protection and respect; and 4) a freestanding right. This typical German understanding of human dignity stands in stark contrast with an alternative understanding held by, for instance, the Israel Supreme Court and the South African Constitutional Court. These courts conceive of human dignity as 1) a relative right; 2) a right subject to constitutional revision; and 3) a supreme constitutional value, though not necessarily the only supreme value.[33] However, it was not clear whether Justice Su's approach could eventually triumph without a more solid constitutional textual base. Yet Justice Su's opinion at least put this agenda on the table. As constitutional amendment later turned out to be very difficult after 2005,[34] the task of developing human dignity jurisprudence would fall on the TCC alone. The subsequent development could be seen as continued negotiation between the radical German agenda and the institutional constraints on the TCC's methodology of constitutional interpretation.

Clear from the beginning is that human dignity was used as a significant constitutional value to give purpose and weight to existent constitutional rights. *JY Interpretation No. 372* involved the right to personal security from domestic violence. Under examination was a Supreme Court precedent maintaining that a spontaneous outburst of abuse upon provocation of inappropriate behavior of the spouse alone does not constitute "unbearable domestic abuse" as a cause for divorce. While upholding this precedent, the TCC added that abuse would become unbearable if it surpasses reasonably bearable degree and begins to invade human dignity and personal security.

JY Interpretation No. 400 (1996) involved the right to property in the context of public easement of private land. The Court opened its holding with an articulation of the significance of the right to property not before seen. The Court stated: "The purpose of Article 15 of the Constitution, which provides that the people's property right shall be protected, is to guarantee each individual the freedom to exercise the rights to use, profit and dispose of property for the duration of the this right, and to prevent infringements from public power and other parties upon such freedoms, so that he/she may develop his/her personality and maintain his/her dignity."[35] The

---

[32] Ibid., para. 4.
[33] Aharon Barak, *Human Dignity: The Constitutional Value and the Constitutional Right* (Cambridge: Cambridge University Press, 2015), pp. 243–248, 281–286.
[34] In the amendment in 2005, the procedural bar of constitutional amendment was set impracticably high. The additional Article 12 of the ROC Constitution provides: "Amendment of the Constitution shall be initiated upon the proposal of one-fourth of the total members of the Legislative Yuan, passed by at least three-fourths of the members present at a meeting attended by at least three-fourths of the total members of the Legislative Yuan, and sanctioned by electors in the free area of the Republic of China at a referendum held upon expiration of a six-month period of public announcement of the proposal, wherein the number of valid votes in favor exceeds one-half of the total number of electors."
[35] *JY Interpretation No. 400* (1996), Reasoning, para. 2.

Court struck down the administrative order that indemnified the government from compensating landowners burdened with public easement. The association of right to property and human dignity articulated in this Interpretation were repeated in right-to-property decisions, such as *JY Interpretation Nos. 672, 709, 732, 739, and 742.*

In *JY Interpretation No. 445* (1998), the Court struck down provisions in the Assembly and Parade Act which authorized the government to forbid assemblies and parades advocating "communism or secession of territory." In this decision, the Court pronounced the significance of freedom of expression:

> Based on the principle of popular sovereignty, the people enjoy the right to free discussion, and the right to fully express opinions, so as to facilitate pursuit of facts, discovery of truth, and to form public will through democratic procedures in the form of policy and law. Therefore, freedom of expression is one of the most important fundamental rights with regard to the practice of democracy. Further, the state shall protect it with an aim to respect the dignity of individuals and autonomy of free activities.[36]

As liberalization of the marketplace of ideas from overregulation was a critical step in democratic transition, this Interpretation stood in a series of rulings that eventually culminated in *JY Interpretation No. 509*, through which the Court reinterpreted the criminal defamation provision in the Criminal Code and relieved the criminal defamation defendants from the responsibility of proving the truth of the defamatory statement.[37] The significance of inserting dignity into the purpose of freedom of expression is to strengthen it against political expediencies that may be abused in the name of democracy. However, in *Interpretation No. 509* the wording of dignity was replaced with "personal realization," possibly due to influence of the American First Amendment jurisprudence and its lack of dignity in its major forms of articulation.

In *JY Interpretation No. 485* (1999), the Court dealt with the constitutionality of a statute offering military personnel and their descendants the right of priority to buy social housing at a price significantly lower than market price, coupled with the right to sell such housing after five years of possession. This statute was challenged by opposition legislators on the ground that it violated the principle of equality by unfairly benefiting the military personnel's dependents. The Court recognized that social security and welfare is an important part of the state's mission, affirmed in the Preamble, Article 1, the Chapter of Fundamental National Policy (Directives), and Article 10 of the Additional Articles of the Constitution. The Court also recognized that, in the area of social and economic measures, the Legislative Yuan has broad discretion as to what groups could be benefited and how much. However, the purpose of social security and welfare measures is to help "secure the people's

---

[36] *JY Interpretation No. 445* (1998), Reasoning, para. 7.

[37] For a detailed account of this Interpretation and its aftermath, see Jimmy Chia-Shin Hsu, "What Would Happen to the Actual Malice Doctrine in a Severely Polarized Democracy? The Case of Taiwan," *Opinio Juris in Comparatione* 1, no. 1 (2013): 7–16.

basic standard of living so as to preserve human dignity."[38] Significantly, the Court used human dignity not only to buttress the principle of welfare state in the Constitution but also to signify a rough idea of when such benefits may go overboard. The welfare state principle with the purpose of maintaining human dignity would again be affirmed in subsequent Interpretations such as JY Interpretation No. 550 (2002) and No. 694 (2011).

3 SETTING LIMITS ON CONSTITUTIONAL DUTIES

Unlike typical bills of rights of contemporary liberal constitutional democracies, the Second Chapter of the ROC Constitution is entitled "People's Rights and Duties." Alongside fundamental rights, it encompasses three basic duties, namely the duty to pay tax in accordance with law (Article 19), the duty to perform military service in accordance with law (Article 20), and the right and duty to receive civic education (Article 21). The juxtaposition of fundamental rights and duties presents a problem of constitutional interpretation. In cases where the fundamental rights and duties come into conflict, it may be constitutionally implausible to treat the law embodying the basic duty as any other law that infringes fundamental rights, since the basic duties supposedly enjoy the same constitutional status. The issue of how to review a statute concretizing the basic duties presented a challenge to the Court.

In JY Interpretation No. 490 (1999), the Court was presented with the issue of whether the Conscription Act is unconstitutional by not allowing members of Jehovah's Witnesses or any other religious groups to refrain from mandatory military service out of religious beliefs. Typical of male Jehovah's Witnesses believers in Taiwan, the petitioners defied conscription, were convicted and sentenced to prison, were released after serving the sentence, were conscripted again, defied again, were incarcerated again, and continued the cycle until they were officially discharged from military service at the age of forty-five. The Court was faced with the conflict between religious freedom in Article 13 and the duty to perform military service in Article 20 of the Constitution. The Court upheld the Conscription Act by arguing that the Act is based on Article 20 of the Constitution with the legitimate purpose of national security. Further, the Court argued that the Conscription Act is not intended to promote, enhance, or restrict religions, nor does it have such effects, and hence it does not violate religious freedom as protected in Article 13 of the Constitution. Even though the Court upheld the Act, there was an interesting twist in its reasoning. It did not simply take for granted the legitimacy of the tax duty clause of Article 20. When the Court examined the Conscription Act and Article 20 of the Constitution, it maintained that the duty to perform military service in general "does not violate human dignity, nor does it undermine the foundation of the constitutional value system."[39]

---

[38] JY Interpretation No. 485 (1999), Reasoning: para. 1.
[39] JY Interpretation No. 490 (1999), Holding, para. 1.

The Court suggested that "human dignity and the foundation of the constitutional value system" stands above the constitutional text and constitute a limit that cannot be crossed even by constitutionally authorized statutes. This step is significant, because before this Interpretation human dignity was used mainly to underpin fundamental rights by serving only as a purpose of such rights. It was not yet a free-standing constitutional norm. In this Interpretation, the Court began to expand the functions of human dignity. And the next important Interpretation delivered by the Court would demonstrate most clearly such expansion.

4 CONSTITUTING THE ABSOLUTE BOUNDARY OF STATE ACTION

In *JY Interpretation No. 567* (2003), the Court reviewed a special statute left over from the authoritarian era, *Disciplinary Measures for the Prevention of Repeat Offenses by Communist Espionage Criminals during the Period of National Mobilization for the Suppression of the Communist Rebellion*. This Act authorized the highest police authority in times of "national mobilization against the communist rebellion" to extend the length of detention and forced labor of communist espionage offenders beyond the official judicial sentence, simply on the finding that such offenders "have not been reformed in his/her thoughts and behaviors." This case arose not from a petitioner held in such detention, for the statute had not been in use ever since the onset of democratization ended the state of "national mobilization against communist rebellion." The grievance that led to the constitutional petition involved a more recent statute that mandated the government to compensate citizens whose fundamental rights were unlawfully violated by the government under the Martial Law. The issue was whether such detention falls within the compensable categories of grievances. Although the "Disciplinary Measures" was no longer in use, it was still valid law. The Court seized the opportunity to review its constitutionality.

The Court stated that the disciplinary detention infringes not only personal physical liberty but also freedom of thoughts, since such detention and forced labor is imposed for the purpose of thought reform. The Court first recognizes that "while the state may impose more restrictions on individual rights during extraordinary periods and under extraordinary circumstances, such restrictions must not exceed the boundaries of minimum human rights protection."[40] The Court then continues to elaborate the significance of freedom of thoughts: "Freedom of thought safeguards the spiritual activities of the people. It is the root of human civilization, the foundation of freedom of expression, and the most fundamental human dignity the Constitution intends to protect. It is hence of extraordinary significance to the continuation of the liberal democratic constitutional order."[41] Based on the extraordinary significance of freedom of thought, the

---

[40] *JY Interpretation No. 567* (2003), Reasoning, para. 3.
[41] Ibid.

Court states that human dignity constitutes the minimum human rights which the state shall not infringe for whatever reason or in whatever manner, even in times of emergencies.

In this Interpretation, the Court identified freedom of thoughts with the most "fundamental human dignity," which requires absolute protection. State actions infringing this minimum sphere of human rights should be struck down without any proportionality review or balancing. In this Interpretation, the Court further expanded human dignity from one constitutional value to be served by fundamental rights to a constitutional norm constituting the absolute boundary of state action. This is a significant development in the TCC jurisprudence of human dignity, and it most clearly showcases the influence of German constitutional jurisprudence on the TCC.

The absolute boundary entailed by human dignity, however, raises new problems. If human dignity is absolute and inviolable, as is human dignity in Article 1 of German Basic Law, arguably any fundamental right associated with it could be seen as inviolable. So interpreted, human dignity would come into conflict with the general limitation clause of Article 23, which subjects all fundamental rights to proportionality review. Less than two years after the Court delivered *JY Interpretation No. 567*, one justice took up this issue in her concurring opinion in *JY Interpretation No. 588* (2005). This Interpretation involves the constitutionality of the detention provisions of the Administrative Execution Act. The issues are whether and to what extent administrative detention is justified as a measure to compel payment of administrative fines. The petitioner made human dignity an important argument for the unconstitutionality of administrative custody for the said purpose. However, the Court did not address this particular argument in its holding and reasoning. Nor did it explain why. The Court upheld administrative detention for enforcing payment, but it struck down some of the stipulated purposes as not proportional. Justice Peng Feng-Chi seized the opportunity to clarify what the status of human dignity should be, in response to the issue raised by *JY Interpretation No. 567*. In view of the petitioner's human dignity argument and Justice Peng's concurring opinion, it is reasonable to infer that the Court's silence on human dignity was deliberate. If we treat Justice Peng's concurring opinion as her response to the issue that in her eyes led to the Court's silence, then the most reasonable explanation for such silence is that the Court had not decided on how to reconcile the absolute protection accorded to human dignity and the necessity of proportionality review.

In her concurring opinion, Justice Peng gave the most extensive discussion of human dignity since Justice Su Jyun-Hsiung's concurring opinion in *JY Interpretation No. 372*. Drawing heavily on German constitutional jurisprudence, she first discussed the content of human dignity. She recognized from the outset that human dignity varies according to the history, culture, and religions of the society in which it is situated. Nonetheless, she affirmed the relevance of German constitutional jurisprudence and introduced the *Objektformel* (object formula) employed by the German Constitutional Court, while recognizing the inherent vagueness of this formula.[42] In lieu of her discussion of the content of human dignity, she proceeded to address the issue faced by the TCC: since the Court elevated human dignity to be absolutely inviolable, not subject to balancing, what is its relationship with all the fundamental rights that are subject to the general limitations of Article 23?

Her solution to this issue can be summarized as follows. First, human dignity is the supreme constitutional value. Functionally, it can be used as an objective value that affects how fundamental rights are interpreted, and it can also be used as a subjective right that can be invoked against state intrusions. Moreover, it constitutes the core area of the constitutional order that is not subject to constitutional amendment. Second, as a supreme constitutional value, human dignity should be concretized through individual fundamental rights. Fundamental rights can be seen as "special law" that in principle takes precedence over the "general law" of human dignity in constitutional interpretation. When fundamental rights take precedence, they are subject to proportionality review. Third, human dignity as a supreme value does not recuse from cases in which fundamental rights take precedence in application. Human dignity is best conceived as *Schranken-Schranke*, the "limitation of limitation." In other words, human dignity should constitute the narrow core area of fundamental rights, infringement of which is not justifiable through balancing or proportionality review.[43]

5 GENERATING UNENUMERATED RIGHTS

On the basis of the extraordinary weight accorded to human dignity in *JY Interpretation* No. 567, the Court went on to expand its usage. The most important in the following years is to use human dignity to ground unenumerated fundamental rights. This usage confirms that human dignity has come to be seen as a supreme constitutional value that underpins the whole system of fundamental rights. Further, it reflects a refined methodology of human dignity jurisprudence. Since human dignity is accorded extraordinary weight and is absolutely inviolable where it is directly attacked, in principle it is best mediated through other fundamental rights that are subject to proportionate limitation. Given that the Constitution has a very limited list of enumerated rights, to meet challenges unforeseen by the framers, the Court is under pressure to generate new rights, instead of putting human dignity directly to the front line. Human dignity provides the much-needed foundation on which to introduce new rights. It should also be noted that this use of human dignity began to develop mainly after 2003, by a new term of grand justices who were

---

[42] *JY Interpretation* No. 588, Justice Peng Feng-Chi partly concurring partly dissenting opinion, para. 5–6.
[43] Id. para. 7–10.

nominated by President Chen Shui-bian, the first non-KMT president in ROC constitutional history and a once-imprisoned political dissident and democratic opposition leader.

5.1 Right to Privacy

In *JY Interpretation No. 585* (2004), the Court for the first time recognized the right to privacy as an unenumerated fundamental right covered by Article 22. The Court justified the incorporation by articulating that the right to privacy "is necessary to preserve human dignity, personal autonomy, and the development of personality, as well as to safeguard the private life sphere from interference and the autonomous control of personal information." The right to privacy was only a side issue in this Interpretation.[44] Nonetheless, the Interpretation paved way for the next major decision on the right to privacy. In *JY Interpretation No. 603* (2005), the Court was asked to review the new provisions in *Household Registration Act*, which required all citizens to be fingerprinted before receiving the new national identification card. The Court affirmed the right to privacy as a fundamental right and reiterated the human dignity grounds for it. The Court then specified that the right to privacy includes information privacy, a right to control one's own information. The information privacy right, the Court explained, "protects the people's right to decide whether or not to disclose their personal information, as well as to what extent, at what time, in what manner and to what people such information will be disclosed. It also includes the people's right to know and control how their personal information will be used, as well as the right to correct any inaccurate entries contained in such information."[45] However, the Court continued to point out that "the Constitution does not accord absolute protection to the right of information privacy. The State may impose appropriate restrictions on such right through law in accordance with Article 23 of the Constitution."[46]

The Court then identified fingerprints to be a form of critical personal information that falls within the information privacy right. The Court stated that for the government to require such comprehensive fingerprinting, the law should stipulate clear purposes for the use of fingerprinting, forbid use for purposes other than the lawful ones, require uses to be closely related to the lawful purposes, and establish procedural and organizational safeguards to ensure its lawful use. The Household Registration Act failed to satisfy these requirements, and so the Court ruled the provisions unconstitutional. In the following decade, the Court reaffirmed the

---

[44] At issue in the Interpretation was the constitutionality of "The Act of the Special Commission on the Investigation of Truth in Respect of the 319 Shooting," which authorized the commission to conduct an investigation regarding the shooting of President Chen Shui-bian and Vice President Lu Hsiu-lian that occurred on March 19, 2004.

[45] *JY Interpretation No. 603*, Holding, para. 1.

[46] Ibid.

information privacy right grounded by human dignity in *JY Interpretation* No. 631 (communications surveillance warrants should be issue by the court rather than the prosecutor) and No. 689 (the punishment of stalking as prescribed in the Social Order Maintenance Act does not violate freedom of movement or freedom of the press for newsgathering).

5.2 Right to Reputation

The next unenumerated right to be recognized is the right to reputation. In *JY Interpretation* No. 656 (2009), the Court dealt with the latter half of Article 195, Paragraph 1, of the Civil Code, which prescribes: "those whose reputation is injured may petition for proper remedy to restore their reputation." As a long-standing convention, the courts often order liable libel defendants to publish an apology in major newspapers, particularly in cases where the plaintiff is a public figure. The issue is whether a court order of public apology violates the defendant's freedom of speech (non-speech). In this Interpretation, human dignity plays multiples roles and figures prominently in the Court's reasoning. In the beginning, the Court identified the fundamental rights at stake. Public apology, the Court notes, aims to restore the reputation of the plaintiff. The right to reputation, the Court reasoned, "preserves individual personality and autonomy, which is necessary for the realization of human dignity" and hence is protected by Article 22 of the Constitution.[47] The right to reputation is not the only fundamental right that has human dignity on its side in *JY Interpretation* No. 656. The Court stated that on the other side of the balance in this case is the freedom of non-expression, namely the freedom not to speak. The freedom of non-expression has already been recognized by the Court in *JY Interpretation* No. 577 (2004) as included within the Article 11 freedom of speech clause. However, in that Interpretation, the Court did not associate it with human dignity. In *JY Interpretation* No. 656, the Court strengthened the importance of freedom of non-expression and stated that "while the government may impose limitations on the freedom of non-expression in accordance with law, to the extent that the reasons not to speak involve such inner beliefs and values as about morality, ethics, justice, conscience, and religious faith, this freedom is essential to individual spiritual activities and personal autonomy. It is indispensable for the development of individual personality and moral integrity, and it is closely related to the protection of human dignity."[48] At first sight, one might wonder whether the association of freedom of non-expression and human dignity is necessary. If the Court is concerned about finding a balanced point of departure for its reasoning, it has already accorded fundamental right status to freedom of non-expression by including it in the Article 11 free speech clause, and hence on both sides of the balancing scale are

---

[47] *JY Interpretation* No. 656, Reasoning, para. 1.
[48] *JY Interpretation* No. 656, Reasoning, para. 2.

placed fundamental rights, namely the right to reputation versus the freedom of non-expression. However, given the significant rhetorical power of human dignity, the Court may have been concerned that the scale might be slanted toward right to reputation, grounded by human dignity, if the Court did not associate the counter-weight of human dignity with freedom of non-expression.

The Court's use of human dignity did not stop at giving equal weight to both sides of the scale at the outset of balancing. Human dignity continued to play a role in the process of balancing. Since the court order of public apology in newspapers restricts the freedom of non-expression, it is subjected to proportionality review. The Court's insertion of proportionality review into Article 23 was first seen in its full expression in *JY Interpretation* No. 554 (2002). By proportionality review it is required that the purpose of the reviewed state action be legitimate, that the measure taken must be suitable to the purpose, that no measure less intrusive of the fundamental right is available (necessity), and that the benefit brought about by the measure should be proportional with the restriction of the fundamental right (proportionality *stricto sensu*). The Court considered the purpose of public apology legitimate, since it is aimed at restoring the plaintiff's reputation, which is no less a fundamental right. Further, there is obviously a rational linkage between public apology and restoration of reputation. The critical part of the review is necessity, whether public apology is the least intrusive measure available. The Court opined that such public apology may be necessary, insofar as the courts have taken into account such factors as the gravity of reputation injury and the social and financial status of the defendant and the plaintiff and have come to the conclusion that no other measures can achieve the purpose of restoring the plaintiff's reputation to the same effect.[49] However, the Court continued to set a limit to public apology. It maintained that public apology shall not amount to "self-humiliation or other measures that violate human dignity."[50] Here human dignity is the limit to the limitation of freedom of non-expression. It is Justice Peng's concurring opinion of *JY Interpretation* No. 588 put into practice.

5.3 Right of Personality

In *JY Interpretation* No. 664 (2009), the Court recognized the right of personality as a fundamental right encompassed in Article 22 of the Constitution. In this case, the Court was asked to review provisions in the Juvenile Proceedings Act, which provides that a juvenile who frequently skives or runs away from home but has not yet committed any crime can be placed in a juvenile detention center for no longer than six months by the juvenile court, insofar as the court judges such a juvenile is at the risk of committing crimes, provided that alternative measures such as custody of

---

[49] *JY Interpretation* No. 656, Reasoning, para. 3.
[50] *JY Interpretation* No. 656, Reasoning, para. 3.

a legal guardian, parent(s), next of kin, or a juvenile ombudsman are unavailable or obviously inadequate. The issue is whether it is constitutional to place in-risk juveniles who have not yet committed any crime in juvenile detention center, provided other measures are unavailable or obviously inadequate.

Instead of the right to personal liberty and security, the Court used the right of personality to characterize the primary legal interests at stake in this case. The Court stated: "The right of personality is indispensable for guarding the individual autonomy and free development of character, closely related to the safeguarding of human dignity, and is therefore protected by Article 22 of the Constitution."[51] Even though the phrase "right of personality" is first seen in this Interpretation, the substance is not. The phrase "guarding of individual autonomy and free development of character" or similar ones have already been in use in previous Interpretations to support the right to property (*JY Interpretation* No. 580), the right to privacy (*JY Interpretation* No. 603), the right to secret communication (*JY Interpretation* No. 631), and the right to reputation (*JY Interpretation* No. 656).

The right of personality of juveniles for the Court contains not only a negative element that safeguards the personal liberty of juveniles but also a positive element that requires the government to give special protection to their healthy growth and character development, a positive state obligation supported also by the directive in Article 156 of the Constitution.[52] There is tension between the two elements of the right, as the positive element may require the state to restrain personal liberty of juveniles under certain circumstances. And the Court had no settled methodology for balancing the two elements of the same right that are in tension. In its reasoning, the Court put far more weight on the negative element than the positive, arguing that the provision infringes the personal liberty of the juveniles and should be reviewed under the strict proportionality review. The Court struck down the government's power to temporarily detain at-risk juveniles, on the grounds that it is not the least intrusive protective measure, since the government could place the in-risk juveniles in a regular learning and family environment through a proper welfare or fostering agency.[53]

In this Interpretation, there is a notable development of the Court's human dignity jurisprudence. The Court stated that the right of personality is "closely related" to human dignity. The associative phrase "closely related" seems new. In previous Interpretations, when the Court used human dignity to support a certain fundamental right, whether enumerated or not, it typically stated that "based on human dignity, a certain right is indispensable" (*JY Interpretation* Nos. 585, 603, and 656) or that "in order to preserve and protect human dignity, a certain right is

---

[51] *JY Interpretation* No. 664, Reasoning, para. 2.
[52] Article 156 reads: "The State, in order to consolidate the foundation of national existence and development, shall protect motherhood and carry out the policy of promoting the welfare of women and children."
[53] *JY Interpretation* No. 664, Reasoning, para. 6.

necessary" (*JY Interpretation* No. 631). The problem with these expressions is that the relationship between the particular right and human dignity remains vague. Are the right and human dignity the same thing? If the relationship is one of means–end, are the means and end distinct conceptual objects, or do they occupy different parts of a continuum? The vagueness bears on the absolute protection accorded to human dignity in *JY Interpretation* No. 567. How does the Court reconcile the absolute protection accorded to human dignity and the fact that fundamental rights, even those based on human dignity, may be limited through proportionality review? It seems that the phrase "closely related" is the solution. By saying that a certain fundamental right is "closely related" to human dignity, the Court insinuates that human dignity and the right are two distinct concepts with distinguishable extensions, even though they are in very close relationship. Absolute protection is given when human dignity itself may be violated, while the infringement of most fundamental rights may still be justified through balancing.

5.4 Family-Related Rights

In *JY Interpretation* No. 712 (2013), the Court was asked to review Article 65 Paragraph 1 of the Act Governing the Relations Between People of the Taiwan Area and the Mainland Area. The provision in question proscribes any Taiwanese citizen with a child of his/her own from adopting a child from the Mainland Area (PRC). As a result, a Taiwanese citizen with a child of his/her own is forbidden from such adoption, even if that child is a child of his/her Mainland spouse. The Court has long recognized that marriage and family are constitutionally protected institutions.[54] But this is the first Interpretation in which the Court grounded the protection of family on the foundational values of human dignity, individual autonomy, and free development of personality. Based on the institutional protection of family, the Court went on to argue that adoption is part of the family system that forms a bond between a parent and child not related through blood. The right to adopt a child should be protected as a fundamental right covered by Article 22. The Court affirmed that the purpose of inhibiting excessive inflow of population from the Mainland may be legitimate, and the proscription against adopting a Mainland child is rationally linked to that purpose. However, for the proscription to apply to a Taiwanese citizen seeking to adopt a child of his/her Mainland spouse is obviously out of proportion and cannot pass the review of proportionality *stricto sensu*.

In *JY Interpretation* No. 748, the Court was presented with the issue whether the relevant provisions of marriage in the Civil Code are unconstitutional by limiting it to the union of two persons of the opposite sex, to the exclusion of same-sex couples. The Court identified the fundamental right at stake to be the freedom of marriage. This freedom was first recognized in *JY Interpretation* No. 362, in which the Court

---

[54] *JY Interpretations* Nos. 362, 552, 554, and 696.

maintained that the freedom of marriage includes the freedom to decide "whether to marry" and "whom to marry." What is new in *JY Interpretation No. 748* is that the Court placed this freedom on the foundational values of "sound development of personality, safeguarding of human dignity."[55] The Court argued that exclusion of same-sex marriage violated freedom of marriage:

> Creation of a permanent union of intimate and exclusive nature for the purpose of managing a life together by two persons of the same sex will not affect the application of the Marriage Chapter to the union of two persons of the opposite sex. Nor will it alter the social order established upon the existing opposite-sex marriage. Furthermore, the freedom of marriage for two persons of the same sex, once legally recognized, will constitute the collective basis, together with opposite-sex marriage, for a stable society. The need, capability, willingness and longing, in both physical and psychological senses, for creating such permanent unions of intimate and exclusive nature are equally essential to homosexuals and heterosexuals, given the importance of the freedom of marriage to the sound development of personality and safeguarding of human dignity. Both types of union shall be protected by the freedom of marriage under Article 22 of the Constitution. The current provisions of the Marriage Chapter do not allow two persons of the same sex to create a permanent union of intimate and exclusive nature for the committed purpose of managing a life together. This is obviously a gross legislative flaw. To such an extent, the provisions of the Marriage Chapter are incompatible with the spirit and meaning of the freedom of marriage as protected by Article 22 of the Constitution.[56]

The Court added that such exclusion does not only violate freedom of marriage covered by Article 22 but also violates equal protection of Article 7. The Court recognized that "sexual orientation is an immutable characteristic that is resistant to change" and that "homosexuals, because of the demographic structure, have been a discrete and insular minority in the society. Impacted by stereotypes, they have been among those lacking political power for a long time, unable to overturn their legally disadvantaged status through ordinary democratic process."[57] To protect the discrete and insular minority, the Court subjects the differential treatment to heightened scrutiny. It found the differential treatment without rational basis:

> The Marriage Chapter does not set forth the capability to procreate as a requirement for concluding an opposite-sex marriage. Nor does it provide that a marriage is void or voidable, or a divorce decree may be issued, if either party is unable or unwilling to procreate after marriage. Accordingly, reproduction is obviously not an essential element of marriage. The fact that two persons of the same sex are incapable of natural procreation is the same as the result of two opposite-sex persons' inability, in an objective sense, or unwillingness, in a subjective sense, to procreate. Disallowing two persons of the same sex to marry,

---

[55] *JY Interpretation No. 748*, Reasoning, para. 13.
[56] *JY Interpretation No. 748*, Reasoning, para. 13.
[57] *JY Interpretation No. 748*, Reasoning, para. 16.

for the sake of their inability to reproduce, is a different treatment having no apparent rational basis."[58]

6 CONCLUSION

Since it debuted in *JY Interpretation No.* 372 (1995), human dignity has been consolidated as a supreme constitutional value and fundamental right. It gives purpose to enumerated fundamental rights, sets limit to constitutional duty, constitutes the core of fundamental rights that is inviolable, and gives rise to unenumerated fundamental rights. The development showcases how a constitutional court of a new democracy introduces a new constitutional idea into its jurisprudence, despite the precarious basis in the constitutional text, and skillfully expands its functions. The process reflects the Court's ambition and wisdom, as well as the opportunities bestowed by history. The TCC began its use of human dignity for the least controversial function, namely giving purpose and weight to enumerated fundamental rights, since in this role human dignity is predicated on the constitutionally enumerated rights. Next, human dignity was employed for a slightly stronger role of setting limit to the constitutional duty of performing military services. Then history gave the Court a chance to review the authoritarian disciplinary measures of "thought reform" in *JY Interpretation No.* 567 (2003). The Court seized the opportunity to give human dignity the most consequential role of constituting the absolute boundary of state action. If a state action crosses the boundary, it shall be struck down without having to go through proportionality review and balancing. In the following decade, the primary role of human dignity has been to give rise to new fundamental rights.

In its role of generating new fundamental rights, human dignity has been increasingly associated with "individual autonomy and free development of personality," especially after 2013. Together these three ideas have consistently played the role of organizing principles of the fundamental rights system and have been used primarily to generate new and unenumerated fundamental rights. As the Court has never given a definition of human dignity, the regular association of these three ideas gives human dignity in TCC jurisprudence a clearly liberal overtone based on individual autonomy. It shows that TCC jurisprudence, after Taiwan's democratization, has come a long way from the framers' Confucian communitarianism, which prizes duty as much as right, community as much as individuals. However, one risks being misguided by the rhetoric, if one takes the Court's dignity and autonomy rhetoric at full face value. To use this string of ideas to generate unenumerated right is one thing, but to balance the right against competing values is another. For instance, in *JY Interpretation No.* 656, the Court gave weight to both the right to reputation and the right not to speak. Public apology in newspapers is a serious infringement of the

---

[58] Ibid.

right not to speak, not obviously necessary for the restoration of reputation. Nonetheless, the Court upheld this customary practice with caution. This decision shows an appreciation of tradition and community ritual not obviously reflected in the Court's liberal rhetoric. It is clear that TCC in the democratic era has already departed from the framers' ideas. The most recent *JY Interpretation* No. 748 shows a decisively liberal leaning, by breaking away from thousands of years of tradition and legalizing same-sex marriage. However, how far this new momentum will take the Court toward a liberal approach to human dignity remains to be seen.

5

The Human Dignity Factor

Interpreting the Philippine Constitution

J. R. Robert Real[*]

1 INTRODUCTION

Philippine Supreme Court Justice Sanchez once observed: "A high regard for human dignity is the hallmark of our institutions."[1] Indeed, the Legislature has invoked the pursuit of human dignity in enacting new laws and outlining measures that protect, elevate, assert, or restore one's civil, political,[2] economic, social, and cultural rights.[3] Presidents have also made explicit reference to a person's dignity in the instructions, proclamations, and orders they issued.[4] Meanwhile, the Supreme

---

[*] I thank Christopher McCrudden, Jimmy Chia-Shin Hsu, Jonathan Chow, Melissa Loja, and Ryan Balisacan, as well as my other coauthors in this book, for reading and discussing earlier drafts and giving valuable insights. I especially thank Junefe Payot and Ivy Bernardez for helping me with the entire writing process and providing me with crucial comments. Without them, I would not have been able to write this chapter.

[1] *Manila Railroad Co.* v. *Yatco*, 132 Phil. 223 (1968).

[2] For example, the Safe Spaces Act (2019); the Bangsamoro Basic Law (2018); the Human Rights Victims Reparation and Recognition Act (2013); the Expanded Anti-Trafficking in Persons Act (2013); the Responsible Parenthood and Reproductive Health Act (2012); the Anti-Enforced or Involuntary Disappearance Act (2012); the Free Legal Assistance Act (2010); the Act on Crimes Against International Humanitarian Law (2009); the Anti-Torture Act (2009); and the Rights of Persons Arrested, Detained or Under Custodial Investigation Act (1992).

[3] For example, the Pantawid Pamilyang Pilipino Program (4Ps) Act (2019); the Philippine HIV and AIDS Policy Act (2018); the Filipino Sign Language Act (2018); the Domestic Workers Act (2013); the Expanded Senior Citizens Act (2010); the Magna Carta of Women (2009); the Juvenile Justice and Welfare Act (2006); the Indigenous Peoples' Rights Act (1997); the Migrant Workers Act (1995, 2010); the Mail-Order Bride Law (1990); the Comprehensive Agrarian Reform Law (1988); the Philippine Environmental Policy (1977); the Revised Population Act (1972); and the Civil Code of the Philippines (1949).

[4] For example, Executive Order No. 100 (2019) on the Diversity and Inclusion Program (Duterte); Memorandum Circular No. 48 (2013) on gender equality guidelines for media (B. Aquino); Proclamation No. 586 (2004) on defense of life from the moment of conception (Macapagal-Arroyo); the Memorandum (Dec. 1998) on review of laws and jurisprudence to ensure protection and promotion of human rights (Estrada); Proclamation No. 851 (1996) on support for the national campaign of Amnesty International-Pilipinas (Ramos); Memorandum Order No. 393 (1991) on adherence to principles of human rights and humanitarian law in the conduct of operations (C. Aquino); and Letter of Instructions No. 549 (1977) on environmental quality (Marcos).

Court has considered and employed the dignity language countless times,[5] especially when it is called to rule on challenges against official acts of government.

Scholars, however, have noted the lack of any canonical and universalistic definition of "dignity" in legal discourse.[6] They pointed out how its meaning can be highly context-specific and contingent on local circumstances, which may significantly differ between jurisdictions and even vary within the same jurisdiction. As Waldron recognizes,[7] "if you glance quickly at the way in which 'dignity' figures in the law, you will probably get the impression that its usage is seriously confused," requiring readers to employ patience and thoughtfulness in understanding its meaning and purpose.

This introductory exposition seeks to wade through such confusion by examining the adjudicative function of dignity in the Court's decision-making process. Section 2 traces the historical references to a person's "dignity" by looking into the decisions of the Philippine Supreme Court[8] from the time it was established in 1901 until 1987 when the country promulgated its present Constitution. The selected cases would show that early references to dignity largely involved the significance of one's supposed high-ranking societal status in the application of civil and criminal laws until the more egalitarian conception of dignity had begun to dominate discourse during the drafting of the 1935 Constitution.

Section 3 explores the sociohistorical events and local circumstances that appear to have considerable influence in shaping how dignity would color the Court's interpretation of laws. The cases suggest that certain cultural "traumas" suffered by Filipinos have helped push the further development of an egalitarian conception of dignity. The cases also indicate that other factors such as the nation's dominant religion and non-municipal laws have contributed to the molding of the domestic conception of dignity.

Section 4 will then argue how the justices employ the concept of dignity as a lens through which laws are interpreted, albeit in varying ways: dignity was invoked as a basis to discover or expand the scope of existing rights in limiting governmental action, or as justification for upholding governmental measures that seek to advance or further the people's conditions. Ultimately, dignity empowered the justices to avoid a strict original or textual interpretation of constitutional provisions,

---

[5] A Boolean search at the time of writing suggests that the term "human dignity" appears in 171 Supreme Court decisions since its establishment in 1901. Additionally, other search terms were used such as "dignidad humana," "dangal," "personal dignity," and others.

[6] Jeremy Waldron, *Dignity, Rank, and Rights* (New York: Oxford University Press, 2012), p. 31; Christopher McCrudden, "Human Dignity and Judicial Interpretation of Human Rights," *European Journal of International Law* 19, no. 4 (2008): 698; Oscar Schachter, "Human Dignity as a Normative Concept," *American Journal of International Law* 77, no. 4 (1983): 849.

[7] Waldron, *Dignity*, 31.

[8] I focused on the apex court given that its decisions have precedential value, unlike those of lower-level courts. See *De Mesa v. Pepsi Cola*, 504 Phil. 685 (2005).

increasingly so following the inclusion of an entire article dealing with the "right of all the people to human dignity"[9] under the 1987 Constitution.

Understanding human dignity can certainly be confusing; however, this may only be at the surface. As we look deeper, we will realize that how the court and society understand human dignity is heavily influenced by the cultural trauma and the historical events that are shaping their ways of understanding the relationship between individual and society.

2 HISTORICAL REFERENCES TO DIGNITY

2.1 *Brief Background: the Philippine Supreme Court*

The present Court traces its roots back to the establishment of the Supreme Court of the Philippine Islands in 1901, the highest court created in the new American colony following the Spanish-American War.[10] It was composed of seven members appointed by the US president,[11] the majority of whom were American citizens.[12] Although it was the apex court in the islands, its decisions were nevertheless appealable to the US Supreme Court.[13] Like the American Court, the Filipino Court similarly wielded the power of judicial review to determine whether a branch of government has acted beyond the scope of its powers.[14]

The composition of the Court changed following the promulgation of the 1935 Constitution. The number of justices was increased from seven to eleven, all of whom must be Filipino citizens. The Court's jurisdiction remained largely the same,[15] with its power of judicial review now strongly implied in the new constitution[16] but its decisions still appealable to the US Supreme Court until the Philippines gained its full independence in 1946.[17] The number of justices was increased to fifteen during the martial law regime of

---

[9] Constitution (1987), Article xiii.
[10] Division of Insular Affairs, *Public Laws and Resolutions Passed by the Philippine Commission* (Washington, DC: Government Printing Office, 1901), 5; the Judiciary Act (1901); George Malcolm, "Constitutional History of Philippines," *American Bar Association Journal* 6 (1920): 110–111.
[11] Philippine Organic Act (1902), sec. 9.
[12] Four out of seven Supreme Court justices were Americans. See Division of Insular Affairs, *Public Laws*, p. 737; Malcolm, "Constitutional History," p. 110.
[13] Philippine Organic Act (1902); Philippine Autonomy Act (1916).
[14] *Barcelon v. Baker*, 5 Phil. 87 (1905), citing *Marbury v. Madison*; *In re Patterson*, 1 Phil. 93 (1902); see also Leia Castañeda Anastacio, *Foundations of the Modern Philippine State* (New York: Cambridge University Press, 2016), pp. 116–121; Vicente Mendoza, *Judicial Review of Constitutional Questions*, 2nd ed. (Quezon City: Rex Bookstore, 2013), p. 20; Jose Aruego, *The Framing of the Philippine Constitution Vol. I*, (Manila: University Publishing Co., 1936), p. 493.
[15] Constitution (1935), Article viii, sec. 3.
[16] Ibid., at Article viii, sec. 2. For example, *Angara v. Electoral Commission*, 63 Phil. 139, pp. 156–158 (1936).
[17] Ordinance Appended to the 1935 Constitution, sec. 1(13); Treaty of General Relations between the Philippines and the US (1946). See Mendoza, *Judicial Review*, p. 20.

the deposed dictator Ferdinand Marcos by virtue of the 1973 Philippine Constitution. In view of the lessons learned from Marcos' authoritarian rule, the Court's power of judicial review under the present 1987 Constitution had been expanded to include the ability to scrutinize if the president or Congress gravely abused their discretion in performing their official acts, even those that involve political questions.[18]

2.2 *Dignity and Status: 1901–*

The earliest allusion to a person's dignity involved the application of Spanish colonial-era Civil and Penal Codes.[19] In those codes, the term "dignity" was interpreted to mean one's high social or public rank, stature, or authority, such that a violation of one's dignity (e.g., high position in government) would aggravate the severity of an act committed. This would usually equate to a higher amount of damages or harsher penalty being imposed.

"Dignity" in the context of these codes is reminiscent of *dignitas* – a classical Roman concept that is largely associated with one's "status," which is valued and respected. As Cancik explains, the term denotes "worthiness, the outer aspect of a person's social role which evokes respect, and embodies the charisma and the esteem presiding in office, rank or personality."[20] Honor and respect are thus accorded to those worthy of them because of a particular status that they hold, usually a specific role or rank in a societal system of nobility and hierarchical office. This concept of dignity was said to have been carried on in legal systems based on Roman law.[21] It might be the case that the modern Philippine legal system was one of those that received such alegal concept, entering through the Spanish colonial-era laws.

An example of the Court's use of dignity can be seen in the case of *Pardo de Tavera v. Garcia Valdez* (1902),[22] which affirmed the conviction of the accused for *grave insult* as opposed to the less severe crime of *insult*. According to the Court, the offended person's "condition, dignity, and personal circumstances" as a private prosecutor were material in ascertaining the crime committed and the corresponding penalty pursuant to the Codigó Penal of 1870. In terms of civil claims, *Lilius*

---

[18] Constitution (1987), Article viii, sec. 1; *Saguisag* v. *Ochoa*, 777 Phil. 280 (2016).
[19] E.g., *Legarda* v. *Valdez*, 1 Phil. 562 (1902); *USA* v. *Lucinario*, 6 Phil. 325 (1906); *USA* v. *Ocampo*, 18 Phil. 1 (1910); *Barnuevo* v. *Fuster*, 29 Phil. 606 (1913); *Legare* v. *Cuerques*, 34 Phil. 221 (1916); *US* v. *Bustos*, 37 Phil. 731 (1918).
[20] Hubert Cancik, "'Dignity of Man' and 'Persona' in Stoic Anthropology," in *The Concept of Human Dignity in Human Rights Discourse*, edited by David Kretzmer and Eckart Klein (The Hague: Kluwer Law International, 2002), p. 19. See also McCrudden, "Human Dignity," 656–657; Jeremy Waldron, "Citizenship and Dignity," in *Understanding Human Dignity*, edited by Christopher McCrudden (Oxford: British Academy, 2013), p. 327.
[21] Arthur Chaskalson, "Human Dignity as a Constitutional Value," in *Concept of Human Dignity*, pp. 133–135.
[22] 1 Phil. 468.

v. *Manila Railroad Co.* (1934)[23] demonstrated how the Court took into account the claimant's social and financial standing in appraising the amount of moral damages to be awarded. In justifying granting double the amount of damages compared to an earlier case decided by the Court, the justices reasoned that, among other things, the plaintiff in that earlier case "was neither young nor good-looking, nor had he suffered any facial deformity, nor did he have the social standing that ... Lilius enjoys."

2.3 *Dignity and Social Justice: 1935–*

Following the promulgation of the 1935 Constitution, dignity appeared to have acquired another meaning beyond the context of social rank and status contemplated in the Spanish-era codes. This became evident in the framers' deliberations on the constitutional provisions on social justice and women's suffrage.

According to the framers, the inclusion of a specific constitutional provision on social justice as a "concern of the State"[24] was founded on their understanding that the state should play an active part in promoting and protecting a person's dignity, particularly in alleviating the economic and social conditions of the poor and marginalized. They opined that the state should actively seek the people's "social dignification," the "common good," "social equality," and the "safeguarding of man from the inhumanity of his fellow man" through the promotion of social welfare.[25] The framers saw fit to constitutionally enshrine a governmental policy that favors the poor who have especially sacrificed their "freedom and human dignity" during centuries of oppressive treatment under the prior Spanish colonial government. Thus, in the landmark case of *Calalang v. Williams* (1940),[26] the Court pronounced that its judicial task was to ensure the "humanization of laws and the equalization of social and economic forces by the State so that justice in its rational and objectively secular conception may at least be approximated."[27] The social justice provision was meant to "change the spirit of the laws,"[28] so that they are construed broadly[29] in order to vindicate the people's "just claims to human dignity."[30] Human dignity was the core substance of social justice.[31]

The deliberations on the 1935 Constitution also bared that the framers used the dignity language in discussing the proposal on women's suffrage.[32] However, unlike

---

[23] 59 Phil. 758. Compare *Gutierrez v. Gutierrez*, 56 Phil. 177 (1931). See also *Domingding v. Ng*, 103 Phil. 111 (1958).
[24] Constitution (1935), Article ii, sec. 5.
[25] See *Constitutional Convention Records 1934–1935*, Volume (I), Journal No. (15) (Manila: House of Representatives, 1965–7). Also at (I)(15), (I)(19), (III)(49), (VI)(94), (IX)(128), and (X)(132).
[26] 70 Phil. 726.
[27] Ibid.
[28] Ibid.
[29] *Philippine Sugar Estates v. Prudencio*, 76 Phil. 111 (1946).
[30] *Gallego v. Kapisanan Timbulan*, 83 Phil. 124 (1949).
[31] Reynato Puno, *Equal Dignity and Respect* (Quezon City: University of the Philippines College of Law, 2012), p. 507.
[32] Constitution (1935), Article v, sec. 1.

the unanimous support for the inclusion of the social justice provision, the move to recognize women's right to vote was met with division, as both sides of the aisle invoked dignity in justifying their own positions. On the one hand, anti-suffragists[33] emphasized the societal role of women to remain home and take care of the family, as their "dignity" supposedly dictated that they focus on such responsibility. They also referred to women's dignity, purity, and honor in arguing for the need to protect women from "moral and social degradation" brought about by dirty politics. For them, it was the men's role to worry about governance, while it was the women's to take charge of ensuring peace and harmony at home. On the other hand, those in favor[34] of women's suffrage assailed the very idea of according dignity only to particular persons or classes, arguing that women must be granted "political dignification" as free citizens in a democracy and for, simply, being "part of humankind." They maintained that women must be allowed to achieve freedom from their social roles, "complete" the totality of their "personality," and enjoy the "full" set of rights encompassing civil, political, economic, and social aspects that men had enjoyed. In the end, a compromise solution was reached – a plebiscite was held to ask Filipinas to decide for themselves if they wanted the right of suffrage.[35] That the women were seen as being able to decide for themselves could be seen as a sign of respect for their dignity.

By unpacking their deliberations, we can appreciate how the constitutional framers had also viewed and used dignity beyond the context of one's social rank or status. For them, the pursuit of dignity justified the idea that every person should be able to enjoy the same high level of status and respect, regardless of gender or economic status, simply because they were all human beings inherently imbued with dignity. All persons should equally be able to enjoy the full rights, benefits, and privileges under the law and to live a dignified life. Dignity was a major, underlying basis for the inclusion of the provision on social justice and on women's suffrage. Just as Jimmy Chia-Shin Hsu noted after analyzing the discussions of the framers of the ROC (Taiwan) Constitution when it was first passed in 1946,[36] the Filipino constitutional framers were also familiar with the dignity language although no explicit reference to dignity was made in the final text of the 1935 Constitution.

One might wonder if there is any connection or relation between the classical Roman conception of *dignitas* and human dignity. Waldron theorizes that, perhaps, such a connection/relation can be understood in two general ways: the first is that it tells a story about the human dignity conception prevailing over the *dignitas* conception; while the second is that the *dignitas* conception has morphed into a more egalitarian conception.[37] In the latter story, the connection between dignity

---

[33] See *1935 Convention*, at (IV)(72), (IV)(74), and (IV)(79).
[34] Ibid., at (IV)(72), (IV)(74), (IV)(77), (IV)(78), (V)(78), and (V)(84).
[35] Aruego, *Framing*, 220–221.
[36] See Chapter 4 in this volume by Jimmy Chia-Shin Hsu.
[37] Waldron, "Citizenship and Dignity," 327; Waldron, *Dignity*, 33.

and rank is not broken; rather, there is a "transvaluation of *dignitas*" in which every human person, without exception, is assigned a high-ranking legal, political, and social status – a nobility for everyone. It is unfortunately unclear from the discussions of the framers if they had *dignitas* in mind when they were invoking the term "dignity" or if they had intentionally sought its development toward an egalitarian idea in which every person, "from the highest to the lowest," is invested with dignity.[38] What the constitutional debates did show was that both the social-rank-or-status-based and the egalitarian conceptions of dignity had been strongly considered, especially when the issue of women's suffrage and their role in society was being debated. The resulting compromise solution then suggests that the egalitarian conception gained preference, but without completely superseding the *dignitas* conception.[39]

2.4 Human Dignity as a Tool for Interpretation: 1945–

The cases decided by the justices following World War II served as catalyst for them to begin exploring dignity as a possible lens through which laws are to be interpreted, as opposed to a mere legal term that impacted the severity of an offense. Lacking textual support in the 1935 Constitution, the justices looked to the inclusion of "human dignity" in the preamble of the UN Charter and deemed this fact as recognition that the inherent worth of a human being was a value that must be considered when they rule on the rights to be accorded to accused members and supporters of the invading Japanese Imperial Army. In *Raquiza* v. *Bradford* (1945),[40] for example, they deliberated on what constituted proper treatment that must be extended to detained Japanese military collaborators in the light of the "'dignity of the human person,' which is one of the cardinal principles of democracy for which the [UN] have fought in [the] war." The justices followed through in the 1951 *Deportation Cases*[41] when they quoted Article 1 of the Universal Declaration of Human Rights (UDHR) that "all human beings are born free and equal in dignity and rights" in ultimately ordering the release of Japanese spies who were being detained for an unreasonable period of time pending deportation.

The justices also used the dignity language outside the context of reviewing governmental actions concerning wartime criminals. In *Margolari* v. *Tancinco* (1949),[42] Justice Ozaeta in his concurring opinion invoked one's dignity in explaining why the Court could not force a daughter to return to her mother's custody, as ordering her to do so would amount to a "violence to her dignity as a human person."

---

[38] Ibid.
[39] For example, *Spouses Fernando* v. *Northwest Airlines*, 805 Phil. 501 (2017).
[40] 75 Phil. 50 (Dis. Op. Ozaeta).
[41] *Andreu* v. *COI*, 90 Phil. 347 (1951) (Padilla); *Chirkskoff* v. *COI*, 90 Phil. 256 (1951); *Borovsky* v. *COI*, 90 Phil. 107 (1951); *Mejoff* v. *Director of Prisons*, 90 Phil. 70 (1951).
[42] 84 Phil. 865.

This reflects an interpretative shift from the social-rank-or-status-based understanding of dignity, especially as the Spanish-era Código Civil required the prior consent of one's parents before unmarried daughters under twenty-five years old could leave the parental home. Later, in *Morfe v. Mutuc* (1968),[43] the majority decision considered the dignity and integrity of an individual in justifying a stricter scrutiny of laws that facilitated state intrusion into one's personal life.

2.5 Dignity as a Constitutionally Recognized Concept: 1973–

Although the Court has been employing the egalitarian conception of dignity since the mid-1940s, it made its constitutional debut only in the 1973 Constitution. The first mention of dignity was under the article on the *Declaration of Principles and State Policies*, which formalizes dignity's foundational role in the promotion of social justice: "The State shall promote social justice to ensure the dignity, welfare, and security of all the people."[44] Meanwhile, the second mention of dignity appears under the article on the *Duties and Obligations of Citizens*: "It shall be the duty of every citizen to engage in gainful work to assure himself and his family a life worthy of human dignity."[45]

One of the most important cases decided under the aegis of the 1973 Constitution was *Philippine Blooming Mills* (1973),[46] as it helped reinforce the justices' increasing use of dignity as a tool for judicial interpretation. In that case, the Court invalidated a private employer's decision to dismiss union leaders who induced about 400 workers to leave their workstations and join a solidarity walkout against government officers on the ground that the dismissal violated the workers' freedom of speech and of assembly. While acknowledging that these constitutional guarantees were traditionally invoked against the government, the justices reasoned that it was still the Court's responsibility to preserve and enhance "the dignity and worth of the human personality [which] is the central core as well as the cardinal article of faith of our civilization." Given the "inviolable character of man as an individual," it was the Court's duty to protect an individual "in his thoughts and in his beliefs as the citadel of his person," such that it would not issue any ruling that would put an individual's human rights inferior to another's property rights. Implicitly, the Court pronounced that private individuals are equally obliged to recognize another's dignity, emphasizing that freedoms of expression and of assembly are "essential to man's enjoyment of his life, to his happiness and to his full and complete fulfillment."

The justices also continued to develop, broaden, and strengthen the nexus between human dignity and the various constitutional rights of an individual. As

---

[43] 130 Phil. 415. See *Ople v. Torres*, 354 Phil. 948 (1998).
[44] Constitution (1973), Article ii, sec. 6; *Guijarno v. CIR*, 152 Phil. 286 (1973).
[45] Constitution (1973), Article v, sec. 3.
[46] *Philippine Blooming Mills Employees Organization v. Philippine Blooming Mills Co.*, 151-A Phil. 656 (1973).

I will discuss in the following sections of this chapter, the concept of human dignity has been invoked by Court members even during the martial law era in cases involving due process,[47] admissibility of extrajudicial confessions,[48] national security,[49] and religious freedom.[50]

2.6 *Dignity under the 1987 Constitution*

The forty-year judicial discourse on the egalitarian conception of dignity may have helped pave the way for the express recognition of the right of every person to human dignity in the present 1987 Constitution.[51] For the framers of the 1987 Constitution, the protection of human dignity meant the promotion and protection of a whole gamut of rights "pertinent to the existence of the human person" and those that they may eventually discover.[52] Human rights were not to be considered as ends in themselves but, rather, "as means to achieve greater ends."[53] As a result, the country's current 1987 Constitution ensured the "supremacy of human dignity over things,"[54] so much so that it dedicated the entire Article XIII, composed of sixteen sections, to detailing various forms of social justice reforms that specifically tackle labor, agrarian and natural resources, urban land and housing, health, women, and indigenous peoples. Crucially, it established a Commission on Human Rights for the promotion and protection of human dignity.[55] Some of the important cases decided by the Court under the 1987 Constitution will be discussed in Section 4.

3 FORMING THE PHILIPPINE CONCEPTION OF HUMAN DIGNITY

I have briefly discussed a select number of cases that showed the historical references to dignity in Philippine judicial discourse while foreshadowing the factors that could have helped push its development. In this section I will dig deeper into those factors and, in so doing, refer to Joas's claim[56] on the effect of cultural trauma to a people's commitment to values as a useful framework.

---

[47] *Aquino v. Military Commission*, 159-A Phil. 163 (1975) (Dissenting Opinion, Teehankee) (Concurring Opinion, Barredo).
[48] *Magtoto v. Manguera*, 159 Phil 611 (1975) (Dissenting Opinion, Castro) (Concurring Opinion, Antonio).
[49] *In Re: Parong v. Enrile*, 206 Phil. 392 (1983) (Dissenting Opinion, Teehankee).
[50] *Victoriano v. Elizalde Rope Workers' Union*, 158 Phil. 60 (1974) (Concurring Opinion, Fernando).
[51] Constitution (1987), Article xiii, sec. 1; Article ii, sec. 11.
[52] See Record of the Constitutional Commission of 1986, Volume No. (II), Record No. 46; also at (II)47, (III)66, (IV)81, (IV)84, (IV)87, and (IV)89. The proceedings of the 1971 Constitutional Convention were never published.
[53] Ibid., at (III)66.
[54] Ibid., at (IV)89.
[55] Constitution (1987), Article xiii, secs. 17–19.
[56] Hans Joas, *The Sacredness of the Person* (Washington, DC; Georgetown University Press, 2013), p. 5.

3.1 Cultural Trauma

According to Hans Joas, analyzing sociohistorical events would reveal that a significant portion of our commitment to values and our notion of what is valuable emerged from violent experiences suffered by communities or entire cultures for which they feel a collective trauma. This "cultural trauma" occurred when "members of a collectivity feel they have been subjected to a horrendous event that leaves indelible marks upon their group consciousness."[57] These violent experiences eventually led to "motivational and sensitizing effects" that impelled communities to mobilize and transform the value generated from such traumatic events into universal value commitments.

Proceeding from Joas' proposition, the following can be considered as relevant "culturally traumatic" events that have impelled the nation to commit to and institutionalize human dignity: the Filipino people's suffering from the more than three centuries of Spanish colonial oppression; the Japanese wartime atrocities; and the twenty-one-year authoritarian rule of President Marcos. These experiences involved subjugation, discrimination, and oppression in various forms that, I argue, contributed to the expansion of the domestic conception of dignity in judicial discourse.[58]

The motivational effect of Spanish colonization, as cultural trauma, is undeniable; in fact, the framers of the 1935 Constitution have extensively deliberated on correcting the discriminatory treatment of Filipinos under Spain. For example, the Spanish introduction of the *impuesto de cédula personal* (community tax) was viewed as one of the colonial authority's instruments of tyranny whereby a fixed amount of tax was imposed regardless of an individual's economic standing. It also conveniently provided a justification for imprisoning rebels who refused to pay them.[59] The framers, therefore, sought to redress the colonial injustices by introducing reforms that would consider the "dignity of the free people ... the dignification of man himself."[60] They carefully crafted a constitution that would afford high and equal regard to every person, with the specific provision on social justice being a way to seek social equality, as well as equal recognition and respect of dignity regardless of race.

The atrocities of the Imperial Japanese Army had also left an indelible mark on the Filipino conception of dignity. The Philippines was considered the foremost victim of the Japanese armed aggression in the Pacific War, with Manila assessed to be, after Warsaw, the most devastated city during the Second World War.[61] Japanese

---

[57] Ibid., at p. 79; see also Jeffrey C. Alexander, "Toward a Theory of Cultural Trauma," in *Cultural Trauma and Collective Identity*, edited by Jeffrey C. Alexander, Ron Eyerman, Bernhard Giesen, Neil J. Smelser, and Piotr Sztompka (Oakland: University of California Press, 2004), p. 1.

[58] Joas, *Sacredness*, 80.

[59] See 1935 Convention, at (I)(19), (V)(84).

[60] Ibid., at (I)(15), (I)(19), (III)(49), (IV)(94), (IV)(94), (IX)(128), and (X)(132).

[61] Thomas Zeiler, *Unconditional Defeat: Japan, America, and the End of World War II* (Wilmington, DE: Scholarly Resources, 2004), pp. 130–131; Takushi Ohno, *War Reparations & Peace Settlement: Philippines–Japan Relations 1945–1956* (Manila: Solidaridad Publishing

brutality in the islands was infamous – they slaughtered thousands of innocent and defenseless persons, razed towns and cities, and even put thousands of women in a system of military sexual slavery,[62] so much so that the Filipino people could have been expected to respond with unbridled vengeance. Instead, at the hour of reckoning for Japanese military leaders and those accused of collaborating with them, the justices chose to uphold the respect for their dignity as human persons as expressed in the Preamble of the UN Charter.[63] Such choice could be seen as particularly telling of an institution's commitment to the value generated in the light of the Court's very own chief justice, José Abad Santos, having been previously executed for refusing to cooperate with the Japanese during the latter's occupation. In *Peralta v. Director of Prisons*,[64] Justice Ozaeta explained the ruling of the Court against the implementation of a summary criminal procedure and subsequent imposition of harsher penalty by emphasizing that such treatment was "repugnant to the humanitarian method of administering criminal justice" and inconsistent with the "dignity and worth of the human person" enshrined in the UN Charter. As discussed in Section 2.4, the judicial review of the treatment of prisoners of war became a decisive moment for the Justices in understanding how dignity can be used in adjudication, especially dignity's equal and universal application to benefit even a cruel oppressor.

The dictatorial rule of the former president Marcos was another culturally traumatic experience for Filipinos, which led to the 1986 People Power Revolution.[65] The abuses that thousands suffered under his martial rule was universally cited as the main reason for placing stronger emphasis on human rights protection under the present 1987 Constitution. The Constitution is replete with provisions on both the respect for human dignity and the protection of human rights in the light of those who, "during the dark days of Martial Law, were illegally detained, tortured, and even involuntarily disappeared."[66] That is why the constitutional framers crafted a more detailed Bill of Rights, which includes the prohibition against the infliction of cruel, degrading, or inhuman punishment and the abolition of existing laws imposing the death penalty. For good measure, they included the creation of the Commission on Human Rights, to investigate all forms of human rights violations involving civil and political rights, and to monitor the Philippine government's compliance with international treaty obligations on human rights.[67]

House, 1986), p. 4; Teodoro Agoncillo and Milagros Guerrero, *History of the Filipino People* (Quezon City: Garcia Publishing Co., 1974), p. 484.

[62] See *Vinuya v. Romulo*, 633 Phil. 538 (2010); *In re: Vicente Sotto*, 82 Phil. 595 (1949) (Dissenting Opinion, Perfecto); *Yamashita v. Styer*, 75 Phil. 563 (1945); *Duran v. Santos*, 75 Phil. 410 (1945); J. R. Robert Real, "Continuing the Quest for Justice after the Philippine Supreme Court's Decision on the Japanese Military Sex Slaves," *Michigan International Lawyer* 26, no. III (2014): 13.

[63] See Yamashita v. Styer (Concurring Opinion, Perfecto).

[64] 75 Phil. 285 (1945) (Concurring Opinion, Ozaeta).

[65] See *In re: Puno*, 285 Phil. 1055 (1992).

[66] *Enrile v. Sandiganbayan*, 767 Phil. 147 (2015) (Dissenting Opinion, Leonen). See also *Olaguer v. Military Commission*, 234 Phil. 144 (1987) (Concurring Opinion, Teehankee).

[67] Constitution (1987), Article ii, sec. 11, Article xiii, sec. 18.

Congress, later on, established the Human Rights Victims' Claims Board as an acknowledgment of the state's "moral and legal obligation" to provide reparation to the victims of the Marcos dictatorship; to recognize their heroism and sacrifices; and to "restore the victims' honor and dignity."[68]

We can find from the discussions of the constitutional framers and the opinions of the justices that these culturally traumatic experiences significantly contributed to ensuring the sustained use of the egalitarian conception of dignity in Philippine judicial discourse. In turn, these experiences also helped advance the entrenchment of human dignity as a value commitment, with the present 1987 Constitution expressly making it the avowed state policy to "valu[e] the dignity of every human person and guarant[ee] full respect for human rights" and specifically mandating Congress to "give highest priority to the enactment of measures that protect and enhance the right of all the people to human dignity."[69]

While cultural trauma could provide an explanation as to what might have helped impel the further development of dignity towards an egalitarian concept, this may not be enough in understanding the flavor that the domestic conception of dignity has acquired. It is also vital to uncover other contributory factors that helped shape how dignity is conceived by the justices. As I will examine, strong religious beliefs, adherence to international law, and, too, the persuasive value of US constitutional law have significantly influenced the domestic conception of dignity.

3.2 Other Factors

3.2.1 Catholic Teachings

The pervasiveness of Catholic teachings[70] in Philippine legal discourse and in Filipino culture[71] is undeniable. Justice Perfecto once appealed to his colleagues' sense of faith to revisit the denial of bail to a prisoner of war: "Are we Christians? Do we believe in the teachings of the Bible? Have we faith in the biblical doctrines which are the vitalizing essentials of the Democracy?"[72]

The Roman Catholic Church viewed human dignity as an attribute possessed by humans as beings created in the *Imago Dei* – the image and likeness of God. In the writings of Saint Thomas Aquinas, for example, Man is an intellectual and rational being whose ultimate end is to understand God.[73] Interference with this goal through the restriction of Man's freedom and rationality, therefore, would be

---

[68] Human Rights Victims Reparation and Recognition Act (2013), sec. 2.
[69] Constitution (1987), Article ii, sec. 11, Article xiii, sec. 1.
[70] There is no clear evidence of a significant influence of Islamic teachings in judicial discourse. (Note: Justice Bidin was the only Muslim Justice who served at the Court from 1987 to 1995.)
[71] See Chapter 14 in this volume by Jonathan Chow.
[72] *Duran v. Santos*.
[73] See Thomas Aquinas, *Summa Contra Gentiles*.

considered an infringement on human dignity.[74] It is with the concept of *Imago Dei* that the Church characterized the value of human life and dignity: that it is derived from God, because He created Man in His image.[75]

The sway of Catholic teachings is so powerful that justices would openly and expressly invoke it in their decisions. For example, in the death penalty cases (1997/1999), Justice Panganiban (later chief justice) reminded his colleagues that "'Thou shall not kill' is a fundamental commandment to all Christians, as well as to the rest of the 'sovereign Filipino people' who believe in Almighty God" and that the punishment of death should be meted out only "in cases of absolute necessity," quoting Pope John Paul II's encyclical *Evangelium Vitae* and its reference to humans having begin created in the *Imago Dei*.[76] In *Re: Parong v. Enrile* (1983), Justice Teehankee criticized the majority opinion's pronouncement that "the duty of the judiciary to protect individual rights must yield to the power of the Executive to protect the State," while quoting the exhortation of Pope John Paul II to the Filipino nation: "Any apparent conflict between the exigencies of [the security of a nation] and of the citizens' basic rights must be resolved according to the fundamental principle – upheld always by the Church – that social organization exists only for the service of man and for the protection of his dignity, and that it cannot claim to serve the common good when human rights are not safeguarded."

As further discussed by Jonathan T. Chow in Chapter 14, central to the Catholic faith is the preferential respect for the poor and those living on the margins of society.[77] Such Catholic teachings were concurrent with the concept of social justice, which strives to address the inequalities present in society through affirmative action and policies. It is also these considerations of charity and other Christian values that served as guidance for some of the justices. The Court had even acknowledged the influence of the Christian faith in the rejection of the laissez-faire philosophy, explaining that it had been "superseded by the benign Christian shibboleth of live-and-help others to live," thus denouncing biblical Cain's "selfish affirmation that he is not his brother's keeper."[78]

Crucially, Catholic teachings influenced the drafting of the current Constitution. When the dictator Marcos was toppled and the opposition leaders began preparations to advance their reformist agenda, the Catholic Bishops' Conference of the Philippines (CBCP) immediately issued an appeal to the would-be framers of the new constitution to bear in mind the "human dignity of all," the "common good," and the protection of "basic human freedoms won at so

---

[74] See Pope Leo XIII, "Rerum Novarum: Encyclical on Capital and Labor," *The Holy See*, May 15, 1891, www.vatican.va/content/leo-xiii/en/encyclicals/documents/hf_l-xiii_enc_15051891_rerum-novarum.html.

[75] See Chow, "Catholicism and Human Dignity."

[76] *Echegaray v. Secretary of Justice*, 361 Phil. 73 (1999); *People v. Echegaray*, 335 Phil. 343 (1997).

[77] "Catholicism and Human Dignity." See Pope Paul VI, "Octogesima Adveniens," *The Holy See*, May 14, 1971, www.vatican.va/content/paul-vi/en/apost_letters/documents/hf_p-vi_apl_19710514_octogesima-adveniens.html.

[78] *Floresca v. Philex Mining*, 220 Phil. 533 (1985).

hard a price."[79] It also reminded them that the Philippines is a "nation founded on selfless service where [people] are responsible for one another."[80] More significantly, the Church directly influenced the drafting of the Constitution through several respected members of the clergy who served as constitutional framers – Fr. Joaquin Bernas, Bishop Teodoro Bacani, Sr. Christine Tan, and Rev. Cirilo Rigos, among others – securing the Church's ability to ensure the incorporation of Catholic teachings in the nation's fundamental law. Ultimately, the Constitution reflected the Church's position such as a ban on abortion, abolition of the death penalty, a provision for religious instruction in public schools, and an acknowledgment of parental rights in educational and family planning decisions.[81]

3.2.2 International Law

Just like in the Taiwanese constitutional discourse, international instruments such as the UN Charter and the UDHR were also crucial in setting up the stage for human dignity's eventual debut in the Philippine Constitution.[82] I have discussed in Section 2.4 that the justices first relied on these international instruments for textual support in introducing the idea that human dignity was a value that must be considered in the interpretation and application of laws as they dealt with the rights of an accused.[83] Subsequent cases show that the justices continue to cite the UDHR, as well as the International Covenant on Civil and Political Rights and the Convention on the Elimination of all Forms of Discrimination Against Women, in stressing the nation's commitment to valuing the inherent dignity and worth of every human being.[84] Indeed, international legal norms have aided the development of domestic law in various ways, with the justices even using treaties or conventions to which the Philippines is not a party as an underpinning treaty to resolve a legal question.[85]

---

[79] Ricardo Vidal, "Pastoral Exhortation on the Constitutional Commission and Its Work," *CBCP Online*, May 18, 1986, https://cbcponline.net/pastoral-exhortation-on-the-constitutional-commission-and-its-work.
[80] Ibid.
[81] See Ricardo Vidal, "A Covenant Towards Peace," *CBCP Online*, November 21, 1986, https://cbcponline.net/a-covenant-towards-peace.
[82] See Chapter 4 in this volume by Jimmy Chia-Shin Hsu.
[83] *Raquiza v. Bradford*; *Peralta v. Director of Prisons*; *Reyes v. Crisologo*, 75 Phil. 225–271 (1945) (Dissenting Opinion, Perfecto); *Duran v. Santos* (Dissenting Opinion, Perfecto).
[84] See *David v. Senate Electoral Tribunal*, GRN 221538 (2016); *Poe-Llamanzares v. Commission on Elections*, GRN 221697 (2016) (Concurring Opinion, Leonen); *Enrile v. Sandiganbayan*, 767 Phil. 147 (2015); *Government of Hongkong Special Administrative Region v. Olalia*, 550 Phil. 63 (2007); *Government of the United States of America v. Purganan*, 438 Phil. 417 (2002) (Separate Opinion, Puno); *Romualdez-Marcos v. Commission on Elections*, 318 Phil. 329 (1995) (Separate Opinion, Romero); *Hildawa v. Enrile*, 222 Phil. 450 (1986) (Separate Opinion, Teehankee).
[85] Francis Temprosa, "Reflections of a Confluence: International Law in the Philippine Court 1940–2000," *Asian Yearbook of International Law* 19 (2013): 120–121.

3.2.3 US Constitutional Law

The "close and personal contact"[86] of American political institutions in the formative years of the Court fostered the transplantation of American constitutional law in the islands. The extent and potency of this contact can be seen in *Kepner v. United States* when the US Supreme Court reversed a decision made by the Philippine Supreme Court concerning the interpretation of the guarantee against double jeopardy in the Philippine Bill. According to *Kepner*, Philippine courts should "look to the origin and source of the expression and the judicial construction put upon it," which "makes evident the intention of Congress to carry some, at least, of the essential principles of American constitutional jurisprudence to these islands."[87] The American Court reiterated in *Serra v. Mortiga* that "guaranties equivalent to the due process and equal protection of the law clause of the 14th Amendment, the twice in jeopardy clause of the 5th Amendment, and the substantial guaranties of the 6th Amendment, exclusive of the right to trial by jury, were extended to the Philippine Islands."[88] Consequently, these guarantees were interpreted the way US constitutional provisions would have been interpreted, applying "the same criteria which [the US Supreme Court] would apply to a case arising in the United States and controlled by the Bill of Rights expressed in the Amendments to the Constitution of the United States."[89]

While the umbilical cord between the American and Philippine constitutional laws has long been cut,[90] Filipino justices continue to consider opinions of US Supreme Court justices as persuasive, especially in buttressing their own justifications as to how the concept of human dignity should color the interpretation of constitutional issues. For example, in explaining the significance of observing the right of an accused against self-incrimination, the justices have often considered Chief Justice Warren's statement in *Miranda v. Arizona* that "the constitutional foundation underlying the privilege is the respect a government ... must accord to the dignity and integrity of its citizens."[91] With respect to issues involving personal autonomy, justices have several times cited *Lawrence v. Texas* in reinforcing their argument that "matters, involving the most intimate and personal choices a person may make in a lifetime, choices central to personal dignity and autonomy, are central to the liberty protected"[92] by the Philippine Constitution. Filipino Justices

---

[86] See Malcolm, "Constitutional History," pp. 110–111.
[87] *Kepner v. United States*, 195 US 100, 121–122 (1904).
[88] *Serra v. Mortiga*, 204 U.S. 470, 474 (1907).
[89] Ibid. See also Malcolm, "Constitutional History," p. 111.
[90] *Francisco v. House of Representatives*, 460 Phil. 830 (2003).
[91] *Miranda v. Arizona*, 384 US 436, 460 (1966), cited in, for example, *People v. Mojello*, 468 Phil. 944 (2004) (Ynares-Santiago); *Galman v. Pamaran*, 222 Phil. 588 (1985) (Concurring Opinion, Dela Fuente); *People v. Buscato*, 165 Phil. 652 (1976) (Antonio); *Magtoto v. Manguera*; *Pascual v. Board of Medical Examiners*, 138 Phil. 361 (1969) (Fernando).
[92] 539 US 558 (2003) (quoting *Planned Parenthood v. Casey*, 505 US 833 [1992]) cited in, for example, *Zabal v. Duterte*, G.R. No. 238467, February 12, 2019 (Dissenting Opinion, Leonen); *Capin-Cadiz v. Brent Hospital and Colleges*, 781 Phil. 610 (2016) (Concurring Opinion, Jardeleza); *Ang Ladlad*

have also readily referred to scholarly works of US constitutional law experts in examining issues involving searches and seizure,[93] free speech,[94] privacy,[95] and the privilege against self-incrimination.[96]

The purpose of highlighting these factors is to gain a better understanding of the dominant influences that the justices have expressed as they attempted to use dignity as a tool for interpretation. Although these factors are in no case exhaustive considering that the justices may have been influenced by other unwritten considerations, discussing these still provides a richer picture of how the current conception of dignity in Philippine judicial discourse has developed and a better understanding of the flavor it has acquired.

4 THE EMERGENCE OF THE PRESENT CONCEPTION OF DIGNITY

As we have seen so far, the justices appear to be using the dignity language in a variety of contexts, whether it involved social justice, rights of an accused, and even personal relations. My next inquiry, then, is to make sense of these varieties – Clapham's general categorization of the aspects of dignity can be useful in organizing these cases and to contextualize how the justices have referred to and eventually developed the domestic conception of dignity.[97] The four aspects he mentioned are: 1) the prohibition of all types of inhuman treatment, humiliation, or degradation by one person over another; 2) the assurance of the possibility for individual choice and the conditions for "each individual's self-fulfillment," autonomy, or self-realization; 3) the recognition that the protection of group identity and culture may be essential for the protection of personal dignity; and 4) the creation of the necessary conditions for each individual to have their essential needs satisfied. In view of this categorization, it would seem from the cases I will discuss that the justices have been invoking dignity as a basis to discover or expand the scope of existing rights in limiting governmental action or as justification of governmental measures that seek to advance or further the people's welfare. Further, justices seem to have considered the express recognition of dignity in the present 1987 Constitution as a clear basis to avoid a strict textual or original meaning of constitutional provisions.

---

v. *Commission on Elections* 632 Phil. 32 (2010) (Separate Opinion, Puno); *City of Manila* v. *Laguio*, 495 Phil. 28 (2005) (Tinga).

[93] *Villanueva* v. *Querubin*, 150-C Phil. 519 (1972) (Fernando), quoting Jacob Landynski, *Search and Seizure and the Supreme Court* (1966).

[94] *Philippine Blooming Mills Employees Organization* v. *Philippine Blooming Mills Co.*, citing *American Communications Assn.* v. *Douds*, 339 US 382 (1950).

[95] *Morfe* v. *Mutuc*, quoting Thomas I. Emerson, "Nine Justices in Search of a Doctrine," *Michigan Law Review* 64 (1965): 219–234.

[96] *Chavez* v. *Court of Appeals*, 133 Phil. 661 (1968) (Concurring Opinion, Castro) quoting Erwin N. Griswold, *The Fifth Amendment Today: Three Speeches* (1955).

[97] Andrew Clapham, *Human Rights Obligations of Non-State Actors* (Cheltenham, UK: Edward Elgar Publishing, 2006), pp. 545–546.

4.1 Treatment of Others

The first aspect points to how persons are to be treated so that their human dignity is not infringed. As I find that it may be easier to imagine how the dignity of law-abiding citizens would be upheld or infringed, the extent and characterization of the domestic conception of human dignity may be better understood if we instead analyze the treatment accorded to someone accused of committing a crime. In this regard, I will refer to what appears to be the two areas in which the justices extensively considered a person's dignity in their decision-making process: 1) recognition of due process; and 2) imposition of penalties.

4.1.1 Recognition of Due Process

In Philippine judicial discourse, the prevailing view on how much weight should be placed on dignity in upholding an accused's due process rights appears to vary depending on whether or not the issue involves national security.

ISSUES INVOLVING NATIONAL SECURITY. When it comes to those charged with political crimes such as rebellion or subversion, the current view among the justices is that "the duty of the judiciary to protect individual rights must yield to the power of the Executive to protect the State."[98] This thinking had been justified on the belief that "if the State perishes, the Constitution, with the Bill of Rights that guarantees the right to personal liberty, perishes with it."[99] A majority of the justices had thus ruled in favor of the jurisdiction of military courts over civilians,[100] the denial of bail for a political prisoner who had been detained for three months without charges,[101] and the foreign military's detention of alleged spies.[102]

Justices who hold the opposite view have argued for tilting the scales in favor of the preservation of human dignity when weighing the security of the state against the protection of the individual. As discussed in Section 3.2.1, Justice Teehankee in *Parong* had insisted that "the fundamental principle that social organization exists only for the service of man and for the protection of his dignity," further reiterating in another case that "the preservation and enhancement of the dignity and worth of the human personality is the central core as well as the cardinal article of faith of our civilization."[103] Justice Sarmiento follows a similar reasoning in *Marcos v. Manglapus* (1989)[104] in dissenting against the decision of the majority to uphold

---

[98] *Parong v. Enrile*.
[99] Ibid.
[100] *Reyes v. Crisologo*, 75 Phil. 225 (1945). Compare *Olaguer v. Military Commission*.
[101] *Duran v. Santos*.
[102] *Raquiza v. Bradford*.
[103] *In Re: Ilagan v. Enrile*, 223 Phil. 561 (1985).
[104] 258 Phil. 479 quoting Enrique Fernando, *The Bill of Rights* (1972). See also *Genuino v. De Lima*, G. R. Nos. 197930, 199034, and 199046, April 17, 2018.

a presidential order that barred former dictator Marcos from returning to the country amidst constitutional arguments on his right to travel. He emphasized that "a constitution exists to assure that in the discharge of the governmental functions, the dignity that is the birthright of every human being is duly safeguarded."

The *Subversion Cases*[105] continued to adopt this line of thinking when the Court ruled on the application of the martial law–era Anti-Subversion Act, which outlawed mere membership in the Communist Party of the Philippines. In those cases, the majority opinion had found valid the warrantless arrests as it was "founded on an overwhelming public interest in peace and order in our communities." Justice Sarmiento dissented, arguing that the constitutional prohibition against unreasonable seizures of persons should be read in conjunction with the constitutional precept that the state "values the dignity of every human person and guarantees full respect for human rights." He insisted that national security was not a ground for sanctioning the warrantless arrests and reminded his colleagues that such a justification was the "dictator's own excuses to perpetuate tyranny."

As these cases are decades old, it remains to be seen[106] how the justices would consider cases involving national security amidst the increasing references to dignity in adjudication. This is likely to be examined in the pending case of *Almora v. Dela Rosa*, which involves the constitutionality of the government's nationwide system of anonymous reporting of suspected drug users, pushers, and "personalities" – one of the first challenges against President Duterte's "war on drugs." Notably, Justice Leonen asked during the oral arguments if the official creation of a "drug watch list" would also violate the Constitution given that "human dignity should be respected by the State [and that] the State shall respect the human dignity of every person."[107] President Duterte has earlier claimed that drug addicts are "dysfunctional members" of society who can be stripped of their human dignity in the name of protecting the public; and that the government's obligation in upholding the people's dignity is more focused on giving the populace "a decent and dignified future through the social and physical infrastructures necessary to better their lives" than the dignity of suspected criminals.[108] While the case has yet to be decided as of this writing, the Court in the meantime directed the government to release a copy of

---

[105] In Re: Umil v. Ramos, 279 Phil. 266 (1991); Umil v. Ramos, 265 Phil. 325 (1990).
[106] There had been a later case on rebellion – that is, Ladlad v. Velasco, 551 Phil. 313 (2007). The Court made no reference to dignity.
[107] See *Almora v. Dela Rosa* (GRN 234359, 234484), SC Oral Arguments Transcript (November 21, 2017) at p. 148.
[108] See ibid., at pp. 146–149; *State of the Nation Address of the President of the Philippines*, July 23, 2018, https://pcoo.gov.ph/wp-content/uploads/2018/07/2018-State-of-the-Nation-Address-of-Duterte.pdf; *Speech of President Rodrigo Duterte at the Philippines-India Business Forum*, January 26, 2018, https://pcoo.gov.ph/wp-content/uploads/2018/01/20180126-Speech_of_President_Rodrigo_Roa_Duterte__during_the_Philippines-India_Business_Forum.pdf; *State of the Nation Address of the President of the Philippines*, July 25, 2016, https://pcoo.gov.ph/wp-content/uploads/2018/07/2016-State-of-the-Nation-Address-of-Duterte.pdf; Marlon Ramos, "Junkies Are Not Humans," *Philippine Daily Inquirer*, August 28, 2016 (01:59 AM), http://newsinfo.inquirer.net/810395/junkies-are-not-humans.

the watch list in spite of the solicitor general's continued insistence that the matter involved national security.[109] This suggests that a discussion on the impact of human dignity on the legality of alleged national security measures may be forthcoming.

ISSUES UNRELATED TO NATIONAL SECURITY. In contrast, justices appear to be more open to invoking dignity to insist on according treatment in favor of the accused. As early as in *People v. Bagasala* (1971),[110] the Court had already considered the dignity language in interpreting that the constitutional right against self-incrimination necessarily entails the inadmissibility of any evidence forcibly obtained from an accused. According to Justice Fernando (later chief justice), "the imperative requirements of truth and of humanity condemn the utilization of force and violence to extract confessions from unwilling victims" and "[a] decent regard for the dignity that attaches to every human being as such will be satisfied with nothing less."[111] *Bagasala* was a landmark decision, for it effectively recognized the constitutional status of the exclusionary rule even before it was formally written into the 1973 Constitution. As the justices have declared in a number of cases, "even the evil man is a human being" whose dignity must be respected.[112]

Justices applied a similar interpretative approach that benefits an accused in *Enrile v. Sandiganbayan* (2015).[113] Amidst strong insistence from the dissenting justices on the plain reading of the constitutional provision that expressly precludes an accused charged with serious offenses from posting bail "when evidence of guilt is strong," the majority nevertheless granted bail in favor of former Senate President Juan Ponce Enrile (accused of plunder) on humanitarian grounds in view of his "advanced age and frail health." According to the Court, this is in the light of the "national commitment to uphold the fundamental human rights as well as value the worth and dignity of every person." Justice Leonen dissented, explaining that there was no legal provision that compels the Court to grant bail on the basis of the medical condition of the accused and that the "general declaration to uphold the value and dignity of every person . . . does not prohibit the arrest of any accused based on lawful causes nor does it prohibit the detention of any person accused of crimes," as this "only implies that any arrest or detention must be carried out in a dignified and humane manner." Here, we can see that while both the majority and dissenting Justices agree that the dignity of a person requires that he or she be treated humanely, they differ in their understanding of what humane treatment dictates.

---

[109] See *Almora v. Dela Rosa* (GRN 234359, 234484), Resolution (April 2, 2019) at 2, 11–12; Almora Oral Arguments Transcript (December 5, 2017), at 135–137.
[110] *People v. Bagasala*, 148-A Phil. 195 (1971). See *People v. Panopio*, 75 Phil. 767 (1946).
[111] Ibid.
[112] *Chavez v. Court of Appeals*. See also *In Re: Morales v. Enrile*, 206 Phil. 466 (1983) (Opinions of Fernando and Teehankee); *People v. Ong*, 159 Phil. 212 (1975) (Concurring and Dissenting Opinion, Barredo); *People v. Bagasala*; *Manila Railroad Co. v. Yatco*, 132 Phil. 223 (1968).
[113] *Enrile v. Sandiganbayan*, 767 Phil. 147 (2015).

4.1.2 Imposition of Penalties

As Philippine courts have little discretion in imposing statutory penalties,[114] I have instead focused on the aspects of the law in which there is an entry point for a possible dignity analysis. One such entry point, I find, is when justices are called to rule on arguments pertaining to the harshness or disproportionality of the law itself, particularly on grounds that the penalty provided is a "cruel, degrading or inhuman punishment."[115]

In *Echegaray v. Secretary of Justice* (1998),[116] for example, the justices recognized the possibility of reconsidering the constitutionality of the imposition of the death penalty by lethal injection depending on "the evolving standards of decency." According to the Court, "what is cruel and unusual 'is not fastened to the obsolete but may acquire meaning as public opinion becomes enlightened by a humane justice.'" Although the Court eventually found that the entire procedure was not cruel, inhuman, or degrading – especially as compared with previous forms of execution, such as through an electric chair or gas chamber – the justices nevertheless kept the door ajar for a further human dignity analysis. Such possibility is bolstered by the fact that the majority opinion in *Echegaray* strangely adopted the reasoning of pre-1987 jurisprudence, which had involved the earlier constitutional language of "cruel or unusual punishment."[117] It remains to be seen whether the Court would revisit or explain why such analyses remain valid given the change in wording of the constitutional proscription to "cruel, degrading or inhuman punishment" under the present 1987 Constitution.[118]

Corpuz v. People (2014)[119] indicates that the Court has yet to engage (expressly) in a full discussion on how the pursuit of human dignity should impact the scrutiny of punishments provided by law. In upholding the continued constitutionality of an admittedly unjust penalty provided for by an outdated law (1930), the majority opinion explained that "all penalties are generally harsh, being punitive in nature" and that "whether or not they are excessive or amount to cruel punishment is a matter that should be left to lawmakers." In response, Chief Justice Sereno asked the majority to avoid adhering to a literal imposition of the law, emphasizing that the "measure of a just society depends not only on how it apprehends and punishes the guilty" but "also lies in the dignity and fairness it collectively accords convicted persons who, irrevocably, are still members of that society." She reminded her colleagues that the Court, in the past, has "never shirked from its role of interpreting

---

[114] Discretion is mainly limited to length of imprisonment, which must still be within the statutory period.
[115] Constitution (1987), Article. iii, sec. 19(1).
[116] *Echegaray v. Secretary of Justice*, quoting, inter alia, *Weems v. United States*, 217 US 349 (1910). See generally *Perez v. People*, 568 Phil. 491 (2008). (Note: the Philippines has been a state-party to the Second Optional Protocol to the ICCPR on the abolition of death penalty since 2007.)
[117] Constitution (1973), Article iv, sec. 21; Constitution (1935), Article iii, sec. 19.
[118] Constitution (1987), Article iii, sec. 19(1).
[119] 734 Phil. 352.

the law ... to prevent a result that is manifestly unjust" and thus called on them to uphold their duty "not only to dispense justice, but to actively prevent injustice wrought by inaction on the question of the continued justness of the penalties." Meanwhile, Justice Carpio pointed out how the history of the cruel punishment clause was intended to restrain the king "from punishing convicts in ways inconsistent with human dignity." In spite of the references to dignity, the majority opinion felt no need to respond to such argumentations.

As we can observe from these cases, the justices have referred to dignity in ascertaining whether to limit state action and/or to expand the traditional scope of an existing right. They have shown their willingness to engage actively with the dignity discourse when it comes to due process and remedial issues, but have exhibited hesitance when it comes to the issue of imposable penalties and the treatment of an accused. Clearly, however, the Court has yet to employ a more robust dignity analysis on these areas.

4.2 Individual Choice

The second aspect revolves around the concepts of autonomy and of freedom of choice that allow a person to achieve self-fulfillment. Here I will consider two areas of human existence where the Court has expressly used the dignity language to ascertain and balance the extent of allowable government interference that may be seen to encroach upon the person's private sphere: 1) informational privacy; and 2) decisional privacy.

4.2.1 Informational Privacy

The Court characterized the right to privacy as the "embodiment of a spiritual concept – the belief that to value the privacy of home and person and to afford its constitutional protection against the long reach of government is no less than to value human dignity."[120] To violate one's right to privacy, therefore, is to violate one's dignity.

On the strength of its connection to dignity, the Court has recognized the right to privacy as an "unwritten" right having a constitutional status.[121] In *Morfe* (1968),[122] the Court explained that it fully deserved constitutional protection, since an intrusion into one's personal life would amount to an infringement of one's dignity and integrity as an individual. *Morfe* is seminal, for it continues to be regarded as the main basis for recognizing the right to privacy as an unenumerated constitutional

---

[120] *20th Century Fox Film Corp. v. Court of Appeals*, 247 Phil. 624 (1988); *People v. Burgos*, 228 Phil. 1 (1986); *Villanueva v. Querubin*.
[121] *Disini v. Secretary of Justice*, 727 Phil. 28 (2014).
[122] *Morfe v. Mutuc*.

right even as the subsequent 1973 and 1987 Constitutions failed to bestow it its pride of place in the Bill of Rights.[123]

The inclination of the Court to grant a constitutional status to a right (privacy) that has not been expressly mentioned in the Constitution based on a seeming constitutional value (dignity) can be seen as, perhaps, a clear manifestation of what McCrudden describes[124] as the "thick view" of dignity. He explains that having a thick view entails an approach to human rights adjudication that considers dignity as expressing a value unique to itself, helping in the identification and further explication of a catalogue of rights. In contrast, having a "thin view" entails approaching dignity as simply another way of expressing the idea of a catalogue of human rights, neither adding to nor detracting from but coterminous with human rights. Such a thin view adds little to the debate on what rights there are or how they should be interpreted.

4.2.2 Decisional Privacy

Imbong v. Ochoa (2014)[125] offers us a good picture of the debates surrounding the use of dignity in assessing the constitutionality of a law that affects one's personal choice concerning marriage and founding of a family. The case concerned various provisions of the Reproductive Health Law, including a clause that gives a spouse absolute autonomy over medical procedures done to his or her body in view of the constitutionally enshrined state policy to protect and strengthen the family as a "basic autonomous social institution."[126] On one side, Justice De Castro (later chief justice) relied on the dignity of the family in rationalizing the majority's decision to strike down the provision on spousal autonomy, explaining that the law undermined the sanctity of the family and assaulted the family's "inherent dignity as an instrument to God's creation." She argued that the law's guarantee of "universal access to so-called 'medically-safe, non-abortifacient ... reproductive health care services, methods, devices, supplies' ... seriously impairs the constitutional protections extended to the family," especially as the assailed provision does away with spousal consent.

On the other side, Justice Leonen made a connection between personal autonomy and social justice by arguing for the need to even up the playing field and promote the dignity of vulnerable groups such as the women and the poor. He had emphasized the "differential impact of lack of knowledge and access to reproductive health technologies between the rich and the poor" and argued that "informed choices provide greater chances for a better quality of life for families." He then pushed for an interpretation that would provide "choices so that the quality of life

---

[123] See *Ople v. Torres*; *Disini v. Secretary of Justice*.
[124] McCrudden, "Human Dignity," 680–681.
[125] *Spouses Imbong v. Ochoa*, 732 Phil. 1 (2014).
[126] Constitution (1987), Article ii, sec. 12.

improves" and would "assure human dignity" beyond "corporeal existence." It is in these discussions that we can appreciate, firstly, how the justices on both sides engaged with the dignity argument in supporting their diametrical positions (as in the *Enrile* case); and secondly, how they grappled with their opposing understanding of whose dignity should be respected – the family's or the individual's.

We can then compare the analyses of the justices in *Imbong* with the ruling in *People* v. *Jumawan* (2014),[127] which similarly involved issues concerning founding a family and personal autonomy. In *Jumawan*, the Court found the husband guilty of raping his wife, rejecting arguments on the possible recognition of the old common-law marital exemption rule in rape. Writing the majority opinion, Justice Reyes emphasized that "a husband who has sexual intercourse with his wife is not merely using a property, he is fulfilling a marital consortium with a fellow human being with dignity equal to that he accords himself." He explained that the ancient customs and ideologies that justified the irrevocable implied consent theory had already been superseded by "modern global principles on the equality of rights between men and women and respect for human dignity established in various international conventions, such as the CEDAW." He then stressed that rape "is an abhorrence to a woman's value and dignity as a human being."

The ways in which the justices analyzed and employed dignity in these cases reflect an ongoing tug-of-war over how dignity could function in the interpretation of laws that involve personal and joint spousal decisions affecting marriage and founding a family. The unanimous view in *Jumawan* suggests that marriage would not empower the husband to insist on the supposed "marital obligations" of the wife on account of her dignity as an autonomous individual. However, the varying opinions in *Imbong* indicate a competing conception of dignity as it relates to the spouse's personal autonomy to make the final decision on his or her own body, even those that do not involve abortion. It would thus seem in these discussions that, in disputes concerning marriage and family, the question is whether to put a premium on the integrity of a collective (i.e. the couple or family) over the autonomy of the individual – and under what circumstances such preference would be regarded.

Based on these cases, we can see that, when it comes to informational privacy, the Court has considered human dignity to further justify limiting governmental action to the extent that it would recognize the constitutional status of an unwritten right. However, when it comes to decisional privacy, it appears that the Court would be slow to sanction a governmental measure that expressly recognizes individual choice, especially if it would affect marriage and founding a family. Unlike in the issues discussed in Section 4.1 on due process and penalties, however, we can see that justices have been openly teasing out the role of dignity in interpreting various constitutional provisions.

---

[127] 733 Phil. 102 (Reyes). See also *City of Manila* v. *Laguio*, 495 Phil. 289 (2005).

4.3 Group Identity and Culture

In the third aspect, Clapham appears to relate dignity to group identity and culture, suggesting that a person's dignity is also tied to that of a group with which one identifies, such as those defined by their sexuality, culture, or any other collective characteristic. Oftentimes, it is based on these characteristics that the state makes classifications, and equal protection then becomes a paramount concern. Foreign judicial decisions have thus been seen to use dignity in interpreting anti-discrimination laws.[128] For instance, in the landmark case of *Obergefell v. Hodges* (2015),[129] the US Supreme Court drew from the precepts of liberty and equality when it found that the challenged laws prohibiting the recognition of same-sex marriage in certain states "burden the liberty of same-sex couples" and "serves to disrespect and subordinate them." In arriving at this decision, Justice Kennedy traced the evolution of the tradition of marriage – from the acceptance of interracial marriages to the acknowledgment of the unequal power dynamics between husband and wife – pointing out that such differences in treatment were due to the perception that these particular groups of individuals did not have the same "dignity." He then explained that the US Constitution grants same-sex couples "equal dignity in the eyes of the law."

We can also see that members of the Philippine Supreme Court are beginning to use dignity in relation to the struggle of individuals with discrimination, as they seek full expression of their identity. In *Ang Ladlad v. Commission on Elections* (2010),[130] for example, the Court invalidated the commission's denial of accreditation for a political organization representing lesbians, gays, bisexuals, and transgender individuals (LGBTs), reiterating that "homosexual conduct is not illegal in this country" and that "the activity of forming a political association that supports LGBT individuals is protected." Chief Justice Puno, through a separate opinion, further elaborated that freedom of thought, belief, expression, and certain intimate conduct are all protected liberties under the Constitution and that these matters, which are intimate and personal, are central to personal dignity and autonomy, thereby limiting governmental regulations.

The positions taken by the parties in *Falcis v. Civil Registrar General*[131] would also show the relevance of a dignity analysis in the constitutional adjudication of marriage equality.[132] During the oral arguments, the petitioner asserted that to deny LGBT individuals of their right to marry, "a decision so personal, so intimate, and so life-changing," would be to devalue their dignity. He then quoted the majority decision in *Imbong* – that "the right to chart their own destiny together falls within the protected zones of marital privacy, and such state intervention would

---

[128] McCrudden, "Human Dignity," 689–692.
[129] 135 S. Ct. 2584 (2015).
[130] 632 Phil. 32 (2010).
[131] GRN 217910, September 3, 2019.
[132] Oral Arguments Transcript (June 19, 2018) at pp. 10–15, (June 26, 2018) at pp. 44–46.

encroach into the zones of spousal privacy guaranteed by the Constitution." Meanwhile, the solicitor general argued that the intent of the framers of the Constitution – reflecting the Catholic view[133] of marriage as a vehicle to create life – should be paramount. As such, he explained that it was unlikely that the constitutional right to human dignity could be interpreted to allow marriage of same-sex couples, even when read with the provisions on founding a family and equal protection of the laws.

Falcis was dismissed on predominantly technical grounds.[134] However, "aware of the need to empower and uphold the dignity of the LGBTQI+ community," an overwhelming majority of justices[135] made sure to pronounce through Justice Leonen that the plain text of the Constitution "does not define or restrict marriage on the basis of sex, gender, sexual orientation, or gender identity or expression" and that it "is capable of accommodating a contemporaneous understanding of sexual orientation, gender identity and expression, and sex characteristics."

These cases suggest that dignity has in fact helped color the Court's appreciation and interpretation of the equal protection clause of the Constitution. Dignity can be seen to contribute in the interpretation of what restricts governmental action. It is also evident that the textual support provided by the 1987 Constitution has empowered the Justices to analyze open-ended constitutional provisions with due regard to the full realization of one's dignity.

4.4 Satisfaction of Essential Needs

The last category considers the necessities required for a person not only to survive but to realize full potential. As discussed in Section 2.3, the Philippine legal concept of dignity has been closely tied with the concept of social justice. What is particularly notable is how the Court has long appreciated the role of the state in creating opportunities for vulnerable groups so that they could attain a certain standard of living that is deemed worthy of a human being. In fact, justices have used and referred to the protection of human dignity as the central argument for justifying government measures promoting economic and social rights. As the Court said in *Asociacion de Agricultores* v. *Talisay-Silay Milling* (1979):[136] "Whenever any government measure designed for the advancement of the working class is impugned on constitutional grounds ... the imperious mandate of the social justice ... asserts its majesty, calling upon the Courts to accord utmost consideration to the spirit

---

[133] According to the CBCP, "the union of man and woman ... is also ordered towards the procreation and education of children." See Socrates Villegas, "The Dignity and Vocation of Homosexual Persons," *CBCP Online*, August 28, 2015, https://cbcponline.net/the-dignity-and-vocation-of-homosexual-persons.

[134] That is, the case did not present an actual controversy before the Court.

[135] Justice Leonen wrote the majority opinion. Out of the fifteen Supreme Court Justices, only Justice Peralta (later chief justice) presented a contrary analysis.

[136] 177 Phil. 247.

animating the act assailed ... to serve the sacred cause of human dignity, which is actually what lies at the core of those constitutional precepts."

In line with what the Court described as the shifting emphasis to community interest with a view to "affirmative enhancement of human values,"[137] it has upheld and reinforced social legislations and government policies on various subjects, such as on collective bargaining,[138] security of tenure,[139] minimum wages,[140] equal pay,[141] compulsory arbitration,[142] limitation of work hours,[143] requirement of separation pay,[144] social security scheme,[145] and agricultural tenancy.[146] The Court has similarly used the dignity language in upholding more recent issues, such as the regulation of the recruitment and deployment of overseas Filipino workers.[147] Government measures to equalize opportunities for the underprivileged and marginalized, to ensure the preservation of the latter's dignity, are thus almost always upheld by the Court even if these affect property rights.

The Court's continued justification of affirmative actions aimed to uplift the dignity of vulnerable groups is not limited to labor rights. For instance, the Court acknowledges the burdens of senior citizens and persons with disabilities in accessing health care[148] and the plight of the poor. In *Sumulong v. Guerrero* (1987),[149] the Court went on to recognize that housing is a "basic human need," and that "shortage in housing is a matter of state concern" since it directly and significantly affects general welfare. The justices unanimously upheld the expropriation of parcels of land for the government's socialized housing project even though it stood to benefit only "a handful of people," amidst arguments that it was at odds with the traditional conception of "public use."

Merely alleging that a particular issue involves the livelihood of a person does not mean, however, that it would be automatically favored, especially if an issue involves a community interest recognized in the Constitution. For example, in *Zabal v. Duterte* (2019),[150] the Court found valid President Duterte's proclamation ordering the total closure of the island of Boracay for six months to clean up the country's prime tourist destination, since it concerned "the environment and health, safety,

---

[137] *Antamok Goldfields Mining v. CIR*, 70 Phil. 340 (1940). See also *Marcopper Mining v. Ople*, 192 Phil. 368 (1981); *Central Textile Mills v. NLRC*, 179 Phil. 8 (1979); *Alfanta v. Noe*, 152 Phil. 458 (1973).
[138] *Pampanga Bus v. Pambusco Employees Union*, 68 Phil. 541 (1939).
[139] *Globe-Mackay Cable and Radio v. NLRC*, 283 Phil. 649 (1992); *Aris (Phil.) Inc. v. NLRC*, 277 Phil. 282 (1991).
[140] *International Hardwood & Veneer v. Pangil Federation of Labor*, 70 Phil. 602 (1940).
[141] *International School Alliance of Educators v. Quisumbing*, 388 Phil. 661 (2000).
[142] *Antamok Goldfields Mining v. CIR*.
[143] *Philippine Airlines Employees' Association v. Philippine Air Lines*, 120 Phil. 383 (1964).
[144] *Abe v. Foster Wheeler*, 110 Phil. 198 (1960).
[145] *In Re: Catholic Archbishop of Manila v. Social Security Commission*, 110 Phil. 616 (1961).
[146] *Tapang v. El Tribunal de Relaciones Industriales*, 72 Phil. 79 (1941).
[147] *Serrano v. Gallant*, 601 Phil. 245 (2009); *JSS Indochina Corp. v. Ferrer*, 509 Phil. 699 (2005).
[148] *Southern Luzon Drug v. DSWD*, 809 Phil. 315 (2017).
[149] 238 Phil. 462 (1987).
[150] GRN 238467, February 12, 2019.

and well-being of the people." In dissenting against the majority opinion, Justice Leonen insisted that, in the hierarchy of rights, "the right to life and the right to liberty sit higher than the right to property," which was also the import of the constitutional principle that the state should value the dignity of every human person. He then reminded his colleagues that the human dignity and social justice provisions in the Constitution require that the Court apply a stricter judicial scrutiny especially when their everyday livelihood is affected.

OBSERVATIONS. McCrudden argues[151] that the basic minimum content of "human dignity" seems to have at least three elements: first, that every human being possesses an intrinsic worth, merely by being human (an ontological claim); second, that this intrinsic worth should be recognized and respected by others, and some forms of treatment by others are inconsistent with, or required by, respect for this intrinsic worth (a relational claim); and third, that recognizing the intrinsic worth of the individual requires that the state should be seen to exist for the sake of the individual human being and not vice versa (a limited-state claim). Indeed, we have seen manifestations of all of these elements in the cases mentioned, whether or not it involves the aspect of "treatment of others," "individual choice," "group identity and culture," or "satisfaction of essential needs."

McCrudden further posits[152] that courts around the world have used dignity either to express a communitarian ideal or to further individual autonomy, in the sense of advancing individual liberty based upon the choice of the individual. Some courts lean toward one side or the other side, while others appear to be significantly split on the issue. In understanding where the Philippine approach to dignity lies, the recurring theme I found is that the interest of the broader community could restrict individual autonomy under very limited circumstances, such as those involving national security, founding a family, and environmental protection. In other words, while the autonomy of individuals must always be protected, there may be instances in which their freedom of action might be limited in view of the constitutionally recognized interests of the community. The Court has yet to verbalize, however, if the constitutional right to human dignity would amount to a stricter scrutiny of such laws as proposed by Justice Leonen in *Zabal*.

5 CONCLUSION

The Court has been using dignity as a tool for judicial interpretation. Exhibiting a thick view of dignity, the Justices have invoked it as a basis to either: 1) discover or expand the scope of existing rights that limits governmental action; or 2) justify governmental measures that seek to advance or improve people's condition. In both

---

[151] McCrudden, "Human Dignity," 679–680.
[152] Ibid., at pp. 699–700.

instances, the dignity language has provided justices with a conceptual justification for considering the evolving meaning of an existing right, thereby unshackling them from having to adopt a strict textual or original meaning interpretation of constitutional provisions in favor of human dignity.

Based on the cases examined in this chapter, it seems that any possibility of attaining a more common conception of dignity (at least within the same aspect of dignity as categorized in Section 3) would require the confluence of the factors influencing the conception of dignity. For example, we saw the justices speaking with one voice when they discussed how the pursuit of dignity would be realized if the Court were to uphold social legislations that sought to satisfy the people's essential needs. It may be that they reached consensus on this aspect given that the factors they drew from (discussed in Section 2) have aligned in favor of the preferential treatment of the underprivileged and marginalized. In contrast, we have seen how the justices had varying views on how (and whose) dignity should be pursued when it comes to issues on decisional privacy, perhaps because the factors they drew from were not aligned with each other (e.g. varying views on extent of individual autonomy). Indeed, achieving such a common conception even within the same legal system or across all human rights laws beyond the minimum core posited by McCrudden may be difficult. Of course, this is not at all impossible – a comparison of the chapters on the judicial discourse in Indonesia,[153] Philippines, Singapore[154] and Taiwan[155] shows that, up to a certain extent, there are some common grounds in these jurisdictions' conception of dignity, especially in the area of social welfare and security.

FINAL WORDS. Although the use of dignity in judicial interpretation has a long history, it has yet to be consistently and faithfully invoked for what it was meant to be – a standard principle of constitutional interpretation to which Filipino justices must adhere. This is indeed peculiar given that the justices have been using the dignity language for the past eighty years.[156] This is especially so when the Court has now been armed with two key provisions under the 1987 Constitution – the right to human dignity and the expanded power of judicial review – texts that did not exist during the period of *Raquiza* (1945), *Morfe* (1968), *Bagasala* (1971), or *Philippine Blooming Mills* (1973), yet the justices in those cases were still able to exhibit a thick view of dignity.

---

[153] See Chapter 6 in this volume by Nadirsyah Hosen.
[154] See Chapter 8 in this volume by Li-ann Thio.
[155] See Chapter 4 in this volume by Jimmy Chia-Shin Hsu.
[156] For context, most of the names of the jurists who invoked dignity have been mentioned in the footnotes to showcase how very few of the around 150 Supreme Court justices (appointed from the promulgation of the 1935 Constitution) have engaged in the dignity analysis.

The right to human dignity should be treated as a right that evokes a constitutionally mandated interpretative principle that reads laws in favor of allowing every person to pursue one's own happiness and complete fulfillment.[157] It is a directive for the Court to consider removing barriers to aspirational goals, especially if these goals are traceable to constitutional rights. If human dignity is not meant to expand and constantly re-explore the current metes and bounds of other human rights provisions, then what is this constitutional right for?

---

[157] See *Philippine Blooming Mills Employees Organization v. Philippine Blooming Mills Co.*

6

Human Dignity in the Jurisprudence of the Indonesian Constitutional Court

Nadirsyah Hosen

The original version of the 1945 Indonesian Constitution contained no references to basic civil, political rights, or socio-economic rights. Reform of the 1945 Constitution, during the period of 1999–2002, has been one of the most important aspects of the transition to democracy in Indonesia. The amendments have established democratic principles of separation of powers and checks and balances, as well as revising the constitutional framework for executive–legislative relations.[1] More importantly, the amendments have inserted a new chapter on human rights to the 1945 Constitution, which also mandated establishment of a new Constitutional Court (Mahkamah Konstitusi – MK) that has the authority to conduct judicial review of legislation.[2]

The Constitution was based on *Pancasila*, an integralist state ideology embodying communitarian values of harmony and cooperation in all aspects of life.[3] *Pancasila* consists of the five pillars that eventually became the state foundation: Belief in One God, Humanitarianism, National Unity, Representative Democracy, and Social Justice. Accordingly, all articles in the Constitution were inspired by *Pancasila*. It is placed in the Preamble of the 1945 Constitution, providing a set of principles intended to act as the foundation for all Indonesian laws. *Pancasila* is narrated in an abstract way. It can accommodate everything, as reflected in the national motto 'Bhinneka Tunggal Ika' (unity in diversity).

---

[1] See Nadirsyah Hosen, 'Promoting Democracy and Finding the Right Direction: A Review of Major Constitutional Developments in Indonesia', in A. H. Y. Chen (ed.), *Constitutionalism in Asia in the Early Twenty-First Century* (Cambridge: Cambridge University Press, 2014), pp. 322–42; Denny Indrayana, *Indonesian Constitutional Reform 1999–2002: An Evaluation of Constitution Making in Transition* (Jakarta: Kompas Book Publishing, 2008). On the Indonesian Constitution in general, see Simon Butt and Tim Lindsey, *The Constitution of Indonesia: A Contextual Analysis* (Oxford: Hart Publishing, 2012).

[2] On the Indonesian Constitutional Court, see Simon Butt, 'The Indonesian Constitutional Court', in Rosalind Dixon and Adrienne Stone (eds.), *The Invisible Constitution in Comparative Perspective* (Cambridge: Cambridge University Press, 2018), pp. 298–319; and Simon Butt, *The Constitutional Court and Democracy in Indonesia* (Leiden: Brill, 2015).

[3] See Chapter 13 in this volume by Etin Anwar.

The 1999–2002 amendments are a watershed of Indonesian history, but they were not a whole new beginning. The Indonesian Constitution has a high degree of continuity with what came before and after it. Despite the weaknesses in the original 1945 Constitution when it came to serving as the basis for democracy, it was explicitly or implicitly accepted by most major political forces as the framework for the transition in Indonesia, beginning in 1998. Indonesia decided to follow the American practice of constitutional amendment and not write a new constitution. In this respect, Indonesia is different from the Philippines[4] and South Korea.[5] Both countries had a new constitution in 1987 to transition to democracy. The democratization and *Pancasila* struck a new balance. The new conflict and tension is exemplified by the Court's interpretation of human dignity.

In this chapter, I will analyse several Constitutional Court decisions on human dignity. But first, an explanation of the human rights provision in the amendments to the 1945 Constitution will be presented. Afterwards, I will focus on the word 'dignity', which is mentioned three times, in Article 28 G(1), Article 28 H(3), and Article 34(2), respectively. While 'dignity' in Article 28 G(1) is mentioned in the context of the civil and political rights, both Article 28 H(3) and Article 34(2) mention 'dignity' in the context of the rights of social security.

I will demonstrate how the Court interprets the concept of 'dignity' differently in those articles. While the Court has agreed that the exercising of civil and political rights is limited by the law, the rights of others, and also religious values as determined by the limitation clause under Article 28 J(2), the Court has confidently maintained 'dignity' under social security rights. Arguably, the Indonesian Court takes the position that human dignity in terms of individual rights should be limited, but human dignity in terms of socio-economic and cultural rights should be promoted. The different approaches are due to the nature of the 1945 Constitution, which rejects the notion of Western individual liberalism.

1 CONSTITUTIONAL AMENDMENTS

It could be argued that reform of the 1945 Constitution has been one of the most important aspects of Indonesia's transition to democracy that began in 1998. In October 1999, August 2000, November 2001, and August 2002, the People's Consultative Assembly passed the First, Second, Third, and Fourth Amendments, respectively. The People's Consultative Assembly (Majelis Permusyawaratan Rakyat – MPR) is the sole body empowered by the 1945 Constitution to amend it. The MPR consists of 695 members, 500 of whom are national legislators (DPR members); the remainder consist of 130 regional delegates, elected by provincial assemblies, and sixty-five representatives of social organizations, chosen by the

---

[4] See Chapter 5 in this volume by J. R. Robert Real.
[5] See Chapter 3 in this volume by Chaihark Hahm.

Electoral Commission. However, the process of constitutional reform in Indonesia is like playing with building blocks: attempting to protect press freedoms, fix the economy, and have free and fair elections all led to the constitutional amendments.

The process of designing fresh, better constitutional and electoral reforms did not start from scratch. Indonesian reform was expected to meet popular demands in the post-Soeharto[6] era, such as a less powerful presidency, a multi-party system, a more powerful parliament, and a reduction in, or eradication of, parliamentary seats for the military in the People's Representative Assembly (Dewan Perwakilan Rakyat – DPR).[7] There were differing opinions regarding what the necessary first steps were in the reform of Indonesian law. Some scholars suggest a reform of the Mahkamah Agung (Supreme Court) by replacing the chief justice and other judges. The reasons, as the critics said, were that the Supreme Court was subordinated to the executive and suffered from pervasive corruption.[8]

There came an early consensus in November 1999 on three major points:

1) to leave the Constitution's preamble untouched, thereby retaining *Pancasila* as the state ideology;
2) to maintain the basic structure of the state as unitary, thereby thwarting an emerging debate on federalism; and
3) to maintain the basic structure of the government as purely presidential, thereby preventing a debate on the re-establishment of parliamentary government.[9]

Apart from these macro-level issues, all other parts of the Constitution were up for debate. As a result, the four amendments affect the fundamental rules.

Among other changes, the amendments have:

1) established the presidential democratic principles of separation of powers and of checks and balances;
2) substantially revised the constitutional framework for executive–legislative relations;
3) reinforced the principle of civilian supremacy over the military;
4) devolved potentially significant powers to subnational authorities;
5) established a second chamber of the national legislature to represent regional interests;

---

[6] Readers may be familiar the spelling 'Suharto', with the letter 'u' substituting for 'oe'. However, this chapter uses the original spelling of Soeharto's name, as recorded in official Indonesian documents.
[7] See Judith Bird, 'Indonesia in 1998: The Pot Boils Over', *Asian Survey* 39, no. 1 (1999): 29.
[8] Daniel S. Lev, 'Reformasi Hukum Dimulai dari Penggantian Hakim Agung (interview)', *Kompas*, 27 October 1999.
[9] Suharizal, *Reformasi Konstitusi 1998–2002: Pergulatan Konsep dan Pemikiran Amandemen UUD 1945* [*Constitutional reform 1998–2002: The struggle for concepts and thoughts in the Amendment to the 1945 Constitution*] (Padang: Anggrek Law Firm, 2002), p. 80.

6) inserted sweeping guarantees of citizens' civil and political rights into the Constitution; and
7) established a Constitutional Court.

The last of these points is important for the purpose of our discussion. The main reason for establishing a new Constitutional Court was due to the fact that the Supreme Court lacked powers of constitutional interpretation and judicial review. Prior to the passage of the Third Amendment in November 2001, the Article on the judiciary was one of the most inadequate parts of the 1945 Constitution. It said only that there was to be a Supreme Court and other judicial bodies whose make-up and powers would be regulated by law.[10] The Third Amendment made significant progress in resolving many of these issues. It reiterated the power of the Supreme Court to conduct judicial reviews of legal determinations below the level of laws in the hierarchy. It transferred authority over the judicial review of laws from the MPR to the new Constitutional Court. The Third Amendment also indirectly granted the Constitutional Court the power of constitutional interpretation, by stipulating that the court can 'resolve conflicts of authority between state institutions whose powers are established by the Constitution'.[11]

The Constitutional Court (Mahkamah Konstitusi – MK) has the authority to conduct judicial review of legislation; decide on conflicts of interest within state institutions relating to their constitutional powers; regulate activities for the dissolution of political parties; and decide objections to the results of general elections. The Court was officially established with the passing of Law No 24 of 2003. The Court consists of nine justices: three presidential nominees, three Supreme Court nominees, and three House of Representatives nominees. The judges' term of office is five years, and they may be reelected for another term.

2 HUMAN RIGHTS PROVISION

This section deals with human rights provisions in the Second Amendment to the 1945 Constitution. As Tim Lindsey remarks, Articles 28 A–28 J in Chapter XA are 'lengthy and impressive, granting a full range of protections extending well beyond those guaranteed in most developed states'.[12] In the same vein, Gary Bell takes the view that the inclusion of human rights provision in the Second Amendment to the UUD (Undang-Undang Dasar – the Constitution) 1945 "has brought a significant change in the orientation of Indonesian constitutional law."[13] Provisions include the

---

[10] 1945 Constitution, ch. IX.
[11] 1945 Constitution, Article 24 C(1).
[12] Tim Lindsey, 'Indonesia: Devaluing Asian Values, Rewriting Rule of Law', in Randall Peerenboom (ed.), *Asian Discourses of Rule of Law* (London: RoutledgeCurzon, 2004), p. 301.
[13] Gary F. Bell, 'Minority Rights and Regionalism in Indonesia – Will Constitutional Recognition Lead to Disintegration and Discrimination?', *Singapore Journal of International and Comparative Law* 5 (2001): 784.

civil and political rights to life (Art. 28 A) and equal treatment before the law (Art. 28 D); and the economic, social, and cultural rights to improve one's welfare (Art. 28 C), to a healthy environment (Art. 28 H(1)), and to receive medical care (Art. 28 H(1)) and social security (Art. 28 H(3)). The state is obliged to protect, advance, and fulfil these rights (Art. 28 I(4)).[14]

It is worth noting that in August 2002 the Fourth Amendment to the 1945 Constitution placed even more stringent requirements on the state to fulfil economic, social, and cultural rights. For example, 'the state shall prioritise the budget for education to a minimum of 20 per cent of the State Budget' (Art. 31 (4)). The state now has positive duties under the Constitution to take care of impoverished people (Art. 34 (1)); develop a system of social security and empower the underprivileged (Art. 34 (2)); provide public services including medical facilities (Art. 34 (3)); advance science, technology, and the national culture (Art. 31 (5) and 32 (1)); and preserve local languages (Art. 32(2)). A new subsection was also added to Article 33 on the National Economy and Social Welfare, stating that the economy 'shall be conducted on the basis of economic democracy upholding the principles of togetherness, efficiency with justice ... [and] protection of the environment' (Art. 33(4)).

The principle of equality is a primary principle of human rights. Human rights are for everyone – as much for people living in poverty and social isolation as for the visible and articulate. 'All human beings are born free and equal in dignity and rights'[15] – these famous first few words of the Universal Declaration of Human Rights established the basic premise of international human rights law. The principle of non-discrimination prohibits discrimination in the enjoyment of human rights, on any grounds, such as race, skin colour, gender, language, religion, politics or other opinions, national or social origins, property, and birth or other status.[16] The term 'or other status' might include personal circumstances, occupation, lifestyle, sexual orientation, or health status.

Equality requires that all persons within a society enjoy equal access to the available goods and services which are necessary to fulfil basic human needs. Equality before the law prohibits discrimination in law or in practice, in any field regulated and protected by public authorities.[17] Thus, the principle of non-discrimination applies to all state policies and practices, including those concerning

---

[14] Analysis on the 1945 Constitution include Gary F. Bell, ibid.; and also Gary F. Bell, 'Obstacles to Reform the 1945 Constitution – Constitutions Do Not Perform Miracles', *Van Zorge Report on Indonesia – Commentary and Analysis on Indonesian Politics and Economics* 3, no. 6 (2001): 4–13; Tim Lindsey, 'Indonesian Constitutional Reform: Mud Towards Democracy', *Singapore Journal of International & Comparative Law* 6 (2002): 244–301; Bivitri Susanti, 'Constitution and Human Rights Provisions in Indonesia: An Unfinished Task in the Transitional Process', in Tessa Morris-Suzuki (ed.), *Constitutions & Human Rights in a Global Age: An Asia-Pacific Perspective* (Canberra: Australian National University, 2003), pp. 5–14.
[15] Article 1, the Universal Declaration of Human Rights.
[16] Article 2, the Universal Declaration of Human Rights.
[17] Article 7, the Universal Declaration of Human Rights.

healthcare, education, access to services, travel regulations, entry requirements, and immigration.

The Second Amendment forbids discrimination on the basis of gender, race, disability, language, or social status. It stipulates equal rights and obligations for all citizens, both native and naturalized. Article 28 I(2) stipulates: 'Each person has the right to be free from discriminatory treatment on any grounds and has the right to obtain protection from such discriminatory treatment.' Article 28 D(1) states: 'Each person has the right to the recognition, the security, the protection and the certainty of just laws and equal treatment before the law.' This Article guarantees the right to equal treatment 'before the law' and to the protection of human rights and freedoms, without discrimination.

Under Article 28 D(2), anyone, without discrimination, has the right to work and to receive just and appropriate rewards and treatment in their working relationships. Moreover, Article 27 of the original 1945 Constitution has not been changed. This Article clearly guarantees the right to equality by stating that 'all citizens have equal status before the law and in government and shall abide by the law and the government without any exception'.

Indonesia still has a long road to travel to fulfil these economic, social, and cultural rights, as the constitutional amendments require the introduction of many legislative changes, and, clearly, the mere legislating of rights does not ensure their protection and fulfilment.[18] As set out in the Universal Declaration of Human Rights (UDHR) and the International Covenant on Civil and Political Rights (ICCPR), civil and political rights include: the right to life (ICCPR Art. 6; UDHR Art. 3); freedom of speech (ICCPR Art. 19; UDHR Preamble); freedom from torture and cruel or degrading treatment (ICCPR Art. 7; UDHR Ar. 5); and the right to a fair trial (ICCPR Art. 14; UDHR Art. 11).

Economic, social, and cultural rights include the rights to: work (International Covenant on Economic, Social and Cultural Rights (ICESCR) Art. 6; UDHR Art. 23); health (ICESCR Art. 12; UDHR Art. 25); education (ICESCR Art. 13; UDHR Art. 26); social security (ICESCR Art. 9; UDHR Art. 22); and an adequate standard of living (ICESCR Art. 11; UDHR Art. 25), as encapsulated in the ICESCR and the UDHR.

Therefore, in order to ensure that legislation does not contradict the aforementioned human rights provision, a constitutional amendment was also used to establish the Constitutional Court (Mahkamah Konstitusi – MK). The Constitutional Court does not restrict itself to the text of the Constitution in its decisions but also refers to international human rights law. For instance, with respect to the former members of the now-defunct Indonesian Communist Party, the Court declared that every citizen shall have an equal right to elect and to be elected and to participate in

---

[18] Simon Butt and Tim Lindsey, 'The People's Prosperity? Indonesian Constitutional Interpretation', in John Gillespie and Randall Peerenboom (eds.), *Economic Reform and Globalization in Regulation in Asia: Pushing Back on Globalization* (London: Routledge, 2009).

vowing his/her aspiration by referring to Article 25 of the International Covenant on Civil and Political Rights (ICCPR). The Universal Declaration of Human Rights have been used repeatedly as a reference for justices to make their considerations for deciding cases such as the case of the Corruption Court in Manopo (Art. 12 (2)),[19] the case of former President Abdurahman Wahid (Art. 21),[20] and the case of Agus Miftach[21] and the case of Human Rights Court (both Art. 29 (2)).[22] The Court's invocation of international human rights law is not required by the Constitution. But the fact that the Court opens its doors to international human rights law documents indicates its open-mindedness.

3 HUMAN DIGNITY IN THE 1945 CONSTITUTION

The phrase 'human dignity' can be translated loosely as 'martabat manusia' in the Indonesian language. As pointed out by Etin Anwar,[23] the word *martabat* is read in the context of 'derajat' (degree). Linguistically speaking, it is related to status. Not all human beings have *martabat* and *derajat*; therefore, the state must ensure that people are not treated in such way that they lose their dignity as human beings. If we search for the word *martabat* in the text of the 1945 Constitution after the amendments of 1999–2002, we find several mentions. The first time is in Article 24 B(1), specifically in the context of judges (emphasis mine):

Article 24 B
(1) There shall be an independent Judicial Commission which shall possess the authority to propose candidates for appointment as justices of the Supreme Court and shall possess further authority to maintain and ensure the honour, *dignity* and behaviour of judges.

The word *martabat* is also used in Article 28 G(1) and (2), in the context of the civil and political rights (again, emphasis mine).

Article 28 G
1) Each person is entitled to protection of self, his family, honour, dignity, the property he owns, and has the right to feel secure and to be protected against threats from fear to do or not to do something that is part of basic rights.

2) Every person shall have the right to be free from torture or inhumane and degrading treatment that undermines his/her *dignity*, and shall have the right to obtain political asylum from another country

Third, dignity is mentioned in Article 28 H(3) and Article 34 in the context of social security. This can be categorized under economic, social, and cultural rights.

---

[19] Constitutional Court Decision No. 069/PUU-II/2004.
[20] Constitutional Court Decision No. 008/PUU-II/2004.
[21] Constitutional Court Decision No. 020/PUU-I/2003.
[22] Constitutional Court Decision No. 065/PUU-II/2004.
[23] See Chapter 13 in this volume by Etin Anwar.

Article 28 H
3) Every person shall have the right to social security in order to develop oneself fully as a dignified human being.

Article 34
2) The state develops a social security system for everybody and empowers the weak and underprivileged in society in accordance with their dignity as human beings.

I will examine the second and the third categories – namely, 'dignity' under individual rights (the civil and political rights), as mentioned in Article 28 G, and under economic, social and cultural rights, as stated under Articles 28 H and 34 respectively. For the purpose of our discussion, the first category that is specifically mentioned, Article 24 B in the context of judges, will not be discussed.

4 DIGNITY AND INDIVIDUAL HUMAN RIGHTS

The main controversy surrounding individual human rights under the Indonesian Constitution is due to two 'conflicting' articles: Article 28 I(1) on 'non-derogable rights' and Article 28 J(2) on 'limitation'. While the first highlights that there are certain rights that cannot be dismissed or changed in any circumstances (non-derogable rights), the latter mentions that state law can limit the application of human rights (emphases mine):

Article 28 I
1) The right to life, the right to be free of torture, the rights for freedom of thought and conscience, the rights to religion, the rights to be free from slavery, the rights to be treated equal in front of the law, and the rights to not be charged on retroactive laws are *non-derogable rights in any circumstances*.

Article 28 J
2) In exercising his rights and liberties, each person has the duty to accept the limitations determined by law for the sole purposes of guaranteeing the recognition and respect of the rights and liberties of other people and of satisfying a democratic society's just demands based on considerations of morality, religious values, security, and public order.

As can be seen from the formulation of Article 28 J, Indonesian human rights law conceptualizes human rights in the context of a 'balance' between rights and duties, and this fact shaped the court's decision on a number of levels. It contrasts the asserted right to life of those sentenced against both the rights of the victims as individuals and the rights of 'society as victim'.

4.1 Death Penalty Cases

The Indonesian Constitutional Court has at least three times confirmed that the death penalty is not against the Constitution, in decisions numbered 065/PUU-II

/2004, 2–3/PUU-V/2007, and 15/PUU-X/2012. Despite the fact that the Court values the right to life as the most fundamental right in human life, as enshrined in Article 28 I of Indonesia's Constitution, the exception applies as per Article 28 J.

The Indonesian government ratified the International Covenant on Civil and Political Rights (ICCPR) in 2005, committing itself to upholding international human rights law. Indonesia has yet to ratify the optional protocol to abolish the death penalty. However, Indonesia issued Law No 22 of 1997, which allowed the imposition of the death penalty in some narcotics cases, which according to the applicants, contradicted Article 28 I(1).

In the case number 2–3/PUU-V/2007, a 5:4 majority upheld Law No 22 of 1997, finding that narcotics offences were so serious that they could displace the right to life in Article 28 I(1). The majority pointed out that the ICCPR permitted the death penalty being imposed by member states for the most serious crimes. In Indonesia, the Court noted that narcotic offences were classified as such crimes.

The Constitutional Court reasoned that Indonesia is obliged to implement international law as a state party to the United Nations Convention against Illicit Traffic in Narcotic Drugs and Psychotropic Substances (1988). According to the Court, the Narcotics Law imposes the death penalty for limited criminal acts, considered in accordance with Article 3(6) of the Convention, with the objective 'to maximize the effectiveness of law enforcement measures in respect of those offences, and with due regard to the need to deter the commission of such offences'. Thus, the Court has included the possession of narcotics as one of the most serious crimes, along with the crime of genocide and crimes against humanity, because these crimes 'adversely affect the economic, cultural and political foundation of society' and also cause 'a danger of incalculable gravity'.[24] Therefore, the Court read down the 'absoluteness' of the rights to life under Article 28 I(1) by allowing the state to limit such rights as per Article 28 J(2). The minority, however, in separate judgements, found the death penalty to be unconstitutional on the plain reading of Article 28 I(1) that the right to life cannot be diminished under any circumstances.

Natalie Zerial argued that this decision is based on the balance between the rights of individuals and the public welfare that become characteristic of human rights debates in Asia.[25] The Court concluded with the opinion that, in reforming criminal law, a number of matters should be carefully considered: capital punishment shall no longer be a principal punishment, but rather a special and alternative punishment; capital punishment shall be imposed with a probation period of ten years, though if the convicts indicate good behaviour, it may be changed into life imprisonment or twenty years; capital punishment shall not be imposed on underage children; and the execution of capital punishment on pregnant women and

---

[24] Constitutional Court Decision No. 2–3/PUU-V/2007 at 426.
[25] See Natalie Zerial, 'Decision No. 2–3/PUU-V/2007 [2007] (Indonesian Constitutional Court)', *Australian International Law Journal* 14 (2007): 217.

mentally ill persons shall be postponed until the women deliver their babies and the mentally ill recover their sanity.[26]

Cases on the death penalty have not touched the articles on *martabat* or dignity. The sheer fact that these cases have not touched on dignity is significant, given how often and how strongly dignity is regarded as relevant in death penalty constitutionality cases in other jurisdictions, such as the constitutional courts of South Africa and Hungary.[27] I use the death penalty cases mentioned already to illustrate the controversy surrounding Article 28 I(1) (on 'non-derogable rights') and Article 28 J(2) (on 'limitation'). It is worth noting that the right to be free of torture is also mentioned in Article 28 I(1) as one of the rights that cannot be diminished under any circumstances. And even further, Article 28 G(2) highlights again the right to be free from torture in the context of maintaining human dignity.

4.2 *Torture Case*

Can 'the right to be free from torture', in both Articles 28 I(1) and 28 G(2), be limited by the application of Article 28 J(2), just like the right to life in the cases already mentioned?

In the *Firing Squad* case, some of the Bali bombers asked the Constitutional Court to assess whether the way the death penalty is carried out in Indonesia – by firing squad – constituted 'torture' and cruel and inhumane punishment, which are prohibited under the Constitution. This was Constitutional Court decision 21/PUU-VI/2008. The statute under review was Law No 2/PNPS/1964, on the Procedure for Carrying Out the Death Penalty.

Executions in Indonesia are carried out by firing squad and typically take place late at night in secret locations. Condemned prisoners are informed seventy-two hours before their execution is to take place. A police firing squad shoots the prisoner in the heart from a distance of 5–10 metres, upon the signal of a swift downward sword stroke from the squad commander. If the prisoner is still alive, the deputy squad commander then presses the muzzle of his gun on the prisoner's head and fires a 'finishing shot'.

This case dealt only with the means of execution and not the validity of the death penalty itself, as this had been decided in an earlier case. Appellants were convicted of terrorism for their roles in the Bali bombing and sentenced to death by firing squad. They argued before the Constitutional Court that death by firing squad amounts to torture. Instead, by following Shari'a requirement, they requested to be executed by beheading.

The Court ruled that the pain of execution by firing squad was a natural part of the execution process. Finding that this method of execution – firing squad – was in fact

---

[26] Constitutional Court Decision No. 2–3/PUU-V/2007 [2007] at 108.
[27] For South Africa, see *State v. Makwanyane* (CCT3/94) [1995]; for Hungary, see the Constitutional Court of Hungary, Decision 23 (1990).

not torture, the Court took the view that it was not necessary to determine whether the right to be free from torture was absolute. The Court did not discuss the relation between non-derogable rights under Articles 28 I(1) and the limitation of human rights under Article 28 J(2).[28]

Therefore, the issue of whether 'the right to be free of torture that undermines human dignity' could be limited by the state law is far from settled. This means that in one case the Court read down Article 28 I(1), but in a different case it did not use a similar approach.

4.3 Retroactive Law

I have mentioned already the *death penalty* case in which the Court read down Article 28 I(1) ('non-derogable rights'), but in the *Masykur Kadir* case on retroactive law the Court applied a plain reading of Article 28 I(1) and declared that retroactive law was unconstitutional, as this is one of the non-derogable rights under Article 28 I(1) that cannot be diminished under any circumstances. Here is the context of the *Masykur* case.

Without it being known by the Indonesian public, the Indonesian government drafted the Anti-Terrorism Law in April 2002 in response to the events of 11 September 2011 in New York. However, the Bali Bombing on 12 October 2002 forced President Megawati, six days after the attack, to issue the Government Regulation in Lieu of Law (*Peraturan Pemerintah Pengganti Undang-Undang* – PERPU) No 1/2002 and No 2/2002. This was owing to US allegations that Indonesia was one of the most important headquarters of terrorist organizations, especially that of Jemaah Islamiah, an affiliate of Al-Qaeda. The Australian government was also not happy about the Bali bombing, which killed 202 people and injured a further 209, most of whom were Australian. Both the US and the Australian governments asked the Megawati government to take the problem of terrorism seriously and to provide the necessary legal framework to deal with the attack. The Indonesian government therefore treated the attack as an emergency matter and took over the debate within parliament on the Anti-Terrorism Bill.

The argument for issuing the PERPU was that the government is of the view that crimes of terrorism involve many actors, such as planners, doers, funding supporters, and others, as well as requiring a wide-ranging network, exceeding state borders. That is why the government felt the need to create a national law referring to international conventions and other laws related to terrorism. PERPU No. 1/2002 also put in a special regulation on laws of criminal procedure to strengthen the ability of police in combating crimes of terrorism. For the sake of investigation and prosecution, police as investigators have authority to detain a suspect for six months at most. This detainment is obviously much longer than

---

[28] Constitutional Court decision No 21/PUU-VI/2008 at 95.

a usual criminal detainment, where police have authority to detain a suspect for twenty days at most. To gather sufficient preliminary evidence, police investigators can use every intelligence report, on the condition that the report has to be examined and determined by the head or vice-head of the District Court.

PERPU No 1/2002 gives legitimacy to law enforcement agencies that use legal measures different from those available for other criminal offences. Moreover, it imposes severe sanctions on those who commit acts of terrorism. Furthermore, any person found guilty of intentionally providing assistance to any perpetrator by 'providing or lending money or goods or other assets to any perpetrator of criminal acts of terrorism; harbouring any perpetrator of any criminal act of terrorism; or hiding any information on any criminal act of terrorism' is liable to imprisonment for a minimum term of three years and a maximum of fifteen years (Art. 13). This Article is used against Masykur Kadir, as we will discuss.

PERPU expands the scope of criminal liability by providing that anyone who 'conducts any plot, attempt, or assistance to commit any criminal act of terrorism' will be sentenced the same as those who are committing such an act of terrorism (Art. 15). One interesting point to note is that it can also be applied to those who provide any assistance, facilities, means, or information for any criminal acts of terrorism committed extraterritorially. The sentence is the same as for committing the act of terrorism itself (Art. 16). It is argued that ordinary criminal law in Indonesia was inadequate and failed to deal comprehensively with combating criminal acts of terrorism.[29]

According to the Constitution, a PERPU must obtain the approval of the parliament during its next session. The Indonesian parliament approved the two PERPU on terrorism. PERPU No. 1 was adopted by the DPR through Law No. 15 of 2003 on 4 April 2003, whereas PERPU No. 2 of 2002 was by the parliament in the form of Law No. 16 of 2003. PERPU No. 2 of 2002 (or Law No. 16 of 2003) merely states that PERPU No. 1 of 2002 can be used retrospectively, with respect to the Bali bombings. The two anti-terrorism laws have been used as the basis for the arrest, prosecution, and conviction of twenty-five of the now infamous Bali bombers. Given that the laws were enacted only after the bombings had occurred, the suspects were tried and punished for a crime which, according to law, was not strictly a crime at the time it was committed.[30]

Masykur Kadir was alleged to have met with three members of the terror group in the immediate aftermath of the Bali Bombing on 12 October 2002 and was subsequently put on trial for aiding in an act of terrorism. Kadir claimed that he was a tour guide and not involved in the terrorist act. No evidence was presented connecting Kadir to the assembly of the bombs used in the attack. However, he was sentenced to fifteen years in prison under Article 13(a) of Law No. 15 of 2003 for

---

[29] Hikmahanto. Juwana, 'Indonesia's Anti-Terrorism Law', in V. V. Ramraj, M. Hor, and K. Roach (eds.), *Global Anti-Terrorism Law and Policy* (Cambridge: Cambridge University Press, 2005), p. 304.
[30] Juwana, 'Indonesia's Anti-Terrorism Law', pp. 291–3.

assisting the Bali bombers. If he was charged under ordinary criminal law, Kadir would go free. Lawyers for Kadir claimed that he had been investigated, charged, prosecuted, and convicted under an unconstitutional law (Law No. 16 of 2003). They argued that Article 28 I(1) of the Indonesian Constitution provides citizens with a right not to be prosecuted under retrospective laws. The Constitutional Court agreed, exercising its powers of constitutional review to declare Law No. 16 of 2003 to be invalid.[31]

The decision of the Indonesian Court was reached by a majority of five justices to four. The decision demonstrates the potential dilemma faced by the Court. On the one hand, the majority displayed their commitment to upholding the Constitution,[32] but on the other they were criticized for providing an unjust outcome, particularly for the victims of the bombings and their families, both Indonesian and Australian.

The dilemma continues: should all the convicted Bali bombers use the Constitutional Court's decision and the constitutional invalidity of the law as a basis for the appeal? Butt and Hansell report:

> Apparently fearing that the convictions would be lost, Justice Minister Yusril Ihza Mahendra and Constitutional Court Chief Justice Professor Dr Jimly Asshiddiqie announced their own interpretation of the decision to the press. They claimed that the bombers would remain in jail because the Constitutional Court's decision itself could not operate retrospectively. In other words, the decision, whilst binding, only prevents future investigations, prosecutions and convictions being carried out retrospectively. It would not, therefore, impact upon convictions that have already been obtained. This statement, particularly from Asshiddiqie, constitutes an inappropriate politicization of the court. That Asshiddiqie's statement and that of the Justice Minister were announced at around the same time, and conveyed the same view, gives the impression that Asshiddiqie may have collaborated with the government, even though he might not actually have done so.[33]

This is a dilemma. Is it better to keep the terrorists in jail, although they were convicted under an unconstitutional anti-terrorism law, which is basically against the principles of human rights and the rule of law; or to let them go free, which puts the country at higher risk from the bombers themselves and also from the criticism of foreign countries, including the United States and Australia, which certainly will not

---

[31] Simon Butt and D. Hansell, 'The Masykur Abdul Kadir Case: Indonesian Constitutional Court Decision No 013', *Australian Journal of Asian Law* 6, no. 2 (2004): 176–96.

[32] Under international law an exception is sometimes allowed to permit trial or punishment for any act or omission which, at the time it was committed, was criminal according to the general principles of law recognized by civilized countries. This expression is drawn directly from the statute of the International Court of Justice. However, the Indonesian Constitution states in Article 28I: 'The rights to life, freedom from torture, freedom of thought and conscience, freedom of religion, freedom from enslavement, recognition as a person before the law, and the right not to be tried under a law with retrospective effect are all human rights that cannot be limited under any circumstances.'

[33] Butt and Hansell, 'The Masykur Abdul Kadir Case', p. 181.

be happy to see the convicted terrorists walk free? As has been stated, Justice Minister Mahendra and Constitutional Court Chief Justice Asshiddiqie take the view that the Court's decisions effect only the application of the law in the future, and therefore Masykur Kadir and other convicted bombers remain in jail or face execution.

The point for our discussion is that in this Masykur Kadir case the Constitutional Court applied a plain reading of Article 28 I(1) 'non-derogable rights'. The majority did not take the view that Article 28 I(1) 'non-derogable rights' should be limited by the application of Article 28 J(2) 'limitation'. However, the Court's decision cannot be implemented to Masykur Kadir, and he still served fifteen years in jail. The decision about retroactive law can only be applied in future cases. But how about the Court's arguments on plain reading of Article 28I (1) 'non-derogable rights'? Can they sustain the argument when dealing with Article 28 G 'individual rights'? Let us look at different cases.

4.4 Freedom of Opinion and Expression

In Indonesia, the 1999 Press Law allows journalists to freely join associations, guarantees the right of journalists to protect their sources, and eliminates prior censorship of print or broadcast news. Not only that, those found guilty of subverting the independence of the press can be fined or imprisoned. The establishment of the Press Council, an independent body whose mission is to mediate between the press, the public, and government institutions, is also supported. It also guarantees the upholding of an ethical code for journalists and has provisions for the adjudication of disputes.[34]

However, in practice, the 1999 Press Law is often ignored. It has been reported that, out of forty-two suits against the media since 1999, only six were actually handled through the Press Law. In its place, aggrieved parties use provisions in Indonesia's Criminal Code, which offer plaintiffs a much more potent and wide-ranging set of punishments. Most commonly used are articles on criminal defamation and insult.[35]

Article 207 of the Criminal Code states that anyone who intentionally and publicly insults a public official or public body faces up to one year and four months in prison. Similarly, Article 208 provides that anyone who intentionally broadcasts, shows, or displays text or images that insult a public official or public body can be imprisoned for up to four months. Both articles have survived judicial review by the Constitutional Court, which, in cases decided in 2008, held that various

---

[34] More information about Law No 40 of 1999 on Press Law, see Nadirsyah Hosen, *Human Rights, Politics and Corruption in Indonesia: A Critical Reflection on the Post Soeharto Era* (Dordrecht, Netherlands: Republic of Letters, 2010), pp. 194–220.

[35] Sebastian Dettman, 'Blaming the Messenger', *Inside Indonesia*, no. 93, August–October 2008, available at www.insideindonesia.org/blaming-the-messenger.

constitutional free speech rights were overridden by Article 28 G of the Constitution, which gives citizens (including public figures) rights to protection of their dignity and honour.[36]

Freedom of expression was further curtailed in 2008 with the adoption of the Law on Electronic Information and Transactions (ITE). The Law contains provisions that sanction defamation with longer terms of imprisonment and higher fines than those stipulated in the Criminal Code, and media groups expressed concern that this could silence the press.

In September 2008, legislator Alvin Lie initiated defamation proceedings against Narliswandi Piliang, blogger and journalist for Tempo. Piliang had written an article alleging that a coal mining company, PT Adaro Energy, had bribed the National Mandate Party through Lie to influence an investigation by the House of Representatives into the company's initial public offering of shares. Lie reported this to the police, who charged and detained Piliang under Article 27 (3) of the ITE, which prohibits making available electronic information and documents that contain insults or defile the good name of another person. Piliang applied to the Constitutional Court and argued that such provision is against the freedom provision in the Constitution.[37]

Bersihar Lubis, a reporter for *Koran Tempo*, spent a month in jail in early 2008 for writing a piece critical of the attorney general. He criticized the attorney general for banning a high school history textbook because he believed the decision contravened principles guaranteed by the Indonesian Constitution. Yet he found himself charged – and eventually convicted – under article 207 of the Indonesian Criminal Code for 'insulting' the attorney general. Because Lubis' piece was considered opinion, the court said it could not be dealt with under the Press Law. Lubis was charged with defamation of an authority figure, a criminal offence under the Criminal Code.[38]

In December 2004, Risang Bima Wijaya, then the general manager of the Yogyakarta newspaper *Radar Jogja*, was found guilty of criminal defamation and sentenced to six months' imprisonment, which he served from December 2007 to June 2008, after his newspaper printed a number of articles critical of the executive director of another paper, who had been accused of sexually harassing a female staff member at the time the articles were written. Though his reporting was based on police reports and a press conference held by the victim (and was reported by several other news outlets), Wijaya was prosecuted under the Criminal Code for defamation. His appeals were rejected by both the district court and the Supreme Court.[39]

---

[36] Constitutional Court Decisions No 14/PUU-VI/2008 and No 50/PUU-VI/2008.
[37] Butt and Lindsey, *The Constitution of Indonesia*, p. 199.
[38] See Human Rights Watch, 'Turning Critics into Criminals: The Human Rights Consequences of Criminal Defamation Law in Indonesia', 3 May 2010, available at www.hrw.org/report/2010/05/03/turning-critics-criminals/human-rights-consequences-criminal-defamation-law.
[39] Ibid.

Risang Bima Wijaya and Bersihar Lubis together applied for constitutional review of provisions relating to defamation in the Criminal Code considered contrary to the freedom of thought, conscience, speech, and communication. In addition, the applicants argued that the provision was easily misused by those who do not like freedom of thought and opinion, freedoms of expression, and freedom of the press.

In two cases on freedom of press, *Wijaya and Lubis* (decision No. 14/PUU-VI /2008), and *Piliang* (decision No. 50/PUU-VI/2008), the Court surprisingly referred to Article 28 G 'individual rights' on one's honour and dignity. The challenge to Indonesia's defamation laws as applied to journalists was rejected. In both cases, the Court noted that freedom of expression in Article 28 E(2) and 28 D(3) and the right to communicate freely in Article 28 F must, by virtue of Article 28 J(2) 'limitations', be balanced against the protection of other rights.

In its legal reasons, the Constitutional Court stated that the Indonesian Constitution guarantees the rights and freedoms mentioned by the applicants, so the state must protect them. Nevertheless, the state, at the same time, is also obliged to protect the constitutional rights of others, equal to the applicant's rights, as guaranteed by Article 28 G 'individual rights' of the Constitution and international law, under the rights to honour and dignity.

According to the Court, under an obligation to protect the constitutional rights of others, the state is allowed to make restrictions as expressly stated in Article 28 J(2) 'limitations' of the Constitution. Similar decisions by the Constitutional Court can also be found in the Online Defamation cases in 2008. The difference is the provisions reviewed were related to actions conducted in cyberspace. Piliang filed a constitutional review of Article 27 (3) of the ITE, considering it contrary to the principles of the rule of law and the spirit of democracy that hold freedom of the press and freedom of expression as basic human rights. The Constitutional Court ruled that the article is constitutional on the grounds that it is still necessary for balancing between freedom of expression and the rights to honour and dignity of other people, equally guaranteed by the Constitution and international laws, inter alia Article 12 of the UDHR and Articles 17 and 19 of the ICCPR.

The Court made an important observation in the 2009 Bloggers case where several bloggers and NGO activists challenged one more time the validity of Article 27 (3) of the ITE:

> The protection of human rights in the context of the Indonesian community is primarily directed towards the relationship between citizens and the government with the normative-traditional assumption that the interaction will be harmonious and balanced. In other words, the protection of human rights in Indonesia, including freedom of expression and opinion, is particularly directed towards the achievement of harmony and balance within the community.[40]

---

[40] Constitutional Court Decision No 2/PUU-VII/2009 at 134.

As can be seen, the Court takes the strong position about maintaining harmony and balance between the individual rights and community. Here, the Court applied the limitation of those rights by Article 28 J(2) 'limitations' as a balance with the constitutional right to protection of human dignity in Article 28 G 'individual rights'. The limitation contained in Article 28 J(2) is on two limbs: 1) for the sole purposes of guaranteeing the recognition and respect of the rights and liberties of other people; and 2) and of satisfying a democratic society's just demands based on considerations of morality, religious values, security, and public order.

The Constitutional Court related the first limb to Article 28 G ('individual rights') on human dignity. In fact, the Court claimed that, without the rights to honour and dignity that Article 28 G provides, democracy would disintegrate.[41] The Court did not elaborate further on this claim. It simply tried to make a connection between democracy, perceived as guaranteeing freedom, and the human dignity of others, threatened by such freedom. As can be seen, the approach taken by the Court is that individual rights have to be limited by Article 28 J(2) 'limitations' or be balanced with Article 28 G 'individual rights' (protection of dignity for others).

5 DIGNITY AND ECONOMIC, SOCIAL, AND CULTURAL RIGHTS

The Amendments to the 1945 Constitution impose a number of express obligations upon the Indonesian government. One of the obligations is to develop a social security system for all and to empower the weak and impoverished as befits human dignity. This is clearly stated in Article 34 (2). Through this Article, human dignity is placed in the context of ESC (economic, social, and cultural) rights. It is worth noting what Stefanus Hendrianto pointed out:

> The socio-economic rights jurisprudence in the Indonesian Constitutional Court is not based on the notion of individual rights, in which the rights holder can demand enjoyment of the right to be ensured. Rather, the Court has interpreted socio-economic provisions as an obligation on the state to ensure citizens enjoy their rights. Moreover, the Court has conflated the notion of socio-economic rights with the state control over natural resources. Instead of defining socio-economic rights as individual rights, the Court has consistently granted privileges to the State to control natural resources.[42]

I will now provide the cases to argue that the approach taken by the Court that protecting dignity in the community is a higher priority than protecting individual rights.

---

[41] Constitutional Court Decision No 50/PUU-VI/2008 at 100.
[42] Stefanus Hendrianto, 'The Divergence of a Wandering Court: Socio-Economic Rights in the Indonesian Constitutional Court', *Australian Journal of Asian Law* 16, no. 2 (2016): 2. See also Philippa Venning, 'Determination of Economic, Social and Cultural Rights by the Indonesian Constitutional Court', *Australian Journal of Asian Law* 10, no. 1 (2008): 100.

5.1 Education Case

The Second Amendment to the 1945 Constitution provides for a right to education under Article 28 C(1). Not only that, in Article 31 (4), the Constitution mentions that 'the state shall prioritise the budget for education to a minimum of 20 per cent of the State Budget'. It is a bit unusual to mention the budget percentage in the Constitution, but the idea is to promote education for the Indonesian people. However, it is not easy for the government to fulfil such a large percentage as required by the Constitution.

Considering this burden, Law No. 20 of 2003 on the National Education System (Sistem Pendidikan Nasional) states that the constitutionally required education budget, or 20 per cent of the national budget, would be 'achieved in stages'.[43] This led individual activists, elementary and middle school teachers, and college teachers to challenge the National Education Law in the Constitutional Court. The claimants argued that the Law violated the education budget's minimum of 20 per cent as immediately required by the Constitution and that the Constitution could not allow the allocation to be achieved incrementally. Interestingly the claimants also invoked Article 28 H 'ESC rights' of the Constitution as the grounds for their claim: 'Every person shall have the right to social security in order to develop oneself fully as a *dignified human being*' (emphasis mine).

In short, the claimants argued that the Law infringed on their rights to work and to receive fair and proper remuneration and treatment in employment and to enjoy physical and spiritual prosperity, as well as the right to social security.[44] These arguments are based on Articles 28 D(2), 28 H(1), and 28 H(3) of the Constitution respectively. The majority of judges ruled in favour of the plaintiffs and declared that the provision that allowed the national education budget to be fulfilled incrementally was unconstitutional. The Court stated:

> The implementation of constitutional provisions cannot be delayed. The constitution has expressly stated that a minimum of 20 percent of the budget must be prioritised ... and this cannot be reduced by laws below it in the hierarchy.[45]

It is clear that the Court is trying to promote the rights to education as stipulated in the Constitution. This indicates a strong support by the Court for socio-economic rights, as we can also see from the social security cases discussed next.

5.2 Social Security Cases

At least three cases involve Article 34 (2) 'ESC Rights' of the Constitution relating the issue of social security to human dignity. All challenged the validity of two related

---

[43] The elucidation of Article 49(1) of Law No 20 of 2003 on the National Education System.
[44] See Bivitri Susanti, 'The Implementation of the Rights to Health Care and Education in Indonesia', in Varun Gauri and Daniel M Brinks (eds.), *Courting Social Justice: Judicial Enforcement of Social and Economic Rights in the Developing World* (Cambridge: Cambridge University Press, 2008).
[45] Constitutional Court Decision No 011/PUU-III/2005 at 101.

laws, namely Law No. 40 of 2004 on National Social Security (SJSN) and Law No. 24 of 2011 on Social Security Providers (BPJS). In Indonesia, the social security system has undergone significant reform over the past decade. In the past, the social security system was managed by five separate agencies: Jamsostek (Jaminan Sosial Tenaga Kerja – Workforce Social Security) for employees in private companies; Taspen (Dana Tabungan dan Asuransi Pegawai Negeri – Civil Servants Pension Fund) and Askes (Asuransi Kesehatan Indonesia – Indonesian Health Insurance) for civil servants; Asabri (Asuransi Sosial Angkatan Bersenjata Republik Indonesia – Indonesian Armed Forces Insurance) for the police and military; and, after 2005, Jamkesmas (Jaminan Kesehatan Masyarakat – Community Health Insurance) for the poor and near-poor.

Law No. 40 of 2004 on the National Social Security System set in motion major changes to the administration and management of social security. It provided for the establishment of new social security administrative agencies (Badan Penyelenggara Jaminan Sosial – BPJS) (Articles 5(1) and (2)), and extended coverage to all Indonesians (Art. 2), whether employed in the formal or informal sectors. The preamble of the general elucidation of the National Social Security System declares that the law was passed to fulfil the mandates of Articles 28 H and 34 of the Constitution: they are ESC rights. Article 28 H(3) says that everyone shall have the right to social security in order to develop fully as a dignified human being; and Article 34 (2) adds that the state shall develop a system of social security for all of the people and empowers the weak and underprivileged in society in accordance with their dignity as human beings.

In 2011, a new statute was passed to strengthen the legal basis of the BPJS: Law No. 24 of 2011 on Social Security Administrative Agencies (BPJS). The BPJS Law established two new agencies: BPJS Workforce and BPJS Health (Art. 5 (2) of the BPJS Law). Every individual, including foreigners employed for more than six months in Indonesia, must now participate in the social security programme implemented by BPJS (Article 14 of the BPJS Law). Employers must register themselves and their employees as participants in the BPJS system (Art. 15 (1)). Under the previous Jamsostek regime, only employers with ten or more employees or paying wages exceeding Rp 1 million per month were required to participate. Employers that fail to register for the BPJS scheme face administrative sanctions, including written warnings, fines, or denial of certain public services (Art. 17(1), (2)). Employers must pay premiums to BPJS (Article 19).

The Indonesian legislature (DPR) passed the Law on the National Social Security System (Sistem Jaminan Sosial Nasional – SJSN) in 2004. The preamble of the general elucidation of the SJSN declares that the Law was passed to fulfil the mandates of Articles 28 H and 34 of the Constitution. Article 28 H(3) says that everyone shall have the right to social security, and Article 34 (2) adds that the state shall develop a system of social security for all of the people. The SJSN expressly discusses the State's obligations to improve people's welfare and defines social security as the fulfilment of basic needs. In 2013, there was a challenge to the law as the appellants said that they did not want to pay the premium of the insurable as this is the obligation of the government. Any payment should be deemed unconstitutional. The Constitutional Court decided this case in No. 101/PUU-XII/2014.

In 2015, four insurance companies have petitioned the Constitutional Court for a judicial review of articles in the Social Security Providers (BPJS) Law that oblige employees to register for health insurance with the Healthcare and Social Security Agency (BPJS Kesehatan). The petitioners argued that the articles have created monopolies in the health insurance industry. The case was decided in Court decision No. 199/PUU-XIII/2015.

In 2016, Gowa Regency from South Sulawesi province challenged the constitutional validity of the same law on the grounds that the social security system should be decentralized by accommodating different ability and capacity of provinces and regencies, instead of organizing by the national government. This case has been decided under Court decision No. 101/PUU-XIV/2016.

The Constitutional Court rejected all these challenges. The main argument was that the Constitution imposes the obligation upon the government to establish a social security system. The Constitution did not elaborate further which system or model that the government must follow. Therefore, any model or system would be considered constitutional as long as it meets the requirement of Article 34 (2) of the Constitution: it is for all people and to assist people to maintain their human dignity.

Unlike in the cases involving individual rights, the Court did not read down Article 34 (2) 'ESC rights' by limiting its application to Article 28 J(2) 'limitations'. The Court took the view that all items under Article 28 are protecting individual rights, whereas the term 'human dignity' under Article 34 is in the context of state obligation to promote economic, social, and cultural rights.

6 CONCLUSION

In this chapter, I have evaluated the meaning of human dignity as interpreted in different ways in the Indonesian Constitution. Human dignity can be examined under the lenses of individual rights and ESC (economic, social, and cultural) rights. In a number of cases, the Indonesian Constitutional Court (Mahkamah Konstitusi) has applied different approaches to the protection of human dignity. The individual rights have to be limited by state law as determined by the limitation clause under Article 28 J (2) or balanced with Article 28 G on human dignity. However, the Court took the position that human dignity under ESC rights in Articles 28 H(3) and 34(2) should be supported, as this was seen as the state obligation.

Arguably, the different approaches are due to the nature of the 1945 Constitution that rejected the notion of Western individual liberalism. Instead, it provided a balance between rights and responsibility amongst citizens; and also a balance between rights and obligation of the state. As has been explained, the Court takes a position of balancing harmony and honour amongst communities. Therefore, human dignity is acknowledged in the Constitution, but the interpretation and application of human dignity will be treated differently at the individual and community levels.

The balance approach between civil and political rights, on the one hand, and economic, social, and cultural rights on the other has proved to be an empowering force in Indonesia, providing a forum for the intersection of political and human rights discourse. In a way, the Court is in favour of the state's obligation to guarantee socio-economic rights, but it is careful in providing a protection against 'unlimited' individual freedom. It was believed that, while rights relate more to freedom, obligations are associated with responsibility. Despite this distinction, freedom and responsibility are interdependent. Freedom should therefore never be exercised without limits. Without a proper balance, unrestricted freedom is as dangerous as imposed social responsibility. The amendment to the 1945 Constitution clearly states this balance approach in Article 28 J(1): 'Each person has the obligation to respect the fundamental human rights of others while partaking in the life of the community, the nation, and the state.'

In one of the decisions mentioned earlier, the Court stated firmly that 'the protection of human rights in the context of the Indonesian community is primarily directed towards the relationship between citizens and the government with the normative-traditional assumption that such interaction will be harmonious and balanced'.[46] It should be clear by now that, in the Indonesian context, the meaning of human dignity is related to the understanding of human rights.

The Indonesian cases demonstrate that individual rights are protected but that this should not undermine other people's honour and dignity. Therefore, state law can limit such individual rights. At the same time, protecting dignity in the community is a higher priority than protecting individual rights. According to the Court, the state is under the obligation to protect economic, social, and cultural rights. Maintaining harmony and balance is key to the meaning of human dignity in the Indonesian Constitution.

---

[46] Constitutional Court Decision No 2/PUU-VII/2009 at 134.

7

Dignity as a Constitutional Value in Hong Kong

Toward a Contextual Approach?

*Kelley Loper**

1 INTRODUCTION

This chapter considers the development of "dignity" as a constitutional value in Hong Kong, a special administrative region (SAR) of the People's Republic of China (PRC). Hong Kong has maintained a separate legal system since its reversion to Chinese sovereignty in 1997 after more than 150 years as a British colony. The 1984 Sino-British Joint Declaration promised Hong Kong a high degree of autonomy in all areas except foreign affairs and defence. The Basic Law,[1] Hong Kong's constitutional document, sets out the terms of this "One Country, Two Systems" arrangement, including guarantees of fundamental rights. In particular, it provides for the continuing application of the International Covenant on Civil and Political Rights (ICCPR)[2] and the International Covenant on Economic, Social and Cultural Rights (ICESCR).[3] The PRC has not ratified the ICCPR, so its place in Hong Kong's regional constitutional framework is a key feature of the SAR's autonomy. The ICCPR has also been directly incorporated in the Bill of Rights Ordinance (BOR),[4] a statute which has achieved constitutional status. While dignity is not mentioned in the Basic Law, these international standards have supported the judiciary's use of dignity as a core value that underpins constitutional rights and informs a purposive approach to their interpretation.[5]

---

[*] I am grateful to Simon Bronnitt, Patricia Ho, Jimmy chia-Shin Hsu, and Scott Veitch for their valuable feedback on earlier drafts and to participants at international conferences in Copenhagen, Bangkok, and Taipei where I shared some of these ideas. I would also like to thank Anabelle Basterrechea-Jones and Sakshi Chandrasekhar for their research assistance. Portions of the research for this chapter were supported by a General Research Fund grant awarded by the Hong Kong Research Grants Council (Project code: 17613117).

[1] Basic Law of the Hong Kong Special Administrative Region of the People's Republic of China, July 1, 1997.

[2] International Covenant on Civil and Political Rights (adopted 16 December 1966, entered into force 23 March 1976) 999 UNTS 171 (ICCPR).

[3] International Covenant on Economic, Social and Cultural Rights (adopted December 16, 1966, entered into force January 3, 1976) 993 UNTS 3 (ICESCR).

[4] Section 8 (Cap 383).

[5] For a discussion of dignity as a constitutional value, see, for example, Aharon Barak, *Human Dignity: The Constitutional Value and the Constitutional Right* (Cambridge: Cambridge University Press, 2015); and Arthur Chaskalson, "Human Dignity as a Constitutional Value," in *The Concept of Human Dignity in*

Hong Kong courts have considered dignity in cases involving only a limited number of rights, including freedom from cruel, inhuman, or degrading treatment; equality and non-discrimination; transgender marriage; humane treatment in detention; and freedom from slavery or forced labour, among others. Overall, the cases are few in number, and the function of dignity as a constitutional value remains underdeveloped. In some instances, the courts have applied dignity to expand the scope of rights. In others, dignity operates more restrictively. For example, dignity has influenced the courts' determination of which rights are more (or less) "fundamental" and therefore which are subject to more (or less) rigorous judicial scrutiny. This has led to the creation of an implicit hierarchy that prioritizes civil and political rights over economic, social, and cultural rights.

An examination of the Hong Kong courts' reliance on dignity, however limited, allows for a helpful reflection on broader debates about the role of dignity as a value in comparative constitutional law more generally.[6] Some commentators have queried whether such a vague and imprecise term can have any substantive meaning.[7] Can dignity be a useful interpretive tool that produces coherent understandings of the content of constitutional rights? Or is it actually an empty, even dangerous, notion that judges can manipulate inappropriately to increase their discretion?[8] Is dignity so fluid that it can support competing claims?[9] Does it undermine, rather

---

    Human Rights Discourse, edited by David Kretzmer and Eckart Klein (Alphen aan den Rijn, Netherlands: Kluwer Law International, 2002), p. 135. Chaskalson asserts that "treating dignity as a foundational value of a human rights order may give it greater weight than if it were treated merely as an enumerated right."

[6] A sample of the vast literature on human dignity in human rights and constitutional law includes, for example, Barak, *Human Dignity*; Christopher McCrudden, "Human Dignity and the Judicial Interpretation of Human Rights," *European Journal of International Law* 19, no. 4 (2008): 655–724; Samuel Moyn, "The Secret History of Constitutional Dignity," *Yale Human Rights and Development Journal* 39, no. 17 (2014): 39–73; Paolo G. Carozza, "Human Dignity," in *Oxford Handbook of International Human Rights Law*, edited by Dinah Shelton (Oxford: Oxford University Press, 2013); Paolo G. Carozza, "Human Dignity in Constitutional Adjudication," in *Comparative Constitutional Law*, edited by Tom Ginsburg and Rosalind Dixon (Cheltenham, UK: Edward Elgar, 2011), pp. 459–472; and Vicki C. Jackson, "Constitutional Dialogue and Human Dignity: States and Transnational Constitutional Discourse," *Montana Law Review* 65, no. 1 (2004): 15–40; among many others.

[7] McCrudden, "Human Dignity and the Judicial Interpretation of Human Rights"; Mirko Bagaric and James Allan, "The Vacuous Concept of Dignity," *Journal of Human Rights* 5, no. 2 (2006): 257–270; Carozza, "Human Dignity in Constitutional Adjudication," pp. 459–472.

[8] McCrudden, "Human Dignity and the Judicial Interpretation of Human Rights"; Moyn, "The Secret History of Constitutional Dignity"; see also Samuel Moyn, "Dignity's Due," *The Nation*, October 16, 2013, www.thenation.com/article/archive/dignitys-due/. Moyn writes sardonically that "today, human dignity is a principle chiefly for those who admire judges and want to have the power to check the state in the name of basic humanitarian values."

[9] Reva B. Siegel, "Dignity and Sexuality: Claims on Dignity in Transnational Debates over Abortion and Same-Sex Marriage," *International Journal of Constitutional Law* 10, no. 2 (March 2012): 365; Neomi Rao, "Three Concepts of Dignity in Constitutional Law," *Notre Dame Law Review* 86, no. 1 (2013): 189.

than promote, the protection of human rights?[10] Does dignity create an additional hurdle that rights claimants must overcome?[11] While such concerns are understandable, and courts have indeed often construed dignity unevenly, others contend this lack of clarity does not justify abandoning dignity altogether.[12]

This chapter concludes that attention to context can mitigate concerns about dignity's indeterminacy and contribute to its development as a more holistic constitutional value. When divorced from context, dignity is more susceptible to relativistic critiques: that it is external and inappropriately imposed on distinct communities. The circumstances for understanding dignity, however, are universal as well as local. They include dignity's position as a broad-based foundational principle in international human rights law. All universal civil, political, economic, social, and cultural rights derive from dignity and, therefore, interpreting these rights with reference to dignity reveals insights about the interdependence of rights across these categories. For example, the denial of dignity in one area, such as a failure to address extreme poverty, may affect dignity in others, such as violations of the right to life or greater vulnerability to forced labour. In this sense, dignity is cross-cutting and requires measures that allow equal participation in all spheres of life. At the same time, context also encompasses local factors such as a jurisdiction's constitutional framework and empirical realities that impact human dignity in any given setting.

With this in mind, this chapter identifies gaps in the Hong Kong courts' approach to dignity when understood in a holistic sense. At the same time, it considers elements in the jurisprudence that the courts could build upon to strengthen dignity's relevance for resolving a wider array of constitutional issues. The remainder of the chapter proceeds as follows. Section 2 elaborates on the contours of a contextual approach and briefly mentions certain salient features that may influence the development of Hong Kong's nascent dignity jurisprudence. Section 3 examines the Hong Kong courts' invocation of dignity in greater depth. Section 4 concludes with a summary of key findings.

2 A CONTEXTUAL APPROACH TO DIGNITY

As mentioned, the contextual approach this chapter endorses recognizes the universal nature of dignity and its association with international human rights law across *all* categories of rights. In this sense, dignity underpins an inclusive vision that

---

[10] Neomi Rao, "On the Use and Abuse of Dignity in Constitutional Law," *Columbia Journal of European Law* 14, no. 2 (Spring 2008): 204.
[11] See Sandra Fredman, *Discrimination Law* (Oxford: Oxford University Press, 2011), 23–24, explaining that "there is a risk that dignity comes to be regarded as an independent element in discrimination law, requiring a claimant to prove not just that she has been disadvantaged, but that this signifies lack of respect for her as a person." She critiques the Canadian Supreme Court's use of dignity in this way in *Gosselin v. Quebec* [2002] SCC 84.
[12] See, for example, Barak, *Human Dignity*, p. 133, countering common critiques of a broad concept of human dignity that embraces the entire humanity of the person.

implicates the full range of human experience. It also takes account of constitutional and other aspects of the local environment that influence dignity's specific application. Against this backdrop, dignity functions expansively, linking rights and bridging universal values with the domestic sphere. The universal and particular aspects of dignity reinforce each other to create sites for richer deliberations about dignity's interpretive role in human rights adjudication.

2.1 The Universal Nature of Dignity as a Cross-Cutting Value

Schachter observed in 1983 that "political leaders, jurists and philosophers have increasingly alluded to the dignity of human persons as a basic ideal so generally recognised as to require no independent support.... No other ideal seems so clearly accepted as a universal social good."[13] Barak has similarly remarked that the value of "human dignity ... is the factor that unites the human rights into one whole" and "comprises the foundation for all of the constitutional rights. Human dignity is the central argument for the existence of human rights. It is the rationale for them all."[14] Indeed, the identification of dignity as the reason for human rights in international human rights law has fortified its status as a universal value and its translation into domestic constitutions.[15] In particular, dignity takes prominent place in the Universal Declaration of Human Rights (UDHR), the ICESCR, and the ICCPR, which together comprise the International Bill of Human Rights.

The Preamble of the UDHR proclaims that the inherent dignity "of all members of the human family" is "the foundation of freedom, justice and peace in the world".[16] Article 1 provides that "all human beings are born free and equal in dignity and rights." Article 22 stipulates that everyone "is entitled to realisation of the economic, social and cultural rights" that are "indispensable" for human dignity and the "free development" of an individual's personality. Article 23 requires that states safeguard the right to work and necessary means of social protection in order to ensure "an existence worthy of human dignity." The ICCPR and the ICESCR later codified the UDHR rights, repeating the reference to dignity in their own Preambles and affirming that human rights "derive from the inherent dignity of the human person." Article 10 of the ICCPR and Article 13 of the ICESCR also contain references to dignity.[17] Even when not explicitly invoked, dignity, as a guiding principle, is implicit in other rights

---

[13] Oscar Schachter, "Human Dignity as a Normative Concept," *American Journal of International Law* 77, no. 4 (October 1983): 848–849.
[14] Barak, *Human Dignity*, 103.
[15] McCrudden notes that the distinction between international human rights and constitutional rights has become increasingly blurred, especially with regard to constitutions drafted since World War II. See Christopher McCrudden, "Dignity, Rights, and the Comparative Method," in *Modern Constitutions*, edited by Rogers M. Smith and Richard R. Beeman (Philadelphia: University of Pennsylvania Press, 2020), p. 112.
[16] Universal Declaration of Human Rights (adopted December 10, 1948) UNGA res 217 A(III).
[17] ICCPR Article 10 requires states to treat "persons deprived of their liberty" with "humanity and with respect for the inherent dignity of the human person," and ICESCR Article 13 mandates that

provisions.[18] This framework supports an expansive role for dignity. As Schacter notes, the recognition of dignity as "the 'source' of human rights" implies that "we can extend and strengthen human rights by formulating new rights or construing existing rights to apply to new situations."[19] A holistic approach exposes the effects of rights violations that may have otherwise been more difficult to identify and, therefore, to remedy.

Dignity also highlights the connections between rights and prevents their demarcation into arbitrary, distinct categories. The Preambles of the ICCPR and the ICESCR emphasize the importance of all of the rights in both instruments. For example, the ICCPR asserts that conditions must be "created whereby everyone may enjoy his civil and political rights, as well as his economic, social and cultural rights" to achieve the purpose of the treaty.[20] Scott and Macklem explain the significance of including socio-economic rights as well as civil and political rights in a constitution, since "constitutionalising half of the human rights equation ... would be constitutionalising only part of what it is to be a full person."[21] They add that "a constitution containing only civil and political rights projects an image of truncated humanity ... it excludes those segments of society for whom autonomy means little without the necessities of life."[22] Barak also argues that, since human dignity is the foundation for all rights, "there is no justification for viewing [it] narrowly."[23] He adds:

> There is no reason to restrict the value of human dignity to "taboo cases" or to protecting people from humiliation and degradation. The constitutional value of human dignity protects all aspects of the individual and all of his aspirations. Thus, the constitutional value of human dignity should be approached with a "spacious" view, expressing the full complexity of the human being.[24]

As such, dignity is relevant when interpreting "both civil rights and social rights"[25] and when resolving issues that arise at the intersections of those rights. Rather than prioritizing certain rights over others, dignity brings them together under the same umbrella.[26]

education be "directed to the full development of the human personality and the sense of its dignity" and "shall strengthen the respect for human rights and fundamental freedoms."

[18] According to the Vienna Convention on the Law of Treaties (adopted May 22, 1969, entered into force January 27, 1980) 1155 UNTS 331, Article 31, the Preambles of international treaties provide context when interpreting the treaty's substantive provisions in light of its object and purpose. By extension, the Preambles of the ICCPR and ICESCR should be taken into consideration when interpreting domestic constitutional rights that are based on these instruments.

[19] Schachter, "Human Dignity as a Normative Concept," p. 853.

[20] ICCPR, Preamble.

[21] Craig Scott and Patrick Macklem, "Constitutional Ropes of Sand or Justiciable Guarantees? Social Rights in a New South African Constitution," *University of Pennsylvania Law Review* 141, no. 1 (1992): 29.

[22] Scott and Macklem, "Constitutional Ropes of Sand," 29.

[23] Barak, *Human Dignity*, 121.

[24] Barak, *Human Dignity*, 121.

[25] Barak, *Human Dignity*, 107, citing Sandra Liebenberg, "The Value of Human Dignity in Interpreting Socio-Economic Rights," *South African Journal of Human Rights* 21, no. 1 (2005): 1–31.

[26] McCrudden, "Human Dignity and the Judicial Interpretation of Human Rights," 670, points out that dignity was adopted as "the central organising principle" at the Vienna World Conference on Human

Although such a broad understanding of dignity may produce conflicting results, this tension is not necessarily problematic. As Waldron contends, "sometimes clarity and determinacy are over-rated."[27] Terms that lack clear definitions may "operate as sites for some of the thoughtfulness that the rule of law sponsors ... It is a mistake to think of the demand for clarity as though it were supposed to be a way of implacably ruling out thought and argumentation in the law."[28] Indeed, he notes that the concept of dignity in human rights law is still a "work-in-progress."[29] Such contestation may actually be "productive" in the sense that it "might generate for us a richer sense of what the concept involves than we would have with a concept that had been arbitrarily pinned down ... with a stipulative definition."[30]

2.2 Domestic Implementation and Context

Domestic contextual factors also contribute to this process of productive contestation and shape how dignity develops in a given constitutional setting. As many have pointed out, international human rights, while universal, can only be effectively enforced at the domestic level. Human rights, like dignity itself, are generally expressed in vague language that takes on meaning when implemented according to the particular environment. Marks and Clapham explain that "human rights are not just abstract" but "must be made meaningful in specific social conditions, each of them unique in its political institutions, cultural traditions, and economic circumstances."[31] In other words, "the specificity of life in different places – all places – must be taken seriously."[32] Liebenberg similarly observes that "we value human beings by viewing them in the context of the reality of their lives and inquiring what they are actually able to be and to do."[33]

An application of human rights norms in light of local particularities, however, need not be inconsistent with the universal nature of rights and dignity. Bantekas and Oette note that "recognition of the need to be context specific must not necessarily equate with an abandonment of universality, which can still provide a valuable framework of culturally transcendent and genuinely universal

---

Rights, where the global community confirmed that "all human rights are universal, indivisible and interdependent and interrelated." UN General Assembly, "Vienna Declaration and Programme of Action, adopted by the World Conference on Human Rights in Vienna on 25 June 1993," July 12, 1993, A/CONF.157/23, para. 5, available at www.ohchr.org/en/professionalinterest/pages/vienna.aspx.

[27] Jeremy Waldron, "What Do the Philosophers Have against Dignity?," NYU School of Law, Public Law Research Paper Series 14–59, New York University, New York, NY, 2014: 8, http://dx.doi.org/10.2139/ssrn.2497742.
[28] Waldron, "What Do the Philosophers Have against Dignity?"
[29] Waldron, "What Do the Philosophers Have against Dignity?," pp. 9, 10.
[30] Waldron, "What Do the Philosophers Have against Dignity?," p. 12.
[31] Susan Marks and Andrew Clapham, *International Human Rights Lexicon* (Oxford: Oxford University Press 2005), p. 388.
[32] Marks and Clapham, *International Human Rights Lexicon*, p. 388.
[33] Liebenberg "The Value of Human Dignity in Interpreting Socio-Economic Rights," p. 31.

aspirations."[34] In fact, the complex interaction between universal norms and the local settings where they are implemented is a key feature of international human rights law. Hannum observes that "permitting countries to make reasonable decisions based on what ultimately are very different historical, cultural, political or economic circumstances in which they find themselves is a strength of human rights, not a weakness."[35] Although often a gradual process, the internalization of universal values within a society gives them substance. Koh asserts that international norms are enforced "by motivating nation-states to *obey* international human rights law – out of a sense of internal acceptance."[36] Jackson also remarks that "the migration of the idea of human dignity illustrates ... the interaction between new ideas and other elements of the system in which they are embraced. The impact of constitutional text may vary substantially depending on context, development, history and culture."[37] McCrudden points out that dignity helps resolve the "tension in international human rights law" between universality and "respecting the diversity and freedom of human cultures."[38] He also argues that "dignity, in the judicial context, not only permits the incorporation of local contingencies in the interpretation of human rights norms; it requires it. Dignity allows *each jurisdiction to develop its own practice of human rights*."[39]

In other words, attention to context gives life to dignity and the rights that flow from it. The adaptable nature of human rights facilitates their acceptance in societies with diverse cultures and religions, political systems, and socio-economic concerns. In this way, dignity is less likely to be viewed as remote, abstract, or disconnected. Barak contends that, while "human dignity is a contextually dependent value" and "a changing value in a changing world,"[40] this "relativity ... does not diminish its importance. On the contrary ... [it] intensifies the position of human dignity in each society, while expressing the special experiences of the society and influencing its conclusions."[41] Dignity's breadth as a value underpinning universal

---

[34] Ilias Bantekas and Lutz Oette, *International Human Rights Law and Practice* (Cambridge: Cambridge University Press, 2013), p. 39.

[35] Hurst Hannum, "Getting Human Rights Right," interview by *Vital Interests: The United States in a New Global Paradigm*, The Center on National Security at Fordham Law, August 27, 2020, www.centeronnationalsecurity.org/vital-interests-issue-46-hurst-hannum.

[36] Harold Koh, "How is International Human Rights Law Enforced?," *Indiana International Law Journal* 74, no. 4 (1999): 1408. Emphasis in original.

[37] Jackson, "Constitutional Dialogue and Human Dignity: States and Transnational Constitutional Discourse," p. 27.

[38] McCrudden, "Human Dignity and the Judicial Interpretation of Human Rights," p. 719, citing Paolo G. Carozza, "Subsidiarity as a Structural Principle of International Human Rights Law," *American Journal of International Law* 97, no. 1 (2003): 39–79.

[39] McCrudden, "Human Dignity and the Judicial Interpretation of Human Rights," p. 720, citing Carozza, "Subsidiarity as a Structural Principle of International Human Rights Law." Emphasis added.

[40] Barak, *Human Dignity*, p 14, citing Matthias Mahlmann, *Elemente einer ethischen Grundrechtstheorie* (Berlin: Nomos, 2008), p. 5.

[41] Barak, *Human Dignity*, 14, citing Mahlmann, *Elemente einer ethischen Grundrechtstheorie*, pp. 6–7.

human rights norms and its depth and dependence on local specificities go hand in hand to enhance its significance.

2.3 Contextual Factors in Hong Kong

How might such a contextual approach shape the development of dignity as a constitutional value in Hong Kong? Elements of the constitutional context – the text of the Basic Law and the values that inform its purpose – have influenced the courts' reasoning about dignity to some extent. De facto denials of – or potential risks to – human dignity that arise from socio-economic, political, and other realities are also important to consider. Significant socio-economic inequalities in Hong Kong undercut the ability of many people to live a life in dignity[42] and certain groups are particularly marginalized. Immigration from mainland China increased after Hong Kong's reversion to Chinese sovereignty in 1997 and many new immigrants live in relative poverty.[43] The majority are women, and gender can also influence the experience of marginalization.[44] Asylum seekers and refugees also face disadvantage.[45] As will be seen, an analysis of the cases in Section 3 with reference to both constitutional factors and de facto inequalities exposes gaps in judicial reasoning on dignity. At the same time, however, it identifies potential areas for elaboration.

The constitutional context supports an expansive notion of dignity as a value that cuts across a broader range of constitutional rights than currently recognized. As mentioned, the Basic Law sets out the framework for implementing "One Country, Two Systems," the foundational principle designed to facilitate Hong Kong's return to Chinese sovereignty and the functioning of its unique form of regional autonomy.[46] While not expressly mentioned in the Basic Law, its characteristics are evident in provisions that emphasize Chinese sovereignty (one country) and those that specify the components of Hong Kong's autonomy (two systems). For example, Article 1 stipulates that Hong Kong is an inalienable part of the PRC, while

---

[42] Hong Kong's Gini coefficient, a standard measure of income inequality, is one of the highest in the world. See Oxfam Hong Kong, *Hong Kong Inequality Report*, September 25, 2018, www.oxfam.org.hk/en/f/news_and_publication/16372/Oxfam_inequality%20report_Eng_FINAL.pdf.

[43] Kee-Lee Chou, Kelvin Cheung, and Maggie Lau, "Trends in Child Poverty in Hong Kong Immigrant Families," *Social Indicators Research* 117 (July 2014): 811.

[44] See Census and Statistics Department Hong Kong Special Administrative Region, *Women and Men in Hong Kong, Key Statistics* (2020), 29, table 1.14, "Persons from the mainland of China having resided in Hong Kong for less than 7 years by sex and duration of residence in Hong Kong," www.statistics.gov.hk/pub/B11303032020AN20B0100.pdf.

[45] Ada Pui Yim Lai and Kerry J. Kennedy, "Refugees and Civic Stratification: The 'Asian Rejection' Hypothesis and Its Implications for Protection Claimants in Hong Kong," *Asian and Pacific Migration Journal* 26, no. 2 (2017): 206.

[46] In the early 1980s, Deng Xiaoping, China's preeminent leader at the time, introduced this idea during negotiations over Hong Kong's postcolonial future. China Daily, "Deng Xiaoping on 'One Country, Two Systems,'" reproduced from the *Selected Works of Deng Xiaoping*, June 22–3, 1984, www.chinadaily.com.cn/english/doc/2004-02/19/content_307590.htm.

Article 2 authorizes Hong Kong "to exercise a high degree of autonomy and enjoy executive, legislative and independent judicial power."[47]

This autonomy is also reinforced by other guarantees: judicial independence (Art. 85);[48] the continuation of the common law system, which is distinct from the PRC's legal system (Article 8); and the ability of the Court of Final Appeal (CFA) to invite foreign judges to sit as non-permanent judges (Art. 82)[49] and to cite decisions by other common law courts (Art. 84). Article 39 provides that the ICCPR and the ICESCR shall remain in force and be implemented through the laws of Hong Kong. Along with the direct incorporation of the ICCPR in the BOR, Article 39 firmly grounds constitutional rights in international human rights law. Dignity has therefore become an implicit constitutional value and helped open up the interpretative process. The courts' heavy reliance on international and comparative materials for guidance when adjudicating human rights cases has strengthened these developments.[50] The courts have also established a strong tradition of judicial review and a robust proportionality test for determining when limitations on rights are justifiable.[51]

---

[47] Hong Kong Basic Law.
[48] Although judicial independence has been largely respected since 1997, the National People's Congress Standing Committee has the power of final interpretation of the Basic Law (Article 158). Recent legal and political developments, including the controversial introduction of the Law of the [PRC] on Safeguarding National Security in Hong Kong (SAR), which took effect on June 30, 2020, have called judicial independence into question. See Johannes Chan, "Reconciliation of the NPCSC's Power of Interpretation of the Basic Law with the Common Law in the HKSAR," *Hong Kong Law Journal* 50 (2020): 657; Johannes Chan, "A storm of Unprecedented Ferocity: The Shrinking Space of the Right to Political Participation, Peaceful Demonstration, and Judicial Independence in Hong Kong," *International Journal of Constitutional Law* 16, no. 2 (April 2018): 373; and Carole J. Petersen, "The Disappearing Firewall: International Consequences of Beijing's Decision to Impose a National Security Law and Operate National Security Institutions in Hong Kong," *Hong Kong Law Journal* 50 (2020): 633.
[49] For a discussion of the roles and contributions of nonlocal judges, see, for example, the Hon. Mr Justice Joseph Fok, PJ, "Judges from Other Common Law Jurisdictions in the Hong Kong Court of Final Appeal" (the Commonwealth Law Conference, Melbourne, Australia, March 22, 2017), www.hkcfa.hk/filemanager/engagement/en/upload/43/D5_The%20Use%20of%20Non-local%20Judges%20in%20Overseas%20Jurisdictions.pdf.
[50] Hong Kong courts are conscious of their active participation in transnational judicial conversations. For example, the Court of Final Appeal, in *QT v. Director of Immigration* (2018) 21 HKCFAR 324, remarked on "a notable convergence in the approaches of various courts, including our own, to what constitutes discrimination, influenced by international human rights instruments." See Kelley Loper, "The Courts, Public Opinion and the Rights of Lesbian, Gay, Bisexual and Transgender Persons: A Hong Kong Perspective," *Australian Journal of Asian Law* 20, no. 1 (2019). See also, for example, Sir Anthony Mason, "The Place of Comparative Law in Developing the Jurisprudence on the Rule of Law and Human Rights in Hong Kong," *Hong Kong Law Journal* 37 (2007): 299; Albert H.Y. Chen, "International Human Rights Law and Domestic Constitutional Law: Internationalisation of Constitutional Law in Hong Kong," *National Taiwan University Law Review* 4, no. 3 (2010); Simon N. M. Young, "Constitutional Rights in Hong Kong's Court of Final Appeal," *Chinese (Taiwan) Y. B. International Law and Affairs* 67 (2011): 81–82.
[51] See *Leung Kwok Hung & Others v. HKSAR* (2005) 8 HKCFAR 229, para. 33–39.

These features have supported the courts' endorsement of a purposive approach to the interpretation of rights.⁵² The CFA, Hong Kong's apex court since 1997, has acknowledged that "gaps and ambiguities are bound to arise," so in order to ascertain "the true meaning of the instrument, the courts must consider [its] purpose ... and its relevant provisions as well as the language of its text in the light of the context."⁵³ The CFA explained that "the purpose of the Basic Law is to establish the Hong Kong [SAR] ... under the principle of 'one country, two systems.'"⁵⁴ The interpretive process "must avoid" readings of the constitutional text that are "literal, technical, narrow or rigid,"⁵⁵ and the courts "should give a generous interpretation," especially to "the constitutional guarantees for the freedoms that lie at the heart of Hong Kong's separate system."⁵⁶

This framework promotes dignity as a value that should inform the interpretive process across all constitutional rights. As will be discussed, however, the Hong Kong jurisprudence has not fully recognized the implications of dignity for economic, social, and cultural rights or the socio-economic components of civil and political rights. Despite the reference to the ICESCR in Article 39 of the Basic Law, the ICCPR has had more of an impact.⁵⁷ Indeed, the courts have consistently pointed out that the ICESCR has not been as fully domesticated as the ICCPR, which the BOR essentially duplicates word for word.⁵⁸ Nevertheless, dignity could still play a more influential role when considering socio-economic matters than it has so far. For example, when the meaning of a statute is unclear, the courts are likely to interpret its provisions as consistently as possible with Hong Kong's international treaty obligations.⁵⁹ Dignity is also relevant to the interpretation of certain socio-economic rights enumerated in the Basic Law and any statutes that incorporate

---

⁵² In a decision handed down two years after 1997, the newly established Court of Final Appeal clarified that "it is generally accepted that in the interpretation of a constitution such as the Basic Law a purposive approach is to be applied." *Ng Ka Ling v. Director of Immigration* (1999) 2 HKCFAR 4, para. 28–29.

⁵³ *Ng Ka Ling v. Director of Immigration* (1999) 2 HKCFAR 4, para. 28–29.

⁵⁴ *Ng Ka Ling v. Director of Immigration* (1999) 2 HKCFAR 4, para. 28–29.

⁵⁵ *Ng Ka Ling v. Director of Immigration* (1999) 2 HKCFAR 4, para. 28–29.

⁵⁶ *Ng Ka Ling* v. Director of Immigration (1999) 2 HKCFAR 4, para. 28–29.

⁵⁷ See Johannes Chan, "Basic Law and Constitutional Review: the First Decade," *Hong Kong Law Journal* 37 (2009): 411–413.

⁵⁸ In *Comilang Milagros Tecson v. Director of Immigration* (2019) 22 HKCFAR 59, para. 74, the Court of Final Appeal explained that "the ICESCR is an international treaty and under the common law dualist principle is not self-executing. Unless and until made part of Hong Kong domestic law by legislation, the provisions of such a treaty do not confer or impose any rights or obligations on individual citizens." See also *Ubamaka v. Secretary for Security* (2012) 15 HKCFAR 743, para. 42–44; and *GA v. Director of Immigration* (2014) 17 HKCFAR 60, para. 58.

⁵⁹ The Court of First Instance, in *Equal Opportunities Commission v. Director of Education* [2001] 2 HKLRD 690, favourably cited *Garland v. British Rail Engineering Ltd (No 2)* [1983] 2 AC 751, 771, per Lord Diplock, who explained that "the words of a statute passed after [a] Treaty has been signed and dealing with the subject matter of the international obligation of the United Kingdom, are to be construed, if they are reasonably capable of bearing such a meaning, as intended to carry out the obligation, and not to be inconsistent with it."

elements of the ICESCR.[60] The courts could also invoke dignity when identifying the socio-economic aspects of civil and political rights. For example, the UN Human Rights Committee, the expert body that monitors states' implementation of their obligations under the ICCPR, has interpreted the right to life as a "right to life with dignity," and this mandates the introduction of socio-economic measures.[61]

Dignity might also help clarify the connection between human rights and democratic participation in Hong Kong. Although the British colonial government never introduced full democracy before 1997, the Basic Law stipulates that universal suffrage is the ultimate aim for electing both the leader of Hong Kong – the chief executive – and all members of the legislature.[62] It is beyond the scope of this chapter to chronicle ongoing debates about political reform since 1997,[63] but these provisions had not been implemented at the time of writing. As will be discussed, however, dignity might assist with developing a notion of democratic participation that goes beyond particular electoral procedures. A richer meaning of democracy in line with human dignity requires inclusion, backed by the right to substantive equality,[64] other civil and political rights associated with participation, and socio-economic rights.[65]

3 KEY JUDICIAL DECISIONS

Despite this supportive constitutional framework, the development of dignity as a constitutional value in Hong Kong is still in its nascent stages. The courts have infrequently referred to dignity and, when mentioned, the reasoning is fairly brief. Initial steps, however, signal judicial recognition that universal values underpin constitutional rights and suggest potential for a more robust approach. The following discussion illustrates the gaps and possibilities. Dignity has helped extend the

[60] See *Ho Choi Wan v. Housing Authority* (2005) 8 HKCFAR 628, para. 54–67, per Bokhary J., writing, in *obiter*: "If it were necessary to do so in order to establish that the [Housing] Authority is duty-bound to provide affordable housing, it might well be possible to pray the ICESCR powerfully in aid of construing the Housing Ordinance to impose that duty."
[61] See discussion in Section 3.
[62] Basic Law Articles 45 and 68.
[63] See, for example, Michael C. Davis, "Human Rights and Political Opposition in Hong Kong," in *Handbook on Human Rights in China*, eds. Sarah Biddulph and Joshua Rosenzweig (Cheltenham, UK: Edward Elgar, 2019): 588–604.
[64] On the right to substantive equality in Hong Kong constitutional law, see Kelley Loper, "Human Rights and Substantive Equality: Prospects for Same-Sex Relationship Recognition in Hong Kong," *North Carolina Journal of International Law* 44 (2019): 273; and Kelley Loper, "Right to Equality and Non-discrimination," in *Law of the Hong Kong Constitution*, 2nd ed., edited by Johannes Chan and C. L. Lim (London: Sweet and Maxwell, 2015), pp. 991–1012.
[65] For a discussion of how international law supports a fuller understanding of democracy, see, for example, Stephen Wheatley, "Deliberative Democracy and Minorities," *European Journal of International Law* 14, no. 3 (June 2003): 508. Wheatley explains that "the deliberative model conceives of democracy as a free association of equal citizens who engage in a rational discussion on political issues, presenting options and seeking a consensus on what is to be done" and that the "cardinal features" of this model are "equality, participation (i.e. inclusion) and consensus."

human rights canon in some areas (for example, the determination that sexual orientation is an invidious ground of discrimination). In others, however, the courts have overlooked the implications of dignity and raised the bar for judicial intervention when matters of socio-economic policy are at issue.[66] While in some cases, judicial deference to government decision-makers may be appropriate, a fuller evaluation according to an expansive value of dignity would likely result in a richer analysis. The courts could more deliberately differentiate between those aspects of socio-economic policy that engage constitutional rights and those that do not, to produce more nuanced, coherent decisions.

3.1 Cruel, Inhuman, or Degrading Treatment or Punishment

The courts have referred to dignity in a handful of decisions involving the rights of individuals who fear cruel, inhuman, or degrading treatment or punishment (or other types of serious harm) if returned to their countries of origin. These cases demonstrate dignity's capacity to broaden the reach of a particular civil right as well as address socio-economic concerns.

In *Ubamaka v. Director of Immigration*,[67] the CFA invoked dignity when clarifying the threshold for determining cruel, inhuman, or degrading treatment in contravention of Article 3 of the BOR (Art. 7 of the ICCPR). The case involved a Nigerian national who had been convicted of drug offences in Hong Kong and feared he would be tried again in Nigeria when deported after serving his custodial sentence. In establishing whether such double jeopardy might give rise to degrading treatment, the court adopted a test developed by the European Court of Human Rights when interpreting a similar prohibition of inhuman or degrading treatment or punishment in Article 3 of the European Convention on Human Rights:

> Where treatment humiliates or debases an individual showing a lack of respect for, or diminishing, his or her human dignity or arouses feelings of fear, anguish or inferiority capable of breaking an individual's moral and physical resistance, it may be characterised as degrading.[68]

Although the Hong Kong court decided that the applicant's circumstances did not meet this threshold, the judgment prompted the establishment of a government mechanism that considers a range of non-refoulement (non-return) claims.[69] The

---

[66] For a critique of judicial deference in Hong Kong, see Cora Chan, "Judicial Deference at Work: Some Reflections on *Chan Kin Sum* and *Kong Yun Ming*," *Hong Kong Law Journal* 40, no. 1 (2010): 1–14.

[67] (2012) 15 HKCFAR 743.

[68] *Ubamaka v. Director of Immigration* (2012), para. 173, citing *Pretty v. United Kingdom* 35 EHRR 1, 33, para. 52, as cited by the UK House of Lords *R (Limbuela) v. Secretary of State for the Home Department*, [2006] 1 AC 396.

[69] Previously, the system had only considered claims by persons who were at risk of torture if returned to their countries of origin as required by Article 3 of the Convention against Torture and Other Cruel, Inhuman or Degrading Treatment or Punishment (adopted December 10, 1984; entry into force

Court of First Instance subsequently referred to this test when reviewing a failed non-refoulement decision, stating it "is well settled that the Article 3 [of the European Convention] threshold is a very high one ... Ill treatment involves actual bodily harm or intense physical or mental suffering and must attain a minimum level of severity."[70]

In *GA v. Director of Immigration*,[71] the CFA considered whether the refugee applicants had a right to work in Hong Kong.[72] The claims were based partly on the rights to work in Article 6 of the ICESCR and freedom of choice of occupation in Article 33 of the Basic Law.[73] The court ultimately rejected these grounds, noting the lack of domestic incorporation of Article 6 and a reservation to the ICESCR allowing restrictions to the right to work in Hong Kong.[74] The chief justice, however, remarked that if the inability to work posed a substantial and imminent risk of inhuman or degrading treatment in a given case, based on the dignity test in *Ubamaka*, then the director of immigration must grant permission to work.[75] The court expressed the view that there was no "precise formula" and that it must assess the individual facts to determine whether the treatment met the necessary minimum level of severity.

Although the court decided this was unnecessary in the applicants' situation (they had already each been granted temporary permission – though not a "right" – to work on a case-by-case basis), it noted that "all have been in Hong Kong for a long time ... [and] evidence has been adduced by the applicants dealing with their mental condition, referring to their loss of dignity, and feelings of hopelessness and desperation."[76] It also favourably referred to a comment by the Court of Appeal in its earlier judgment that

> it must be recognised that ... the ICCPR emphasise[s] the recognition of human dignity and that its protection is, therefore, one of the fundamental purposes of the ICCPR. Moreover, there is more to cruel, inhuman or degrading treatment and human dignity than either destitution or complete mental breakdown. It seems to

---

June 26, 1987) 1465 UNTS 85. See *Secretary for Security v. Sakthevel Prabakar* (2004) 7 HKCFAR 187. For background on the development of this "Unified Screening Mechanism," see Legislative Council Secretariat, "Report of Subcommittee to Follow Up Issues Relating to the Unified Screening Mechanism for Non-refoulement Claims," Paper for the House Committee meeting on March 1, 2019, LC Paper No. CB(2)874/18–19, www.legco.gov.hk/yr18-19/english/hc/papers/hc20190301cb2-874-e.pdf.

[70] *Mohammad Palash v. William Lam, Esq and Another* (2017) HKEC 272.
[71] *GA v. Director of Immigration* (2014) 17 HKCFA para. 60.
[72] Although Hong Kong provides non-refoulement protection through the Unified Screening Mechanism, it does not grant "status" or any form of temporary residence to successful claimants, who are often left in limbo for many years.
[73] The applicants also tried to argue that the right to work exists at common law.
[74] *GA v. Director of Immigration* (2014), para. 60–68. See also Karen Kong, "Refugees' Right to Work in Hong Kong – or Lack Thereof: *GA v Director of Immigration*," *Oxford University Commonwealth Law Journal* 14, no. 2 (2014): 337–48.
[75] *GA v. Director of Immigration* (2014), para. 45 and 58.
[76] *GA v. Director of Immigration* (2014), para. 54. Emphasis added.

me that it is certainly arguable that an inability to function economically may well give rise to cruel, inhuman or degrading treatment.[77]

This acknowledgment that dignity provides the foundation for all of the rights in the ICCPR opens up possibilities for elaboration in future cases. Dignity already played an expansive role in both *Ubamaka* and *GA*, by supporting: 1) a broader, implicit right to non-refoulement in the BOR; and 2) the connection between the ability to work (a socio-economic right) and the enjoyment of a civil and political right. The court also indicated that the right to work could affect freedom from interference in a person's privacy, family, home, or correspondence.[78]

On the other hand, dignity's association with freedom from inhuman or degrading treatment – an "absolute" right that requires a particularly high threshold to establish a breach – poses some risks. For example, the courts might be tempted to refrain from using dignity when construing nonabsolute rights. Indeed, the relatively few references to dignity in Hong Kong's constitutional jurisprudence overall might contribute to a perception that dignity is only relevant when reviewing more "serious" breaches of so-called fundamental rights. In other words, dignity could be (incorrectly) disengaged from a constitutional context grounded in international human rights law which mandates that all rights be treated "in a fair and equal manner, on the same footing, and with the same emphasis."[79]

3.2 *The Rights to Equality and Non-discrimination and Social Welfare*

The courts have also referred to dignity as a constitutional value when interpreting the right to equality and non-discrimination. In doing so, they have clarified that a breach of equality (or the existence of discrimination) amounts to a denial of dignity. Article 25 of the Basic Law guarantees the right to equality before the law, and Articles 1 and 22 of the BOR (Articles 2(1) and 26 of the ICCPR) require protection from discrimination based on a nonexhaustive list of grounds ("such as race, colour, sex, language, religion, political or other opinion, national or social origin, property, birth or other status"). Dignity has played a role in determining when differential treatment is particularly invidious and where government

---

[77] *GA v. Director of Immigration* (2014), para. 13, citing *MA v. Director of Immigration* [2011] 2 HKLRD F6, para. 76 (Court of Appeal).
[78] *GA v. Director of Immigration* (2014). These rights are set out in Article 14 of the BOR (Article 17 of the ICCPR). The court held that these rights would not apply due to an exception in section 11 of the BOR which excludes challenges to immigration legislation based on nonabsolute rights. The connection between the right to work and the right to privacy might be considered in future cases, however, outside of the immigration context. Before the Court of Appeal, the applicants had argued that earning a living is an element of the right to privacy and family life and that the ability to work is critical to secure respect for human dignity based on the jurisprudence of the European Court of Human Rights. See *Niemietz v. Germany* [1992] 16 EHRR 97, as cited in *MA v. Director of Immigration*, para. 61.
[79] Vienna Declaration and Programme of Action (1993).

justifications for such treatment demand stringent review. As with the cases involving freedom from cruel, inhuman, or degrading treatment or punishment, these cases illustrate dignity's expansive potential. At the same time, they reveal gaps that might be addressed by greater sensitivity to local contextual factors which, in association with dignity, could help identify additional forms of indirect discrimination and substantive inequality.

The CFA first construed the right to equality with reference to dignity in *Secretary for Justice* v. *Yau Yuk Lung*.[80] In this landmark decision, the court held that the criminal offence of committing "buggery otherwise than in private" discriminated on the basis of sexual orientation and was therefore unconstitutional.[81] This was the first time Hong Kong's highest court recognized sexual orientation as a suspect ground of discrimination. The judgment emphasized universality, stating that equality is a "fundamental human right ... enshrined in numerous international human rights instruments ... [and] widely embodied in the constitutions of jurisdictions around the world."[82] It also explained that the occurrence of discrimination can be determined, in part, with reference to dignity (or the lack of dignity). "Discriminatory law is unfair and violates the human dignity of those discriminated against. It is demeaning for them and generates ill-will and a sense of grievance on their part. It breeds tension and discord in society."[83] These passages demonstrate the influence of international and comparative human rights law on the interpretation of rights in the Hong Kong context. They also provided the foundation for subsequent decisions that elaborated on the equality doctrine in terms of dignity.

In one of these cases, *Fok Chun Wa* v. *Hospital Authority*,[84] the applicant – a woman from mainland China who was married to a Hong Kong permanent resident and gave birth in a Hong Kong public hospital – claimed that higher obstetric charges for non-residents were discriminatory. While the courts have frequently granted the government considerable discretion in cases involving socio-economic matters, such as healthcare,[85] the CFA clarified that careful scrutiny may nevertheless be required. When applying the right to equality in particular, the courts have factored dignity into a determination of which types of differential treatment involve an affront to "core-values" and therefore warrant strict judicial review:

> Where ... the reason for unequal treatment strikes at the heart of core-values relating to personal or human characteristics (such as race, colour, gender, sexual

---

[80] *Secretary for Justice* v. *Yau Yuk Lung* [2007] 3 HKC 545.
[81] *Secretary for Justice* v. *Yau Yuk Lung* [2007] 3 HKC 545.
[82] *Secretary for Justice* v. *Yau Yuk Lung* [2007] 3 HKC 545, para. 1.
[83] *Secretary for Justice* v. *Yau Yuk Lung* [2007] 3 HKC 545, para. 2.
[84] *Fok Chun Wa* v. *Hospital Authority* [2012] 15 HKCFAR 409.
[85] For a discussion of judicial deference in Hong Kong, see Cora Chan, "Judicial Deference at Work: Some Reflections on *Chan Kin Sum* and *Kong Yun Ming*," *Hong Kong Law Journal* 4, no. 1 (2010): 1–14; and Cora Chan, "Rights, Proportionality and Deference: A Study of Post-Handover Judgments in Hong Kong," *Hong Kong Law Journal* 48, no. 1 (2018): 51.

orientation, religion, politics, or social origin), the courts would extremely rarely (if at all) find this acceptable. These characteristics involve the respect and dignity that society accords to a human being. They are fundamental societal values.[86]

The court distinguished these "core values" however, from "other characteristics or status."[87] In those circumstances, "the courts will hesitate much more before interfering."[88] Since the distinction in *Fok Chun Wa* was based on residence status *and* involved a socio-economic right, the court allowed policy-makers a greater "margin of appreciation."[89] In the court's view, "the entitlement to social welfare or to subsidised health services is not a fundamental concept ... It is a right that is inextricably bound with socio-economic considerations."[90] Here, the court associated "fundamental concepts" which "go to the heart of any society" exclusively with civil and political rights.[91] "They include, for example, the right to life, the right not to be tortured, the right not to be held in slavery, the freedom of expression and opinion, freedom of religion (among others)" and "the right to a fair trial and the presumption of innocence."[92] Insofar as dignity assists the court in identifying "core values," which may correlate with these "fundamental concepts," it functions as a limiting device. At the same time, a consideration of certain contextual factors might have alerted the court to a fuller range of issues. For example, the policy had a particular impact on pregnant immigrant women and may have indirectly discriminated on the grounds of sex, gender, and/or place of origin. In other words, it might have engaged "core values" after all. The court also did not consider the implications of poverty and dislocation that often affect the dignity of many new immigrants. Dignity in a more expansive sense might prevent these types of missed opportunities.

Similar questions arose in a case involving equality and the right to social welfare (*Kong Yunming v. Director of Social Welfare*).[93] The applicant was a mainland immigrant who had been married to a Hong Kong permanent resident and arrived to settle in Hong Kong the day before her husband died. She became destitute, but the government rejected her application for social welfare since recipients must have resided in Hong Kong for seven years. She also became homeless after the government repossessed her deceased husband's public housing unit.

---

[86] *Fok Chun Wa v. Hospital Authority* [2012], para. 77. Emphasis added.
[87] *Fok Chun Wa v. Hospital Authority* [2012], para. 77.
[88] *Fok Chun Wa v. Hospital Authority* [2012], para. 77
[89] The Hong Kong courts' use of the "margin of appreciation" doctrine is based on the jurisprudence of the European Court of Human Rights. For a critique of this reasoning, see Holning Lau and Derek Loh, "Misapplication of ECHR Jurisprudence in W v. Registrar of Marriages," *Hong Kong Law Journal* 41, no. 1 (2011): 75.
[90] *Fok Chun Wa v. Hospital Authority* [2012], para 80.
[91] *Fok Chun Wa v. Hospital Authority* [2012], para. 79.
[92] *Fok Chun Wa v. Hospital Authority* [2012], para 79
[93] *Kong Yunming v. Director of Social Welfare* (2013) 16 HKCFAR 950 (Court of Final Appeal); *Kong Yunming v. Director of Social Welfare* [2012] HKEC 1223 (Court of Appeal).

Although she contended that these policies violated her rights to equality and non-discrimination as well as social welfare, the CFA eventually decided the case in favour of the applicant on the basis of the right to social welfare alone. The Court of Appeal, however, had earlier considered the relevance of dignity when interpreting the right to equality, applying the proportionality test, and rejecting the claim on that basis. In doing so, it again distinguished between characteristics that involve "core values" and those that do not. First, the court held that the distinction at issue was based on residency status and had a legitimate aim.[94] When considering the next stage of the test – "whether the difference in treatment is no more than is necessary to achieve the legitimate aim" – the court rejected arguments that social security is a fundamental right. As such, "the differentiation" in its application was not "inherently an affront to individual dignity" and therefore was not "amenable to severe scrutiny."[95] The applicants had also attempted to claim that the targeted group had been stereotyped by the reasons for their exclusion: lack of skill and education, a potential burden on society, and a gender-based impact since "most of those excluded are, or are likely to be women."[96] In rejecting the proposition that "the suggested stereotype categorisation" is "of a kind that diminishes the dignity of the excluded individual," the court explained that "the risk of possible offence to dignity is, unfortunately, occasionally a consequence of any immigration policy which chooses to admit some and deny admission to others."[97] It elaborated that "such a denial is not directed at intrinsically objectionable grounds of differentiation"[98] and concluded: "The point is that there are certain grounds for differentiation that strike at the core of our values and at the respect which those values dictate must be accorded the individual."[99]

While the CFA overruled the Court of Appeal's decision, it did not find it necessary to consider the discrimination claim or evaluate the lower court's reasoning on this point. The apex court did, however, consider dignity when concluding that the government had unjustifiably denied the applicant her constitutional right to social welfare.[100] In doing so, it favourably cited the South African Constitutional Court, which held in *Khosa v. Minister of Social Development* that the exclusion from social security "is likely to have a severe impact on the dignity of the persons concerned, who, unable to sustain themselves, have to turn to others to enable them to meet the necessities of life and are thus cast in the role of supplicants."[101] This recognition that the denial of a socio-economic right can affect human dignity

---

[94] *Kong Yunming v. Director of Social Welfare* [2012] HKEC 1223 (Court of Appeal), para. 88.
[95] *Kong Yunming v. Director of Social Welfare* [2012], para. 94.
[96] *Kong Yunming v. Director of Social Welfare* [2012], para. 94.
[97] *Kong Yunming v. Director of Social Welfare* [2012], para. 97.
[98] *Kong Yunming v. Director of Social Welfare* [2012], para. 97.
[99] *Kong Yunming v. Director of Social Welfare* [2012], para. 98.
[100] Articles 36 and 145 of the Basic Law.
[101] *Khosa v. Minister of Social Development* (2004) (6) SA 505, at para. 80, as cited in *Kong Yunming v. Director of Social Welfare* (2013) (Court of Final Appeal), para. 184.

suggests possibilities for a more expansive approach. As Chan observes, this decision marked the first time a Hong Kong court applied the proportionality test to scrutinize a restriction on the right to social welfare.[102]

Others have noted, however, that the standard of review in this case was in fact relatively weak. Ip argues that it resembled the proportionality test only "in form but definitely not in spirit" and did not differ substantially from a weaker Wednesbury irrationality review.[103] In many ways the court reaffirmed its doctrine of deference when assessing socio-economic policies. As Chan comments, the court did not explicitly acknowledge the right to social welfare as a "fundamental right" despite its inclusion in the list of "fundamental rights" in the Basic Law.[104] It also maintained its "longstanding distinction between cases involving fundamental concepts or core values, where the rigorous 'minimal impairment' proportionality standard would apply, and cases involving socio-economic policies, where the less demanding 'manifestly unreasonableness' proportionality standard would apply."[105]

In more recent cases involving the rights of same-sex couples, the courts have elaborated on the role of dignity when evaluating differential treatment. Although these cases also concern policies with resource implications, the courts reiterated that they will still stringently review differential treatment based directly or indirectly on a suspect ground that affects a person's dignity. In addition, they have clarified that indirect, as well as direct, discrimination is a violation of equality.

In *QT v. Director of Immigration*,[106] the applicant was a UK citizen in a valid same-sex civil partnership (recognized in England) with a woman who was granted an employment visa to work in Hong Kong. The CFA held that the decision to deny QT a dependent visa to join her partner was directly based on marital status but amounted to indirect sexual orientation discrimination. When considering the nature of discrimination, the CFA cited *R (Carson) v. Secretary of State for Work and Pensions* per Lord Walker of Gestingthorpe,[107] who explained: "In the field of human rights,

---

[102] Cora Chan, "Focus: *Kong Yunming v. Director of Social Welfare*, Introduction," *Hong Kong Law Journal* 44, no. 1 (2014): 2.
[103] See Eric C. Ip, "*Kong Yunming* Manifest Unreasonableness: The Doctrinal Future of Constitutional Review of the Welfare Policy in Hong Kong," *Hong Kong Law Journal* 44, no. 1 (2014): 56. Ip notes: "In letter and spirit, the new test that the *Kong Yunming* Court propounded for gauging the constitutionality of limits on the right to social welfare is narrow, deferential, and devoid of any appeal whatsoever to social ideals." For another view, see Po Jen Yap and Thomas Wong, "Public Welfare and the Judicial Over-Enforcement of Socio-Economic Rights in Hong Kong," *Hong Kong Law Journal* 44, no. 1 (2014): 41.
[104] Chan, "Focus: *Kong Yunming*," p. 2.
[105] Chan, "Focus: *Kong Yunming*," p. 3. Abeyratne observes that the courts have, in recent years, extended this lower standard of review (manifest unreasonableness) beyond the context of socio-economic rights adjudication. See Rehan Abeyratne, "More Structure, More Deference: Proportionality in Hong Kong," in *Proportionality in Asia*, edited by Po Jen Yap (Cambridge: Cambridge University Press, 2020), pp. 45–48.
[106] *QT v. Director of Immigration* (2018) 21 HKCFAR 324.
[107] Lord Walker was sitting as a non-permanent foreign judge on the Hong Kong bench in the *QT* case (*QT v. Director of Immigration* (2018) 21 HKCFAR 324).

discrimination is regarded as particularly objectionable because it disregards the fundamental notion of human dignity and equality before the law."[108] The court confirmed that sexual orientation is among the "core values" or "suspect or prohibited grounds" that are "especially pernicious" as "personal characteristics ... which an individual cannot change ... and which, if used as a ground for discrimination, are recognised as particularly demeaning for the victim."[109]

In *Leung Chun Kwong v. Secretary for the Civil Service*,[110] the CFA held that excluding same-sex couples from civil service spousal benefits and joint tax filing is also discriminatory. Although it did not invoke dignity in its judgment, the court relied on its reasoning in *QT v. Director of Immigration*. Both lower courts had also mentioned dignity, although each had come to a different conclusion.[111] The Court of First Instance had favourably cited Lady Hale's view (citing Ackermann J of the South African Constitutional Court), in *Rodriguez v. Minister of Housing of Gibraltar*, that the impact of the differential treatment in this case "constituted a crass, blunt, cruel and serious invasion of their dignity."[112] Although the Court of Appeal accepted the government's justification for the differential treatment, it also affirmed that "when an individual's fundamental right to equality is engaged on [a] suspect ground such as sexual orientation, the court needs to subject the encroaching measure to stringent scrutiny."[113]

3.3 Right to Transgender Marriage

While the courts have not determined whether "gender identity" also falls within the "core values" category of suspect grounds,[114] the CFA invoked dignity when

---

[108] *QT v. Director of Immigration* (2018), para. 27.

[109] *QT v. Director of Immigration* (2018), para. 107, citing *R (Carson) v. Secretary of State for Work and Pensions* [2006] 1 AC 173, para. 55. The court also cites Iacobucci J in *Law v. Canada (Minister of Employment & Immigration)* [1999] 1 SCR 497: "Human dignity is harmed by unfair treatment premised upon personal traits or circumstances which do not relate to individual needs, capacities, or merits" (as cited in *QT v. Director of Immigration* (2018), fn 137).

[110] *Leung Chun Kwong v. Secretary for the Civil Service* (2019) 22 HKCFAR 282.

[111] *Rodriguez v. Minister of Housing of Gibraltar* [2017] 2 HKLRD 1132.

[112] *Rodriguez v. Minister of Housing of Gibraltar* [2017], para. 55, citing *National Coalition for Gay and Lesbian Equality v. Minister of Home Affairs* [2000] 4 LRC 292, para. 54.

[113] *Leung Chun Kwong v. Secretary for Civil Service* [2018] HKCA 318 (Court of Appeal), para. 127. The Court of First Instance has also invoked dignity when ruling that the exclusion of same-sex couples from public housing designated for "ordinary families" was unconstitutional. See *Infinger v. Hong Kong Housing Authority* [2020] 3 HKC 41, para. 43, quoting *Fok Chun Wa v. Hospital Authority* [2012], para. 77–79.

[114] The Court of First Instance, however, considered whether refusing to allow three transgender men (who had not undergone gender affirmation surgery) to change the gender marker on their identity documents amounted to sex discrimination under the Sex Discrimination Ordinance (Cap. 480). Although the court rejected this argument, it did reiterate the "core values" language and dismissed the government's view that a wide margin of appreciation be granted since gender recognition impacts broad societal interests and socio-economic policy. See *Q v. Commissioner of Registration* [2019] 1 HKLRD 1244, para. 45 and 46, citing *Fok Chun Wa v. Hospital Authority* [2012], para. 76–79.

interpreting the right to marry to include transgender persons.[115] In this sense, dignity functioned expansively. In W v. *Registrar of Marriages*, the majority of the court held that a post-operative transgender woman had the constitutional right to marry in her acquired gender. In support, it cited the European Court of Human Rights, which had explained that "society may be reasonably expected to tolerate a certain inconvenience to enable individuals to live in dignity and worth in accordance with the sexual identity chosen by them at great personal cost."[116] Even the sole dissenting judge in Hong Kong acknowledged the difficulties facing transgender persons and recommended that the government undertake a comprehensive review of relevant legislation. In doing so, he also favourably cited a reference to dignity in a dissenting opinion in another European Court of Human Rights case, *Cossey* v. *United Kingdom*:

> The principle which is basic in human rights and which underlies the various specific rights spelled out in the [European] Convention is respect for human dignity and human freedom. Human dignity and human freedom imply that a man should be free to shape himself and his fate in the way that he deems best fits his personality. A transsexual does use those very fundamental rights. He is prepared to shape himself and his fate.[117]

3.4 The Right to Be Treated with Dignity When Deprived of Liberty

The courts have also considered a number of cases involving Article 6 of the BOR (Art. 10 (1) of the ICCPR), which mandates that "all persons deprived of their liberty ... be treated with humanity and with respect for the inherent dignity of the human person."[118] As noted earlier, this is the only substantive provision in the ICCPR that explicitly mentions dignity. The Human Rights Committee has clarified in its General Comment on Article 10 (1) that this protection of dignity is separate from, but complements the right to be free from torture and other forms of cruel, inhuman, or degrading treatment or punishment in Article 7 (Art. 3 of the Hong Kong BOR):

> Not only may persons deprived of their liberty not be subjected to treatment that is contrary to article 7 ... but neither may they be subjected to any hardship or constraint

---

[115] W v. *Registrar of Marriages* (2013) 16 HKCFAR 112.
[116] *Goodwin* v. *the United Kingdom* (2002) 35 EHRR 18, para. 91 as cited in W v. *Registrar of Marriages* (2013), para. 77(g).
[117] *Cossey* v. *United Kingdom* (1990) 13 EHRR 622, as cited in W v. *Registrar of Marriages* (2013), per Chan PJ in dissent, para. 195.
[118] In *Abid Saeed* v. *Secretary for Justice* [2015] 2 HKC 187, the District Court held that repeated strip searches of the plaintiff had been unlawful and undignified and violated a range of civil rights including Article 6, freedom from cruel, inhuman or degrading treatment, among others. See also *Shafqat Ali* v. *Secretary for Justice* [2013] HKEC 1830.

other than that resulting from the deprivation of liberty; respect for the dignity of such persons must be guaranteed under the same conditions as for that of free persons."[119]

The Hong Kong cases that follow have produced mixed results and represent some missed opportunities for the courts to extend their reasoning about dignity and consider more fully what dignity (or the lack of dignity) means in the situation of incarceration.

In *Navarro Luigi Recasa v. Commissioner of Correctional Services*,[120] a transgender woman, convicted of drug trafficking offences, challenged her treatment in detention. She had not undergone sex reassignment surgery (now frequently referred to as gender affirmation or confirmation surgery), so still had male genitalia, but presented and identified as a woman. She was not allowed to intermingle with female or male prisoners, had been subjected to body searches by male officers, and was denied hormone replacement therapy. She claimed these conditions were unlawful under the Sex Discrimination Ordinance[121] and the Disability Discrimination Ordinance[122] and unconstitutional under various rights in the BOR, including Article 6 as well as the rights to privacy and freedom from cruel, inhuman, degrading treatment or punishment. The government had argued that nonabsolute or nonderogable provisions in the BOR would not apply in the context of detention because of a reservation made to the ICCPR in its application to Hong Kong.[123] The presiding judge, Hartmann J, did not ultimately rule on this point but did express "some reservations."[124] He noted that the right of all persons deprived of their liberty to be treated with humanity and with respect for the inherent dignity of the human person "seems at least to be intended to cover the very circumstances of lawful detention."[125] He added that it is "a far-reaching proposition that a 'restriction' ... even for custodial discipline could permit persons who are lawfully detained by the authorities not to be treated with and with respect for the most basic humanity and human dignity."[126] He ruled, however, that her separation from the prison population was "imposed to protect the very security and safety of [the applicant] and other non-transsexual female inmates. In those measures, [she] had also been treated with dignity and humanity by seeking to protect her from the risks of being seen exposed and harassed by other non-transsexual male [prisoners]."[127]

---

[119] UN Human Rights Committee, ICCPR General Comment No. 21: Article 10 (Humane treatment of persons deprived of their liberty), 1992, para. 3.
[120] *Navarro Luigi Recasa v. Commissioner of Correctional Services* [2018] 4 HKLRD 38.
[121] Cap. 480.
[122] Cap. 487.
[123] Incorporated into section 9 of the BRO: "persons lawfully detained in penal establishments ... are subject to such restrictions as may be authorised by law from time to time for the preservation of ... custodial discipline."
[124] *Navarro Luigi Recasa v. Commissioner of Correctional Services* [2018], para. 139.
[125] *Navarro Luigi Recasa v. Commissioner of Correctional Services* [2018], para. 139.
[126] *Navarro Luigi Recasa v. Commissioner of Correctional Services* [2018], para. 139.
[127] *Navarro Luigi Recasa v. Commissioner of Correctional Services* [2018], para. 153.

A more comprehensive analysis may have also taken into account the effects that isolation from the general prison population can have on a person's dignity, such as the psychological trauma that arises from exclusion from prison life.[128] This may have opened up consideration of other less severe measures that might have been used to ensure her safety instead. For example, the court may have looked to the Yogyakarta Principles, an influential soft-law document which details the application of international human rights law in relation to sexual orientation, gender identity, gender expression, and sex characteristics. This document clarifies that protective measures put in place for "prisoners vulnerable to violence or abuse on the basis of their ... gender identity" must "involve no greater restriction of [the] rights of [transgender persons] than is experienced by the general prison population" and that "protective" solitary confinement may amount to unjustifiable harm on the grounds of gender identity.[129]

On the other hand, the court held that a requirement that body searches be conducted by an officer of the same sex – which meant the applicant was searched by a male officer – could violate Article 6 if applied too stringently. It explained that this rule was only general and that police officers have discretion to determine how a search should be conducted lawfully, considering all relevant circumstances including "the need to protect the detained person's fundamental human rights to respect to dignity and privacy."[130] A strip search by a male officer of an inmate who identifies as female would be prima facie interference with both the rights to privacy and dignity. The court suggested the authorities develop guidelines related to custody searches of pre-operative transgender prisoners.

Leung Kwok Hung (also known as "Long Hair") v. Commissioner of Correctional Services[131] also involved the rights of prisoners. In this case, the Court of First Instance missed opportunities to consider the possible connections between dignity and political identity in greater depth. The applicant claimed that a policy requiring the cutting of male (but not female) prisoners' hair was a violation of their right to be treated with dignity in prison according to Article 6 of the BOR. Although at first instance, and eventually before the CFA, the applicant succeeded on the basis of provisions in Sex Discrimination Ordinance, the court rejected the argument that cutting a male prisoner's hair undermines human dignity as understood in Article 6.[132] The applicant

---

[128] See Douglas Routh, Gassan Abess, Davis Makin, Mary K. Stohr, Craig Hemmens, and Jihye Yoo, "Transgender Inmates in Prisons: A Review of Applicable Statutes and Policies," *International Journal of Offender Therapy and Comparative Criminology* 61, no. 6 (2017): 650–651.

[129] The Yogyakarta Principles and the Yogyakarta Principles Plus 10, Principle 9 Relating to the Right to Treatment with Humanity while in Detention, available at https://yogyakartaprinciples.org/principles-en/.

[130] *Navarro Luigi Recasa v. Commissioner of Correctional Services* [2018], para. 222.

[131] [2017] 1 HKLRD 1041 (Court of First Instance).

[132] The Court of Appeal did not consider arguments related to dignity which had not been cross appealed by the applicant. *Leung Kwok Hung v. Commissioner of Correctional Services* [2018] 2 HKLRD 933. It did allow the Commissioner of Correctional Services' appeal of the sex discrimination decision, overturning the Court of First Instance's ruling that the haircut requirement

had contended that the general public recognized his long hair as part of his identity as a prominent political activist and that cutting it "amounts to a particularly serious insult to his dignity."[133] The court stated that there was no basis "to suggest that the hair-cutting requirement for male prisoners would undermine 'the inherent dignity of the human person.'"[134] It distinguished Leung's case from the European Court of Human Rights' decision in *Yankov v. Bulgaria*[135] that the forced shaving of a prisoner's hair violated a similar provision in the European Convention on Human Rights.

The court did not appear to take Hong Kong's political context or Long Hair's identity as a political activist into consideration. A forced haircut for no justifiable reason might very well engage the dignity of a person like him whose hair is so inextricably bound up with his political identity. An apt analogy is the connection between hair and a Sikh's religious or cultural identity. In many jurisdictions, prison officials make exceptions that allow Sikhs to keep their long hair and wear a turban when incarcerated. It is worth noting that "political opinion," like "religion," is a prohibited ground of discrimination in Articles 1 and 22 of the BOR (Art. 2 (1) and 26 of the ICCPR). Dignity could play a role when courts consider how best to balance the needs for prison conformity and discipline and unjustifiable restrictions on individual prisoners' rights.

3.5 *Human Trafficking and Slavery*

In ZN v. *Secretary for Justice and Others*,[136] the Court of First Instance held that the lack of a government policy dealing with human trafficking violated Article 4 of the BOR (Article 8 of the ICCPR), which prohibits slavery or forced or compulsory labour. The court used dignity to expand the scope of Article 4 to include human trafficking. In doing so, Zervos J stated that "human trafficking in all its forms is unquestionably an affront to human dignity and a denial or curtailment of personal autonomy from which springs the most fundamental human rights and freedoms."[137] In coming to this conclusion, the court cited the UDHR[138] and the European Court of Human Rights, which had held that "there can be no doubt that trafficking threatens the human dignity and fundamental freedoms of its victims and cannot be considered compatible with a democratic society and the values

---

discriminated on the basis of sex. The CFA, however, reversed this and held the requirement violated the Sex Discrimination Ordinance. *Leung Kwok Hung v. Commissioner of Correctional Services* [2020] HKCFA 37 (CFA). Neither the Court of Appeal nor the CFA revisited the dignity arguments based on Article 6.

[133] *Leung Kwok Hung v. Commissioner of Correctional Services* [2017] (Court of First Instance), para. 112.
[134] *Leung Kwok Hung v. Commissioner of Correctional Services* [2017] (Court of First Instance), para. 114.
[135] *Yankov v. Bulgaria* (2005) 40 EHRR 36, cited in *Leung Kwok Hung v. Commissioner of Correctional Services* [2017] (Court of First Instance), para. 113–114.
[136] *ZN v. Secretary for Justice and Others* [2016] HKCU 3130.
[137] *ZN v. Secretary for Justice and Others* [2016], para. 4.
[138] *ZN v. Secretary for Justice and Others* [2016], para. 170.

expounded in the Convention."¹³⁹ The Court of Appeal reversed this decision, however, and the CFA rejected the applicant's appeal.¹⁴⁰ The CFA construed the prohibition of slavery more narrowly, excluding human trafficking from its ambit, and characterized the European Court of Human Rights' references to dignity as having used an overly "broad brush." Although the higher courts ultimately rejected the Court of First Instance's conclusions, the case nevertheless highlights dignity's potential to clarify the meaning of an additional ICCPR right.

3.6 Other Opportunities

The cases discussed reveal gaps, but they also suggest opportunities for construing a more diverse collection of constitutional rights with reference to dignity. Indeed, the use of dignity in many jurisdictions is often evolutionary, and the growing global judicial dialogue about dignity may well influence the direction of Hong Kong's human rights jurisprudence.

One area that has not yet been, but could be, explored is the relationship between dignity and the right to life as expressed in Article 2 of the BOR (Art. 6 of the ICCPR). The UN Human Rights Committee has interpreted this provision expansively to include a range of socio-economic interests. In its General Comment 36, the Committee explains that the "right to life ... should not be interpreted narrowly. It concerns the entitlement of individuals to ... enjoy a life with dignity."¹⁴¹ Such scope creates duties on the state "to take appropriate measures to address the general conditions in society that may give rise to direct threats to life or prevent individuals from enjoying their right to life with dignity."¹⁴² Measures may be needed to tackle a range of issues, such as "high levels of criminal and gun violence, pervasive traffic and industrial accidents, degradation of the environment ... extensive substance abuse, widespread hunger and malnutrition and extreme poverty and homelessness."¹⁴³ The General Comment also mentions access "to essential goods and services such as food, water, shelter, health-care, electricity and sanitation ... bolstering of effective emergency health services, emergency response operations ... and social housing programs."¹⁴⁴

Hong Kong courts have rarely invoked the right to life, however.¹⁴⁵ The Court of First Instance heard, but dismissed, a judicial review application challenging

---

¹³⁹ ZN v. *Secretary for Justice and Others* [2016], para. 250, citing *Rantsev v. Cyprus & Russia* (2010) 51 EHRR 1.
¹⁴⁰ ZN v. *Secretary for Justice and Others* [2018] HKCA 473 (Court of Appeal); ZN v. *Secretary for Justice and Others* (2020) 23 HKCFAR 15 (CFA).
¹⁴¹ UN Human Rights Committee, General Comment No. 36: Article 6 (right to life), CCPR/C/GC/36, September 2018, para. 3.
¹⁴² Human Rights Committee, General Comment No. 36, para. 26.
¹⁴³ Human Rights Committee, General Comment No. 36, para. 26.
¹⁴⁴ Human Rights Committee, General Comment No. 36, para. 26.
¹⁴⁵ In other jurisdictions, dignity has contributed to the reasoning in cases involving the death penalty, but Hong Kong formally abolished capital punishment in 1993 and has not carried out an execution since 1966.

government policies on air pollution.[146] The applicants claimed that policy responses had failed to ensure the best possible healthcare to Hong Kong residents and argued for a broad construction of the right to life. Hartmann J declined to extend the right to life beyond the context of detention, trial, and punishment. Again, he carved out socio-economic rights, ruling that the executive and legislative branches of government have "wide discretion" to "make difficult decisions in respect of competing social and economic priorities."[147] Drawing on an expansive notion of dignity to construe the right to life, consistent with a purposive approach and taking the Human Rights Committee's position into consideration, might have allowed a fuller evaluation of the issues.

As with the right to life, dignity may also assist in increasing the scope of civil and political rights related to democracy and political participation. The Court of First Instance set the stage in *Chan Kin Sum v. Secretary for Justice*,[148] when ruling that limitations on prisoners' right to vote were unconstitutional. In doing so, it favourably cited the South African Constitutional Court, which noted that "the vote of each and every citizen is a badge of dignity and of personhood. Quite literally, it says that everybody counts."[149] Dignity is also associated with democracy beyond procedural rights. As Schachter explains:

> Respect for the dignity and worth of all persons, and for their individual choices, leads, broadly speaking, to a strong emphasis on the will and consent of the governed. It means that the coercive rule of one or the few over the many is incompatible with a due respect for the dignity of the person.[150]

According to Dupré, "a new type of democracy" that has emerged since World War II, "with respect for human dignity at its heart," and this new type has challenged "a purely procedural, i.e. majoritarian democracy."[151] She adds, therefore, that "the concept of human dignity is much more than the individual (intuitive and elusive) sense of self-respect and respect of others, it positions human beings at the heart of democracy, determining thus the exercise of political power."[152]

---

[146] *Clean Air Foundation Ltd & Another v. Government of HKSAR* [2007] HKEC 1356.
[147] *Clean Air Foundation Ltd & Another v. Government of HKSAR* [2007].
[148] *Chan Kin Sum v. Secretary for Justice* [2009] 2 HKLRD 166.
[149] Para. 181, citing *August v Electoral Commission* 1999 (3) SA 1, para. 17. The Hong Kong court also cited the Canadian Supreme Court in *Sauvé v. Canada (Chief Electoral Officer)* [2002] 3 SCR 519, which had also referenced the South African Court's explanation of dignity and democracy. For a discussion of the issue in Hong Kong prior to the CFI's decision, see Wing Hong Chui, "Prisoners' Right to Vote in Hong Kong: A Human Rights Perspective," *Asian Journal of Social Science* 35, no. 2 (2007): 170–194.
[150] Schachter, "Human Dignity as a Normative Concept," p. 850.
[151] Catherine Dupré, "Dignity, Democracy, Civilisation," *Liverpool Law Review* 33 (2012): 264, citing Peter Häberle, *Europäische Verfassungslehre*, 6th ed. (Baden–Baden: Nomos, 2002), p. 289.
[152] Catherine Dupré, "Dignity, Democracy, Civilisation," citing Peter Häberle, *Europäische Verfassungslehre*.

This type of democracy mandates nondiscriminatory inclusion for everyone in all areas of life, including political activity. The right to equality in international human rights law requires remedies for de facto discrimination such as the removal of systemic barriers to participation for certain marginalized groups. As discussed, greater attention to context can reveal the existence of such disparities. Other rights that support democracy include the freedoms of association, assembly, expression, and belief and religion, among others. For example, the Human Rights Committee has clarified that the right to peaceful assembly "together with other related rights ... constitutes the very foundation of a system of participatory governance based on democracy, human rights, the rule of law and pluralism."[153] Similarly, the Canadian Supreme Court, in a case concerning hate speech, made the connection between dignity, human rights, and democracy:

> Freedom of expression is a crucial aspect of the democratic commitment, not merely because it permits the best policies to be chosen from among a wide array of proffered options, but additionally because it helps to ensure that participation in the political process is open to all persons. *Such open participation must involve to a substantial degree the notion that all persons are equally deserving of respect and dignity.*[154]

Inclusion also demands attention to socio-economic rights. In the context of South Africa, Liebenberg notes that

> access to basic social services is crucial not only to people's physical survival, but also to enable the development of their potential to shape their own lives and to be active agents in the shaping of our new society. Human dignity as a relational concept requires society to respect the equal worth of the poor by marshalling its resources to redress the conditions that perpetuate their marginalization.[155]

4 CONCLUSIONS

Hong Kong courts have used dignity as a constitutional value to both expand and restrict the scope of rights. Although judicial reasoning about dignity is still evolving, some elements of the jurisprudence discussed in this chapter suggest possibilities for a more holistic approach. Taking account of certain contextual factors could enable the development of a "spacious" view of dignity that cuts across and connects civil, political, economic, social, and cultural rights. These include the universal nature of dignity, its function as a foundational principle in international human rights law, and domestic constitutional, social, economic, and political features. The Hong Kong jurisprudence has developed within a constitutional framework and

---

[153] UN Human Rights Committee, General Comment No. 37, Article 21: Right of Peaceful Assembly, CCPR/C/GC/37, September 2020, para. 1.
[154] *R v. Keegstra* [1990] 3 SCR 697, para. 764 (emphasis added).
[155] Liebenberg, "The Value of Human Dignity in Interpreting Socio-Economic Rights," p. 1.

culture that embraces universal values and illustrates the internalization of globally recognized norms. As a result, Hong Kong is well placed to contribute to the convergence of norms and transnational judicial conversations about dignity in the human rights arena.[156]

Despite this outward-looking orientation, however, the principle of "One Country, Two Systems" may also produce countervailing tensions that influence the Hong Kong rights jurisprudence. Striking the right balance is often a fraught exercise. In particular, perceived threats to Hong Kong's autonomy may cause courts to use dignity strategically to buttress judicial independence and distinguish Hong Kong's legal system and culture from that of mainland China. It could also support deference and limit judicial discretion, however, in an attempt to pre-empt an interpretation of the Basic Law by the National People's Congress Standing Committee that would be binding on Hong Kong courts. Indeed, as the relationship between Hong Kong and Beijing continues to develop, dignity reasoning may highlight conflicts among potentially competing values; it may also further clarify and refine the nature of Hong Kong's "high degree of autonomy." As Ghai points out, one of Hong Kong's key distinguishing characteristics vis-à-vis mainland China is its perception of human rights ... as "inherent in individuals, whether derived from some higher law or essential to human dignity (and therefore universal and inalienable)."[157]

---

[156] For a discussion of dignity and judicial dialogue, see Jackson, "Constitutional Dialogue and Human Dignity: States and Transnational Constitutional Discourse"; and Holning Lau and Hillary Li, "American Equal Protection and Global Convergence," *Fordham Law Review* 86, no. 3 (2017): 1251–1302.

[157] Yash Ghai, *Hong Kong's New Constitutional Order: The Resumption of Chinese Sovereignty and the Basic Law* (Hong Kong: Hong Kong University Press, 1998), p. 401.

8

Human Dignity and Relational Constitutionalism in Singapore

Li-ann Thio

1 INTRODUCTION

In contemporary legal thinking, the idea of "human dignity" carries the weight of an axiomatic proposition; it has been constitutionalized in various jurisdictions as a fundamental value[1] and internationalized as the basis of universal and regional human rights law.[2] It is a subject of philosophical and theological enquiry, as well as broader parliamentary and public discourse;[3] it is rhetorically invoked to advance ideological agendas and operates as an interpretive principle giving rise to varied meanings[4] within adjudicatory settings[5].

"Human dignity" is a concept with rich antecedents in and beyond the Euro-American world; however, its content remains indeterminate and contested. It seeks to prevent and remedy dignitary harms; it may implicate obligations of self-restraint, reciprocal duties to recognize and respect others. Universally appealing yet ambiguous, it may be misused as an empty container to serve the political cause *du jour*. In apprehending how "human dignity" is understood and used, much turns on the

---

[1] Article 1(1). German Grundgesetz; Articles 39(f), 51A(c) Constitution of India; Article 38, Constitution of the People's Republic of China; Article 24, Constitution of Japan; see Doron Shulztiner and Guy E. Carmi, "Human Dignity in National Constitutions: Functions, Promises and Dangers,"*American Journal of Comparative Law* 62, no. 2 (Spring 2014): 461–490.

[2] The Universal Declaration of Human Rights refers to dignity five times: twice in the Preamble and in Articles 1, 22, and 23(3). The ASEAN Human Rights Declaration (2012) refers to dignity once in the Preamble and in Article 1. See Jeremy Waldron, "Is Dignity the Foundation of Human Rights," *New York University Public Law and Legal Theory Working Papers*, Paper 374 (2013), http://lsr.nellco.org/nyu_plltwp/374.

[3] Matthias Mahlmann, "Human Dignity and Autonomy in Modern Constitutional Orders," in *Oxford Handbook of Comparative Constitutional Law*, edited by Michel Rosenfeld and András Sajó (Oxford: Oxford University Press, 2012), pp. 371–396.

[4] Christopher McCrudden, "Human Dignity and Judicial Interpretation of Human Rights," *European Journal of International Law* 19, no. 4 (July 2008): 655–724.

[5] See generally Marcus Duwell, Jens Braarvig, Roger Brownsword, and Dietmar Mieth, eds., *The Cambridge Handbook of Human Dignity: Interdisciplinary Perspectives* (Cambridge: Cambridge University Press, 2014).

understanding of what it means to be human[6] and what human flourishing constitutes. In a plural, postmodern world, this enquiry elicits competitor visions.

Two primary conceptions of human dignity may be identified: the first is associated with the contemporary human rights movement. Human dignity is foundational to the architecture of the universal human rights regime; "in the shadow of genocide the light of human dignity shone forth," heralding the advent of "dignitarian constitutionalism"[7] and equal rights. Where the dominant vision of human rights embodies a brand of liberal individualism,[8] a liberal-humanistic conception of human dignity is an individual-oriented norm predicated on the intrinsic worth of individuals who have autonomist,[9] experimental, and choice-oriented dispositions. This sustains a rights-generating egalitarian vision of human dignity, where the liberal "neutral" state facilitates human agency and capabilities and where individuals determine "the good life." The voluntarist metric of individual autonomy measures the realization of human dignity by the capacity to make choices one considers highly important. In respecting human dignity, the state should refrain from curtailing human rights unless restrictive measures are reasonable or proportionate.

Three caveats are apposite: firstly, the liberal state is not neutral but advances its own liberal ideology of the good; it seeks not only to protect but to constitute liberal citizens. In prescriptive and descriptive terms, this does not exhaust the range of state–citizen relations within modern constitutional democracies. Other philosophies hold that certain choices should not be chosen, that any theory of choice has limits.[10] In valorizing *choice*, the idea that society can champion a *chosen* norm is rejected, which is itself an ideological position. Second, human rights law transcends autonomy-maximizing negative rights to encompass positive state action to secure basic material needs[11] or respect for intangible individual and group identity claims, portending a clash of values. Third, where dignity is understood as the basis

---

[6] For example, is an unborn child or fetus recognized as having human dignity and the right to life, or is it a thing subject to reproductive autonomy?
[7] Samuel Moyn, "The Secret History of Constitutional Dignity," *Yale Human Rights and Development Journal* 17, no. 1 (2014): 40.
[8] Makau Mutua, "The Ideology of Human Rights," *Virginia Journal of International Law* 36 (Spring 1996): 589.
[9] Oscar Schachter, "Human Dignity as a Normative Concept," *American Journal of International Law* 77, no. 4 (October 1983): 848.
[10] For example, while same-sex marriage in some jurisdictions is considered a dignity-based right of privacy or respect for differences based on lifestyle liberationism, religions like Islam see this as contrary to its view, shared by the Abrahamic religions, that "human dignity is marriage of a man and a woman." See Miklos Maroth, *"Human Dignity in the Islamic World,"* in *The Cambridge Handbook of Human Dignity: Interdisciplinary Perspectives,* edited by Marcus Duwell, Jens Braarvig, Roger Brownsword, and Dietmar Mieth (Cambridge: Cambridge University Press, 2014), pp. 155–162.
[11] "Transforming Our World: The 2030 Agenda for Sustainable Development," G.A. Res 70/1 of September 25, 2015, provides: "We are determined to end poverty and hunger, in all their forms and dimensions, and to ensure that all human beings can fulfil their potential in dignity and equality and in a healthy environment."

for the full moral status of human beings, the intrinsic worth of an individual may rest on theological or humanistic bases, such as the Judeo-Christian idea of *imago dei/tzelem Elohim*[12] or the Kantian vision of treating human beings, possessed of rationality,[13] as ends not means. These factors caution against assuming that human dignity is "inextricably linked to a liberal-individualist view of human beings as people whose life-choices deserve respect."[14] Alternative theistic visions of dignity such as *imago dei i* postulate the existence of transcendent values beyond liberalism's predilection to freedom, fueling the constitutionalist idea of restraints on government;[15] secular humanists may demur and argue against the anti-egalitarian bent of certain theocratic visions of human dignity that do not translate into equal rights for men and women.[16] One's worldview will determine one's vision of human dignity.

While the first conception is a universal attribute of personhood, the second conception is an aspect of social relationship, relating to an elevated status or rank within a hierarchically ordered society. Deference is owed to a person of high rank or office who possesses some ideal of moral virtue, personal excellence, or other social merit. This sustains an ethos of elitism,[17] where dignity is not inherent but ascribed to a social role or something attained.[18] It is socially embedded and resonates with the Roman idea of *dignitas*, of having an elevated social status commanding special honor. In this nonliberal or communitarian setting that may be based on religious or secular constitutionalism, human dignity is differentiated, a form of relational property possessed by individuals. Individual autonomy is not valorized in constructing and interpreting rights and

---

[12] Caritas Singapore, "Dignity of the Human Person," at www.caritas-singapore.org/catholic-social-teaching/cst-human-person/#.WkINqzcRWUk. In the Ancient Near East, only the king and his offspring had the exalted stage of being made in the image of God, legitimating their right to rule. Judaism democratizes this idea by pointing to the glory of the human race: Yair Lorberbaum, "Human Dignity in the Jewish Tradition," in *The Cambridge Handbook of Human Dignity: Interdisciplinary Perspectives*, edited by Marcus Duwell, Jens Braarvig, Roger Brownsword, and Dietmar Mieth (Cambridge: Cambridge University Press, 2014), pp. 135–144; Joshua A. Berman, *Created Equal: How the Bible Broke with Ancient Political Thought* (Oxford: Oxford University Press, 2008).

[13] This opens up questions of whether unborn persons, the mentally handicapped, or comatose persons possess dignity.

[14] David Feldman, "Human Dignity as a Legal Value," *Public Law* (1999): 685.

[15] This "faith in the worth of each human being" flows from "the Christian doctrine of personality. The insistence upon the individual as the final value, the emphasis upon the transcendental importance of each man's soul, creates an insoluble conflict with any sort of absolutism." Carl J. Friedrich, *Limited Government: A Comparison* (Hoboken, NJ: Prentice-Hall, 1974), pp. 12–13.

[16] Article 6, OIC Cairo Declaration of Human Rights in Islam, states: "Woman is equal to man in human dignity" but not in equal rights. This conception of human dignity is theocentric ("The true religion is the guarantee for enhancing such dignity along the path to human integrity").

[17] Jeremy Waldron and Meir Dan-Cohen, *Dignity, Rank and Rights* (Oxford: Oxford University Press, 2012).

[18] For example, a dignified person is one who follows the Dao: Qing-Ju Qiao, "Dignity in Traditional Chinese Daoism," in *The Cambridge Handbook of Human Dignity: Interdisciplinary Perspectives*, edited by Marcus Duwell, Jens Braarvig, Roger Brownsword, and Dietmar Mieth (Cambridge: Cambridge University Press, 2014), pp. 182–188.

choice prerogatives. Further, rather than being "neutral," governments in non-liberal states actively espouse a communal vision of the good based on factors like national identity and religious or moral solidarity.[19] This, however, raises concerns about state paternalism.

Most constitutional orders are "mixed," having both liberal and nonliberal elements. This is not to treat the "constitution" as a purely descriptive term but to broaden the ambit of constitutionalism beyond liberal constitutional orders.[20] Mixing liberal and nonliberal elements to attain a "principled constitutional mixture" of "rival legitimacy principles"[21] serves the constitutionalist goal of constraining absolute rulers or rules of every persuasion and of articulating and realizing fundamental principles and objectives through norms, institutions, and processes.

Context is key as an understanding of human dignity draws on the worldview or political philosophy and sociopolitical matrix within which it operates as a public value. This chapter explores how human dignity is apprehended as a public value within the Singapore constitutional order, to contribute to the global discourse on human dignity, pluralizing the concept to better understand what it means, as well as how and why it is invoked in Asia and beyond. The Constitution, based on the Westminster system of parliamentary government, with autochthonous modifications, makes no explicit reference to "human dignity." However, while chary of the politicized misuses of human rights, the government has endorsed the Universal Declaration of Human Rights, which identifies human dignity as a foundational idea.[22] In additional to parliamentary debates and civil society discourse, "human dignity" has been directly or indirectly invoked in constitutional rights and criminal law cases.

Singapore's Constitution may be described as a communitarian one, with statist and liberal elements;[23] the parliamentary executive secured eighty-three of eighty-nine elective seats after the 2015 general election and faces no real constraint in driving its agenda and in amending and proactively developing the Constitution[24]

---

[19] Graham Walker, "The Idea of Nonliberal Constitutionalism," *Ethnicity and Group Rights* 39 (1997): 154–184.

[20] Li-ann Thio, "Constitutionalism in Illiberal Polities," in *The Oxford Handbook of Comparative Constitutional Law*, edited by Michel Rosenfeld and András Sajó (Oxford: Oxford University Press, 2012), pp. 133–152.

[21] Graham Walker, "The New Mixed Constitution: A Response to Liberal Debility & Constitutional Deadlock in Eastern Europe," *Polity* 26, no. 3 (Spring 1994): 503–515.

[22] Foreign Minister Wong Kan Seng, "The Real World of Human Rights," Speech, Vienna World Conference on Human Rights 1993, reproduced in [1993] SJLS 605.

[23] See Li-ann Thio, "We Are Feeling Our Way Forward, Step by Step," in *Constitutionalism in Asia in the Early Twenty-First Century*, edited by Albert H. Y. Chen (Cambridge: Cambridge University Press, 2014), pp. 270–294; Li-ann Thio, "Principled Pragmatism and the 'Third Wave' of Communitarian Judicial Review in Singapore," in *Constitutional Interpretation in Singapore: Theory and Practice*, edited by Jaclyn L. Neo (Abingdon, UK: Routledge, 2016), pp. 75–116.

[24] Article 5(2) of the Singapore Constitution provides that a two-thirds parliamentary majority is generally required to alter the Constitution.

as a "living document,"[25] aside from parliamentary scrutiny and public debate. While constitutional rights are justiciable entitlements, the judiciary avoids activist values-based interpretive approaches, as social engineering and juristocracy is considered anathema to the rule of law and separation of powers.[26] In favoring a "green light" approach toward judicial review, the judiciary, rather than combatively checking the executive, seeks to encourage good governance "through the political process and public avenues."[27]

"Human dignity" and cognate ideas like honor, integrity, benevolence, and moral virtue have been invoked in the context of Singapore public law, in both the streams of "dignity as autonomy" and "dignity as status." As human dignity essentially relates to the question of how we should treat each other, this is influenced by the confluence of political, cultural, economic, and other factors that shape social relationships.[28] Equal and special dignity may coexist, insofar as all citizens have inherent or equal dignity, while individuals occupying certain social positions or offices, like judges, may be accorded special dignity in the form of privileges and immunities. In addition, within Singapore's secular state and multireligious society, what may be described as a form of "relational constitutionalism" is practiced. This views the function of a constitution as not only to constrain government power but to promote

> the relational well-being of individuals and groups and to preserve sustainable relationships in a polity where disparate religious groups and their members are able to co-exist, maintain their distinct identities, while being unified by a national identity and a shared commitment to the common good.[29]

The government actively articulates the common good, fundamental values relating to humanity and solidarity, most notably in the shared values white paper;[30] certain

---

[25] PM Lee Hsien Loong, Parliamentary Debate on the Constitution (Amendment) Bill, November 8, 2016.

[26] Li-ann Thio, "Between Apology and Apogee, Autochthony: The Rule of Law beyond the Rules of Law in Singapore," *Singapore Journal of Legal Studies* (July 2012): 269. See *Mohammad Faizal bin Sabtu v. Public Prosecutor* [2012] SGHC 163 at [16].

[27] *Jeyaretnam Kenneth Andrew v. AG* [2014] 1 SLR 345 at [48], quoting an extra-judicial article by former chief justice Chan Sek Keong, "Judicial Review – From Angst to Empathy," *Singapore Academy of Law Journal* 22, no. 2 (September 2010): 469.

[28] If an anti-corruption law were read as requiring the government to "keep surveillance on Singaporeans wherever in the world they might live or work," this would connote an Orwellian, paternalistic state, demeaning "the nobility of Parliament and the dignity of citizenship." Karthigesu JA, *Taw Cheng Kong v. PP* [1998] SGHC 10 at [62]. This judicial statement observes that, to maintain dignity, the state should not be over-interventionist.

[29] Li-ann Thio, "Relational Constitutionalism and the Management of Religious Disputes: The Singapore 'Secularism with a Soul' Model," *Oxford Journal of Law and Religion* 1, no. 2 (October 2012): 446–469. For an alternative view of relational justice as nurturing subordinate political voices, see Peggy Cooper Davis, "Towards a Relational Constitutionalism," in *Dignity, Freedom and the Apartheid Legal Order: The Critical Jurisprudence of Laurie Ackermann*, edited by A.J. Barnard-Naudé, Drucilla Cornell, and François du Bois (Cape Town: Juta Law, 2008), pp. 239–253.

[30] Cmd 1 of 1991 (Parliament of Singapore).

ones, such as "racial and religious harmony," are regularly referenced or reflected in constitutional practice; these articulated norms serve as "soft constitutional law,"[31] a form of formally nonbinding but influential norms that are widely publicized and shape expectations of how constitutional actors should act.

In affecting how these actors relate to each other through the lens of a commitment to communitarianism and relationism, the issue of human dignity in various incarnations is implicated and explored in this chapter. One may reflect on the capacity of human dignity to function as the cornerstone for the universal human rights discourse, where the dominant vision is couched in particularist, liberal terms. Indeed, insofar as liberal democracy is presented as the "end of history," Singapore strikes a discordant note, manifesting a form of "paternal democracy" that adapts to the changing nature of governor–governed relationships. Once authoritarian and increasingly communitarian, having secured First World levels of development Singapore did not choose a "liberal" model of human dignity within its constitutional order but evolved its own autochthonous blend of liberal and nonliberal elements, according varying emphasis to values of autonomy, identity, moral solidarity, and honor.

Section 2 sets the political and cultural context of Singapore, examining how human dignity operates beyond the courts in public discourse and how it operates in relation to relational constitutionalism; Section 3 examines relevant case law. Section 4 offers concluding observations.

2 THE POLITICAL AND CULTURAL CONTEXT OF SINGAPORE AND HUMAN DIGNITY

2.1 *The Evolving Political-Legal Culture and Changing Mode of Governance: Father, Elder Brother, Servant Leader?*

Singapore is a secular democracy with a multiracial and multireligious society.[32] Some have pejoratively described it as having an "authoritarian constitution,"[33] where considerations of utility, in having an efficient, effective government, predominate over ideals. After seceding on August 9, 1965, from the Malaysian Federation, this "improbable nation"[34] certainly focused on economic development.

---

[31] Li-ann Thio, "Soft Constitutional Law in Non-Liberal Asian Constitutional Democracies," *International Journal of Constitutional Law* 8, no.4 (October 2010): 766–799.
[32] Singapore is the most religiously diverse country in the world according to a 2014 Pew Research Centre report. According to the Singapore Demographics Profile 2018, the religious composition is: Buddhist (33.9 percent); Christian (18.2 percent); Muslim (14.3 percent); Hindu (5.2 percent); Other Faiths (9.7%); and Religiously Unaffiliated (16.4 percent). Its population is approximately 5.9 million people, as of January 2018: "Singapore Population," http://countrymeters.info/en/Singapore#religion.
[33] Mark Tushnet, "Authoritarian Constitutionalism," *Cornell Law Review* 100, no. 2 (2015): 391.
[34] Sundaresh Menon, "The Rule of Law: The Path to Exceptionalism," *Singapore Academy of Law Journal* 28, no. 2 (September 2016): 413, para. 3.

This was driven by Prime Minister Lee Kuan Yew's "authoritarian pragmatism"[35] which was "cloaked in anti-ideological garb" where philosophical schemes were eschewed and pragmatic realism preferred.[36]

From Independence until 1981 when it lost a byelection, the People's Action Party (PAP) commanded a parliamentary monopoly; it was interventionist and unabashedly paternalistic in its version of an elective dictatorship. This was reflected in national campaigns, from the 1970s onward, directing Singaporeans how to conduct their lives in relation to population growth ("girl or boy, two is enough"),[37] public health ("let's not feed the pigeons, they bring disease";[38] "don't urinate in lifts";[39] "don't bring AIDS home" and "no spitting"[40]) and prohibitive rules governing the minutiae of life (chewing gum bans, prescribed hair lengths for men), as an antidote to Western "hippie culture."[41]

Buoyed by self-confidence and economic achievement, the government in the 1990s became known on the international stage as one of the most vocal proponents of the "Asian values" or trade-off theory, articulated in rarefied diplomatic discourse.[42] This posits that, in the early stages of a country's development, social discipline and political stability, entailing the curtailment of civil-political rights, should be prioritized over democracy and expressive freedoms, in order to provide a legal environment conducive to foreign investment and trade within an export-oriented economy. Economic growth, it was argued, was foundational to "any system that claims to advance human dignity" anchored by the "order and stability needed for development."[43] The government anticipated that with economic growth and a more literate and demanding citizenry, the balance would be adjusted to cater to increased demands for political participation.

The localized expression of the internationalized Asian values debate was comprehensively concretized in the 1991 shared values white paper, authored by the

---

[35] Carlton Tan, "Lee Kuan Yew Leaves a Legacy of Authoritarian Pragmatism," *The Guardian*, March 23, 2015, www.theguardian.com/world/2015/mar/23/lee-kuan-yews-legacy-of-authoritarian-pragmatism-will-serve-singapore-well.
[36] Mark Jacobson, "The Singapore Solution," *National Geographic*, January 2010, www.nationalgeographic.com/magazine/2010/01/singapore-malaysia-indonesia/.
[37] "Two Is Enough: Salleh Sariman," www.iremember.sg/index.php/2014/07/two-is-enough-salleh-sariman/.
[38] Tiziano Terzani, *A Fortune Teller Told Me: Earthbound Travels in the Far East* (London: Flamingo, 1997), p. 157.
[39] Clement Yap, "Woman caught urinating in Pinnacle lift," *AsiaOne*, 20 June 2014, www.asiaone.com/singapore/woman-caught-urinating-pinnacle-lift-0.
[40] It is an offence under Section 17(1)(g) to "spit any substance or expel mucus from the nose upon or onto any street or any public place": Environmental Public Health Act (Cap 95).
[41] The 1992 ban on chewing gum was lifted in 2004: "Singapore Loosens 12-Year Chewing Gum Ban," Associated Press, May 26, 2004, www.nbcnews.com/id/5066384/ns/world_news-weird_news/t/singapore-loosens-year-chewing-gum-ban/#.XuM-WEUzYa4.
[42] Francis Fukuyama, "Asia's Soft Authoritarian Alternative," *New Perspectives Quarterly* 9, no.2 (Spring 1992): 60.
[43] Seng, "The Real World of Human Rights."

government in a prescriptive fashion as "a national ideology which Singaporeans of all races and faiths can subscribe to and live by." This was a response to concerns that "traditional Asian ideas of morality, duty and society" were "giving way to a more Westernized, individualistic and self-centered outlook on life."[44] While Singapore was open and cosmopolitan in orientation, the cultural heritage of each community needed to be preserved, as did "certain common values which capture the essence of being a Singaporean." To proactively and consciously develop a "coherent Singaporean identity,"[45] five values were proposed to enable future generations to "prosper and live in peace among themselves"[46] and regional neighbors:

1) Nation before community and society above self
2) Family as the basic unit of society
3) Regard and community support for the individual
4) Consensus instead of contention
5) Racial and religious harmony

This white paper was subject to parliamentary debate but not popular consultation, as was typical of policymaking in the 1990s. It advocated socially conservative values like the upholding of the traditional family as the basic unit of society[47] and "trusting" political leaders as Confucian *junzi* (gentlemen) rather than treating them as Humean knaves pursuant to the "liberalism of fear"[48] that dominates Western constitutionalism.

Some of these principles have become influential and acquired the status of "soft constitutional law," influencing the conduct of government-citizens and between citizens and shaping the content of constitutional concepts like "public order," particularly in the context of regulating religious expression and activity. Indeed, this executive reading of the scope of religious freedom has been elaborated in the Maintenance of Religious Harmony white paper of 1989,[49] and it is regularly referenced in the event of incidents implicating religious freedoms and order, as

[44] Cmd 1 of 1991 (Parliament of Singapore), para. 2.
[45] Ibid., para. 3.
[46] Ibid., para. 6.
[47] "In recent decades many developed societies have witnessed a trend towards heavier reliance on the state to take care of the aged, and more permissible social mores, such as increasing acceptance of 'alternative lifestyles,' casual sexual relationships and single parenthood. The result has been to weaken the family unit. Singapore should not follow these untested fashions uncritically." Ibid., para. 13. In 2007, the prime minister stated that "by 'family' in Singapore, we mean one man, one woman, marrying, having children and bringing up children within the framework of a stable family unit." 83 Singapore Parliament Reports, Penal Code (Amendment) Bill, October 23, 2007, col 2354 ff.
[48] Judith N. Shklar, *Political Thought and Political Thinkers*, edited by Stanley Hoffman (Chicago, IL: University of Chicago Press, 1998), p. 3.
[49] Cmd 29 of 1989. See Li-ann Thio, "Control, Co-optation and Co-operation: Managing Religious Harmony in Singapore's Multi-Ethnic, Quasi-Secular State," *Hastings Constitutional Law Quarterly* 33, no. 2 (2006): 197–253; Li-ann Thio, "Irreducible Plurality, Indivisible Unity: Singapore Relational Constitutionalism and Cultivating Harmony through Constructing a Constitutional Civil Religion," *German Law Journal* 16, no. 3 (2019): 1007–1034.

a guideline to appropriate or expected behavior. These principles also affect how human dignity is understood. For example, in terms of material needs, there was recognition that "rationality and economic efficiency" was not the end-all and be-all as it was important to assist the needy, not through handouts but through educational opportunities and skills upgrading, to broaden the pool of economic growth beneficiaries. Showing community support for individuals through volunteer welfare work, "will keep Singapore a humane society" while avoiding "the dependent mentality and severe social problems" suffered by many developed welfare states.[50]

Other values identified in the white paper are also reflected, at least implicitly, in judicial reasoning when it comes to weighing "group interests more heavily than individual ones"[51] or theorizing free speech in relation to political defamation, as discussed in Section 3.1.

In formulating these shared values that frame political culture, the government was careful not to contradict the tenets of any major religion in Singapore;[52] while impossible to synthesis the diverse heritage of Singaporeans into "a single comprehensive doctrine," diversity had to be turned into "a source of strength."[53] The approach was to "identify a few key values" common to all major groups drawing on the "essence of each of these heritages." It had to allay concerns of non-Chinese Singaporeans that the shared values were not "a subterfuge for imposing Chinese Confucian values on them."[54] Indeed, these concerns about legitimating authoritarian governance were shared by non-Confucianist Chinese. The government's pragmatic approach in selectively appropriating cultural tenets is evident in how it approved and jettisoned values associated with Confucianism, which has "no monopoly of value." Indeed, its patriarchical ethos is inconsistent with the gender egalitarianism promoted by human rights treaties like the Convention for the Elimination of All Forms of Discrimination (CEDAW), which Singapore acceded to in 1995.[55] Therefore, some of the tenets of Confucianism[56] as a code of conduct had to be updated and "reconciled with other ideas which are also essential parts of our ethos."[57] The Confucian concept of family ties leading to nepotism was rejected in the interests of having an incorrupt bureaucracy, and it was noted that "strictly

---

[50] Cmd 1 of 1991 (Parliament of Singapore), para. 31–38.
[51] Ibid., para. 26. The white paper notes that, while "stressing communitarianism," the rights of individuals "should be respected and not lightly encroached upon," as seeking a balance between community and the individual was the goal: para. 30.
[52] Ibid., para. 8–9, 18–19.
[53] Cmd 1 of 1991 (Parliament of Singapore), para. 7.
[54] Ibid., para. 39.
[55] Li-ann Thio, "She's a Woman, but She Acts Very Fast: Women, Religion and Law in Singapore," in *Mixed Blessings: Law, Religions, and Women's Rights in the Asia-Pacific Region*, edited by Carolyn Evans and Amanda Whiting (Leiden: Brill, 2006), pp. 241–277.
[56] Luo An'xian, "Human Dignity in Traditional Chinese Confucianism," edited by Marcus Duwell, Jens Braarvig, Roger Brownsword, and Dietmar Mieth, *The Cambridge Handbook of Human Dignity: Interdisciplinary Perspectives* (Cambridge: Cambridge University Press, 2014), 177–181.
[57] Cmd 1 of 1991 (Parliament of Singapore), para. 42.

hierarchal" family relationships were giving way to "a parent–child relationship" shaped by "respect rather than absolute subordination," where sons and daughters "are increasingly treated equally."[58] Modifications to accommodate modernist sensibilities and exigencies were made, like deploying legal sanctions to require children to maintain their parents, rather than relying on filial piety.[59] Notably, one Confucian norm that was retained and affirmed was that ordering relations between the ruler and ruled, which critics may consider a self-serving apology for power:

> 41. Many Confucian ideals are relevant to Singapore ... The concept of government by honourable men [君子 – *junzi*], who have a duty to do right for the people, and who have the trust and respect of the population, fits us better than the Western idea that a government should be given as limited powers as possible, and should always be treated with suspicion unless proven otherwise.[60]

This presumption of trust is reflected in both constitutional and statutory canons of construction. In *Ramalingam Ravinthran v. AG*,[61] the Court of Appeal noted that, in reviewing the basis of executive decisions of individuals occupying "high constitutional offices," courts should apply a presumption of legality, such as where bad faith was alleged, as encapsulated in the maxim *omnia praesumuntur rite esse acta* (all things are presumed to have been done rightly and regularly; i.e. in conformity with the law). Given the attorney-general's high constitutional status, the courts should presume that "he acts in the public interest" when exercising prosecutorial discretion. This presumption, albeit a weaker one, also applies to nonconstitutional public officials.[62] As we will discuss, the idea of governors as honorable personages shapes judicial reasoning.

These shared values provide a basis in attempts to forge a national identity, a Habermasian sense of constitutional patriotism in a nonliberal setting. To build a "Singaporean" tribe[63] out of a nation composed primarily of immigrants who lack a shared history, language, culture, or religion, focus is placed on nurturing a vision of a common future.

Political culture is not static, and one may discern three "waves" in the evolution of governance styles, which reflects a form of "Paternal Democracy"[64] as distinct from paternalism. While the latter reflects a certain style of rule or ideology, the former refers to an evolving relationship such as that between father and child; children go through a period of tutelage and in due course mature into adults, where the relationship transforms into one between two adults, on a more equal footing.

---

[58] Ibid., para. 43–44.
[59] Maintenance of Parents Act (Cap 167B).
[60] Cmd 1 of 1991 (Parliament of Singapore), para. 41.
[61] [2012] 2 SLR 49 at [45].
[62] Ibid., [46]–[47].
[63] "PM Goh's Vision: Nation Free of Racial Tribes," *South China Morning Post*, May 6, 1999.
[64] Li-ann Thio, *A Treatise on Singapore Constitutional Law* (Orlando, FL: Academy Publishing, 2012), p. 758.

The tenor of governance during the first wave under Prime Minister Lee Kuan Yew, Singapore's acknowledged founding father,[65] was likened by its second prime minister, Goh Chok Tong, to that of a "stern father" who ruled through diktat rather than persuasion, based on a mandate drawn from elections. Prime Minister Goh, who represents the second wave, described his role as that of the "elder brother" whose job was to persuade Singaporeans to accept the house rules of the family.[66] Around that time, government ministers admonished citizens as the "junior party" to relate to them as the "senior party," with deferential respect in conducting debate, reflecting a social hierarchy.[67]

Things have changed in twenty-first-century Singapore, as economic liberalization has given rise to modest political liberalization. When Prime Minister Lee Hsien Loong took office in 2004, he adopted a more consultative "third-wave" approach in encouraging active citizenry and engagement with government officials with respect to laws and policies, to satisfy citizen demands for greater political participation. Prime Minister Lee urged people to "debate issues with reason, passion and conviction, and not be passive bystanders in their own fate." He adopted a conciliatory tone in urging that "disagreement does not necessarily imply rebellion" and that unity of purpose did not require homogeneity of thought. Debate over national issues should be rigorous and robust, "issued-focused, based on facts and logic, and not just on assertions and emotions," in order to find "the best way forward for the country."[68] What further galvanized change was the loss of the Aljunied Group Representation Constituency in the 2011 general elections, which saw the ouster of a strong PAP team including two ministers. This accelerated the reform of governance style from the dictatorial mode of technocratic superiors instructing passive citizens to one more akin to that of servant leadership, where politicians could admit mistakes and offer apologies while continuing to seek to persuade citizens as rational persons while attempting to make emotional connections.[69] Government members of parliament (MPs) were told there was no job security in politics, and they opted for moral informal methods of relating to their constituents, discarding expectations of red carpet treatment and feudal mentalities.[70] This consultative governance style and active engagement of the demos through national conversations proved effective in the post-deferential era: the PAP secured almost 70 percent of the votes at the 2015 general election.

[65] Warren Fernandez, "Singapore's Founding Father Mr Lee Kuan Yew Dies Aged 91 at 3.18 am on Monday," *Straits Times*, March 23, 2015, www.straitstimes.com/singapore/singapores-founding-father-mr-lee-kuan-yew-dies-aged-91-at-318am-on-monday.
[66] "PM Goh on His Role as 'Elder Brother,'" *Straits Times*, October 20, 1994, p. 4.
[67] Minister for Information and the Arts George Yeo, "Debate Yes, but Do Not Take on Those in Authority as 'Equals,'" *Straits Times*, February 20, 1995, p. 1.
[68] Lee Hsien Loong, "Building a Civic Society," Harvard Club of Singapore 35th Anniversary Dinner (2004).
[69] Lydia Lim, "PM Says Sorry," *Straits Times*, May 4, 2011.
[70] "MPs Tell Residents: No Need to Stand, Clap for Us," Yahoo News, June 19, 2011.

Within the brand of nonliberal secular democratic constitutionalism in Singapore today, the government's propensity to be inclusive, to consult and address citizens as "coauthors"[71] of the Singapore story, marks a shift, but not a total departure, from a "deference" society; this is a society where a nonelite considers an elite to be of a "superior status and culture to their own," considering their political leadership "to be something normal and natural." Deference, conditioned by tradition, is a product not of coercion but of "conditioned freedom," where the deferential "freely accept" a "follower role in a society hierarchically structured."[72] The question is whether a wholly egalitarian conception of human dignity now prevails or continues to coexist with a hierarchical conception.

2.2 *How Human Dignity Is Used in Public Discourse*

To treat someone with dignity is to attribute to them the highest status, to affirm their intrinsic worth or rank. The term "human dignity," though, can be deployed both to raise the status of subordinate beings and to legitimate superior–subordinate relational orderings. The latter may speak to the proper place one occupies in a divine/natural order and "invites an account of the proper place of human beings in the world, and what their essential, valuable characteristics are."[73] The former relates to an egalitarian conception of human dignity, but this raises the question of whether dignity is secured by equal or different treatment. Is human dignity realized or thwarted by according religious minorities some degree of autonomy from general law through a system of legal pluralism? Like dignity, "equality" is, as Peter Westen[74] pointed out, an empty concept parasitic on an independent substantive philosophy. Its rhetorical invocation may occlude the important question of what should be treated as equal to what and for what purposes.

In Singapore, over and above inherent human dignity, the dignity of high constitutional office holders and the conduct expected of them has been spoken of. For example, the president, who is elected and possesses limited veto powers over certain government financial transactions, is meant to personify the state and is "a symbol of the dignity and honor of our people, a symbol of the unity and values of our country."[75] Thus, as a symbol of the multiracial polity, any divisiveness that elections may throw up is to be modulated by rules governing presidential elections campaigning. While parliamentary elections involved a "vigorous contest of ideas" as the winner will be charged with formulating national policies, the president has

---

[71] PM Lee Hsien Loong, Swearing-in Ceremony, October 1, 2015. Debates over what this story should contain would take place "in civil society and Parliament."

[72] J. G. A. Pocock, "The Classical Theory of Deference," *American Historical Review* 81, no. 3 (June 1976): 516.

[73] Michael Rosen, "Dignity Past and Present," in *Dignity, Ranks and Rights*, edited by Jeremy Waldron and Meir Dan-Cohen (Oxford: Oxford University Press, 2012), p. 90.

[74] Peter Westen, "The Empty Idea of Equality," *Harvard Law Review* 95, no. 3 (January 1982): 537.

[75] *Tan Cheng Bock* v. *AG* [2017] SGHC 160 at [43].

"no policy agenda to advance." A 2016 constitutional commission tasked with proposing recommendations to specific aspects of the presidency suggested that acts that "inflame emotions, cause divisiveness or encourage invective,"[76] such as rallies, be excluded or discouraged, in favor of state-sponsored televised outreaches. New rules applied to the 2017 presidential elections: as the office was the highest position in the land, election campaigning should "be dignified and above the political fray."[77] This flowed from the experience of the 2011 presidential elections in which candidates made unrealistic promises and campaigned combatively. Candidates in 2017 therefore were asked to voluntarily fill in a form promising to campaign in a "dignified and decorous manner."[78] Similarly, rules on contempt of court are not meant to "protect the dignity of judges" but to serve the public interest in ensuring public confidence in the administration of justice,[79] which requires maintaining "the dignity and authority of the court" to ensure a fair trial.[80] Public respect for judges is key to this, such that criticism may be directed at judgments but should not descend to denigrating judges.

The plasticity of the concept of human dignity is evident in the varied manner in which it is invoked in Singapore's public discourse. The government has firstly invoked "dignity" as a term to underscore the importance *of securing a material condition of living,* such as facilitating employment for the elderly by raising the re-employment age so they can "age with dignity."[81] The government views work and earning one's keep as being "the best form of welfare" as it "enables dignity and self-respect"; the importance of individual self-reliance, of standing on one's own two feet and living "a life of dignity," is central to its rejection of socioeconomic rights and welfare handouts and focus on programs to promote social welfare by "enabling those who can work to work"; this empowers individuals and helps them retain their dignity.[82] Part of the social compact based on "our shared values" were policies "to improve social mobility" to ensure "all of us can lead lives with dignity and meaning and participate and contribute in our own ways."[83]

---

[76] Constitutional Commission Report (2016), 7.13.
[77] Elections Department, Prime Minister's Office, Press Release, Campaigning Guidelines for the Presidential Elections, August 29, 2017.
[78] Charissa Yong, "Presidential Election 2017: New Rules to Ensure Candidates Act with Dignity," *Straits Times,* August 30, 2017.
[79] *Shadrake Alan* v. *AG* [2011] SGCA 26 at [21].
[80] *Lee Shieh-Peen Clement* v. *Ho Chin Nguang* [2010] SGCA 34 at [44].
[81] Singapore National Report, Universal Periodic Review, A/HRC/WG.6/24/SGP/1 at para. 40. Various MPs pointed out that seniors lost their dignity when viewed as societal burdens, reminding the House that the economic benefits the present generation enjoyed were built on the sweat of the previous, who deserved to "enjoy their golden years in dignity," urging that the "neglect or abuse of such seniors by their adult children" was not to be condoned. 94 Singapore Parliament Reports, parliamentary motion, February 6, 2018.
[82] Tan Chuan Jin, 94 Singapore Parliament Reports, March 8, 2017, Budget (Ministry of Social and Family Development).
[83] Desmond Lee, Singapore Parliament Reports, 2018 Budget (Ministry of Social and Family Development).

Nongovernment organizations have linked human dignity and poverty issues in contending that a basic standard of living was necessary for a dignified existence;[84] the mission of some NGOs extends to restoring the dignity of the elderly indigent by improving their living conditions through cleaning and refurbishment of their homes; others like Dignity Kitchen[85] allow the disabled and those with low-income to earn a dignified living through operating food stalls. Being part of the workforce promotes their inclusion in mainstream society, empowering the poor and disabled to "live with dignity, be empowered and have the opportunity to fully and effectively participate in society as integral members."[86]

Second, the government has extended protective legislation with respect to situations where individuals may horizontally violate the human dignity of other individuals through insult, contempt, causing expressive or symbolic dignitary harms; the state has sought to proscribe these intangible harms through laws like the Protection from Harassment Act (POHA), which seeks to help "innocent Singaporeans" to "protect their dignity, protect themselves against ... some very malicious-intent people out there."[87] Soft guidelines on managing workplace harassment, which can "violate a person's dignity" have been provided in a Tripartite advisory authored by the government, labor, and employers.[88]

Third, the government publicly admonished acts characterized as violating human dignity, signaling the transgression of community norms. For example, government ministers have criticized sexually offensive university orientation games that humiliated female students as disrespecting human dignity.[89] The courts too have signaled the boundaries of acceptable conduct by describing a professor who sexually seduced an undergraduate student who gave him gifts for higher grades

---

[84] Claire Pascua, "GK Singapore helps restore dignity to the indigent elderly in Singapore," GK1World (Singapore) Ltd., www.gk1world.com/portal/country/sg/Articleviewer.aspx?ID=131798#.

[85] The work of Dignity Kitchen (the world's first hawker center run by the disabled) has been endorsed by the president of Singapore: http://dignitykitchen.sg/; Aqil Hamzah, "Dignity Kitchen Lends a Helping Hand to the Underprivileged," *New Paper*, February 26, 2018.

[86] Ministry of Social and Family Development, Enabling Masterplan 2012–2016 at 116 [1]. Singapore acceded to the Convention on the Rights of Persons with Disabilities in 2013, advancing the goal to make it a "caring and inclusive society." Article 3(a) states that a basic principle shall be "respect for inherent dignity, individual autonomy including the freedom to make one's own choices, and independence of persons."

[87] Tin Pei Ling, Second Reading, Protection from Harassment Bill, 91 Singapore Parliament Reports, March 13, 2014. See Yihan Goh, "The Case for Legislating Harassment in Singapore," *Singapore Academy of Law* 26, no. 1 (2014): 68–97.

[88] Olivia Ho, "Tripartite Advisory Advocates Zero Tolerance for Workplace Harassment," *Straits Times*, December 23, 2015.

[89] "Inappropriate Orientation Games Cannot Be Tolerated: Ong Ke Yung," *Channel News Asia*, July 28, 2016. Minister Ong stated that "pretending to ejaculate into the face of a fellow student" plays no part in university education, while "goading others to act out a rape scene" trivializes the suffering of rape victims and humiliates female students. His criticism was motivated not by prudishness but by championing "respect for human dignity." "Minister Ong Ye Kung Slams Sexualized University Orientation Activities in Facebook Post," *Stomp*, July 28, 2016, https://stomp.straitstimes.com/singapore-seen/singapore/minister-ong-ye-kung-slams-sexualised-university-orientation-activities-in.

as a "man without honor," even if he was cleared of corruption charges.[90] Dignity is related to meeting certain standards of behavior and is lost where these are breached.

Fourth, the need to protect the "dignity" of the vulnerable is underscored in such acts as the Mental Capacity Act (MCA), amended in 2016 and described as a "Law for Dignified Living," enabling Singaporeans to plan ahead and exercise decisional autonomy by making provision for such time when they might lose their mental capacity. The MCA allows one to choose a trusted person to make decisions on one's behalf through a Lasting Power of Attorney, respecting how a person wishes to be treated.[91] It operates on a presumption of mental capacity, setting the fundamental tone of the MCA that "a person's autonomy and dignity must be respected."[92] The MCA was a "mirror for all of us," reflecting how we want to live and be treated "across the generations," to treat family members with respect and dignity and to give effect to the duty to protect the "most vulnerable members in our society" and to "respect their wishes and "to enable them to live with dignity."[93] A government minister identified the importance of values, attitudes, and responsibility when the Act was introduced, stating that this legislation as a safety net would seek to ensure "our community continues to treasure people who are old . . . [who are not] disposable, as the "old, disabled or mentally incapacitated have value and dignity and deserve protection and choice."[94] The Vulnerable Adults Act of 2018 seeks to protect individuals who cannot protect themselves from abuse, neglect, or self-neglect because of a physical or mental disability, by allowing government social services to intervene. Abuse was related to loss of personal dignity, a proffered example being that of a caregiver failing to dress an adult after bathing her, leaving her unclothed in a room with open windows and visible to neighbors.[95] The Prevention of Human Trafficking Act also seeks to protect and support the rehabilitation of a vulnerable group, to "restore their dignity."[96] Under the Advanced Medical Directive Act, terminal patients with no prospect of recovery may give directions against artificially prolonging the dying process and so "pass on in peace and dignity."[97]

[90] *Tey Tsun Hang v. PP* [2014] SGHC 39 at [330].
[91] Tan Chuan Jin (Minister for Social and Family Development), Second Reading, Mental Capacity (Amendment) Bill, 94 Singapore Parliament Reports, March 14, 2016.
[92] "Ageing with Grace," *Business Times*, June 7, 2016, www.businesstimes.com.sg/focus/magazines/wealth-june-2016/ageing-with-grace.
[93] Ibid.
[94] Vivian Balakrishan (Minister for Community Development, Youth and Sports), Second Reading, Mental Capacity Bill, 85 Singapore Parliament Reports, September 15, 2008.
[95] Desmond Lee (Minister for Social and Family Development), Vulnerable Adults Bill, 95 Singapore Parliament Reports, March 18, 2018.
[96] Christopher de Souza, Second Reading, Prevention of Human Trafficking Bill, 92 Singapore Parliament Reports, November 3, 2014.
[97] Heng Chee How (Minister of State for Health), Singapore Parliament Reports, Budget (Ministry of Health), 2008. See generally Toh Puay San and Stanley Yeo, "Decriminalizing Physician-Assisted Suicide in Singapore," *Singapore Academy of Law Journal* 22, no. 1 (March 2010): 379; Tan Seow Hon, "The Case against Physician-Assisted Suicide and Voluntary Active Euthanasia: A Jurisprudential Consideration," *Singapore Academy of Law Journal* 29, no. 2 (September 2017): 375.

Political claims invoking human dignity, frequently formulated and sometimes recognized as rights, inform critiques that humans are degraded by commodification or that the death penalty violates human dignity;[98] they fuel humanist efforts[99] at promoting lifestyle liberationism and sexual preference rights as well as assisted suicide.[100] These relate both to human dignity as an intrinsic value and to "dignity as autonomy" claims, demonstrating its rhetorical force.

2.3 Relational Constitutionalism, Respect, and Racial and Religious Harmony

Singapore's communitarian constitutionalism sustains a government that is actively interested in the character of its citizens and in building a Singaporean identity based on key values. Understandings of human dignity are shaped by ideas of relational autonomy, which takes into account the importance of autonomy and agency as principles of liberal justice; these eschew the hyper-individualism associated with liberal accounts of the individual as autonomous person by incorporating an understanding of how the "self" is socially embedded, "the fundamentally relational nature of our motivations and the overall social character of our being." This perspective goes beyond the reductionist view of the atomistic individual shorn of ethnic, religious, and cultural traits and is sensitive to "relations of care, interdependence and mutual support" shaping human relations; it holds forth a vision of a person as a "free self-governing agent who is also socially constituted" and whose value commitments are shaped by "interpersonal relations and mutual dependencies."[101] It also moderates the anti-paternalism associated with liberal autonomy by valuing the need for an overarching national identity and sense of community vision, conscience, and identity, while guarding against subjugating individuals to authoritarian rule.

Article 15 of the Singapore Constitution protects the right of a person to "profess, practice and propagate" his religion. This model of religious freedom is voluntarist in terms of religious affiliation, "premised on removing restrictions to one's choice

---

[98] Gabriel Seow, "Ensure Respect for Dignity of Human Life," *Straits Times*, November 8, 2010; Kong Soon Tan, "Death Penalty Undermines Human Dignity and Right to Life," *Online Citizen*, July 11, 2012, www.theonlinecitizen.com/2012/07/11/death-penalty-undermines-human-dignity-and-right-to-life/; Lester Lim, "Does a Legalized Market for Kidneys in Singapore Violate Human Dignity?" Kentridge Commons, August 31, 2009, http://kentridgecommon.com/does-a-legalized-market-for-kidneys-in-singapore-violate-human-dignity/.

[99] Grace Boey, "A Summary of Human Worth and Dignity Talk," Singapore Humanist Society, August 10, 2014, http://humanist.org.sg/a-summary-of-human-worth-and-dignity-talk/.

[100] Philip Yap Lin Kiat, "Lets talk about Advance Care Planning to Die with Dignity," *Straits Times*, December 16, 2017, www.straitstimes.com/opinion/lets-talk-about-advance-care-planning-to-die-with-dignity; "Letting the Terminally Ill Die with Dignity," *Asiaone*, www.asiaone.com/health/letting-terminally-ill-die-dignity.

[101] John Christman, "Relational Autonomy, Liberal Individualism, and the Social Constitution of Selves," *Philosophical Studies* 117, no. 1/2 (January 2004): 143.

of religious belief," a form of "accommodative secularism"[102] that is anti-theocratic rather than anti-theistic. While the *forum internum* is absolute, consonant with the rights-oriented conception of "dignity as autonomy," the *forum externum*, religious practice and propagation, is subject to considerations of "public order, morality and health" and open to communitarian or statist readings of the scope of these liberties. The courts have recognized the legislative premium placed on public order and are aware of the threat of fissiparous tendencies that exist within a multiracial and multireligious society.

To that end, the content of "public order" and the rule of law is informed by the imperative of "maintaining racial and religious harmony" that is considered "the fundamental bases for our social stability, cohesion and security."[103] While public order relates to the absence of disorder and encompasses "danger to human life and safety and the disturbance of public tranquility,"[104] the idea of "racial and religious harmony" goes further, beyond civil peace. It speaks to the goals of relational constitutionalism and its core concern with the sustainability of relationships beyond mere tolerance, implicating rights, duties, and public goods that inform a vision of community where social trust is nurtured. This relates to relations between government and citizen, and between citizens, and how legal institutions and practices can contribute toward generating and sustaining common understandings and aspirations toward standards of basic humanity and moral solidarity. Maintaining relational well-being requires that we treat each other with human dignity, which requires reciprocal respect and a certain generosity of heart in the event of social conflicts.

The methods of relational constitutionalism seek to protect rights without promoting rightism and the agonistic social relations this engenders, favoring informal methods of regulation and dispute management to smooth over strained social ties; this could be through promoting dialogical venues to build social bonds and appealing to nonbinding normative instruments as the common reference point. This has a regulatory and socializing function in cultivating expectations about social and anti-social conduct. This is best exemplified in the management of ethnoreligious disputes: the government strives to be even-handed in dealing with the various race and religions. It uses a mix of formal and informal methods, legal sanction, hortatory persuasion, and social pressure to punish, deter, and promote the kind of reconciliation needed for durable relationships. This is illustrated by examining how two events involving racial and/or religious conflict were managed.[105]

---

[102] *Nappalii Peter Williams v. Institute of Technical Education* [1999] 2 SLR 569 at [28].
[103] S. Jayakumar, "Applying the Rule of Law," *International Lawyer* 43, no. 1 (Spring 2009): 85.
[104] *Tan Boon Liat v. Menteri Hal Ehwal Dalam Negeri Malaysia* [1976] 2 MLJ 83 at 86D-F, cited in *Vijaya Kumar s/o Rajendran v. Attorney-General* [2015] SGHC 244 at [31].
[105] Li-ann Thio, "Singapore Relational Constitutionalism: The 'Living Institution' and the Project of Religious Harmony," *Singapore Journal of Legal Studies* (March 2019): 72–102.

To contextualize this discussion, two things should be borne in mind. First, the government has at its disposal a pool of "hard" and "soft" legal norms to deploy.[106] Penal sanctions can be imposed through various laws such as the Sedition Act for action which promotes "feelings of ill-will and hostility between different races or classes of the population of Singapore," with "race" often been conflated with "religion" as far as Malays, who are 99 percent Muslim, are concerned. Thus, a Christian couple was convicted in *Public Prosecutor v. Ong Kian Cheong*[107] for distributing seditious publications in the form of Christian tracts carrying titles like "Who is Allah?" and "The Little Bride" to persons with Malay names,[108] which had "the tendency to promote feelings of ill-will and hostility between Christians and Muslims in Singapore." This limitation of free speech shows how maintaining peace and deferring to religious sensitivities trumps speech and the argument from truth. While it is a constitutional right to propagate one's religion, the court's tone was largely condemnatory in criticizing the accused's acts of "distributing tracts with callous denigratory, offensive and insensitive statements on religion with aspersions on race," which had the tendency "to cause social unrest thereby jeopardizing racial and religious harmony," betraying a lack of "sensitivity, tolerance and mutual respect for another's faith and religious beliefs."[109] This is one-sided, as an equally rational way of responding when receiving a tract with information one dislikes rather than making a police report, is to throw it away, recognizing the greater good of robust free speech in matters of ultimate significance.[110] However, Singapore's horizontal sedition laws that relate to "feelings" cater not only to the hoped for assumption of the "rational man" but also the possibility of the "emotional man." "Hard" legal sanctions that have a punitive, deterrent effect lack a relational quality; their effect may be educative in drawing a "red-line" against anti-social behavior, as in *Benjamin Koh v. PP*[111] where an online post consisting of anti-Malay and anti-Muslim remarks and the offensive juxtaposition of a pig's head next to a halal logo was found seditious. Richard Magnus SDJ stated that "independent of any legal duty" it was "only appropriate social behavior" for all citizens and residents to ensure "nothing is said or done" that might incite racial strife and violence.[112] The appeal to

---

[106] Eugene K. B. Tan, "From Clampdown to Limited Empowerment: Hard and Soft Law in the Calibration and Regulation of Religious Conduct in Singapore," *Law and Policy* 31, no. 3 (June 2009): 351–379.
[107] [2009] SGDC 163.
[108] District Judge Roy Neighbour in *Ong Kian Cheong*, ibid., noted at [48]: "Though a name does not reveal a person's religion, but in our multi-racial society, it would give rise to an inference of a person's religious beliefs." This is in principle contrary to a voluntarist conception of religious identity.
[109] Ibid., [82].
[110] The district judge characterized a Muslim woman's police report – that she had received a publication which made her angry and that could inspire Muslim feelings of ill will and hostility against Christians if it fell into the wrong hands – as a matter of "acting rationally." Ibid., [13].
[111] [2005] SGDC 272. See "Jail Terms, Fines – and a Warning," *Today*, October 8, 2005, p. 3.
[112] [2005] SGDC 272 at [8].

rationality is apparent where citizens are urged to observe unwritten social duties in responsibly exercising free speech. Dignity-based rationales may clash, where free speech, an expression of "dignity as autonomy,"[113] may be at odds with the dignity of the group in the sense of its subjective feelings or self-esteem. "Human dignity" in this context will be colored not just by rights but responsibilities, shaped by cultural and cosmopolitan norms.

Prosecuted sedition cases have all related to the potential impact of expression on Muslims, while similar expressions directed against Christians have merely received stern warnings.[114] Where reconciliation is an important goal, "soft law" norms are more likely to be utilized, providing guidance for the exercise of religious freedoms. Widely publicized instruments containing soft law norms such as the 1989 maintenance of religious harmony white paper[115] and 2004 declaration on religious harmony[116] are influential as executive-authored interpretations of the scope of constitutional rights and duties. For example, while there is a constitutional right to propagation, this must be exercised "very sensitively" and not offensively denigrate another's faith. This is why the government "has always discouraged Christian groups from aggressively evangelizing among the Malay Muslim community."[117] The use of soft law, to promote the objectives of relational constitutionalism, including principles of humanity, human dignity and social harmony, is further discussed in Section 2.3.

Second, institutions can provide forums for dialogue which can moderate relations between religious groups. The Presidential Council for Religious Harmony (PCRH)[118] was created to advise the Government on "how best to deal with sensitive religious issues" and to play a role in the check and balance scheme regulating the minister's powers under the Maintenance of Religious Harmony Act to issue restraining or "gag" orders to religious leaders or other persons for committing or attempting to commit acts which might cause "feelings of enmity, hatred, ill-will or hostility between different religious groups."[119] At least two-thirds of the PCRH members are to be "representatives of the major religions in Singapore," while the remainder are persons who have "distinguished themselves in public service or community relations in Singapore."[120] The relational aspect of this is reflected in

---

[113] "There are different philosophical justifications for the right to free speech. Three primary arguments can be identified: the argument from truth, the argument from democracy, and the argument from human dignity." *Lee Hsieng Loong v. Roy Ngerng Yi Ling* [2015] SGHC 320 at [97].
[114] "Government Drops Charges against Blogger Who Posted Jesus Cartoons," Reporters without Borders, July 20, 2006.
[115] Cmd 29 of 1989.
[116] Li-ann Thio, "Constitutional 'Soft' Law and the Management of Religious Liberty and Order: The 2003 Declaration on Religious Harmony," *Singapore Journal of Legal Studies* (December 2004): 414–443.
[117] *Supra*, note 49, para. 15
[118] Section 3, Maintenance of Religious Harmony Act (Cap 167A).
[119] Sections 8 and 9, ibid.
[120] Section 3(2), ibid.

Prime Minister Lee's own commitment to regularly meet and maintain close touch with religious leaders and exchange views on how to maintain harmony to "keep the line warm and the confidence on both sides"; if a problem arises, "we are not dealing with strangers but with somebody we know and trust." He has alluded to how the government has relied "on mutual trust and the wisdom of our religious leaders to defuse tensions" over "specific difficult issues," without publicity.[121]

Against this backdrop, we turn to a discussion of how tensions involving religious groups are managed and examine how human dignity is negotiated through specific instances where one's behavior is seen to give rise, or does give rise, to social tensions. These cases may or may not attract legal prosecution, but the overriding intent of the government is to promote reconciliation between the religious parties; in this, a certain protocol or public reconciliatory ritual seems to be followed.

The first case involved Muslims and Christians/Jews. One Nalla Mohamed, a Muslim imam of Indian citizenship pleaded guilty to and was convicted of a charge under section 298A(b), Penal Code (Cap 224), for committing an act prejudicial to the maintenance of harmony between different religious groups in Singapore, which was likely to disturb public tranquility. At a mosque service in 2017, he recited a prayer in Arabic stating: "God help us against Jews and Christians." He later took steps to meet and apologize to various religious representatives and all Singaporeans; the judge noted Nalla's "great remorse,"[122] expressed through his acts of contrition. These reconciliatory meetings with Christian, Jewish, and other religious leaders, as well as a breakfast with the law minister, were widely publicized in the media. The press published photographs of Minister Shanmugam hugging Nalla,[123] which testifies to a rift repaired. The Home Affairs ministry, in a conciliatory tone, noted the decision to repatriate the imam was taken with "some regret," as Nalla who had "worked diligently" at the mosque for seven years and had "not been deliberately malicious."[124] In a subsequent press statement, Nalla testified that Christian and Jewish leaders had received him graciously, stating "all mortal men make mistakes" and that "we must move forward consciously for the sake of social trust and religious cohesion."[125] This showed rapprochement; the matter was capped by the Muslim affairs minister's Facebook post thanking non-Muslims for accepting the apology offered, noting that grace and forgiveness

---

[121] Prime Minister Lee Hsien Loong, National Day Rally Speech 2009, Part 3 – Religious Harmony.
[122] Ibid., 4.
[123] Toh Yong Chuan, "Minister Meets Imam Who Was Fined for Making Offensive Remarks and Will Be Headed Home," *Straits Times*, April 5, 2017, www.straitstimes.com/singapore/minister-meets-imam-who-was-fined-for-making-offensive-remarks-and-will-be-heading-home.
[124] Toh Yong Chuan, "Imam Who Made Offensive Remarks about Jews and Christians Will Be Asked to Leave Singapore," *Straits Times*, April 3, 2017, www.straitstimes.com/singapore/imam-who-made-offensive-remarks-against-christians-and-jews-charged-in-court.
[125] Toh Yong Chuan, "Shanmugam Appreciates Imam's Sincere Apology," *Straits Times*, April 6, 2017, www.straitstimes.com/singapore/shanmugam-appreciates-imams-sincere-apology.

reflected "the Singapore way" of upholding "mutual respect and harmony for our common good."[126]

The second type of case also involved online media publications that stirred interreligious tensions between Christians and Muslims, spurred by an irreligious conflict entrepreneur who disliked a Christian church's public stance on certain moral issues. Building on past experience, it appears this was the latest manifestation of actors in such crises adhering to the convention or "soft law" norm of exercising good faith in seeking reconciliation and offering forgiveness, forming a sort of constitutional practice.[127]

In 2018, Lou Engle, an American preacher invited to speak at a conference organized by a local church, allegedly made an "anti-Islam remark."[128] Lim, a christophobic[129] secular humanist, had bought a $220 ticket to attend this conference, after which he made a complaint against the Home Affairs Ministry's decision to grant the preacher a miscellaneous work pass and published a provocative article on Rice Media. The church in turn filed a police report alleging that the article constituted a "scurrilous attack" and was inflammatory, with the effect of "stirring up religious tensions and promoting feelings of ill-will and hostility between Christians and Muslims." The article also had a "seditious tendency" and "denigrated the Christian faith."[130] The article and police reports sparked investigations by the police and the Home Affairs Ministry.[131]

---

[126] "Imam Who Made Offensive Remarks to Be Repatriated; Stern Warnings for Two Others: MHA," *Today*, April 3, 2017, www.todayonline.com/singapore/imam-who-made-offensive-remarks-be-repatriated-stern-warnings-two-others-mha.

[127] This appreciates that the Constitution as a living institution can be developed not just by formal amendment or judicial interpretation but also by the consistent action of constitutional actors: Karl Llewellyn, "The Constitution as Institution," *Columbia Law Review* 34, no. 1 (January 1943): 15, 17.

[128] Lou Engle apparently stated: "The Muslims are taking over the south of Spain. But I had a dream, where I will raise up the church all over Spain to push back a new modern Muslim movement." A church spokesman said this referred to rising ISIS propaganda in Europe, including Spain; it was unclear from the one-and-a-half-minute audio clip posted by Rice Media whether ISIS was mentioned. Jeanette Tan, "Church in Spore Makes Police Report against Rice Media for Scurrilous Attack in Article," *mothership*, March 27, 2017, https://mothership.sg/2018/03/preacher-lou-engle-cornerstone-church-anti-islam/.

[129] The article written by Lim demonstrates animus against the stand taken by the church and Lou Engle on issues like abortion and homosexuality, which may have motivated his hostility, beyond any apparent concern for religious harmony. Lim alleged that Engle had a political agenda; Lim expressed fears of politicized religious communities and criticized Engle for "apparently targeting" Muslims; Engle had not referred to Muslims in Singapore but had prayed that Muslims in Spain would have dreams of Jesus. This could be an instance of manufacturing indignation against an ideological opponent, through a form of conflict entrepreneurship. See Benjamin Lim, "Lou Engle: An American Threatens a Christian-Muslim divide in Singapore," RICE, March 25, 2018, http://ricemedia.co/current-affairs-features-lou-engle-american-threatens-christian-muslim-divide-singapore/. See also Cherian George, *Hate Spin: The Manufacture of Religious Offense and Its Threat to Democracy* (Cambridge, MA: Massachusetts Institute of Technology Press, 2016).

[130] Jeanette Tan, "Church in S'pore Makes Police Report against Rice Media for 'Scurrilous Attack' in Article," Mothership.sg, March 27, 2018, https://mothership.sg/2018/03/preacher-lou-engle-cornerstone-church-anti-islam/.

[131] Ibid.

Evidently, religious tensions were stirred; the church pastor issued both a written apology and a personal one when he requested a meeting with Muslim leaders, including the Mufti, to express his apologies, because Engle's speech had "been the cause of considerable distress and misunderstanding, particularly among the Muslim community." The Mufti and Muslim leaders accepted the pastor's sincere apologies, declaring their intention to "move on and look forward to a more constructive and healthy relationship." The Muslim Affairs minister then gave the seal of ministerial approval through a Facebook post stating that he appreciated the pastor's apology and his taking responsibility for the invitation. The media published photos of the pastor and Mufti warmly shaking hands.[132] Shortly afterwards, former nominated MP Zulkifli Baharudin organized a lunch between leaders of the church and Ba'akwie Mosque, with both sides affirming that "these sorts of things can be easily resolved ... by meeting together." Among the dignitaries attending was the husband of President Halimah Yacob. Baharudin realistically observed that these sorts of disputes could not be avoided completely and that the "only guarantee" was that when it happened "there is enough goodwill among us. But goodwill starts from personal relationships." Reflecting an approach committed to relationism, he urged that religious communities should welcome those "who have made mistakes, with love, with care, as a brother," adding that he thought "Singaporeans should be like that, and Muslims in Singapore are capable of that."[133] The National Council of Churches in Singapore (NCCS) also issued a public statement affirming the "measured response" of the Islamic Religious Council and their "gracious acceptance" of the pastor's apology as actions worthy of emulation, which generate expectations of future similar conduct. The pastor reciprocated by inviting members of the mosque to visit his church, declaring a commitment to proactively build bridges of trust through regular meetings between faith leaders; he reportedly stated that out of this controversy "we have found ourselves new friends from the Muslim community."[134]

This speaks of cordiality and friendship. As the Singapore High Court noted in *Kalpanath Singh v. Law Society*, a possible "common value" is "forgiving those who have trespassed against us."[135] Forgiveness is a way of treating a person with human dignity; rather than earning endless demonization and social exile, the offending

---

[132] Zhaki Abdullah, "Police Ask US Preacher to Return for Interview," *Straits Times*, April 5, 2018, www.straitstimes.com/singapore/police-ask-us-preacher-to-return-for-interview.
[133] Low De Wei, "Regular Meetings Can Resolve Religious Controversies Say Muslim and Christian Community Leaders," *Straits Times*, April 13, 2018, www.straitstimes.com/singapore/regular-meetings-can-help-resolve-religious-controversies-say-muslim-and-christian.
[134] Rahimah Rashith, "Church Tightens Procedures for Inviting Speakers," *Straits Times*, July 9, 2018, www.straitstimes.com/singapore/church-tightens-procedures-for-inviting-speakers.
[135] [2009] 4 SLR(R) 1018 at [23].

person, after acts of atonement, is received back into the community as a member of good standing. Government approval is given to acts taken between religious groups to preserve friendly relations, which is duly publicized, while attempts to stir ill will and opprobrium against a group are not encouraged.

Thus a soft law norm has been developed in the form of consolidated and legitimized expectation that, after religious offence is caused, sincere apologies and forgiveness should be extended and received by the relevant parties; this is to be sealed by a ministerial-level expression of public approval, presenting an occasion for all concerned to reaffirm their joint commitment to preserving religious harmony. In the meantime, goodwill is to be cultivated by developing relations, dialogue, and quiet diplomacy, the methods of relational constitutionalism.

3 HUMAN DIGNITY AND JUDICIAL REVIEW

Human dignity is not an express right or principle in the Singapore Constitution, as this has few explicit normative values. Part IV (Fundamental Liberties) does not contain any socioeconomic rights nor provide for the horizontal application of rights. Social engineering from the bench is avoided as a violation of the rule of law and separation of powers, unlike the Indian Supreme Court, which has used the reference to dignity in the Indian constitutional preamble to drive a values-based interpretation of the right to life, which encompasses living with adequate nutrition, clothing, and shelter.[136]

The text and historical intent is taken seriously in constitutional interpretation, particularly in reading Article 9 (1), which prohibits the deprivation of "life and personal liberty save in accordance with law." The Court of Appeal rejected the expansive interpretative approach toward Article 21 of the Indian Constitution, the equivalent of Article 9 (1); while this was "understandable having regard to India's economic, social and political conditions"[137] it was not possible to read Article 9 (1) similarly. Insofar as international human rights law, which is based on a conception of human dignity, might influence judicial interpretation, Singapore adopts a dualist system; treaties do not apply domestically unless expressly incorporated by statute, and any recognized customary international law rule bears the status of a common law norm.[138]

Failed arguments related to "human dignity" have been raised in several constitutional law cases relating to the mandatory death penalty[139] and to criminalization

---

[136] Upendra Baxi, "The Place of Dignity in the Indian Constitution," in *The Cambridge Handbook of Human Dignity: Interdisciplinary Perspectives*, edited by Marcus Duwell, Jens Braarvig, Roger Brownsword, and Dietmar Mieth (Cambridge: Cambridge University Press, 2014), pp. 429–436.
[137] *Yong Vui Kong* v. *Public Prosecutor* [2010] 3 SLR 489 at [83]. See *Yong Vui Kong* [2015] 1 SLR 26 at [47].
[138] *Yong Vui Kong* v. *Public Prosecutor* [2015] 2 SLR 1129, [26]–[38].
[139] In *Yong Vui Kong* v. *Public Prosecutor* [2010] 3 SLR 489, it was argued that the mandatory death penalty was an inhuman punishment in precluding judicial assessment of the offender's moral

of homosexual sodomy. In *Lim Meng Suang* v. *AG*[140] the Court of Appeal refused to read a right to privacy and personal autonomy into "life and personal liberty" under Article 9 (1). Defense counsel argued that life and personal liberty at their core had to include a "right of personal autonomy allowing a person to enjoy and express affection and love toward another human being."[141] While this feelings-based argument may have succeeded in more juristocratic settings, it fell flat in Singapore as what was couched as a limited privacy right was a claim that was "not only vague and general" but also contained within it the "seeds of an unlimited right." The claimed right to personal autonomy so formulated "could be interpreted to encompass as well as legalize all manner of subjective expressions of love and affection, which could (in turn) embody content that may be wholly unacceptable from the perspective of broader societal policy."[142] These issues fell to legislative determination as the courts refrain from legislating new rights in the guise of constitutional interpretation.

The resort to human dignity can be used to preserve a social hierarchy, to "level up" or "level down" someone's status or situation. "Human dignity" has been expressly invoked in Singapore criminal cases involving vulnerable groups, namely female domestic workers, and implicitly informs the presumptions underlying free speech and reputation in political libel cases.

3.1 *Preserving Social Hierarchy: The Junzi Syndrome*

Relational Constitutionalism raises the question of what manner of relationship between governor–governed and between citizens is normative. Within a democratic order, the focus is on the equal status of citizens and expressive freedoms, including political speech, as the lifeblood of democratic society. In Euro-American jurisdictions,[143] political speech is accorded paramountcy where balanced against the reputational interests of politicians or public figures. Given its

---

blameworthiness in the sentencing process. Offenders were dehumanized by being treated as a faceless, undifferentiated mass and deprived of human dignity: [38]. However, there is no constitutional clause prohibiting inhuman punishment, nor could one be implied, given the drafting history where such a clause was contemplated but not included in Part IV: [87]–[92].

[140] [2015] 1 SLR 26.
[141] [2015] 1 SLR 26 at [43]. Counsel directed linked privacy, human dignity, and individual autonomy with "the human need for an intimate personal sphere," presented as a self-evident proposition, in challenging the same law in *Tan Eng Hong* v. *AG* [2012] SGCA 45. These matters are contested, not immutable verities.
[142] Ibid., [49]. Every moral theory of consent or autonomy has its limits. A recognition of a person's autonomous choice in sexual matters, which is violated by an act of rape, has been recognized in terms of an "inalienable right not to be a victim of predatory sexual aggression" and is related to "respect for the dignity, privacy and free will of a person." *Ng Kean Meng Terence* v. *PP* [2017] SGCA 37 at [46]. The justification for the scope and limits of consent must rest on a substantive basis other than a bare invocation of "consent" or "autonomy."
[143] For example, *New York Times* v. *Sullivan* 376 US 254 (1964); *Lingens* v. *Austria* App No 9815/82, July 8, 1986, European Court of Human Rights.

importance to democratic society, political speech warrants greater protection such that "the limits of acceptable criticism are accordingly wider"[144] for politicians, compared to private individuals. Where the right to reputation and the associated idea of honor is recognized as part of the right to privacy, a coequal right, this affects the balancing process.[145] Political culture will shape the conception of reputation in any one jurisdiction, and local conditions will determine the value judgments made in adjudicating expressive freedoms and reputational rights.[146]

In Singapore, a hierarchical conception of social status operates in the backdrop of defamation law. Singapore courts have rejected the US public figure doctrine and hold instead that politicians or public office holders "are equally entitled to have their reputations protected as those of any other person."[147] Citing the nineteenth-century Canadian case of *Campbell* v. *Spottiswoode*, the Court of Appeal asserted that "the law of defamation protects the public reputation of public men as well."[148] Criticisms about public men that would be "destructive of their character and honor" should not be allowed, unless "well founded."[149] The court recognized a public interest in maintaining the public character of public men, as it would be a social loss if "sensitive and honorable men were deterred from seeking public positions of trust and responsibility," if their reputational interests were inadequately protected owing to an extensive privilege for alleged libel.[150] The Singapore position is that allegedly libeled public men are to enjoy equal protection with private men, because to moderate damages "purely on the basis that the successful plaintiff is a politician" or where the case has a "political flavor" would violate the Article 12 equality guarantee.[151] However, it appears that, rather than treating public men on par with private persons, the courts treated the fact that a libel suit involves "prominent public figures" as a relevant consideration in increasing damages, as "the public perception of their integrity will affect their effectiveness and standing" and they would have "the capacity to damage the reputations of those they speak ill of."[152]

Subsequent cases elaborated upon the theory underlying reputation, which resonates with the idea of the trustworthy Confucian gentleman, or *junzi*; moral superiority is expected of such men, and their reputation will suffer greatly in breaching social norms.[153] Even though Confucius is never explicitly referenced,

[144] *Lingens* v. *Austria*, para. 42. See *Gertz* v. *Robert Welch Inc* 418 US 323 (1974).
[145] Article 11, American Convention on Human Rights (1969).
[146] *Review Publishing Co Lt* v. *Lee Hsien Loong* [2010] 1 SLR at 177 [271].
[147] *Jeyaretnam Joshua Benjamin* v. *Lee Kuan Yew* [1992] 2 SLR 332H-I.
[148] (1863) 32 LJ QB 185 at 333A.
[149] Cockburn CJ, ibid., at 200.
[150] Citing Clement Gatley, *Gatley on Libel and Slander*, 8th ed. (London: Sweet & Maxwell, 1981); [1992] 2 SLR 332H–I at 333I.
[151] *Tang Liang Hong* v. *Lee Kuan Yew* [1998] 1 SLR 97 at 137–139.
[152] *Goh Chok Tong* v. *Chee Soon Juan No 2* [2005] 1 SLR 573. The two parties were the prime minister and a prominent opposition politician.
[153] For example, the Speaker of Parliament resigned his seat after his adulterous affair became public: Tessa Wong, "The Woman in Michael Palmer Affair Identified," *Straits Times*, December 12, 2012,

Justice Ang's reasoning in *Lee Hsien Loong* v. *Singapore Democratic Party*[154] resonates with Confucianist values. She explained that defamation law "presumes the good reputation of the plaintiff," which is "of utmost importance to one's personal and professional life," as people tend to listen to those they trust. The learned judge invoked the Greek rhetorician Isocrates for the proposition that "the stronger a man's desire to persuade his hearers, the more zealously will he strive to be honorable and to have the esteem of his fellow citizens." She stated that, sans public vindication, the plaintiffs, which included the prime minister, would suffer "immense and lasting damage on their political reputation and their moral authority as leaders." Defamation law protects the "essential dignity and worth of every human being";[155] it defines and enforces the boundaries of social civility, for, when the rules of civility are breached, this undermines the dignity of respect and self-respect one enjoys from full membership within the community. Defamation law seeks to remedy reputational harm through various remedies, including apologies and damages; it affirms the dignity of reputation by confirming that individuals are part of a community that suffers when one of its members is libeled.

The Court of Appeal underscored in *Review Publishing Co Ltd* v. *Lee Hsien Loong*,[156] the importance of reputation by endorsing Lord Nicholls' statement in *Reynolds* v. *Times Newspaper*[157] that reputation composed "an integral and important part of the dignity of the individual," though protecting reputation was also "conducive to the public good." Consonant with the vision of honorable governors, the court stressed that "there is no place in our political culture" for falsely defaming the reputation of persons, particularly public office holders, for "the purposes of scoring political points," as a "heavy emphasis" is placed "on honesty and integrity in public discourse on matters of public interest," including governance issues.

The clearest articulation of social ranking is found in the scheme for calculating damages after a fourfold category of defamed persons in *Lim Eng Hock Peter* v. *Lin Jian Wei*.[158] This reflects a "deference" society,[159] which is distinct from a market society where reputation is created, as preserving honor in a deference society goes beyond protecting mere individual interests. The honor due to rank is "not created by individual labor" but by "shared social perceptions" and is a public good. As Post

    www.straitstimes.com/politics/the-woman-in-michael-palmer-affair-identified. Opposition parties like the Worker's Party have applied similar standards to their MPs: "Hougang MP Yaw Disappears amid Affair Rumors," *AsiaOne*, January 28, 2012. See also Chua Chin Hon, "Few Public Signs of Trouble before Alleged Affair Prompted David Ong to Resign as MP," *Today*, March 12, 2016, www.todayonline.com/singapore/few-public-signs-trouble-alleged-affair-prompted-david-ong-resign-mp?fb_comment_id=1012594882129226_1012847902103924.
[154] [2009] 1 SLR 642 at [690[.
[155] *Rosenblatt* v. *Baer*, 383 US 75, 92 (1966), Stewart J, concurring.
[156] [2010] 1 SLR 52 at [279]
[157] [2001] 2 AC 127 at [201].
[158] [2010] SGCA 26; [2010] 4 SLR 357.
[159] Robert C. Post, "Social Foundations of Defamation Law: Reputation and the Constitution," *California Law Review* 74 (1986): 691.

argues, protecting honor involves maintaining societal consensus "with regard to the order of precedence," such that defamation law "must define and enforce the ascribed status of social roles."[160]

Both the social status of defamer and defamed are relevant in computing damages. In *Lee Hsien Loong* v. *Roy Ngerng*, the High Court accepted that a "discount" for damages should be given to a defamer "of low credence"[161] whose libel would be less grave as it was less likely to be believed. Private blog writings, for example, would be less credible than articles published on a well-established newspaper company's institutional website.[162] As Ngerng was a person of "modest standing,"[163] the judge gave him a 50 percent discount ($150,000 SGD) from the typical general and aggravated damages awarded to defamed ministers over the last twenty years.

Where the defamed person was concerned, the courts differentiated between categories of plaintiffs in determining the quantum of damages. The Court of Appeal in *Lim Eng Hock Peter* articulated four categories determining rank or social standing, based on attainment not ascription, for purposes of gradating damages. Higher damages were appropriate where public leaders were involved, for "the greater damage done not only to them personally, but also to the reputation of the institution of which they are members."[164] The term "public leaders" applied to three subcategories and not to merely people "merely famous in the public eye, such as footballers or singers and people in the entertainment industry." Their devotion to public service and high standing in Singapore society warranted higher damages.[165] This reflects a form of reputation as honor, which attaches to a social role the individual personally identifies with, who receives the estimation society accords that role. These include:

1) Political public leaders in the government
2) Non-political leaders in the public sector
3) Private sector leaders who serve the public and augment public welfare

While a prominent businessman, Peter Lim was not a public leader in the business fraternity, as contended. He was "in business for himself and not for the public welfare" and was not a "public figure" with elevated standing for purposes of defamation law.[166] However, he ought to get "a higher sum than ordinary individuals" because of damages done to his professional reputation, which conceives of reputation in the marketplace as a sort of property right earned by individual effort and labor.[167]

---

[160] Ibid., 702.
[161] [2015] SGHC 320 at [34].
[162] Ibid., at [55].
[163] Ibid., at [116].
[164] [2010] SGCA 26; [2010] 4 SLR 357 at [11].
[165] [2010] 4 SLR 357 at [12]
[166] Ibid., [29].
[167] This sort of reputation varies with market conditions and conceives of individuals as equal in that the laws of the market apply to all: Post, "Social Foundations of Defamation Law," p. 696. Professional reputation can be lost where ethical standards are transgressed. Singapore doctors swear an oath to

The court underscored the seriousness of defaming Singapore political leaders as this "damages the moral authority of such a person to lead the people and the country." While leaders could be criticized for matters like incompetence or ignorance, the critique should not "go to the extent of besmirching their integrity, honesty, honor"[168] and other qualities composing a person's reputation, like loyalty, courage, and achievement. In addition, defaming a public leader damages both his personal reputation and the corporate reputation of Singapore as a state "whose leaders have acquired a worldwide reputation for honesty and integrity in office and dedication to service of the people."[169] Higher damages reaffirm to society the importance of these particular social roles: vindication of a public leader cannot be purely pecuniary, as the defamed must enjoy a "status rehabilitation ceremony" while the convicted defamer, denounced for his wrongdoing, suffers a "status degradation ceremony."[170]

The graded approach toward quantifying damages reflects a stratified vision of human dignity; as a baseline, libelous damages suffered by an ordinary individual and private person apparently rests on his essential inherent dignity, which is fixed. For public leaders, their social role and contribution to public weal elicits higher damages, reflecting the higher social regard their role attracts, as befits the special dignity given the office. This links identity to institutional role, though the honor of those occupying the role may be forfeited by improper behavior falling short of expectations associated with that social position.[171]

3.2 Protecting the Vulnerable: The Ward Syndrome and Principles of Humanity

Human dignity as a public law value has been most explicitly articulated in cases involving the maltreatment of foreign female domestic workers (FDWs), an economically subordinate class. These cases do not directly involve government actors, relating to "horizontal relations" between private actors, where the workplace is the "private" home. There is a shameful tendency to treat FDWs badly by

---

practice medicine "with conscience and dignity"; exploiting patients through overcharging is subject to disciplinary proceedings: *Lim Mey Lee Susan v. Singapore Medical Council* [2013] SGHC 122, [39], [136]. Left unchecked, the misconduct of errant lawyers would "inexorably undermine the dignity of the legal profession": *Law Society of Singapore v. Leong Pek Gan* [2016] SGHC 250.

[168] [2010] 4 SLR 357 at [13].
[169] Ibid., at [12]. The importance of national dignity based on the integrity of public institutions and the persons entrusted with running them was emphasized in *Chee Siok Chin v. Minister of Home Affairs* [2006] 1 SLR (R) 582 at [133]. In the Islamic conception, good reputation is part of human dignity, and defamation is a "major sin whether against Muslim or dhimmi." Miklos Maroth, "Human Dignity in the Islamic World," in *The Cambridge Handbook of Human Dignity: Interdisciplinary Perspectives*, edited by Marcus Duwell, Jens Braarvig, Roger Brownsword, and Dietmar Mieth (Cambridge: Cambridge University Press, 2014), pp. 155–162.
[170] Post, "Social Foundations of Defamation Law," p, 704.
[171] Ibid., pp. 700–701.

commodifying them, as reflected in advertisements that market them like merchandise with promotional rates, placing the biodata of maids for hire on shop windows. The Manpower Ministry was prompted by a critical news article in 2014 to issue an advisory responding to disrespectful marketing practices like putting maids on display in mock living rooms doing domestic tasks; this required agencies to ensure advertisements accorded maids "basic respect and human dignity."[172] The ministry warned that action would be taken against agencies engaged in "insensitive advertising and inappropriate display."

The particular vulnerability of FDWs to the abusive treatment of employers has been described thus:

> Domestic maids are female, work within the confines of their employers' home for 24 hours of the day, and except during their time-off, are isolated from the rest of society nearly all the time, and depend on their employer for food and lodging. Maids are therefore more vulnerable to abuse by employers and their immediate family members, than any other category of employees. All employers have an obligation to treat their maids humanely and decently. The great majority of employers treat their maids well, but a small minority behave as if their maids are slaves ... Maid abuse runs counter to Singapore's aspiration to become a gracious and civil society. Abuse of foreign domestic maids can also damage our international reputation and bilateral relations.[173]

To signal the seriousness of maid abuse, the Penal Code was amended to provide that certain offences perpetrated upon a FDW by an employer or his household would carry 1.5 times the normal maximum penalties.

The judiciary has both shamed and imposed enhanced penalties on employers falling short of basic standards of decent treatment, reinforcing the communal view of unacceptable behavior. In *PP* v. *Lim Choon Hong*,[174] employers were convicted of violating a condition of the Employment of Foreign Manpower (Work Passes) Regulations 2012 in not providing adequate food to their FDW. The public prosecutor characterized this as a "denial of her basic human rights to adequate nutrition," in demanding the maximum 12 months of imprisonment.[175] Owing to a "bizarre

---

[172] Amelia Tanthe, "Treat Maids with Dignity in Ads," *Straits Times*, July 18, 2014; Samantha Boh, "Maid Agencies Remove Ads Likening Domestic Workers to Goods," *Straits Times*, September 11, 2014, www.straitstimes.com/singapore/maid-agencies-remove-ads-likening-domestic-workers-to-goods.

[173] Wong Kan Seng (Home Affairs Minister), Second Report, Penal Code (Amendment) Bill, 68 Singapore Parliament Reports, April 20, 1998.

[174] [2017] SGHC 237. See Benjamin Joshua Ong, "Offences against Foreign Domestic Workers in Singapore: Vindicating the Victim's Right to Dignity," Research Collection School Of Law (2017), http://ink.library.smu.edu.sg/cgi/viewcontent.cgi?article=4359&context=sol_research.

[175] The chief justice noted a prosecutorial "misstep" that lead to the appeal, in charging the employers under the Employment of Foreign Manpower Act, which carried lighter sentences, compared to the offence of voluntarily causing hurt (two to ten years' imprisonment) under the Penal Code. [2017] SGHC 237 at [7].

feeding regime,"[176] the victim suffered severe undernourishment and lost 40 percent of her body weight.

Chief Justice Sundaresh Menon emphasized that maids were vulnerable victims and that it was imperative to accord them "the sort of guarantees of human dignity that we would accord to any human being."[177] The respondents' "deplorable" conduct was highlighted and the "settled jurisprudence"[178] was to apply deterrence and retributive sentencing principles in cases concerning the ill treatment of FDWs. Deterrence was particularly important since FDWs "usually do not have a voice," being in a foreign land; it is also harder to detect abuses taking place within a private home. Further, to keep their jobs, maids may not report their maltreatment. FDWs were "in an inherently unequal position of subordination in relation to their employers," in many ways "dependent"[179] on their employers' good faith.

Menon CJ found the respondents had "subjected the victim to systematic cruelty and the denial of her basic human dignity,"[180] warranting the most stringent punishment. He stated the issue of whether Singaporeans accorded decent treatment to foreign workers was particularly important because of "what this says about ourselves as a society";[181] it was a matter that "defines our humanity":[182]

> If we as a progressing nation do not set our face firmly against the treatment of our fellow human beings in a way that reasonable people would regard as not being in keeping with the most basic standards of decency, then we have condemned ourselves.[183]

This serves as a compass to what should be normative standards of treatment. Indeed, in 2018, the Supreme Court signalled the need in maid abuse cases for upward revision of sentencing benchmarks. In identifying key sentencing factors, the Court appreciated the vulnerable position of maids who faced both physical and emotional harm; due weight should be accorded psychological harm, caused by humiliating or degrading treatment[184] and relentless, deliberate abuse; mental anguish would now become an aggravating sentencing consideration, while remorse could have mitigating effect. Offences involving serious harms would attract sentences between twenty and thirty months.[185]

---

[176] Ibid., [18].
[177] Ibid., [2].
[178] Ibid., [3]–[4].
[179] *Janardana Jayasankarr v. Public Prosecutor* [2016] 4 SLR 1288 at [3]–[4].
[180] [2017] SGHC 237 at [20].
[181] Ibid., at [2].
[182] Ibid., at [21].
[183] Ibid., at [2].
[184] Examples of humiliating or degrading treatment of the victim discussed in *Tay* [2018] SGHC 42 at [72] include placing ice cubes in the victim's underwear and kicking her (*Ong Ting Ting v. Public Prosecutor* [2004] 4 SLR(R) 53) and forcing a victim to strip naked and puncturing her with a sewing needle (*Soh Meiyun* [2014] 3 SLR 299).
[185] Shaffiq Idris Alkhatib, "Supreme Court Sets Sentencing Framework for Maid Abuse Cases," *Straits Times*, March 2, 2018, www.straitstimes.com/singapore/courts-crime/supreme-court-sets-sentencing-framework-for-maid-abuse-cases.

This framework was motivated by the facts of *Tay Wee Kiat* v. *Public Prosecutor*[186] where a maid was subject to "humiliating and degrading" treatment that included being forced to place herself in a push-up position when Tay kicked her. Tay was charged with voluntarily causing hurt to the victim. The district judge found it aggravating that the victim had been put through humiliating punishments, such as being subject to abusive language and forced to slap another maid and make a "humiliating confession" about stealing food.[187] Upon appeal, Tay's original sentence of twenty-eight months was increased to forty-three months as "an important signal that a maid's dignity must be considered";[188] the court factored in the egregious psychological harm inflicted, including Tay bullying his Muslim and Christian maids into bowing before a Buddhist altar 100 times, which violates religious freedom.[189]

Courts adopt a protective posture in handling FDW abuse cases, recognizing maids as "a category of persons in need of constant protection"[190] on whose behalf the "law steps in."[191] Thus, FDWs are treated as state "wards" rather than agents to be empowered. Human dignity is preserved by punishing those who subject their maids to "blatant displays of violence, cruelty and humiliating and demeaning (even dehumanising) behaviour."[192] Strongly worded condemnations such as describing subjecting domestic maids to "slave-like" working conditions and treating the victim "as chattel"[193] have educative value in identifying unacceptable behavior. Employers dehumanize their employed help insofar as some

> reduce them to their function of providing domestic help instead of seeing them as human beings with aspirations, interests, intellect and more. These employers might treat their maids as second-class persons who ought to endure uncomplainingly conditions at which they themselves would be aghast.[194]

In this context, judicial invocations of the fundamental principle of human dignity involve a call to "level up" by duly respecting the human dignity of vulnerable persons. This appeal to conscience attempts to remind employers to see maids not as quasi-slaves who employers claim a "right" to slap[195] but as fellow human beings deserving decent treatment. It also warns that those who flout these standards of civilized, humane treatment will be punished. This upholds moral solidarity by

---

[186] [2018] SGHC 42.
[187] [2018] SGHC 42 at [12].
[188] Shaffiq Idris Alkhatib, "Getting Tougher on Maid Abusers," *Straits Times*, March 8, 2018, www.straitstimes.com/singapore/courts-crime/getting-tougher-on-maid-abusers.
[189] [2018] SGHC 42 at [78].
[190] ADF v. PP [2010] 1 SLR 874 at [61].
[191] *Janardana Jayasankarr* v. *Public Prosecutor* [2016] 4 SLR 1288 at [4].
[192] Ibid., [66].
[193] [2018] SGHC 42 at [69].
[194] Chao Hick Tin JA, *Soh Meiyun* v. *Public Prosecutor* [2014] 3 SLR 299 at [44].
[195] *Public Prosecutor* v. *Rosman bin Anwar* [2015] 5 SLR 937 at [50].

elaborating on what common moral standards require, which informs the identity and character of the community itself.

4 CONCLUDING OBSERVATIONS

Inherent or contingent, egalitarian or elitist, source of rights or of duties, it is clear that there are divergent conceptions of human dignity; what is required to realize this varies on a global scale. Understandings of human dignity, whether based on a substantive conception that identifies what a dignified/undignified life[196] is or a more "procedural one" prioritizing individual choice and agency may not be reconcilable but may coexist and clash. Courts have, for example, recognized "self-determination, personal autonomy, self-respect, feelings of self-worth and empowerment" as being "the stuff and substance of essential human dignity."[197] Human dignity has been invoked to support claims for material state assistance to realize a dignified existence, correlating with the goal of socioeconomic rights. It has grounded the basis for resisting the state to secure maximum autonomy, which correlates with civil-political rights. It has been utilized to support claims for recognition of differences and inclusion in the community and to prohibit words or forms of conduct that affect the self-esteem of groups and generate feelings of exclusion or second-class citizenship.[198]

Which conception assumes precedence will be influenced by whether a polity is committed to liberal or communitarian values (or a mix thereof), whether religious or secular criteria is applied. This points to the open-textured nature of "human dignity" and its malleability in political claims and legal argumentation. Invoking human dignity does not solve many of the old debates between individual and group rights, liberty and equality, such as whether a ban on religious dress like the burqa vindicates or undermines women's dignity.

In Singapore, human dignity as the basis for universal human rights has legitimized the discourse globally but brings with it disputes over what are genuinely universal core human rights and what claims are contested. Dignity discourse brings to the fore the fundamental question of "what type of respect can a person demand from others and from the state?"[199] This implicates questions of personhood, community identity, and public values. Singapore's communitarian-oriented relational

---

[196] For example, dwarf throwing is considered an affront to human dignity, even if the dwarf chooses to allow this: *Wackenheim v. France* CCPR/C75/D/854/1999 (July 26, 2002) at 4.5.

[197] *Gosselin v. Quebec* 2002, SCC 84, para. 65 (Can).

[198] "A person's sense of human dignity and belonging to the community at large is closely linked to the concern and respect accorded the group to which he or she belongs." *R v. Keegstra* [1990] 3 SCR 697 at 746–747 (Can). Section 298 of the Singapore Penal Code makes it an offence to utter words with deliberate intent "to wound the religious or racial feelings of any person," which may be related to this conception of dignity.

[199] Neomi Rao, "Three Concepts of Dignity in Constitutional Law," *Notre Dame Law Review* 86, no. 1 (2011): 186.

constitutionalism sustains a vision of human dignity distinct from liberal, autonomist,[200] and egalitarian conceptions of human dignity, though this does not preclude a mix of "liberal" and "nonliberal" visions of human dignity within the same polity. Agency is not the sole value, as communitarians conceive of human dignity as a value that binds a group together by setting community-defined limits to individual freedom and defining anti-social action by criminalizing conduct or advocating preferred norms of conduct. This could relate to the goal of promoting relational solidarity, such as committing to forgive repentant disruptors of racial and religious harmony, or give effect to cultural norms where "virtuous" political leaders enjoy special respect, as reflected in defamation laws.

Both egalitarian and hierarchical conceptions of human dignity coexist in Singapore; all persons may enjoy equal dignity, but special dignity may attach to a social status or role, such that degrees of dignity exist in the social realm. To deny these important aspects of human nature and society may be destructive. The egalitarian strain flows from a conception of citizens as political equals who participate in a system they can shape to secure individual and collective welfare; it may also derive from the idea of dignity as inherent in all human being, stemming from "core" universal human rights. This may come into tension where a system adopts methods like legal pluralism or special rights to respect differences, such as establishing religious courts that apply gender inegalitarian religious laws over specific matters like inheritance laws, contrary to human rights standards.[201]

Ultimately the concept of human dignity that a sociopolitical community wants to promote and protect is an act of self-definition, of deciding who belongs and is excluded from the community, how its members are to interrelate, how the government treats citizens and foreigners, and the shape of the common good. This foregrounds the long-standing debate over what the "good life" constitutes and how human flourishing is best achieved, which bare invocations of human dignity cannot resolve.

---

[200] Oscar Schacter, "Human Dignity as a Normative Concept," *American Journal of International Law* 77, no. 4 (October 1983): 848.
[201] Thio, "She's a Woman, but She Acts Very Fast."

9

Personal Dignity under Chinese Constitutional Law

Xiaobo Zhai[*]

Article 38 of the Constitution of the People's Republic of China reads: "The personal dignity [*renge zunyan* 人格尊严][1] of citizens of the People's Republic of China is inviolable. Insult, libel, false charge, or frame-up directed against citizens by any means is prohibited." The ratification of Article 38 was unprecedented in the almost 100 years of constitution-making history in China. It was intended to be a record of the painful lessons of, and a direct response to, the totalitarian atrocities of the Cultural Revolution (1966–76, hereafter CR). This chapter has two tasks. Section 1 discusses the correct understanding of Article 38. Section 2 considers the implementation of Article 38 in modern China.

1 THE MEANING OF ARTICLE 38

There are two prevalent readings of Article 38 in China. In the first, the term "personal dignity" is not synonymous with "human dignity" – as the latter is typically construed under German Basic Law – but much more limited in its scope. According to this reading, personal dignity refers to typical personality rights, including the right to one's name, likeness, reputation, honors, and privacy, or to the general personality right.[2] In the second reading, the right of personal dignity is

---

[*] I would like to express sincere gratitude to Pritam Baruah, Jimmy Chia-Shin Hsu, and Chris Riley for their helpful suggestions and comments and to Yanfeng Zhang for his research assistance.

[1] This term is literally susceptible to three different translations: "personhood and dignity"; "the dignity of personhood"; and "personal dignity." "Personal dignity" is the most common translation and will be adopted throughout the present chapter.

[2] Lin Laifan, "Ren de zunyan yu renge zunyan [Human dignity and personal dignity]," *Zhejiang shehui kexue* [*Zhejiang Social Sciences*], no. 3 (2008): 49, 52; also Lin Laifan, *Cong Xianfa guifan dao guifan xianfa* [*From constitutional norms to normative constitution*] (Beijing: Shangwu Yinshuguan, 2017): 183–187. Wang Kai, "Lun xianfa shangde yiban rengequan jiqi dui minfa de yingxiang [The general personality right in the Constitution and its influence on civil law]," *Zhongguo faxue* [*China Legal Science*], no. 3 (2017): 103–104, 108. Wang Liming, Yang Lixin, and Yaohui, *Rengequan fa* [*Law of Personality Rights*] (Beijing: Falv Chubanshe, 1997): 19. Li Zhang, "The Emergence of Human Dignity in China: From a Private Right to a Constitutional Principle," in B. Feuillet-Liger and K. Orfali (eds.), *The Reality of Human Dignity in Law and Bioethics* (New York: Springer, 2018), p. 237. Supreme

a constitutional right that ought to be protected against the state and the use of its public power, rather than a civil law right that might be invoked by one private citizen against another.³

These two prevalent readings of Article 38 will be challenged in this chapter, which argues that personal dignity under Article 38 is indistinguishable from human dignity as typically understood in German Basic Law⁴ and that it imposes duty upon both the state and private individuals.

1.1 *Official Interchangeability*

"Personal dignity" and "human dignity" are used interchangeably in official Chinese legal texts. In its report entitled *Progress in Human Rights over the 40 Years of Reform and Opening Up in China* of December 2018, for instance, the State Council declared that "for the past forty years, Chinese Communist Party has always respected the value and dignity of humans (人的价值与尊严), and promoted the full development of humans."⁵ In *The Annual Report of the Rule of Law in China* (2010), the China Law Society (中国法学会), an official organization, pointed out that "the protection of human dignity (人的尊严) became an important guiding idea of China's rule-of-law construction."⁶ In his speech at Yale University in 2006, China's former president Hu Jintao (胡锦涛) announced that "Chinese civilization has always taken people as its foundation (以民为本), and respected the

---

People's Court, "Quanguo minshi anjian shenpan zhiliang gongzuo zuotanhui jiyao [A Summary of National Symposium on Quality of Civil-Case-Trials]" [no. 231, 1999], in The Supreme People's Court and The Supreme People's Procuratorate, *Judicial Interpretations & the Queries and Replies: Civil Law Volume* (Sifajieshi yu qingshidafu) (Beijing: Zhongguo Fazhi Chubanshe, 2006), p. 1100. On the official position of the Chinese government, see Guo Wuyuan Xinwen Bangongshi (The State Council Information Office), *Gaige kaifang sishinian zhongguo renquanshiye de fazhan* jinbu (Progress in Human Rights over the 40 Years of Reform and Opening Up in China) (December 2018), www.gov.cn/zhengce/2018-12/12/content_5347961.htm, accessed June 13, 2020.

³ Xie Libin, "Zhongde bijiao xianfa shiyexia de renge zunyan [Personal Dignity: A Comparison between German and Chinese Constitutions]," *Zhengfa Luntan* [*Tribune of Political Science and Law*], no. 4 (2010): 61–2. Wang Kai, "Lun xianfa shangde yiban rengequan," p. 117.

⁴ Under German Basic Law, human dignity is "the foundational value of the social order, a basic norm that appears behind the more concrete guarantees in the Bill of Rights, but also behind the structural and organizational provisions of the constitution such as democracy and the rule of law." Dieter Grimm, "Dignity in a Legal Context and as an Absolute Right," in Christopher McCrudden (ed.), *Understanding Human Dignity* (Oxford: Oxford University Press, 2013), p. 386; also Werrner Heun, *The Constitution of Germany* (Oxford: Hart Publishing, 2011), p. 201: human dignity is "the highest value of the Basic Law, the ultimate basis of the constitutional system and the foundation of all guaranteed rights ... the normative foundation of the Federal Republic, the essence of its statehood." For the idea of human dignity in German Basic Law, see Donald Kommers and Russell Miller, *The Constitutional Jurisprudence of the Federal Republic of Germany* (Durham, NC: Duke University Press, 2012), pp. 355–373.

⁵ Guo Wuyuan, *Gaige kaifang sishinian*.

⁶ Zhongguo Faxuehui (The China Law Society), *Zhongguo Fazhi Jianshe Niandu Baogao* [*The Annual Report of the Rule of Law in China*] (2010), www.pkulaw.com/chl/fbc11b59d117210fbdfb.html, accessed June 13, 2020.

dignity and value of humans (人的尊严和价值)."[7] At the opening ceremony of the 4th Beijing Forum on Human Rights in 2011, Luo Haocai (罗豪才), former vice chairman of the Chinese People's Political Consultative Conference and former president of the China Society for Human Rights Studies (CSHRS), gave a speech entitled "Different Cultures can Equally Respect Human Dignity," in which he claimed that "protecting and improving human dignity has already become the starting point and the ultimate goal of the work of our government."[8] In his congratulatory letter to a symposium marking the seventieth anniversary of the Universal Declaration of Human Rights in Beijing, China's current president Xi Jinping (习近平) pledged that "Chinese people will work with people of other countries to uphold the common values of peace, development, equality, justice, democracy and freedom, and to safeguard the dignity and rights of humans (人的尊严与权利)."[9] In his speech at the same symposium, Qiangba Puncog (向平巴措), vice chairman of the Standing Committee of the 12th National People's Congress and current president of the CSHRS, used the phrases "human dignity" and "personal dignity" interchangeably in the same paragraph.[10] On each of these occasions, leading authorities who were familiar with Article 38 opted to utilize the term "human dignity" and did not make any distinction between human dignity and personal dignity. It may safely be assumed that they believed both were interchangeable and therefore that both were equivalent to one another in the interpretation and implementation of the content of Article 38.

According to the official constitutional ideology in China, legislation or lawmaking works as a major way of interpreting and implementing the Constitution. In Chinese legal texts, the term "personal dignity" is more frequently used than human dignity, but the term "human dignity" is not absent entirely. For instance, the *Law of China's Red Cross Society* (2017) states that its purpose is to "protect human life and health, and safeguard human dignity."[11] The *Regulation on the Ethical Review of Biomedical Research Involving Humans* (2016), as enacted by the National Committee of Health and Family Planning, also stipulates that its purpose is to

---

[7] Hu Jintao, "Zai Yelu Daxue de yanjiang [A speech at Yale University]," http://news.sina.com.cn/c/2006-04-22/054687604135.shtml. The translation is mine. An English version of his speech is available at www.wsj.com/articles/SB114566179560133020, accessed June 13, 2020.

[8] Luo Haocai, "Buyiyang de wenhua keyi yiyang zunzhong rende zunyan [Different cultures can equally respect human dignity]," www.humanrights-china.org/cn/zt/qita/rqzz/2011/6/t20120112_838631.htm, accessed June 13, 2020.

[9] Xi Jingping, "Jianchi zou fuhe guoqing de renquan fazhan daolu, cujin ren de quanmian fazhan [Adhering to the path of human rights development with Chinese characteristics, and promoting the comprehensive development of humans]," www.xinhuanet.com/politics/leaders/2018-12/10/c_1123831503.htm, accessed June 13, 2020.

[10] Qiangba Puncog, "Zai jinian shijie renquan xuanyan fabiao 70 zhounian zuotanhui shang de jianghua [A speech at the Symposium Commemorating the 70th Anniversary of the Universal Declaration of Human Rights]," www.humanrights.cn/html/2018/2_1211/40928.html, accessed June 13, 2020.

[11] Article 1, www.gov.cn/banshi/2005-07/12/content_13743.htm, accessed June 13, 2020.

"protect human life and health, and safeguard human dignity."[12] The Supreme Court in its *Unified Regulation on Evidence (A Proposal)* (2008) provides that "the confession obtained by means of measures impairing human dignity should be excluded."[13] In Taiwan's legal and political discourse, human dignity (人性尊严, literally "the dignity of human nature") is predominant – but here, too, "personal dignity" is commonly used interchangeably with "human dignity." For instance, one of the amendments to the Taiwan's Constitution reads: "The state should safeguard the personal dignity of women."[14] The Taiwan Constitutional Court stipulates in its constitutional interpretation No. 372 that "personal dignity ... is enshrined in the Universal Declaration of Human Rights" and that "personal dignity" is "the foundational idea underlying our constitutional provisions of liberties and rights."[15]

In official documents, the term "personal dignity" is translated as "human dignity." The National People's Congress (NPC), China's highest lawmaking authority, has failed to provide an official translation of the Chinese Constitution into English. In spite of this, Article 38 was copied directly by the NPC into Article 30 of Macau Basic Law, which was enacted bilingually in both Chinese and Portuguese. In the official Portuguese version of the text, "personal dignity" has been transliterated as "dignidade humana" – that is, human dignity. This demonstrates that the NPC, which also has the power to interpret the Constitution, does not think that there is any distinction between personal dignity and human dignity. Similarly, in the preamble of the *Charter of the United Nations* (1945), "the dignity ... of the human person" in English corresponds to personal dignity in the Chinese version of the text. In unofficial contexts, translating "human dignity" into "personal dignity" is also common. "Human dignity" in a number of foreign constitutions around the world has been widely translated as "personal dignity."[16]

1.2 *Ordinary and Technical Uses*

Of the word "personal" (人格) in the term "personal dignity," there are two alternative uses, namely the ordinary use by the public and the technical use by lawyers. As lawyers' jargon, "personal" or personality encompasses a set of civil law rights: the right to life; the inviolability and integrity of one's person; the right to one's name,

---

[12] Article 1, www.nhc.gov.cn/fzs/s3576/201610/84b33b81d8e747eaaf048f68b174f829.shtml, accessed June 13, 2020.
[13] Zuigao Renmin Fayuan (The Supreme Court), "Renmin fayuan tongyi zhengju guiding (sifa jieshi jianyigao) [Unified Regulation on Evidence (A proposal)], http://lawinfochina.com/display.aspx?id=24fb066fb8eded79bdfb&lib=law, accessed June 13, 2020.
[14] Article 10 of the Additional Articles, https://law.moj.gov.tw/LawClass/LawSingle.aspx?pcode=A0000002, accessed June 13, 2020.
[15] Judicial Yuan Interpretation No. 372, http://cons.judicial.gov.tw/jcc/zh-tw/jep03/show?expno=372, accessed June 13, 2020. For an in-depth analysis of this seminal constitutional interpretation, see Chapter 4 in this volume by Jimmy Chia-Shin Hsu.
[16] See Chen Yunsheng, "Gongmin de renge zunyan bushou qinfan [The personal dignity of citizens is inviolable]," *Faxue Yanjiu* [*Chinese Journal of Law*], no. 1 (1983): 17.

image, reputation, honor, privacy, and personal data; and also the general personality right.[17] Given that, among those who drafted the Chinese Constitution in 1982, no one boasted sufficient legal expertise, the terms "personal" or "personality" (人格) cannot have been understood in a legalistic sense, as construed in civil law.[18] The Constitution was drafted and ratified by politicians and addressed to the Chinese people, and therefore personality should be understood in its ordinary, lay sense, as shared by politicians and the general public.

Although the majority of constitutional scholars now identify personal dignity in Article 38 with personality rights, its ordinary, nontechnical use has been adopted by those who were involved in the writing of the Constitution and who therefore better understood its meaning. According to these individuals, the inviolable nature of personal dignity demands the protection of personality rights, but the former is more foundational and broader than the latter. For instance, in 1982, Chen Yunsheng asked "What is citizens' personal dignity?" and he explained that it was "the dignity or status of being a person, which includes one's status, reputation, image, title, and prestige, etc."[19] An essay that was published in *Worker's Daily* in the same year argued that "personal dignity means that one's personhood ought to be respected and protected. Personhood is the status by which a person, as a person, must have," and "denying one's personhood is denying that he is a person, and in law it means denying all of his rights."[20] This explanation was repeated by Wang Xiangming and Xu Chongde in their coauthored textbook entitled *Lectures on Chinese Constitution* in 1987.[21]

1.3 *Etymologically Kantian*

If the ordinary, lay use of the term "personal dignity" ought to be adopted, what does it mean?[22] In the present and next subsections, this question will be answered first etymologically and then historically.

[17] For the general personality right, see Corinna Coors, "Headwind from Europe: The New Position of the German Courts on Personality Rights after the Judgment of the European Court of Human Rights," *German Law Journal* 11, no. 5 (2010): 529; Adrian Popovici, "Personality Rights – A Civil Law Concept," *Loyola Law Review* 50, no. 2 (2004): 353.
[18] On the specialized, Germanic civil law reading, see Wangkai, "Lun xianfa shangde yiban rengequan," p. 104.
[19] Chen Yunsheng, "Gongmin de renge zunyan," p.15.
[20] *Gongren Ribao* (*Worker's Daily*) (Augus 10, 1982).
[21] *Zhongguo Xianfa Jiangyi* (Beijing: Zhongguo Guangbo Dianshi Daxue Chubanshe, 1987): 372. Other influential authors who wrote in 1982 and 1983 and did not treat personal dignity as a legal jargon include Xu Chongde, *Xinxianfa Jianghua* [*Lectures on New Constitution*] (Hangzhou: Zhejiang Renmin Chubanshe): 107; and Lin Hengyuan, "Citizens' Basic Rights and Duties," in *Xinxianfa shier jiang* [*Twelve Lectures on New Constitution*] (Nanjing: Jiangsu Renmin Chubanshe, 1983), p. 67.
[22] In its ordinary usage, 人格 also has two other meanings: first, it means a person's morality (see Deng Xiaomang, "Renge bianyi [An analysis of the meanings of personality]," *Jianghai Xuekan* [*Jianghai Academic Journal*], no. 3 (1989): 10; and second, it is a technical term in psychology. These two meanings are not relevant to Article 38 of the Chinese Constitution.

"Dignity" (尊严) is a traditional Chinese term, which means the inviolability of one's respectable, honorable, and dignified status or identity.²³ Personality (or personhood, 人格) is not a common word in traditional Chinese vocabulary, and it was not included in *Ciyuan* (辞源), a major modern Chinese dictionary, first published in 1915.²⁴ In a rare early example, philosopher Chen Guangtao (陈光焘) used the term "personal dignity" (人格尊严) in a poem entitled "Three Saints Meeting Each Other" to mean the sacredness of personhood and humanity, and the quality which distinguishes human beings from brute beasts. Chen Guangtao emphasized in this poem that personal dignity is a universal value shared by a number of major religions, including Confucianism, Buddhism, and Christianity.²⁵ The Chinese words 人格, and 人格尊严, in their modern uses, may very likely, as do many other Chinese moral, political, and legal terms, have their origins in Japanese from the late Qing Dynasty (1840–1912).²⁶ In Japanese, there are also two phrases which correspond to Chinese vocabulary in this context: namely, 人間の尊厳, meaning human dignity, and 人格の尊厳, meaning personal dignity, both of which may be used interchangeably. When referring to human dignity, or *persönlichkeit* in the Kantian sense, 人格の尊厳 is often preferred.²⁷ With this in mind, it is probably safe to suggest that, as an etymological matter, personal dignity in Article 38 has a somewhat Kantian origin. Chinese philosopher and Kantian scholar Deng Xiaomang (邓晓芒) has interpreted personhood this way,²⁸ stating that it is what, quoting Kant,

> elevates a human being above himself (as a part of the sensible world). ... It is nothing other than personality, that is, freedom and independence from the mechanism of the whole of nature, ... a capacity of a being subject to ... pure practical laws given by his own reason, so that a person as belonging to the sensible world is subject to his own personality insofar as he also belongs to the intelligible world.²⁹

By virtue of his personality, according to Kant, "a human being alone, and with him every rational creature, is an end in itself: by virtue of the autonomy of his freedom he is the subject of the moral law, which is holy."³⁰ The Kantian tone of the Chinese

---

²³ See also Chapter 4 in this volume by Jimmy Chia-Shin Hsu.
²⁴ *Ciyuan* (Beijing: Shangwu Yinshuguan, 1915).
²⁵ Chen Guangtao "Sansheng juhuitu tishi [A Poem on Three Saints Meeting Each Other]," *Xueheng* [*The Critical Review*], no. 70 (July 1929): 13.
²⁶ According to Qu Wei, the Chinese word 人格, in its legal sense, originally came from Japan. See his *Renge zhi mi* [*The Mystery of Personality*] (Beijing: Zhongguo Renmindaxue Chubanshe, 1991): 8.
²⁷ I thank Michihiro Kaino for his clarification on this point.
²⁸ Deng Xiaomang, "Renge bianyi" and "Guanyu person he personlichkeit de fanyi wenti [On the translation of person and personlichkeit], *Zhexue Dongtai* [*Philosophical Trends*], no. 10 (2015).
²⁹ Immanuel Kant, "Critique of Practical Reason," in *Practical Philosophy*, translated and edited by Mary J. Gregor (Cambridge: Cambridge University Press, 1999), p. 210.
³⁰ Ibid. See also Immanuel Kant, "The Groundwork of the Metaphysics of Morals," in *Practical Philosophy*, p. 84: "Morality is the condition under which alone a rational being can be an end in itself ... Morality, and humanity insofar as it is capable of morality, is that which alone has dignity."

understanding of personal dignity is abundantly clear in the aforementioned speech by Luo Haocai:

> Human dignity denotes the inherent nobleness and sublimity of humans, the basic capacities by means of which humans are humans. ... Human dignity is based upon the rationality and morality of humans, and it includes the recognition of the importance of the worth of humans, requires equal treatment, and opposes discrimination and unfairness.[31]

Civil law scholar Zhu Qingyu (朱庆育) has also suggested that lawyers only began to discuss personality rights in earnest after Kant's philosophy had penetrated legal theory and that the development of personal dignity as a legal construct was based upon Kant's ethical idea of personality.[32]

1.4 *The Historical Rationality of Article 38*

The Kantian understanding of personal dignity is further confirmed by the historical rationale that gave rise to Article 38 itself. As already alluded to, it is widely acknowledged that this article was a reaction to the bitter lessons of the CR. The meaning of Article 38, therefore, must be understood in the context of the CR itself and the broader ideological Maoism from which the CR was inseparable. The CR, formally called the Great Proletarian Cultural Revolution, was a ten-year movement (1966–76) launched by Mao, "during which, at his command, the mass of the Chinese people engaged in an orgy of violence. They humiliated, beat, and killed anyone suspected of being opposed to Mao."[33] The CR is a banned topic in present-day China, but, according to the official narrative of the Chinese government, it was a "great disaster" that "caused the most severe setback and the heaviest losses to the Party, the state, and the people since the founding of the People's Republic." It was a serious "domestic turmoil which was initiated mistakenly by a leader and capitalized on by counter-revolutionary cliques," and it "brought severe catastrophe upon the Party, the state and the whole people."[34] During the CR, "state institutions, including the police, procuratorates, and courts, were completely smashed, democracy and laws were flagrantly trampled on, and the country was thrown into a serious political and social crisis." After the CR had ended, "social atmosphere was much worse than before, and people's morality plummeted."[35] According to historian

---

[31] Luo Haocai, "Buyiyang de wenhua."
[32] Zhu Qingyu, *Minfa Zonglun* [*The General Theory of Civil Law*] (Beijing: Beijing Daxue Chubansshe, 2016), pp. 400–401.
[33] Michael Lynch, *The People's Republic of China 1949–1976* (London: Hodder Education, 2008), 72.
[34] Zhonggong Zhongyang Dangshi Yanjiushi, *Liangge Lishiwenti de Jueyi ji Shiyijie Sanzhongquanhui yilai dang dui lishi de huigu (jianming zhushi ben)* [*Two Resolutions on CPC History and CPC's Reviews of History since the Third Plenary Session of the Eleventh Central Committee*] (Beijing: Zhonggong Dangshi Chubanshe, 2013), 75, 100.
[35] Ibid., p. 175.

Tong Tekong, in the last two decades of Mao's rule, "tens of millions suffered unnatural death.... The whole of China had been pushed into a bottomless abyss of complete shamelessness and immorality."[36]

The CR was an unprecedented human tragedy, and one that far exceeded the imaginations of many people in China and around the world.[37] It was not merely the mistake of its initiator or of its leaders but rather the eruption of collective madness and brutality at the instigation of a tyrannical leader,[38] who had been glorified as a god and who abused millions of ordinary people – particularly the official and intellectual elite – in furtherance of his own personal grandeur. A substantial proportion of the Chinese people enthusiastically participated in or contributed to his evildoing, brutally persecuting their friends, relatives, and fellow citizens.

During the CR, tens of millions of people were persecuted extrajudicially – scores of innocent people, including children and newborn babies, were murdered: shot, beheaded, pushed off cliffs, hacked to death with farming implements, or cannibalized.[39] Many more were beaten and crippled. Anyone could be violently dragged out in public before jeering crowds: cursed, tortured, insulted, humiliated, or imprisoned. People were arbitrarily labeled with derogatory epithets – "ox ghost and snake spirit" (牛鬼蛇神), "son of a bitch" (狗崽子), "capitalist running-dog," "counterrevolutionary," "traitor," and "spy" – or were classified into "five black categories" (黑五类), including landlords, rich farmers, counterrevolutionaries, bad elements, and rightists (地富反坏右). Intellectuals were labeled as "the stinking number nine" (臭老九).[40] People were forced to betray, humiliate, or even kill their loved ones, including their parents, spouses, children, teachers, friends, and colleagues. Hundreds of thousands of others committed suicide or suffered mental breakdown. Houses were searched and personal property was confiscated or destroyed, without any legal basis.

---

[36] Tong Tekong, *Mao Zedong Zhuanzheng Shimo* [*A History of Mao's Dictatorship*] (Taiwan: Yuanliu Chubanshe, 2005), p. 224.

[37] See Andrew G. Walder, "Cultural Revolution Radicalism: Variations on a Stalinist Theme," in W. Joseph, C. Wong, and D. Zweig (eds.), *New Perspectives on the Cultural Revolution* (Cambridge, MA: Harvard University Press, 1991), p. 42. See also Roderick MacFarquhar, *Origins of the Cultural Revolution, Volume I: Contradictions among the People* (New York: Columbia University Press, 1974), p. 3; Xu Youyu, "Wenhua dageming shi shenme? [What is the Cultural Revolution?]," in Jean Hung, Song Yongyi, and Yu Kwok Leung (eds), *Zhongwai Xuezhe Tan Wenge* [*Cultural Revolution: Recollections, Reconstructions, and Reflections*)] (Hong Kong: Chinese University of Hong Kong Press, 2018), p. xlviii.

[38] Wang Xiaobo, *Chenmo de Daduoshu* [*The Silent Majority*] (Beijing: Zhongguo Qingnian Chubanshe, 1997), p. 17; Michael Linch, *The People's Republic of China 1949-76*, p. 102.

[39] See Y. Su, *Collective Killings in Rural China during the Cultural Revolution* (Cambridge: Cambridge University Press, 2011); Xu Youyu, "Wenhua dageming shi shenme," p. xl.

[40] The term originated during the Yuan Dynasty (1279–1368). The Mongol conquerors classified the population into ten ranks: bureaucrats, officials, Buddhist monks, Taoist priests, physicians, workers, hunters, prostitutes, Confucian scholars, and beggars. Scholars were the ninth in this hierarchy, only above beggars. See also Kwok-sing Li, *A Glossary of Political Terms of PRC*, trans. M. Lock (Hong Kong: Chinese University of Hong Kong Press, 1995), 27.

Anne Thurston has characterized the effects of the CR on its victims by the word "loss": "loss of culture and of spiritual values; loss of status and honor; loss of career and dignity; loss of hope and ideals; loss of time, truth, and of life; loss, in short, of nearly everything that gives meaning to life ... [loss] of trust and predictability in human relations."[41] Chinese writer Feng Jicai (冯骥才) has also provided a vivid description of the extensive and lasting damage of the CR:

> Within ten years, a civilization whose abundant roots reach back into antiquity suddenly all but vanished: people turned on each other in a barbarous performance of blood-letting; goodness and beauty went underground, ugliness and evil were given wanton release; ... everything that contributes to the nobility of man – ... humanity, ... human dignity and value – was ridiculed and abused. ... The frailty of human nature, manifested in jealousy, timidity, selfishness, and vanity, as well as such human strengths as courage, loyalty, and devotion, all were capitalized on and transformed into a monstrous driving force.[42]

According to Wang Hanbin (王汉斌), one of the leading members of the Committee for Amending the Constitution (宪法修改委员会副秘书长 (1980–2)), it was Peng Zhen (彭真) who insisted that the inviolability of personal dignity be enshrined in the Constitution.[43] This seems to contradict Wang Kai (王锴)'s claim that personal dignity is "a right of low importance" under the Chinese Constitution and only one component part of personal freedom.[44] Peng Zhen was the first Politburo member to be purged during the CR. As the vice chairman of the Committee for Amending the Constitution, Peng Zhen explained that the newly added Article 38 was a lesson that had been taught by the CR.[45] Undoubtedly, there were widespread violations of people's personality rights in the years of the CR, but its lesson was much more wide-ranging. The monstrosities of the CR consisted mainly in its systemic and comprehensive dehumanization – it was a massacre of the rationality and morality by virtue of which humans may be conceived as human.[46] As a lesson of and reaction to the dehumanizing effects of the CR, Article 38 requires that the humanity – that is, the *rationality and morality* by

---

[41] Anne Thurston, "Victims of China's Cultural Revolution: The Invisible Wounds: Part I," *Pacific Affairs* 57, no. 4 (1984–1985): 605–606.
[42] Feng Jicai, *Yibai ge ren de shinian* [*Ten Years of One Hundred People*] (Nanjing: Jiangsu Wenyi Chubanshe, 1991): 1–3. The translation is based on that of Howard Goldblatt in *Ten Years of Madness: Oral Histories of China's Cultural Revolution* (San Francisco, CA: China Books and Periodicals, Inc., 1996), pp. v–vi, viii, but with some revisions and additions.
[43] Zhao Lei, "Renda Yuan Fuweiyuanzhang Wang Hanbin: Renda Changweihui ying xingshi weixian shenchaquan [NPCSC Ought to Exercise Its Power of Constitutional Review]," *Southern Weekly* (April 18, 2013).
[44] Wang Kai, "Lun xianfa shangde yiban rengequan," p. 108.
[45] Peng Zhen, "Guanyu zhonghua renmin gongheguo xianfa caoan de baogao [Report on the Draft of the Revised Constitution of the People's Republic of China]" (November 26, 1982), www.people.com.cn/item/xianfa/08.html, accessed June 13, 2020.
[46] Xu Youyu, "Wenhua dageming shi shenme?", pp. xl, xlvi.

means of which humans are humans and have equal worth – be respected and protected and that humans be treated "as an end, and never as a mere means."

Another familiar way of talking about the violations of human dignity during the CR concerns how China's social and official elites were treated in this period. The CR, in the mind of its leaders, was meant to be a revolution against authorities and intellectuals.[47] During the CR, leading cadres of the Party and of government organizations at all levels were overthrown or subjected to persecution, and, as already alluded to, many accomplished intellectuals were labeled as "ox ghost and snake spirit" and attacked.[48] A common form of persecution that was suffered by these elites was being forced to perform jobs which, in Chinese culture, were regarded as the dirtiest and basest occupations, such as cleaning latrines, and were hence particularly demeaning and humiliating for those who were involved. A common belief among the Chinese people is that, morally and legally speaking, people ought to be treated equally – but that, as the result of extraordinarily hard work and self-cultivation, some people make great achievements and thus become more virtuous, enjoying higher social standing as a consequence, and deserve special respect from their fellow citizens. In this context, what was violated during the CR, aside from the *human* dignity of these elites, was the dignity of these elites *qua* elites – a special, elevated form of dignity, befitting professors, artists, and leading statesmen. It should be noted that this type of dignity (i.e. the idea of *dignitas*, meaning the special status attached to, and special respect owed to, a certain social standing) is not considered to be a part of the personal dignity under Article 38, which emphasizes that the inviolable personal dignity is that of ordinary citizens. Here, even those who might be regarded as the basest, most despicable or unintelligent of Chinese citizens have inviolable personal dignity, simply by virtue of their being human.

1.5 A Basic Constitutional Right and Principle

Thus far in the present chapter the foundational idea of the inviolability of personal dignity under Article 38 has been examined. Now it remains to look in greater detail at its concrete constitutional meaning, followed by an analysis of its implementation or the lack thereof.

In the Constitution itself, Article 38 is placed in Chapter 2, entitled "The Fundamental Rights and Duties of Citizens," and hence personal dignity is undoubtedly a fundamental constitutional right of the Chinese people. The right to human dignity includes the right of reputation, which is embodied in the second sentence of Article 38: "Insult, libel, false charge or frame-up directed against citizens by any means is prohibited."

---

[47] See J. K. Fairbank and M. Goldman, *China: A New History* (Cambridge, MA: Harvard University Press, 2006): 359–364.
[48] CPC, "Guanyu jiangguoyilai dang de ruogan lishiwenti de jueyi."

Chinese scholar Lin Laifan (林来梵) has claimed that "the first sentence of Article 38 can be roughly and arguably understood as announcing a key and fundamental constitutional value or principle which forms the core of human rights."[49] This is to treat Article 38 in the same way as constitutional lawyers in Germany treat the first sentence of Article 1 of German Basic Law. Lin's reading was criticized by Xie Libin (谢立斌) as oversimplified, farfetched, and unconvincing.[50] One obvious reason for this criticism is the location of Article 38 in the Constitution.[51] Under German Basic Law, the inviolability of human dignity is established in the first sentence of Article 1 of Chapter 1, entitled "Basic Rights." Under the Chinese Constitution, however, it is stipulated in Article 38, which is the sixth article in Chapter 2, preceded by the freedom of one's person and preceding the violability of one's home. The question, therefore, is how important the place of a provision is in the Constitution when determining its overall gravity. There is little doubt that the place does matter and that personal dignity under the Chinese Constitution is not exactly equivalent to what human dignity is under German Basic Law. However, unwarranted is the view that the place of Article 38 shows that personal dignity is only one constitutional right, no more important than the other rights contained within Chapter 2.[52] First, as shown above, this view is inconsistent with the intention of the Constitution-makers when they composed Article 38.[53] Second, regarding the interpretation of Article 38, its positioning is only one – and far from the most important – of the many factors that determine its meaning and importance.[54] For instance, the market economy is the most important principle of China's economic system, but it does not appear until Article 15 of Chapter 1, following Article 14 on labor productivity and followed by Article 16 on the autonomous managerial power of state enterprises.

Third, this view contradicts China's current official position on personal or human dignity. In December 2018, for example, the State Council Information Office stated that "universal human rights are grounded in the dignity and worth of humans."[55] Luo Haocai, in his opening speech to the 4th Beijing Human Rights Forum, announced:

> [To respect] human dignity includes the recognition of the important worth of humans, the equal treatment of humans, and the protection against discrimination and unfairness. Human dignity is the foundation by virtue of which humans are humans, and it is the ground and foundation of all other human rights. The

---

[49] Lin, "Ren de zunyan yu renge zunyan," p. 51.
[50] Xie Libin, "Zhongde bijiao xianfa shiyexia de renge zunyan," p. 60.
[51] See Wang Kai, "Lun xianfa shangde yiban rengequan," p. 108.
[52] Lin Laifan, "Ren de zunyan yu renge zunyan," p. 50.
[53] See Peng Zhen, "Guanyu zhonghua renmin gongheguo xianfa caoan de baogao."
[54] For a notable critique of the importance of the place of a provision in a larger charter in which it is included, see Bai Bin, "Xianfa zhong de rengezunyan guifan ji qi tixi diwei [The constitutional norm of personal dignity and its systemic status]," in *Caijing Faxue* (*Law and Economy*), no. 6 (2019).
[55] Guo Wuyuan (the State Council), *Gaige kaifang sishinian*.

realization of human rights ultimately aims at human dignity. To recognize and respect human dignity is the starting point and basic principle of international human rights law, and it is also the basic position of our government.[56]

Quoting the *Charter of the United Nations*, the *Universal Declaration of Human Rights*, the *International Covenant on Civil and Political Rights*, and the *International Covenant on Economic, Social and Cultural Rights*, Luo stressed that "basic human rights originate from the core value of human dignity."[57] Such high-profile official discourse should be presumed to be conforming to the official understanding of Article 38.

These opinions demonstrate that the inviolability of personal dignity under Article 38 is not just one of many constitutional rights: it is a basic *principle* and a cornerstone of human rights in China, which may be used to interpret other rights or to generate new rights that are contained in the wider notion of human dignity.

As a basic right under Article 38, the right to personal dignity is absolute. As well as in Article 38, as quoted earlier, the word "inviolable" appears in the context of the protection of one's private property (Art. 13), one's personal freedom (Art. 37), and one's home (Art. 39). While the Constitution somewhat contradictorily allows that these three so-called "inviolable" rights can be limited according to law, personal dignity is an exception, with Article 38 emphasizing that any kind of insult or humiliation, defamation or libel, or false accusation against citizens is absolutely prohibited.

If, therefore, personal dignity is a basic right under the Chinese Constitution, who are the duty-bearers? The dominant view in China is that they are the public authorities, or the holders of state power. The reason for this is that the right of personal dignity is a constitutional right, and a constitutional right is the right that is possessed by citizens against the state.[58] By interpreting Article 38 against the historical background of the CR, it is soon revealed that the main duty-bearers also include private citizens, because most of those atrocities against human dignity during the CR were conducted by private citizens – albeit at the instigation and with the support of the supreme leaders. This does not entail that the constitutional provision directly binds private individuals, but, for many scholars, especially those specializing in civil law, it does mean that this article will partly rely upon civil law to be implemented.

As a basic right, personal dignity refers to a bundle of personality rights, including the general personality right. Then what constitutes personal dignity as a basic

---

[56] Luo Haocai, "Buyiyang de wenhua."
[57] Ibid.
[58] Xie Libin, "Zhongde bijiao xianfa shiyexia de renge zunyan," pp. 61–62; and Wang Kai, "Lun xianfa shang de yiban rengequan," pp. 117, 121. This is also the dominant view in Germany. According to Grimm, "all holders of public authority in Germany or all state agents are the addressees of the norm. They are bound by it. ... Hence, only state agents can violate the constitutional guarantee." See Grimm, "Dignity in a Legal Context," 382.

principle? Luo Haocai recently declared that to respect "human dignity includes the recognition of the important worth of humans, the equal treatment of humans, and the protection against discrimination and unfairness."[59] Similarly, philosopher James Griffin has famously claimed:[60]

> Out of the notion of personhood we can generate most of the conventional list of human rights. We have a right to life (without it, personhood is impossible), to security of person (for the same reason), to a voice in political decision (a key exercise of autonomy), to free expression, to assembly, and to a free press (without them, exercise of autonomy would be hollow), to worship (a key exercise of what one takes to be the point of life). It also generates, I should say (though this is hotly disputed), a positive freedom: namely, a right to basic education and minimum provision needed for existence as a person – something more, that is, than mere physical survival. It also generates a right not to be tortured, because, among its several evils, torture destroys one's capacity to decide and to stick to the decision. And so on. It should already be clear that the generative capacities of the notion of personhood are quite great.

All of these rights are, in one form or another, embodied in China's Constitution. Recently, the Chinese government declared: "All human beings are born free and equal in dignity and rights. Human dignity is related to both human freedom and the all-round development of human beings."[61] What seems to characterize present-day China's approach is its clear advocacy of James Griffin's so-called positive freedom, which has been explained as follows:

> The right to subsistence and the right to development are the primary basic human rights ... [We] should pay special attention to safeguarding the people's right to subsistence ..., especially to achieve a decent standard of living, adequate food, clothing, and clean drinking water, the right to housing, the right to security, work, education, and the right to health and social security.[62]

The Chinese government has also stressed:

> All human rights are inseparable and interdependent. Civil and political rights cannot be realized without the simultaneous acquisition of economic, social and cultural rights; both types of rights are equally important and interrelated.[63]

China appears to have accepted, at least according to Luo Haocai, that "human dignity is the foundation by virtue of which humans are humans" – that is, moral and rational agents – and that "it is the ground and foundation of all other human rights",

---

[59] Luo Haocai, "Buyiyang de wenhua."
[60] James Griffin, *On Human Rights* (Oxford: Oxford University Press, 2008), p. 33.
[61] The First South-South Human Rights Forum, "Beijing Declaration" (December 8, 2017), www.xinhuanet.com//politics/2017-12/08/c_1122081753.htm, accessed June 14, 2020.
[62] Ibid.
[63] Ibid.

the realization of which is paramount to the guarantee of human dignity. Luo continued to say:

> In order to further protect and promote human dignity, it is necessary to eliminate all social conditions which jeopardize human's inherent nobility and stateliness, and to ensure the rights to equal development and participation for all members of society.... We should guarantee citizens' liberty and rights by means of the rule of law: every citizen shall receive equal legal protection, and citizens' freedoms and rights must be guaranteed by the Constitution and laws. Human dignity must be institutionalized.[64]

Regarding the relationship between human dignity and human rights, China's view – as a matter of discourse – appears to be no different from that adopted by the German Constitutional Court, when it declared in 1995 that "all fundamental rights of the Constitution are concretizations of human dignity."[65]

2 THE PROBLEM OF IMPLEMENTATION

The Chinese government has claimed that human dignity is protected by certain human rights, that the civil and political rights of the Chinese people are equally as important as their economic, social, and cultural rights, and that these rights are already guaranteed by the Constitution. The fundamental problem with these assertions lies in the fact that China's Constitution is not justiciable. China does not have an effective judicial system of constitutional review, which means that all of its constitutional provisions cannot be utilized by its citizens to challenge, nor by its courts to review, the constitutionality of legal and political decisions or of state actions. In other words, China's Constitution is not a normative constitution,[66] which is a highly significant factor when considering the practical implementation of Article 38. The basic principle of human dignity can be invoked neither by citizens nor by the courts, thus creating a substantial chasm between the claim that human dignity is respected in China and the reality of how the Chinese state treats its citizens. Even if the promise to guarantee the human dignity of the Chinese people is a sincere one, it is very far from being fulfilled.[67] The problem with the guarantee of human dignity in present-day China is not a theoretical but a practical

---

[64] Luo Haocai, "Buyiyang de wenhua."
[65] Grimm, "Dignity in a Legal Context," p. 390: "Every right has a dignity core." See also Werner Heun, *The Constitution of Germany*, p. 204.
[66] According to Loewenstein, a normative constitution "determines who will become the power holders, and it truly regulates the exercise of power and the relationship between the power holders. Its normative force is internalized by the political actors who take seriously the rules stipulated in the constitution, respect them, and abide by them." Karl Loewenstein, *Political Power and the Governmental Process* (Chicago, IL: University of Chicago Press, 1957), pp. 148–149.
[67] Perry Keller, "The Protection of Human Dignity under Chinese Law," in M. Duwell, J. Braarvig, R. Brownsword, and D. Mieth (eds), *The Cambridge Handbook of Human Dignity* (Cambridge: Cambridge University Press, 2014), p. 414.

one. In this context, it is useful to delineate personal dignity into its political and its nonpolitical forms – bearing in mind that the dividing line between the two is not always clear. The difficulty in the full implementation of Article 38 mainly concerns its political aspect – that is, the dignity to which an individual is entitled against any undue infringements by the state. The features that are commonly considered central to human dignity, such as personal autonomy, civil and political rights, liberal democracy, and the rule of law, are either extremely weak or nonexistent in China.

2.1 General Improvements in Nonpolitical Dignity

This is not to deny, however, that relative progress has been made in China in recent years. The concept of personal dignity, as embodied in Article 38, has begun to play a greater role in Chinese legal discourse, and it has made a tangible difference to some people's lives. As China's Law Society has declared, "the protection of human dignity has become an important guiding idea of China's rule-of-law construction since 2010."[68] As mentioned, the tenor of Article 38 represents the hope that Chinese lawmakers at different levels would begin to make laws or bylaws that protect personal dignity – both in the positive sense, by actively making laws to guarantee the goods to which dignity is intricately connected, and in the negative sense, by prohibiting measures infringing upon human dignity. But while in only a few areas of the Chinese state has this hope been realized to a satisfactory degree, the human dignity of the Chinese people – particularly their private or nonpolitical dignity – may be said to be improving.[69]

Since the end of the CR, for instance, the Chinese leadership has started to liberalize China's economy and society, and the government has withdrawn from many aspects of the private domain, causing the sphere of personal autonomy to expand. Owing to this movement toward liberalization, the process of public power has been largely revolutionized according to the principles of procedural justice and publicity (including public participation), especially in the areas of public administration and criminal law. The *Administrative Litigation Law* of 1989, effective from 1990, has allowed citizens to bring litigation against officials for the first time in Chinese history, something which has greatly improved the likelihood that individuals will be treated with dignity by the state. The *Administrative Penalty Law* of 1996 provides that any citizens who are to be punished shall have "the right to state their cases and the right to defend themselves" (Art. 6) and that "any administrative penalty without legal grounds or violating legal procedures shall be void" (Art. 3). The *Law of Administrative Penalties of Public Security* of 2005 provides that, when imposing administrative penalties in the name of public security, "human

---

[68] Zhongguo Faxuehui, *Zhongguo Fazhi Jianshe Niandu Baogao*.
[69] For a general and largely reliable overview of this situation, see Guo Wuyuan Xinwen Bangongshi, *Gaige kaifang sishinian zhongguo renquanshiye de fazhan jinbu*.

rights shall be respected and safeguarded, and the personal dignity of citizens shall be protected" (Art. 5). *Directives on Improving Fair Market Competition and Maintaining Good Market Order* (《国务院关于促进市场公平竞争维护市场正常秩序的若干意见》), ratified by the State Council in 2014, requires the administration "not to treat citizens rudely, and not to violate their personal dignity."

In the field of criminal law, many reforms have strengthened procedural protections for suspected criminals over the course of the past four decades. Torture was forbidden by the *Criminal Litigation Law* of 1979, and reported instances of torture have been reduced by the recent exclusionary rules that apply to illegally obtained evidence. These rules state that confessions or statements obtained by means of torture, force, or threat should be excluded from all prosecutions. The Supreme People's Court (SPC), in its *Unified Regulation on Evidence (A Proposal)* (2008), provides that "the confession obtained by measures impairing *human dignity* should be excluded."[70] The SPC's *Interpretation of the Civil Litigation Law* of 2015 requires that courts respect people's privacy and dignity when examining or investigating evidence or sites (Art. 124). During the past two decades, the presumption of innocence, the right against self-incrimination, and the right to counsel have been largely established, and the indignified practices of sheltering for examination (收容审查), custody and repatriation (收容遣送), and re-education through labour (劳动教养), have gradually been abolished. In 1998, the SPC outlawed parading criminals through streets or violating the personality of criminals. Regarding the death penalty, "less and prudent" (少杀慎杀) has become its official policy. The power to review and approve death sentences was withdrawn by the SPC from the local High Courts (高级法院) in 2007. The number of capital offenses has been reduced as a consequence, and executions have gradually declined by a half or even two-thirds in most regions, with those executions that do still take place being performed more frequently by lethal injection and less frequently by firearms.[71]

China is attempting to prioritize the positive or economic dimension of dignity, and there is little doubt that China has made some headway in this respect. Over the past four decades, China has made great leaps from poverty to moderate prosperity, and ordinary people's material lives have markedly improved. As Perry Keller has noted:

> In one dimension of human dignity, the state's responsibility to ensure the basic economic and social well-being of its citizens, China has become a global model.

---

[70] Emphasis added.
[71] Lin Wei, "Zhongguo sixing qishinian [Death Penalty in China: A Survey of Seven Decades]," https://wemp.app/posts/28f9da4a-bc4c-4f2a-a153-877624b56e29?utm_source=bottom-latest-posts, accessed June 14, 2020.

Since the Cultural Revolution, the Party has created the conditions for an unprecedented rise in household and personal well-being.[72]

Moreover, "China has built the largest-scale social security system covering the largest population of the world, raising the world social security coverage rate by 11 percentage points" in the relatively short time of thirty years.[73] As a recognition of these efforts, the Chinese government was given the prestigious Award for Outstanding Achievement in Social Security by the International Social Security Association (ISSA) in 2016.[74] In Section 2.2, the focus turns to the civil law protection of personal dignity and the legal protection of the personal dignity of special groups.

2.2 *The Civil Law Protection of Human Dignity*

The relationship between the right of human dignity and civil law personality rights is a complex and sophisticated one that cannot be explored in detail here. Although human dignity was enshrined in the Constitution in 1982, civil law scholars had not been interested in it. This indifference only started to change in the late 1990s. In 1999, civil law judges in China reached a consensus that the "general personality right is the inviolable right of personal dignity explicitly recognized in the Constitution."[75] As leading Chinese civil law scholar Wang Liming (王利明) has stated, "the core value that is served by personality rights is personal dignity."[76] Wang and others have also claimed that the right of personal dignity can be used to generate, supplement, and explain enacted concrete personality rights.[77] Chen Xianjie (陈现杰), a SPC judge who was one of those who drafted *the Interpretation on Emotional Compensation for Tort* in 2001, wrote that "personality is the dignity and value that make humans human."[78] Civil law scholar Zhu Qingyu also claims that human dignity has various manifestations, each of which can be enacted as rights, and that personality rights are its direct manifestations in contrast

---

[72] Perry Keller, "The Protection of Human Dignity under Chinese Law," p. 418.
[73] World Social Security Forum, "Government of China Receives International Social Security Award," www.issa.int/en/-/government-of-china-receives-international-social-security-award, accessed June 14, 2020.
[74] Ibid.
[75] Supreme People's Court, "Quanguo minshi anjian shenpan zhiliang gongzuo zuotanhui jiyao," p. 1100. See also Zhang Jianwen, "Zuowei xinxingquanli sifabaohu fangfa de yiban rengequan [The general personality right as a new judicial method of protecting new rights]," *Faxue Zazhi* [*Law Science Magazine*], no. 6 (2019): 68.
[76] Wang Liming, *Rengequan Fa Yanjiu* [*On Law of Personality Rights*] (Beijing: Zhongguo Renmindaxue Chubanshe, 2018), pp. II.
[77] Ibid., pp. 152–154. Shekeyuan Faxuesuo (ed.), *Falv Cidian* [*Law Dictionary*] (Beijing: Falv Chubanshe, 2004), p. 525. For a similar view, see also Wang Zejian, *Minfaxueshuo yu Panli Yanjiu* [*Civil Law: Doctrines and Cases*], vol. 3 (Beijing: Beijing Daxue Chubanshe, 2015), 623, 637.
[78] Chen Xianjie, "Zuigao renminfayuan guanyu queding minshi qinquan jingshen sunhai peichang zeren ruoganwenti de jieshi de lijie yu shiyong [Correctly understanding and applying 'SPC's Interpretation on Emotional Compensation for Tort]," www.npc.gov.cn/zgrdw/huiyi/lfzt/qqzrfca/2008-12/21/content_1462859.htm, accessed June 14, 2020.

to property rights, which are its indirect forms.[79] It is now commonly acknowledged that the most important manifestation of the principle of human dignity, or at least the most important implementation of Article 38 of the Chinese Constitution, is civil law protection of personality rights.[80]

The CR was a chaos of sheer lawlessness: the independent personhood of individuals was entirely denied, and even the nonpolitical dignity of individuals was nonexistent. After the end of the CR, China embarked upon a project of extensive lawmaking. *General Principles of the Civil Law* (民法通则, GPCL hereafter) enacted in 1986 established for Chinese citizens six personality rights – namely the rights to life and health (i.e. physical personality rights), name, portrait, reputation, honor, and marital autonomy (i.e. spiritual personality rights). To this list, *Tort Law* (2009) added the right to privacy. Article 101 of the GPCL provides that "citizens and legal persons shall have the right of reputation, the personal dignity of citizens shall be protected by law, and damaging citizens' or legal persons' reputation by insult, defamation and other means shall be prohibited."

The SPC has maintained that a citizen's reputation refers to the external or social evaluations or opinions that are generally held about his or her character, ability, credibility, and so forth, whereas personal dignity denotes a citizen's internal self-understanding, self-evaluation, or self-respect regarding his or her social status.[81] This understanding seems to presuppose a subjectivist concept of human dignity. In a case in 1998,[82] Qian Yuan, who was suspected of stealing commodities, was illegally searched and forced to unbutton and pull down her trousers in front of a female security guard and a female clerk of Shanghai Watson's Commodity Co Ltd. Qian Yuan subsequently filed a lawsuit, in which she claimed that her right to reputation was violated. The Court decided the case in Qian Yuan's favor, but pointed out that the right that was violated here was not the right to reputation but the right to personal dignity. The Court applied directly Article 38 of the Constitution, alongside Article 101 of GPCL.

The SPC's *Interpretation on Emotional Compensation for Tort* (《最高人民法院关于确定民事侵权精神损害赔偿责任若干问题的解释》) of 2001 explicitly established personal dignity as a legal right. Chen Xianjie wrote that

---

[79] Zhu Qingyu, *Minfa Zonglun*, p. 402.
[80] Wang Liming, "Shilun minfazongze dui rengezunyan de baohu [On the Protection of Personal Dignity in the General Part of Civil Code]," *Zhongguo Renmin Daxue Xuebao* [*Journal of Renmin University of China*], no. 4 (2017): 4; Wang Liming, "Rengequan fa de fazhan yu wanshan [The Development and Improvement of the Law on Personality Rights]," *Falvkexue* [*Science of Law*], no. 4 (2012); Yang Lixin, "Dui minfadian guiding rengequan fa zhongda lunzheng de lixing sikao [A Rational Reflection on Personality Rights in Civil Code]," *Zhongguo Falv Pinglun* [*China Law Review*], no. 1 (2016); Wang Kai, "Lun xianfa shangde yiban rengequan," pp. 117, 121; Zhu Qingyu, *Minfa Zonglun*, p. 402.
[81] *Ni Peilu and Wang Ying v. China World Trade Center*, http://gongbao.court.gov.cn/Details/9eef491516ee0e2b67f01f73ec2eb0.html, accessed June 14, 2020.
[82] *Qian Yuan v. Shanghai Watsons' Commodity Co Ltd*, www.dffyw.com/sifashijian/jj/201307/32892.html, accessed June 14, 2020.

it is worth noting that "the right to personal dignity" refers to "the general personality right," and it epitomizes the value of personality rights. It therefore has an important role of supplementing the defects or gaps of statutes on specific personality rights.[83]

Since this interpretation was published, however, Chinese courts has seldom grounded its decisions upon "the right to personal dignity." In one case, the Court held that a husband's personal dignity was violated when he found that the child he had raised was born from his wife's adultery with another man.[84] In other cases, the Court found that personal dignity was infringed by actions violating public order and morals – for example, destroying people's ancestral tombs.[85] In these cases, the idea of personal dignity was used to protect the new type of personality rights or interests that were not formerly covered by specific personality rights.

The *Interpretation* of 2001 also extends personality rights to the deceased, including their names, portraits, reputations, honor, and privacy. *The Regulation on Organ Transplantation* (《人体器官移植条例》) of 2007, ratified by the State Council, requires "the dignity of the dead" to be respected. According to Chen Xianjie,

> the deceased do not have personality rights. But, as a result of the relationship between close relatives, the elements of one's personality – after his death – will have influence on his spouse, parents, children and other close relatives who survive, and constitute important spiritual and emotional interests of the living. These spiritual and emotional interests embody the brilliance of human nature ... Therefore, the violation of the personality of the deceased is in truth a direct violation of the spiritual and emotional interests and the personal dignity of the living. .... The true purpose [of protecting the personality of the deceased] is to protect the human dignity and spiritual interests of the living.[86]

The latest and perhaps the most important development in the civil law protection of personal dignity is the Chinese Civil Code that is currently in the making,[87] Chapter 5 of the general part of which concerns civil rights. In this chapter, personality rights precede property rights, and the first article (i.e. Article 109) reads: "Natural persons' personal freedom and personal dignity shall be protected by law." The location and wording of this article displays the fundamental importance that the Civil Code attaches to personal freedom and personal dignity. Chapter 5 then provides a list of personality rights, including the right to life, physical integrity, health, name, portrait, reputation, honor, privacy, and marital autonomy. It also provides that "personal data shall be protected by law. Any organization or individual who needs to obtain personal data of others shall obtain

---

[83] Chen Xianjie, "Minshi qinquan jingshen sunhai peichang."
[84] See Zhu Qingyu, *Minfa Zonglun*, pp. 404–405.
[85] See Zhang Jianwen, "Zuowei xinxingquanli," p. 70.
[86] Chen Xianjie, "Minshi qinquan jingshen sunhai peichang."
[87] "China's Draft Civil Code to Be Submitted to NPC Annual Session for Review," www.xinhuanet.com/english/2019-12/28/c_138663610.htm, accessed June 14, 2020.

them according to law, and shall guarantee the safety of personal data. It is not allowed to illegally collect, use, process, transfer, buy or sell, supply, or publish personal data of others."[88]

What has been extolled as a great innovation is that China's Civil Code will have a separate part on personality rights. According to Shen Chunyao (沈春耀), the current director of the Legislative Affairs Commission of the Standing Committee of the NPC, the country's top legislature:

> Regarding whether to add a separate part on personality rights, we believe that personality rights ... concern each person's personal dignity, and are therefore the most basic and important rights of civil subjects. Protecting personality rights, and safeguarding personal dignity is an important task of our rule of law construction in China. ... In order to implement the Constitution's requirement that "citizens' personal dignity shall not be violated," ... we believe that it is appropriate and desirable to add a separate part on personality rights in Civil Code. This part on personality rights is mainly about personality rights of civil law, and it does not touch upon the civil, political, and social rights.[89]

The draft of this part, following its third reading in August 2019, contains six chapters, namely General Provisions, the Right of Life, Physical Integrity and Health, the Right of Name, the Right of Portrait, the Right of Reputation and Honour, and the Right of Privacy and Personal Data. The following provisions are particularly innovative and worthy of attention.

In General Provisions, following a list of the major types of specific personality rights, Article 774 stipulates that, "apart from these listed personality rights, a natural person shall enjoy other personality interests which are generated by personal freedom and personal dignity." This provision explicitly indicates that personal dignity can generate specific personality rights and that personal dignity can be used to fill the legislative gaps regarding specific personality rights.

Chapter 2 concerns the right of life, physical integrity, and health. Article 783 emphasizes that all natural persons have the right to protect their lives and physical integrity. Article 788 prohibits the purchase or sale of human cells, tissues, organs, or remains in any form and voids the acts of purchase or sale in question. Article 789 requires clinical trials be approved of by government, reviewed and authorized by ethical committees, and be consented to by the subjects of the trials or their guardians, who must be informed of the purpose, use, possible risks, and other details of the trials. In this respect, the *Regulations of Quality Management of Clinical Trial of Medical Devices* (《医疗器械临床试验质量管理规范》) and the *Regulations of Quality Management of Clinical Trial of Medicine* (《药物临床试验质量管理规范》), both of 2016, take the rights of research subjects as their

---

[88] *Minfa Zongze* (General Part of Civil Code, 2017), www.npc.gov.cn/zgrdw/npc/xinwen/2017-03/15/content_2018907.htm, accessed June 14, 2020.

[89] "Minfa fenbian caoan shouci qiting shenyi [Civil Code Draft to be submitted for review]," www.npc.gov.cn/npc/c183/201808/f1672691d1a3438ba525d9e941daa9ab.shtml, accessed June 14, 2020.

primary concern, which should outweigh the concerns for science and social benefits, and thus require that clinical trials be conducted according to the *WMA Declaration of Helsinki: Ethical Principles for Medical Research Involving Human Subjects* (2013), which provides that it is the duty of physicians to protect the dignity, integrity, right to self-determination, privacy, and confidentiality of personal information of research subjects. As a response to the notorious incident of He Jiankui (贺建奎)'s gene-edited babies,[90] Article 789 provides that those who are engaged in activities related to human genes and embryos "shall obey laws, by-laws (i.e. administrative regulations), and relevant state provisions, and must not ... harm human health, violate ethics and morality, or harm [the] public interest." Article 791 prohibits sexual harassment – an act which is defined as "conducted against people's will, and by means of language or action", and imposes upon employers the duty to prevent and stop its occurrence.

Chapter 4 concerns likeness rights. It defines likenesses as "visualizations (including images, statues, and drawings) from which particular natural persons can be identified", which transcends the traditional approach of defining likeness as representing the characteristics of a person's face. As a response to the recent development of so-called deepfakes, it also prohibits faking people's likeness by using information technology. These protections of likeness rights also apply to people's voices. Chapter 6 concerns privacy and personal information. It defines privacy as natural persons' private space, activities, information, and so forth, which they are unwilling to disclose to others. One type of enacted violations of privacy is "disturbing people's quiet and peaceful life by means of text messages, phone calls, instant messaging, emails, flyers, etc." Personal information is defined as "any information by means of which a particular natural person can be identified, including name, the date of birth, identity number, personal bio-metric identification information, address, phone number, email address, whereabouts, etc." These seemingly very humane and detailed provisions only raise the question, however, of how they will be implemented in practice.

2.3 *Dignity of Special Groups*

Other than protecting citizens' personal dignity in general, there are many laws in China that single out special groups and emphasize the special importance of their personal dignity.[91] The first type of these special groups includes the disabled, organ recipients, persons with mental disorders, minor-students, women, the elderly, and

---

[90] "China Confirms Birth of Gene-Edited Babies, Blames Scientist He Jiankui for Breaking Rules," www.scmp.com/news/china/science/article/2182964/china-confirms-gene-edited-babies-blames-scientist-he-jiankui, accessed June 14, 2020.

[91] I draw on Hu Yuhong, "Woguo xianxingfa zhong guanyu rende zunyan zhi guiding de wanshan [Improving Our Law on Human Dignity]," *Fashang Yanjiu* [*Studies in Law and Business*], no. 1 (2017): 4–5.

so on. These people are the weak in society, and personal dignity for them has much to do with equal treatment or nondiscrimination. For example, the *Law of the Protection of Disabled Persons* (《残疾人保障法》) (2008) prohibits discriminating, insulting, and abusing the disabled, and the mass media is prohibited from derogating their personality (Art. 3). The *Law of Compulsory Education Law* (《义务教育法》) (2006) requires teachers "to respect pupils' personality, not to discriminate them, and not to impose corporal punishment, explicitly or in disguise" (Art. 29).[92] The *Law of the Protection of Women's Rights and Interests* (《妇女权益保障法》) (1992) prohibits violating women's dignity by means of insulting, libelling, or publicizing matters related to women's privacy. In much the same way as with the protection of the disabled, this law prohibits the media from derogating women's personality (Article 39). *Nyotaimori* (i.e. body sushi) and surrogacy were prohibited in China on the grounds that, in these cases, a woman's body was used as a tool for the furtherance of the interests of others and their dignity was thereby violated.[93] The second type are those who are vulnerable under particular situations. Chinese law requires the personal dignity and ethnic customs and habits of consumers and tourists to be protected.[94] Also singled out for protection is the personal dignity of mental health workers, tour guides, medical practitioners, nurses, doctors in undeveloped villages, witnesses, teachers, and so forth. Finally, Chinese law requires the state to adopt effective measures to protect the personal dignity of servicemen, diplomats, consuls, judges, and so on. Personal dignity for them means privileged protection, which serves to honour their occupations.

3 CONCLUDING REMARKS

The Chinese Constitution aims to protect human dignity, which it considers not only as a foundational right but also as a basic principle. The basic rights that are necessary to implement this basic principle are all enshrined in the Constitution. China has made notable progress in protecting the nonpolitical dignity of Chinese citizens, in creating positive material conditions for its citizens to flourish, and in developing a legal framework for providing remedies when its people's rights of nonpolitical dignity are infringed upon. The political dignity of Chinese citizens – something which is essential to their independence and autonomy – however remains unprotected in practice. There remain tens of millions of people living in undignified conditions of poverty, people are still treated radically differently as

---

[92] The Law of Minors Protection of 2012 (中华人民共和国未成年人保护法) and the Law of Minor Crimes Prevention of 1999 (预防未成年人犯罪法) have similar provisions.
[93] See Houyu, *Ren de Zunyan zhi Faxue Sibian* [*The Jurisprudence of Human Dignity*] (Beijing: Falv Chubanshe, 2018); "Daiyun xieyi wuxiao" (Contract of Surrogacy Voided), http://news.sina.com.cn /0/2010-08-12/071717952869s.shtml, accessed June 14, 2020.
[94] Law of Consumer Protection (1993) (消费者权益保障法): Articles 14, 43, and 50; Law of Tourism (2013) (旅游法): Article 10.

a consequence of their household registration,[95] and their treatment also relies heavily upon whether or not they are members of the Communist Party. Far greater efforts are required in order to reduce the rapidly widening gaps in personal wealth and the flagrant, degrading inequality of the people who live in China. The dignity-protecting laws that it currently has are poorly implemented, and practices such as humiliating forced televised confessions prior to a citizens' court appearance still take place.[96] There is still a long way to go for China to transform the constitutional dream of inviolable human dignity into a reality.

[95] Lu Yilong, "Hukou haiqi zuoyong ma? huji zhidu yu shehui fencing he liudong [Does Hukou Still Matter? The Household Registration System and Its impact on Social Stratification and Mobility in China]," *Zhongguo Shehui Kexue* (*Social Sciences in China*), no. 1 (2008).

[96] Steven Jiang, "Trial by Media? Confessions Go Prime Time in China," https://edition.cnn.com/2016/01/26/asia/china-television-confessions/index.html, accessed June 14, 2020.

10

Virtue, Dignity, and Constitutional Democracy

A Confucian Perspective

Sungmoon Kim[*]

Is the discourse of human dignity an exclusive asset of the Western moral and political tradition? In the West, the ideal account of human dignity (and one's *natural rights*) is deeply embedded in ancient Greek philosophy and early Christian thought in which a human being is believed to possess the moral power of rational self-control or to be created after the image of God and thus critically distinguished from animals. In more recent Western political theory, Kantian liberals single out the capacity of rational autonomy as the moral ground of human dignity, which gives rise to membership in the "Kingdom of Ends,"[1] while neorepublicans recast human dignity in terms of freedom as nondomination, understanding equal status as the defining characteristic of human beings with profound normative import.[2] Attempting to bring the two traditions together, Jeremy Waldron further argues for the concept of human dignity as an elevated social rank that is underpinned by law and equally protected in terms of rights.[3] And yet, liberal individualists such as George Kateb justify human dignity on pre-moral and purely "existential" terms by deriving the intrinsic value of humanity from the uniqueness of humans, which factually and normatively separates them from nature.[4]

If we take rational autonomy or freedom as nondomination, or legally protected social status (or right) as the authoritative reference, only in the light of which the moral ideal of human dignity can be identified, then non-Western traditions that do not embrace "the eyeball test," valorize individual autonomy, or develop rule of law as the litmus test for human dignity would accordingly have no claim to it. This would be especially true of Confucianism, which, notwithstanding its recognition of the moral distinction between humans and animals, understands the core of

---

[*] This work was partially supported by a grant from the Research Grants Council of Hong Kong Special Administrative Region, China (CityU 11670216).
[1] Christine M. Korsgaard, *Creating the Kingdom of Ends* (Cambridge: Cambridge University Press, 1996).
[2] Philip Pettit, *Republicanism: A Theory of Freedom and Government* (Oxford: Oxford University Press, 1997).
[3] Jeremy Waldron, *Dignity, Rank, and Rights* (New York: Oxford University Press, 2015).
[4] George Kateb, *Human Dignity* (Cambridge, MA: Belknap Press, 2011).

personhood in reference to social relationships in which one is embedded and the social roles that one plays, and it thus stresses virtues such as caring, ritual propriety, humility, and deference that are often believed to sit uneasily with equal freedom and/or rational autonomy. After all, traditional Confucians never generated the conception of rights, commonly affiliated with the idea of human dignity, nor did they endorse the (popular) right to political participation, the "right to have rights," according to Waldron.[5] But does that necessarily entail that Confucianism has no conception of human dignity?

In the past two decades, Confucian philosophers have vigorously explored the ideal of human dignity in the Confucian tradition by reinterpreting key classical Confucian texts such as the *Analects of Confucius* (*Lunyu* 論語) and especially the *Mencius* (*Mengzi* 孟子). As a result, the Western presumption that human dignity is an exclusive asset of the Western tradition has been successfully debunked, and, more significantly, two contending philosophical (and moral) theses with regard to the Confucian account of human dignity have emerged. One group of scholars strongly inspired by Confucian virtue ethics argue for the notion of human dignity as an achievement. Understanding human dignity as the outcome of a painstaking process of moral self-cultivation, scholars in this vein find wanting the account of human dignity concentrated on universally shared human nature, character traits, or moral potentiality and instead uphold moral and, by extension, social hierarchy between morally developed persons (called *junzi* 君子) and those who have completely neglected or failed, despite some efforts, in their moral development (called *xiaoren* 小人).[6] In this view, the dignity that one deserves is proportional to the virtue he has cultivated, and thus it belongs, in principle, only to the *junzi* and, to a lesser extent, to those who are striving to become one, leaving quite ambiguous whether a petty man deserves human dignity. Though not completely rejecting the importance of virtue to dignified personhood, however, some scholars disagree with the "strong" virtue-based account of human dignity and shift attention to universal moral potentiality. This group of scholars' most common canonical inspiration is Mencius, most famous for his claim that human nature is good, and they assert that as long as one is born with "a set of innate virtues unique to the human race and the capacity for fully realizing [the] virtues that make him a mature person,"[7] he or she should be regarded as a dignified person, regardless of his or her moral self-cultivation or achievement of virtue.

---

[5] Jeremy Waldron, *Law and Disagreement* (Oxford: Oxford University Press, 1999), chap. 11.
[6] Most eminently, see Peimin Ni, "Seek and You Will Find It; Let Go and You Will Lose It: Exploring a Confucian Approach to Human Dignity," *Dao* 13, no. 2 (2014): 174-198; Tongdong Bai, *Against Political Equality: The Confucian Case* (Princeton, NJ: Princeton University Press, 2000), 98–106. Also see Joseph Chan, *Confucian Perfectionism: A Political Philosophy for Modern Times* (Princeton, NJ: Princeton University Press, 2014), pp. 32–5, which justifies a person's moral worth in reference to one's contribution to the other's well-being.
[7] Qianfan Zhang, "The Idea of Human Dignity in Classical Chinese Philosophy: A Reconstruction of Confucianism," *Journal of Chinese Philosophy* 27, no. 3 (2000): 315.

This chapter aims to reinforce the second group's position, but my approach to that effect is notably different from the way in which the core argument of this group has been developed. Instead of focusing on Mencius, I pay attention to Xunzi, commonly considered Mencius' archrival given his view of human nature as bad. Recall that scholars belonging to the second group advance their potential-based account of human dignity by paying close attention to Mencius' argument on innate virtues, possessed by all human beings as moral potential. Xunzi denies the innateness of virtue and, not surprisingly, emphasizes the critical importance of moral self-cultivation via a fundamental re-formation of the self from bad to good, strongly vindicating the notion of human dignity as achievement. And thus, if Xunzi is also found to potentially support the idea that human dignity is universally available, even to those who have yet to develop morally or have hopelessly failed in one's moral training, there will be an additional, much stronger, basis for the second interpretation that highlights human dignity as an essential component of one's moral personhood.

After establishing the Xunzian case for human dignity, I revisit the recent debate between Confucian meritocrats and Confucian democrats with regard to the right to political participation. I argue that the Confucian case for human dignity, as vindicated in this chapter in terms of universal moral potential, has strong potential to support the popular right to political participation. I conclude the chapter by discussing the constitutional implications of what I call "Confucian egalitarian dignity" and the Confucian right to political participation.

1 CONFUCIAN VIRTUE ETHICS AND HUMAN DIGNITY

Despite ongoing controversy over the nature of Confucian ethics, a consensus seems to be emerging among the students of Chinese philosophy that Confucian ethics can be best understood as a sort of virtue ethics. At the heart of Confucian virtue ethics, it is often said, are the interrelated postulates: 1) humans have innate virtues as moral potential; 2) realization of moral potential produces a formidable moral character; 3) formation of a formidable moral character requires an arduous process of moral self-cultivation; 4) moral self-cultivation is internally motivated; 5) virtue, understood as stable character traits resulting from moral self-cultivation, generates the deepest joy and happiness, making it valuable for its own sake; and, therefore, 6) a person of formidable character lives a flourishing moral life despite or in the face of "situational variations."[8]

These six postulates formulate an argument for Confucian dignity as achievement. The argument goes in the following steps. First, the telos of human life is human (moral) excellence and flourishing. Second, therefore, a life that is not

---

[8] For how Confucian virtue ethics (especially of the Mencian strand) can effectively meet the situationist challenge, see Edward Slingerland, "The Situationist Critique and Early Confucian Virtue Ethics," *Ethics* 121, no. 2 (2011): 390–419.

flourishing is less valuable. Third, a flourishing moral life is attained only when one values the intrinsic worth of moral life and takes joy in the course of living it. Fourth, the capacity to take joy in living a moral life requires a sustained period of cultivation. And finally, fifth, only one who has cultivated such a capacity, thus possessing a formidable moral character, can live a dignified human life. In the scheme of Confucian virtue ethics, therefore, the gist of human dignity does not lie in the ontological fact that humans are born with innate virtues, however important they are in motivating one to become good; rather, what makes humans morally dignified is that, unlike animals, they are capable of actually *becoming* good. That is, "the more one is able to develop [moral] potentiality, the more dignity the person has."[9]

Though Confucian virtue ethics, understood in this way, is sometimes attributed to both Mencius and Xunzi,[10] it is Mencian virtue ethics that is fully compatible with all six postulates just introduced. According to Mencius, human nature is good not in the sense that humans are born fully moral or virtuous but in the sense that humans possess the "sprouts" (*duan* 端) of morality – such as the heart of compassion (as the sprout of benevolence or *ren* 仁), the heart of shame (as the sprout of righteousness or *yi* 義), the heart of courtesy and modesty (as the sprout of ritual propriety or *li* 禮), and the heart of right and wrong (as the sprout of wisdom or *zhi* 智) – the careful development of which makes them virtuous.[11] As suggested by the image of the sprout, Mencius explains the process of moral self-cultivation by using the agricultural metaphor, implying that what differentiates humans, equally endowed with Heaven-bestowed nature, is their differing moral efforts to become good.

> In years of plenty, most young men are gentle; in years of poverty, most young men are violent. It is not that the potential that Heaven confers on them varies like this. They are like this because of what sinks and drowns their hearts. Consider barley. Sow the seeds and cover them. The soil is the same and the time of planting is also the same. They grow rapidly, and by the time of the summer solstice they have all ripened. Although there are some differences, these are due to the richness of the soil and to unevenness in the rain and in human effort.[12]

What, then, does Mencius mean by "human effort"? For Mencius, the sprouts of virtue provide seminal moral motivation for moral action, sometimes leading even

---

[9] Ni, "Seek and You Will Find It; Let Go and You Will Lose It," p. 180.
[10] Ni, for instance, finds no significant difference between Mencius and Xunzi in their accounts of human nature by interpreting Xunzi as basically agreeing with Mencius that humans possess the sense of morality (ibid., p. 179). This, however, is a serious misrepresentation of Xunzi, who believes that humans do not possess any innate sense of morality. Instead of assimilating Xunzian virtue ethics to its Mencian counterpart, I take Xunzi's claim that human nature is bad seriously and examine what normative implications can be drawn from it in relation to human dignity.
[11] *Mencius* 2A6.
[12] *Mencius* 6A7. Throughout this chapter, the English translations of the *Mengzi* 孟子 are adapted from *Mengzi: With Selections from Traditional Commentaries*, trans. Bryan W. Van Norden (Indianapolis, IN: Hackett, 2008). Also see 2A2; 6A8; 6A9.

uncultivated people toward proper behavior. For example, as Mencius shows, it is not hard to imagine one being motivated (naturally, by the sprout of compassion) to save a baby who is about to fall into a well.[13] However, this happy congruence between moral motivation and moral action is hardly stable or reliable because it is based on untutored moral intuition, which is prone to lead one to bad judgment and improper behavior.[14] When left untutored and uncultivated, one's heart (xin 心), the inner faculty that enables one to make moral decisions, can easily be ensnared by external conditions.[15] By human effort, therefore, Mencius means nothing more than one's effort to put the heart on the right track, as internally motivated by the sprouts of virtue, and to make moral judgment or engage in moral action in a stable and consistent manner.

For Mencius, what is central to putting the heart on the right track is one's capability of "reflection" or "concentration" (si 思). To si is to concentrate on one's moral sprouts and make sure they "grow" healthy and strong so that the heart is steadily focused on moral goodness. As Van Norden aptly puts it, the result of this process of concentrating is that "one 'extends' one's moral actions and reactions to more and more situations." That is, "by concentrating, one extends one's moral feelings, so that instead of just maintaining one's integrity in some things ... one maintains one's integrity in all situations."[16] Indeed, Mencius explicitly attributes moral inequality among men to their differing capabilities of si.

> It is not the function of the ears and eyes to reflect, and they are misled by things. Things interact with other things and simply lead them along. But the function of the heart is to reflect (si). If it reflects, then it will get it. If it does not reflect, then it will not get it. This is what Heaven has given us. If one first takes one's stand on what is greater [i.e. the reflective heart], then what is lesser [i.e. what the ears and eyes want] will not be able to snatch it away. This is how to become a great person.[17]

Si, however, is far from the top-down rationality Kant associates with moral agency and, by implication, human dignity. One of the distinctive features of si as a mode of moral reasoning is that reflective attention to nascent moral feelings and assiduous practice of moral action engender a profound sense of joy, which in turn strengthens otherwise feeble moral sprouts and helps one's attention to fixate on what is good, ultimately contributing to the formation of a formidable moral character.[18] Thus

---

[13] Mencius 2A6.
[14] For an insightful discussion on the congruence between moral motivation and moral action in Mencius' moral philosophy, see David Nivison, *The Ways of Confucianism: Investigations in Chinese Philosophy*, edited by Bryan W. Van Norden (Chicago, IL: Open Court, 1996), chap. 7.
[15] See *Mencius* 6A8.
[16] Bryan W. Van Norden, "Mengzi and Xunzi: Two Views of Human Agency," in *Virtue, Nature, and Moral Agency in the Xunzi*, edited by T. C. Kline III and Philip J. Ivanhoe (Indianapolis, IN: Hackett, 2000), pp. 103–134, at p. 113.
[17] Mencius 6A15.
[18] For the importance of a profound sense of joy in Mencian virtue ethics, see Eric L. Hutton, "Moral Connoisseurship in Mengzi," and Philip J. Ivanhoe, "Confucian Self Cultivation and Mengzi's

understood, "a great person" is a person of formidable moral character who finds virtue intrinsically appealing. It is for this reason that Mencius regards formidable moral character as an honor given by Heaven and distinguishes it from honor given by other humans.[19] The critical difference between Heavenly honor and human honor lies in the fact that human honor can be given and taken away (by the ruler in particular), while Heavenly honor cannot be taken away once it is given, as long as one persists in the moral life that warrants it. As such, in Mencian virtue ethics, moral character is the single greatest source of human dignity; like moral character, human dignity is an honor that can only be obtained by the strenuous practice of virtue.

Two points can be gleaned from the discussion thus far. First, for Mencius and in Confucian virtue ethics generally, the morally salient feature of *human* dignity does not lie in the moral distinction between human beings and animals. To be sure, Mencius acknowledges that there is a subtle distinction that morally differentiates humans from animals. But in noting such a distinction, Mencius' real concern is not so much with the moral superiority of humans over animals – mainly the way in which human dignity has been conceptualized in the Western moral tradition –[20] but with the moral distinction between the gentleman (or the great man) and the common man (the petty man, more accurately) – that is, between one who preserves (*cun* 存) one's inner moral heart and one who has abandoned (*qu* 去) it.[21] And it should be reminded that, in Mencian virtue ethics, one cannot preserve one's moral heart without arduously cultivating the moral sprouts of virtue and developing a formidable moral character.

Second, and relatedly, Confucian dignity, though initially starting from the assumption of universal possession of innate virtues, allows differing degrees of moral development and this justifies moral inequality among the people. Donald Munro has once captured moral inequality understood in this way in terms of *evaluative inequality* and distinguished it from natural inequality that denies similar endowment and potential among the people.[22] Insomuch as the central concern of

---

Notion of Extension," both in *Essays on the Moral Philosophy of Mengzi*, edited by Xiusheng Liu and Philip J. Ivanhoe (Indianapolis, IN: Hackett, 2002), pp. 175 and 224 respectively.

[19] "There are Heavenly honors, and there are human honors. Benevolence, righteousness, devotion, faithfulness, delighting in goodness without tiring – these are Heavenly honors. Being a duke, High Minister, or Chief Counselor – these are human honors. The ancients cultivated Heavenly honors, and human honors followed upon them. Nowadays, people cultivate Heavenly honors because they want human honors. So when they have obtained the human honors, they cast away the Heavenly honors. This is the extreme confusion!" (*Mencius* 6A16).

[20] Kateb's understanding of human dignity still adheres to this old Western paradigm of anthropocentrism when he says: "The core idea of human dignity is that on earth, humanity is the greatest type of beings – or what we call species because we have learned to see humanity as one species in the animal kingdom, which is made up of many other species along with our own – and that every member deserves to be treated in a manner consonant with the high worth of the species" (*Human Dignity*, p. 3).

[21] *Mencius* 4B19.

[22] Donald J. Munro, *The Concept of Man in Early China* (Stanford, CA: Stanford University Press, 1969).

Confucian virtue ethics lies in moral self-cultivation and it identifies human dignity as "moral esteem" attached only to the truly moral human beings,[23] its attitude toward natural moral equality is at best ambiguous. If human dignity is essentially a moral achievement, how much normative weight should be given to natural equality that is grounded on Heaven-given moral potential? Yet, if too much attention is given to natural equality and natural equality is understood as another form of moral equality, the whole project of Confucian moral self-cultivation would be critically undermined – if all humans, as they are, are worthy of moral esteem, what would be the point of moral self-cultivation? One way to interpret Confucian virtue ethics, therefore, is that natural equality has little moral significance, and its moral importance is strictly limited to moral motivation. In this interpretation, natural equality provides the condition for human dignity but is not thought to be equal to it. Not surprisingly, the recent argument for Confucian dignity as achievement is premised on this normative distinction between natural equality and moral inequality.

2 HUMAN DIGNITY AS ACHIEVEMENT?

In his recent essay, Peimin Ni challenges the discourse of human rights grounded on the assumption of *Menschenwürde* (universal human dignity) that attributes the gist of human dignity to properties, qualities, or capabilities that are universally shared by all human beings. In Ni's judgment, the idea of universal human dignity encounters two serious problems. First, if human dignity is understood in reference to properties presumably common to human nature, it would risk excluding some people who do not actually possess such alleged common properties, thus practically discriminating against them. The second problem is that, insomuch as human dignity is defined as a value that needs protection, *Menschenwürde* is self-contradictory, as it is constructed around "inalienable" human tenets and qualities. If human dignity is inalienable, why does it need protection? Even if it is accepted that the inalienability of human dignity is a purely normative claim and it simply means that human dignity ought not to be violated, the inalienability claim's special normative force is lost because it fails to offer a substantive moral ground for protection.[24]

For Ni, Confucian virtue ethics provides an alternative conception of human dignity, focused not on what humans supposedly share but, as we have seen earlier, on moral qualities or virtues that humans can achieve. More specifically, instead of reading Mencius' claim that human nature is good not as a description but as a prescription, Ni shows that Mencius' real concern is with encouraging people to actually *do* the things that *make* them worthy of dignity.

---

[23] Van Norden, "Mengzi and Xunzi," p. 114.
[24] Ni, "Seek and You Will Find It; Let Go and You Will Lose It," pp. 177–178.

The moral appeal of the notion of human dignity as achievement comes precisely from its ability to avoid the two problems affiliated with *Menschenwürde*. To take the second problem first, since it is a moral achievement, it is not vulnerable to the weakness of the inalienability claim. Human dignity has special normative force that warrants moral protection precisely because it is *alienable*; in Mencius' expression, it can be let go, unless we preserve or cultivate it. Second, more importantly for Ni, human dignity understood as achievement does not risk discriminating against others because it is not constructed around certain core human features or properties such as rational autonomy, which we may use as a litmus test for *others'* entitlement to it. Instead, the Confucian ethic of self-cultivation demands self-reflection or self-perfection when we are tempted to discriminate against others on the basis of some features that we believe they ought to possess as a human being; it brings us to ask if "we lacked adequate understanding, compassion, patience, and whole-hearted devotion toward [them]."[25] Ni calls this a "Copernicus turn," transforming the issue from "one of determining the external scope of universality of human dignity to an issue about internal moral cultivation, and from judging other people to demanding one's own moral integrity, compassion, and responsibility."[26]

What is fascinating about Ni's virtue-ethical reconstruction of Confucian dignity is that, by making human dignity something that can be let go or alienable, he simultaneously renders it something that can be inalienable by making it ultimately dependent on oneself. As Ni puts it, "as long as we are able to maintain what is human ourselves, no one can do anything about it."[27] Understood in this way, human dignity can be alienable only either by self-abandonment or by external calamities. Since external calamities pose an eminent threat to our ability to preserve and develop our moral sprouts, the ideal of human dignity requires humans to be effectively protected from them. But, as Ni admits, external calamities per se do not diminish human dignity as, again, it is dependent on or internal to one's virtue. What they do instead is merely deprive the vital conditions necessary for a dignified life.[28] In this way, Ni reinforces the virtue-dependent character of Confucian dignity.

Is this a plausible account of human dignity? We can tackle this question from two different viewpoints. First, is Ni's account of Confucian dignity faithful to the core stipulations of (Mencian) Confucian virtue ethics by which he is strongly inspired? As we have seen, Confucian virtue ethics generates the idea of human dignity in terms of "merit" (i.e. whether one deserves the Heavenly honor). Put differently, in Confucian virtue ethics one who is entitled to human dignity is one who has made him/herself worthy of it by properly cultivating him/herself, and his/her moral dignity is pronounced in contradistinction to one who has failed in moral self-cultivation, namely

---

[25] Ibid., p. 182.
[26] Ibid., p. 183.
[27] Ibid., p. 184.
[28] Ibid., pp. 184–185.

the petty man. This virtue-based moral inequality is the defining feature of the Confucian account of human dignity. Yet Ni's account only implies moral inequality and never explores its normative implications for the Confucian account of human dignity. For instance, Ni never discusses whether one who has failed in moral self-cultivation deserves human dignity at all and/or how the Confucian gentleman should engage with the petty man. Since, presumably, a petty man does not deserve human dignity – or deserves only a modicum degree of it, in the case he has made some effort to cultivate himself but ultimately failed in moral growth – can (or should) a Confucian gentleman treat him with disrespect or even disdain? If not, is it reasonable to attribute the Confucian gentleman's respectful treatment of the petty man who is undignified solely to his inner desire for moral perfection?

This leads to the second way to evaluate Ni's account – whether it offers a viable normative alternative to universal human dignity as he claims. When approaching human dignity in terms of achievement, Ni's concern is solely with what he calls *internal moral cultivation*, which is concerned with one's ability to cultivate one's self and become compassionate and responsible toward others, without asking whether the "others" in question deserve moral esteem. But, if we take Confucian virtue ethics seriously, why should we take random "others" to be worthy of our compassion and responsibility? Ni's strategy seems to be that we simply forget about the moral qualification of others to be worthy of human dignity and the respect it entails and just concentrate on self-perfection by exercising virtue toward others (i.e. random others who are mostly indignified). Apparently the guiding concern of internal moral cultivation is one's deep moral anxiety about whether one becomes a dignified person, regardless of what others do to him/her or whatever the circumstances are that can be beyond one's control.

The trouble is that Ni's account says nothing about whether or why others are to be counted as persons deserving moral respect. It is all about how one becomes a virtuous person, and in this preoccupation with self-perfection the "others" tend to be relegated to the social backdrop against which one's heroic engrossment in moral development is pronounced. But "others" here do not seem to have real identities or voices. We are left not knowing who they are, why we owe them our moral responsibility (except for our moral desire to become better by doing good to "them" whose identities are unspecified), and whether they have a moral status or right to make a claim *to us* about their well-being and basic interest. Ni's account of human dignity as achievement takes only the perspective of a moral agent who is engaged in moral self-cultivation, leaving unexplained what is or is not achieved for *others* (again, we do not know whether they are equally engaged in moral self-cultivation or they are just petty), though intimate and sustained relationship with them is required for *our* moral growth.

In short, though offering a powerful practical prescription for moral *self-cultivation* as well as a penetrating insight into its nature and scope, involving deep and extensive self-reflection, Ni, unfortunately, hardly comes to terms with human dignity as a moral ideal that holds a normative grip on all human beings or as the foundational value for constitutional politics. By "normative grip on all human beings," I do not mean that universal human dignity as inscribed in the idea of *Menschenwürde*, which is a fundamentally egalitarian (and metaphysical) ideal, is the only valid way to conceptualize human dignity. Moreover, as Confucian virtue ethics clearly demonstrates, human dignity can have a normative grip on all humans as well, although in inegalitarian and meritocratic terms, by ascribing dignity to *any* person who has become virtuous in light of an objective moral standard, such as the Way (*dao* 道). On Ni's account, however, the scope of *human* dignity becomes too narrow as it neither presents human dignity as a universal moral ideal, equally applying to all humans, nor explicitly acknowledges moral inequality implied in its meritocratic presupposition by failing to bring "others" back in the scope of human dignity in a morally meaningful way.

Therefore, although *human dignity as achievement* does capture an important aspect of the Confucian virtue-ethical account of human dignity, it seems necessary to differentiate between Ni's specific understanding and the meritocratic account generally supported by Confucian virtue ethics. I call this latter, more general meritocratic account of Confucian dignity "Confucian inegalitarian dignity." Confucian inegalitarian dignity encompasses Ni's internal conception of Confucian dignity as one of its special instantiations, and what makes it special lies precisely in its remarkable ability to turn our attention away from the unequal *relations* between the Confucian gentlemen and the petty men, on which it is predicated.

3 CONFUCIAN DIGNITY AS POTENTIAL AND THE XUNZIAN CHALLENGE

My own view is that *Menschenwürde* and Confucian inegalitarian dignity present two viable ways to understand human dignity, justified on different moral grounds – one egalitarian and the other meritocratic. While the first undergirds a liberal and democratic notion of human dignity, the latter advances an aristocratic notion of human dignity. Both accounts take human dignity as intrinsically valuable, and to this extent they both understand human dignity as having a normative grip on all human beings.

That being said, what if we do not subscribe to the meritocratic interpretation of Confucian virtue ethics? What if we judge that the kernel of Confucianism as an ethical tradition lies in natural equality among those whose nature is "good" (*shan* 善) in the sense Mencius understands the term and that natural equality thus understood is itself a kind of moral equality? Insomuch as Mencian Confucianism is employed as the foundation of Confucian dignity, it does not seem implausible to use its faith in natural moral equality as an inspiration and to support the universalist account of human dignity that draws on shared human moral potential or capacity.

In fact, this is how scholars such as Qianfan Zhang and Irene Bloom justify human dignity in Confucian, predominantly Mencian, terms. Let us call this position *Confucian dignity as potential*.

Bloom, for instance, asserts that "the [Mencian] emphasis on a common human potential implies a respect for persons that goes beyond, and tends to undermine, class distinctions."[29] In a similar spirit, Zhang claims that "the belief in human dignity presupposes an irreducible worth attached to every person insofar as he or she is a human being. This is best illustrated by the Mencian theory of human nature, which enables Mencius to develop a positive doctrine of human value."[30] What is striking is how these scholars reinterpret Mencius' otherwise meritocratic notion of Heavenly honor in a way that reinforces his egalitarian side. More specifically, Bloom encourages us to approach *Mencius* 6A16, where Mencius distinguishes Heavenly honor – in Chinese *tianjue* 天爵, which Bloom translates as "the nobility of Heaven" – from human honor, with reference to what Mencius calls "good honor" (*lianggui* 良貴) in *Mencius* 6A17 in contradistinction with "the honor that derives from men (*ren zhi suo qui zhe* 人之所貴者)" or, simply, human honor. Bloom comments on *lianggui* (and by implication, *tianjue*) in the following way:

> Mencius's use of the term *liang* as "good honor" is noteworthy. It is the same word he used in explaining the source of human moral potential, a potential that all human beings share through an endowment of Heaven expressed in their "good ability" and "good knowledge." In the present context Mencius uses the term *liang* to identify the "good honor" that all human beings have within themselves.... As in the case of Mencian equality, Mencian dignity is based on moral potential and, more particularly, on the psychological awareness of that potential within the minds of individuals.[31]

Bloom's point is that there is a good textual ground to understand "Heavenly honor" and "good honor" as interchangeable, as they are both presented in contrast to "human honor"; and, since in Mencius the term "*liang*" is intimately associated with Heaven-bestowed natural ability or knowledge, Heavenly honor as good honor denotes nothing less than the moral potential that all humans are born with. In Bloom's interpretation, Heavenly honor is not moral esteem that is *achieved* as a form of merit only after one's moral self-cultivation, as the virtue-ethical interpretation of Mencian Confucianism suggests. On the contrary, Heavenly honor is what one as a human being naturally possesses, making him/her dignified irrespective of whether or not he/she has cultivated virtue. Zhang echoes Bloom by claiming that "humanity [*ren* 仁] and justice [*yi* 義] are true nobility, which is endowed by Heaven

---

[29] Irene Bloom, "Mencius and Human Rights," in *Confucianism and Human Rights*, edited by Wm. Theodore de Bary and Tu Wei-ming (New York: Columbia University Press, 1998), p. 98.
[30] Zhang, "The Idea of Human Dignity," p. 309.
[31] Bloom, "Mencius and Human Rights," p. 107.

and cannot be substituted by human nobility (such as high social status and comfortable material life). Whereas human nobility is contingent on individual fortune and limited necessarily to a few, the inherent nobility of Heaven is absolute and universal to all human beings."[32]

By emphasizing that *all* human beings possess natural moral dignity, therefore, the advocates of Confucian dignity as potential shift our attention from the moral hierarchy between the gentleman and the petty man to the moral distinction between humans and animals. The attention to this distinction, however, is not to valorize the moral superiority of humans over animals. What it entails is the moral encouragement that *anyone* can experience moral growth and even become a sage, the culmination of moral self-cultivation.

As such, this alternative reconstruction of Confucian dignity as potential is possible only if it is presupposed that human nature is good, equipped with "good ability," "good knowledge," and "good honor." Only if it is assumed that people equally possess innate moral sentiments can it follow that they are morally equal, thus equally and universally entitled to moral respect, regardless of how they turn out in the course of their life. That is, the case for Confucian dignity as potential only stands when we give normative priority to what people share as humans over the extent to which they can part company as individuals with regard to moral development.

But what if humans do not possess innate virtues? The problem with the account of Confucian dignity as potential is that it is mainly based on Mencian Confucianism and is completely incommensurable with Xunzian Confucianism, which is premised on the assumption that human nature is bad.

As is well known, Xunzi challenges Mencius by claiming that his "human nature is good" thesis is mistaken and even dangerous as it is likely to lead to a false belief that moral self-cultivation requires no external training or education proffered by ritual and teachers.[33] According to Xunzi, human nature is bad in the sense that it is driven by desire for profit, which then naturally disposes all humans to struggle and contention. Xunzi famously says:

> People's nature is bad. Their goodness is a matter of deliberate effort. Now people's nature is such that they are born with a fondness for profit in them. If they follow

---

[32] Zhang, "The Idea of Human Dignity," p. 310. In a recent article, Xu modifies this universalist Confucian account of human dignity by drawing attention to ritual (*li*) as an objective institutional arrangement that can impart to human dignity a distinctive material form. See Keqian Xu, "Contemporary Re-Examination of Confucian Li 禮 and Human Dignity," *Frontiers of Philosophy in China* 13, no. 3 (2018): 449–464. Though I find Xu's institutional approach interesting, Xu's *li*-based account of Confucian human dignity can be understood as yet another version of Confucian inegalitarian dignity given the fact that Confucian ritual order is hierarchical and, more alarmingly for us the moderns, deeply gendered. Like other advocates of Confucian inegalitarian dignity, Xu does not extend his *li*-based account of Confucian dignity to political and constitutional theory, leaving unanswered precisely what form of constitutional arrangement can best realize Confucian dignity in modern China.

[33] *Xunzi* 23.2a.

along with this, then struggle and contention will arise, and yielding and deference will perish therein. . . . If they follow along with their inborn dispositions and obey their nature, they are sure to come to struggle and contention, turn to disrupting social divisions and order, and end up becoming violent. So, it is necessary to await the transforming influence of teachers and models and the guidance of ritual and *yi*, and only then will they come to yielding and deference, turn to proper form and order, and end up becoming controlled.[34]

In asserting that "human nature is bad," therefore, Xunzi's purpose is not so much to demonstrate the radical evilness of humans but to reject the existence of innate virtues or moral resources as well as to argue for natural proneness toward disorder. Xunzi's argument is that humans are driven by desire for profit, completely devoid of moral sentiments, and that they lack innate motivation to behave morally or to become good. Thus, they must be externally motivated toward goodness, and for that purpose a painstaking process of drastic moral self-transformation is necessary, which involves re-forming oneself according to the models and norms established by ancient sage-kings.[35] In this view, morality is an artifice and has no foundation in human nature.[36]

What is important in the present context is that Xunzian Confucianism fully supports Confucian dignity as achievement without allowing for an alternative Confucian account of human dignity as potential like Mencian Confucianism. Roughly, Xunzian Confucian virtue ethics takes the following steps: 1) human nature is bad; 2) in order to become good, a person must undergo moral self-transformation; 3) since there is no moral sentiment or potential within the self,

---

[34] *Xunzi* 23.1a. The English translations of the *Xunzi* 荀子 are adapted from *Xunzi: The Complete Text*, trans. Eric L. Hutton (Princeton, NJ: Princeton University Press, 2014).

[35] *Xunzi* 19.1a. On Xunzi's "re-formation model of moral self-cultivation," see Philip J. Ivanhoe, *Confucian Moral Self Cultivation* (Indianapolis, IN: Hackett, 2000), pp. 29–42.

[36] As noted earlier in n 10, Ni brushes away the fundamental difference between Mencius and Xunzi in their accounts of human nature. The point to which Ni draws attention is Xunzi's controversial claim that humans have a sense of appropriateness/rightness (*yi*) in addition to vital energy (*qi* 氣), life, and awareness that are possessed by plants or nonhuman animals (*Xunzi* 9.16a). Despite his disagreement with Ni, Zhang, too, interprets Xunzi here as believing in the innate sense of justice ("The Idea of Human Dignity," p. 309), thereby assimilating Xunzi to Mencius. Unfortunately, I do not have the space to examine the plausibility of this line of interpretation of Xunzi's statement, advanced first in the Anglophone academic world by Donald Munro (see Donald J. Munro, "A Villain in the *Xunzi*," in *Chinese Language, Thought, and Culture: Nivison and His Critics*, edited by Philip J. Ivanhoe [Chicago, IL: Open Court, 1996]). It suffices to say that Ni's and Zhang's misunderstanding was caused by their failure to capture Xunzi's nuanced conceptualization of *yi*, not as an innate sense of morality but as a social norm or a pattern of social organization. On this account, that humans have *yi* implies that they have an ability to form community and organize it by following their social allotments and roles created by the sage-kings. For an argument for *yi* as a social norm, see Eric L. Hutton, "Ethics in the Xunzi," in *Dao Companion to the Philosophy of Xunzi*, ed. Eric L. Hutton (Dordrecht: Springer, 2016), pp. 71–74. Also see Eric L. Hutton, "Does Xunzi Have a Consistent Theory of Human Nature?" in *Virtue, Nature and Moral Agency in the Xunzi*, edited by T. C. Kline III and Philip J. Ivanhoe (Indianapolis, IN: Hackett, 2000) for a forceful refutation of Munro's assimilation of Xunzi to Mencius.

one must re-form himself to become good and produce morality by following the models and norms established by the sage-kings (in their prudential desire to avoid chaos and poverty);[37] 4) while one who has successfully re-formed one's self and accumulated virtues becomes a gentleman, one who has failed in moral self-transformation remains a petty man;[38] 5) there is a moral hierarchy between the gentleman and the petty man; and finally, 6) human dignity is a merit that only the gentleman deserves.

In Xunzian virtue ethics, therefore, Confucian dignity as achievement is the only account of human dignity that can be justified. Even though Xunzi, like Mencius, presupposes natural equality in the sense that all humans are bad prior to the rise of ritual order, it is far from moral equality in the way that Mencian natural equality can be, because there is no morality before ritual and *yi* (as a social norm). In fact, Xunzi points out radical equality of men in the state of nature as the single greatest cause of political disorder and social chaos:

> If people's authority is all equal, then they cannot be unified. If all the masses are equal in status, then they cannot be put to use … As for the fact that two nobles cannot serve each other, and two base men cannot employ each other, this is the Heavenly order of things. If people's authority and position are equal and their desires and dislikes the same, then goods cannot be made sufficient for them, and they will certainly struggle. If they struggle then there will certainly be chaos, and if there is chaos then they will be impoverished. The former kings hated this chaos, and so they established ritual and *yi* in order to divide up mankind, so as to cause ranking of poor and rich and noble and base, so that they might take charge of them. This is the basis for nourishing all under Heaven.[39]

Thus, for Xunzi, natural equality is a state of affairs that ought to be overcome. Accordingly, human dignity is not a value that can be derived from natural equality as it holds no moral worth. It is an honor achieved by one who has successfully cultivated himself. To use the Mencian language, the honor in question is "Heavenly honor" because it denotes the moral desert or merit that represents one's accumulated virtue. What is interesting about Xunzi is that he wants to achieve perfect congruence between virtue and "human honor" by proposing a merit-based social order and government structure. Consider the following statement by Xunzi:

> Promote the worthy and the capable without waiting for them to rise through the ranks. Dismiss the unfit and the incapable without waiting for even a single moment. … Even the sons and grandsons of kings, dukes, gentry, and grand ministers, if they cannot submit to ritual and *yi*, should be assigned the status of commoners. Even the sons and grandsons of commoners, if they accumulate

---

[37] *Xunzi* 8.11.
[38] "By birth, people are originally petty people. Without a teacher and the proper model, they will seek only benefit" (*Xunzi* 4.10).
[39] *Xunzi* 9.3.

culture and learning, correct their person and conduct, and can submit to ritual and *yi*, should be assigned the status of prime minister, gentry, or grand ministers. ... Encourage [the people] with accolades and rewards, and discipline them with punishments and penalties. If they rest secure in their occupations, then nurture them. If they do not rest secure in their occupations, then abandon them.[40]

For Mencius, Heavenly honor and human honor are two different kinds of honor that are independent of each other. Of course, as a virtue ethicist Mencius does not deny the importance of achieving the congruence between Heavenly honor and human honor, but his main point is that, even if this happy congruence does not obtain, one deserves moral esteem as far as one possesses Heaven-given moral capacities and potential, the most profound source of human dignity. In contrast, Xunzi is convinced that Heavenly honor must be singularly grounded in virtue alone achieved by good conduct. As long as (accumulated) virtue is the only source or sign of Heaven's blessing – he calls it "Heavenly virtue" (*tiande* 天德)[41] – Heavenly honor must not be confused with inner moral potential, whose existence Xunzi rejects, and should, in principle, be understood as the single ground for human honor.

For Xunzi, therefore, human dignity is a merit and as such it ought to be accompanied by relevant social veneration or rank. From Xunzi's perspective, Mencius' "human nature is good" thesis not only creates two sources of morality (moral potential and virtue) but further generates a fundamental tension between natural equality and moral inequality (in virtue or achievement) by rendering the former as a kind of moral equality, resulting in the troubling situation that (natural) moral equality leads to moral inequality. His alternative account of Heavenly honor or human dignity does not succumb to this problem because it allows the single ground for Heaven honor (i.e. virtue) and attaches no normative value to natural equality. The result is a happy congruence between moral meritocracy and political meritocracy in which political inequality tracks moral inequality. In this way, Xunzian virtue ethics presents a coherent and universally applicable account of Confucian dignity that is meritocratic and inegalitarian without getting embroiled with the problems internal to Ni's purely subjective account of Confucian dignity as achievement.

4 THE SERVICE CONCEPTION OF POLITICAL RIGHT

One of the most salient features of the Confucian virtue-ethical account of human dignity as achievement is that it does not acknowledge political right as one's moral

---

[40] *Xunzi* 9.1.
[41] "For the gentleman's cultivation of his heart, nothing is better than integrity. When you have achieved integrity, there is nothing more to do than to cling to *ren* and to carry out *yi*. If you cling to *ren* with a heart of integrity, then you will come to embody it. If you embody it, then you will have spirit-like power. With this spirit-like power, you can then transform things. If you carry out *yi* with a heart of integrity, then you will become well-ordered. If you are well-ordered, then you will become enlightened. When you are enlightened, then you can adapt to things. To transform and adapt in succession is called *Heavenly virtue*" (*Xunzi* 3.9a, emphasis added).

entitlement. Xunzi's argument for the congruence between moral inequality (or moral meritocracy) and political inequality (or political meritocracy) clearly attests to this feature. Therefore, it is hardly surprising that some contemporary advocates of Confucian political meritocracy (hereafter "Confucian meritocrats") espouse a political theory (and political system) that explicitly rejects the intrinsic value of political equality and justifies the so-called "service conception of political right." Among others, Joseph Chan presents perhaps the most sophisticated argument for this view.

Chan's argument faithfully tracks the core stipulations of Confucian virtue ethics when he justifies the service conception as an alternative conception of political right against its dominant liberal counterpart:

> [In Confucianism] political authority exists to serve the ruled, and the political rights attached to this authority are justified instrumentally by the contribution they make to the betterment of people's lives. These political rights are not fundamental moral rights that belong to individuals but are more on a par with the rights of officials such as the police, who have rights because their proper exercise of them can protect and promote the well-being of the people. ... The general view is that the distribution of political rights or powers, and the institutional form that these rights or powers take, should be evaluated by the service conception. A person possessing political rights or a share in an institution of political authority must have this possession justified by reference to the good of the people. In this sense there is no natural right to political power as such.[42]

Chan's reasoning proceeds in the following steps: 1) the ultimate end of Confucianism is to enhance the well-being of the people; 2) in Confucianism, political authority or the "power" to influence others is justified by its service to the well-being of the ruled; 3) political rights are the power held by the people to influence the well-being of others; 4) as power, political rights, like political authority, must be justified by the service conception; 5) holding only instrumental value in its service to the well-being of the people as the ruled, political right is neither a natural right nor a moral right; 6) as justified by the service conception, political rights can be exercised only by those who have contributed to the well-being of others, namely those who are virtuous; 7) on the flip side, one who has failed to contribute to the well-being of others is not entitled to possess political rights; and finally, 8) the more one contributes to the well-being of others, the more political rights one can have.

Evidently, there is remarkable parallelism between Chan's reasoning and Xunzian virtue ethics. First, there is no natural equality understood as moral equality. Second, there should be significant overlapping between moral/virtue inequality and political inequality. And third, as human dignity is not grounded in

---

[42] Chan, *Confucian Perfectionism*, p. 32.

moral equality, in principle, human dignity is compatible with moral inequality and by extension political inequality.

To be fair, it is far from clear whether Chan fully commits himself to Xunzian virtue ethics by accepting the purely meritocratic justification of human dignity because he does distinguish human right from political right, although without explaining the normative ground for this important distinction.[43] Without further complicating the issue, the point that I am trying to make here is that Chan's service conception of political right can be best understood against the backdrop of traditional Confucian virtue ethics, especially the Xunzian version, in which the moral worth of natural equality is denied. So, as far as Chan and company present the service conception as a matter of textual interpretation– that is, as a response to the purely speculative philosophical question of what kind of political right can be derived from the Confucian ethical tradition – there should be little controversy. The problem is that Confucian meritocrats advocate the service conception of political right in contemporary East Asian societies of the Confucian heritage as a normative claim and with prescriptive purposes, refuting both natural moral equality and the one person one vote (OPOV) principle that is predicated on it.

However, rejection of moral and political equality comes with far-reaching political and constitutional implications. First, it implies that the political structure undergirded by the service conception is not a constitutional democracy in which political equality is derived from natural moral equality and which relies on OPOV as the institutional expression of political equality and popular sovereignty. Not surprisingly, Confucian meritocrats either outright reject constitutional democracy or embrace minimal democracy (mainly elections) within the otherwise meritocratic political system to the extent that it can be conducive to the nondemocratic political or moral ends that they promote.[44] The specific constitutional designs suggested by Confucian meritocrats vary from scholar to scholar, but the general consensus is to establish a second chamber (or the meritocratic upper house) in the legislature composed of the so-called the best and the brightest, who are nondemocratically selected through examination or recommendation and possess a (permanent) veto power over the decisions made by the democratically elected lower house.[45]

---

[43] See Chan, *Confucian Perfectionism*, chap. 5. In my view, while appealing to ethical perfectionism à la Joseph Raz for the service conception of political right, Chan relies on Waldron's fallback theory of right when he embraces basic human rights, which does not have the perfectionist justification. On this inconsistency in Chan's political theory, see Sungmoon Kim, "Confucian Authority, Political Right, and Democracy," *Philosophy East and West* 67, no. 1 (2017): 3–14.

[44] See, among others, Daniel A. Bell, *The China Model: Political Meritocracy and Its Limits of Democracy* (Princeton, NJ: Princeton University Press, 2015); Jiang Qing, *A Confucian Constitutional Order: How China's Ancient Past Can Shape Its Political Future*, trans. Edmund Ryden (Princeton, NJ: Princeton University Press, 2013); Bai, *Against Political Equality*.

[45] Unlike most other Confucian meritocrats advocating the meritocratic upper house, however, Chan leaves the moral and legal status of the second chamber as the lawmaking institution deeply ambiguous by giving it only an advisory function as well as expecting it to be a role model of public deliberation for politicians and citizens (*Confucian Perfectionism*, p. 108).

The central goal of instituting the meritocratic upper house is to constrain popular sovereignty as much as to produce laws that can serve (what the political elites deem to be) "true" public interests.

Second, rejection of core democratic principles renders the purpose of separation of powers, the independent judiciary in particular, helplessly ambiguous. Admittedly, the core moral assumption that underlies democracy as a political system is that (universal) human dignity naturally entails moral equality among the people as humans and moral equality in turn underpins political equality among the people as citizens. In a constitutional democracy the purpose of separating powers is to ensure that citizens can govern themselves effectively by prohibiting the concentration and arbitrary use of the state's coercive power so that it can be exercised in ways respectful of citizens' equal moral and public status.[46] Independent judiciary plays a special role in constitutional democracy by protecting citizens – their equal status and basic rights, more precisely, which are ground on the foundational value of human dignity – from the unjustified public use of coercive power in mediation of law.

However, both the meritocratic account of human dignity, concentrated on accumulated virtue and the service conception of political right, emphasizing one's contribution to the well-being of others, are critically limited in justifying a consistent form of constitutionalism and independence of the judiciary in particular. Thorny questions arise. If human dignity is understood in meritocratic terms and thus the intrinsic value of (natural) moral equality is rejected along with political equality, on what ground can it be claimed that coercive public power ought to be justified to citizens? Given that the role of the judiciary lies in determining the justness (and justifiability) of the state's coercive power expressed by law in light of public equality and basic rights, if the value of moral equality is rejected, how can an independent judiciary be justified? Confucian meritocrats might respond by arguing that, without positing moral equality and by extension political equality, an independent judiciary can still be justified with reference to the well-being of the people alone. Specifically, they may claim that the justness of state power can be determined by examining whether or not one's well-being has been violated by it, and, for that purpose, the judiciary as the institution whose central function is to subject state power to the justifiability test must entertain an independent constitutional status vis-à-vis other branches of the government.

---

[46] This understanding of constitutional democracy may not be strictly consistent with some versions of liberal constitutionalism, which pay far more attention to protection of rights and freedoms than their "equal" protection or understand separation of powers in relation to individual rights and freedoms rather than in relation to democratic self-government. That said, my understanding of constitutional democracy is largely consistent with the various accounts of constitutional democracy suggested by the following scholars: Philip Pettit, *On the People's Terms: A Republican Theory and Model of Democracy* (Cambridge: Cambridge University Press, 2012); Christopher L. Eisgruber, *Constitutional Self-Government* (Cambridge, MA: Harvard University Press, 2001); Stephen Macedo, *Liberal Virtues: Citizenship, Virtue, and Community in Liberal Constitutionalism* (Oxford: Clarendon, 1990).

The problem is that, without positing egalitarian dignity and, by extension, moral equality, it is impossible to make sure that the court's justifiability test can be *equally* available for all citizens regardless of the virtue they possess or the past contributions that they made to others' well-being. The meritocratic justification of human dignity (as achievement) logically entails that the more virtuous one is, the more one is entitled to moral esteem and, therefore, political authority. Confucian meritocrats tend to appeal to this line of reasoning in justifying the virtuous people's lawmaking power in the meritocratic upper house. However, they do not seem to realize that the same reasoning can be exploited to support unequal treatment of the people in the court, as the court is likely or even encouraged to give priority to protecting the well-being of the (more) virtuous than those who are not or less virtuous. Otherwise stated, in Confucian political meritocracy, law is expected to discriminate between the gentleman and the one who falls short of this ideal, not only in authorizing one's political power to rule but also in subjecting one to the court's justifiability test with regard to the state's coercive power. And in Confucian political meritocracy such otherwise morally controversial judgments as who is more or less virtuous, whether one is subject to punishment, and how much or what kind of punishment one deserves are (entirely?) up to the putatively virtuous political elites who possess the lawmaking power. In short, in Confucian political meritocracy, the power to make law and the authority to test law's justifiability is potentially entrusted to the unified body of the undemocratically selected ruling elite. Seen in this way, Bell's advocacy of "the China model," where the judiciary does not enjoy full institutional autonomy from the party-state (that Bell judges to be meritocratic), is the logical corollary of the service conception.[47]

Insomuch as the contemporary proposals of Confucian political meritocracy are intended to reinstate Confucian virtue politics, their ambivalence toward an independent judiciary, let alone their refutation of a constitutional democracy, is hardly surprising. After all, Confucian virtue politics, operating on the assumption of meritorious rulership, was never predicated on the principle of separation of powers, and it never acknowledged the nexus between (natural) moral equality and political equality. However, precisely for this reason, Confucian virtue politics is not compatible with protection of basic rights, nor is it compatible with constitutional democracy. Likewise, Confucian political meritocracy does not offer an unequivocal defense of basic rights, including the right to political participation. If one's political right is covariant with one's virtue,[48] on what ground can *equal* protection of basic

---

[47] It is not surprising that, in redesigning China's constitutional structure, Jiang Qing pays attention solely to the legislature with a view to constraining the will of the people by the so-called "sacred authority of the House of *Ru* (Confucian Scholars)," while being completely silent on the independence of the judiciary or separation of powers in general. The same problem applies virtually all Confucian meritocrats including Tongdong Bai, Joseph Chan, and Ruiping Fan.

[48] Without denying this covariation between right and virtue, Chung-ying Cheng further claims that we can derive implicit rights from explicit virtues by turning moral duties correlated with virtues into the rights of the people to whom the virtues are owed. However, as Cheng himself admits, this suggestion

rights be morally justified?[49] Again, it is not accidental that Confucian meritocrats such as Bell single out the right to subsistence as the only right recognized and recognizable in the Confucian tradition while downplaying the importance of civil and political rights as if they could be traded off.[50] Though Confucian meritocrats do not explicitly associate their dismissal of civil and political rights with Confucian virtue ethics, it does seem to have a strong moral foundation in their (sometimes implicit) understanding of human dignity as achievement.

Here arises a question. Even though there is no reason to believe that constitutional democracy is the only right way to organize our political life, if our conception of human dignity is critically limited in justifying public equality, equal protection of basic rights, and an independent judiciary, all of which are indispensable to effective protection of the people's well-being, does this not generate an important reason to pursue constitutional democracy, which can integrate all these elements, as well as democratic values such as collective self-government and public freedom, within a coherent institutional structure?[51] If the answer is "yes," this means that the constitutional democracy that is being pursued here cannot be grounded in the traditional form of Confucian virtue ethics in which human dignity is envisioned in relation to virtue as achievement. Rather, an alternative vision of Confucianism is required, and, following Bloom and Zhang, I argue that such an alternative vision can be inspired by the Mencian commitment to human dignity as potential.

But can we justify our alternative vision of Confucianism toward constitutional democracy from a Xunzian standpoint as well? If it turns out that Xunzi's philosophy can also lend support to the account of Confucian dignity as potential or Confucian

has critical limitations as a theory of right as it cannot come to grips with the right to political participation. See his "Transforming Confucian Virtues into Human Rights: A Study of Human Agency and Potency in Confucian Ethics," in *Confucianism and Human Rights*, edited by Wm. Theodore de Bary and Tu Wei-ming (New York: Columbia University Press, 1998), p. 146. For a similar view, see Ruiping Fan, *Reconstructionist Confucianism: Rethinking Morality after the West* (Dordrecht: Springer, 2010), pp. 58–59.

[49] Chenyang Li, another Confucian meritocrat, proposes the general participation principle along with the qualification/exclusion principle in his effort to enact Confucian political meritocracy. He advocates what he calls "proportional equality," another version of Confucian moral inequality based on virtue, but fails to explain how the general participation principle can be derived from Confucianism in a way consistent with the Confucian account of qualitative equality that can otherwise justify the qualification/exclusion principle. See his "Equality and Inequality in Confucianism," *Dao* 11, no. 3 (2012): 295–313.

[50] See Daniel A. Bell, *Beyond Liberal Democracy: Political Thinking for an East Asian Context* (Princeton, NJ: Princeton University Press, 2008), pp. 242–243. In the same vein, Bai claims that "for a Confucian, it is good trade-off that by giving the competent people a higher political and social status, they share more of their wealth with the masses and try to help the masses economically" (*Against Political Equality*, p. 105). For my criticism of Bell, see Sungmoon Kim, "Confucianism, Moral Equality, and Human Rights: A Mencian Perspective," *American Journal of Economics and Sociology* 74, no. 1 (2015): 174–178.

[51] This reason does not have to be an absolutely compelling one in a moral sense. Notice that what I am suggesting here is not the complete disvalue of political meritocracy but the possibility of an alternative institutional model to it and a sufficient, but not necessary, reason to support constitutional democracy as such an alternative.

egalitarian dignity without doing away with its underlying assumption that human nature is evil, we can secure a firmer philosophical ground for constitutional democracy justifiable in Confucian terms, although how constitutional democracy can actually be justified by the Xunzian perspective is a wholly different matter, requiring another venue for investigation. In the remainder of this chapter, I attempt to justify human dignity as potential from a Xunzian perspective as a first step toward the philosophical justification of Confucian constitutional democracy.

5 A XUNZIAN CASE FOR HUMAN DIGNITY AS POTENTIAL

One way to make our task simpler is to reinterpret Xunzi's "human nature is bad" thesis in a way consistent with the presence of innate goodness, and this is indeed precisely what Ni and Zhang do, despite their different accounts of Confucian dignity (as achievement versus potential), by asserting, in reference to *Xunzi* 9.16a, that Xunzi implicitly concedes that humans have the innate sense of justice and/or righteousness. But even if we, following Hutton and others, assume that Xunzi's account of human nature is coherent and philosophically robust[52] – that is, without doing away with Xunzi's own claim that human nature is bad – can we still find in Xunzi's philosophy resources by which to justify the universalist and egalitarian conception of human dignity as potential applicable to all humans? Consider the following statement by Xunzi:

> Heaven did not favor Zengzi, Minzi Qian, and Xiao Yi and excluded the masses. Then why is it that only Zengzi, Minzi Qian, and Xiao Yi were rich in the true substance of filial piety and were perfect in their reputation for filial piety? It is because they exerted themselves to the utmost in ritual and *yi*. Heaven does not favor people of Qi and Lu and exclude the people of Qin. Then why is it that with regard to the *yi* between father and son, and the distinction between husband and wife, the people of Qin are not as good at filial reverence and respectful good form as those of Qi and Lu? It is because the people of Qin follow along with their inborn dispositions and nature, take comfort in utter lack of restraint, and are lax in regard to ritual and *yi*. How could it be because their nature is different?[53]

Xunzi's argument is that it is not because Heaven favored certain people and made them virtuous that they are virtuous; it is because, even if Heaven created all equally, some have become virtuous and others have not. As we have discussed, for Xunzi the fact that people are born equally holds no moral significance because they are all born equally bad. What is interesting about Xunzi's statement here is that Heaven

---

[52] For Hutton's position, see n 36. Also see Philip J. Ivanhoe, "Morality as an Artifact: The Nature of Moral Norms in Xunzi's Philosophy," in *Oxford Handbook of Chinese Philosophy*, edited by Justin Tiwald (New York: Oxford University Press, forthcoming). For a nuanced disagreement with this view, see Siufu Tang, *Self-Realization through Confucian Learning: A Contemporary Reconstruction of Xunzi's Ethics* (Albany: State University of New York Press, 2016).
[53] *Xunzi* 23.4b.

does not discriminate among people when it comes to one's *ability* to become virtuous. Put differently, Xunzi not only believes in equal ability of moral self-cultivation (even if whether or how much one actually exercises it depends on one's commitment to the Way), but, more importantly, he imparts to this ability strong normative import by grounding it on Heaven's impartiality. This Heaven-given ability to transform one's self does not presuppose humans' innate goodness and for Xunzi "follow[ing] along with [one's] inborn dispositions and nature" means nothing more than self-abandonment. Let us call this *the equal ability proposition*.

Xunzi's belief in equal moral ability of self-development is most clearly addressed in the following statement where Xunzi claims that *everyone* is capable of becoming a sage:

> Anyone on the streets can become a Yu [a legendary sage-king]. How do I mean this? I say: that by which Yu was Yu was because he was *ren*, *yi*, lawful, and correct. Thus, *ren*, *yi*, lawfulness, and correctness have patterns that can be known and can be practiced. However, people on the streets all have the material [*zhi* 質] for knowing *ren*, *yi*, lawfulness, and correctness, and they all have the equipment [*ju* 具] for practicing *ren*, *yi*, lawfulness, and correctness. Thus, it is clear that they can become a Yu. ... Now it is the case that anyone on the streets can know the *yi* of father and son within the family, and can know the proper relations of lord and minister outside the family. Thus, it is clear that the material for understanding these things and the equipment for practicing them is present in people on the streets. Now if people on the streets were to use their material for understanding these things and the equipment for practicing them to base themselves upon the knowable patterns and practicable aspects of *ren* and *yi*, then is it clear that anyone on the streets could become a Yu.[54]

Two points are worth noting here. First, not only is the ability of moral development equally available to everyone, but sagehood, the final destination of moral self-cultivation, is equally accessible to *everyone*, regardless of one's social pedigree. This finding is of pivotal importance because, while the equal ability proposition does not necessarily imply moral perfectibility of all humans (it only conveys possible moral inequalities resulting from different degrees of moral self-cultivation), what can be called *the equal perfection proposition* informs that the ideal state of moral self-cultivation is equally achievable by everyone and that humans are radically equal from the perspective of moral perfectibility. So Xunzi does not merely say that people can become a Yu. When he says that "anyone on the street" can become a sage like Yu, he certainly reveals his moral egalitarianism, highlighting the *equal* moral potential for human perfectibility.

Second, his belief that human nature is bad notwithstanding, Xunzi admits that the path toward morality is known to and practicable by everyone because all humans possess the inner "material" (*zhi*) and "equipment" (*ju*) by which to know

[54] *Xunzi* 23.5a.

and practice morality. To be sure, unlike Mencius, Xunzi does not present the inner (epistemic and practical) capacity that enables one to acquire moral sensibilities in terms of moral sprouts or sentiments that are internal to human nature. For Xunzi, in order to acquire moral sensibilities one must undergo moral education by means of ritual and *yi*, and since ritual and *yi* are institutional models and social norms rather than moral sentiments, morality is definitely an artifact. And insomuch as morality is an artifact, people come to possess or construct different kinds of moral artifact in ways corresponding with their different levels of moral training. What we learn additionally from Xunzi's statement on the inner material and equipment is that, unless we posit certain inner capacity, which may be morally contentless, morality cannot be created even with one's deliberate effort and education. Xunzi's argument is that such inner capacity that lacks moral content is equally shared by everyone. So, according to Xunzi, one may not be *ren* and *yi* by nature, but everyone is capable of knowing and practicing *ren* and *yi* under necessary external circumstances. Let us call this *the inner capacity proposition*.

The equal ability proposition, the equal perfection proposition, and the inner capacity proposition may be limited in fully supporting the egalitarian account of human dignity as an independent moral proposition. When combined, however, they can undergird the egalitarian conception of human dignity as potential. Of course, this Xunzian conception of Confucian dignity as potential does not replace or supersede its virtue/achievement-based counterpart, as both Xunzian-Confucian accounts of human dignity are incommensurable with each other, and each can be a viable interpretation depending on one's broader political and constitutional theory, as part of which Confucian dignity is (and should be) reconstructed in the first place. What I intend to do here is to propose an alternative Xunzian account of human dignity focused on moral potential universally and equally available to all humans, as opposed to one concentrated on virtue that is unequally achieved among the people. One salient advantage of this alternative Xunzian conception of human dignity is that it can explain Xunzi's unmeritocratic, quite universalist concern with the well-being of the people:

> If the common people are uneasy with the government, then the gentleman will not feel secure in holding his position. ... When the common people are uneasy with the government, then nothing works better than treating them generously. ... Take in those who are orphaned or widowed. Assist those who are poor and in dire straits. If you do this, then the common people will feel at ease with the government, only then will the gentleman feel as ease in holding his position. There is a saying, "The lord is the boat. The common people are the water. The water can support the boat. The water can also overturn the boat." This expresses my meaning.[55]

In this statement Xunzi draws the ruler's attention to the critical importance of the people's well-being in relation to the stability of his government. Xunzi's seemingly

---

[55] *Xunzi* 9.4.

instrumentalist approach to the well-being of the people in the present context, however, should not prevent us from appreciating the unmeritocratic dimension of his political thought. A purely meritocratic conception of Confucian dignity (as achievement) cannot account for Xunzi's argument that the ruler ought to take seriously the well-being of those who are most destitute and indiscriminately take care of the people at large. If virtue is the sole basis of merit on which one's human dignity rests, as Ni suggests, logically speaking there can be no compelling *moral* reason (in addition to the instrumental consideration of stability) for the Xunzian ruler to take care of, let alone give priority to, the well-being of the worst-off without first assessing whether they are actually worthy of human dignity and *deserve* government support.[56]

Likewise, when Xunzi asserts that common people are the water that can overturn (or support) the boat (i.e. the ruler), he does not grant them this remarkable collective political power based on the service conception of political right. Nor does he make a vivid political distinction among the people, between active subjects (e.g. ministers) and the laypeople, an important distinction for Mencius as far as his political theory is concerned.[57] According to Xunzi, common people as a whole deserve the governmental protection of their well-being, and common people as a whole – irrespective of each individual's contribution to the well-being of others – possess a significant degree of political power sufficient to overthrow a bad ruler.

While the Xunzian account of human dignity as virtue/achievement is critically limited in accounting for Xunzi's unmeritocratic justification of the people's well-being and common people's collective political power, our alternative Xunzian conception of human dignity as potential can lend strong support to both the protection of the people's well-being and their political power (though not *equal* power). The fact that all humans possess inner capacity to develop moral sensibilities (when properly educated), all humans have equal ability to improve themselves morally, and all humans can become morally perfect leads to the conclusion that all humans are dignified regardless of their virtue or service to the well-being of others and that common people are worthy of public protection of their well-being or basic interests as humans. These three propositions of the Xunzian-Confucian idea of

[56] Compare Xunzi's egalitarian conception of human dignity with that of Han Fei, a famous Legalist and Xunzi's own student, which takes a purely meritocratic approach to social justice: "Once, when Qin had a great famine, Marquis Ying petitioned His Majesty, say[ing], 'The grass, vegetables, acorns, dates, and chestnuts in the Five Parks are sufficient to save the people. May Your Majesty give them out?' In reply King Zhao Xian said, 'In accordance with the law of our country the people shall be rewarded for merits and punished for crimes. Now, if I give out the vegetables and fruits of the Five Parks, I will in so doing reward men of merit and no merit equally. To be sure, to reward men of merit and no merit equally, leads to disorder. Indeed, instead of giving out the products of the Five Parks and thereby inviting confusion, we may as well discard the fruits and vegetables and thereby maintain order'" (*Hanfeizi* 35). The English translation is adopted from *The Complete Works of Han Fei Tzu: A Classic of Chinese Legalism*, vol. 2, trans. W. K. Liao (London: Arthur Probsthain, 1959), pp. 126–27.
[57] See Sungmoon Kim, "Confucian Constitutionalism: Mencius and Xunzi on Virtue, Ritual, and Royal Transmission," *Review of Politics* 73, no. 3 (2011): 371–99.

human dignity also create a moral ground for common people's collective power as the members of political community to overthrow a bad ruler who miserably fails to fulfill the moral responsibility to serve the well-being of the people, which divests them of the sufficient material condition in which they can engage in moral self-cultivation.[58]

6 CONCLUSION

This last point brings us back to our earlier discussion on the possibility of Confucian constitutional democracy. The Xunzian account of Confucian dignity as potential clearly vindicates that a Confucian political meritocracy premised on the Confucian conception of human dignity as achievement is not the only way to conceive of a constitutional structure in Confucian terms in modern East Asia. Despite intimate affiliation between Xunzian virtue ethics and Confucian political meritocracy, our alternative Xunzian conception of Confucian dignity as potential decouples one's *right* to be included in the political system as a citizen from his virtue and regards even the "petty man" as being worthy of equal respect as a human being by focusing on his moral potentiality and perfectibility.[59] This alternative Xunzian conception of Confucian dignity further supports the sustained institutional structure that at once allows people to participate in public decision-making processes in both formal political forums and civil society and protects their basic interests, although I admit that additional moral and social conditions should be met for there to be a robust connection between Confucian egalitarian dignity and the right to political participation.[60]

"Basic interests," however, should not be understood purely in terms of material well-being. Under modern circumstances of politics, where citizens hold different values, ideas, faiths, and moral interests and their social lives are significantly

[58] For Xunzi's endorsement of tyrannicide, see *Xunzi* 13.9; 18.2. That being said, in these passages Xunzi is seen to endorse the sagacious ministers' action of regicide, not the rebellion of the common people as such. But his analogy between the common people and the water does open the theoretical possibility that common people can engage in a rebellion against a tyrannical ruler unless we interpret *shu ren* 庶人, translated as "common people" here, differently.

[59] Therefore, I largely agree with Zhang, when he says, "To be consistent with the Confucian assumption of natural equality, however, even *xiaoren* ['littleman'] is, after all, a *ren* (person) and must be treated as a human being with the inborn potential virtues.... Even a littleman deserves some respect for his innate nobility by virtue of being a human – better, nobler, and more worthy than other animals" ("The Idea of Human Dignity," p. 319). The important difference between Zhang and me is that I arrive at a similar conclusion from the Xunzian perspective, thus without positing the presence of "inborn potential virtues." I also do not share Zhang's anthropocentric conception of human dignity.

[60] Elsewhere, I call such conditions that help establish a robust moral connection between Confucian egalitarian dignity and the right to political participation "the circumstances of modern politics" in East Asia and pay close attention to value pluralism and moral disagreement. See Sungmoon Kim, *Public Reason Confucianism: Democratic Perfectionism and Constitutionalism in East Asia* (New York: Cambridge University Press, 2016), chap. 6.

marked by moral disagreement, what one deems to be one's basic interest is often inextricably intertwined with one's moral interest; and basic interest understood in this complex sense, reflecting one's own conception of the good life, cannot be dictated by the state or by a handful of political elites. In our alternative Xunzian Confucianism, one's vital interest in public protection of one's basic interest gives rise to a moral claim to basic rights including, first and foremost, the right to political participation and freedoms of speech, expression, association, religion, and so on, which cannot be violated by the state without providing "compelling" public justification (and the judgment as to whether or not the justification being offered by the state is compelling is up to citizens). Confucian constitutional democracy undergirds an intricate political structure of public justification as well as a legal system that subjects the state to the justifiability test in its exercise of coercive power.

The attraction of Confucian constitutional democracy does not stop with public justification and protection of basic interests or rights. Though Confucian constitutional democracy does not subscribe to a strong form of state perfectionism of the kind that is embedded in the core stipulations of Confucian virtue politics, it does encourage citizens to exercise their constitutionally protected rights responsibly as well as intelligently, to cultivate civic virtues that help balance one's private interest and public interest, and to create the socioeconomic conditions in which they and others who may hold different faiths, values, or moral ideals can co-grow morally, thereby realizing a more expansive ideal of the Confucian Way. Ultimately, Confucian constitutional democracy creates an institutional structure of rights (for both protection and reciprocity) that is simultaneously aimed at moral development of its citizens and their collective self-government. In this way, the Confucian conception of human dignity as potential is being reunited with the traditional Confucian concern with virtue (now recast as civic virtue) and moral growth, while balancing the inherently inegalitarian side of virtue with the egalitarianism of human dignity and basic rights.

11

Buddhist Philosophical Approaches to Human Dignity

Anton Sevilla-Liu

1 INTRODUCTION

Can we ground "human dignity" within Buddhist thought? While the origins of the idea of human dignity may be Western, today it forms the foundation of human rights and various transnational and transcultural forms of legislation – a foundation that may prove to be empty and meaningless, or biased, or, perhaps, a potential ground for dialogue between very different traditions.

In this chapter, I will begin with a review of the prior research on human dignity and human rights in Buddhism. This will show the present state of affairs and certain challenges that have left the discussion deadlocked. Then, I will attempt to go past this deadlock by examining certain critical shifts in how Buddhism views the human condition and the path toward freedom. I will begin by examining early (or classical) Buddhism, then proceed to examine Mahāyāna Buddhism. Next, I will examine two very common forms of Buddhism that are often neglected in rights/dignity discourses – salvific Buddhism (Pure Land) and Confucian Buddhism. These will show us four distinct but related ways of viewing the relationship between Buddhism and human dignity. Finally, I will examine one key caveat – the parts of Buddhism that go beyond or *against* ethics – the trans-ethical. This final discussion hopes to offer a key critique of the very presuppositions of our discussion.

One brief explanation before I begin. I will primarily be drawing from Buddhist *philosophy* in order to dialogue with the idea of dignity. Any attempt to analyze Buddhist ideas runs into several problems. First, there are very many schools of Buddhism, and they are theoretically very different. Buddhism is traditionally divided into Theravāda, Mahāyāna, and Vajrayāna schools, but even within Mahāyāna there is an astounding amount of difference, for example between Zen and Pure Land approaches. Second, there is a gap between what Buddhologists and philosophers say and how religion is *lived* (as an anthropology of religion might reveal). Because of these numerous sources of plurality, I chose several thinkers who form certain "archetypes" for how to approach Buddhist spirituality. I particularly focus on four Japanese thinkers – Nishitani Keiji, Tanabe Hajime, Watsuji Tetsurō, and Sueki Fumihiko – for the ideas of enlightenment, salvation, community, and trans-ethics. But they could easily be substituted for other thinkers from other countries or other time periods.

2 THE QUAGMIRE OF HUMAN RIGHTS AND DIGNITY IN BUDDHISM

The question of the relationship between Buddhism and human rights or human dignity is not new. Allow me to examine the present state of the discussion on these three ideas.

I begin with the question "What is human dignity?" In the long introduction to Christopher McCrudden's voluminous *Understanding Human Dignity*, he begins with a simple but useful definition: "The power of the concept of human dignity is unquestionable. It appears to present a simple command to all of us: that we (individually and collectively) should value the human person, simply because he or she is human."[1] When we get into the specifics of human dignity, things get much more complicated. Is human dignity a "conversation stopper" (3), a "non-interpreted thesis" or "placeholder" (7), an "empty or flawed signifier" (11), or perhaps, more promisingly, "a vehicle for attempting to secure consensus in the face of disagreement about comprehensive positions or starting points" (14)? Should we approach it through its political, institutional, or conceptual/emotional functions (13)? How do we trace its genesis in Western society, Christianity, and Enlightenment ideals?

In the following discussion, I will momentarily abstract from the local origins of the concept of human dignity, harboring the hope that dignity is indeed a vehicle for attempting to secure consensus, and seek out where, in the various views of Buddhism, we can find something resembling human dignity – an unconditional call to value the human being insofar as the human being is human.

Jens Braarvig writes one of the few articles focused on the idea of dignity in Buddhism. He writes: "Although in a strict sense there exists no 'self,' one could say that in classical Buddhism nonetheless we find a notion of dignity grounded precisely in the freedom of individuals to liberate themselves from the suffering which the circle of eternal birth causes them."[2]

One could ground Braarvig's claim textually via the "*Chiggala Sutta*: The Hole" from the *Saṃyutta Nikāya* of the Pali Tipitaka of Buddhism. Allow me to quote it in full:

"Monks, suppose that this great earth were totally covered with water, and a man were to toss a yoke with a single hole there. A wind from the east would push it west,

---

[1] Christopher McCrudden, "In Pursuit of Human Dignity: An Introduction to Current Debates," in *Understanding Human Dignity*, edited by Christopher McCrudden (Oxford: Oxford University Press, 2013), p. 1.
[2] Jens Braarvig, "Buddhism: Inner Dignity and Absolute Altruism," in *The Cambridge Handbook of Human Dignity*, edited by Marcus Düwell, Jens Braarvig, Roger Brownsword, and Dietmar Mieth (Cambridge: Cambridge University Press, 2014), p. 171.

a wind from the west would push it east. A wind from the north would push it south, a wind from the south would push it north. And suppose a blind sea-turtle were there. It would come to the surface once every one hundred years. Now what do you think: would that blind sea-turtle, coming to the surface once every one hundred years, stick his neck into the yoke with a single hole?"

"It would be a sheer coincidence, lord ..."

"It's likewise a sheer coincidence that one obtains the human state. It's likewise a sheer coincidence that a Tathagata [one who has thus gone, the Buddha], worthy & rightly self-awakened, arises in the world. It's likewise a sheer coincidence that a doctrine & discipline expounded by a Tathagata appears in the world. Now, this human state has been obtained. A Tathagata, worthy & rightly self-awakened, has arisen in the world. A doctrine & discipline expounded by a Tathagata appears in the world.

"Therefore your duty is the contemplation, 'This is stress [suffering] ... This is the origination of stress ... This is the cessation of stress.' Your duty is the contemplation, 'This is the path of practice leading to the cessation of stress.'"[3]

This idea finds its way into different views of Buddhism, for instance in Japanese Zen Master Dōgen's *Shushōgi* (What Is Truly Meant by Training and Enlightenment).[4] The idea is simple: it is rare to be born as a human being, thus having the opportunity to hear the teachings of the Buddha and the challenges to spur us on to realize these teachings in our own lives. Thus, it is our *duty* to contemplate and realize the way to freedom from suffering. This potential and this duty become the source of our *dignity* as human beings.

However, Braarvig warns us of the limits of this idea: "This is conceptualized in a radically individualistic fashion ... This philosophical notion of dignity was not reflected as a social/moral dignity: persons did not hold individual rights.... [Monks] should focus on the search from freedom *from* – not in – this world."[5] Enlightenment was a personal, private affair of some very gifted individuals. And the way to enlightenment was deliberately by moving *away* from the public sphere. Thus, Braarvig warns that early Buddhism had a very limited view of human dignity.

He then moves on to suggest that it is Mahāyāna Buddhism that comes closer to our view of human dignity. By seeing all beings as having "Buddha-nature" and by aspiring to be a *bodhisattva* who tries to save all living beings, one thus has a stronger sense of dignity – bolstered both by this innate capacity for Buddhahood and by this strong sense of compassion for others – that links this potentially solitary practice into the community of all human/living beings.

I will discuss the specifics of Braarvig in the next few chapters. Reading Braarvig alone, it may seem that the question of human dignity in Buddhism has been

---

[3] "Chiggala Sutta: The Hole" (SN 56.48), translated from the Pali by Thanissaro Bhikkhu. *Access to Insight (BCBS Edition)*, July 1, 2010, www.accesstoinsight.org/tipitaka/sn/sn56/sn56.048.than.html.
[4] P. T. N. H. Jiyu-Kennett, *Zen Is Eternal Life* (Mount Shasta, CA: Shasta Abbey Press, 1999), p. 94.
[5] Braarvig, "Buddhism: Inner Dignity and Absolute Altruism," p. 171.

answered. But if we turn to the more extensive discourse on human *rights* in Buddhism, we find that things are much more confusing than they seem.

Most of the dialogue between Buddhism and human dignity comes not directly but by way of discussions on human rights. Damien Keown, Charles Prebish, and Wayne Husted's *Buddhism and Human Rights* (1998) provides a dense discussion of both critiques and defenses of human rights in Buddhism, including by the 14th Dalai Lama himself. Allow me to summarize the points on human rights in Buddhism that apply to the problem of human dignity.

First, Kenneth Inada warns:

> The Western view on human rights is generally based on a hard relationship. Persons are treated as separate and independent entities or even bodies, each having its own assumed identity or self-identity.... This dualistic perspective has naturally filtered down into human relationships and has eventually crystallized into what we refer to as the nature of a hard relationship.[6]

Inada suggests that this individualistic view is incompatible with the "soft," interconnectionist view of the person found in Buddhism, where the individual exists only in relation with all things. This critique is seconded by Craig Ihara, who takes a role relational view of Buddhism versus individualism. Buddhism is about playing one's role in this soteriological dance and not a closed sense of individual rights. This criticism applies to human dignity as well. Dignity tends to be associated with the *individual* being made "in the image and likeness of God" or the *individual's* autonomy as a rational being. A purely individualistic view of dignity would, contrary to what Braarvig suggests, run contrary to Buddhism.

A response to these criticisms and an overall defense of human rights in Buddhism is given by Damien Keown and is presented in an updated version in the *Oxford Handbook of Buddhist Ethics*.[7] First, Buddhism (in the Vinaya) has an extensive discussion on our duties to the monastic community and to each other, which reflects the rights (and dignity) of the recipients of these duties. Second, just because the self is "empty" (as suggested by the "soft" view) does not mean that this self has no dignity. Keown writes:

> The doctrine of no-self (anātman) only denies the existence of a transcendental self (ātman), not of a phenomenal, empirical self. It does not deny the existence of human individuals with unique self-shaped identities, and if such identities provide an ontological foundation stable enough for the attribution of duties, as the Buddha clearly believed, presumably they also do for rights.

---

[6] Damien Keown, Charles Prebish, and Wayne Husted, *Buddhism and Human Rights* (Surrey, BC: Curzon Press: 1998), p. 4.
[7] Damien Keown, "Human Rights," in *Oxford Handbook of Buddhist Ethics*, edited by Daniel Cozort and James Mark Shields (Oxford: Oxford University Press, 2018), pp. 531–551.

So from the point of view of human dignity, it is possible to attribute dignity to the individual who is capable of seeking enlightenment, even if this individual is fundamentally without self and one with all things (in a mystical sense).

Third, while Keown defends human rights, he also prescribes care in how we connect human rights to Buddhism. In particular, he is critical of Inada's suggestion that the interrelation of persons should be the foundation of rights:

> The assumption is often made that interdependency provides a ground for moral respect on the basis that once we understand the nature of our deep dependence on others, moral feelings will spontaneously arise. [But as a counter-example,] Children who are trafficked have an interdependent relationship with their traffickers, but the well-being of children in such situations depends on severing the interdependent relationship in question. Sevilla is therefore right to point out that interrelationship is important "not on the level of ontology but on the level of soteriology. We are interrelated not merely in what we are, but in our struggle to become what we ought to be."

Merely saying that people are interrelated does not give sufficient ground to any respect for the dignity of others. Keown is similarly critical of the idea of compassion, for it fails to sufficiently consider other aspects of Buddhism like wisdom.

If not interdependency or compassion, what then grounds our duty toward others and the dignity this presupposes? The fourth contribution made by Keown is his connection of dignity and rights to the four noble truths. These four truths are considered to be "the most basic Buddhist doctrinal foundation of all." The first noble truth is that we all suffer. The second is that this suffering is caused by our own attachments. But Keown's focus is on the third and fourth: that we can be free from this suffering; and that there is a way to this freedom.[8] As it said in the *Chiggala Sutta*, human dignity lies in our opportunity to free ourselves from suffering and our duty to realize this path.

The previous discussion not only gives us the present state of the discussion: it shows the enormity of the task we have at hand. The extensive dialogue on human rights and Buddhism has shown the dangers of introducing individualism into a fundamentally relational view of Buddhism. But conversely, it has also shown the danger of having a flimsily argued view of relationality. It showed that the four noble truths – particularly the last two truths of the freedom from suffering and the path – can ground human rights and human dignity. But conversely it showed that there is no reason for this human dignity to connect with any form of social respect – that early Buddhist practice was even more individualist than the discourse of human rights.

What is the cause of our confusing state of affairs? Braarvig, Inada, Ihara, and Keown all talk of freedom from suffering, relations, compassion, and so on. But I get

---

[8] For more on the four noble truths, see Paul Williams, Anthony Tribe, and Alexander Wynne, *Buddhist Thought: A Complete Introduction to the Indian Tradition* 2nd ed. (Oxford: Routledge, 2012), chap. 2.

the feeling they end up talking past each other, as if they have very different meanings for these key ideas. Perhaps the danger lies in presuming that there is *one* Buddhism we are all talking about. In Keown's conclusion, he writes:

> Focusing on individual teachings may be unnecessarily exclusive: approaches that emphasize compassion, for example, have little to say about wisdom. It might be thought that a successful foundation for human rights should be comprehensive, as well as rooted in the core teachings of Buddhism accepted by all schools. It would thus seem desirable for any proposed foundation to meet the criteria formulated by Evans, namely: (1) Simplicity: ordinary Buddhists must be able to understand the argument; (2) Universality: it must be based on principles that all Buddhists accept; (3) Authority or dignity: the theory must articulate the moral inviolability, or its equivalent, of the human person; and (4) It must integrate Buddhist "resignation" (acceptance of the reality of suffering) with human rights advocacy.[9]

What if grounding human rights/dignity in a way that is applicable to *all Buddhisms* is simply too ambitious? Perhaps the answer is in Buddhism as it is in interreligious debate – dignity is at worst an empty signifier we use to vie for hegemony, at best a space for dialogue between disagreeing positions.

In order to get this dialogue going, I turn to the details. If our potential to free ourselves from suffering is the key to dignity, what are the different ways we see this freeing? Is it individual? Does it need social respect or protection? Is it even visible to others? And to do this, I turn to certain philosophical accounts of enlightenment.

3 ENLIGHTENMENT IN EARLY BUDDHISM

Let me begin with a "textbook" understanding of the process of enlightenment, as would be discussed, for example, in Paul Williams' introductory text.

Human beings suffer – that is, they feel distress as they flee from things they dislike and toward things they like (first noble truth). But Buddhism claims that the source of this suffering is *taṇhā*, attachment. Because we are attached to what we like and we refuse what we dislike, then these cause us distress (second). If we could look at the world with a sense of detachment, it would become possible to be free from suffering (third). But concretely, the way to free ourselves from suffering and attachment is to avoid recreating those patterns of attachment in our actions (*śīla*), develop our ability to see our inner landscape (*samādhi*), and recognize how our suffering actually arises from this attachment (*prajñā*). This *insight* is what allows us to be free from suffering.

However, as we might all intuit, this is easier said than done. In early Buddhism, doing this required a lifetime (or lifetimes!) of hard practice, in a community living separately from the attachments (and defilements) of secular society. Most people merely remain mired in their own attachments, unable to see how they are causing

---

[9] Keown, "Human Rights," p. 141.

themselves to suffer, unable to let go. That means that this potential for freedom remains at least partially, if not fully, dormant in most cases. As Braarvig writes, "by the practice of the Buddhas teachings, he can attain the status of an *arhat*, sainthood, or rather *dignity*, and reach *nirvana* at death. We can say, then, that classical Buddhism teaches *inner* dignity, that can be attained by religious practice, but it is not an *inherent* dignity."[10]

This has several implications. First, unlike the Western notion of human dignity, where the *imago dei* is present in our ability for rational thought (our autonomy, as Kant says), this ability for insight (or wisdom) is not easily demonstrated. The ability to make decisions, not merely on the basis of desires but on the basis of universalizable principles, becomes a concern for many people after they enter high school (developmental psychologist Lawrence Kohlberg's "postconventional morality"). When one shows but the most rudimentary forms of practical reason as an adult, people around are likely to notice. The ability to see where suffering comes from and the ability to completely renounce attachments, however, are not parts of a citizen's everyday life.

This leads us to Braarvig's concern: Does this potential require respect? Or conversely, for someone who cares nothing for the way, what is the point of respecting this potential? This is an important question for Keown, I believe, and his assertion that the ground of dignity is the third and fourth noble truths. For Braarvig, we cannot answer in the affirmative for early Buddhism – that needs to wait for Mahāyāna.

However, I think there is a way out of this quandary, by bringing the focus back to the first noble truth: life is suffering. While the origin, freedom from, and way out of suffering are a mystery to the majority of people, suffering is not. Thus, any suffering person wants some sort of solution to this suffering, and the possibility that this person before me might be capable of resolving this suffering is reason for me to respect his dignity. (This is not to say that I have utilitarian reasons for respecting another's dignity but that I have this capacity in me to recognize that dignity as worthy of respect, due to my suffering.)

However, this leads me to another question: I know that I suffer, but do I recognize that the other suffers? And what is the relationship between my suffering and that of others? If the relationship was such that, by other people suffering, I would suffer less, or that the suffering of others had nothing to do with mine, then yet again suffering and the path would not lead to any form of dignity and respect. Thus we see that dignity requires not merely the capacity of each for enlightenment but the universality of suffering and the connection between the suffering of each. Perhaps it is a weak form of dignity, but it is not nothing.

As I have shown, "human dignity" connects to various concepts in early Buddhism: "human existence" (*manuṣya*), "the truth of the path leading to the

---

[10] Braarvig, "Buddhism: Inner Dignity and Absolute Altruism," p. 172.

cessation of suffering" (*dukkha-nirodha-gamini patipada*), "the urge to better oneself" (*chanda*), "*arhat*" (one who is worthy), and so on. All these concepts point to something that is of intrinsic worth in a human being and that can, to a certain degree, be worthy of respect (especially in the case of a monk). They also have the added function of urging practice to increase this inner worth.

I am not in a position to carefully argue for concrete examples for this, but allow me to give an example where (arguably) we can see this sense of human dignity demonstrated. First, when B. R. Ambedkar argued against discrimination of Dalits (a class of former "untouchables" in India), he drew from Buddhism and its rejection of the Hindu institution of caste (as can be found, for example, in the *Vāseṭṭha Sutta* in the Middle Discourses) and the possibility of anyone, regardless of caste or gender, to work toward enlightenment.[11] Here, the possibility of walking the path becomes a source of dignity for all human beings, and we see this at play in the actuality of history.

4 ENLIGHTENMENT IN ZEN

For Braarvig, the idea of dignity gets stronger in Mahāyāna Buddhism:

> The so-called "Mahāyāna Buddhism" paved the way for a more egalitarian conception of dignity. In parts of Mahāyāna Buddhism, we find a view that attributes dignity to all living things equally, not only human beings, but also gods, animals, spirits and the inhabitants of Hell participate in the "Buddha-nature" or the "nature of the Awakened."[12]

Braarvig cites the shift in ideals from the *arhat* (one who awakens himself to the truth) to the *bodhisattva* – "the person who has vowed to give all living beings happiness and spiritual maturity, and is reborn in every cycle of the universe to help those who suffer before thinking about himself."[13]

But conceptually, where does this shift come from? Why think about everyone as equally having the capacity for enlightenment? Why should we deliberately concern ourselves with the suffering of others? One way of understanding this shift in a way that connects with the four noble truths is through the ideas of Nishitani Keiji (1900–90). Nishitani was a lay Zen Buddhist, a student of Martin Heidegger, Nishida Kitarō (the founder of the Kyoto School of Philosophy), and Tanabe Hajime (the cofounder, whom we will discuss next). He made great contributions to philosophy of religion and interreligious dialogue.

Nishitani's view of enlightenment in *Religion and Nothingness* is the process of moving from the standpoint of consciousness (attachment) to the standpoint of

---

[11] Sallie B. King, *Socially Engaged Buddhism* (Honolulu: University of Hawaii Press, 2009), pp. 145–146.
[12] Braarvig, "Buddhism: Inner Dignity and Absolute Altruism," p. 172.
[13] Ibid.

nihility (negating attachment) and to the standpoint of emptiness (freedom).[14] In this process, he gives an *ontological* rereading of the idea of the four noble truths: "It might not be wide of the mark to suggest that Buddhism's explanation of suffering as one of its Four Noble Truths ... be regarded as an advance beyond the existential *awareness* of suffering to an existential *interpretation* (in Heidegger's sense) of being-in-the-world."[15]

In the discussion in Section 3, suffering and attachment were seen as individual experiential phenomena, whose mechanism is potentially identical to that of other people. Furthermore, they are phenomena (albeit very common) *within* the world. However, for Nishitani, suffering is not a part of the world: it is interwoven into the very structure of the world. The very way we see the world, where "A is A" ("a pen is a pen" or, if we draw from Nishitani's more controversial discussions of morality, "a Nazi is a Nazi"), gives rise to suffering, to the inability to live life in a depth that is irreducible to rationality. We insist on figuring out the world, figuring out ourselves, while at the same time living as ourselves, in the world, a reality irreducible to "figuring out." The result of this is a deep sense of meaninglessness and suffering.

Key here is that this suffering is not individual, because this way of seeing the world is not individual. In his reading of the notion of *karma*, Nishitani argues that this way of seeing the world is something we learn in society and live in society as part of our "fate." He writes: "Since our Dasein, determined by the karma of an unlimited past, in its turn determines the karma of an unlimited future, the essence of our present voluntary actions (karma) comes into perspective against the backdrop of a causality of fate without end."[16] Thus suffering is something we not only have in common with others, but, in a sense, *we are all suffering the same suffering*.

Therefore, the path of facing up to the meaninglessness of things, while strongly individuating, is not individualistic. It is not about merely dealing with my own suffering but with an ontological suffering all human beings share. It is a response to others just as much as it is to myself. In this way, the *arhat* and the *bodhisattva* are linked – both of them struggle with suffering that is shared with others. The difference is that the *arhat* merely has things in common with the suffering of others. The *bodhisattva*'s suffering *is* the suffering of others.

In this way, compassion acquires a different hue. In early Buddhism, there was a split between wisdom and compassion. The contemporary Buddhist philosopher Sueki Fumihiko explains this through the parable of Brahmā's Request (*Bonten kanjō*):

> When Buddha attained enlightenment, he thought that the people of the world would never understand what he had realized anyway, and he considered simply enjoying this state of bliss until his final days, without bothering to teach it to

---

[14] Nishitani Keiji, *Religion and Nothingness*, trans. Jan Van Bragt (Berkeley: University of California Press, 1982).
[15] Ibid., p. 169; emphases in original.
[16] Ibid.

anyone. But the chief god of Earth, Brahmā, thought that if Buddha dies without teaching what he had finally realized, many suffering people will remain unsaved. And so he implored Buddha to teach, and after three rounds of heartfelt begging, Buddha finally relented and agreed.[17]

Here, the Buddha's suffering is not identical to the suffering of others, and so wisdom does not necessitate compassion. But the shift in Mahāyāna makes it so that the *bodhisattva*'s suffering is identical to that of others, thus there is no need to unite the paths of wisdom and compassion – they are identical.

This shared suffering and shared path of enlightenment is reflected in the idea of "Buddha-nature" that is shared by most Mahāyāna schools (with exceptions like the Mind Only Hossō school). The Buddha-nature of sentient beings implies the possibility of each to awaken – a source of inner worth. But deeper than that, it becomes an existential unity between various beings who share the same suffering and the same path of liberation. It therefore can be a deep source for respect and compassion.

I argue that the nature of "connection/relation" lies behind the disagreement between Inada and Keown – Keown is looking at our interrelationship from a classical Buddhist standpoint. There are good and bad relationships: the other can tempt me, vex me, torment me. But Inada is talking about a more mystical interconnection rather than a factual interconnection. This results in his refusal of rights as "individualist."

From the point of view of dignity, then, dignity here is about the capacity of each to wrestle with the suffering that we all share – and though nobody might succeed entirely, we might slowly unravel the knots of this suffering existence. We see this in various ideas like "Buddha-nature" (*busshō* 仏性), "original enlightenment" (*hongaku* 本覚), "bodhicitta" (*bodaishin* 菩提心), "bodhisattva" (*bosatsu* 菩薩), and "compassion" (*jihi* 慈悲). There is no separation between monk and layperson here, or even between humans and nonhumans. Therefore, there is a clear sense not only of dignity but of an inalienable dignity that is worthy of *respect*. And this dignity is not *individual* dignity but the dignity of humankind as the clearing of being itself (to use a Heideggerian phrase).

This constellation of views may function to urge practice (by letting each know that "you too can attain enlightenment"), but, as we will see in Section 7, it can also have the opposite effect. It may also lead to respect for and compassion for all living beings, no matter how "low." One possible historical example of how this functions can be seen in Thich Nhat Hanh's socially engaged Buddhism and its opposition to the Vietnam War. He wrote: "Take the situation of a country suffering war. . . . Try to see that every person involved is a victim. . . . See that two sides in a conflict are not

---

[17] Sueki Fumihiko, *Religion and Ethics at Odds: A Buddhist Counter-Position*, trans. Anton Luis Sevilla (Nagoya: Chisokudō Publication, 2016), chap. 4.

really opposing, but two aspects of the same reality."[18] Here, the sense of existential connectedness in suffering and liberation functions as the fount of human dignity.

5 SALVATION IN BUDDHISM

Braarvig's discussion deals only with early Buddhism and Mahāyāna Buddhism. But there is a glaring lack in his view of Mahāyāna Buddhism – his focus is on the practice of the *bodhisattva* that realizes the truths of no-self and emptiness, for the sake of saving others. However, the majority of Buddhists in Japan, for instance, do not view themselves as *bodhisattvas*. Instead, the most common form of Buddhism is Pure Land Buddhism – the belief that the only way one can be saved is by entrusting oneself to the vow of Amida Buddha and being brought to the Pure Land, where one will have better chances at attaining enlightenment. In this view, there seems to be no clear drive to liberate oneself from suffering at all, making the previous discussion of dignity seem incredibly partial. There is another form of Buddhism that is similar – belief in salvation by reading, intoning, transcribing, or teaching the *Lotus Sutra*.[19] Both of these traditions can be called "other-power" (*tariki*) traditions, in opposition to "self-power" (*jiriki*) traditions like Zen.

To represent other-power Buddhism, I examine its philosophical expression in Tanabe Hajime's *Philosophy as Metanoetics*. In this book, Tanabe (1885–1962) criticizes the Zennist inclinations of his colleague Nishida (and his student Nishitani), calling these "the path of sages" – a difficult path, fit only for those who are wise enough to see through the veil of illusion. However, Tanabe thinks that he (and most people for that matter) are too ignorant for the path of sages.[20] Most people are not capable of dispelling their ignorance and their sinfulness. What they can do, however, is become aware of their own failings and *repent* (*zange* 懺悔). Tanabe explains the way of *zange* as follows: "The term 'metanoetics' helps express these ideas clearly in that metanoetics implies, on the one hand a self-awakening through a 'way' of repentance, a 'thinking-afterward' (metanoia), and on the other, suggests a self-conscious transcending of intuition and contemplation (metanoesis)."[21]

From the point of view of Tanabe, dignity as arising from the human potential to achieve enlightenment is overconfident. Instead, dignity here can be seen as the fact that we *are saved*. The mark of divinity is not our *imago dei* but our sinfulness, through which human beings become open to the possibility of redemption.

---

[18] Cited in King, *Socially Engaged Buddhism*, p. 77.
[19] This is an important movement that is gaining influence as a new religion. For more on its sources, see Paul Williams, "The *Saddharmapuṇḍarīka Sūtra* and Its Influences," in *Mahāyāna Buddhism: The Doctrinal Foundations*, 2nd ed. (Oxford: Routledge, 2009), pp. 149–171.
[20] Historically, this is called *Mappō Shisō*, the theory of the degenerate age 2,000 years after Buddha's death, when no amount of practice could lead to enlightenment.
[21] Tanabe Hajime, *Philosophy as Metanoetics* (Berkeley: University of California Press, 1990), p. 3.

However, there is another way that dignity arises in Tanabe's thought. People are not merely the recipients of salvation but the *mediators* of salvation. He writes: "Nothingness [the Absolute] cannot, however, exist directly ... Nothingness must manifest itself in the mediation of negative transformation."[22] Other-power as nothingness does not act in the world as an independent force (like being). Rather, absolute other-power only manifests through the self-negation of finite beings in their *zange*.

Not only is the other saved: the other, in his/her ability to repent, can become a means of the salvation of others – including myself. This is the *only way* other power is manifest. Tanabe writes: "The self is restored to a state of 'empty being' as a mediator of absolute nothingness. In our gratitude the self is led to cooperate in a mediating function in the absolute's work of saving other relative beings."[23]

These two movements – being saved and saving others as a mediator – form the core of dignity, which is expressed in Pure Land terminology as "*ōsō*" (往相, going to the Pure Land) and as "*gensō*" (還相, returning from the Pure Land).

This view of dignity has similarities to Gushee's Protestant approach, as referenced by McCrudden.[24] Gushee sees the sacredness of human life as the will of God – something unfathomable by our minds. It is also similar to Margalit's Jewish reading. In McCrudden's words, "the value of humans is the reflected glory that human beings have, but they do not have intrinsic value. They have a value only as icons of something else that deserves adoration."[25] In Tanabe, as in these two thinkers, dignity is tempered by the humility of the saved.

As we have seen, human dignity connects to various concepts like "repentance" (*zange* 懺悔), "going to the Pure Land" (*ōsō* 往相), "returning from the Pure Land" (*gensō* 還相), "the right opportunity of evil persons" (*akunin shōki* 悪人正機, that even evil people can be saved), and "practice-faith-witness" (*gyō shin shō* 行信証). These all function to support self-acceptance, moral humility, tolerance, forgiveness, and compassion. One possible historical example of this is Takagi Kenmyō's "socialist Amidism" that attempted to protect discriminated people in Japan as an expression of Amida's love.[26]

6 CONFUCIAN BUDDHISM

There is another equally common form of Buddhism that is present in East Asia and many diasporic communities around the world: a Buddhist-Confucian worldview. In this way of thinking, Buddhist self-renunciation is combined with the Confucian communitarian sense of social order. This has a long, complex history

---

[22] Ibid., p. 272.
[23] Ibid., p. 256.
[24] McCrudden, "In Pursuit of Human Dignity," p. 28.
[25] Ibid., p. 29.
[26] See Sueki, *Religion and Ethics at Odds*, chap. 8.

in China, one that I am not qualified to discuss. But in Japan, one classic representative of this view is Suzuki Shōsan. And a modern philosophical proponent of this is Watsuji Tetsurō (1889–1960), who was for a time affiliated with the Kyoto School of Philosophy.

A comprehensive discussion of Watsuji's ethics can be found in my monograph.[27] As I suggest there, Watsuji had a complex relationship to both Buddhism and Confucianism – sometimes these elements were combined, and sometimes they resisted each other. But one very common reading of Watsuji is as a philosopher of relationality (*aidagara*).

In criticizing Western individuality, Watsuji saw the core of ethics as emptying the self (of selfish attachments and egoism) – not to achieve some abstract enlightenment but in order to serve society. In his wartime publications, he discussed for instance how this "selflessness" might be reflected in each level of society – from the mutual trust of husband and wife to filial piety amongst parents and children to becoming a full-fledged member of society, all the way to loyalty to the state. This pattern of "layers of community" is one that traces back to the *Doctrine of the Mean* of Confucianism.

In this version of Buddhism, selflessness is contextualized within a finite community. So while wisdom and compassion are unified (as in Zen), compassion is not for an abstract community but for particular concrete communities – my family, my city, my country. Thus, dignity is recast as this potential to be free from oneself *for* community.

This view of dignity is similar to Ihara's, who writes: "I maintain that the notion of Dharma may be part of a vision of society in which human life is ideally a kind of dance with well defined role-responsibilities. This is a view that I believe is common to many traditional cultures, Confucian China for example."[28] His resistance to "individualism" is distinct from Inada's mystical approach. But all the same it refuses the early Buddhist "individualism" along with the individualism of human rights (as evidenced by the Asian Values Debate).

Here, human dignity connects to ideas like "moral community" (*jinrin* 人倫), "trust and sincerity" (*shinrai seijitsu* 信頼 誠実), and "benevolence" (*jin* 仁). It critiques selfishness and urges service to community, thus to some extent promoting the respect of individuals – but only insofar as they are members of one's community. An example of this functioning in history would be the case of Suzuki Shōsan, who taught service to one's community and faithfulness to one's duties, in a way backed by a Buddhist notion of selflessness.[29] However, due to the clash between communitarianism and very liberal visions of human dignity, I must concede that

---

[27] Anton Luis Sevilla, *Watsuji Tetsurô's Global Ethics of Emptiness: A Contemporary Look at a Modern Japanese Philosopher* (Cham: Palgrave Macmillan, 2017).
[28] In Keown, Prebish, and Husted, *Buddhism and Human Rights*, p. 47.
[29] For more on this, see Winston L. King, *Death Was His Kōan: Samurai-Zen of Suzuki Shōsan* (Fremont, CA: Asian Humanities Press, 1986).

the connection of these concepts and examples with contemporary "human dignity" discourses is likely very weak (albeit difficult to ignore given the historical melding of Buddhism and Confucianism).

7 CONCLUSION, AND BEYOND ETHICS

In this chapter we have seen that, while the view of the human condition and liberation points the way for a view of Buddhism and human dignity, the view of the human condition and liberation varies *essentially* from early Buddhism to self-power forms of Mahāyāna to other-power faiths and to communitarian approaches. Human dignity seems to have at least four definitions: the worth that arises intrinsically due to

1) the ability of each individual to free oneself from suffering;
2) the ability to free everyone from an ontologically shared suffering;
3) the ability to repent, witness to other-power, and support the repentance of others; and
4) the ability to free oneself from egoism in order to serve community.

Even within the same religion, there is so much diversity in how adherents view the intrinsic worth of human beings. But one thing they do have in common – which may put them in diametric opposition with many contemporary secular views of human dignity – is that they are *not* about the freedom of a rational subject to maximize utility but rather about the "moral" freedom *from* egoistic desire. There is a strong transcendent moment to be found in the views of dignity explored here.

However, I must end with a caveat. Looking at the discussion in this chapter, it seems that the different views of the human condition and liberation in Buddhism support, if not contribute to, the discourse on human dignity and the rights that are founded on it. While I am hopeful for these, it is necessary to be careful not to reduce Buddhism to this-worldly ethical concerns. There are aspects of this same "dignity" that are nonethical and some that may even be *unethical*.

This idea was developed by Sueki Fumihiko in his two recent books, *Religion and Ethics at Odds* and *Philosophizing in Japan*. He writes:

> All I wish to say is that there are problems that cannot be explained away by ethics, science, politics, economics, or law. Perhaps the true problems of humanity lie at the very point where we deviate from that domain of rationality. Objectively speaking, until now, it is what we call "religion" that has most deeply involved itself with these kinds of problems.[30]

He calls this domain beyond rational ethics "trans-ethics" (*chō rinri* 超倫理).

Each of the views quoted earlier seem to contribute to the discourse of human dignity. But a majority of this discourse has to do with political and practical

---

[30] Sueki, *Religion and Ethics at Odds*, pp. 10–11.

effects – ways to reduce oppression, combat dehumanizing practices, promote mutual responsibility, and so on. All of these effects can be understood and measured in a rational way. However, Buddhism is not just an ethical system: it is a religion, focused on the problem of existential liberation. There is a part of this liberation that reveals itself ethically (*śīla*), but, Sueki argues, there is a part that does not.

As the Buddhologist Tamura Yoshirō suggests, Buddhism (especially early Buddhism) can be criticized as a form of "seclusionism" (*tonseishugi* 遁世主義), overly focused on mystical insight.[31] The core duty of a monk trying to become an *arhat* is to realize the core of his/her own suffering, and often this means keeping away from the contaminating influence of society. Thus, as Braarvig suggests, instead of this dignity flourishing within and under the protection of society, it withdraws from society, caring little for whatever respect society might have to offer.

This trans-ethical element is also present in Mahāyāna as well. This is clearly demonstrated in the idea of "original enlightenment" (*hongaku*):

> Broadly defined, *hongaku* theory refers to the Buddhist thought, which developed in medieval Japan, that affirms the present reality as it is. More specifically, it refers to the trend that developed particularly during the Middle Ages in the Tendai school, and is also called Tendai hongaku theory.
>
> In other words, this impermanent world, as impermanent, realizes eternal enlightenment. There is no need to search anew for enlightenment outside of it. Sentient beings are fine as they are; they do not need to become buddhas. Hell is fine remaining as hell, and human beings are fine remaining as human beings.[32]

If everything expresses the capacity for enlightenment, then the light of "Buddha-nature" already shines within everything, and everything can be affirmed as it is. On the one hand, this view can lead to a deep sense of acceptance of reality as it is. On the other hand, this can lead to a laziness and a refusal to commit to spiritual practice.

In Pure Land Buddhism, this shows as the "opportunity of evil persons" (*akunin shōki*):

> If all were unconditionally saved by Amitābha Buddha then one would fall into the problematic notion of the "unobstructed creation of evil" wherein one could wreak whatever havoc one pleases. This kind of thinking is also deeply connected to hongaku thinking. The well-known theory, found in the Lamentations of Divergences (Tannishō), of the opportunity of evil persons (*akunin shōki*, which states that evil people have a unique opportunity to be saved by Amitābha), was also born out of this tendency. If everything in the present world was affirmed, then wrongdoings, and the reasons why wrongs should be opposed, would all disappear.

The very dignity that can lead to a sense of repentance and respect for others can lead to a lackadaisical, anything-goes attitude.

[31] Ibid., pp. 23–24.
[32] Ibid., p. 26.

Finally, Sueki also directly criticizes Confucianized thinkers like Suzuki Shōsan and Watsuji Tetsurō, pointing out how they tend to support the status quo as is and how the dignity of selflessly serving the whole becomes an opportunity for totalitarianism.

Perhaps at this point one might be feeling a sense of frustration. Are these ideas from Buddhism useful for dignity or not? Are there perhaps some things wrong with certain kinds of Buddhism that need to be fixed to make them more ethical? But perhaps, as we take part in this interdisciplinary dialogue on religious and judiciary approaches to human dignity, Sueki is pointing out something more essential:

> Religion, to put it concisely, is what is constituted in the place that binds in a tensional relationship both the inter-personal and that which transcends the inter-personal. It teaches what deviates toward the world beyond the inter-personal, from within the inter-personal. But at the same time, religion does not remain within this deviation, but rather tries to retrieve the inter-personal. It is in the tensional relationship in the boundaries of both domains that religion comes to be.[33]

Human dignity has, in a sense, a dual pedigree. It is a religious concept, but it is also a philosophical concept and an ethical-political one. The latter pedigree means that it can be helpful in preserving and improving the order of human society, with a rational function. But the former pedigree means that it can reflect deep human irrationalities – both the beautiful and the ugly: our need for space from society's demands, our potential to come to terms with our own limitedness, our need to withdraw into the bosom of an accepting whole. Perhaps we are called to be sensitive to both the rational and the irrational, as we try to make this concept a space of genuine dialogue.

In this volume, as we examine the overlap between law, philosophy, and culture (religion), there is a tendency to over-focus on the part of culture/religion that is rational, ethical, and interpersonal. But this tends to neglect the very part of religion that resists being reduced to law or philosophy – the existential, nonrational, trans-ethical shadow that responds to very deep human needs. It is my hope that we keep both sides in mind as we explore the possibilities and limits of the idea of human dignity and its praxis in the contemporary world.

---

[33] Ibid., pp. 217–218.

12

Dignity and Status in Ancient and Medieval India

Timothy Lubin[*]

1 DIGNITY AND "HUMAN DIGNITY" IN SOUTH ASIAN TERMS

If one goes looking for a Hindu analogue of what today is called "human dignity," it is not clear what to look for. "Human dignity" is a modern ethical and legal concept, with its roots in Greco-Roman classical thought and later Christian (especially Roman Catholic) theology as well as Kant's moral philosophy, but with its branches spreading worldwide today. One of the aims of this project was to take account of resources of classical philosophical and religious traditions of Asia, resources that might be brought to bear on the discussions about human dignity today. This chapter looks to premodern Indian sources,[1] especially those of the family of traditions that come under the label Hindu in modern times.

When people today speak of human dignity, they generally presume that such talk concerns a general ideal of fairness and intrinsic worth based on an egalitarian conception of humanity and human rights. Yet one of the distinctive features of the Indian cultural sphere is a very deeply rooted social convention, supported by a long tradition of doctrine and theory, that rank is intrinsic to human existence in the world. It is a convention that has been subject to extensive treatment, from different angles, in Indian philosophy, religion, law, and literature over more than three millennia. And although modern cosmopolitan norms of egalitarianism and human rights have (in varying degrees) been made the basis of the state legal order across South Asia today, framed largely in the terms of Euro-American thought and constitutional law imbibed during and after the colonial era, the situation on the ground, and in some areas of Hindu public and religious discourse, retains some

---

[*] Besides the stimulating input from my fellow participants in the Taipei conference, I thank Donald R. Davis Jr. for valuable suggestions. The research and writing were supported by a grant from the Lenfest Foundation, and a substantial rewrite was done as a fellow of the National Endowment for the Humanities and of the American Council of Learned Societies. The chapter includes research supported by the DHARMA Project, European Research Council grant no. 809994.

[1] "Ancient" covers through the end of the sixth century, the close of the Gupta era; "medieval" roughly covers 600–1200 (early medieval) and 1200–1600 (late medieval, beginning with the establishment of Muslim-ruled states and ending with the beginnings of a European presence).

very inegalitarian features.² Norms of hierarchy (based on caste, gender, and other social statuses) continue to cause or legitimize harms and indignities great and small suffered by those deemed lower, at the hands of the higher.

Earlier scholars who have tried to apply the modern concept of "human dignity" or "human rights" to Hindu sources have mostly relied on a selective rendering of "the tradition," sometimes coupled with an idealized interpretation of its history that is designed to minimize or excuse its inequities.³ Some studies seek to show either that caste is not central to Hinduism⁴ or that, properly understood (i.e. by an innocuous interpretation of a putative "original" *varṇa* doctrine), it was a system that classified nonhierarchically by personal aptitude and family tradition rather than by hierarchy of birth.⁵ Apart from the fact that such arguments tend to

---

² This was poignantly noted by B. R. Ambedkar, the Dalit leader who headed the committee that drafted the Constitution of India, just as it was about to come into effect: "On the 26th January 1950, we are going to enter into a life of contradictions. In politics we will have equality and in social and economic life we will have inequality. In politics we will be recognising the principle of one man one vote and one vote one value. In our social and economic life, we shall by reason of our social and economic structure, continue to deny the principle of one man one value" (Final Speech to the Constituent Assembly, November 25, 1949).

³ See, for example, Ved P. Nanda, "Hinduism and Human Rights," in *Hindu Law and Legal Theory*, edited by Ved P. Nanda and Surya Prakash Sinha (New York: New York University Press, 1997), pp. 237–247; Arvind Sharma, *Hinduism and Human Rights: A Conceptual Approach* (New Delhi: Oxford University Press, 2004); and Arvind Sharma, *Hindu Narratives on Hindu Rights* (Santa Barbara, CA: Praeger/ABC-CLIO, 2010); the latter volume interprets Hindu narratives as illustrating or implying a conception of human rights. Carman (John B. Carman, "Duties and Rights in Hindu Society," in *Human Rights and the World's Religions*, edited by Leroy S. Rouner [Notre Dame, IN: University of Notre Dame Press, 1988], pp. 113–128) takes a balanced approach that points to the focus on duties rather than rights in Hindu culture and the weight of status differences in calibrating those duties. Braarvig (Jens Braarvig, "Hinduism: The Universal Self in a Class Society," in *The Cambridge Handbook of Human Dignity*, edited by Marcus Düwell et al. [Cambridge: Cambridge University Press, 2014], pp. 163–169) briefly discusses three landmark Sanskrit scriptures, but he does not explain what he sees as dignity therein, apart from an "accentuated individualism [that] coexists with a social system which is programmatically unequal ... [and] does not necessarily create social conventions that promote the principle of inherent and equal dignity for all human beings" (168). Werner Menski, "Hinduism and Human Rights," in *Religion and Human Rights: An Introduction*, edited by John Witte Jr. and M. Christian Green (Oxford: Oxford University Press, 2011), pp. 71–86, is a meandering essay that does not address Hindu perspectives directly, instead depicting an East–West culture war. In his view "aggressive human rights rhetoric from hegemonic or cosmopolitan and neo-colonial sources" reflecting "a rabid anti-Hindu stance in global academia, which probably also pleases various Muslim lobbies" (etc.) generates "defensive Hindu responses [that] use exaggerated rhetoric to stake their claims and may resort to violence." What is needed, he argues, is more tolerance of difference from Western norms.

⁴ Foreign observers are sometimes accused of making more of caste than Hindus do themselves, or even of "inventing" caste, or of rigidifying it (and thereby making it more noxious) through the creation of colonial administrative policies and Orientalist knowledge. Alternatively, blame for harsher application of caste strictures and control of women has sometimes been attributed to incursions (after 1000), and widespread rule (after 1200) by Muslims of central Asian origin.

⁵ Mohandas Gandhi famously promoted a version of this argument: that every person is born into a *varṇa* (as distinct from a "caste," which is a status-category) that correlates with a distinctive social function, all of equal dignity, inherited according to a "natural law," though individuals may, by their personal aptitudes, move between them (and be recognized in their new role). For such views,

misrepresent history and derail serious inquiry by obscuring or explaining away the unsavory aspects of caste prejudice, they also raise what strike me as interesting and important questions:

- Can there be a concept of human dignity operating within an inegalitarian social order, and if so, what does it mean?
- Would it convey something useful to wider discourse about human dignity?

2 THE GENEALOGY OF THE CONCEPT OF HUMAN DIGNITY

It has been noted that "human dignity" as a concept appeals to the Roman notion of *dignitas*. Jeremy Waldron has argued that "human dignity" is a generalization of a previously particular sort of social rank enjoyed only by elites.[6] In classical Rome, certain individuals enjoyed respect, protections, and rights unavailable to others. By a "leveling-up process," the notion of a dignity shared by all humans by virtue merely of their being human replaced the older ethos in which dignity was the privilege only of particular ranks:[7] "every man a Brahmin."[8]

One way to look at this is that "human dignity" puts forward the status of humanity itself as a generic status *intrinsically endowed with* or *having a just claim to* a certain basic dignity conceived of in terms of fundamental rights. It is a dignity shared by rank, but the rank is no longer a rank in society but rather one in nature. Humans share a common dignity among themselves without distinction, but it is particular to them all in contrast to other living things. In a sense, this generalized used of the term is (or begins with) a metaphorical or figurative extension of the older notion of dignity.

Whether this dignity is an intrinsic endowment or an ethical or legal claim has been a matter of philosophical debate. On the related subject of freedom, Jeremy Bentham, with his characteristic asperity, ridiculed as "absurd and miserable non-sense" the claim that human beings are intrinsically free: "It is from

---

B. R. Ambedkar, *Annihilation of Caste, with a Reply to Mahatma Gandhi*, edited by S. Anand (London: Verso, 2016 [1936]), took him to task.

[6] Jeremy Waldron, *Dignity, Rank, and Rights*, edited by Meir Dan-Cohen (Oxford: Oxford University Press, 2012), pp. 12–29. This may not be compared with Cicero's proposition in *De officiis* I, pp. 105–107, that human beings possess a shared human *dignitas* to be protected unsullied by the practice of Stoic virtues. Giltaij (Jacob Giltaij, "*Existimatio* as 'Human Dignity' in Late-Classical Roman Law," *Fundamina* 22, no. 2 [2016]: 233) points out that for Cicero this is "an obligation, not a right"; compare Hubert Cancik, "Dignity of Man and Persona in Stoic Anthropology: Some Remarks on Cicero, De officiis I," in *The Concept of Human Dignity in Human Rights Discourse*, edited by David Kretzmer and Eckart Klein (The Hague: Kluwer Law International, 2002), pp. 19–40.

[7] Waldron borrows this concept from James Whitman, "Human Dignity in Europe and the United States: The Social Foundations," in *Europe and US Constitutionalism*, edited by G. Nolte (New York: Cambridge University Press, 2005), pp. 108–124.

[8] Gregory Vlastos, "Justice and Equality," in *Theories of Rights*, edited by Jeremy Waldron (New York: Oxford University Press, 1984), p. 54.

beginning to end so much flat assertion ... It lays down as a fundamental and inviolable principle whatever is in dispute."[9] Waldron avoids this fallacy by proposing not that dignity is an intrinsic worth but rather that it is a *status*, something that can be *accorded* (under an ethical or legal regime) or *violated* – and can be *demanded* when it is not accorded or when it is violated.[10]

Ancient India has left us a vast written record that deals in various ways with the nature of the human being, the pursuits of life, the proper ordering of society, and the legal, religious, and ethical norms that ought to be observed. The largest portion of this literature was composed in Sanskrit, mainly by males of the rank of Brahmin, a hereditary class defined by its priestly and scholastic functions. Though diverse in genres and schools of thought, with widely differing views on many subjects, this Brahmanical literature in Sanskrit generally affirmed the special dignity and claimed privileges (and corresponding duties) of Brahmin status, as well as assigning particular criteria to other ranks: Kṣatriyas (those assigned to rule and protect), Vaiśyas (producers and merchants), Śūdras (those supposed to serve the higher ranks – e.g. as laborers), and some other stigmatized groupings that lay outside and below the ideal four-rank model. This literature also recognizes unfree statuses, both servile and penal, though these were not (necessarily) set by birth. Women as a sex were characterized as having rights circumscribed in many ways by the superior authority of male family members.

Beside the Brahmanical sources are works composed by adherents of mendicant orders (since antiquity classed together as *śramaṇa*s), most prominently the early Buddhists and Jainas but also some others commonly classed today as Hindu; such groups promoted perspectives on many ethical questions that often opposed the Brahmanical version of hierarchy without necessarily denying the validity of innate hierarchy of some sort. The third major stream was the intensely devotionalist *bhakti* movement that appeared in Sanskrit form near the beginning of the Common Era and then, in vernacular media, gradually permeated all of South Asia, roughly from south to north, from around the middle of the first millennium onward. None of these discourses produced a concept quite analogous to human dignity – which is a concept whose particular contours were set by particular developments in European thought and sociopolitical history – but they do offer views on the intrinsic, innate character of human beings and on the factors bearing on status of human beings in the world. From these, we can triangulate to assess the implications of these views for contemporary reflection on human dignity.

---

[9] Jeremy Bentham, *Supply without Burthen; or Escheat vice Taxation* (London, 1795); reprinted in *Jeremy Bentham's Economic Writings*, ed. W. Stark, vol. 1 (Abingdon: Routledge, 1952), p. 335.

[10] See especially Waldron, *Dignity, Rank, and Rights*, pp. 18–20, 50–51. In making this argument he is building on H. L. A. Hart's "choice theory" of rights (H. L. A. Hart, "Are There Any Natural Rights?" *Philosophical Review* 64 (1955): 175–191) and Joel Feinberg's theory of claims (Joel Feinberg, "Duties, Rights and Claims," *American Philosophical Quarterly* 3 [1966]: 137–144; "The Nature and Value of Rights," *Journal of Value Inquiry* 4 [1970]: 243–257).

3 BRAHMANICAL RELIGIOUS LAW

I am impartial to all creatures, and no one is hateful or dear to me;
but men devoted to me are in me, and I am within them.
If he is devoted solely to me, even a violent criminal
must be deemed a man of virtue, for his resolve is right.
His spirit quickens to sacred duty (*dharma*), and he finds eternal peace;
Arjuna, know that no one devoted to me is lost.
If they rely on me, Arjuna, women, commoners, men of low rank,
even men born in the womb of evil, reach the highest way.[11]

Thus speaks Kṛṣṇa, divinity incarnate, to the warrior prince Arjuna in the *Bhagavad Gītā* (9.29–32). This didactic poem is embedded in the *Mahābhārata* epic at the point when Arjuna and his brothers (the sons of the abdicated king Pāṇḍu) face their usurping cousins on the battlefield, at the start of a devastating war. These stanzas exemplify the distinctive outlook of classical *bhakti*, Hindu devotionalism as expressed in Sanskrit works. Our divine narrator alludes to the sorts of distinctions that divide humanity – gender, rank, legal status – and then affirms that, in the sight of God, all are intrinsically equal, and all have access to the divine presence on the same terms. The force of this promise comes from the context within which it is made: a discourse on *dharma* and *adharma* (right and wrong)[12] addressed to a society riven by ranked castes and other statuses. The *Gītā* proposed that true devotion (*bhakti*) to the Lord, expressed through selfless, pious observance of the duties proper to one's status in the world, was the ultimate criterion of right and that it ennobled even the low-born in the end.

This offered a counterpoint to the canonical religious law of *varṇa-dharma*, duties according to social class. The latter was an already-well-established doctrine that human beings are born into hierarchically ranked group-statuses that correlate with divinely ordained social functions. This doctrine was developed over centuries by theorists of groups who called themselves *Brāhmaṇa*, Brahmin in English. While theories of social hierarchy by rank are known from many cultures around the world (including the "three estates" of medieval Europe), the distinctive character of the South Asian caste system derives from the way it was theorized by Brahmins and reinforced by rulers and other elites who embraced the theory to rationalize and legitimize their own statuses. The Brahmanical model placed Brahmins at the apex

---

[11] *Bhagavad Gītā* 9.29–32, as translated by Babara Stoler Miller, *The Bhagavad-Gita: Krishna's Counsel in Time of War* (New York: Bantam Books, 1986), pp. 89–90: "samo 'haṃ sarvabhūteṣu na me dveṣyo 'sti na priyaḥ | ye bhajanti tu māṃ bhaktyā mayi te teṣu cāpy aham || 9.29 || api cet sudurācāro bhajate mām ananyabhāk | sādhur eva sa mantavyaḥ samyag vyavasito hi saḥ || 9.30 || kṣipraṃ bhavati dharmātmā śaśvacchāntiṃ nigacchati | kaunteya pratijānīhi na me bhaktaḥ praṇaśyati || 9.31 || māṃ hi pārtha vyapāśritya ye 'pi syuḥ pāpayonayaḥ | striyo vaiśyās tathā śūdrās te 'pi yānti parāṃ gatim || 9.32 ||."

[12] "Dharma," a key term in Hindu religion, is used in a range of meanings: "right" or "justice"; or (often in the plural) "ordained rule" or "duty." It was also used to refer to collectively to the doctrines and practices of a particular doctrine, approaching the sense of English *religion*, as will be explained.

of society as a class of priests and scholars, vessels of the timeless words of the Veda, mediators between gods and men, innately pure (but ever at risk of pollution), calling themselves "gods among men." Below them in purity if above them in material power are the Kṣatriyas, repositories of earthly might and authority, assigned the responsibility to protect and govern. The third estate, the Vaiśyas ("commoners"), were conceived to be the productive class of society – herders and farmers in the oldest *dharma* texts but also merchants and businesspeople in the later ones. These three ranks are classified as "Ārya" (roughly, the "noble" or "worthy" ones), culturally unified by their eligibility and duty to learn the Veda and to honor Brahmins. Below them all are ranked the Śūdras, whose assigned role is to serve and be supported by the higher classes.

The oldest sacred text of the Veda, the *Ṛg Veda*, includes a hymn (10.90) that depicts this social order as arising as part of the creation and ordering of the natural world, accomplished through a primordial rite of sacrifice, during which a "man" comprising the whole unformed universe is dismembered, with the Brahmin emerging from his mouth, the Kṣatriya from his arms, the Vaiśya from his thighs, and the Śūdra from his feet. The respective body parts symbolized the ideal functions of the four groups: the mouth representing the Brahmin's dual roles as reciters of the Veda and eaters of the offerings; the arms signifying the Kṣatriya's duty to protect (by bearing the scepter of rule which is simultaneously the rod of punishment or club of battle); the thighs conveying the fruitfulness of the loins and sustaining strength; and the feet supporting the rest. This vignette of society embodied is reproduced many times in subsequent sources down through the centuries to reaffirm the divine origin and naturalness of the arrangement and the harmonious complementarity of the organic whole. (The actual multiplicity of distinct social groups in India has since antiquity been explained as the result of various intergroup marriages, with offspring of some of these pairings being deemed to occupy intermediate or even lower statuses.)

As a model of social hierarchy, the key innovation of the Brahmanical theory was its formulation as *varṇāśrama-dharma*, canonized in the *Mānava Dharmaśāstra* (commonly known as *The Laws of Manu*). This work, compiled circa 150 CE[13] – that is, roughly the same time as the *Bhagavad Gītā* – was intended to resolve a long-standing tension within Brahmanical circles between those who advocated marriage and the cycle of domestic rites and those who pursued one of a set of ascetical modes of life (as lifelong celibate acolyte of a teacher, as forest hermit, or as wandering mendicant). The ascetic movements had been ascendant since the era of the Maurya empire, and while most Brahmins, as heirs to the hereditary priesthood that looked back to the Veda, continued to affirm the values of family life and worldly aspirations, some among them had adopted a world-rejecting path. Between

---

[13] Patrick Olivelle, *Manu's Code of Law: A Critical Edition and Translation of the Mānava-Dharmaśāstra* (Oxford: Oxford University Press, 2005), pp. 18–25.

the Maurya era and the advent of the Gupta dynasty in 320 CE, ascetic orders attracted a lot of veneration and patronage and thus rivaled the prestige and religious authority claimed by Brahmin groups.

In fact, the Dharmaśāstra codes and the *Bhagavad Gītā* represent two alternative solutions to this problem. The authors of the earliest *dharma* codes, the four *Dharmasūtras* (late third century BCE–first century CE), proposed that the life of a rigorously observant Vedic householder constituted a religious discipline (an *āśrama*) just as much as that of an ascetic (*śramaṇa*) monk or mendicant – and was even superior to those disciplines.[14] These rulebooks thus established a system whereby a life of *dharma* (using the word as the *śramaṇa* orders did) meant learning the Veda in youth and then choosing one of four *āśramas* (vocations or disciplines), with emphasis placed on the home-based profession in preference to the others. Brahmins who modeled domestic piety were thus able to put themselves forward *as a caste that doubled as a religious profession* by virtue of its elaborate regimen of discipline and standards of purity – standards modeled in fact on those that bound specially consecrated worshipers and Veda-students. This doctrine presupposed a divinely ordained vision of society in which Brahmins mediated between divinity and the rest of humanity, who were enjoined to adhere to sacred norms taught as appropriate to their social rank (*varṇa*), with many of these norms having been adapted (using graduated distinctions) from those applying to Brahmins.

However, this still left open the question of which *āśrama* should be chosen after graduation from Veda study and, more generally, about the relative value of the various *āśramas*, in spite of the Dharmasūtras' common refrain that the householder was the best, supporting all the others. The *Mānava Dharmaśāstra* removed this problem by proposing a sequential version of the system: individuals (viz. males of the three "Ārya" *varṇas* eligible for Veda study and ritual agency) were now supposed to pass from studentship in youth to married householdership, followed in later life by transition first to the life of the forest-hermit and finally to status of wandering mendicant.[15] This is the classical ideal of *varṇāśrama-dharma* presupposed by almost all later Brahmanical sources.

The *Bhagavad Gītā*, by contrast, demoted the world-rejecting forms of asceticism (lumped together as *jñāna-yoga*, the discipline aimed at gnosis) in favor of worldly engagement and attention to class-specific social duties. Just as the Dharmaśāstrins innovated by metaphorically redescribing domestic life as an ascetic vocation (an *āśrama*), the author of the *Bhagavad Gītā* redescribed worldly activity (*karman*) as a form of spiritual discipline (a *yoga*, viz. *karma-yoga*, and, by a further theological turn, *bhakti-yoga*, the discipline of devotion). The ascetic professions were not altogether invalidated but were shown to be unnecessarily difficult. Thus, both

---

[14] For the best account of the emergence of this doctrine, see now the studies collected in Patrick Olivelle, ed., *Gṛhastha: The Householder in Ancient Indian Religious Culture* (Oxford: Oxford University Press, 2019).
[15] The option of lifelong student was silently elided.

these seminal Sanskrit works were aimed, in different but potentially complementary ways, at reaffirming a pious life in the world that coopted and "domesticated" the radical challenge posed by otherworldly asceticism. They both acknowledged the authority of Vedic learning and the Brahmanical model of the social order, though the *bhakti* element of the *Bhagavad Gītā* provided a language for transcending the hierarchy implicit in that order, at least so far as access to God is concerned. The *Śivadharmaśāstra*, a scripture composed around the late sixth century, followed the lead of the *Bhagavad Gītā* but was even more radical in envisioning a society of Śiva-devotees adhering to an overarching Śiva-*āśrama* in which distinctions of birth-status were largely (though not totally) overwritten for devotees.[16]

These approaches to *dharma* – the status-based and the devotion-based – appear fairly compatible in the *Bhagavad Gītā*. Kṛṣṇa urges Arjuna to fulfill his proper duty as a leading member of the Kṣatriya *varṇa*, the class with the responsibility to rule, protect, and (when necessary) fight. But, as in the quoted stanzas, the promise is also made that distinctions of birth are irrelevant to one's spiritual condition once the element of *bhakti* is present. In the later "*bhakti* literature" – composed not just in Sanskrit or Prakrit but in regional vernaculars, often with a marked confessional tone – the language of caste is often explicitly and deliberately subverted, and low-caste spiritual heroes are elevated to receive honor even from Brahmins. This devotionalist discourse never becomes caste-blind; the effect is often to invert the scale by taking intensity of devotion as the determinant of high status, rather than birth, inherent purity, and ritual observance.

4 ROYAL POLICY AND BRAHMANICAL DISCOURSE ON THE LAW OF THE STATE

So far I have presented the ancient Hindu social doctrine as it appears in Vedic sacred lore and in Sanskrit normative and doctrinal works that attained scriptural status in Brahmanically oriented forms of Hinduism. The literature of Dharmaśāstra, which is often described as "Hindu law" or "Brahmanical law," was developed out of two or three somewhat distinct steams. Like most religious legal traditions, it comprises a combination of ritual, ethical, and more narrowly legal material (in the secular modern sense). Most of the material relating to *varṇāśramadharma* belongs to the sphere that the tradition itself called *ācāra*, the norms of pious conduct, which includes precepts on ritual activity, purity and penance, and personal behavior; these topics may be seen as an extension of priestly expertise to

---

[16] On this tradition, see the "Introduction" to Peter C. Bisschop, Nirajan Kafle, and Timothy Lubin, *A Śaiva Utopia: The Śivadharma's Revision of Brahmanical Varṇāśramadharma: Critical Edition, Translation & Study of the Śivāśramādhyāya of the Śivadharmaśāstra* (Naples: UniorPress, 2021). The tenth chapter of the *Kalpadrumāvadānamālā*, a Buddhist work thought to be composed in the seventh or eighth centuries in a similar style of verse, fully repudiated the *varṇa* doctrine in notably Dharmaśāstric terms: "This whole world is of one class [*ekavarṇa*] because it came into being as an emanation of Brahman [*ekavarṇam idaṃ sarvaṃ brahmasṛṣṭisamudbhavam*] [10.130ab]."

daily life. The other major topics dealt with in Dharmaśāstra are *vyavahāra* (the adjudication of disputes at law) and *daṇḍanīti* (governance, including criminal law). This seems to have been a separate tradition of expertise that was gradually subsumed within Dharmaśāstra. The oldest and almost only integral book standing outside that literature was Kauṭilya's *Arthaśāstra* (initially compiled around the first century CE and revised around the third or fourth century).[17] But much similar material, probably deriving from that tradition, was integrated in increasing volume into the Dharmaśāstras. These chapters (and the *Arthaśāstra* itself) generally recognize the Brahmanical *varṇa* social model, but we do find here some intimations of more generally applicable standards of fairness, decency, and equity that show up at moments when the needs of good governance come to the fore.

Actually, we have one suggestive window onto early Indian governmental policy that probably predates any surviving example of Dharmaśāstra or Arthaśāstra (in the form in which we have them): the famous edicts of Aśoka.[18] The third-century BCE Mauryan emperor Aśoka, an avowed lay devotee of the Buddha but also a nonpartisan patron of Brahmins and ascetics (*śramaṇa*s) in general, stands out as an early and singular proponent of a generalized ethics applicable to all people without distinction. The Indian historian Romila Thapar called Aśoka's policy "a plea for the recognition of the dignity of man."[19] Even prisoners awaiting execution were to be shown some clemency: three days' respite so that "their relations may plead for their lives, or, if there is no one to plead for them, they may make donations or undertake a fast for the sake of the next world. For it is my wish that they should gain the next world."[20] Aśoka does not frame his reasons in terms of any inherent "dignity" or "worth" inhering in a human or anyway living being, though something like this may be thought to be implicit in his concern that even the worst ought to have the chance of redemption and may well seize that chance. Aśoka, though, stands out as an exception to the norm.

By contrast, status-dignity is a central concern of Brahmanical normative works, especially those concerned to promote the ideals of *varṇāśrama-dharma*. Members

[17] Patrick Olivelle, *King, Governance, and Law in Ancient India: Kauṭilya's Arthaśāstra* (Oxford: Oxford University Press, 2013), pp. 28–31.

[18] According to much later tradition, the *Arthaśāstra* was the work of a Brahmin minister to Aśoka's grandfather Candragupta, but the consensus of the best scholarship today is that the text as we have it, even if it incorporates some authentically Maurya-era traces, was produced centuries later and does not accord in detail with the structure of the Mauryan state as we discern it in the edicts; for a discussion of these issues, see the introduction to Olivelle, *King, Governance, and Law*. Meanwhile, there are indications that the oldest Dharmaśāstric work, the *Āpastamba Dharmasūtra*, was composed not far in time from Aśoka or soon thereafter; the use of the term "dharma" in that work seems to have been inspired by Aśoka's use of it (which in turn likely reflects Buddhist usage).

[19] Romila Thapar, *Aśoka and the Decline of the Mauryas* (Oxford: Oxford University Press, 1961), p. 3.

[20] Pillar Edict 4; adapted from the translation by Thapar, *Aśoka*, 263: "baṃdhanabaddhānaṃ munissānaṃ tīlitadaṃdānaṃ pattavadhānaṃ tiṃni divasāni me yote diṃne. nātikā va kāni nijjhapayissanti jīvitāye tānaṃ nāsaṃtaṃ vā nijjhapayitā dānaṃ dāhaṃti pālattikaṃ upavāsaṃ va kaccaṃti. icchā hi me hevaṃ niluddhassi pi kālassi pālattaṃ ālādhayevū ti." Jules Bloch, *Les inscriptions d'Asoka* (Paris: Société d'Édition "Les Belles Lettres," 1950), p. 165.

of the four status ranks are systematically assigned different duties and privileges. In the case of crimes and torts, penalties are graduated in severity. An offense by a lower-ranked person against one of higher rank entails double or triple sanction (depending on the distance between their ranks), and vice versa. Brahmins are uniquely exempt from capital punishment; only fines or banishment may be applied. In a case of nonpayment of debt, Manu specifies that, if the debtor is of the same or lower status as the creditor, he may pay his debt in labor, but repayment by installments is the only option if the debtor be of higher status (*Mānava Dharmaśāstra* 8.177). The perhaps-eighth-century commentator Bhāruci explains:

> "One of higher caste" must be excused in case he cannot make payment, because he is entitled to respect. He should never be forced to labour like one of equal or inferior caste, out of impatience.[21]

Yet even this literature is not wholly devoid of allusions to underlying universal standards of basic dignity. Just two stanzas later, in discussing the law of deposits, Manu proposes that "a wise man should entrust a deposit to a man who is born in an illustrious family, has an impeccable character, knows the Law, speaks the truth, has a large following, is wealthy, and is respectable/an Ārya" (*Mānava Dharmaśāstra* 8.179).[22] This mixes status-based and character-based criteria, but it is again interesting to note that in his commentary Bhāruci, after noting that "good family" means superior caste, goes on to assert:

> "Respectable" will include even a Śūdra who behaves in such a fashion, because his nature is without deformity. But there are some who (wrongly) say that "respectable" literally means a twice-born, and that that expression is used for an unseen purpose.[23]

Although he acknowledges that some authorities take the word *ārya* to be a birth-status label, Bhāruci deduces from the fact that the next stanza frames its rule in general terms that it was not meant to apply only to people of high birth:

> The following should be understood from the use of the word "a man" [in 8.180]: in the previous verse the word *ārya* ("respectable") must have referred to all castes and was not restricted to the twice-born.[24]

In other words, although many authoritative rules specify distinctions based on rank and dignity, rules that do not do so explicitly apply without distinction – in this case,

---

[21] Tr. Derrett, p. 149.
[22] Olivelle's translation has only "an Ārya"; Derrett (8.178 in his edition) translates this word as "respectable" in accordance with Bhāruci's explanation. See J. Duncan and M. Derrett, *Bhāruci's Commentary on the Manusmṛti* (*The Manu-Śāstra-Vivaraṇa, Books 6–12*), 2 vols (Wiesbaden: Steiner, 1975). In the *Arthaśāstra* (3.13.1), Śūdras are in fact classed as Ārya.
[23] Tr. Derrett, p. 150.
[24] Tr. adapted from Derrett, p. 150.

entailing that *ārya* be treated as a moral attribute rather than an attributive status, as in fact the Buddhist and Jain traditions used the word.

Kauṭilya's *Arthaśāstra* occasionally evinces an implicit recognition of a basic human dignity that should not be transgressed. Although he proposes calibrated punishments for offenses against members of different social ranks, certain penalties apply without distinction for particularly depraved offenses (e.g. sale of human flesh: *Arthaśāstra* 4.10.15). Similarly, Kauṭilya forbids degrading mistreatment of unfree persons: "When a man given as a pledge is made to handle a corpse, urine, feces, or leavings, or when women given as pledges are made to bathe a naked man, are subjected to corporal punishment, or are raped, it causes the loss of the capital; the same acts also cause the freeing of nurses, female attendants, sharecroppers, and maidservants" (*Arthaśāstra* 3.13.9). Although the specified penalty is "merely" monetary, it means that maltreatment of this dire sort negates whatever right the perpetrator had to possess or control the victim.

Similarly, a general standard of human worth appears to be presupposed (though never explicitly stated) in many sections of the rules governing *vyavahāra*. Verbal and physical assaults are classified by gravity of the act itself, without reference to the status of the victim or perpetrator:

7. For both of these there are five different situations when it comes to assigning innocence or guilt:
8. If an assault arose out of rage and both parties are agitated, the one who calms down is to be admired and the one who carries on is to be punished.
9. If two persons are engaged in an assault on one another and no difference in their behavior is obvious, they should both receive the same punishment.
10. The one who starts the fracas is certainly at fault, and the one who responds is also wrong, but the former receives the heavier penalty.
11. When both are equally involved, the one who keeps at it is the one who is punished, whether he started it or not.[25]

In fact, only four situations are described. However, the rest of the section (vv. 12–31) is of an entirely different character: the subject shifts to how distinctions of status factor into offenses and punishments, with draconian penalties prescribed for the low-born, some of them (vv. 23–28) prescribing grisly mutilation as punishment for a Śūdra who insults, strikes, or offends the dignity of a Brahmin. The contrast between these two sequential passages is a stark instance of what I perceive to be a thoroughgoing bifurcation running unacknowledged through much of the Sanskrit normative literature.

The basic duty of the sovereign is to protect those within the realm. This duty is to be discharged without bias or corruption, and the litmus test is whether the

---

[25] *Nārada Smṛti*, pp. 15–16; tr. Lariviere.

powerless can be protected from the powerful. This duty is a moral duty to protect all subjects of whatever social rank from harms of all sorts, including property loss:

> The king must restore to individuals of all classes any property of theirs stolen by thieves; if the king retains it for himself, he incurs the sin of its thief.[26]

Medhātithi, a couple of centuries later, adds that "all castes" includes Caṇḍālas, representing the lowest of the low. Part of that duty, though, includes recognizing and enforcing the positive or customary laws (*dharma*s) adopted by particular groups within the realm:

> He who knows the Law should examine the Laws of castes, regions, guilds, and families, and only then settle the Law specific to each.[27]

Bhāruci explains:

> The "law of castes" is well known. "Caste" means Brahmin, etc. This is considered fixed [*nitya*] because it is defined in the sacred teachings [*śāstra*s]. "Of regions" means laws set by convention, relating to the grazing of cattle and protection of water, which do not have the *śāstra*s as their authority. The "law of guilds" is propounded by merchants, artisans, and minstrels to order to foster their respective activities. This is the law [*dharma*] that the king must uphold. He should not nullify them on the grounds that they are merely set by convention. If the king disregards the laws set by convention there will be a breach of established law [*vyavasthā*], and the Rule of the Fish (*mātsya-nyāya*) will prevail.

In other words, Bhāruci makes a distinction between *jāti-dharma*s, "caste laws," which he takes to be divinely ordained, and the norms of other social groups, which he takes to be examples of positive law. Other authorities, however, treat even the *jāti-dharma*s as based on human convention rather than scripture.[28]

Similar themes of wisdom and good policy, presented as advice to princes, appear in didactic narratives that, though composed in Sanskrit or other literary idioms, often speak of the vicissitudes of life in terms that that seem to pertain to humanity in general. For example, the *Pañcatantra* is a collection of fables deployed to teach the

---

[26] MDh 8.40; tr. Olivelle, p. 169.
[27] MDh 8.41; tr. Olivelle, p. 169.
[28] On this point, see Patrick Olivelle, "Patañjali and the Beginnings of Dharmaśāstra: An Alternative Social History of Early Dharmasūtra Production," in *Aux abords de la clairière: Études indiennes et comparées en l'honneur de Charles Malamoud* [At the edge of the clearing: Indian and comparative studies in honor of Charles Malamoud], edited by Silvia D'Intino and Caterina Guenzi (Turnhout: Brepols, 2012), pp. 117–133; Timothy Lubin, "Customary Practice in the Vedic Ritual Codes as an Emergent Legal Principle," *Journal of the American Oriental Society* 136, no. 4 (2016): 669–687.

art of government, and "its stories depict human life with all its ambivalences."[29] Misfortune can have a degrading effect even on the mighty:

> 2.39 cd–40: Palpable ignominy, the seat of calamity, it robs proud people of their dignity! That is what beggary does to wise men. I see no difference between that and hell. [39] When he has no wealth, a man feels ashamed; Clothed in shame, he's bereft of dignity; Without dignity, he suffers insults; Suffering insults, he becomes depressed; When he is depressed, he suffers anguish; And anguished at heart, he loses his mind; Losing his mind, he's totally destroyed; the lack of wealth is, alas, the source of all misfortunes! [40][30]

"Dignity" here is *tejas*, a luminous quality that elicits respect and need not align with a particular caste or rank but is associated with worldly power and wealth. It is destroyed, we are told, by *lāghavam* (disrespect, ignominy) or penury, which bring shame. And the *Pañcatantra* voices "the age-old debate between nature and character, whether a man is who he is because of his birth and caste or because of his conduct and talents, whether a king should judge a man by his character or his pedigree" (Olivelle, *Pañcatantra*, xxxv). The strongest form of the non-caste view is voiced thus:

> 1.v166: A man's excellence is not a matter of birth [*jāti-dharma*]; Mortal men's honor is based on their behavior. Disgrace and in its train a web of disasters, hundreds of them, Hound a man who is an ingrate, both in this world and in the next.[31]

Nevertheless, in general, the work reaffirms the putative "naturalness" of innate moral differences, by comparing them to those that separate species of animal: herbivores will never eat meat (part I, p. 44); a cow will not mate with a stallion.[32]

Courtly literature includes collections of *subhāṣita*, epigrams in verse; many of these pearls of wisdom distill aspects of common humanity. One of the most famous became a popular motto in India:

> 'Is he one of us or is he an outsider?' – so ask small-minded men. Those of noble mind take the whole world for family.[33]

---

[29] Patrick Olivelle, *Pañcatantra: The Book of India's Folk Wisdom* (Oxford: Oxford University Press, 1997), p. xxxii.

[30] "mūrtaṃ lāghavam āśrayaś ca vipadāṃ tejoharaṃ māninām |
arthitvaṃ hi manasvināṃ na narakāt paśyāmi vastv antaram || 39
nirdravyo hriyam eti hrīparigataḥ prabhraśyate tejaso
nistejāḥ paribhūyate paribhavān nirvedam āgacchati |
nirviṇṇaḥ śucam eti śokamanaso buddhiḥ paribhraśyate
nirbuddhiḥ kṣayam ety aho nidhanatā sarvāpadām āspadam || 40."

[31] "na jātidharmaḥ puruṣasya sādhutā caritramūlāni yaśāṃsi dehinām |
akīrtir āpacchatajālakarṣaṇī kṛtaghnam anveti paratra ceha ca || 1.v166."

[32] Olivelle, *Pañcatantra*, pp. xxxv–xxxvi.

[33] "ayaṃ nijaḥ paro veti gaṇanā laghucetasāṃ | udāracaritānāṃ tu vasudhaiva kuṭumbakam ||." Daniel H. H. Ingalls, trans., *Sanskrit Poetry, from Vidyākara's "Treasury"* (Cambridge: Belknap Press, 1968), 347 (v. 1241), discussed in Donald R. Davis Jr., "Justice Demands Facts: Law, Narrative, and Poetry in Classical India," *Antiquorum Philosophia* 11 (2017): 23.

Other stanzas evoke similar sentiments. A verse from the *Mahābhārata* epic (13.114.8) provides an Indian avatar of the "golden rule":

> One should not offer to another what is disagreeable to oneself. This, in brief, is *dharma*; anything else arises from desire.[34]

Verses like these seem to undercut the caste-wise division of humanity into high and low, "us and them," that otherwise is so obtrusive in ancient Indian texts, particularly those in Sanskrit. A similar tension shows up in literary depictions of courtroom justice: to the magistrates, justice is a standard that applies to all regardless of birth. In the play "The Little Clay Cart" (circa seventh century), the king's wicked brother-in-law seeks to accuse Cārudatta, an innocent and virtuous man, of murder. When the haughty prince brags of his royal stature, the judge replies with an aphorism that rejects the claim that birth can be a sufficient basis for assigning merit:

> 9.7: Why bring up your family? Character is all that matters here. Thorn trees thrive especially well in a good field.[35]

When Cārudatta is convicted and sentenced to execution, he tries to play his status card to escape death: he mentions the Dharmaśāstra-based rule that Brahmins are exempt from capital punishment. But the magistrate dismisses this status claim and sends him off to his execution (9.39.5) anyway, from which he is saved only by the reappearance of the supposed victim, safe and sound.[36]

In each of these genres – norms for the administration of justice, didactic works on good policy, and courtly literature – we find that the gradations of privileges and penalties by social rank that were promoted by Brahmin apologists for *varṇa* hierarchy competed with a distinct ethos that applied standards of public morality and justice as generally applicable.

5 ASCETIC DISCOURSE

It was the ascetic movements that were the first to propose a view of the person that utterly ignored social status, at least so far as "absolute reality" was concerned. A direct cognition of soul, the innermost aspect of the person – the immutable Self (*ātman*) of the Hindus, or vital stuff (*jīva*) of the Jains, or, for Buddhist theorists, simply the ephemeral composite nature of sentience itself – constituted a perception of that reality, in which caste, gender, and all the conventional distinctions of this world become irrelevant, for they pertain only to worldly concerns.

[34] "na tat parasya saṃdadyāt pratikūlaṃ yad ātmanaḥ | eṣa saṃkṣepato dharmaḥ kāmād anyaḥ pravartate || ."
[35] "kiṃ kulenopadiṣṭena śīlam evātra kāraṇam | bhavanti nitarāṃ sphītāḥ sukṣetre kaṇṭakidrumāḥ || 9.7."
[36] Davis, "Justice Demands Facts," pp. 11–25 discusses a few of the numerous laments about injustice appearing in Sanskrit fables; he argues that narratives depicting concrete situations were common as a way of addressing in concrete terms the issues of injustice and the indignities to which human beings are so often subject.

These movements continued to recognize some social distinctions on the grounds that one's bodily condition, whether determined by birth (caste and sex) or adventitious (e.g. disease or disability), could pose a greater impediment to liberation from worldly bondage. For the Buddhists and Jains, feminine gender was a greater hindrance than male, but in principle at least they did not stress other distinctions of birth. But Brahmanically orthodox groups viewed Brahmin status, or at least Ārya status (membership in one of the three highest social ranks), as necessary for advancement, on the grounds that knowledge of the Vedic revelation was a prerequisite, and that was open by definition only to those ranks. And in any case, distinctions of dignity were often taken simply to be symptomatic of the vicissitudes of *saṃsāra*. Thus the eighth-century Vedānta theorist Śaṅkarācārya wrote:

> Although one and the same Self is hidden in all beings movable as well as immovable, yet owing to the gradual rise of excellence of the minds which form the limiting conditions (of the Self), Scripture declares that the Self, although eternally unchanging and uniform, reveals itself in a graduated series of beings, and so appears in forms of various dignity (*aiśvarya*) and power.[37]

In wrestling with the seeming paradox that Brahman, the intelligent creator and actual nature of the Self within all beings (according to Śaṅkara's school of thought), would bring about harmful effects in the world, Śaṅkara addresses the objection that the existence of suffering disproves the existence of an intelligent creator:

> For we know that no free person will build a prison for himself, and take up his abode in it. Nor would a being, itself absolutely stainless, look on this altogether unclean body as forming part of its Self. It would, moreover, free itself, according to its liking, of the consequences of those of its former actions which result in pain, and would enjoy the consequences of those actions only which are rewarded by pleasure.[38]

Śaṅkara evades this objection only by reiterating that the sufferings affect only the illusory personal self and not the soul per se.

This absolute equality or even sameness at the core does not wholly cancel the inequality of condition of those in the grip of illusion (or those subject to the bondage of *karma*, according to the dualist schools of thought, which take material existence to be real if still ephemeral). The differences of birth matter insofar as they affect one's capacity to attain liberation in the present lifetime. But the ascetic thinkers often did recognize a species-wide status vis-à-vis lower life forms. The *Nārada Parivrājaka Upaniṣad* says: "'[Brahman] is one and I am another' [quoting *Bṛhadāraṇyaka Upaniṣad* 1.4.10]: those who think thus are animals; they do not

---

[37] *Vedānta Sūtra Bhāṣya* 1.1.11; Thibaut, p. 63. "yady apy eka ātmā sarvabhūteṣu sthāvarajaṅgameṣu gūḍhas tathāpi cittopādhiviśeṣatāratamyād ātmanaḥ kūṭasthanityasyaikarūpasyāpy uttarottaram āviṣkṛtasya tāratamyam aiśvaryaśaktiviśeṣaiḥ śrūyate ... "

[38] *Vedānta Sūtra Bhāṣya* 2.1.21; tr. Thibaut, pp. 343–344.

behold their true nature" (6.117–118). Buddhists observe that a human birth is actually the best; those below us have too-limited cognition to attain liberation, and divine beings feel too powerful and too comfortable even to recognize their own impermanence.

In practice, of course, most of these ascetic orders (even the most egalitarian in spirit) came to be dominated by one or another segment of society; and among the laypeople, sectarian allegiance had a tendency to be passed down in families and thus to become part of one's group identity. Even so, the theoretical orientation of the ascetic traditions tended to emphasize the commonalities of the human condition that transcend any given status, and indeed the stories used to illustrate their teaching frequently make precisely the point that one's birth and social position do not matter as much as one's personal choices and virtues.

In any case, this philosophical or soteriological universalism – relating as it did to an otherworldly spiritual condition – had little application in society or in law. Moreover, the definition of soul was so radically abstract that it did not belong only to human beings. A soul might be born into the womb of any sentient being, from an ant to a heavenly being, depending on its balance of accumulated *karma* (the residual effects of actions in past lives). In that sense, all sentient beings are subject to the same litany of woes and can aspire to the same liberation from them – at least they can when fortunate to be born in a form endowed with reason, which Kant took to be the prerequisite for the moral autonomy that is the basis of human dignity. This perspective on the nature of the soul and the machinations of *karma* has the tendency to elevate the lowliest creatures in dignity and to humble the pride of the mighty. Indra, the hero-god of the Veda, is informed, in the *Brahmavaivarta Purāṇa* (Kṛṣṇa. 47.96–122), that he is but one of an infinite line of Indras who have held sway over heaven in the past and will do so in the future, for even the gods die and are reborn at the transition from one great eon to the next.

Ascetical discourse did contribute an important element to Hindu religious law more widely: a concept of a "universal" (*sādhāraṇa*) or "general" (*sāmānya*) dharma equally applicable to all humanity. This took the form of a set of rules of self-discipline (*yama*s and *niyama*s) appearing in overlapping lists in Hindu[39] as well as Buddhist and Jain[40] scriptures for ascetics: not causing harm (*ahiṃsā*); not stealing (*asteya*); truthfulness (*satya*); celibacy (*brahmacarya*); forebearance; non-acquisitiveness; and the like. In its strongest form, enjoined upon ascetics, this dharma requires total celibacy and renunciation of possessions, but a milder variant was ordained for laypeople as well, substituting "restraint of the organs"

---

[39] For example, *Yoga Sūtra* 2.30, 32; Kauṇḍinya's *Pañcārthabhāṣya* on *Pāśupata Sūtra* 1.9.

[40] The "great observance" (*mahāvrata*) for Jain ascetics, identical with the *Yoga Sūtra*'s five *yama*s: for example, *Ācārāṅga Sūtra* 2.15; compare the "five precepts" of Buddhist monastics: for example, *Aṅguttara Nikāya* 8.39.

(*indriyanigraha*) in place of celibacy.[41] The *Mānava Dharmaśāstra* interrupts its long exposition of the mixing of classes and the degraded statuses arising therefrom to list five such rules: "this, Manu has declared, is the gist of the dharma for the four classes" (10.63).[42] Vijñāneśvara, a twelfth-century commentator on the *Yājñavalkyadharmaśāstra*, affirms that these rules apply to all, even Caṇḍālas (the archetypal lowest-status caste).[43] All other rules of *dharma* are the "particular" (*viśeṣa*, *sva*) rules correlated with one's status (*varṇa* and *āśrama*). Many of the latter run afoul of modern egalitarian norms of human rights and human dignity, while the general rules seem unimpeachable, which is why they are often appealed to as a Hindu basis for egalitarian, universal norms.[44]

Accordingly, Gandhi appealed to Indians to embrace these ideals both personally and as a nation when he translated many of them into political activism: nonharm (*ahiṃsā*) as nonviolence, holding fast to truth (*satyāgraha*) in resisting tyranny, and self-determination (*svātantrya*) as an extension of mastering the senses. Accordingly, he responded in his magazine, *Harijan* (July 11 and 18, 1936), to "Dr. Ambedkar's Indictment" of his efforts to excuse the concept of *varṇa* from the sins of casteism by asserting that hierarchy is a distortion of the original Hindu social structure and a violation of Hinduism's essential laws:

> It would be wrong and improper to judge the law of varna by its caricature in the lives of men who profess to belong to a varna whilst they openly commit a breach of its only operative rule. Arrogation of a superior status by any of the varnas over another is a denial of the law. And there is nothing in the law of varna to warrant a belief in untouchability. (The essence of Hinduism is contained in its enunciation of one and only God as Truth and its bold acceptance of ahimsa as the law of the human family.)

These general ideals, derived from the ascetic orders but normally considered to apply to all Hindus or even to all humanity, express general ethical precepts of

---

[41] For example, in the *Mānava Dharmaśāstra* (6.91–93 and 10.63); *Śivadharmaśāstra* (10.137–138; cf. 11.46–47); *Viṣṇudharma* 100.2–3.

[42] "ahiṃsā satyam akrodhaḥ śaucam indriyanigrahaḥ: etaṃ sāmāsikaṃ dharmaṃ cāturvarṇye' bravīn manuḥ." Many manuscripts have *asteyam* instead of *akrodhaḥ*. Note, however, that in 6.91–93, most of these appear in a longer list of ten rules prescribed only for Brahmins or other higher-ranked Ārya classes, not for all – in other words, not as a universal dharma. But other authorities extend the rules more broadly; see the next note.

[43] "Not causing harm, etc., constitute universal *dharma*. The universal *dharma* 'one should not seek to harm any creature' applies even to the Caṇḍāla" ("sādhāraṇdharmo 'hiṃsādiḥ; na hiṃsyāt sarvā bhūtāni ity ācaṇḍālaṃ sādhāraṇo dharmaḥ," ad YDh 1.1). The *Śivadharmaśāstra* (1.28) extends its "great observance" (*mahāvrata*) even to foreign barbarians: "When this eight-fold *bhakti* is present even in a barbarian, he [may be deemed] the best of Brahmins, an illustrious sage, an ascetic, a scholar!" ("bhaktir aṣṭavidhā hy eṣā yasmin mlecche 'pi vartate | sa viprendro muniḥ śrīmān sa yatiḥ sa ca paṇḍitaḥ"); Bisschop, Kafle, and Lubin, *A Śaiva Utopia*, p. 30.

[44] Sharma (*Hinduism and Human Rights*, pp. 14–20, 154–155; *Hindu Narratives*, pp. 144–148) does so; Carman ("Duties and Rights," pp. 126–127) alludes to Gandhi's promotion of these principles of general dharma.

virtuous practice, perhaps even general duties, and as such might be taken as marking out all people as held to a common moral standard, implying that each person owes the other respect for person and property. Insofar as these general norms designed for ascetic virtuosi were adapted as suitable to apply to all humanity, we may see this as a "leveling up" (in Whitman's and Waldron's terms), implying a shared human capacity (and thus a duty?) to live up to the highest moral ideals (though still no explicit sense that particular rights are implied).

Yet when we see the Dharmaśāstras and many other Sanskrit works addressing the particulars of good conduct, of civil law, and of crimes and sins, the calculus of rank and status is everywhere. The greater the disparity between the statuses of offender and offended, the heavier the punishments prescribed for the lowly and the lighter those for the elite. Violating status boundaries is itself the source of innumerable offenses. Such rules are elaborated at vast length, and the general *dharma* is mentioned only in passing, except where spiritual or general moral virtues are the focus.

6 VERNACULAR *BHAKTI* DISCOURSE

So far as premodern sources are concerned, it was only with the emergence of medieval devotional *bhakti* lyric and narrative works – especially those composed in the regional languages of the subcontinent, in a generally less formal register of the language than that used for learned discourse – that we can speak of a direct affirmation of something like human dignity *in contrast to* (and even as a repudiation of) Brahmanical rank-and-status-based dignity. This vernacular *bhakti* tradition begins with intensely confessional poems expressing personal connection to the divinity. The poets are treated like saints who have a special intimacy with the gods whom they praise, and their lives form the subject of hagiographies.

This new tradition offers the nearest thing to a systematic Indian model of human dignity. In light of Whitman and Waldron's view that human dignity implies a "leveling up" of the classical status-based dignity, it is worth noting that for the *bhakti*-inspired poets, in many cases, "equality is equalising downwards on the social scale, a downward mobility, almost a seeking of dishonour as among the Cynics of Greece and the Pāśupatas of India, debasing themselves so that they may be cleansed of pride."[45] In other words, it is not so much a democratization of dignity as its inversion in light of an ascendant ethics of humility. Thus the female saint Mīrābāī, when told she could not meet with a leading male theologian because she was a woman, retorted that, among devotees of Lord Kṛṣṇa, there is only one man – Kṛṣṇa himself; all his mortal devotees share the status of the herdswomen (*gopīs*)

---

[45] A. K. Ramanujan, *Collected Essays* (Oxford: Oxford University Press, 1999), p. 285.

who were in love with Kṛṣṇa and thus modeled the all-consuming devotion aspired to in Kṛṣṇa worship.

Similarly, the seventeenth-century Maharashtrian saint Tukārām lamented the unfairness with which he was treated: "I was born in a Śūdra family, so I am illtreated by the proud ... I was not allowed to learn sacred words. In all respects, lowly, Tuka says, I am an outcaste" (Abhaṅg 2766, 65). He ridicules the hypocrisy and shallow orthodoxy of the Brahmins, whose concern for ritualism and purity mask an inward impurity: "He is sensitive about the pure and impure, But in his innermost heart, anger has polluted his soul" (Abhaṅg 2855, 66). Similar sentiments are expressed by other low-caste saints like Ravidās, Kabīr, Nāmdev, and Dādu Dayāl.

The other side of the coin, though, is that when Brahmins told the stories of poet-saints' lives (as they do in the *Bhaktamāla* of Priyadās, ca. 1600, and the *Bhaktavijaya* of Mahipati, 1774), the outwardly low-caste saints, of which there are quite a few, end up being presented as Brahmins in a past life, or inwardly Brahmin, in order to justify the paradox of their being revered by those socially superior in rank to them. This is the reason that Ravidās, a so-called untouchable leather worker, is said to have opened his chest to reveal the sacred thread of a Brahmin, to show that he is worthy to dine beside the Brahmins.[46] Even when no explicit claim to inner Brahminhood is made, the biographies include miraculous confirmations that the low-caste saints' devotion put them on a par with Brahmins – vindication in the court of God. Thus when a Brahmin decrees that Tukārām's writings be cast into a river because as a Śūdra he has no authority to preach on the message of the *Bhagavad Gītā*, Tukārām fasts until the river goddess returns his work intact.

A similar inversion happens on the gender axis. Out of her intense love of God, the Tamil female saint Āṇḍāḷ would put on the garlands that her father prepared daily for worship. When he discovered this, he scolded her for polluting the pure offering by using it before the god did, but later the deity came to him in a vision to ask why the specially blessed garlands were no longer being offered. Other female saints refused to marry, or repudiated their unwished-for human husband, in order to devote themselves wholly to the divine object of their love.[47] In all these cases, behavior that defies the rules of Brahmanical purity or propriety within a hierarchical social order is deemed justified on account of the subject's authentic and single-minded *bhakti*.

Bhakti is a standard that can override or invert hierarchy, but it does not erase it. It is capable of conferring a sense of dignity upon those otherwise denied it in the dominant order of things, but it is most often a dignity sensed inwardly by oneself or

---

[46] John Stratton Hawley and Mark Juergensmeyer, *Songs of the Saints of India*, 2nd ed. (New York: Oxford University Press, 2006), 15.
[47] A. K. Ramanujan, "On Women Saints," in *The Divine Consort*, edited by J. S. Hawley and Donna Marie Wulff (Boston, MA: Beacon Press, 1982), pp. 316–324.

recognized within one's peer group or religious society, not one that has been effectively wielded to assert a social or legal claim.[48] It is very hard to find any example of explicit premodern legal or administrative recognition of such dignity. Courtroom trial scenes appearing in the *bhakti* hagiographies tend to depict the low-caste *sant* (holy man) being treated unjustly by Brahmin authorities. Moreover, the message of inner equality can get undercut, first by the fact that the injustice hinges largely in the saint's special sanctity, which may be said to mitigate the stigma of low birth; this has the effect of neutralizing any implication that the caste prejudice on display would be wrong if directed to other, less saintly members of the caste (though the complementary claim that the high-born tend to be unworthy usually holds). Moreover, at least in some cases, the *sant* acquiesces in his injustice. Such may be said to be the case with Cakradhar in the *Līḷācaritra*. On trial before a Brahmin council led by the learned Dharmaśāstra authority Hemādri, in the presence of many other social dignitaries, he is condemned for what we take to be a specious charge of improper relations with women, in a process that is depicted as not being quite above-board, but in spite of these irregularities at the end of the trial he offers his nose to be cut off. This self-mortifying act might have been intended to show that he was not really at the mercy of the Brahmins. The fact that he later consoles his caste-fellows and restores their "pride" by miraculously growing a new nose does not compensate for his public degradation in which he himself was complicit.[49] In another story, the *sant* Jñāndev, born of Brahmin parents who had been stripped by a Brahmin court of their caste status for the ritual fault (but saintly virtue) of premature renunciation, rejects the legal remedy that would restore his and his brother's status because they claim to have transcended social distinctions. Yet he goes on in a sermon to endorse the importance of maintaining Brahmanical caste norms taught in the Sanskrit *śāstras*. Here again, personal transcendence of status concerns fails to translate into a new social or legal normative standard.[50]

---

[48] The limited aspirations of *bhakti* social critique are summed up well by O'Hanlon (Rosalind O'Hanlon, *Caste, Conflict, and Ideology: Mahatma Jotirao Phule and Low Caste Protest in Nineteenth-Century Western India* (Cambridge: Cambridge University Press, 1985), 61):

> Indian religious life had, of course, its own traditions of debate. But in the past these had tended always to address themselves to the limited audience of a particular *sampradaya* or individual religious sect. This was true, for example of the *bhakti* devotional cults of western India. Much of the work of the Marathi saint–writers of this religious tradition contained a strong dislike of any rigid equivalence of spiritual merit with high caste status. It placed the individual's love of God as a virtue that stood above all, regardless of caste or secular position. This was particularly true of the seventeenth-century *bhakti* poet Tukaram. Yet these kinds of criticism never burgeoned into a self-conscious intellectual attempt to confront and refute religious values that emphasised the caste hierarchy and religious pre-eminence of the Brahman. They remained a spiritual solace for individual believers, rather than the ground for a direct challenge to the position of the Brahman as the mediator between the Hindus and the high gods in ritual, and the arbiters of religious rectitude in their role as interpreters of the Hindu scriptures.

[49] See the discussion in Christian Novetzke, *Quotidian Revolution* (New York: Columbia University Press, 2016), pp. 204–209 and 246.

[50] Novetzke, *Quotidian Revolution*, pp. 288–290.

Nevertheless, some social reformers of the colonial era appealed to the teachings or example of the *bhakti* saints: in western India there were the Prarthana Samaj, which looked to Tukārām, and the Satyashodhak Samaj, founded by Jyotirao Phule (1827–90), which took inspiration from the weaver Kabīr.[51] Religious movements with a strongly anti-caste-prejudice message included the Mahānubhavs and the Kabīr Panth. However it was more common for social reformers to approach their task from a secularist approach looking to Western models or to posit (as did Dayananda Sarasvati and Mohandas Gandhi) a revisionist ideal of "Vedic" tradition that depicted caste prejudice and social abuses as historical corruptions of an originally pure and harmonious dharma.

7 CONCLUSIONS

When one attempts to make room in a culture for a modern notion of universal human dignity, it is not enough to search for an "indigenous" analogue on which to anchor it and to deploy against nonegalitarian status norms. And one must also come to terms with the capacity of dissonant ethical norms to persist in tension. Promoting human dignity then becomes a matter of expanding the range of contexts in which human dignity is accepted as the proper standard to apply. In classical Hinduism, the proponents of *varṇāśrama-dharma* generally succeeded in setting the agenda for most purposes; the vernacular *bhakti* movement pushed back against it and, in modern times, helped provide a home-grown idiom for talk of human dignity.

A Hindu argument for human dignity might also amplify the "undercurrent" of universal justice that I have pointed to that runs through Sanskrit works dealing with general virtues, good policy, and just governance – especially since, unlike most devotional or ascetic teachings, they are explicitly aimed at giving shape to a fair society and a good polity. But making such an argument should not involve a denial or minimizing of the obtrusive and persistent role of *varṇa*-ideology in Sanskrit discourse. The tension between them should be acknowledged and historically contextualized. Proponents of human dignity have had to come to terms with the brute facts of human history: in most times and places, a conception of human dignity has been absent, denied, or ignored in practice, and this was generally the case in ancient and medieval India.

The strands of Hindu religious discourse reviewed here show that, in some contexts, universally shared aspects of the human condition – susceptibility to suffering, subjection to law of karma, the expectation of a fair hearing in court – come to the surface, but the theme of ranked ascriptive status by birth is rarely far from sight. This has usually been taken as evidence that caste obligations (*jāti-dharma*), together with their theological and religious legal doctrinal justification (*varṇāśrama-dharma*), are definitive of Hindu religion. It certainly reflects the

---

[51] O'Hanlon, *Caste, Conflict, and Ideology*, pp. 220–230.

tremendous influence that Brahmin authors and their elite patrons have had, over two or three millennia, in shaping public discourse and social practices. However influential it has been, this is the voice of a minority of Hindus. Those strands of discourse that diverge from the theme of *varṇāśrama-dharma* sometimes nevertheless do so, perhaps inevitably, within the terms set by caste or birth-class. Ascetic discourse asserts that the soul itself has no caste, which belongs only to things of this passing, karma-generated world of woe, which afflicts all people (albeit in varying degrees). Ascetic norms promoted a set of general rules of discipline, originally intended for those aspiring to spiritual perfection, that were generalized to constitute a general dharma for all – a sort of "leveling up." *Bhakti* discourse, particularly in its vernacular forms, asserts that true devotion or divine grace can invert the scale, elevating the saint above the self-righteous priest or showing that all are equally lowly before God. These two ways of thinking have tended to recognize a shared human dignity mainly within a personal, even interior sphere of experience, or anyway within the bounds of a sect or religious community. These modes of discourse, especially the *bhakti* discourse, certainly can provide an idiom for a social, political, or legal articulation of human dignity – and have, in modern times, done so. But this potential was only occasionally and very hesitantly realized in earlier eras.

Least often noted, but quite interesting, is what I find to be an undercurrent of thought (even in Brahmanical sources) on the subject of the dharma of the king, wise policy, and jurisprudence that suggests an overarching ideal of equity, proposes general standards of right and wrong, and hints that even the lowest of society should not be subjected to wanton degradation. This line of thought seems to be particularly associated with depictions of or prescriptions for the exercise of good governance. Most of the sources in which these traces have been preserved (with the exception of Aśoka's edicts) are in fact Sanskrit works, thus likely authored by Brahmins; indeed, in other passages of these same works, Brahmanical norms of social hierarchy are clearly endorsed. But it is worth noting that, even in an intellectual tradition famed for its endorsement of strict inegalitarianism and protection of the special dignity of the highly ranked, there is room for a notion of equity and common dignity that cuts across or bypasses rank. This apparent dissonance may be an artifact of the convergence of two distinct streams of thought in early India: the priestly social model promoted by the Brahmins who wrote the first Dharma codes; and the political philosophy espoused by rulers and their ministers (some but certainly not all of them Brahmins, with different concerns from those of the priestly authors). These two streams flowed together in the classical Sanskrit literature to the point that their distinct origins have been obscured.

We began by asking what a careful consideration of Hindu sources might contribute to discussions about human dignity. The fact that such divergent views of human worth and status could coexist and could be cited even side by side suggests that, in practice, ethical and legal orders find ways to "compartmentalize," affirming common humanity with common concerns in one breath and sorting people into birth-ranks deserving different "fair shares" in the next. The formulation of a notion of human dignity does not automatically sweep the field clear of other, more ancient conceptions of special dignity associated with ascriptive status, just as the formulation of a concept of universal human rights did not (and indeed still has not) done away with social norms and political institutions that appear incompatible with such a concept. That is how the founders of the United States of America could proclaim it a self-evident truth "that all men are created equal, that they are endowed by their Creator with certain unalienable Rights" including "Life, Liberty and the pursuit of Happiness"[52] yet fail to extend those rights to enslaved Blacks when drafting the Constitution and the Bill of Rights – and, in fact, continue to recognize and preserve in statute law the institutions of slavery and the general subordination of people of African or Native American descent.[53]

[52] Declaration of Independence, signed July 4, 1776, America's Founding Documents, National Archives, www.archives.gov/founding-docs/declaration.
[53] These statutes included the slave codes of the colonies before independence and of fifteen southern states thereafter, but also many other laws such as those in New York and New Jersey that prohibited free Blacks from owning real estate. In the Constitution, slaves were obliquely alluded to as "other persons," who would count for "three fifths" of a "free person" for purposes of calculating representation and taxation by population. Even after Emancipation via the Thirteenth Amendment to the Constitution (1865), "Jim Crow" laws at the state and local level maintained the segregation of Blacks in public spaces in many parts of the United States until 1965. The Supreme Court decision in *Plessey v. Ferguson*, 163 US 537 (1896), upheld the constitutionality of such laws on the grounds that legal equality did not necessarily entail the prohibition of discrimination or separation of races.

13

Human Dignity, *Pancasila*, and Islam

Contexts and Contestations in Indonesia

Etin Anwar

1 INTRODUCTION

The term "dignity" (*martabat*)[1] within Indonesian contexts is usually paired with the word "degree" (*derajat*).[2] Both terms intersect in the pursuit of human becoming as they are situated within the context of progress (*kemajuan*) of the nation and its people before and after Independence. The discourses of human dignity emerged during colonialism and was cemented in the Declaration of Independence on August 17, 1945. Following the Declaration of Independence, the Constitution of the Republic of Indonesia was introduced on August 18, 1945. The 1945 Constitution frames human dignity in terms of rights for Indonesian people in order to live a decent life. Later on, the governmental policies on national development reconfigured the pursuit of human dignity and the nation through developmental goals, programs, and policies. For instance, the New Order regime introduced the concept of the integrated development of human being (*pembangunan manusia seutuhnya*) as the core of its policy. In the process of formulating developmental policies that were aligned with the 1948 Universal Declarations of Human Rights, the New Order government and its successors amended the 1945 Constitution. As indicated by Nadirsyah Hosen (see Chapter 6 in this volume), the term "dignity," especially in the post-Suharto era, is formulated in accordance with human rights provisions.

The debates and policies associated with the pursuit of human dignity and the degree of its fulfillment have evolved following local challenges and global interactions. These discursive narratives and practices of human dignity reinforce the importance of humans as inviolable beings. Hasan argues that human dignity is something innate to each individual and is irreducible.[3] The association of dignity with human inviolability leads to the emphasis of respect for others on the part of

---

[1] W. J. S. Poerwadarmita, *Kamus Umum Bahasa Indonesia* [General Indonesian Dictionary] (Jakarta: Balai Pustaka, 2003), p. 748.
[2] Ibid., p. 284.
[3] Moh. Hasan, *Harkat and Martabat Manusia Indonesia dalam Negara Pancasila* [Indonesian Human Dignity and Dignity in the Pancasila State] (Jakarta: Markas Besar Angkatan Bersenjata, Republik Indonesia, Lembaga Pertahanan Nasional, 1984), p. 2.

individuals and the fulfillment of individual rights on the part of the state. It is true that individual dignity is ingrained in the cultural and social scripts; however, human dignity in terms of the fulfillment of citizens' rights is only achievable within the mechanism of an independent state. This is to say that the state has the ability to institutionalize human dignity through policies that guarantee some degrees of prosperity for its citizens.

The important role of the state in fulfilling rights associated with human dignity has long ignited heated debates among secular and Muslim nationalists. These debates revolved around issues of progress for the new nation both during colonialism and after, as well as the need to modernize Indonesia. The pursuit of a nation came to fruition with the Declaration of Independence. Post-Independence, a series of Indonesian governments have utilized the guiding principles inscribed within *Pancasila*[4] and the 1945 Constitution of the Republic of Indonesia in order to uphold human dignity and fulfill the rights of citizens. Here, the role of *Pancasila* in the pursuit of human dignity is important to note. While the founding fathers of the Indonesian Republic established *Pancasila* as the foundation of the state, its politicization during the New Order (1966–98) muddled Islam's role in state governance and the actualization of human dignity. The New Order perceived Islam as a political ideology as a threat to *Pancasila* and the state. This strenuous relationship has brought to the fore the perennial question of whether Islam is truly compatible with *Pancasila*. In this chapter, I will show how the affinity between Islam and *Pancasila* is reflected in values, such as the belief in God, inclusive humanity, unity, consensus, and social justice and how these values shape the formulation of human dignity.

As ethical values drawn from Islam and *Pancasila* mutually reinforce the inviolability of humans, I will examine the pattern of how human dignity has been contextualized, debated, and contested both before and after Independence. In Section 2, I will contextualize the discursive narrative of human dignity among secular and Muslim nationalists and link it to the local challenges of colonialism and the debates on the need for national sovereignty. I will also trace the importance of human dignity in Sukarno's speeches on *Pancasila* as well as the 1945 Constitution of the Republic of Indonesia. In Section 3, I will show how the legacy of *Pancasila* and the 1945 Constitution orients the nation's aspiration in modernizing the country, ensuring rights, and promoting human dignity. At the same time, I will also discuss how the New Order's politicization of *Pancasila* impacted the debates and the practices of human dignity and the formulation of Islam as ethics and politics. I will end the chapter by focusing on the overlapping consensus between Islam and *Pancasila* in formulating human dignity as the fulfillment of rights.

---

[4] *Pancasila* refers to the five philosophical foundations of the state. They are: the belief in the one God; a just and civilized humanity; the unity of Indonesia; democracy; and social justice for all Indonesians.

2 HUMAN DIGNITY AND THE PURSUIT OF A NATION

Dutch colonialism stripped human dignity and decency from the Indonesian people, aside from the few individuals who benefited from colonial policies and its politics. For over 350 years, from 1509 to 1942, different Western powers invaded and colonized what is now called Indonesia, the Dutch being the longest colonizer.[5] From 1942 to 1945, Japan colonized Indonesia until it was defeated by the US-led Allied army. Within the Dutch colonial context, citizenship was racially defined. Locher-Scholten shows how Dutch citizenship in 1892 was limited to individuals born of Dutch descent and later on was expanded to the wives of the Dutch men.[6] By 1910, the colonized people were defined as the Dutch subjects[7] and were called natives to differentiate them from the Dutch, Europeans, foreign Orientals, Moors, Chinese and other foreign Muslims, and Pagans.[8] The racial distinction was expanded to social, political, cultural, and economic divides with various degrees of accessibility depending on race, class, and gender.[9] Within this colonial state, pioneering men and women in Indonesia pursued dignity for their people and their future nation. In this section, I will discuss how the secular and Islamic nationalists, especially the founding fathers, namely Sukarno and Muhammad Hatta who became the nation's first president and vice president respectively, promoted human dignity. I also link the debates on human dignity to the local challenges of modernizing the country and pursuing the idea of sovereignty as the condition for enacting such dignity.

The Dutch colonial policies directly and indirectly contributed to the genesis of the modern Indonesian concept of human dignity. The promotion of the colony's dignity came about as a result of the implementation of the Ethical Policy during which the fundamental changes emerged in the colonial environment.[10] This Ethical Policy sought to promote the well-being of the colony by repurposing colonial policies and practices to support the political and economic hegemony of the colonials. The Ethical Policy, however, originally developed as a result of the opposition of the Dutch liberal middle class to the *cultuurstelsel* policy and its oppressive impact on the natives, as documented in a famous literary work, entitled *Max Haveelar*, written by a former colonial official, Eduard Douwes Dekker (1820–87) in 1860. The promotion of the natives' well-being also came from C. Th. Van Deventer, a lawyer, who visited Indonesia from 1880 to 1897 and who made the argument that "the Netherlands owed the Indonesians such a debt for all

---

[5] For more information on the history of Indonesia, see M. C. Ricklefs, *A History of Modern Indonesia* (London: Macmillan, 1981).
[6] Elsbeth Locher-Scholten, *Women and the Colonial State: Essays on Gender and Modernity in the Netherlands Indies 1900–1942* (Amsterdam: Amsterdam University Press, 2000), p. 38.
[7] Ibid.
[8] A. Massier, *The Voice of the Law in Transition: Indonesian Jurists and Their Languages, 1915–2000* (Leiden: Brill, 2008), p. 79.
[9] Locher-Scholten, *Women and the Colonial State*, p. 38.
[10] Ricklefs, *A History of Modern Indonesia*, p. 143.

the wealth which has been drained from their country."[11] This humanitarian concern led to the realization on the part of colonialists that colonial subjects were not only human capital required for economic exploitation and the extraction of natural resources but also were customers. As the Ethical Policy was rooted in humanitarian concern and a realignment of economic colonial advantage, it drove changes in education, irrigation, and immigration.[12] It should be noted that this concern for the natives as customers did not translate into their recognition as full human beings. Instead, the Dutch strengthened their hold over their colony by instituting the administrative structure of the *bupatis* (district head) and other local official positions that represented the colonial power when dealing with local administrative affairs. They also expanded Dutch education to commoners and counted on the disappearance of an old elite bureaucracy, power, and authority.[13] To that effect, the Ethical Policy paved the way for a new model of colonialism where economic interest intersected with a civilizing mission.

The success of the colonial civilizing mission came with the increase of the natives' education. Exposure to education beyond aristocratic families brought about a generation of intellectuals and activists who cared for the promotion of human dignity, societal well-being, and the vision of a new nation. In the beginning of 1878, chief schools (*hoodebscholen*) were built to educate sons of the upper elites, but later on they branched out to offer vocational curricula to other classes. As the sons of the *bupatis* (district's leaders) were not always interested in succeeding their parents' position, the Dutch expanded administrative office positions to a select group of individuals who achieved their standing by individual merit (*priyayi*).[14] Ricklefts notes: "In the twentieth century, the new *priyayi* were destined to play a crucial role. Those who remained in the bureaucracy joined the older *priyayi* to become the backbone of first Dutch, then Japanese, then Indonesian administrations. Those who turned their backs on government service led the anti-colonial movements and created the independent state."[15]

The making of modern indigenous bureaucracy to administer the Dutch colonial policy and practice intersected with mass education that was available from 1890s onward. At the elementary school levels, the educational system was racially divided. The First Class schools were founded for the upper class natives, whereas the Second Class schools were designed for the general population.[16] In 1914, the Dutch established a more extensive primary school (*Meer uitgebreid lager onderwijs*, or MULO) for upper class Indonesians, Chinese, and Europeans. Later in 1919, a middle school level (*Algemene Middelbare scholen*, AMS) was founded to train students for

[11] Ibid., p. 143.
[12] Ibid., pp. 143–144.
[13] Ibid., p. 124.
[14] Ibid., p. 123.
[15] Ibid.
[16] Ibid., p. 150.

university education. A number of Indonesians joined the European senior high schools (*the Hoogere burgerschool*, HBS) that prepared students to study in the Netherlands. The university educational level for the natives began only with the opening of the Technische Hoogeschool (technical college) in Bandung in 1920, a Rechtshoogeschool (law college) in Batavia in 1924, and STOVIA (the School tot Opleiding van Inlandsche Artsen, or School for the Training of Native Doctors) in 1927.[17] Although the Dutch educational system was racially divided and far from being fair to the colonial subjects, it produced able and loyal native officials who prolonged colonialism and, at the same time, inspired a few dissatisfied elites to pursue human dignity of the natives.[18]

While few native men were officially admitted to schools, women were left behind. Pioneering women, such as Raden Adjeng Kartini (1879–1905), Dewi Sartika (1884–1947), and Rahmah El-Joenesijjah (1900–69), struggled to promote women's dignity through the right to education. Although these women differed in their class, religious background, and geographical location, they exemplified efforts to value both men and women as human beings with dignity and rights. In Central Java, Raden Adjeng Kartini (1879–1905) is especially important as she struggled to free herself from her own seclusion. Not only did Kartini oppose cultural practices that were oppressive against women, but she also aspired for human equality between aristocrats and commoners and between men and women. Kartini lamented women's fate as they were "[perceived as] nothing – women were created for men, for their pleasure; they could do with them as they willed."[19] She wanted women to achieve their dignity through education. To this end, she opened a school in her own town. In West Java, Dewi Sartika (1884–1947) also promoted women's dignity through education. Sartika fought the cultural assumption that education was forbidden for women.[20] Likewise, Rahmah El-Joenesijjah (1900–69) introduced rights to education in Muslim conservative settings where women were expected only to get married and to become wives and mothers.[21] Although pioneering women differed in their background and strategies, they attempted to address the injustice directed toward women and their environment by promoting girls' education. They saw the correlation between the level of women's education and their understanding of rights. With education, women could contribute to progress in Indonesia.

---

[17] Ibid.
[18] Ibid., p. 154.
[19] For Raden Adjeng Kartini's life and thought, see *Letters for a Javanese Princess*, translated by Agnes Louise Symmers, with a foreword by Louis Coopers (Kuala Lumpur: Oxford University Press, 1976), p. 64.
[20] Yan Daryono, *Sang Perintis: R. Dewi Sartika* (Jakarta: Yayasan Awika and PT. Grafitri Budi Utarna, 1996), pp. 82, 86.
[21] Junaidatul Munawarah, "Rahmah el-Yunusiah: Pelopor Pendidikan Perempuan," in *Ulama Perempuan Indonesia* (Jakarta: Gramedia Pustaka Utama, 2002), pp. 2–6.

The promotion of human dignity found more support within youth, religious, communist, and women's movements. These movements brought about a new awareness among activists that invoked a sense of belonging to a nation. At the same time, they also bridged communication as well as brought discord among the elites who supported the colonial regime. In the early 1900s, many organizations were oriented toward the advancement of their respective group interest, ethnicity, and religious affiliation. Among these pioneering group were the Budi Utomo (Yogyakarta, 1908); the Sarekat Dagang Islamiyah (Islamic Trade Union) (Batavia, 1909), which later became the Sarikat Islam (1912); the Sarekat Ambon (Ambonese Union, 1920); the Jong Java (Youth of Java, 1918); the Pasundan (1914); and others. Religious organizations also emerged in various parts of Indonesia, but they were local initiatives, except for a few organizations such as the Muhammadiyyah (The Muhammadan Way), founded by Kyai Haji Ahmad Dahlan (1868–1923) in Yogyakarta in 1912, and the Persatuan Islam (The Islamic Unity), founded by merchants such as Haji Zamzam (1854–1952) and Haji Muhammad Yunus in Bandung in 1923. The Nahdlatul Wathan ("Awakening of the Nation"), the precursor to the Nahdhatul Ulama, was founded Abdul Wahab Hasbullah (1888–1971) in 1916. The Nahdhatul Ulama ("the Awakening of Religious Scholars") was founded by the Javanese scholar Hasyim Asyari (1871–1947) in 1926 as a reaction to more puritan trends in Indonesia, namely the Muhammadiyah and Persatuan Islam. The communist movement found supporters among Muslims as well. The Indies Social Democratic Association (ISDV) was initially for the Dutch only, but it eventually recruited members of Sarekat Islam, creating a variant of an Islamic communism.[22] Women were also actively pursuing their dignity within the colonial landscape and male-dominated spaces. Most women's groups were initially founded as a wing of a male organization, such the Putri Mardhika (1912) of the Budi Utomo; Aisyiyah of Muhammadiyyah (1914); Jong Islamieten Bond Dames Afdeeling ("Young Muslim League Women's Section," JIBDA) of the well-known of Jong Islamieten Bond; Sarekat Perempuan Islam Indonesia ("Federation of the Muslim Women of Indonesia of Sarekat Islam"); and Natdatoel Fataat (1920).[23] Other women's organizations include the Pajiwatan Wanito of Magelang (1915), the Percintaan Ibu kepada Anak Temurun ("Mother's Love for Her Offspring," 1917) of Menado, and the Sarekat Kaum Ibu Sumatra ("Association of Sumatranese Mothers," 1920) of Bukit Tinggi.[24] The emergence of youth, religious, communist, and female movements raised the indigenous people's awareness of the injustices of Dutch colonialism. While groups sometimes clashed with each other and were subjected to close

---

[22] Ricklefs, *A History of Modern Indonesia*, p. 166.
[23] Susan Blackburn, ed., *The First Indonesian Women's Congress of 1928* (Clayton, Australia: Monash University Press, 2008), pp. 1–26.
[24] Sukanti Suryochondro, *Potret Pergerakan Wanita di Indonesia [Portrait of the Women's Movement in Indonesia]* (Jakarta: Rajawali, 1984), pp. 85–86.

scrutiny from the Dutch administration, this first phase of national revival provided a foundation for the blossoming of regional identity.[25]

The later pursuit for dignity bolstered efforts for national unity among activists through congresses, active political participation at the Volksraad (People's Council),[26] students' organizations both locally and internationally, and publications. The Youth Congress held on October 28, 1928, in Batavia planted the seed for the pursuit of the nation's dignity by pledging one's loyalty to one motherland, one nation, and one language, namely Indonesia. A few months afterward, on December 28, 1928, women from many parts of Indonesia joined the chorus in uniting their efforts to promote the dignity of women. Although male and female congresses fueled optimism for the progress and dignity of the nation and its people, the natives' representation at the Volksraad remained rare. At the international level, from 1922 onward, students studying abroad were also actively mobilizing their efforts to promote Indonesian nationalism especially through a youth organization called Perhimpunan Indonesia (the Indonesian Association).[27]

Two youth leaders – namely Sukarno, the founder of Perserikatan Nasional Indonesia (PNI, the Indonesian Nationalist Association), and Mohammad Hatta, the leader of Perhimpunan Indonesia (the Indonesian Association) – are worth noting. These two figures would eventually play a critical role in the pursuit of the Indonesian independence.[28] They were also known for their contribution to the political and literary discussions on the importance of having a sovereign nation for Indonesians. In 1933, Sukarno published an article entitled "Achieving Indonesia's Independence" (*Mencapai Indonesia Merdeka*), in which he defined independence (*merdeka*) in terms of political independence.[29] He regarded national sovereignty as a "bridge" that can pave the way for achieving true societal prosperity and human dignity.

Sukarno, the future president, and Hatta, the future vice president, represented secular nationalist voices in promoting the importance of a new nation. Sukarno was particularly important to mention as he was largely credited for introducing the term *Pancasila*. This term emerged within the discourse of what the foundation of the state should be within the context of political sovereignty. These debates came about as a result of the colonial Japanese administrative effort to assist the independence of Indonesia. The colonial Japanese administration established the Committee for the

---

[25] Ricklefs, *A History of Modern Indonesia*, p. 171.
[26] The Volksraad (People's Council) was founded in 1918 and served as an advisory body with a limited legislative capacity on budget and internal legislation within the Dutch administration. Although the organization was initially set up for the colonial defense of the Indies, it attracted nationalists and activists to engage in political awakening and modernizing the country. Ibid., p. 153.
[27] Ibid., p. 174.
[28] Ibid.
[29] Tim Penerbitan Buku Pancasila, *Pancasila Bung Karno: Himpunan Pidato, Ceramah, Kursus, dan Kuliah* [Bung Karno's Pancasila: Collection of Speeches, Lectures, Courses, and Lectures] (Jakarta: Paksi Bhineka Tunggal Ika, 2005), p. 5.

Preparatory Work for Indonesian Independence (*Dokuritsu Junbi Chosa-kai* or Badan Penyelidik Usaha-Usaha Kemerdekaan Indonesia) (BPUKI) in May 28, 1945. Following its inauguration, members of BPUKI held a three-day conference to discuss the preparation needed to achieve independence. This included intense debates over the foundation of the state. Muh. Yamin gave a talk on May 29, 1945, Prof. Dr. Supomo on May 31, 1945, and Ir. Sukarno on June 1, 1945.[30] Sukarno's talk is important to mention as he was hailed as the founder of the term *Pancasila*. Sukarno elaborated on what independence meant and on what he believed should be the foundation of the new state. He reiterated the meaning of independence (*merdeka*) in terms of political independence. By declaring the nation's independence, he argued that Indonesians would strive toward a free society, alleviate the burden of colonialism from their heart, improve their health, and train the youth. Sukarno envisioned an Indonesian independence that was strong, healthy, and everlasting based on the foundation of *Pancasila*.[31] He listed five principles that constitute the foundation of the state, namely nationhood, internationalism, democracy, social justice, and the belief in One God.[32]

Infused in Sukarno's formulation of *Pancasila* as the foundation of the state was the inherent value of human dignity that the Indonesian people had long aspired to achieve. The first principle of nationhood invoked the sense of belonging for all individuals within the geography of Indonesia in which various ethnicities were valued as equal. While he emphasized the sense of belonging to a nation, he envisioned a second principle, namely the significance of internationalism where each individual cultivates a sense of universal kinship (*sentimen kekeluargaan*). To become a people with their own nation, Indonesian independence was necessary in order to establish their own personhood and humanity. Sukarno held that the innate dignity of human beings was achievable only within the framework of a nation. Sukarno also espoused his vision for human equality within the principles of democracy. He introduced democracy as the third principle of Pancasila. He argued that all individuals, regardless of ethnicity, religion, and social status, need to have their voices heard and represented in government through the house of representatives. This body would represent all groups from across Indonesia and would discuss important issues to arrive at a consensus. In this sense, democracy would ensure the fulfillment of social justice for everyone. Sukarno envisioned social justice as the fourth principle. This principle is intended to guide the process of achieving consensus among representatives and to ensure that all citizens are treated fairly. The belief in One God is the final principle that Sukarno believed should govern the state. Thus, for him, human dignity was integral to the state formation through which the rights of individuals would be ensured.

---

[30] Nugroho Notosusanto, *Proses Perumusan Pancasila Dasar Negara* [The Process of Formulating the Basic Pancasila of the State] (Jakarta: PN Balai Pustaka, 1981), p. 20.
[31] Tim Penerbitan Buku Pancasila, *Pancasila Bung Karno*, p. 7.
[32] Ibid., p. 21.

Sukarno's establishment of *Pancasila* as the foundation of the state was well-received, but the ordering of the principles was slightly changed when it was inducted in the 1945 Constitution of the Republic of Indonesia. The new order of *Pancasila* runs as follows: the belief in the One and Only God; a just and civilized humanity; the unity of Indonesia; democratic rule that is guided by the strength of wisdom resulting from deliberation and representation; and social justice for all Indonesians. This new order of *Pancasila* represented a compromise between the secular and Islamic nationalists. Deliar Noer, a historian, argues that *Pancasila* as stated in the 1945 Constitution represents the concerted effort by representatives from Muslim and secular nationalists who were members of the Committee for the Preparatory Work for Indonesia's Independence (Panitia Persiapan Kemerdekaan Indonesia) in prioritizing the unity of Indonesia in their work.[33] Initially the Committee for the Preparatory Work for Indonesian Independence appointed a Small Committee (Panitia Kecil) or the Committee of the Nine (Panitia Sembilan) with four Muslim representatives (Haji Agus Salim, Kyai Wahid Hasjim, Abikusno, and Abdoul Kahar Moezakkir), one Christian (A. A. Maramis), and four secular nasionalists (Sukarno, Mohammad Hatta, Achmad Subarjo, and Muhammad Yamin. The Committee of Nine was tasked with formulating the foundation of the state as already discussed during the conference hosted by the Committee for the Preparatory Work for Indonesian Independence. The Committee agreed on the formulation of the first principle of *Pancasila* stating "the belief in God with the obligation to carry out Islamic law for its adherents."[34] Although representatives from Muslims and Christians agreed on this formulation, Hatta informed the Muslims that Christians from Eastern Indonesia would not join the newly independent country if this formulation remained. Eventually, Muslim representatives agreed to a new formulation of the first principle of *Pancasila* stating "the belief in the Oneness of God."

The new formulation of *Pancasila* appears in the Constitution of the Republic of Indonesia following Independence and was issued on August 18, 1945. Like *Pancasila* that defines the foundational values of human dignity, such as religious virtue, just humanity, unity, democracy, and social justice, the Constitution also grants equal rights for citizens. The Constitution treats everyone equally before the law (Art. 27). It also gives right to assembly (and later this right was amended to include human rights provision (Art. 28, 28 A–J). The right to practice religion is also granted in Article 29. The rights to education (Art. 31), to participate in economic advancement (Art. 33), and to accept social welfare (Art. 33) are also included. With the recognition of rights, both *Pancasila* and the Constitution of the Republic of Indonesia advocate for human dignity within the context of a new state.

---

[33] Deliar Noer, *Partai Islam di Pentas Nasional* [Islamic Party on the National Stage] (Jakarta: Grafiti Press, 1987), pp. 36–40.
[34] Noer, *Partai Islam di Pentas Nasional*, p. 36.

Although the newly independent state was eager to promote human dignity, it faced new challenges. The Dutch made a series of attempts to recolonize the country between 1945 and 1949, with the support of Allied armies from Britain and Australia. Many revolutionary and local *laskar*s (armies) were involved in defending the dignity of the nation and its people from further foreign encroachment. Wars broke out in many parts of Indonesia as the Dutch attempted to reconquer Indonesia by planning to impose a federal state with a Dutch president. During one of the battles in Surabaya in October–November 1945, Muslim leaders of Nahdatul Ulama and Masyumi called for *jihad* (in the sense of armed struggle) to defend the motherland.[35] The call for armed struggle demonstrates the seriousness in upholding the dignity of the state as well as the fight against colonialism. For Indonesians, the dignity of humans depends on the dignity of the state. The disappearance of the newly founded state would lead to the absence of freedom and the ability to exercise the rights to human equality before law, education, livelihood, and assembly. For this reason, human dignity is discursively and nondiscursively linked to the nation's progress and development.

3 HUMAN DIGNITY AND *PANCASILA* INTERPRETATIONS IN DEVELOPMENT SETTINGS

The discourses of human dignity in the post-Independence period revolve around questions of how to improve the level of prosperity of the nation and how to develop wholesome human beings. These questions were addressed through various models of governance, from a parliamentary system (1950–7), a guided democracy (1957–65), and a *Pancasila* democracy (1965–98) to democratic reformation (1998–onward). At the heart of these changing political landscapes were efforts to keep up with values and practices derived from *Pancasila* and the Constitution of the Republic of Indonesia and to guarantee the rights of citizens. While both the Old and New Orders aspired to fulfill the promise of Independence in improving the human condition of Indonesian people, their authoritarian practices caused more harm than good. The competing interest between improving the democratization of politics, the need for economic development, and advancing human condition is the backdrop of the debates on the dignity of individuals and the nation. In this section, I will show how the authoritarian New Order's regime of politicizing *Pancasila* leads into a rich debate of how human dignity is appropriated within the Indonesian settings.

The New Order regime came to power after Major General Suharto, a commander of Kostrad (Komando Strategis Angkatan Darat, the Armies' Strategic Reserve), defeated a failed military coup on September 30, 1965.[36] The coup killed

---

[35] Ricklefs, *A History of Modern Indonesia*, p. 207.
[36] Stefan Eklöf, *Power and Political Culture in Suharto's Indonesia: The Indonesian Democratic Party (PDI) and Decline of the New Order (1986–98)* (Copenhagen: NIAS Press, 2004), p. 44.

six generals in an attempt to replace them with those who would support Sukarno and the Communist Party of Indonesia (Partai Komunis Indonesia, PKI). Eklöf describes the attempted coup as "a pretext to eliminate the PKI." To respond to the attemped coup, Suharto and his army "initiated the concerted campaign against the party, in which the PKI was portrayed as treacherous and morally corrupt."[37] Certainly Suharto, as Noer describes, had by 1966 replaced the Old Order, a period of presidency led by Sukarno. After the military coup, Suharto became the new president with an order from the former president Sukarno on March 11, 1966, known as the *Supersemar*.

President Suharto stayed in power for the next thirty years and retained his presidency through a series of highly controlled democratic elections from 1971 to 1997. His presidency implemented the developmental policy called the Broad Guidelines of State Policy (*Garis-Garis Besar Haluan Negara*, GBHN), restructured political parties with *Pancasila* as the state ideology, and simultaneously transformed the state bureaucratization of the private and public spheres. Honna shows how Suharto's core ideological basis of the New Order was based on the military "with a rationale that identified political stability as the precondition for development."[38] Suharto's military approach along with the installment of *Pancasila* as the state ideology aimed at safeguarding national development.

The overall goal of the national development, as stated in the 1988 Broad Guidelines of State Policy (Garis-Garis Besar Haluan Negara, GBHN), was to achieve a certain degree of prosperity for individuals and society.[39] Ancok notes that GBHN envisions a society that is modern, peaceful, physically and spiritually prosperous, and harmonious in regard to human relations with God, other humans, nature, and society. Only within these interdependent qualities is human dignity achievable. To this end, Nimpoeno argues that the Indonesian development has to be conducive to cultural and social changes.[40] Such changes require "social flexibility" and "cultural permeability" in order for both individuals and society to be able to address challenges and to find new opportunities with the goal of improving

---

[37] Ibid.
[38] Jun Honna, "Military Ideology in Response to Democratic Pressure during the Late Suharto Era: Political and Institutional Contexts," in *Violence and the State in Suharto's Indonesia*, edited by Benedict Richard O'Gorman Anderson (Ithaca, NY: Cornell Southeast Asia Program, 2002), p. 55.
[39] Djamaludin Ancok, "Kualitas Masyarakat dan Pembangunan: Mencari Tolok Ukur Dampak Pembangunan terhadap Kualitas Masyarakat [Community Quality and Development: Finding Benchmarks of Development Impacts on Community Quality]," in *Membangun Martabat Manusia: Peranan Ilmu-Ilmu Sosial dalam Pembangunan* [Building Human Dignity: The Role of Social Sciences in Development], edited by Sofian Effendi, Sjafri Sairin, and M. Alwi Dahlan (Jogjakarta: Gadjah Mada University Press and HIPIIS cabang Yogyakarta, 1992), p. 40.
[40] John S. Nimpoeno, "Kualitas Manusia dan Masyarakat menurut Disiplin Ilmu Psikologi Sosial dengan Penekanan Pada Alur Pikir Metodologs [Quality of Humans and Society According to the Discipline of Social Psychology with Emphasis on Methodologists' Line of Mind]," in *Membangun Martabat Manusia: Peranan Ilmu-Ilmu Sosial dalam Pembangunan* [Building Human Dignity: The Role of Social Sciences in Development], edited by SofianEffendi, Sjafri Sairin, and M. Alwi Dahlan (Jogjakarta: Gadjah Mada University Press and HIPIIS cabang Yogyakarta, 1992), p. 54.

the dignity of society and the nation. The New Order relied on the utility of *Pancasila* as the foundation for "social flexibility" and "cultural permeability."

Pancasila as an ethical framework provides the foundational values that would form the basis of the dignity of humans, societies, and the nation. As Suharto indicates, there is a need for *Pancasila* to be embodied and reinterpreted so that it becomes understandable and applicable to daily behaviors.[41] He considers the embodiment of *Pancasila* in everyday life as the key for achieving the dignity (*martabat*) of individuals, society, and the nation. In achieving this end, Suharto and his New Order government implemented policies that reinforced *Pancasila* as the foundation of the state. At first, the New Order introduced a Guideline for Instilling and Implementing *Pancasila* into Practice (*Pedoman Penghayatan dan Pengamalan Pancasila*, P4). This Guideline was enacted by the People's Consultative Assembly (Majlis Permusyawaratan Rakyat, MPR) in 1978 with regulation number II/MPR/1978.[42] Five years later, in 1985, the People's Consultative Assembly declared Pancasila as the sole basis (*azas tunggal*) of the state, "superseding all loyalties to religion, region, ethnicity or any other political program."[43]

In an attempt to strengthen *Pancasila* as the social and political ideology of the state, Harjana notes that Suharto strategically linked the embodiment of *Pancasila* to the national development programs and instituted

> a National Agency for Educating, Promoting, Implementing, Guiding, Internalizing, and Practicing Pancasila (BP7/Badan Pembinaan, Pendidikan, Pelaksanaan, Pedoman Penghayatan dan Pengamalan Pancasila). In addition, he made Pancasila a compulsory subject in all primary, secondary, and tertiary levels of formal education. Moreover, a Pancasila certificate was needed for any job attainment and promotion. Pancasila was, then, the core element of Suharto's developmentalism – that is development as an ideology – and became the most effective tool for maintaining power.[44]

Suharto used *Pancasila* to unite Indonesian citizens. This political move was intended to dissipate the tension left behind by the failed coup of the Communist Party of Indonesia (Partai Komunis Indonesia, PKI) on September 30, 1965. Suharto characterized his government as the opposite of the Communist Party of Indonesia

---

[41] Suharto, "Pancasila sebagai Sistem Filsafat dan Masyarakat Perguruan Tinggi [: [Pancasila as a Philosophical System and Higher Education Society]," in *Pemikiran Para Pemimpin Negara tentang Pancasila* [Thoughts of State Leaders on Pancasila], edited by Ika Dewi Ana, Singgih Hawibowo, and Agus Wahyudi (Yogyakarta: Universitas Gajah Mada, 2006), p. 76.

[42] Michael Wood, "Has Pancasila Ever Been Relevant: An Historical Inquiry," in *Pancasila's Contemporary Appeal: Re-legitimizing Indonesia's Founding Ethos*, edited by Thomas J. Connors, Mason C. Hoadley, Frank Dhont, and Kevin Ko (Yogyakarta: Yale Indonesia Forum and Indonesian History Studies Center, 2010), pp. 124–125.

[43] Wood, "Has Pancasila Ever Been Relevant," p. 125.

[44] André A. Hardjana, "Pancasila's Contemporary Appeal and Mass Communications," in *Pancasila's Contemporary Appeal: Re-legitimizing Indonesia's Founding Ethos*, edited by Thomas J. Connors, Mason C. Hoadley, Frank Dhont, and Kevin Ko (Yogyakarta: Yale Indonesia Forum and Indonesian History Studies Center, 2010), p. 199.

(Partai Komunis Indonesia, PKI), whom he considered to be antithetical to *Pancasila*. He created a paradigm of how his government would act as the defender of *Pancasila* and how it would perceive its enemies, especially the extreme left (the PKI) and religious rights (Islamist groups, as will be discussed in next section).

Suharto's policy on the implementation of *Pancasila* as an ideology provides the context for how human dignity is discussed during national development. This policy led to the political life of *Pancasila* as a site for contestation. As the New Order used *Pancasila* as a tool to maintain the political status quo for more than thirty years, from 1966 to 1998, this provided the grounds for a conversation about human dignity. On the one hand, the meaning of *Pancasila* as the foundation of the state is contextualized in an attempt to achieve developmental goals; on the other hand, the politics of *Pancasila* authorized the state to use a security approach to deal with social and religious organizations that have had Islam as the basis for their activities. At this juncture, between *Pancasila* as the foundation of the state and as a political force, is where the debate of human dignity during the New Order is located. In what follows, I will discuss the relevance of each *Pancasila* principle in relation to human dignity.

The first principle, the belief in One God (*Ketuhanan Yang Maha Esa*), plays a significant role in shaping human dignity as it serves as the foundation for individual morality and nation building. It recognizes an individual's right to practice his or her religion as well as its importance in the social, religious, and even political spheres. Drawn from diverse religions in Indonesia, the principle of "the belief in One God" upholds human beings' equality before God. It also upholds their equality with other human fellows, given that all humans are created by God. Embedded in this equality is the dignity of humans as God's creature, individuals, and members of society. In other words, dignity as a process of becoming is exercised within the contexts of human relationship where the rights of individuals are granted and respected on the basis of the inviolability of human beings.[45] As humans have both a horizontal relationship to other human beings and a vertical relationship to God, they seek to create a civilized society that guarantees their dignity within the contexts of a nation and its relation to other nations.

The dignity of individual provides a site from which the second principle of "a just and civilized humanity" (*Kemanusiaan yang adil and beradab*) takes root. The second principle of *Pancasila* reflects the historical and contemporary pursuit of human equality. Indonesia achieved independence in 1945 but was formally recognized by the United Nations in 1949. As mentioned earlier, the period between 1945 and 1949 was a period of immense difficulty for the new nation, as the Dutch, with the help of Allied forces, attempted to recapture Indonesian territory. While Indonesian leaders and citizens were participating in revolutionary struggle, Indonesian delegates and student activists, especially those living overseas, engaged

---

[45] Hasan, *Harkat and Martabat Manusia Indonesia dalam Negara Pancasila*, pp. 13–15.

with what Latif calls a "diplomatic revolutionary."[46] These humanitarian efforts gained momentum as Indonesia received its recognition for its Independence, especially from the Middle Eastern and South Asian countries as well as from the United Nations. The recognition for Indonesian Independence shows how the dignity of the people and the nation was a matter of a shared humanity. By this recognition of Independence, Indonesians felt that their humanity had been recognized: as human beings with inviolable rights, they felt connected to other people as citizens of the world. Such rights include the right to self-determination, to treat each other with fairness, and to receive equal treatment before the law. The second principle of *Pancasila*, therefore, demands the recognition of Indonesians as inviolable human beings and to be recognized as part of an inclusive humanity.[47]

The second principle morphs into the third principle, "the unity of Indonesia." The virtue of unity tells a story of how all members of Indonesian society, from kings, leaders, and activists to students, supported the unity of Indonesia through their blood and sweat. This shared historical past allowed Indonesians to develop a strong sense of nationalism. The sense of unity among the youth was long sown during the 1928 Youth Pledge, which declared loyalty to one homeland, one nation, and one language, namely Bahasa Indonesia. Although Independence came almost twenty years later, it had its roots among Islamic and secular supporters who viewed "Indonesia" as a site for how unity was to be exercised. Within this context, the unity of Indonesia is a prerequisite for ways in which Indonesians can achieve dignity. The role of the state is important in achieving human dignity as the state itself is a historical manifestation of the efforts toward achieving the dignified status of an independent nation. Hassan notes that the state has obligations to protect the dignity of its citizens and the nation, to increase its welfare, to promote peace, to prevent conflicts, to uphold justice, and to promote diversity (*bhineka tunngal ika*, unity in diversity).[48]

One of the mechanisms necessary for maintaining the unity of Indonesia is good governance. The fourth principle of *Pancasila*, "democratic rule that is guided by the strength of wisdom resulting from deliberation/representation," speaks to that job precisely. The democratic system warrants the state's ability to govern its citizens and to uphold their equality in the private and public spheres. Hasan interprets the fourth principle of *Pancasila* as showing how: 1) the Indonesian state acknowledges people's sovereignty – which is delegated through representatives in the People's Consultative Assembly (Majlis Permusyawaratan Rakyat, MPR) that deliberates based on a voting system; and (2) the Indonesian state was founded as a state law

---

[46] Yudi Latif, *Mata Air Keteladanan: Pancasila dalam Perbuatan* [The Spring of Example: Pancasila in Action] (Bandung: Mizan, 2012), p. 141.
[47] Hasan, *Harkat and Martabat Manusia Indonesia dalam Negara Pancasila*, p. 20.
[48] Ibid., p. 21.

(*negara hukum*) on the basis of the 1945 Constitution.[49] Hatta, one of the founding fathers of Indonesia, explains that the concept of people's sovereignty means that the people of Indonesia have the rights to determine how they want to govern and to be governed.[50] Once the House of Representatives reaches a decision, the government receives the mandate to govern. For this reason, the people's sovereignty creates a pathway for governing the Indonesian state according to their power, yet at the same time, it entrusts the government to enact their policies.

As the government is trusted with governing the people, it becomes the responsibility of the state to pursue and implement justice for all citizens. The fifth principle of *Pancasila* encourages the fulfillment of social justice in both private and public spheres. Hasan indicates that the fifth principle invokes the state's responsibilities in providing economic justice, managing natural resources for public good, providing a just life physically and spiritually, offering affordable education, and developing human capacity comprehensively.[51] Such responsibilities stem from a historical narrative of colonialism in which various global forces led to injustices being committed against the colonized peoples. Latif argues that the struggle for economic justice and the dream of equality (*kesederajatan*) run parallel with political democracy.[52] If the fourth principle of *Pancasila* lays the groundwork for political participation in democratic settings, the fifth principle pursues a just society and social justice for everyone.

Pancasila as the foundation of the state provides a blueprint for achieving the dignity of human beings and nations. Suharto's New Order was successful in introducing the concept of human dignity at a new level in Indonesia. The dignity of human beings is perceived to be constitutive of the dignity of the nation within the contexts of national development. Unfortunately, in the process of implementing this policy, the New Order pressed for the homogenization of ethnicity, religious life, and political expression. The politicization of *Pancasila* played a key role in homogenizing ethnicity by socializing the concept of diversity (*bhineka tunggal ika*, unity in diversity). On the surface, such a concept promoted diversity, but at the practical level it failed to cultivate an appreciation for diverse cultures due to its emphasis on Java ethnicity in state bureaucracy and cultural programs. *Pancasila* as the sole ideological foundation of the state (*azas tunggal*) also created distrust for various expressions of Islam, especially for political and social organizations that used Islam as the foundation of their organizations, all of which caused contestations among Muslims about the relationship between Islam and *Pancasila*.

---

[49] Hasan, *Harkat and Martabat Manusia Indonesia dalam Negara Pancasila*, p. 20.
[50] S. Suryoutoro, *Sukarno, Hatta, Suharto Menggembleng Bangsanya* [Sukarno, Hatta, Suharto Galvanized the Nation] (Surabaya: Bina Ilmu, 1980), 31.
[51] Hasan, *Harkat and Martabat Manusia Indonesia dalam Negara Pancasila*, p. 22.
[52] Yudi Latif, *Negara Paripurna: Historisitas, Rasionalitas, and Actualitas* [The Plenary State: Historicity, Rationality, and Actuality] (Jakarta: Gramedia, 2011), p. 527.

4 HUMAN DIGNITY AS THE FULFILLMENT OF RIGHTS: AN OVERLAPPING CONSENSUS IN *PANCASILA* AND ISLAM AS AN ETHICAL FRAMEWORK

The contestation between *Pancasila* and Islam not only leads to the political debate on whether or not *Pancasila* is compatible with political expressions of Islam, but it also drives the discursive narrative of how to incorporate Islam into the public sphere. Efforts to incorporate Islam into the social and political fabric go hand in hand with a particular understanding of the role of Islam in life. Islam, for its followers, confers significant meaning onto political, social, and ritualistic realms. Politically oriented Islam (Islamism) emphasizes the role of Islam as a political force and perceives it as the only legitimate foundation of the state. The political tendency among this group varies from articulating Islam as a political ideology that demands Islam be implemented as a legal system – the pursuit of an Islamic state – to the refusal of the use of *Pancasila* as the foundation of social or political organizations. Moderate Islam, on the other hand, perceives the role of Islam as being part of the social fabric of Indonesia and argues that, hence, Islamic values should permeate every aspect of life without necessarily being political. Ritualistic Islam perceives both private and public spheres as units for which Islamic values are to be exercised. This is commonly indicated by the increased use of Arabic names, dress, and rituals in public. Given the variations among Muslims in expressing the importance of Islam, the New Order offered a reconciliatory model, called cultural Islam, *Pancasila* Islam, or Islamic formalism. This model is inclusive of both moderate and ritualistic Islam and is suspicious of political Islam. While Muslims have had divergent opinions on the relationship between Islam and *Pancasila*, they fundamentally agree on the importance of achieving the dignity of humans and the nation. To this end, *Pancasila* and Islam play a role as an ethical paradigm in shaping human dignity as the fulfillment of rights.

Pancasila and Islam as ethical frameworks mutually reinforce the individual's dignity in practicing religious rights and duties. The first principle of *Pancasila*, "the belief in the oneness of God," undergirds citizens' right to have religious freedom and to practice the religious life according to individual belief. The belief in the Oneness of God (*tawḥīd*) is the foundational teaching of Islam. It establishes a link between faith and human agency. By simply declaring that there is no deity but God, Muslims affirm their innate disposition with tendency to know God (*fiṭrah*). This innate tendency materializes through the voluntary choice of testifying one's belief in God (*imān*), as exemplified by the Prophet Muhammad, who became the model for spiritual excellence (*iḥsān*).[53] Since becoming a Muslim is a voluntary choice, she or he has the freedom to submit or not to submit to God. Sachiko Murata and William Chittick define freedom as the freedom to submit to God and the freedom

---

[53] Sachiko Murata and William C. Chittick, *The Vision of Islam* (New York: Paragon House, 1994), p. 9.

from anything that hinders one's ability to worship God.⁵⁴ Such freedom is granted within the *Pancasila* state.

Even when the New Order implemented *Pancasila* as the ideology of the state, Islam as a ritual performance flourished. *Pancasila* Islam paved the way for how Islam was embodied at the individual, social, and political levels. Individually, Muslims' rights to religious expression and freedom became front and center as the government built so-called *Pancasila* mosques in many districts throughout Indonesia. The bureaucratization of Islam permeated religious life, especially in mosques, families, schools, and other social institutions. It was also expanded to the political sphere, where *Pancasila* functioned as the ideology of the state. It is within the political sphere that the belief in God is perceived to be in conflict with *Pancasila*. For some radical Islamist groups, such as Jama'ah Tabligh (1974), Darul Arqom (1980s), Hizb al-Tahrir (1978), and the remnants of Darul Islam (1948), the dignity of Muslims should include the ability to exercise Islam in political matters. The Islamic political argument for the unity of state and religion is grounded in the Prophetic tradition where the Prophet Muhammad established the state of Medina based on Islamic teachings. Within the Indonesian state, as previously mentioned, the founding fathers of the Indonesian nation drafted an agreement on *Pancasila* as the foundation of the state and added the phrase "with the obligation to carry out the Islamic law for its adherents" to the first principle thereof.⁵⁵ Despite the fact that this phrase was dropped from the official version of the 1945 Constitution, politically oriented Muslims still desire to implement Islamic law (*sharī'a*) at the political level. This contestation will continue to shape the relationship between Islam and *Pancasila* for politically oriented individuals and groups.

At the heart of the belief in One God in Islam as well as in *Pancasila* is respect for individuals regardless of religious, social, ethnic, and sexual differences. Islam frames such difference as natural and desirable. Diversity in humans is expected and purposeful. The Quranic discourse on the diversity of humans is closely linked to the story of how human beings come into being. While the story of the male father, Adam, dominates the discourse of humanity in Islam, the Quran also offers the story of creation of human beings out of "a single self" (*nafs wāḥidah*).⁵⁶ Not only do humans come from a common origin, but they are also made out of biological materials, such as dust (soil, [22:5]) and tin (clay [6:2]). For feminists, the common ontological and biological origin of men and women points to the

---

[54] Ibid., p. 115.
[55] Ibid., p. 31.
[56] "O mankind, fear your Lord, who created you from one soul and created from it its mate and dispersed from both of them many men and women. And fear Allah, through whom you ask one another, and the wombs. Indeed, Allah is ever, over you, an Observer" (Quran, 4:1). See https://quran.com/4/1 (accessed January 30, 2020).

equality of humans.⁵⁷ This equality is further cemented with the equality of dignity that human beings possess as inviolable beings.⁵⁸ Human beings as moral agents position themselves in the honorable status as they carry the mission as God's representative on earth with the responsibility of care toward fellow human beings and the universe.

The Islamic teaching of an inclusive humanity intersects with the second principle of *Pancasila*, "a just and civilized humanity" (*Kemanusiaan yang adil and beradab*). Humanity consists of people with various political, sexual, social, religious, and cultural orientations. In order to protect all interests that humans share, Islam emphasizes the merit of moderation. The term moderation or *al-wasaṭ* carries the meaning of being selected (*khiyār*) to a central position, being moderate in performing religion, and being committed to justice.⁵⁹ As the ethics of moderation is tied into the commitment for justice and the eradication of injustice, it functions to protect the dignity of human beings from abuses, violence, and oppression. Such protection is important given that violence in the private and public spheres could rob a person's dignity and is corrosive to humanity in general. As the challenges to the dignity of humanity are rooted in injustice, both *Pancasila* and Islam are clearly invested in the protection of the inviolability of human beings and find common ground in nurturing a just humanity.

The efforts to strike a balance between protecting human dignity and accepting diversity are well-founded in the third principle of Pancasila. The principle of "unity of Indonesia" (*Persatuan Indonesia*) provides the foundation for working together (*gotong royong*) and tolerance. Islam as a religion teaches how its adherents may work together and develop tolerance as the necessary condition for nurturing the dignity of human beings and the nation. Ali shows that Indonesia as a *Pancasila* state does not separate religion and the state, but it facilitates the growth of religious morality and the development of religious institutions and prevents any social and political situations that are contradictory to religious values or are discriminatory toward religious people.⁶⁰ In this spirit, it is important to embrace religious principles that nurture the unity of Indonesia, such as *tasāmuḥ* (tolerance), *ta'addudiyah*

---

57 For further reading, see Riffat Hassan's "Feminism and Islam" in Arvind Sharma and Katherine K. Young (eds.), *Feminism and World Religions* (Albany: State University of New York Press, 1999), pp. 248–278; and Hassan, "The Issue of Woman-Man Equality in the Islamic Tradition," in Kristen E. Kvam, Linda S. Schearing, and Valarie H. Ziegler (eds.), *Eve and Adam: Jewish, Christian and Muslim Readings on Genesis and Gender* (Bloomington: Indiana University Press, 1999), pp. 464–476. See also Amina Wadud-Muhsin's writings in *Qur'ān and Women* (Kuala Lumpur: Fajar Bakti Sdn, 1992); and Asma Barlas, *"Believing Women" in Islam* (Austin: University of Texas Press, 2002).
58 "And we have certainly honored the children of Adam and carried them on the land and sea and provided for them of the good things and preferred them over much of what We have created, with [definite] preference" (Quran, 4:1). See https://quran.com/4/1 (accessed January 30, 2020).
59 'Alī b. Muḥammad b. Ḥabīb al-Māwardī al-Baṣrī, *Al-Nukat wa al-'Uyūn: Tafsīr al-Māwardī*, vol. 1 (Beirut: Dār al-Kutub al-'Ilmiyyah, n.d.), pp. 198–199.
60 As'ad Said Ali, *Negara Pancasila: Jalan Kemashlahatan Berbangsa* [Pancasila State: The Way of the Nation's Prosperity] (Jakarta: LP3S, 2009), pp. 146–152.

(plurality), *tawassuṭ* (moderation), and *tawāzun* (balance). The concept of tolerance provides the basis for which Muslims and adherents of other religions carry out their duties and their traditions without fear of discrimination. The cultivation of a respectful and tolerant attitude toward others is important in cultivating respect for human dignity. Similarly, an appreciation for the diversity of religious and cultural expressions leads to peaceful coexistence among citizens. As for the virtues of moderation and balance, both provide the framework through which the dignity of human beings is linked to the overall well-being of the country. In this sense, any challenge to the unity of the country is a threat to the dignity of the nation and its people.

Islam as a religion is neither a challenge to *Pancasila* nor a threat to democracy. The organization Indonesian NGOs for Democracy notes in their report that the real challenge faced by Indonesians is the New Order authoritarian regime. This government heavily relied on the "security approach" to 1) facilitate their economic and political interest of their own patronage network in the military, bureaucracy, and business; 2) suppress opposition, the right to organize, and the freedom of the press; and 3) abuse the democratic system and process to support the status quo.[61] This suppression of citizens led to the violation of human dignity due to arrests, imprisonment, and even death –

> even such as the January 15 movements of 1974, the 1978 students' movements, the August 5 Action of 1989, students convicted in the Yogyakarta study group subversion case in the late 1980s, the mysterious killings in 1983, the Tanjung Priuk Incident in 1984, the Lampung Affair in 1989, and the Dili Massacre on 1991.[62]

While few Muslims were involved in many of these incidences, they were not the only responsible parties. The neoliberal economy in the developmental era opened the floodgates for the privatization of the economy, greatly enriching the government's cronies. Additionally, the military regime maintained the status quo and supported it by hijacking the democratic process. The neoliberal economy, the military regimes, and the lack of democracy cemented the radical Islamist grievances against the state. In the process, they sacralized their violent reaction in the name of Islam.

This association of Islam with violence creates a discursive narrative of Islam as lacking commitment to human dignity. The image of Islam as a violent religion comes from the assumptions that the religion encourages violent behavior and that Muslims are violent people. Such assumptions are drawn from the actions of extremists who engage in terrorism in the name of Islam. This reputation of Islam as a violent religion influences how Islam is perceived in the private and the public

---

[61] Indonesian NGOs for Democracy, *The Other Portrait of Indonesia: The Struggle for Democracy and Human Dignity: A Country Report* (Jakarta: Indonesian NGOs for Democracy, 1995), pp. 5–8.
[62] Ibid., p. 5.

spheres. Such discourse rests on the differentiation between the value of violence committed in the name of religion and the state. Cavanagh argues:

> The argument that religion causes violence sanctions a dichotomy between, on the one hand, non-Western, especially Muslim, forms of culture, which – having not yet learned to privatize matters of faith – are absolutist, divisive, and irrational, and Western culture, on the other, which is modest in its claims to truth, unitive, and rational. This dichotomy, this clash-of-civilizations world view, in turn can be used to legitimate the use of violence against those with whom it is impossible to reason on our own terms. In short, their violence is fanatical and uncontrolled; our violence is controlled, reasonable, and often regrettably necessary to contain their violence.[63]

Islam, in Western eyes, falls into this category because of the Islamist insistence on the unity of faith (*dīn*) and state (*dawlah*), the pursuit of an Islamic state, and the installment of *shari'a* (Islamic law) through violent means. With this in mind, violent acts of terror by Muslims came to be perceived as resulting from the inherently violent teachings of the religion. Ironically, the discursive narrative of violence committed by modern states is justified in the name of world security and often receives internal and international supports.

It is true that extremist Muslims find meaning in the sacralization of their violence, but their choices are only meaningful to themselves as the bearers of such action. The claim of being "Islamic" as a motive for engaging in violence comes from a personal justification. The intention, the action, and the motive of violence solely belong to the makers who make violent choices. Ahmed argued:

> As long as the Muslim actor is making his act of violence meaningful to himself in terms of Islam – in terms of Pre-Text, Text, or Con-Text of Revelation – then it is appropriate and meaningful to speak of that act of violence as Islamic violence. The point of the designation is not that Islam causes this violence; rather it is that the violence is made meaningful by the actor in terms of Islam – just as the prodigious violence undertaken by soldiers of democratic nation-states is made meaningful for them and by them in terms of the nation-state, and may, therefore, meaningfully be called "democratic violence" or "national violence" (or may meaningfully be designated in terms of the particular nation-state as "American violence" or "Israeli violence").[64]

In this sense, the assumed violence by Muslims needs to be put into wider contexts where the majority of Muslim countries have: 1) restructured their economic orientation by adopting a neoliberal model – one that protected the rich and, in the process, reduced or even ended social assistance to the poor; and 2) used

---

[63] William T. Cavanaugh, *The Myth of Religious Violence* (New York: Oxford University Press, 2009), pp. 17–18.
[64] Ahmed Shahab, *What Is Islam? The Importance of being Islamic* (Princeton, NJ: Princeton University Press, 2017), p. 452.

a military approach to sustain it. Indonesia during the New Order authoritarian regime did not escape this fate.

Research by Indonesian NGOs for Democracy also shows that the New Order "regime has aggressively promoted the ideology of Pancasila, the guiding principles of state ideology along with the term such Demokrasi Pancasila (Pancasila democracy), Persatuan and Kesatuan (unity and diversity), and kekeluargaan (the state based upon family principles)" to consolidate and advance the interests of the state's elite programs by implementing a "strategy which has led to the widespread abuses of human rights and the suppression of democracy."[65] As the state plays an important role in either advancing or hindering the dignity of the nation and its people, it goes without saying that the government ought to be responsible and accountable for the fulfillment of human rights.

Despite the fact that the New Order's legacy was tainted with corruption, cronyism, and authoritarianism, the state policies on developmentalism were directed toward the improvement of the totality of individuals. The government achieved some measures of poverty reduction, improved distribution and access to education through elementary schools (SD Inpress), and enacted economic policies that were oriented toward the common people (*ekonomi kerakyatan*). With the emergence of the middle and educated classes during the thirty years of Suharto's reign, the degree of the quality of life improved in comparison to when the New Order started in 1967.

The emergence of intellectuals especially played a key role in the debates on the compatibility between *Pancasila* and Islam within democracy. The government did well in translating *Pancasila* into practical guidance. However, the policy of making *Pancasila* the sole ideology of the state made clear to Muslims where the New Order's perception of *Pancasila* stood in relation to Islam. *Pancasila* was put above religion, and any use of religion as the foundation of social and political organizations was framed as anti-*Pancasila*. The duality between *Pancasila* and non-*Pancasila* brought the contentious relationship between Islam and the state to the fore. Scholars like Nurcholish Madjid (2005) and Abdurrahman Wahid (2005) agree that Islam in Indonesia coexists with *Pancasila*. Madjid proposes to treat Islam within the contexts of the *Pancasila* state as an ethical framework. He argues that politics is not an integral part of Islam[66] and urges Muslims to separate religion from politics. The state deals with worldly affairs, whereas religion pertains to spiritual and private matters. Islam as ethics undergirds both state affairs and individual life. In the same vein, Wahid, the former president of Indonesia and a well-known public intellectual, argues that a state with an ideology such as *Pancasila* falls into the category of *dar al-sulḥ* (the territory of peace) as the government facilitates the application of *sharīʿa*, understood in terms of Islamic jurisprudence and social

---

[65] Indonesian NGOs for Democracy, The Other Portrait of Indonesia, pp. 5–6.
[66] Dedy Djamaludin Malik and Idi Subandy Ibrahim, *Zaman Baru Islam Indonesia: Pemikiran dan Aksi Politics* [The New Age of Indonesian Islam: Political Thought and Action] (Bandung: Zaman Wacana Mulia, 1998), 168–169.

ethics.⁶⁷ For this reason, Muslims ought to obey the government and live out an Islamic life to their fullest. Thus, both Wahid and Madjid value Islam within the *Pancasila* state as a framework for ethical living.

By positioning Islam as an ethics, it offers values that are compatible with the pursuit of human dignity within a democratic context in accordance with the fourth principle of *Pancasila* (i.e. democratic rule that is guided by the strength of wisdom resulting from deliberation/representation). The invocation of Islamic values that support democracy goes hand in hand with the need for good governance. Azra, a scholar of Islam, argues for a new construction of "democratic, credible governance to restore the faith of Muslims in democracy" and to

> reconcile the "Islamicness" of many Muslims with supposed unity between din [religion] and dawlah [state] through a kind of "substantification" of politics with the universal values of Islam in contemporary politics. "Substantification" of politics simply means the adoption of universal values of Islam, such as al-musawa (equality), al-'adalah (justice), shura (deliberation), tasamuh (tolerance of plurality) as well as Islamic ethics – that had been emphasized time and again by Muslim political thinkers – in contemporary political concepts, systems, and practices.⁶⁸

By looking at the ethical values of equality, justice, deliberation, and tolerance toward diversity, Islam supports the most basic requirement that would allow human dignity to manifest within the state context. The ethics of equality among human beings undergirds the ontological view of human beings as ends in themselves. Such equality manifests in the just treatment of each other and equal access to the basic needs that are required to maintain their dignity. Within the Indonesian context, *Pancasila* democracy guarantees the implementation of Islam as an ethical system in the private and public spheres.

Although a democratic model of governance promises dignity to the nation and its people, giving social justice to all citizens remains an elusive challenge. The fulfillment of social justice is an inherent goal of the state as it is part of *Pancasila*. The fifth principle promises "social justice for all people of Indonesia." This principle of social justice intersects with the Islamic values of profit-sharing, alms-giving, charity, endowment, and other forms of social welfare that contribute to the public good. The fulfillment of social justice heavily relies on economic prosperity due to people's need for material fulfillment. Human dignity in the context of justice as fairness correlates to the basic rights for livelihood, workforce, education, and healthcare. It is in this process of fulfilling one's livelihood that violations of human dignity occur. Fakih, Indrianto, and Presetyo argue that the capitalist emphasis on global trade and the market caused the New Order to implement state-led development by maintaining the status quo through the depoliticization of the masses, using

---

⁶⁷ Ibid., p. 170.
⁶⁸ Azyumardi Azra, *Indonesia, Islam, and Democracy: Dynamics in a Global Context* (Jakarta: Solstice Publishing, 2006), p. 26.

the military to support developmental programs, and involving international institutions that promoted free market ideology and policies such as the World Bank, the International Monetary Fund, and the World Trade Organization.[69] This neoliberal economic model advantaged the rich and oppressed the poor. The poor, the majority of whom are women, face the end of social assistance; higher prices for gas, electricity, and water; lack of employment; and oftentimes eviction. These compound factors have led to an absence of social justice. Even now, the pursuit of human dignity remains a work in progress.

As both *Pancasila* and Islam as ethics play a role in formulating the epistemological foundation of human dignity, both mutually reinforce the status of humans as equal before God and the law. *Pancasila* as the state's foundation undergirds state affairs, whereas Islam provides a framework of how to carry oneself in the private and public spheres. While both *Pancasila* and Islam provide the foundations and motives for the pursuit of human dignity, its fulfillment in terms of rights belongs to the affairs of the state. The state conceives and enacts what rights, duties, and responsibility citizens have. The Indonesian state has coined the dignity of the human being and the nation in the 1945 Constitution. This Constitution is the foundation of the state, which all citizens must consult in order to arrive at the balanced means by which the government may attain its goal of ensuring that the nation and its people are respected.

5 CONCLUSION

The realization of human dignity is tied into the story of Indonesia during its various stages of development as a nation. The Indonesian state gained sovereignty in 1945 and eventually become a secular country, although one that is religiously oriented. The first principle of *Pancasila* recognizes the right to religious belief and the right to enact such beliefs within the private and public spheres. For Muslims, the ability to enact their faith in life is the site where human dignity resides. The pursuit of the dignity of humanity is a contested site, as Islam came to be understood as being either more ethically or politically oriented. Islam as ethics frames human dignity in terms of rights, duties, and responsibility to God, oneself, humans, and nature, whereas Islam as a political force contextualizes human dignity in relation to the political and the implementation of Islamic law (*shari'a*). While the voice of political Islam expresses grievances toward injustice by proposing change in the structural system, Islam as ethics offers a framework on how to engage with Islamic sources contextually and how to lead a meaningful Islamic life. Though Islam as ethics is receptive to a new form of interpretation and contextualization within the

---

[69] Masour Fakih and Antonius Maria Indrianto, *Menegakkan Keadilan dan Kemanusiaan: Pegangan Untuk Membangun Gerakan Hak Asasi Manusia* [Upholding Justice and Humanity: A Handbook for Building a Human Rights Movement] (Yogyakarta: Insist Press, 2003), pp. 20–21.

context of a nation, the relationship between the state and religion will continue to be important.

The state takes charge of how to realize human dignity through regulations and policies. The state's accountability for enacting human dignity is situated within both local and international forces. Locally, the government's decision regarding democratizing politics and economics is tied to aspirations drawn from *Pancasila*, the 1945 Constitution and its various amendments, and indigenous cultural and religious wisdom. Globally, international financial organizations, such as the World Bank, the International Monetary Fund, the Asian Development Bank; international political and economic institutions, such as the United Nations bodies and the World Trade Organization; and the multilateral corporation, such as the Association of Southeast Asian Nations (ASEAN) have the power to orient Indonesia's economic and political policies and programs. Both local and global factors intersect with the state's interest in pursuing its developmental goals as well as the dignity of human beings and the nation.

The fulfillment of human dignity in terms of rights reaches a more mature state with the involvement of Indonesian women and government in transnational women's movements and international programs. While women's movements in Indonesia existed long before Independence, they have continued to promote better social, economic, and political condition for women as they attempt to challenge the patriarchy. Women's exposures to various international programs, such as the United Nations policies on women in development (WID) and later women and development (WAD) and the Convention on the Elimination of all Forms of Discrimination Against Women (CEDAW) by the Ministry of Women's Empowerment and Child Protection (1980) helped to define their status and rights in family and society. Similarly, Indonesia's involvement in UN conferences along with the growing collaborations between women's organizations in Indonesia and international nonprofit organizations from the West and the Muslim world empower women in the private and public spheres. This exposure to international agencies advanced women's engagement with global human rights issues, including the status of human dignity in Indonesia. While the pursuit of human dignity remains debated, the discursive narratives surrounding it has continued to change depending on the intersection of local and global factors.

14

Catholicism and Human Dignity in the Philippines

Jonathan T. Chow[*]

In Catholic teaching, human dignity stems from the belief that among all creatures, humans alone are created in the image and likeness of God (the *imago Dei*). Consequently, they are never to be exploited as mere resources but instead treated as ends in themselves. Human dignity also encompasses *solidarity*, an orientation that seeks to promote the common good rather than one's narrow self-interest; the *preferential option for the poor*, which demands that justice be provided to all but especially to those most in need of it; and the *sanctity and dignity of human life*. In the Catholic view, taking human dignity seriously requires a radical humanization of the "other" when cultural forces conspire to promote dehumanization instead. This has potentially dramatic implications for reorienting social practices and institutions.

The Philippines is one of only two Asian countries (the other being Timor-Leste) where the majority of the population identifies as Roman Catholic. Moreover, it contains the world's third-largest Catholic population (after Brazil and Mexico).[1] The Catholic Church has played an important cultural and political role throughout the archipelago's history, from its colonization by the Spanish to post-independence struggles for democracy to contemporary matters of social change and globalization. For Catholic proponents of human dignity, the Philippines presents numerous challenges. Exploitative structures and activities are widespread, from political corruption and economic inequality to extrajudicial killings and an

---

[*] I am grateful to Romina Abuan for excellent research assistance. For helpful comments on earlier drafts, I wish to thank Jimmy Chia-Shin Hsu, Shao Kai Tseng, J.R. Robert Real, and the other participants in the "Human Dignity in Asia" conference. I am also indebted to Fr. Franz Gassner, SVD; Fr. Eric Genilo, SJ; Fr. Eugene Trainor; and Dr. Bernardo Villegas, for invaluable comments and research advice. All errors, of course, are solely my responsibility. Research for this paper was conducted in part while I was a visiting fellow at the Ateneo Center for Asian Studies (ACAS) at Ateneo de Manila University in May and June 2018. I am grateful to ACAS Director Violet Valdez and Maia Tangco for arranging my affiliation. Funding for this research was provided in part by a Multi-Year Research Grant from the University of Macau (MYRG2017–00165–FSS).

[1] "Table: Christian Population in Numbers by Country," Pew Research Center (December 19, 2011), www.pewforum.org/2011/12/19/table-christian-population-in-numbers-by-country/.

economy that depends heavily on sending workers overseas – and separating families – for months or years at a time. While the Church has often embraced the language of human rights in its efforts to promote human dignity, it treats the former as a means to achieve the latter rather than as an end in itself. Hence, it has at times clashed with human rights advocates, notably in matters pertaining to reproductive rights.

This chapter surveys how the leadership of the Catholic Church in the Philippines – specifically, the Catholic Bishops' Conference of the Philippines (CBCP) – has conceptualized and applied the idea of human dignity to various social issues. As the official body representing the Catholic hierarchy in the Philippines, the CBCP plays an important agenda-setting role for the Church through its various pastoral statements issued on behalf of all Filipino bishops. Section 1 reviews the Catholic Church's teachings on human dignity and human rights; and Section 2 briefly discusses the Philippine cultural context and the Church's role in Philippine society. Next, Section 3 examines CBCP interpretations of human dignity in public documents from 1990 through 2017 and describes how it has linked Catholic teachings on human dignity to various social issues and sought to shape societal norms and policies. To engage Philippine society on such a wide basis, the Catholic Church requires abundant moral authority. However, although the Church enjoyed moral authority following the 1986 "People Power" Revolution that deposed the martial law regime of Ferdinand Marcos, that moral authority has been diminishing. This is imposing new constraints on the Church's ability to reshape social structures that exploit human dignity. Section 4 considers how the Church's moral authority and sociopolitical influence seem to be declining, particularly under the administration of President Rodrigo Duterte, and how this development is generating new challenges to the Church's efforts to promote human dignity.

1 CATHOLIC TEACHINGS ON HUMAN DIGNITY AND HUMAN RIGHTS

In the Catholic tradition, each person is created in God's image and likeness (the *imago Dei*); this is the source of human dignity.[2] Human dignity does not derive from ability, merit, or behavior, nor can it be lost, even by committing murder.[3] Underlying this conception is Thomas Aquinas' (1225–74) view of man as a distinctly intellectual and rational creation of God. For Aquinas, rationality enabled humans to achieve their ultimate end: to understand God. Yet rationality was insufficient unless humans were also free from both passions (necessitating moral virtues and

---

[2] Genesis 1:26–27. On the development of the *imago Dei* as a concept, see James Hanvey, "Dignity, Person, and *Imago Trinitatis*," in *Understanding Human Dignity*, edited by Christopher McCrudden (Oxford: Oxford University Press, 2013), pp. 209–228, from which this section draws substantially.
[3] Pope John Paul II, *Evangelium Vitae* (1995), §9.

prudence) and external disorder.[4] The Church acknowledges that both rationality and freedom are elements of human dignity[5] but avers that free decisions are not automatically moral or in keeping with human dignity. Rather, human dignity is only affirmed through free cooperation with God's grace and will, through which human beings can attain their ultimate purpose.[6]

Today, Catholic teaching often connects human dignity to human *rights*, but although the Church has long upheld the former, it was initially reluctant to embrace the latter. Because the Church held that people could never fully achieve their purpose in this world, it tended to regard poverty, inequality, social injustice, and the like as temporary burdens to be endured until Jesus Christ's return. Additionally, the anticlericalism of the French Revolution and the rise of secular nationalism across nineteenth-century Europe led popes to distrust democracy, liberalism, and universal rights.[7]

Pope Leo XIII's landmark 1891 encyclical *Rerum Novarum* foreshadowed the Church's growing receptiveness of human rights. Driven by Leo's concern for the grim conditions of industrial laborers, *Rerum Novarum* argued that people possess rights that precede the state, particularly the right to provide for one's own present and future needs.[8] Leo invoked the *imago Dei*: "It is the soul which is made after the image and likeness of God; it is in the soul that the sovereignty resides in virtue whereof man is commanded to rule the creatures below him and use all the earth and the ocean for his profit and advantage."[9] This common *telos* of the soul, he continued, was God-given, made all people equal in dignity, and could never be legitimately impeded:

> No man may with impunity outrage that human dignity which God Himself treats with great reverence, nor stand in the way of that higher life which is the preparation of the eternal life of heaven. Nay, more; no man has in this matter power over himself. To consent to any treatment which is calculated to defeat the end and purpose of his being is beyond his right, he cannot give up his soul to servitude, for it is not man's own rights which are here in question, but the rights of God, the most sacred and inviolable of rights.[10]

Leo did not view this position as one defending human rights in the modern sense but instead as one respecting *God's* destiny for each individual. Hence, he argued, man must never be treated as an instrument but rather as an end in himself.[11] To ensure the soul's achievement of its ultimate purpose, Leo concluded that workers should be granted Sunday rest, reasonable amounts of labour, a living wage, and the

---

[4] Thomas Aquinas, *Summa Contra Gentiles*, edited by Joseph Kenny (New York: Hanover House, 1955–7), bk. III, chs. 25, 37.
[5] *Catechism of the Catholic Church*, 2nd ed. (Vatican City: Libreria Editrice Vaticana, 1997), par. 1730.
[6] *Catechism of the Catholic Church*, par. 308.
[7] See, for instance, Pope Gregory XVI, *Mirari Vos* (1832), §13–§20. Pope Pius IX, *Syllabus of Errors* (1864), §15–§18, §63, §77–§80.
[8] Pope Leo XIII, *Rerum Novarum* (1891), §7.
[9] Ibid., §40.
[10] Ibid., §40.
[11] Ibid., §20.

right to join unions.¹² The state, he continued, must uphold and protect individual rights, regard the working class and the wealthy as equal citizens (though the poor, he emphasized, often required more assistance from the state than the wealthy), and uphold the common good.¹³ Though *Rerum Novarum* did not explicitly invoke human rights, it anticipated the Church's future linkage of human rights to human dignity.

World War II, the Holocaust, and the mainstreaming of international human rights finally led the Church to connect human rights explicitly to its teachings on human dignity. In 1942, Pope Pius XII declared that respect for human dignity necessitated respect for a number of "fundamental personal rights," including the rights to worship, marry, work, and choose freely one's state in life.¹⁴ In 1963, Pope John XXIII formally linked human dignity to human rights in his landmark encyclical, *Pacem in Terris*. It argued that human beings were by nature "endowed with intelligence and free will," giving rise to rights and duties that were "universal and inviolable, and therefore altogether inalienable."¹⁵ It also enumerated rights that in many ways paralleled the Universal Declaration of Human Rights,¹⁶ including the rights to live, to "food, clothing, shelter, medical care, rest, and ... necessary social services";¹⁷ to worship God privately and publicly according to one's conscience;¹⁸ to a living wage;¹⁹ and to free association, freedom of movement, and protection through the rule of law.²⁰ Yet while both the Church and the UDHR asserted that human rights derived from humankind's inherent dignity, the Church also emphasized that human rights were still subordinate to divine moral law.²¹ Embedding human rights within that moral law gives rise to another important concept in Catholic social teaching: the idea of *integral human development*. As expressed in *Populorum Progressio* (1967), development cannot be solely economic but must instead be oriented toward the development of each individual as a whole – physically and morally as well as economically.²²

The rapid technological and societal changes and growing socioeconomic inequality of the late twentieth century stimulated further papal reflection on their implications for human dignity. In *Octogesima Adveniens* (1971), Pope Paul VI wrote of humanity's growing aspirations for *equality* and *participation*, which he describes

---

[12] Ibid., §41–§49.
[13] Ibid., §33, §37, §40.
[14] Pope Pius XII, *The Internal Order of States and People (Christmas Message)* (1942).
[15] Pope John XXIII, *Pacem in Terris* (1963), §9.
[16] On the Catholic provenance of the UDHR, see Mary Ann Glendon, "The Sources of 'Rights Talk,'" *Commonweal* 128, no. 17 (October 12, 1999): 11–13.
[17] Pope John XXIII, *Pacem in Terris*, §11.
[18] Ibid., §14.
[19] Ibid., §20.
[20] Ibid., §23–§27.
[21] "*Gaudium et Spes:* Pastoral Constitution on the Church in the Modern World" (December 7, 1965), §41.
[22] Pope Paul VI, *Populorum Progressio* (1967), §14.

as "two forms of man's dignity and freedom."[23] Paul referred explicitly to equality in the context of economic, cultural, and political inequalities among nations, equality before the law, and equal rights of all (especially women) to participate in cultural, economic, social, and political life.[24] Yet, he continued, formal equality must be buttressed by a "deeper feeling of respect for and service to others," lest it become "an alibi for flagrant discrimination, continued exploitation and actual contempt."[25] By linking recognition of equality and participation to human dignity, *Octogesima Adveniens* provided a moral basis for democracy and for those living on society's margins to demand a greater say in shaping their circumstances. This included "preferential respect due to the poor and the special situation they have in society."[26]

The *preferential option for the poor* is a central principle of liberation theology, which grew out of the experience of Latin American churches in the late 1960s and early 1970s and theological efforts to make Christianity's salvific message resonate with the many Christians enduring crushing poverty and systematic injustice.[27] *Preferential option* implies a free and deliberate choice to stand in solidarity with the poor, who include not only those facing economic privation but also those suffering systematic injustices and violations of fundamental political, cultural, or religious rights.[28] Although the Church excludes no one, liberation theology emphasizes that Jesus, as God made incarnate on earth, shared in humanity's poverty through his life, suffering, and death. "For this reason alone, the poor deserve preferential attention, whatever their moral or personal situation may be."[29] In practice, the preferential option for the poor demands the Church's renunciation of materialist values and a commitment to dismantle unjust social structures. It seeks to locate the Christian community and God's actions within a concrete historical context.[30] Finally, liberation theology emphasizes the need for ecclesial leadership to come from the poor and not only the clergy, as illustrated by its focus on "basic ecclesial communities" (BECs): small grassroots faith communities that pray and study scripture together. Though typically connected with the institutional Church, the relatively decentralized nature of BECs facilitated local empowerment and flexible responses to local injustices.[31]

---

[23] Pope Paul VI, *Octogesima Adveniens* (1971), §22.
[24] Ibid., §2, §13, §16, §23.
[25] Ibid., §23.
[26] Ibid., §23–§24.
[27] Roger Haight, *Christian Community in History: Comparative Ecclesiology*, vol. 2 (New York: Continuum, 2005), p. 414.
[28] Donal Dorr, "Poor, Preferential Option for the," in *The New Dictionary of Catholic Social Thought*, edited by Judith A. Dwyer (Collegeville, MN: Liturgical Press, 1994), p. 757.
[29] Conferencia General del Episcopando Latinoamericano, "La evangelización en el presente y en el futuro de América Latina" (1979), §1141–§1142.
[30] Haight, *Christian Community in History: Comparative Ecclesiology*, 2, pp. 414–415. Compare Pope Paul VI, *Octogesima Adveniens*, §3–§4.
[31] Liberation theology has sometimes been criticized in the Church for overemphasizing worldly justice to the detriment of proclaiming the Gospel, as well as for its association with socialist movements. See, for instance, Pope John Paul II, *Redemptoris Missio* (1990), §17–§19.

The preferential option for the poor grows out of the broader concept of *solidarity*, which refers to "a firm and persevering determination to commit oneself to the common good; that is to say to the good of all and of each individual, because we are all really responsible for all."[32] Solidarity begins with the anthropological observation that human beings are interdependent and move through history together, not just as individuals.[33] This is consistent with the theological concept of the "mystical Body of Christ" in which all members of the Church – those living on this earth, those who have died and are undergoing purification, and those who have already entered into heaven – are united with Christ.[34] According to this doctrine, suffering in any part of the body wounds the whole Church and, by extension, Christ. In *Sollicitudo Rei Socialis* (1987), Pope John Paul II wrote that

> solidarity helps us to see the "other" – whether a person, people or nation – not just as some kind of instrument, with a work capacity and physical strength to be exploited at low cost and then discarded when no longer useful, but as our "neighbour," a "helper," to be made a sharer, on a par with ourselves, in the banquet of life to which all are equally invited by God.[35]

By requiring people to see each other as part of the same whole, solidarity imposes an ethical obligation to understand the causes of suffering and injustice, to dismantle "structures of sin," and to cultivate human rights.[36] Christian solidarity demands a further step: to regard the other – even if an enemy – as created in the *imago Dei* and loved by God. The imperative goes so far as to state: "For that person's sake one must be ready for sacrifice, even the ultimate one: to lay down one's life for the brethren."[37]

A final aspect of Catholic teachings on human dignity regards the *sanctity and dignity of human life*. This became especially prominent during the moral battles surrounding abortion in the last quarter of the twentieth century and the pontificate of Pope John Paul II, who also linked it to capital punishment, euthanasia, and contraception. In *Evangelium Vitae* (1995), John Paul II described how growing moral relativism threatens inviolable human dignity as a foundational value. While human dignity "demands respect, generosity and service," he argued, modern society makes it possible to justify killing society's weakest members because it exalts individual choice above human solidarity or moral truth and reduces human worth to "efficiency, functionality, and usefulness."[38] Hence, it was more important than ever to uphold the sanctity and dignity of human life as a paramount value.

---

[32] Pope John Paul II, *Sollicitudo Rei Socialis* (1987), §38.
[33] Pope Paul VI, *Populorum Progressio*, §17.
[34] *Lumen Gentium: Dogmatic Constitution on the Church* (1964), §7–§8, §49–§50.
[35] Pope John Paul II, *Sollicitudo Rei Socialis*, §39.
[36] Gerald J. Beyer, "The Meaning of Solidarity in Catholic Social Teaching," *Political Theology* 15, no. 1 (2016): 15–17.
[37] Pope John Paul II, *Sollicitudo Rei Socialis*, §40. Compare Matthew 5:43–48, Luke 6:27–36, 1 John 3:16.
[38] Pope John Paul II, *Evangelium Vitae*, §19–§20, §23.

In sum, the Catholic Church teaches that all human beings have inherent dignity because they are created in God's image. Hence, they must be treated with respect and not exploited as mere instruments. To ensure that people can fulfil their nature as free and rational creatures, the Church has endorsed human rights but maintains that they must always be subordinate to human dignity and not absolutes in themselves, lest they undermine human dignity. Particularly since Vatican II, the Church has also called for reshaping social structures that systematically violate human dignity. This has led to growing lay participation in Church leadership and diverse expressions of Church teaching on human dignity. This is no less true in the Philippines, where the application of the Church's teachings on human dignity has taken on distinct local characteristics.

2 THE PHILIPPINE CONTEXT

The Philippines is unique among Asian countries both for the size of its Catholic population and for the Catholic Church's deeply embedded societal role. Catholicism arrived in the Philippines in the sixteenth century as Spain colonized the archipelago. Under Spanish rule, which lasted until 1898, the Church – and especially clergy belonging to religious orders like the Augustinians, Franciscans, and Jesuits – played a central role in the colonial administration. Key clerical positions were appointed by the Spanish Crown under the *patronato real* (royal patronage) system. Spanish clergy, eager to preserve their own privileges and often disdainful of native Filipinos, strongly resisted calls by the Spanish Crown to cultivate Filipino clergy. This deprived the Church of clergy with local cultural knowledge who could administer the sacraments and enforce doctrine throughout the archipelago's highly decentralized communities.[39] It also contributed to the growth of a "folk Catholicism" that continues to be expressed in pious traditions that do not necessarily emanate from (and sometimes violate) official Catholic teaching. Examples of folk Catholicism can be seen today in depictions of Mary and the baby Jesus ("Santo Niño") emblazoned on the jeepneys used for public transit, in the wearing of talismans (*anting-anting*) depicting Catholic imagery but intended to grant supernatural protection or magical powers, in bloody Passion plays on Good Friday (some of which involve actors allowing themselves to be literally nailed to crosses), or in the annual procession of the Black Nazarene statue in Manila's Quiapo district, which some believe to grant healing powers to cloths that are wiped over its surface.

Spain's cession of the Philippines to the United States following its defeat in the Spanish American War of 1898 marked the start of a dramatic shift in the Philippines' developmental trajectory. After waging a vicious, racially tinged war

---

[39] John Leddy Phelan, *The Hispanization of the Philippines: Spanish Aims and Filipino Responses: 1565–1700* (Madison: University of Wisconsin Press, 2011), pp. 84–87.

to suppress the Philippine independence movement and cement colonial rule, the United States adopted an attitude of paternalistic tutelage toward Filipinos, whom the territory's governor William Howard Taft described as "our little brown brothers."[40] The United States established a new political system based on its own government, with separate executive, legislative, and judiciary branches and elections for public office. However, the absence of land reform or meaningful economic redistribution meant that wealth and political power remained concentrated in an oligarchy of landowning dynasties, while tenant farmers frequently incurred intergenerational debt to landowners. Under US rule, the Philippines was tightly bound to the American economy as an inexpensive source of sugar, coconut oil, and other agricultural products. The US administration established English-language public schooling, paving the way for the present-day use of English as an official language alongside Filipino. Newly arrived Protestant missionaries began to establish congregations in the Philippines. Although Catholicism retained its traditional place in Philippine society, disestablishing the Church and ending the *patronato real* system (thereby bringing the Church under direct administration of the Catholic hierarchy) greatly weakened its political influence. In 1935, the Tydings-McDuffie Act bestowed US commonwealth status on the Philippines with the aim of granting full independence in ten years. Although delayed by Japan's invasion and occupation from December 1941 to September 1945, the Philippines gained full independence from the United States in 1946. However, the 1947 Military Bases Agreement and Military Assistance Agreement, as well as the 1951 Mutual Defence Treaty, ensured a large continuing US military presence in the Philippines until the end of the Cold War.

An important element of contemporary Philippine society is the country's economic underdevelopment. The World Bank classifies the Philippines as a "lower middle-income country." Since the beginning of the 2000s, the economy has maintained positive growth, with mean annual GDP growth at 5.67 percent and mean GNI growth at 5.91 percent between 2008 and 2018.[41] Nevertheless, poverty remains a serious problem. Official statistics estimate that, in 2015, 18.0 percent of Filipinos had incomes that placed them below the poverty line; that figure fell to 12.1 percent in 2018.[42] Yet these figures are misleading because they do not measure actual household consumption and because the government has lowered the poverty threshold to unrealistic levels.[43]

---

[40] Stanley Karnow, *In Our Image: America's Empire in the Philippines* (New York: Random House, 1989), p. 174.

[41] World Bank, "World Development Indicators Database" (World Bank Group, 2020), data .worldbank.org/indicator.

[42] Philippine Statistics Authority, "2015 and 2018 Updated Official Poverty Statistics" (June 4, 2020), www .psa.gov.ph/sites/default/files/2015%20and%202018%20Updated%20Official%20Poverty% 20Statistics_04June2020.xlsx.

[43] Arsenio M. Balisacan, "Poverty and Inequality," in *The Philippine Economy: Development, Policies and Challenges*, edited by Arsenio M. Balisacan and Hal Hill (New York: Oxford University Press, 2003),

Stubbornly high levels of unemployment and underemployment provide a steady supply of Filipinos willing to work abroad, often in harsh and dangerous conditions. In 2019, these overseas Filipino workers (OFWs) numbered an estimated 2.2 million, 56 percent of whom were women.[44] The largest share of OFWs (39.6 percent) worked in physically demanding "elementary occupations,"[45] followed by service and sales workers (18.0 percent) and plant and machine operators and assemblers (12.2 percent).[46] In 2018, remittances from OFWs reached $32.2 billion, equivalent to 9.7 percent of the Philippines' GDP.[47] Abuses of OFWs by employers are common, while OFWs' lengthy absences from the Philippines often strain family relationships.

The Philippines' underdevelopment has historically been attributed to its export-led industrialization, which involved rapid trade and investment liberalization in the 1970s and 1980s and high levels of foreign direct investment and loans but lacked a broader strategy for technological upgrading or the cultivation of hometown champions that could compete overseas.[48] Hence, the Philippines' manufacturing and industrial sectors have stagnated, along with the agricultural sector, which also suffers from chronic underinvestment. Agriculture's share of employment declined from 51.4 percent in 1980 to 25.4 percent in 2017, while manufacturing's share declined from 10.6 percent in 1980 to 8.6 percent in 2017.[49] In contrast, the service sector's share of employment grew from 36.5 percent in 1980 to 56.3 percent in 2017, largely because of retail and consumer sectors, whose growth is fuelled by OFW remittances.[50] However, such jobs tend to be lower-paying and less secure than in other sectors. There is also a large informal sector estimated to encompass somewhere between roughly 40 percent and 77 percent of

---

p. 317; Mahar Mangahas, "No Meat Allowed for the Poor," Inquirer.net (October 7, 2011), http://opinion.inquirer.net/14829/no-meat-allowed-for-the-poor; Mahar Mangahas, "Unrealistic Official Poverty," *Philippine Daily Inquirer* (November 12, 2016), http://opinion.inquirer.net/99161/unrealistic-official-poverty; David Michael M. San Juan and Prince Jhay C. Agustin, "Poverty, Inequality, and Development in the Philippines: Official Statistics and Selected Life Stories," *European Journal of Sustainable Development* 8, no. 1 (2019): 290–304.

[44] Philippine Statistics Authority, "Total Number of OFWs Estimated at 2.2 Million" (June 4, 2020), psa.gov.ph/statistics/survey/labor-and-employment/survey-overseas-filipinos.

[45] The Philippine Statistics Authority defines "elementary occupations" as "simple and routine tasks which may require the use of hand-held tools and considerable physical effort." Philippine Statistics Authority, "Philippine Standard Occupational Classification," https://psa.gov.ph/classification/psoc/technical-notes.

[46] Philippine Statistics Authority, "Total Number of OFWs."

[47] Bangko Sentral ng Pilipinas, "Overseas Filipinos' (OF) Remittances" (June 11, 2020), www.bsp.gov.ph/statistics/keystat/ofw.htm; World Bank, "World Development Indicators Database."

[48] Rene E. Ofreneo, "Growth and Employment in De-Industrializing Philippines," *Journal of the Asia Pacific Economy* 20, no. 1 (2015): 118–121.

[49] *Poverty in the Philippines: Causes, Constraints, and Opportunities* (Mandaluyong City, Philippines: Asian Development Bank, 2009), p. 44. "Employed Persons by Major Industry Group, Philippines: 2016-July 2018," http://psa.gov.ph/sites/default/files/attachments/cls/Tab5_11.pdf.

[50] *Poverty in the Philippines*, p. 44. "Employed Persons by Major Industry Group, Philippines: 2016-July 2018," http://psa.gov.ph/sites/default/files/attachments/cls/Tab5_11.pdf.

employed workers.⁵¹ Other factors contributing to underdevelopment include high levels of corruption, population growth that outpaces economic growth, political instability, poor infrastructure, and the country's vulnerability to natural disasters.

3 CATHOLIC BISHOPS' INTERPRETATIONS OF HUMAN DIGNITY IN THE PHILIPPINES

To understand how the Catholic Church in the Philippines has interpreted and applied the concept of human dignity, it is useful to examine official statements by the Catholic Bishops' Conference of the Philippines, which represents the Catholic hierarchy. The issuance of statements, which articulate the Philippine bishops' collective position on a given issue, is one of the CBCP's most visible activities. Certain pastoral statements deemed especially important are read aloud in churches around the country. CBCP statements can play an agenda-setting role by drawing public attention to issues of importance to the Church hierarchy and signaling its position on such issues, thereby prompting responses by other clergy, members of religious orders, and laity. Although other Philippine Catholic organizations such as the Association for Major Religious Superiors of the Philippines, religious orders like the Jesuits or Dominicans, lay groups such as El Shaddai or Couples for Christ, and individual dioceses might adopt their own positions on moral issues, it is virtually never the case that they would directly contradict the moral positions taken by the CBCP. Thus, examining how the CBCP has employed human dignity can give us a window into how the wider institutional Church in the Philippines understands it.

Official statements published by the CBCP between January 1990 and July 2017 and available from the CBCP website (a total of 222 statements) were inputted into NVivo.⁵² The vast majority of these were pastoral letters and statements addressed to various audiences within the Church and Philippine society at large. Also included were specialized texts such as the "Catechism on the Church and Politics" that, while not technically pastoral letters, served a similar hortatory purpose. While the pastoral statements downloaded do not represent the complete set of statements issued by the CBCP or its officers, they nevertheless represent what the CBCP leadership deems most important to publicize.

All of the analyzed documents were published in English, though the CBCP posts particularly important documents in Filipino and other local dialects in addition to

---

⁵¹ Based on estimates respectively by the Philippine Bureau of Labor and Employment Statistics (2010) and the Employers' Confederation of the Philippines (2006). The latter estimate includes underemployed workers. Rene E. Ofreneo, "Precarious Philippines: Expanding Informal Sector, 'Flexibilizing' Labor Market," *American Behavioral Scientist* 57, no. 4 (2013): 424–425.

⁵² The website in question was www.cbcpwebsite.com. As of June 2020, that website is no longer in service and its contents are hosted at www.cbcponline.net. While most of the documents on the old website were transferred, several that are cited in this chapter now appear to be missing. For access to the original dataset, please contact the author.

English. In such cases, only the English-language version was downloaded. The word "dignity" and all of its cognates (e.g. "indignities," "dignification") were located using text search queries. This allowed for searching not only the term "human dignity" but also variants such as "dignity of the human person" or "dignified human life." From the initial pool, 83 sources contained at least one cognate of the word "dignity." Instances of the search terms and the surrounding text were analyzed and coded for issues and themes.

3.1 Overall Trends in CBCP Statements on Human Dignity

The results of the analysis demonstrate both the wide range of issues related to human dignity and a high degree of consistency in how the CBCP invokes the concept. The CBCP frequently describes human dignity as a sacrosanct good, though it does not always define its precise meaning in a given context. Human dignity is respected when people are treated as ends in themselves rather than as means to some other good. Human dignity is violated whenever people fail to regard other human beings as individuals created in the *imago Dei* and thus to be treated with love and reverence. Such violations can take many forms and emanate from individuals as well as dehumanizing social structures, but at their core each treats other human beings as resources to be harnessed (whether for their votes, labor, land, or bodies) or as undesirables to be discarded (such as in the cases of criminals, the poor, or unwanted children). Likewise, the CBCP's prescribed remedies share a similar central element: to build solidarity and regard for the other as a fellow human being made in the *imago Dei* and thus another self. The following sections briefly illustrate how the CBCP has connected the concept of human dignity to various social issues in the Philippines.

3.2 Electoral Politics

The CBCP has served as an important force for shaping Philippine politics. This was perhaps most iconically illustrated by its role in the 1986 People Power Revolution that ousted former president Ferdinand Marcos' martial law regime following the 1983 assassination of his political rival Benigno "Ninoy" Aquino, Jr. Under CBCP leadership, the Church rallied support for Aquino's widow, Corazon Aquino, after Marcos called for snap elections to be held in February 1986. When Marcos declared himself the winner of the election despite widespread reports of fraud, the CBCP mobilized Catholics to undertake nonviolent resistance that, along with resistance by other civil society organizations and the support of the military, led to the toppling of the Marcos regime on February 25 and the elevation of Aquino to the presidency.[53] Subsequently, Church leaders helped to draft the 1987 Philippine

---

[53] Teodoro C. Bacani, Jr., *The Church and Politics* (Quezon City: Claretian Publications, 1987), 84–85.

Constitution. Cardinal Jaime Sin, the charismatic archbishop of Manila and a leading figure in the People Power Revolution, remained a close personal adviser to Aquino throughout her presidency.

In the realm of electoral politics, the CBCP has been heavily concerned with preserving integrity in the midst of widespread corruption. In September 1997, the CBCP issued a pastoral exhortation about Philippine politics as the 1998 national and local elections approached. It began by painting a dim portrait of Philippine politics, pointing to corruption, patronage, constitutional abuses, pork barrel projects, electoral fraud, the transformation of public offices from public trusts into private dynasties, and widespread cynicism toward the political system. In articulating a vision for a reformed Philippine politics, the CBCP referred to human dignity and solidarity as "a first principle of politics." Reiterating the Church's teaching that human dignity derives from the *imago Dei*, the Pastoral Exhortation declares: "Politics must respect and promote human dignity and the fundamental human rights that flow from such dignity."[54] Hence, "when politicians exploit their fellow citizens and deny their will in electoral processes through fraud and violence, when they promote their own vested interests through any means, fair or foul, because of greed for power or possessions at the expense of others, they thereby brazenly dismiss the human dignity of their fellow human beings."[55] Politics driven by a desire to build a dynasty and accumulate rents from holding office violates human dignity by treating the electorate not as a population to be served but rather a source of votes that can be obtained through fraud or violence. Aside from being by itself corrupt, this instrumentalist attitude also undermines solidarity by converting an office of public trust into a clientelist relationship in which a few benefit at the expense of the many.

Vote buying in local and national elections is widely understood to be common practice. For many impoverished Filipinos, the promise of food, clothing, or cash can be a strong incentive to vote for a candidate (or in some cases to abstain from voting so as not to help an opposing candidate). The practice is enabled by weak monitoring, lax enforcement, and inadequate provision of public services.[56] The Catholic Church has regularly condemned the buying and selling of votes as violations of human dignity. In 1992, during the first election of the post-Marcos era, the CBCP exhorted voters to "vote with dignity and freedom" and not to "dishonour" themselves or "betray" the Philippines by selling their votes. "Your votes are sacred. Guard them."[57] In 1995, the

---

[54] Catholic Bishops' Conference of the Philippines, *Pastoral Exhortation on Philippine Politics* (September 16, 1997), www.cbcponline.net/pastoral-exhortation-on-philippine-politics/.
[55] Catholic Bishops' Conference of the Philippines, *Pastoral Exhortation on Philippine Politics*.
[56] See, for instance, Tristan A. Canare, Ronald U. Mendoza, and Mario Antonio Lopez, "An Empirical Analysis of Vote Buying among the Poor: Evidence from Elections in the Philippines," *South East Asia Research* 26, no. 1 (2018): 58–84. Frederic Charles Schaffer and Andreas Schedler, "What Is Vote Buying? Empirical Evidence," in *Elections for Sale: The Causes and Consequences of Vote Buying*, edited by Frederic Charles Schaffer and Andreas Schedler (Boulder, CO: Lynne Rienner, 2007).
[57] Catholic Bishops' Conference of the Philippines, "Pre-Election Statement of the Catholic Bishops' Conference of the Philippines" (May 5, 1992).

CBCP warned electoral candidates that vote buying was "a particularly degrading form of cheating. You do not start serving people by corrupting them and degrading their dignity."[58] In 1998, it offered a more detailed explanation of how vote buying harmed human dignity:

> The person who sells his vote shows that his choice can be bought, and that he is willing to sell his and the country's future to the vote-buyer. In so doing he confirms the vote-buyer's low opinion of him. The person who buys the vote makes clear that he will not hesitate to demean the dignity of the voters to obtain an elective position, and by this fact shows he does not deserve to be elected.[59]

In the CBCP's view, each side's willingness to compromise their integrity and exploit one another for material gain causes them to violate their human dignity.

3.3 Labour and Poverty

The CBCP has also emphasized the importance of human dignity for labour and especially the abuses that the most vulnerable workers suffer at the hands of employers and others in power. Such issues are inextricably linked to matters of poverty and economic inequality. On the one hand, the Church teaches that voluntary poverty and detachment from material comforts emulate Jesus' life and allow one to focus more on God. On the other hand, the Church also recognizes that a poverty that leaves one unable to meet basic needs is fundamentally inconsistent with human dignity.[60] Such poverty is worsened when it arises from unjust actions and societal structures that subordinate the common good and individuals' dignity to profit motives.

In multiple pastoral statements and letters since the 1990s, the CBCP has decried poverty and the societal conditions that help to keep people impoverished. The 1991 Conciliar Document issued by the CBCP's Second Plenary Council declared: "The concentration of economic wealth and political power in the hands of the few is an affront to human dignity and solidarity."[61] While the CBCP does not condemn profit seeking, it warns that profit must not come at the expense of individual dignity. Hence, the CBCP declares, "the first community of persons that the firm must serve should be its own workers" and "serious questions have to be raised on the basic attitudes of businesses regarding labour unions, collective bargaining and just wages

---

[58] Catholic Bishops' Conference of the Philippines, "Do Everything in the Name of the Lord Jesus: A Call to Christian Participation in the Elections" (April 9, 1995).
[59] Catholic Bishops' Conference of the Philippines, "Pastoral Exhortation on the 1998 Elections" (January 31, 1998).
[60] Catholic Bishops' Conference of the Philippines, "Poverty That Dehumanizes, Poverty That Sanctifies" (March 5, 2014).
[61] Catholic Bishops' Conference of the Philippines, "The Conciliar Document of the Second Plenary Council of the Philippines," in *Acts and Decrees of the Second Plenary Council of the Philippines* (Pasay City, Philippines: Paulines, 1991), §296.

in terms of 'family living wage,' working conditions and retrenchment of workers, to name a few."[62]

Similarly, the CBCP regards with ambivalence the Philippines' heavy reliance on OFWs. In a 1995 pastoral letter on migrant workers, the CBCP acknowledged that OFWs' remittances had contributed enormously to their own families and to national development. Yet it observed that OFWs often paid heavy prices, including "loss of life and human dignity, inhuman abuse and maltreatment, exploitation, moral degradation, broken families, loss of Faith, loneliness, and other sufferings."[63] The letter argued that the Philippine government should not promote overseas employment unless "protective measures" were in place to safeguard OFWs' "dignity and human rights."[64] Underscoring the need to prioritize human dignity above economic gain, the letter stated: "Some price is too high for just a better salary. Loss of life, loss of human dignity, moral degradation, or a broken family is too high a price."[65]

The CBCP has also spoken out on the relationship between international inequality and human dignity. Several of its statements have highlighted the role of globalization in perpetuating economic privation in the Philippines. In 1990, it issued a statement declaring that it was a violation of human dignity for creditor countries to force debtor countries into abject poverty over their debts. Even if the demands of creditors were by themselves just, the CBCP argued that, citing the Pontifical Commission on Justice and Peace, they could not be just if complying with them would harm human dignity. It questioned, for instance, the large payments owed to creditors, most of which would go toward paying interest instead of the principal. Instead, the CBCP called for "a debt relief strategy 'with a humane face'" that accounted for not only the debt itself but also equity, employment and people's needs, as well as the need to protect domestic food supplies and support investment in human capital.[66] The CBCP also emphasized the need for integral human development in the Philippines and condemned the growth of prostitution, sex tourism, and other industries that oppressed workers' human rights, as well as "the excessive external and foreign dependence that diminishes our dignity and sovereignty, and erodes international solidarity."[67]

---

[62] Catholic Bishops' Conference of the Philippines, "Pastoral Exhortation on the Philippine Economy" (July 10, 1998).
[63] Catholic Bishops' Conference of the Philippines, "Comfort My People, Comfort Them: A Pastoral Letter on Migrant Workers" (July 10, 1995).
[64] Ibid.
[65] Ibid.
[66] Catholic Bishops' Conference of the Philippines, "CBCP Statement on the Foreign Debt Problem" (September 19, 1990).
[67] Catholic Bishops' Conference of the Philippines, "The Conciliar Document of the Second Plenary Council of the Philippines," §294.

3.4 Reproductive Health and Contraception

Perhaps the CBCP's most controversial invocations of human dignity in recent years were those condemning legislation mandating universal access to reproductive health services throughout the Philippines. Such legislation required government health clinics to make artificial (but nonabortifacient) contraceptives freely available and mandated sexual and reproductive health education in public schools. Proponents emphasized that the Philippines had endorsed major human rights documents, including the 1994 Program of Action of the International Conference on Population and Development, the 1995 Beijing Platform for Action, and the UN Millennium Development Goals, all of which defined access to reproductive health – including modern family planning methods – as a human right. They also noted that, without a unified national policy on reproductive health, there existed a patchwork of wildly differing local laws, with some localities offering comprehensive reproductive health services and others outlawing the sale of contraceptives altogether. Finally, some proponents argued that the Philippines' population growth was a factor contributing to sustained poverty, as well as high unemployment and underemployment. Making family planning services available to all, they argued, could help to alleviate the Philippines' poverty.

Catholic doctrine forbids the use of artificial contraceptives on the basis that they interfere with the procreative aspect of marital intercourse. According to this teaching, God designed sex for procreation and not only the pleasure of the two spouses. Moreover, it is not humans who create life but rather God with the cooperation of human beings. By precluding the possibility of pregnancy, artificial contraception excludes God's design for sex and usurps God's authority.[68] For the CBCP, however, this was not the primary justification for opposing a national reproductive health law. Rather, it was the fear that enshrining access to contraceptives as a right would lead inexorably to the legitimization of abortion. The 1987 Constitution declares: "[The state] shall equally protect the life of the mother and the life of the unborn from conception," a provision that had emerged from a constitutional commission that included prominent Catholic clergy, religious, and lay leaders.[69] The Revised Penal Code of the Philippines also mandates imprisonment for anyone who procures or assists in an abortion, with theoretical exceptions in cases where the life of the mother is at stake or of rape.[70] Nevertheless, in multiple documents regarding

---

[68] Pope Paul VI, *Humanae Vitae: Encyclical of Pope Paul VI on the Regulation of Birth* (July 25, 1968), §13.

[69] Constitution of the Republic of the Philippines (1987), Article 2, §12. On the Catholic provenance of this article, see Joaquin G. Bernas, *The Intent of the 1986 Constitution Writers* (Manila: Rex Book Store, 1995), pp. 118–120.

[70] The Revised Penal Code, 3815, Article 256–Article 259 (December 8, 1930). On mitigating circumstances, see Article 11, par. 4, and Article 12, par. 6. These have not yet been tested by the court. Jihan Jacob and Melissa Upreti, "The Philippines' Criminal Restrictions on Abortion and the CEDAW Committee's Role in Strengthening Calls for Reform," *Canadian Woman Studies* 33, no. 1, 2 (2018): 232.

reproductive health legislation, the CBCP refers to the "fundamental dignity and worth of human life."[71] They also mention the dangers of what Pope John Paul II called a "contraceptive mentality" – that is, a selfish attitude that regards children as an impediment to a hedonistic lifestyle rather than an absolute blessing and their births as something to be prevented by contraception or, failing that, abortion.[72] The logic was that, by placing one's material comfort (or, for that matter, national development) above the possibility of bringing a new *imago Dei* into the world, one denigrated the dignity of human life. Making artificial family planning services available to all, the CBCP argued, would normalize this mindset within Philippine society and pave the way for legalized abortion.

The battle over reproductive health legislation began in 2001 under the presidency of Gloria Macapagal Arroyo (2001–10) with the first reproductive health bill in the Philippine House of Representatives. Arroyo sought the Church's backing in the face of declining popular support and calls for her ouster following allegations in 2005 that she had rigged the 2004 presidential election in her favour.[73] Thus, she promoted natural family planning and refused to allocate government funds for the purchase of artificial contraceptives.[74] Arroyo's stance won plaudits from the CBCP, which notably refrained from supporting calls for her ouster. Archbishop Paciano Aniceto, the chair of the CBCP's Episcopal Commission on Family and Life, declared that the Arroyo government was the only one that "made clear its principle to respect the family life principles of the Church, especially on the natural family planning."[75] This was not the case with President Benigno "Noynoy" Aquino III (2010–16), who openly supported a national reproductive health law in defiance of Church criticism and vowed to push it through. In December 2012, with the support of a congressional majority, Aquino signed into law the Reproductive Health and Responsible Parenthood Act.

During both presidencies, the CBCP and its allies engaged in extensive advocacy and pressure against reproductive health legislation. At times, they attempted to mobilize Catholics to vote lawmakers who supported it out of public office. In one high-profile case, the Diocese of Bacolod in central Philippines hoisted large

---

[71] Catholic Bishops' Conference of the Philippines, "The Christian Family: Good News for the Third Millennium" (December 2, 2002); Catholic Bishops' Conference of the Philippines, Catholic Bishops' Conference of the Philippines, "Proclaim Life ... In Season and Out of Season" (July 11, 2011); Catholic Bishops' Conference of the Philippines, "Choosing Life, Rejecting the RH Bill" (July 22, 2011).

[72] Compare Pope John Paul II, *Evangelium Vitae*, §12–§13.

[73] Yusuke Takagi, "Policy Coalitions and Ambitious Politicians: A Case Study of Philippine Social Policy Reform," *Philippine Political Science Journal* 38, no. 1 (2017): 36.

[74] Romeo B. Lee, Lourdes P. Nacionales, and Luis Pedroso, "The Influence of Local Policy on Contraceptive Provision and Use in Three Locales in the Philippines," *Reproductive Health Matters* 17, no. 34 (2009): 100; Rina Jimenez David, "Living with Sin: The Catholic Hierarchy and Reproductive Rights in the Philippines," *Conscience* (June 22, 2003).

[75] Leslie Ann G. Aquino, "Church Supports GMA on Use of Funds for Natural Family Planning," *Manila Bulletin*, November 4, 2005.

banners in front of San Sebastian Cathedral for the 2013 Senate election listing candidates and party lists that had opposed the 2012 reproductive health law (which the Diocese labelled "Team Buhay" or "Team Life") and those who had supported it (labelled "Team Patay" or "Team Death"). In other cases, Catholic clergy threatened to withhold the sacrament of Holy Communion from politicians who supported the legislation.[76] Not all Catholic clergy supported these heavy-handed tactics, with some arguing that reproductive health legislation did not force Catholics to use contraception or condemning the Church's decision engage in partisan politics,[77] but in general the Church's response to reproductive health legislation was defensive.[78]

Unlike its advocacy regarding economic justice and political corruption, the CBCP's opposition to reproductive health legislation increasingly placed it at odds with popular opinion. Polls indicated that a majority of Filipinos consistently supported government provision of contraceptives.[79] After the Reproductive Health Law passed, opponents quickly petitioned the Supreme Court to rule it unconstitutional. Yet, in 2014, the Court only struck down part of the law, leaving intact the main provisions mandating government provision of contraceptives and reproductive health education and affirming women's right to post-abortion care.[80] Undeterred, in 2015 a Catholic organization successfully petitioned the Supreme Court for a temporary restraining order to prevent the law's implementation, arguing that the contraceptives to be distributed by the government were abortifacient. In 2017, however, the Food and Drug Administration certified that the contraceptives were in fact not abortifacient, clearing the way for implementation.

Despite summoning the full might of the Church's moral authority to halt reproductive health legislation, the CBCP suffered a major defeat. Sociologists Anne Raffin and Jayeel Cornelio describe the reaction of the Church's leadership as a manifestation of "institutional panic" triggered by its diminishing societal influence amidst growing functional differentiation in Philippine society, specifically by the encroachment of the state on matters of private morality.[81] The

---

[76] Anne Raffin and Jayeel Serrano Cornelio, "The Catholic Church and Education as Sources of Institutional Panic in the Philippines," *Asian Journal of Social Science* 37 (2009): 790.

[77] See, for example, Eric O. Genilo, *A Different Paradigm: Critical and Constructive Engagement Amending the Reproductive Health Bill*, Loyola School of Theology (Quezon City, November 2, 2008); Joaquin G. Bernas, "RH Bill: Don't Burn the House to Roast a Pig," *Philippine Daily Inquirer* (August 6, 2012), http://opinion.inquirer.net/34153/rh-bill-dont-burn-the-house-to-roast-a-pig; Joel Tabora, "Team Patay, Team Buhay: Unconscionable," *Rappler* (February 25, 2013), www.rappler.com/thought-leaders/22511-team-patay,-team-buhay-unconscionable.

[78] For a helpful parsing of the various responses within the Church to the reproductive health debate, see David T. Buckley, "Catholicism's Democratic Dilemma: Varieties of Public Religion in the Philippines," *Philippine Studies: Historical and Ethnographic Viewpoints* 62, no. 3/4 (September–December 2014): 327–332, www.jstor.org/stable/24672315.

[79] Mahar Mangahas, "Unity on the RH Law," *Philippine Daily Inquirer*, April 15, 2014.

[80] *Imbong v. Ochoa*, Philippines G.R. No. 204819 (2014).

[81] Raffin and Cornelio, "The Catholic Church and Education as Sources of Institutional Panic in the Philippines," pp. 788–789.

reproductive health battle left the Church with significantly diminished moral authority and invited further challenges to its teachings.

3.5 Capital Punishment

The CBCP has mirrored the Holy See's strong preference for abolishing capital punishment. Strictly speaking, Catholic doctrine does not proscribe the death penalty "if it is the only possible way of defending human lives against the unjust aggressor."[82] However, since Pope John Paul II, the Church has maintained that, under modern penal systems, such situations are "very rare, if not practically non-existent."[83] Punishment without resort to execution, the Church teaches, is more in line with the common good and conforms to the dignity of the human person.[84] Pope Francis has been even more vocal in his opposition to the death penalty. Whereas John Paul II admitted the possibility that there might be extreme cases that warranted capital punishment, Francis has called it "an offense to the inviolability of life and to the dignity of the human person" and stated that the death penalty "contradicts God's plan for individuals and society, and his merciful justice."[85]

Under the Bill of Rights of the 1987 Constitution, capital punishment was abolished (albeit with the option for Congress to restore it "for compelling reasons involving heinous crimes") and all existing death sentences commuted to life imprisonment.[86] In his 1986 sponsorship speech for the Bill of Rights, constitutional commissioner Fr. Joaquin Bernas – a Jesuit priest, constitutional law scholar, and president of Ateneo de Manila University – described capital punishment as "inhuman" and argued: "Assuming mastery over the life of another man is just too presumptuous for any man."[87] Likewise, Bishop Teodoro Bacani, the auxiliary bishop of Manila and also a constitutional commissioner, referenced a 1979 statement by the CBCP opposing capital punishment on the grounds that there were other effective moral means for protecting the community from criminals. While acknowledging that the Church did not forbid the state from imposing capital punishment, Bacani argued: "The development of the moral sense of the people" indicated that the time was ripe for a constitutional prohibition of capital punishment.[88] These statements reflected Pope John Paul II's position on the death penalty.

---

[82] *Catechism of the Catholic Church*, §2267.
[83] Pope John Paul II, *Evangelium Vitae*, §56.
[84] Ibid.
[85] Quoted in Catholic Bishops' Conference of the Philippines, "Ethical Guidelines on Proposals to Restore the Death Penalty" (September 14, 2016).
[86] Constitution of the Republic of the Philippines (1987), Article III, §19.
[87] "R.C.C. No. 32 (July 17, 1986)," in *Record of the Constitutional Commission: Proceedings and Debates* (Manila: Republic of the Philippines Constitutional Commission of 1986, 1986), p. 676.
[88] "R.C.C. No. 32 (July 17, 1986)," p. 712.

Following a number of high-profile violent crimes in the early 1990s, the administration of President Fidel Ramos reinstated capital punishment in 1993. However, the first death sentence was only pronounced in 1996 and carried out it 1999 under the presidency of Joseph Estrada. In 2000, facing heavy lobbying by a civil society coalition supported by the Catholic Church leadership, Estrada imposed a moratorium on capital punishment in commemoration of the Church's Jubilee Year of Mercy, this despite a majority of Filipinos supporting the death penalty.[89] In 2006, President Gloria Macapagal Arroyo repealed the death penalty once again, announcing it during a visit to the Vatican to meet Pope Benedict XVI. The following year, the Philippines acceded to the Second Optional Protocol of the International Covenant on Civil and Political Rights (ICCPR), in which it promised not to reinstate the death penalty.

Efforts to bring back capital punishment received a major boost in 2016 with the election of President Rodrigo Duterte, the former mayor of Davao City who built a political reputation on ruthlessly hunting down criminals. Duterte openly called for a return to capital punishment and vowed to use it extensively.[90] Faced with communities riddled by violence and a corrupt legal system, voters largely supported Duterte's "get tough" approach, seeing it less as a violation of human dignity than an acknowledgment of the realities of Philippine society. In July 2016, a Pulse Asia survey found that 81 percent of Filipinos supported reinstating the death penalty, with only 11 percent opposed.[91] That same month, the new Congress met for the first time; the first bill to be proposed was HB 1, calling for the reinstatement of the death penalty. It was quickly passed by the House of Representatives but never taken up by the Senate.

In 2016, following Duterte's election, the CBCP issued "Ethical Guidelines on Proposals to Restore the Death Penalty." It began by stating: "Every man and woman is a person redeemed by God's own Son, made an adopted son or daughter of God, and heir to the promise of the Resurrection."[92] Capital punishment, the CBCP declared, violated this dignified status. The CBCP also noted that the Philippines was obligated under the ICCPR's Second Optional Protocol not to restore the death penalty. On January 30, 2017, following the House's passage of HB 1, CBCP President Archbishop Socrates Villegas condemned efforts to restore capital punishment: "Though the crime be heinous, no person is ever beyond redemption, and we

---

[89] A poll by the *Philippine Daily Inquirer* conducted around the time of the first execution under the Estrada administration found that eight out of ten Filipinos supported capital punishment for "heinous crimes." Arlie Tagayuna, "Capital Punishment in the Philippines," *Explorations* 5, no. 1 (2004): 1–24.

[90] "Catholics Fight Duterte's Death Penalty Pledge," *Daily Telegraph* (London), December 20, 2016, News.

[91] "Filipinos' Support for Death Penalty Wanes – Survey," *Rappler* (May 5, 2017), www.rappler.com/nation/168939-filipinos-support-death-penalty-wanes-pulse-asia.

[92] Catholic Bishops' Conference of the Philippines, "Ethical Guidelines on Proposals to Restore the Death Penalty."

have no right ever giving up on any person. When we condemn violence, we cannot ourselves be its perpetrators, and when we decry murder, we cannot ourselves participate in murder, no matter that it may be accompanied by the trappings of judicial and legal process."[93] Yet the CBCP's calls went unheeded by most congressional representatives. Members of the ruling coalition who dared to vote against the death penalty bill found themselves removed from House leadership positions, including former president Arroyo, who was ousted as Speaker of the House, while in the May 2019 midterm elections Duterte's allies won an overwhelming majority in the Senate. Legislation to restore capital punishment for certain drug-related offenses passed the House of Representatives in March 2021. Surprisingly, though, it stalled in the Senate by late 2021 after three key senators – Manny Pacquiao, Panfilo Lacson, and Vicente Sotto III – abruptly reversed their long-standing support for capital punishment. Lacson claimed that he had changed his mind after watching *The Life of David Gale*, a fictional film about the death penalty.[94] Sotto declared that life imprisonment in regional penitentiaries was a superior alternative to capital punishment.[95] Pacquiao expressed support in principle for capital punishment but stated that judicial reform was needed first.[96] Significantly, Pacquiao and Lacson were running for president in the 2022 election, while Sotto was seeking the vice-presidency as Lacson's running mate, suggesting that they may have been motivated in part by electoral considerations. The CBCP openly welcomed Lacson and Sotto's new opposition to capital punishment, declaring that it would "boost the Church's advocacy."[97] Other leading presidential candidates, including Vice-President Leni Robredo and Manila Mayor Francisco "Isko Moreno" Domagoso, also expressed opposition to the death penalty, though, as of early February 2022, apparent frontrunner Senator Ferdinand "Bongbong" Marcos, Jr., had not decided whether he would oppose or support it.[98] Thus, the fate of capital punishment in the Philippines remains uncertain.

[93] Yuji Vincent Gonzales, "CBCP on Death Penalty: 'No Person Is Beyond Redemption,'" Inquirer.net (January 31, 2017), https://newsinfo.inquirer.net/866825/cbcp-on-death-penalty-no-person-is-beyond-redemption.
[94] Kurt Dela Peña, "3 key advocates see light on death penalty, give push to pro-life campaign," *Inquirer.net* (November 11, 2021), newsinfo.inquirer.net/1513577/3-key-advocates-see-light-on-death-penalty-give-push-to-pro-life-campaign. John Eric Mendoza, "Lacson on shifting stance on death penalty: Is it wrong to change your mind if awakened with truth?" *Inquirer.net* (January 22, 2022), newsinfo.inquirer.net/1543682/lacson-on-shifting-stance-on-death-penalty-is-it-wrong-to-change-your-mind-when-awakened-with-truth.
[95] "Lacson, Sotto reverse long-standing support for death penalty," *PhilStar.com* (November 4, 2021), www.philstar.com/headlines/2021/11/04/2139033/lacson-sotto-reverse-long-standing-support-death-penalty.
[96] Aika Rey, "From being a staunch supporter of death penalty, Pacquiao says 'Not now'," *Rappler* (January 27, 2022), www.rappler.com/nation/elections/from-staunch-supporter-death-penalty-manny-pacquiao-says-not-now-january-2022.
[97] "Church welcomes Lacson-Sotto turnabout on death penalty," *GMA News Online* (November 7, 2021), www.gmanetwork.com/news/topstories/nation/809982/church-welcomes-lacson-sotto-turnabout-on-death-penalty/story/.
[98] Lian Buan, "Marcos Jr. backs abortion 'for severe cases' like rape and incest," *Rappler* (January 26, 2022) www.rappler.com/nation/elections/ferdinand-bongbong-marcos-jr-okay-abortion-severe-cases-rape-incest/.

4 CATHOLICISM AND HUMAN DIGNITY IN THE PHILIPPINES: AN UPHILL STRUGGLE

The Catholic Church's conception of human dignity derives from its belief that humankind has a divine destiny. Hence, its standard for respecting human dignity is a lofty one – to treat every person, without exception, as having been created in the image of God and therefore entitled to all the things necessary to achieve their divinely ordained purpose. Insofar as human rights facilitate that, the Catholic conception of human dignity embraces them. More fundamentally, the Catholic conception of human dignity demands that people never treat one another as mere instruments but rather as ends in themselves. This is a sweeping vision that demands nothing less than a transformation of societal relations, particularly when such relations are defined by systematic exploitation.

In the Philippines, where economic inequality, corruption, and poverty both sustain and are sustained by exploitative practices, the Church's call for human dignity is countercultural. Given that the Philippines is a Catholic-majority country and that Catholicism has long enjoyed a privileged status in Philippine society, why have Catholic conceptions of human dignity failed to win the day on reproductive health and capital punishment, issues that emphatically concern the sanctity and dignity of human life? While a definitive answer would exceed the scope of this chapter, several observations may shed some light on this matter.

First, the Church's political role is changing. Because of the role it played during the "People Power" revolution in 1986 and in rallying support for Corazon Aquino, the Church assumed the role of a moral authority that could pronounce upon the legitimacy of political leaders. It could therefore shape constitutional language regarding the family and the equal protection of mothers and the unborn from conception, cementing in place policies against divorce and abortion. While it would be an exaggeration to say that the Church's pronouncements *determined* the government's legitimacy, most political leaders recognized that the Church's moral authority was a powerful weapon and generally sought to avoid antagonizing the Church, as illustrated by President Estrada's decision to suspend the death penalty and President Arroyo's endorsement of the Church's views on family planning. When Estrada faced allegations in 2000 that he had profited from an illegal gambling racket, the CBCP and Cardinal Jaime Sin mobilized public opinion against him, with the latter proclaiming to him, "Do not be afraid of the truth. The truth is you have lost the moral ascendancy to govern us."[99] Thousands of Filipinos joined in supporting Estrada's ouster, including the military leadership, members of the business community, former presidents Cory Aquino and Fidel Ramos, and Gloria Arroyo (who was Estrada's vice president at the time), leading ultimately to Estrada stepping down from office in January 2001.

---

[99] Dirk Beveridge, "Philippines Opens Impeachment Trial," Associated Press, December 7, 2000.

In the years following Estrada's ouster, the Church pulled back from its willingness to intervene in national politics. Reasons for doing so include the 2005 death of Cardinal Sin, who had been so instrumental in organizing the two People Power revolutions;[100] concerns that further revolutions would weaken the Philippines' democratic institutions,[101] and directives from the recently elected Pope Benedict XVI declaring that the Church could not replace secular politics in the quest for a more just society.[102] When President Arroyo faced calls for impeachment over a major corruption scandal in 2006, the CBCP pointedly declined to support them, arguing in a pastoral letter that while the Church maintained "a duty to pass moral judgments even in matters political … it is not her responsibility to provide any political blueprint for the just ordering of society."[103] By embracing its role as a moral advocate and civil society actor, the CBCP ceded more space to secular political leaders. While the CBCP remains highly engaged in political lobbying and the politics of moral legitimacy, it has done so within the confines of existing political institutions rather than seeking to circumvent them. It is notable, for instance, that, during the rancorous struggle over reproductive health legislation, the CBCP issued numerous condemnations and sought to frame its congressional supporters as "pro-death," but when the legislation passed it did not declare that lawmakers were illegitimately elected; rather, it sought relief through litigation. The Church has increasingly become a normal political actor, but this also means that its efforts to shape moral norms, including those regarding human dignity, have taken place within a decidedly more competitive environment.

Without privileged access to the political sphere, the Church has also become more vulnerable to attacks against its moral authority. Nowhere has this been more visible than in the Duterte presidency. In the six months after Duterte took office on June 30, 2016, police and unidentified attackers killed over 7,000 people in the war on drugs, according to official statistics.[104] However, there is strong reason to suspect that such data significantly understates the number of deaths.[105] In numerous cases, innocent civilians and children have been killed by police in raids. Duterte has openly dismissed such killings as "collateral damage" and rejected the idea that law

---

[100] Rhoderick John S. Abellanosa, "The CBCP and Philippine Politics: 2005 and After," *Asia-Pacific Social Science Review* 8, no. 1 (2008): 73–88.

[101] Dante B. Gatmaytan, "It's All the Rage: Popular Uprisings and Philippine Democracy," *Pacific Rim Law and Policy Journal* 15, no. 1 (February 2006): 1–37.

[102] Pope Benedict XVI, *Deus Caritas Est* (December 25, 2005), §28.

[103] Catholic Bishops' Conference of the Philippines, "Shepherding and Prophesying in Hope: A CBCP Pastoral Letter on Social Concerns" (July 10, 2006), www.cbcponline.net/shepherding-and-prophesying-in-hope-a-cbcp-pastoral-letter-on-social-concerns/.

[104] Amnesty International, "*If You Are Poor, You Are Killed*": *Extrajudicial Executions in the Philippines' "War on Drugs"* (London: Amnesty International, 2017), p. 6.

[105] Sheila Coronel, Mariel Padilla, David Mora, and the Stabile Center for Investigative Journalism, "The Uncounted Dead of Duterte's Drug War," *The Atlantic* (August 19, 2019), www.theatlantic.com/international/archive/2019/08/philippines-dead-rodrigo-duterte-drug-war/595978/.

enforcement should be liable.[106] In response to Catholic criticisms of the drug war, Duterte has called clergy "sons of bitches,"[107] declared the Church to be "the most hypocritical institution in the Philippines,"[108] and publicly threatened to behead an unnamed bishop.[109] In August 2019, the Philippine National Police levelled sedition, cyber libel, libel, and obstruction of justice charges against two priests and four bishops over a viral video claiming that Duterte's son Paolo and Duterte's close ally Senator Bong Go were involved in the drug trade. The charges alleged that the Catholic leaders were part of a conspiracy to oust Duterte that also included vice president and opposition leader Leni Robredo.[110] Though the Duterte administration denied any involvement with the case, many observers suspected that this was a brazen attempt to silence opposition to Duterte's policies. In February 2020, the Philippine government dropped the charges, admitting that it had no evidence, but the episode strongly suggests that Duterte believed his position to be sufficiently assured that he could directly attack the Church.[111]

Discouragingly for the CBCP, public opinion polls have demonstrated mixed views on the illegal drug campaign. In September 2017, a nationwide Social Weather Stations survey found that 46 percent agreed and 35 percent disagreed with the statement "It cannot be avoided that there are innocent citizens who will die in order to completely eradicate the illegal drug problem."[112] Despite this, quarterly polls between September 2016 and June 2018 showed overwhelming satisfaction with the Duterte administration's campaign against illegal drugs, dropping from a high of 85 percent in December 2016 to a steady average of 77 percent between March 2017 and June 2018.[113] In December 2018, a Social Weather Stations survey found that 66 percent of Filipino adults believed that it was "definitely" or "probably true" that police were involved in the extrajudicial killing of illegal drug suspects, with only 5 percent believing that it was "definitely" or "probably not

[106] "Duterte Says Children Killed in Philippines Drug War Are 'Collateral Damage,'" *The Guardian* (October 17, 2016), www.theguardian.com/world/2016/oct/17/duterte-says-children-killed-in-philippines-drug-war-are-collateral-damage.
[107] Patrick Winn, "Does Duterte's Wrath Against the Catholic Church Have No Limit?," *Public Radio International* (January 22, 2019), www.pri.org/stories/2019-01-22/does-duterte-s-wrath-against-catholic-church-have-no-limit.
[108] Winn, "Does Duterte's Wrath."
[109] Judy Quiros, "Duterte Threatens to Have Bishop's Head Cut Off," Inquirer.net (November 27, 2018), https://newsinfo.inquirer.net/1057402/duterte-threatens-to-cut-off-bishops-head.
[110] Eimor Santos, "CBCP Head: Sedition Case vs. Bishops Unbelievable," CNN Philippines (July 20, 2019), www.cnnphilippines.com/news/2019/7/20/CBCP-head–Sedition-case-vs.-bishops-unbelievable-.html.
[111] "Sedition Charges Dropped Against 4 Bishops in Philippines," *Catholic News Agency* (February 12, 2020), www.catholicnewsagency.com/news/sedition-charges-dropped-against-4-bishops-in-philippines-53080.
[112] "Third Quarter Social Weather Survey: 46% agree and 35% disagree 'it cannot be avoided that there are innocent citizens who will die in order to completely eradicate the illegal drug problem,'" news release, November 1, 2017, www.sws.org.ph/downloads/media_release/pr20171101%20-%20Campaign%20against%20illegal%20drugs_Report%207%20(Special%20Report).pdf.
[113] "June 27–30, 2018 Social Weather Survey: Satisfaction with National Admin's campaign against illegal drugs at net +65," news release, September 23, 2018, www.sws.org.ph/swsmain/artcldisppage/?artcsyscode=ART-20180923090232.

true."[114] The data seemed to suggest that most Filipinos were satisfied with the war on drugs even though they believed that extrajudicial killings were being used to prosecute it. Such a line of thinking is diametrically opposed to the Church's view that human dignity demands that people not be treated as expendable means to some greater end. It also suggests a lack of solidarity with fellow Filipinos. Thus, while the Church continues to call for the defence of human dignity, its rhetoric is in increasing competition with a discourse that seeks to normalize the rejection of inherent human dignity and instead make it contingent upon prevailing social and political attitudes. Such developments raise troubling questions for the Catholic Church about how to ensure the continuing relevance of not only human rights but also the intrinsic value of human dignity and human life.

---

[114] "Fourth Quarter Social Weather Survey: 28% of Filipinos Do Not Believe Police Claims of 'Nanlaban' 28% Believe, and 44% Are Undecided," news release, February 27, 2019, www.sws.org.ph/swsmain/artcldisppage/?artcsyscode=ART-20190227175911.

15

Protestantism and Human Dignity in South Korea

JinHyok Kim

1 INTRODUCTION

The purpose of this chapter is to examine the relationship between Protestantism and human dignity, contextualizing it within the country's modernization and democratization. South Korea is a multireligious country where the major world religions, including Christianity, Buddhism, Confucianism, and Islam, coexist with indigenous religions. According to the recent government's statistics in 2015, Protestantism has the largest population (19.7 percent),[1] although Koreans' first contact with it was later than other major religions. As a religion introduced from the West in the late nineteenth century, Protestantism functioned as a vehicle of the country's modernization and played an indispensable role in introducing the Western notion of dignity.

It is commonly assumed that the Christian doctrine of humanity affected the development of the idea of human dignity. Although one cannot find the word "dignity" in the Christian Scriptures, the biblical story that God created the first human beings as the *imago Dei* (the image of God) in Genesis 1:26–28 has been regarded as the basis for acknowledging and protecting the intrinsic value of human persons on the theoretical and popular level.[2] Furthermore, the early church's acceptance of the Stoic formula of natural law, as distinctively presented by Cicero's connection of it with human nature, encouraged medieval Catholicism to embrace and develop the doctrine of human dignity in theory and ministry.

Protestantism appeared in the sixteenth-century Europe as a wide-ranging theological and cultural reactions to late medieval Catholicism's doctrine and practice, but it did not reject medieval moral theology's emphasis on dignity. Rather,

---

[1] See the official report announced by Statistics Korea: "성별/연령별/종교별 인구," 「국가통계포탈」 ["The Nation's Religious Populations by Sex and Age," KOSIS], http://kosis.kr/statHtml/statHtml.do?orgId=101&tblId=DT_1PM1502&vw_cd=&list_id=&scrId=&seqNo=&lang_mode=ko&obj_var_id=&itm_id=&conn_path=K1, accessed June 11, 2018.

[2] For further and more detailed analysis of the relationship between the concept of dignity and the doctrine of the image of God, as well as its practical implication for Catholic social teaching, see Chapter 14 in this volume by Jonathan Chow.

Protestants accommodated it within newly changed historical and social settings. As Protestantism's missionary movement arose in the nineteenth century, the Christian faith was introduced to Asia, Africa, and the Pacific. In the process of evangelizing non-Christian populations, Protestant missionaries implicitly or explicitly introduced their lifestyle, science, technology, medicine, social etiquettes, and morality – including the Western idea of human dignity – on a nearly global scale. Contacting with Protestantism in the late nineteenth century, Koreans were exposed to a foreign notion of dignity, although their traditional religions also had an idea of the intrinsic value of human life. Moreover, as the concept of human rights and the language of dignity entered into South Korea's constitutional text in the mid-twentieth century (respectively in 1948 and in 1962), they have left indelible marks on South Koreans' legal judgment, moral imagination, and social life. Protestants in the country have taken a certain stance on the issue of human dignity since then, negotiating between its theological conception and constitutional interpretation.

In this light, this chapter will survey how Protestantism influenced the way the notion of human dignity was introduced and accommodated in the course of South Korea's modernization process. Because there are multiple voices within Protestantism,[3] and because the meaning of dignity is difficult to grasp, it is nearly impossible to offer an overarching framework in which their relationship is clearly presented. Instead of treating denominational differences on the issue of human dignity in detail,[4] this chapter will illustrate how Korean Protestant churches adopted and practiced the idea of human dignity for the first 100 years, mainly focusing on their responses to the country's unstable political and social situations. Despite the risk of oversimplification, to avoid being entangled with historical details and diverse theological claims the following sections will divide the history of modern Korea into the three distinct periods: 1) from early evangelism to Japanese colonization, 1884–1945; 2) from independence to the Korean War, 1945–53; and 3) from postwar national reconstruction to democratization, 1953–87.[5] Before investigating these issues, the next section will briefly illustrate premodern Korea's religious

[3] According to the recent government report, there are 374 Protestant denominations in South Korea. It is beyond the purpose and scope of this chapter to deal with these Protestant churches' diverse stances on the concept of dignity in detail. See the following official report: "2018년 한국의 종교현황," 「문화체육관광부」 ["Status of Religion in Korea, 2018," Ministry of Culture, Sports and Tourism], www.mcst.go.kr/kor/s_policy/dept/deptView.jsp?pDataCD=0406000000&pSeq=1731, accessed March 30, 2020.

[4] In general, Korean Christians have treated denominational differences as less important compared to Europeans and North Americans. It is partly because the history of Korean Protestantism is far shorter and less complicated. It is also partly because the first missionaries in early twentieth-century Korea tended to cooperate with one another despite their different denominational backgrounds.

[5] After the massive and nationwide demonstrations against South Korea's dictatorial regime, the June 29 Announcement was declared in 1987. As the outcome of this announcement, the ninth revised Constitution specified the direct popular election of the president, the five-year presidency, and no possibility of reelection. Although a civilian regime was established in 1993, ending more than thirty years of military rule, 1987 marks the turning point in Korean history as the authoritarian regime's surrender to democracy.

situations for a better understanding of the context in which Protestantism was introduced and developed.

2 THE KOREAN RELIGIOUS LANDSCAPE BEFORE THE ARRIVAL OF PROTESTANTISM

As mentioned earlier, South Korea is a multireligious country, and its religious plurality is a historical outcome of Koreans' interaction with other civilizations for thousands of years.[6] This short section will briefly survey Korea's religious situation before the entry of Protestantism. Protestantism's first contact with Korea was much later than those of Buddhism, Confucianism, and Catholicism, but it grew rapidly during the country's modernization in the past century. Protestantism played an indispensable role in introducing the Western notion of dignity, but traditional religions also developed their own unique ways of recognizing the intrinsic value of humanity. Because each traditional religion is a highly complicated belief system, treating it as a single unitary tradition cannot do justice to its nuanced faith and practice. Instead of evaluating, comparing, or categorizing these religions from a certain theological or historical perspective, this section limits its aim to a very broad sketch of Korea's premodern religious landscape.

After Korea's long prehistoric times, the first kingdom *Gojoseon* (고조선 古朝鮮 Old Joseon, ca. 108 BCE) was founded in what is today Northern Korea and Southern Manchuria. Its founding myth shows that ancient Koreans worshipped Heaven and implicitly linked their respect for Heaven with reverence of human beings.[7] According to the myth, the kingdom was established by the descendent of the top-ranked heavenly god, not merely for the flourishing of his people but for *hongikingan* (홍익인간 弘益人間 universally benefiting humankind). Some scholars claim that this myth is the origin of Korean indigenous spirituality, in which the veneration of Heaven plays a central role, forming ancient Koreans' humanistic tendency.[8]

The era of *Gojoseon* was followed by the period of the conflicts among small tribal kingdoms. The three powerful kingdoms Goguryeo (고구려 高句麗), Baekje (백제 百濟), and Silla (신라 新羅) eventually survived and coexisted until *Shila* unified them (57 BCE–668 CE). During the three-kingdom era, Buddhism was introduced from India through China. Buddhism quickly gained prominence among the ruling elite and grasped the mind of ordinary men and women. Buddhism remained the official religion of the next kingdom Goryeo (고려 高麗, 918–1391 CE). Its teaching of

---

[6] About the diversity of religion in Korea, see David Kang, *Syncretism: The Religious Context of Christian Beginnings in Korea* (Albany: State University of New York Press, 2001); Don-ku Kang, "Traditional Religions and Christianity in Korea: Reciprocal Relations and Conflicts," in *Critical Reading on Christianity in Korea*, vol. 3, ed. Donald Baker (Leiden: Brill, 2014), pp. 1055–1081.

[7] See J. Gordon Melton, *Faiths across Time: 5,000 Years of Religious History*, vol. 1 (Santa Barbara, CA: ABC-CLIO, 2014), p. 31.

[8] See Hyung-kon Kim, *The Idea of Human Dignity in Korea: An Ethico-Religious Approach and Application* (Lampeter, UK: Edwin Mellen Press, 2007), pp. 131–136, 162–166.

nondiscrimination of every living being and emphasis upon the Buddha-like nature of all humankind influenced the way the innate worth of humanity was conceived and respected.[9]

Buddhism began to decline in the late Goryeo as the religion's extravagant nationwide rituals squandered the wealth of the country and as its unqualified monks corrupted doctrines and exploited the people. The next kingdom, and the last kingdom of Korea, Joseon (조선 朝鮮, 1392–1897) intentionally repressed Buddhism. Instead, Joseon adopted Neo-Confucianism as its main religious ideology, whose status as the state religion lasted for nearly 500 years. Neo-Confucianism's emphasis upon Heaven as the ground of human being and the author of virtues, coupled with its practical wisdom to cultivate humanity, provided an enhanced view of the value of the human person.[10] However, Joseon's strict social hierarchy, supported by Neo-Confucianism, led many people to yearn for a new society and religion.

In the late Joseon period, Koreans faced varied political, economic, and moral challenges within and from outside the country, but Neo-Confucianism could not function well enough to accommodate them. As a result, indigenous religions and farmers' revolts arose across the country. Among them, *Donghak* (동학 東學, Eastern learning) started in 1860 as a critique of the state's Neo-Confucian ideology and as a nationalistic reaction to a newly rising "Western" religion – Catholicism.[11] It radically claimed that the sacred element of Heaven resides within human nature, even identifying the two in a nearly pantheistic manner. Drawing the idea of equality from this anthropology, the participants of the *Donghak* rebellion challenged Joseon's oppressive social hierarchy and called for a fundamental reformation of the country.

Protestantism entered the Korean peninsula in the late nineteenth century, when the country was marked by political instability and religious diversity. Although Korea's traditional religions valued the worth of human life on their own, the Christian concept of human dignity was based on different theological and philosophical grounds. Its practical implications for modern society were already intensively and extensively investigated and tested through the democratization of Europe and North America. Soon after Protestant mission activities reached Korea, the Christian idea of dignity played a pivotal role both in the growth of Protestantism and in the modernization of the country, as the next sessions will show.

---

[9] About Buddhism's view of human dignity, see Chapter 11 in this volume by Anton Luis Sevilla. It should be noted that Korean Buddhism has its own unique developmental trajectory, but it is beyond the scope and the purpose of this chapter to delve into this issue.

[10] About Confucianism's view of human dignity, see Chapter 10 in this volume by Sungmoon Kim. The uniqueness of Joseon's Neo-Confucianism needs further explanation, but it is beyond the limit of this chapter.

[11] Ki-baik Lee, *A New History of Korea*, trans. Edward W. Wagner (Cambridge, MA: Harvard University Press, 1984), pp. 258–259, 281–288.

3 HUMAN DIGNITY AND PROTESTANTISM IN KOREA

3.1 *Introducing Christian Conceptions of Human Dignity*

It is normally assumed that both Catholicism and Protestantism came to Asia from Europe or North America, but they arrived in Korea in different ways. Catholicism was first introduced in the early seventeenth century through the Korean envoys to China of the late Joseon Dynasty, who encountered the new Western religion in Beijing. These learned people's study of the Chinese translations of Catholic books marked the beginning of Korean Catholicism. After their serious self-study of this "Western teaching," and under the government's tolerance (and ignorance about this strange religion), some believers boldly decided to be baptized and founded churches in the late eighteenth century. As Catholic populations grew and its doctrines seriously questioned Confucianism's ancestral rites and social hierarchy in the nineteenth century, the Joseon government suppressed Catholicism by force. It was also a dangerous time when European imperialism swept Asia. As a result, French missionaries' entry into Korea and Korean Catholics' close connection with Western countries were regarded as threats to the country's security. The government's systematic and brutal persecutions resulted in the death of thousands of Catholics and caused the tragic war with the French navy in 1866.[12]

In contrast, Protestantism was brought mostly by North American and European missionaries, although there were some early contacts with Western missionaries residing in China. In 1883, the first Protestant church – Sorae Church – was established in the northern part of Korea under the leadership of Suh Sang Yoon (서상윤), who became a Christian and participated in the translation of the Christian Bible while in Manchuria, and his brother Suh Kyong Jo (서경조).[13] It was even before the first Protestant missionary, Horace Newton Allen, officially came to Korea in 1884. When foreign missionaries landed on the Korean peninsula, they had to deal with the complicated political and religious situations of the late Joseon society, including the state's organized persecutions of Catholics, the peasants' revolts against the corrupted and weak government, the elite groups' keen interest in modernization, and Japan and other nations' colonial threat. The first Protestant missionaries in Korea were very

---

[12] For further study on the persecution of Catholics in nineteenth-century Korea, see the following articles collected in *Critical Readings on Christianity in Korea*, vol. 1., ed. Donald Baker (Leiden: Brill, 2014): Ki-bok Ch'oe, "The Abolition of Ancestral Rites and Tables by Catholicism in the Chosun Dynasty and the Basic Meaning of Confucian Ancestral Rites," pp. 63–80; Franklin Rausch, "Like Birds and Beasts: Justifying Violence Against Catholics in Late Chosun Korea," pp. 101–130; and Andrew Finch, "The Pursuit of Martyrdom in the Catholic Church in Korea before 1866," pp. 131–157.

[13] See Kyoung Bae Min, *A History of Christian Churches in Korea* (Seoul: Yonsei University Press, 2005), p. 130. However, some church historians claim that the church was established in 1884.

careful not to be entangled with the country's complicated politics.[14] As In Soo Kim summarizes:

> Activities that missionaries undertake in mission fields could be categorized into the three areas. The first is evangelization, the second civilization and the third modernization .... As seen in the Christian history of Korea, medical and educational services, which represent civilization and modernization as a whole, prove to be most useful tools when the freedom of evangelization is not fully granted.[15]

Protestant missionaries in Asia generally tended to keep their distance from politics at the time, but "this was especially true in Korea where political factionalism and power struggles were many."[16] They were well aware that Korean Catholics' conflicts with the Confucian government and that Catholic missionaries' entanglement with European colonial expansion unfortunately resulted in bloody persecutions.[17] Thus, Protestant evangelism was integrated mostly with medical work, education, famine relief, and modernization projects.[18] Consequently, Korea's encounter with the Protestant faith was deeply related to its experience of modernity and exposure to Western culture.

It seems that Protestant missionaries strategically eschewed political engagement to avoid the state's suppression and to obtain favor from the people. Nevertheless, their missional activities embodied the Christian ideal of human dignity. It may be true that they did not have a sophisticated idea of what human dignity is. Christians used the term "dignity" more as a practical notion,[19] even when lacking a well-crafted philosophical and theological definition. Jesus' radical identification of the poor and the marginalized with himself, as shown in his saying "Truly I tell you, just as you did it to one of the least of these who are members of my family, you did it to me" (Matthew 25:40, NRSV), shaped their moral imagination. As a result, medicine, education, and poverty relief were deeply connected to the church's mission of

---

[14] In the following text, we can identify key tactics used by early foreign missionaries in Korea, including approaching the working class (rather than the higher class), targeting women and girls, and focusing on elementary education. See C. C. Vinton, "Presbyterian Mission Work in Korea," *Missionary Review of the World* 16 no. 9 (September 1893): 671.

[15] In Soo Kim, *History of Christianity in Korea* (Seoul: Qumran, 2011), p. 132.

[16] Wi Jo Kang, *Christ and Caesar in Modern Korea: A History of Christianity and Politics* (New York: State University of New York, 1997), p. 17. See also Chapter 3 in this volume by Chaihark Hahm.

[17] See Min, *A History of Christian Churches in Korea*, p. 82.

[18] Cho explains the difference between Catholic and Protestant missions in the nineteenth century as follows: "Catholic missionaries kept a certain distance from the civilization discourse .... They saw the fall of humanity in modern civilization, given the elements of atheism and the destruction of the community values of a rural society .... Protestant missionaries, on the other hand, saw the progress to civilization as a positive pursuit, and kept no distance from it." Cho Hyeon Beom, "A Study on the Protestant Discourse of Civilization in Early Modern Korea," in *Critical Readings on Christianity in Korea*, vol. 1., p. 281.

[19] For example, see a theological account of "dignity as task" in James Hanvey, "Dignity, Person, and Imago Trinitatis," in *Understanding Human Dignity*, ed. Christopher McCrudden (Oxford: Oxford University Press, 2014), pp. 227–228.

enhancing a dignified life of people, especially the life of the miserable and the oppressed.[20] These were a means not merely for a flourishing life but also for forming one's personality in the likeness of God in this temporal life. This line of thought was an effective missionary strategy in the late Joseon Dynasty. Not a small number of the foreign missionaries had medical background, so they opened hospitals, trained doctors, and treated a broad range of patients from the royal family to the beggar. They helped the development of modern education, founding schools even for women, who had little opportunity to receive proper education and had been hindered from public life.[21] They contributed to modernizing the country and bettering its living conditions by introducing Western science and technology. Consequently, Protestantism was even seen at the time as equivalent to "modern civilization."[22]

Protestant churches could spread widely and grow rapidly in Korea thanks to the success of these missions, although Korea's contact with Protestantism was much later than other Asian countries. Through Protestant missions, Koreans were exposed to an unprecedented circumstance in which the dignity of every person was respected regardless of their social rank, education, and gender. Koreans were surprised and impressed by the ways Western missionaries treated the socially marginalized with love and respect.[23] For these foreign missionaries, the rigid hierarchy of Confucianism was a serious moral and social problem of Korean society:

> The evil of this [Confucian] custom is that it denies the right of every man to freedom and creates a class standard of blood and ancestry instead of merit.... It cheapens human life, while custom secures the noble the possession of his goods, immaturity from fortune and a regard for his person, not so the luckless low man ....

---

[20] About the church's mission of enhancing a dignified life of the poor and the miserable in early Christianity, see Peter Brown, *Poverty and Leadership in the Later Roman Empire* (Hanover: Brandeis University Press, 2002), pp. 118–120; Patriarch Kirill of Moscow, *Freedom and Responsibility: A Search for Harmony – Human Rights and Personal Dignity* (London: Darton, Longman and Todd Ltd., 2011), pp. 118–120.

[21] Protestant missionaries not only founded schools for girls and women; they also trained local women, especially widows, and assigned them special roles in assisting male church leaders and even in organizing churches. See Sebastian C. H. Kim and Kristeen Kim, *A History of Korean Christianity* (Cambridge: Cambridge University Press, 2015), pp. 68–69, 76–79. The following essays collected in *Critical Readings on Christianity in Korea*, vol. 3., succinctly illustrate Korean Protestantism's effort to enhance women's life: Hyo-Chae Lee, "Protestant Missionary Work and Enlightenment of Korean Women," pp. 757–785; Lee-Ellen Strawn, "Korean Bible Women's Success: Using the *Anbang* Network and the Religious Authority of *Mudang*," pp. 787–813.

[22] Jang Sukman, "Protestantism in the Name of Modern Civilization," in *Critical Readings on Christianity in Korea*, vol. 1, pp. 293–295.

[23] The relationship between early foreign missionaries and native Koreans was complicated. Missionaries treated Koreans with respect and love *in principle*, but they also established a hierarchy *in reality* which caused discontents and conflicts. See Paul S. Cha, "Unequal Partners, Contested Relations: Protestant Missionaries and Korean Christians, 1884–1907," in *Critical Readings on Christianity in Korea*, vol. 1, pp. 233–266.

This cheapens [cheapness] of human life and disregard of the sacredness of the human body is, after all, not so much a result of the caste as a different effect of heathenism itself.[24]

The early foreign missionaries' contribution to awakening a sense of dignity should neither be ignored nor exaggerated. On the one hand, not all Koreans were enamored by the Christian idea of dignity, and thus its impact had been limited until the clause on dignity became part of Korea's modern constitution in the mid-twentieth century. On the other hand, although many foreign missionaries implicitly or explicitly presupposed the Christian idea of dignity in their mission, they did not want to challenge the political and social order of the late Joseon Dynasty. It should be noted here that not a small number of Koreans learned to recognize an intrinsic worth within every person by their own reading of Scripture. They were impressed by the idea of equality in Christianity, thereby liberating slaves, distributing their property, and teaching the illiterate. The Japanese occupation since 1910 decreased the influence of missionaries as the colonial government restricted their mission by surveilling and even expelling them. Until missionaries came back after Korea's independence, Korean Protestants had to seek their own theology and to redefine the task of the Korean church. The early Korean Protestantism was shaped and developed through their endeavor to discover their identity as Christians and struggle to keep the faith against Japan's persecution.

3.2 Human Dignity Tragically Veiled by Anti-Communism

As the previous section shows, the Christian ideal of human dignity contributed to introducing and developing Protestantism in Korea, albeit not explicitly. It was a crucial aspect of Christian belief the early missionaries and the converts could not ignore, but it was rarely at the center of their moral language. The lack of reflection on its nature and function justified the marginalization of it when other urgent issues, including the protection of sound doctrine or social order, were at stake. As a result, the history of Korean Protestantism has often been marked by its connivance to, or complicity in, the inhuman suppression of dignity by authoritarianism, distorted nationalism, and economic developmentalism. This section will demonstrate how the idea of dignity was tragically overshadowed by anti-communism in the early stage of the nation's democratization. The idea of basic human rights entered into the first constitution in 1948, but the government understood human rights within the limit of its anti-communist policy. Many Protestants played a pivotal role to spread and radicalize the era's notorious anti-communism, failing to conceive of the importance of human dignity.

---

[24] George H. Jones, "Open Korea and Its Methodist Mission," *The Gospel in All Lands* (September 1898): 384, quoted in Chung-Shin Park, "Protestantism in Late Confucian Korea," in *Critical Readings on Christianity in Korea*, vol. 1, pp. 323–333.

Immediately after Korea's independence from Japan in 1945, the country was divided along the thirty-eighth parallel: the zone north of the parallels was occupied by Soviet troops, and the zone south by Americans. The thirty-eighth parallel was not intended to be a national border, but both sides of Korea established their own governments in 1948 as the occupation troops withdrew. Despite strong oppositions to the separation of the country, Rhee Syngman (이승만, 1875–1965) became the first president of South Korea and Kim Ilsung (김일성, 1912–94) the first supreme leader of North Korea. This division was followed by fierce ideological and military conflicts. It also left a tremendous effect on Korean Christianity, especially on both Catholicism and Protestantism above the thirty-eighth parallel. Donald N. Clark summarized the situation as follows:

> Protestants and Catholics both suffered terribly in North Korea before and during the war. By 1949, Christian congregations in North Korea had been shattered and major church establishments ... were experiencing great difficulties and persecution.... Leading Christians in the north had been arrested and some had disappeared without a trace. Likewise, in areas of South Korea that experienced several communist-led insurrections in 1948–49, Christians fared badly as alleged "running dogs" of American and Japanese imperialism and enemies of the people.[25]

In contrast to North Korea's anti-Christian policy, Protestantism was a crucial part of Rhee's regime in South Korea. A large number of the first generation of its political leaders were Protestants, and their affinity with the United States was an invaluable resource to build up a new nation. It even seemed, as Kang said, that "the United States had occupied Korea for the advancement of Christianity in Korea. Korean Christians were totally committed to the support of US policy in Korea."[26] Influenced by America's post-WWII anti-communism and facing the threat of North Korea, Protestant churches played a vital role in spreading and strengthening anti-communism. Among multiple factors that affected the emergence of anti-communist faith, two need to be specially mentioned.

First, along with the entry of the idea of basic human rights into the first constitution, a legal concept of the freedom of religion was introduced.[27] This liberal notion might have intrigued people from different religious backgrounds to reflect on and practice together the idea of dignity in new political and cultural settings. However, it ironically resulted in competition among religions, not only to increase the number of their members but also to secure the support of the government.

---

[25] Donald N. Clark, *Christianity in Modern Korea* (Lanham, MD: University of America Press, 1986), 16.
[26] Kang, *Christ and Caesar in Modern Korea*, p. 74.
[27] Religious liberty was already supported by the Constitution of the Empire of Japan, to which Western missionaries in Korea appealed when the Japanese administration suppressed churches, mission schools, and believers. This is one of the main reasons many missionaries in Korea took the pro-Japanese stance. See Wi Jo Kang, "Church and State Relations in the Japanese Colonial Period," in *Christianity in Korea*, edited by Robert E. Buswell Jr. and Timothy S. Lee (Honolulu: University of Hawaii Press, 2006), pp. 97–115.

There were no explicit oppression or persecution of a certain religion in this new democratic regime, but the president's and political elites' option for one specific religion gave it enormous benefits. Many Protestants eagerly supported the leadership of Rhee, who was a devout Methodist, striving to take "advantage of political powers by taking pro-government stance and following anti-Communist ideology,"[28]

Second, the growth of Christianity in South Korea was immensely indebted to the refugees from North Korea. The North government ruthlessly persecuted Christians, eliminated any public form of Christianity in the territory, and identified it with an ally of American imperialism.[29] To escape oppression and to keep the freedom of belief, many Christians came down to South Korea. They had to survive in the politically chaotic and economically poor South. These refugees could get help from churches, through which American Protestant churches sent a huge amount of relief goods. They founded churches in major cities as the center of their faith and refugee life.[30] The harder their life was, and the more aid they received from America, the more intensified their anti-communism and pro-Americanism were.

During the presidency of Rhee, anti-communism emerged and widely spread in South Korea, and it soon overshadowed the idea of human dignity in the church. The young Rhee studied from 1895 to 1897 at the Methodist mission school Pai Chai (배재) before going to study at Harvard and Princeton. At this school, he converted and became a devout Christian. He also became an active nationalist, facing the immediate threat of Japanese colonization. Christianity and modern political philosophy were the two primary sources through which he accepted Western moral values. The young Rhee showed interest in the biblical view of human dignity, a remarkable idea he found a parallel of within the liberal concept of human rights.[31] The humiliating and painful colonial experience led him to take this notion as a theoretical basis for his struggle against the oppressive rule of Japan. After independence, his main target quickly changed to another totalitarian regime, North Korea, which threatened the security of South Korea and the pursuit of human rights alike. In the process of rising to power, his hostility toward the North increased, even

---

[28] Kim, *The Idea of Human Dignity in Korea*, p. 220.

[29] In Kim Ilsung's speech in 1949, the nationalist assumption of his anti-Christian policy was explicitly shown as follows: "Even though Christians continue to believe in God, they should not believe in the God of other nations but in the God of Joseon." Kim quoted in Kim and Kim, *A History of Korean Christianity*, p. 167.

[30] 윤정란 (Jeong-Ran Yoon), 『한국전쟁과 기독교』 [*Korean War and Christianity*] (Paju: Hanul, 2016), pp. 97–113, 220–226.

[31] Despite the young Rhee's liberal political view, he also believed that it was too early for Koreans to receive the Western liberal idea of the individual. Some scholars argue that this is a reason Rhee preferred a centralized authoritarian government in his real politics. See 오영달 (Young-Dahl Oh), "대한제국기 이승만의 서구 인권 및 주권론 수용: 그의 『독립정신』에 나타난 정치사상을 중심으로 ["Young Syngman Rhee's Introduction of Western Concepts of Human Rights and Sovereignty towards the Period of Daehan Empire]," 「한국민족문화」 [*Korean Studies*] 31 (2008): pp. 430–431.

arguing for the unification by military force if necessary.[32] In his addresses and notes in the 1950s, we can see how his anti-communism was colored by the language of his Christian faith:[33] Korea's reunification by the invasion of the North is a part of God's providential will; the Korean War is not merely an anti-communist war, but it is a divine instrument, like the Crusades, to fulfil God's justice against evil in history.

In the time of intense ideological, economic, political, and military competition with the North, the fear of communism became the most plausible and compelling excuse for the authoritarian government to restrict or suppress human rights. Rhee nearly equated the pursuit of human rights with the conquest of communism.[34] This tendency was justified and strengthened when he felt the threat of war or revolt. The Jeju 4.3 incident (1948–54) is a notable example of how anti-communism easily suppressed the ideal of dignity during Rhee's presidency. This tragic event started in Jeju about two years before the Korean War (1950–3) and ended about one year after. Jeju is Korea's biggest island, lying in the southwestern part of the territory. The background and the cause of the incident are too complex to explain in this limited section. To put it very simply, it first started with the Jeju people's peaceful demonstration on March 1, 1947, to denounce the first presidential election scheduled in May 1948. At the time, many South Koreans were against the election because it would confirm the separation of the South and the North. However, six innocent Jeju civilians were killed by the police on the day, and the demonstration turned into a severe conflict between the police and angry people. After a series of clashes, the armed uprising started as South Korea Labor Party's Jeju branch attacked police offices on April 3, 1948. The situation became worse and more complicated as Korean and US army troops arrived in Jeju to suppress the uprising under the authorization of Rhee's administration.

Rhee conceived of the incident as a communist rebellion, saying in public that it should be "mercilessly" suppressed. The state's use of military force even escalated into near full-scale war. During this incident, approximately between 14,000 and 30,000 people died – nearly 10 percent of Jeju's population.[35] Among 14,231 identified casualties, 11,929 were killed by the state's violence,[36] and nearly 40,000 escaped to Japan to survive. Most massacres and property damages took place between October 11, 1948, and March 1, 1949, under martial law. Indiscriminate killings,

---

[32] Kang, *Christianity and Caesar*, 78–79; 최종원 (Jong-Won Choi), 『이승만의 기독교 수용과 기독교국가건설론 연구』 [*A Study on Rhee Syngman's Reception of Christianity and His Theory of Establishing a Christian Nation*] (Seoul: Booklab, 2014), pp. 315–316.

[33] See 최종원 (Choi), 『이승만의 기독교 수용과 기독교국가건설론 연구』 [*A Study on Rhee Syngman's Christianity and His Theory of Establishing a Christian Nation*], pp. 287–289.

[34] For example, see Rhee's speech to celebrate South Korea's human rights week in 1950: "10일은 인권 공동선언일 [It Is Human Rights Day on 10th]," 「조선일보」 *The Chosunilbo*, December 10, 1953.

[35] Kim Hun Joon, *The Massacre at Mt. Halla: Sixty Years of Truth Seeking in South Korea* (Ithaca, NY: Cornell University Press, 2014), pp. 13–41.

[36] This is the second-highest death toll in modern Korean history after the Korean War. See Jeju 4.3 Peace Foundation, *The Jeju 4.3 Incident Investigation Report* (Jeju: National Committee for the Investigation of the Truth about the Jeju April 3 Incident, 2003), pp. 451–467.

massacres of civilians, mass arrests, detentions, torture, beatings, forced relocations, and large-scale destructions of villages and public facilities turned the beautiful island into a land of horror, agony, and death. The victims' families have been deprived of the life of dignity until recently. They had to repress their painful memory in order not to be misconceived as communists; they were forced to keep silence to live in one village with the people who killed their family; and they even lost their civil liberties due to the guilt-by-association system.

Rhee's administration not only used military force to suppress the incident but also approved the Seobuk (서북, Northwest) Youth Association to participate in military and police acts.[37] Its members came down from the North to avoid the communist party's inhuman persecutions. They established this right-wing group in November 1946, and their churches became main places for supporting their refugee life and sharing their victimized memory.[38] As the Jeju uprising was not easily suppressed, more than 1,000 members of the Seobuk were dispatched to Jeju, and most of them were filled with anti-communist anger. The chair of the Jeju chapter of the Seobuk even called the island "Little MOSCOW."[39] They were officially neither South Korean armies nor police officers, but they participated in military operations wearing police or military uniforms. The Seobuk's violent activity is reported as follows:

> Jeju Island was indeed the land of the Seobuk Youth Association. Even though they committed horrible atrocities, there were no organizations to punish them. Fischgrund, the American advisor, said, "In the United States police officers work in their hometown, but I didn't understand why members of The Seobuk Young Men's Association defecting from North Korea worked as police officers in Jeju." There were, however, the US Army and Rhee Syng-man behind the Seobuk Young Men's Association. The fact that the US Army supported the association is proved by an intelligence report of the US Army.[40]

The Jeju 4.3 incident and the Seobuk's involvement have posed hard questions about the issue of dignity and its relation to religion. One of the main reasons the members of the Seobuk left North Korea was to protect the life of dignity, especially their religious freedom. In Jeju, however, most of them participated in imprisoning, torturing, and even killing innocent civilians, while worshipping and praying to the Christian God whom they believed to be the creator of all humankind and the endower of dignity. What made them keep the dignity of their religious conscience

---

[37] 윤정란 (Yoon), 『한국전쟁과 기독교』 [*Korean War and Christianity*], pp. 217–257. The *Seobuk* was officially dismissed in December 1948, but their activities continued for a while.

[38] 강인철 (Cheol Kang), 『전쟁과 종교』 [*War and Religion*] (Osan: Hanshin University Press, 2003), pp. 177. Especially, the *Seobuk* made *Youngrak* Church (영락교회) in Seoul a basis for their refugee life. See 김병희 편저 (Byung-Hui Kim, ed.), 『한경직목사』 [*Pastor Han Gyungjik*] (Seoul: Kyujang, 1982), pp. 55–56.

[39] Jeju 4.3 Peace Foundation, *The Jeju 4.3 Incident Investigation Report*, p. 179.

[40] Jeju 4.3 Peace Foundation, *The Jeju 4.3 Incident Investigation Report*, p. 336.

on the one hand and crush the dignity of others' lives on the other? How could these young men live with the inner split within themselves? Do we need a more careful and nuanced distinction between human dignity in peacetime and that during war (or revolt)?

The threat of communism and the strong need for fighting against it resulted in the state violence and the *Seobuk*'s participation in it. In this sense, one may argue that the Jeju incident needs to be interpreted in light of the just war theory, although this Christian doctrine cannot be overused to legitimize violence toward civilians during the Cold War era. It is unlikely that Rhee's martial law was the result of his serious reflection of the just war theory, and it hardly fulfilled the fundamental principles of the just war.[41] Nevertheless, one cannot simply deny a possibility that those dispatched to Jeju had just causes in their mind, although deeply intermingled with their hostility toward communism. This tragic history demonstrates to us how human vulnerability affects the way dignity is conceived and practiced in real life and how difficult it is to do justice to the complexity of political and social situations.

Conclusively speaking, anti-communism during Rhee's regime needs to be understood in close relation to Korea's unique situation in the mid-twentieth century. Even Korean political leaders and intellectuals at the time had little interests in the issue of human rights,[42] so the country's anti-communism could easily weaken moral reflections and deliberations. Especially, says David Suh, "Korean Christians had no power or intellectual resources to think and act in light of . . . the poor and the oppressed . . . in the rapid social changes that had taken place immediately after liberation. The official anti-communist stance of the church and the government in the South barred the church from becoming conscious of [them]."[43] The history of the Jeju 4.3 incident remains as an indelible agonizing memory shared by many Koreans. It shows that when the Protestant faith was

---

[41] As mentioned earlier, Rhee's speech at the time rarely reflected the language of the just war; rather it seemed to be closer to fundamentalists' appeal for the notion of holy war. Many scholars argue nowadays that seven principles constitute the just war: "war must have *a just cause*, be waged by *a proper authority*, and with *a right intention*, be undertaken only if there is reasonable chance of success and . . . *overall proportionality*. It must also be used as a *last resort* and be waged in the *pursuit of peace*." See Charles Reed and David Ryall, "Introduction," in *The Prince of Peace: Just War in the Twenty-First Century*, edited by Charles Reed and David Ryall (Cambridge: Cambridge University Press, 2007), p. 3.

[42] This view will undoubtedly invite criticisms. Recent scholarship shows, however, that Korean intellectuals after liberation rarely used the term "human rights." Instead, they paid more attention to the rights of people as a collective. This is perhaps because the Western idea of rights was first introduced within the context of Korea's struggle with colonization and thus was attached to patriotism and nationalism. See 이정은 (Jung-Eun Lee), "해방 후 인권담론의 형성과 제도화에 관한 연구, 1945-1970년대 초" ["The Formation and Institutionalization of Human Rights Discourses after the Liberation, 1945–1970s] (PhD diss., Seoul National University, 2008); 손승호 (Seung Ho Son), 『유신체제와 한국기독교 인권운동』 [*The Yushin Regime and the Human Rights Movement of Korean Christianity*] (Seoul: Institute of the History of Christianity in Korea, 2017), pp. 46–51.

[43] David Kwang-sun Suh, *The Korean Minjung in Christ* (Eugene, WI: Wipf and Stock Publisher, 1991), p. 59.

attached to a specific ideology, the dignity of life or the well-being of the other could be sacrificed for the seemingly higher purpose. A crucial step was made, however, by the next generation of Protestants, who took the biblical idea of human dignity and the constitutional notion of human rights as crucial bases for protesting against military dictatorships.

3.3 Protestantism's Struggle for Human Dignity and Democracy

The Korean War (1950–3) provided critical momentum for intensifying South Korea's anti-communism. During the war, communist troops targeted Christianity, killed believers, tortured church leaders, and destroyed churches. "It is the reason," Clark writes, "why Christianity and communism are mortal enemies in Korea, and it helps explain why the majority of the Korean Church – Catholic and Protestant – is loyal to the anti-communist government in Seoul, and why the government, in turn, invites and welcomes church support."[44] The threat of and the competition with the North quickly justified the state's restriction of human rights for the sake of national security and economic development. The Cold War politics of the world strengthened Korean Christians' fear of communism and their connivance to the authoritarian government. Nonetheless, under the influences of biblical and theological anthropologies, and with the help of modern theories of human rights, progressive Christians provoked renewed interests in human dignity, protesting against the government and caring for the miserable and the persecuted. Their resistance to the authoritative regime left a crucial mark in South Korea's democracy movement.[45] This section will pay special attention to the activity of the National Council of Churches of Korea (한국기독교교회협의회 NCCK) during the country's democratization.[46]

The failure of economic policy and the endemic political corruption under Rhee's leadership after the Korean War resulted in a series of nationwide protests. He had to step down in 1960, ending his nearly twelve-year presidency. The next generation of political elites inherited the legacy of his anti-communism. Some tried to overcome its ideological character, while others used it as a means to achieve power. After the chaotic period that lasted for about a year, General Park Chung-hee (박정희, 1917–79) led a military coup on May 16, 1961, claiming that it was necessary

---

[44] Clark, *Christianity in Modern Korea*, p. 17.
[45] For an overview of Protestantism's contribution to South Korea's democratization in the 1970s, see Yun-Shik Chang, "The Progressive Christian Church and Democracy in South Korea," in *Critical Readings on Christianity in Korea*, vol. 2, ed. Donald Baker (Leiden: Brill, 2014), pp. 553–582.
[46] The NCCK is an ecumenical organization founded in 1924 as the National Christian Council in Korea (조선예수교연합공의회). It became a member of the World Council of Churches (WCC) in 1960 and actively participated in South Korea's democratization movement in the 1970s and the 1980s. After 1988, other Protestant interdenominational organizations, including the Christian Council of Korea (한기총, CCK), the United Christian Churches of Korea (한교총, UCCK), and the Communion of Churches in Korea (한교연, CCIK), were established. Compared to these recent ones, the NCCK has taken a more liberal and progressive stance on theological and political matters.

and legitimate to protect the unstable South from the North. The coup was followed by the fifth revision of the Constitution in 1962, which included the clause on human dignity.[47] The revised Constitution also strengthened the authority of the president (Art. 63, 69, 73, 75, 84, and so on), leaving open a possibility of conflict between the exercise of presidential power and the civilians' pursuit of human dignity.

Park governed through the junta for two years and then became the president of South Korea in 1963. Through controversial procedures, Park was reelected in 1967 and 1971. He eventually installed a repressive authoritarian regime, the Yushin (유신 revitalization reform) on October 17, 1972. Park's emergency decree controlled media communications, universities and colleges, and political activities, seriously limiting fundamental human rights. An amended Constitution was installed in the same year, which invested the president with sweeping powers over all branches of government, extended the period of presidency from four to six years, and even allowed unlimited reelection. Nevertheless, the fast-growing economy and the constant threat of the North led many citizens to keep supporting the regime.

Korean churches' response to Park's government was never monolithic,[48] and his rule certainly had a polarizing effect.[49] On the one hand, many church leaders explicitly supported Park's presidency, conceiving of it as a defender from communism and a good helmsman of economy.[50] For them, the military dictatorship was safer than communism, and unfreedom was more bearable than hunger and poverty. The Korean National Prayer Breakfast (KNPB), for example, started as an unofficial organization allowing political and church leaders to pray together for the nation in March 1966.[51] Although Park was a Buddhist, his appearance in the meeting in 1968 made it a quasi-national event. The attendants prayed for Park's authoritative regime, even seeing it as God's ordained power. Since then, the KNPB became an annual event South Korean presidents have attended regardless of their

---

[47] About the entry of the article on human dignity into South Korea's Constitution, see Chapter 3 in this volume by Chaihark Hamh.

[48] Analyzing each denomination's population and official political attitude in 1972, Kang categorized Protestant churches' response to Park's dictatorial regime as follows: support (24–32.8 percent), resistance (6.4–31.2 percent), and others. 강인철 (Cheol Kang), 『저항과 투항: 군사정권들과 종교』 [Resistance and Reddition] (Seoul: Hanshin University Press, 2013), pp. 265–268.

[49] The majority of Korean Protestantism had remained silent to the dictatorial government since the early years, while only some had actively opposed the state's injustice and persecution. Under Park's regime, however, the tension between the state and the church, and between progressive and conservative churches, increased, and their relationship entered into a new chapter. See Wi Jo Kang, "The Relationship between Christian Communities and Chung-Hee Park's Government in Korea," in Critical Readings on Christianity in Korea, vol. 2, pp. 541–552.

[50] It is noteworthy that "the extent to which the church has stood up for human rights is inversely proportional to the extent to which it has wielded official political power." Richard Amesbury and George M. Newlands, Faith and Human Rights: Christianity and the Global Struggle for Human Dignity (Minneapolis, MN: Fortress Press, 2008), p. 11.

[51] "연혁 [History]" 『(사)대한민국국가조찬기도회』 [Korea National Prayer Breakfast], www.wknpb.org/home/history, accessed June 6 2018.

religion. It has been frequently criticized as a Korean version of a backscratching alliance of politics and religion, especially when the regular meetings were held during dictatorial regimes.[52]

On the other hand, questioning the legitimacy of Park's presidency and observing the increasing oppression of basic human rights, dissident churches rigorously protested against the authoritative state and actively participated in the country's democratization movement. Especially, Park's martial law in 1972 provoked their nonviolent protests, including prayer meetings, all-night vigils, demonstrations, fasting, and many others. In 1973, a group of theologians and church leaders secretly drafted the "Korean Christian Manifesto," beginning with the strong statement that the Christian faith denounces dictatorship. It accused Park's regime, appealed to world churches and citizens for solidarity, and declared for the freedom of conscience, religion, and speech. It was made public in Singapore in May, and its English version was published in July.[53] Although lacking substantial theological reflections,[54] it drew Christians' more active involvement with the anti-government protest and the human rights movement. Following this underground manifesto, the NCCK officially issued the "Human Rights Declaration" in November, demonstrating that the mission of the church is to protect and pursue human rights.

The next year can be marked as a turning point for Protestantism's human rights movement in South Korea. The NCCK established the Human Rights Committee in April, and the sixty-six Christian leaders signed and issued the "Theological Statement of Korean Christians" in November. It is one of the most critical documents Christians made to protest against Park's regime. The following are excerpts from its section on human rights:

> Human rights are endowed by God, and the Christian believes that human rights belong to God. Therefore, Christians are responsible for protecting human rights. Men and women are made in the image of God, and they are God's creation (Genesis 1:27). Thus, if any power other than God steps on them, it is the intrusion of God's realm .... Because humankind has dignity as the image of God, so he or she cannot be used as instruments. No institution can impinge on equality among people .... Institutions and the law are legitimate insofar as they serve to guarantee human rights. Institutions and the law are for human beings, not human beings for them. In this sense, Jesus said "The Sabbath was made for man, not man for the

---

[52] For example, see the messages preached by notable Protestant leaders to support Park's dictatorial regime in 최태욱 (Tae-Yuk Choi), "초창기(1965–70)의 국가조찬기도회[Korea National Breakfast Prayer in Its Early Years (1965–70)]" 「기독교사상」 [Christian Thought] 713 (2018), www.clsk.org/bbs/board.php?bo_table=gisang_special&wr_id=1103&main_visual_page=gisang_new, accessed June 11, 2018.
[53] See "Korean Christianity Manifesto," Christianity and Crisis, July 9, 1973, p. 140.
[54] For example, the manifesto even made no mention of the notion of humanity as God's image, a fundamental (and well-known) biblical basis for the concept of human dignity and rights.

Sabbath. Man is Lord of the Sabbath" (Mark 27:28). This is the first manifesto for human rights against any oppressive institution or law.[55]

According to this document, the church's struggle against Park's dictatorial rule and Christians' care for the poor and the oppressed are not options but necessities.[56] The statement grounds human rights in God's creation, interprets Christians' political protest in light of Jesus' ministry, and boldly applies these theological ideas to the current problems of the state's violence.[57]

At the time, Park's government interpreted and applied the constitutional articles on human rights in a nationalistic and collectivist way. His "Korean-style democracy" imposed and publicized a "Korean version of human rights." It was a twist of the Universal Declaration of Human Rights (UDHR) for the Yushin regime, subsuming human dignity under national sovereignty and basing human rights on nationalistic collectivism.[58] In contrast, the dissident Christian leaders construed the concept of human rights in terms of individual autonomy bestowed by the Creator. They even reinterpreted the mission of the church in close relation to the practice of human rights. For example, in the NCCK's "Human Rights Declaration," the greatest mission of the church is not defined according to the "last" saying of Jesus in Matthew 28:19 ("Go therefore and make disciples of all nations, baptizing them in the name of the Father and of the Son and of the Holy Spirit," NRSV), but in terms of the protection of human rights, reflecting Jesus' deep concern for the poor, the oppressed, and the prisoner in his "first" sermon (Luke 4:18).[59] Hence, they placed at the center of their protest the right to life, freedom of speech, assembly, and religion – key concepts also advocated by secular human rights theorists and activists. This

[55] The following quotation is my translation from "한국 그리스도인의 신학적 성명 [Theological Statement of Korean Christians]," 『1970년대 민주화 운동 I』 [*Democratization Movement in the 1970s*], edited by the NCCK's Human Rights Committee, vol. I. (Seoul: NCCK, 1987), p 406.

[56] The statement was initially made as a critique of Prime Minister Kim Jong-Pil's arbitrary use of Scripture on behalf of Park's regime. However, it begs further reflection as to whether the authors of this anti-government statement interpreted Scripture with a balanced theological stance. For example, Jesus' saying quoted in the statement is not Mark 27:28 but Mark 2:27–28. According to the Markan text, moreover, it is the Son of Man (Jesus), not "man" in general, who is the lord of Sabbath. One may find the partial translation of "Theological Statement of Korean Christians" in English in Kang, *Christ and Caesar in Modern Korea*, pp. 167–169.

[57] Although Korean dissident theologians used the term "individual autonomy," it was not exclusively construed in light of Western individualism; rather, some argued that the "public" dimension of God's entire creation is a context in which human rights should be situated. See 안병무 (Byung Mu Ahn), "인권에 대한 신학적 조명 [Theological Investigations on Human Rights]," in 『민중사건 속의 그리스도』 [*Christ in the Minjung Event*] (Seoul: Korea Theological Study Institute, 1989), pp. 186–188; 최형묵 (Choi Hyung-Mook), "안병무의 인권사상 [Ahn Byung Mu's Thought of Human Rights]," 「신학사상」 [*Theological Thought*] 160 (2013): pp. 168.

[58] For example, see "인권주간을 맞는 소회 [Some Thoughts for Human Rights Week]," 「경향신문」 [*Kyunghyang Shinmun*], December 9, 1972. I owe the discovery of this text to 손승호 (Son), 『유신체제와 한국기독교 인권운동』 [*The Yushin Regime and the Human Rights Movement of Korean Christianity*], p. 42.

[59] See "인권선언 [Human Rights Declaration]" quoted in 조이제 (Yi-Je Cho), 『한국교회 인권운동 30년사』 [*30 Years of Korean Churches' Human Rights Movement*] (Seoul: NCCK, 2005), pp. 59–61.

radical identification of the task of the church with the pursuit of human rights was controversial, drawing criticisms from both conservative Christians and Park's government.

The dictatorial regime responded harshly to progressive Protestantism's more organized resistance, arresting church leaders, inspecting prayer meetings, and using conservative churches to attack and check dissident Christians.[60] For example, at a Breakfast Prayer Meeting for the prime minister in November 1974, Kim Jong-Pil (김종필, 1926–2018), the prime minister at the time and the spokesperson for the state's human rights policy, critiqued progressive church leaders obsession with this-worldly matters, "thereby losing the truth and the purity of their conviction."[61] The fall of South Vietnam in 1975 intensified the fear of communism, and Park's government quickly used it as an excuse to restrict civil liberties and attempted to silence the church's call for human rights.

As a response, dissident church leaders, especially those who belonged to the NCCK, critiqued that Park's administration made wrong use of the liberal separation of politics and religion. They claimed that "considering the doctrinal idea of the image of God and human dignity, [the church] must have a relationship with politics."[62] When appealing to the idea of the individual autonomy created by God, they especially underlined the freedom of religion, a fundamental human right endorsed by the UDHR and supported by world Christians and citizens, as a shield for the NCCK's human rights movement against the state's oppression. They further construed freedom of religion mainly in terms of freedom of mission, conceiving of political resistance as a critical part of the church's social responsibility.[63]

To understand the NCCK's view of human dignity in this period more comprehensively, it worth mentioning the following two issues. First, despite the frequent use of the notion of human rights, one can see in the NCCK's earlier documents little theoretical interest in the nature of human rights, while appreciating its practical importance. The founding members and executive leaders of the NCCK's Human Rights Committee recollected after the nation's democratization that they chose and used the "strange" term "human rights" simply because it "sounded" more fundamental than political democracy.[64] They studied and clarified its meaning through the course of their political activities and anti-government

---

[60] In opposition to the NCCK, the Korean Christian Leaders' Association (KCLA) was established in 1975. Nineteen conservative church leaders formed this organization to support Park's regime, claiming that they represented more churches in South Korea than did the NCCK. They also issued the "Declaration of the Korean Churches," which endorsed Park's government. See Kang, *Christ and Caesar in Modern Korea*, p. 96.
[61] Kim quoted in Chang, "The Progressive Christian Church and Democracy in South Korea," p. 573.
[62] 한국교회협의회 (NCCK), 1976 교회와사회위원회 회의록 [NCCK's Church and Society Committee's Annual Report, 1976], p. 40 (my translation).
[63] 손승호 (Son), 『유신체제와 한국기독교 인권운동』 [*The Yushin Regime and the Human Rights Movement of Korean Christianity*], pp. 84–85.
[64] Ibid., p. 118.

protests.⁶⁵ This may explain why the language of dignity has scarcely appeared – and why its meaning remained unsettled in Protestants' struggle for democratization.

One notable exception is the NCCK's official document entitled the "Declaration on Human Dignity," which is the outcome of Catholic–Protestant dialogue in 1976. In their pro-democracy struggles, progressive Protestants opted to cooperate with Catholics rather than conservative Protestants. The rich tradition of Catholic moral theology empowered Protestant churches' ongoing protests to some extent. From 1974 to 1977, for example, "the Annual Conferences on Human Rights Issues" were hosted by the NCCK's Human Rights Committee. The annual conferences gave explicit priority to praxis,⁶⁶ so their official documents did not clearly mention what the Christian notion of human rights or dignity means except the third conference in 1976. As the outcome of the three-day discussion under the theme of dignity, the participants drafted a theologically rich document, entitled "Declaration on Human Dignity."

The overall theme of the third conference was well presented in the opening sermon, delivered by Catholic Bishop Daniel Tji Hak-soun (지학순, 1921–93). It impressively drew insights from biblical anthropology and from Catholic moral teachings alike, including Thomas Aquinas' natural law theory and Pope John XXIII's encyclical *Pacem in terris* (*Peace on earth*). According to Bishop Tji, "human rights are grounded upon the fact that God created man and woman in God's image; human dignity is confirmed by the fact that God endowed them rights to be united with God and to dialogue with God."⁶⁷ The fundamental value of human beings, therefore, cannot be violated or restricted by any institution or organization in any circumstance. Along with many biblical themes that eagerly call for social justice, Christian moral tradition demonstrates that, if any law infringes human conscience or threatens the common good, it is merely illegitimate violence and has to be resisted. In this sense, human dignity and rights are vital democratic values Christian churches should fight for and defend against the

---

⁶⁵ Borrowing the four categories Christopher McCrudden offered (individual autonomy, freedom from humiliation, protection from discrimination, and satisfaction of basic human needs), the NCCK understood the notion of human dignity mainly in terms of individual autonomy. I owe the discovery of McCrudden's categorization to Hahm's Chapter 3 in this volume. See Christopher McCrudden, "Human Dignity and Judicial Interpretation of Human Rights," *European Journal of International Law* 19, no. 4 (2008): 685–694; Hahm, "Constitutional Discourse on Human Dignity in South Korea." As mentioned earlier, however, some theologians were aware of the risk of individualism embedded in the liberal conception of autonomy, striving to contextualizing it within the Korean cultural context.

⁶⁶ The title of the first conference was "Human Rights and Freedom," the second "The Church and Human Rights," the third "Human Dignity," and the fourth "The Human Right Field and The Church's Responsibility." See 손승호 (Son), 『유신체제와 한국기독교 인권운동』 [*The Yushin Regime and the Human Rights Movement of Korean Christianity*], pp. 209–210.

⁶⁷ 지학순 (Hak-soun Tji), "제3회 인권문제협의회 개회설교 [Opening Sermon for the Third Conference on Human Rights Issues]," in 『1970년대 민주화운동 III』 [*Democratization Movement in the 1970s*], vol. III, edited by the NCCK's Human Rights Committee (Seoul: NCCK, 1987), p. 909; my translation.

inhuman and oppressive state. Bishop Tji also proposed strong cooperation between Catholics and Protestants despite their doctrinal and historical distances, which would in turn facilitate solidarity among the divided people. For this, he suggested founding a human rights organization and establishing a fund for the democracy movement.

Second, the NCCK's human rights movement in the 1970s was influenced by a new conception of mission in terms of *missio Dei* (the mission of God), understanding the Christian mission primarily as participating in and responding to God's mission in history.[68] This missiological stance, endorsed by the Uppsala Assembly of the World Council of Church (WCC) in 1968, took up at its core humanization as being expressed not only in the church but also in the world, not only in the sinner's turning toward God but also in "the worldwide struggle for meaning, dignity, freedom, and love."[69] This inclusive approach integrated social thinking and practice with Christian mission: the restoration of humanity in Jesus Christ cannot be separated from the vision of a fully human life, which in turn requires justice, peace, freedom, and dignity. Influenced by the idea of *missio Dei*, the NCCK struggled for democracy and was involved in varied social justice movements,[70] particularly looking after rights of the industrial workers, farmers, prisoners of conscience, and the poor.

In addition, the NCCK's connection with the WCC enabled it to introduce a Western theology of human rights to Korean churches, to receive financial aid for human rights activities, to expose the reality of Park's dictatorial regime to domestic and foreign people, and to help prisoners of conscience. The NCCK's Human Rights Committee was founded when establishing a nongovernmental human rights organization was nearly impossible in South Korea. To protect the Human Rights Committee from the state's surveillance and oppression, its leaders strongly appealed to the constitutional right to religious freedom and the UDHR's article on it. They brought both Christians and non-Christians to discuss human rights issues, organize protests, support the persecuted and their families, and collaborate with other social organizations. Moreover, the Human Rights Committee also utilized Protestantism's worldwide network, through which Christians in other nations could pray for, financially support, and be in solidarity with dissident churches and the oppressed in South Korea. For example, the NCCK

---

[68] For an illustration of how the notion of *missio Dei* is connected to the political formation of Christians and why it cannot be something that exclusively belongs to liberal theology, see David E. Fitch and Geoffrey Holsclaw, "Mission amid Empire: Relating Trinity, Mission, and Political Formation," *Missiology* 41, no. 4 (2013): 389–401.

[69] Norman Goodall, ed., *The Uppsala Report 1968: Official Report of the Fourth Assembly of the World Council of Churches, Uppsala July 4–20, 1968* (Geneva: WCC, 1968), pp. 27–28.

[70] David Suh argues that a theology of *missio Dei* enabled Korean churches to find their social roles in the secular world, overcoming their fundamentalist tendency. However, Suh ignores that it also widened a gap between liberal and conservative churches. See Suh, *The Korean Minjung Christ*, p. 63.

initiated the "International Conference on National Security – Human Rights – Peace" in Seoul in 1976. After intense discussions during the three-day conference, delegates from churches and countries in Europe, Asia, and North America signed the petition letter to President Park, asking for amnesty to be granted to prisoners of conscience in South Korea.[71]

Park's regime ended with his sudden assassination in 1979, soon followed by General Chun Doo-hwan's military coup. This marked the beginning of another military dictatorship, and dissident churches kept fighting for South Korea's democratization. The NCCK's Human Rights Committee continued to play a crucial role in protecting and promoting human dignity. However, its explicit and continued link between the biblical view of dignity and the democratization movement risked reducing Protestantism's dignity-account as a tool for fighting against the oppressive state. Moreover, those who participated in its human rights movement were limited to a small number of leaders and selected organizations. As Chang keenly observes, "they played a key role in the transition from authoritarianism to democracy ..., [providing] resources and space for pro-democracy struggles. But they did not attempt to mobilize the entire church community to get involved."[72] Accordingly, human dignity had been away from the center of the moral language and reflection of the Protestant majority. Furthermore, the church's struggle against authoritarianism was not successfully extended to an effort to challenge the oppressive power structure within the church.

After South Korea's democratization, the NCCK's Human Rights Committee became less active and influential than before. There are varied reasons for this – the growth of nonreligious (but more specialized) human rights organizations, the burgeoning of the public sphere, the unsmooth transition of leadership within the NCCK, the expansion of conservative churches and the decline of progressive churches, and so on.[73] The Human Rights Committee tried to expand the scope of its activity, including arguing for the abolition of death penalty and taking positions that were anti-industrial pollution, anti-war, and in favor of women's rights; but it has left relatively smaller impacts on these areas.[74] While the NCCK's role in leading and forming moral discourses has somewhat decreased, the social role of megachurches and evangelical groups has definitely increased in recent years. Nevertheless, the NCCK's Human Rights Committee continues to acknowledge and deal with urgent

---

[71] 한국교회협의회(NCCK), "1976 교회와사회위원회 회의록 [NCCK's Church and Society Committee's Annual report, 1976]," p. 85; my translation.
[72] Chang, "The Progressive Christian Church and Democracy in South Korea," p. 581.
[73] For an analysis of the main reasons the NCCK's social activities have declined after Korea's democratization, see 손승호 (Seung Ho Son), "민주화 이후 에큐메니컬 운동의 침체와 활로 모색: 한국기독교회협의회를 중심으로 [The Stagnation of Ecumenical Movement after Democratization and Search for Breakthroughs – Focusing on the National Council of Churches in Korea]," 「한국기독교와 역사」 [Christianity and History in Korea] 48 (2018): 31–68.
[74] See 조이제(Cho), 『한국교회 인권운동 30년사』 [30 Years of Korean Churches' Human Rights Movement], pp. 73, 363, 469. See also the website of the NCCK: www.kncc.or.kr/.

yet controversial human dignity issues, including abortion, homosexuality, and human trafficking.

4 CONCLUDING OBSERVATIONS

As a religion that emphasizes the dignity of every person as God's creation, Protestantism has functioned as a cradle for developing and practicing the notion of human dignity. This chapter has explored Protestantism's relationship with human dignity in South Korea during the nation's transition from premodern kingdom to liberal democracy. This crucial theme was examined against the backdrop of Korea's modern history from the early stages of Protestant mission to the country's democratization movement.

Although most constitutions and religions all over the world respect the intrinsic value of humanity, the concept of human dignity itself is nearly impossible to conceptualize with clarity and precision. As a result, there are always confusions about, and conflicts over, how to understand and practice the idea of dignity. In particular, South Koreans had to go through a very rapid modernization process in the past century and thus did not have sufficient time and resources to accommodate the concept of dignity within its cultural and historical contexts. They could not be exposed to a long democratization process, through which the moral and political concept of dignity could develop together with the growth of rights consciousness. Moreover, South Korea's constitutional clause on human dignity has been overused to justify certain groups' or individual's interests, leaving an uncontrollably wide range of interpretations of what dignity means.[75] Protestants' lack of clarity in using the notion during their anti-government protest also caused more ambiguity in its conception and application.

Despite these difficulties, Protestant churches in South Korea need to continue their social mission by wrestling with the slippery concept of human dignity. The language of dignity, inserted in moral theology and the Constitution alike, will keep influencing their thoughts and acts in a way that requires expressing respect for others as dignified beings.[76] The concept of dignity shows that human beings should never be treated as a means to an end. However, the concept itself has to be a means to an end – achieving the good life or securing the common good.[77] In this sense, Protestant churches' missional priority may not lie in specifying the meaning of dignity but in promoting human flourishing, although the latter explicitly or implicitly requires the former. Protestantism in South Korea needs to keep contributing to human dignity discourse, negotiating the gap between the constitutional value of dignity and its real application, as it did during the country's

---

[75] See Chapter 3 in this volume by Chaihark Hahm.
[76] Michael Rosen, *Dignity: Its History and Meaning* (Cambridge, MA: Harvard University Press, 2012), pp. 156–157.
[77] I owe this insight to Li-ann Thio; see Chapter 8 in this volume.

modernization and democratization periods. By drawing wisdom from its deep theological resources and utilizing its domestic and global network, Protestant churches are still called to play a crucial role in a liberal democratic society where citizens' rights consciousness is constantly growing and the government has to meet the varied range of right claims.

Index

Abe, Shinzo, 7
abortion, 1, 3, 17, 19, 47, 48, 49, 78, 79, 123, 132, 337, 346, 347, 352, 377
adultery, 13, 73, 238
affirmative action, 122, 135
anti-communism, 91, 363, 364, 365, 366, 367, 368, 369
Aquinas, Thomas, 121, 333, 374
Arendt, Hannah, 2
Asian values, 4, 5, 6, 10, 11, 193, 281
Aśoka Maurya, 293, 306
Asshiddiqie, Jimly, 151, 152
Association of South East Asian Nations (ASEAN), 6, 331
authoritarian pragmatism, 193
authoritarianism, 6, 14, 19, 20, 76, 93, 95, 99, 108, 113, 119, 192, 195, 202, 317, 328, 363, 366, 369, 376
   authoritarian regime, 88, 326, 328, 370
autonomy, 3, 18, 30, 32, 38, 47, 48, 50, 51, 60, 74, 97, 108, 130, 131, 160, 164, 167, 168, 186, 188, 192, 198, 201, 202, 218, 232, 241, 275, 300
   individual, 9, 13, 14, 15, 22, 30, 31, 44, 47, 50, 72, 103, 105, 106, 108, 125, 132, 136, 137, 188, 189, 243, 272, 372, 373
   institutional, 261
   liberal, 202
   personal, 30, 32, 47, 49, 102, 103, 124, 131, 132, 133, 182, 210, 218, 234
   rational, 243, 244, 250
   relational, 202

Baxi, Upendra, 24
benevolence, 191
Bentham, Jeremy, 287, 288
Buddhism, 5, 17, 225, 269, 270, 271, 272, 273, 274, 275, 276, 277, 278, 279, 280, 281, 282, 283, 284, 356, 358, 359

Amida Buddha, 279
arhat, 275, 276, 277, 283
bodhicitta (*bodaishin* 菩提心), 278
bodhisattva (*bosatsu* 菩薩), 271, 276, 277, 278, 279
Buddha-nature (*busshō* 仏性), 271, 276, 278, 283
Chiggala Sutta, 270, 273
compassion (*jihi* 慈悲), 271, 273, 274, 277, 278, 280, 281
Confucian Buddhism, 17, 269, 280
Dōgen's Shushōgi, 271
emptiness, 277, 279
enlightenment, 270, 271, 273, 274, 275, 276, 277, 278, 279, 281, 283
karma, 277, 291, 299, 300, 305, 306
Lotus Sutra, 279
Mahāyāna, 17, 269, 271, 275, 276, 278, 279, 282, 283
nirvana, 275
no-self (*anātman*), 272, 279
salvific Buddhism (Pure Land), 17, 269, 279, 280, 283
seclusionism (*tonseishugi* 遁世主義), 283
suffering, 17, 270, 271, 273, 274, 275, 276, 277, 278, 279, 282, 283
the right opportunity of evil persons (akunin shōki 悪人正機), 280, 283
Theravāda, 269
Vajrayāna, 269
Zen, 17, 269, 271, 276, 279, 281

capital punishment. *see* death penalty
caste, 18, 30, 276, 286, 287, 289, 291, 292, 294, 296, 297, 298, 299, 301, 304, 305, 306, 363
   varṇa, 286, 289, 291, 292, 293, 298, 301, 305
CEDAW (Convention on the Elimination of All Forms of Discrimination against Women), 123, 132, 195, 331

379

Chan, Joseph, 258, 259
Chang, Peng-Chun, 87
Chen, Shui-bian, 102
Chiang Ching-Kuo, 88
Chiang Kai-shek, 88
China, 8, 227, 281, 358, 360
China, People's Republic of (PRC)
  Civil Code, 238, 239
  Constitution (1982), 4, 16, 220, 222, 223, 224, 228, 229, 230, 231, 232, 233, 236, 237, 239, 241
  Cultural Revolution, 5, 16, 220, 226, 227, 228, 229, 231, 234, 236, 237
  Law of Compulsory Education Law (《义务教育法》) (2006), 241
  Law of the Protection of Disabled Persons (《残疾人保障法》) (2008), 241
  Law of the Protection of Women's Rights and Interests (《妇女权益保障法》), 241
  National People's Congress Standing Committee, 186
Chinese Communist Party, 88, 221, 242
Chinese Nationalist Party (KMT/ Kuomintang), 91, 94
Christianity, 5, 17, 225, 270, 336, 356, 363, 364, 365, 369
  Catholic Church, 2, 15, 19, 121, 332, 333, 338, 341, 343, 350, 352, 355
  Catholicism, 5, 15, 19, 121, 122, 123, 134, 285, 332, 333, 334, 335, 337, 338, 339, 341, 346, 348, 349, 352, 356, 358, 359, 360, 364, 374
  Protestantism, 5, 19, 356, 357, 358, 359, 360, 362, 363, 364, 369, 371, 373, 375, 376, 377
civil society, 190, 215, 267
colonialism, 3, 19, 308, 309, 310, 311, 312, 313, 315, 317, 322, 357, 365
  decolonization, 8
common law, 168, 209
communitarianism, 37, 108, 189, 190, 192, 203, 218, 219, 281
Confucianism, 5, 16, 74, 195, 225, 243, 244, 252, 253, 254, 255, 258, 262, 268, 281, 282, 356, 358, 359, 360, 362
  Analects of Confucius (*Lunyu* 論語), 244
  Confucian political meritocracy, 258, 261, 267
  dao 道 (the Way), 252, 264
  filial piety, 76, 77, 196, 263, 281
  head of household, 13, 42, 75
  junzi 君子, 194, 196, 210, 211, 244, 251, 252, 254, 256, 261
  li 禮, 246
  marriage prohibition, 74
  moral achievement, 16, 249, 250
  moral development, 244, 248, 251, 254, 264, 268
  moral potentiality, 244, 267
  moral self-cultivation, 16, 244, 245, 246, 249, 250, 251, 253, 254, 264, 267
  moral self-transformation, 255, 256
  ren 仁, 246, 253, 265
  xiaoren 小人, 244
constitutionalism, 1, 3, 60, 189, 190, 194, 260
  communitarian, 202
  democratic, 198
  dignitarian, 188
  relational, 12, 191, 192, 202, 203, 205, 209, 210, 219
counter-majoritarian difficulty, 61
cronyism, 328
cultural trauma, 112, 118, 119, 121

Daly, Erin, 3
Daniel Tji Hak-soun, Bishop, 374
death penalty, 13, 15, 17, 19, 35, 56, 77, 94, 120, 122, 123, 129, 146, 147, 148, 149, 202, 209, 235, 294, 298, 337, 349, 350, 351, 352, 376
defamation, 12, 46, 54, 79, 80, 97, 152, 153, 154, 195, 211, 212, 213, 219, 231, 237
democracy
  constitutional, 16, 40, 259, 260, 261, 262, 263, 267, 268
  democratization, 5, 6, 17, 20, 88, 93, 94, 99, 108, 302, 317, 356, 357, 359, 363, 369, 371, 373, 374, 376, 377, 378
  third-wave democratization, 1, 5, 8, 10
dignity
  as anti-humiliation, 3
  as autonomy, 4, 9, 191, 202, 203, 205
  as concrete right, 67, 71
  as status, 3, 191, 243
  communal understanding of, 32, 33, 37
  Confucian egalitarian understanding of, 245, 263, 267
  dignitas, 113, 115, 116, 189, 229, 287
  egalitarian, 16, 111, 116, 117, 118, 121, 188, 198, 218, 219, 252, 261, 276
  hierarchical, 189, 198, 211, 219
  individual, 13, 15, 31, 32, 33, 34, 40, 41, 43, 44, 45, 46, 47, 48, 50, 51, 52, 53, 54, 55, 56, 57, 58, 59, 60, 61, 63, 76, 176, 212, 278, 309, 344
  inherent, 3, 17, 80, 115, 123, 131, 163, 179, 180, 182, 191, 198, 214, 219, 275, 293, 335, 338, 355
  inner, 17, 275
  intrinsic worth, 2, 3, 22, 36, 37, 136, 188, 189, 198, 276, 282, 285, 288, 363
  Menschenwürde, 249, 250, 252
  meritocratic, 16, 17, 252, 257, 259, 260, 261, 266
  of dead persons, 33, 83, 238
  of legal persons, 79, 80, 83
  of state, 317

discrimination, 30, 32, 56, 72, 119, 133, 143, 144, 173, 174, 176, 177, 178, 180, 182, 226, 230, 232, 276, 326, 336
  de facto, 45, 185
  racial, 3
  sex, 89, 180, 181
  sexual orientation, 171, 174, 175, 177, 178
due process, 35, 36, 47, 118, 124, 126, 130, 132
Dürig, Günter
  Objektformel (object formula), 85, 101
Duterte, Rodrigo, 6, 19, 127, 135, 333, 350, 353
duty
  moral, 296
  state, 70, 82, 85
  to pay tax, 98
  to perform military service, 98, 108
Dworkin, Ronald, 37

egalitarianism, 195, 264, 268, 285, 306
Elazar, Daniel J., 9
elective dictatorship, 193
elitism, 12, 189, 218
equality
  de facto inequality, 167
  differential treatment, 107, 173, 174, 177, 178
  equal protection, 4, 48, 58, 61, 107, 124, 133, 134, 211, 261, 262, 352
  gender, 11, 13, 59, 89, 90
  inequality, 9, 19, 59, 174, 242, 247, 248, 249, 251, 252, 257, 258, 259, 299, 332, 334, 335, 344, 345, 352
  male domination, 43, 313
  marriage, 133
  moral, 247, 248, 249, 251, 252, 256, 257, 258, 259, 260, 261
  natural, 248, 249, 252, 256, 257, 258, 259
  of the sexes, 43, 44, 50, 55, 56, 58, 59, 63, 76
  political, 258, 259, 260, 261
  social, 43, 114, 119
  substantive, 170
ethos, 95, 189, 195, 287, 298
euthanasia, 1, 32, 33, 37, 337
  assisted suicide, 202

family
  household system, 44
  naming system, 45
  parental coercion, 43
federalism, 141
fraternity, 12, 21, 24, 26, 213
free will, 73, 74, 335
freedom
  from humiliation, 72
  of belief, 47, 133, 185, 323, 365
  of choice of occupation, 172
  of expression, 7, 28, 29, 46, 54, 97, 99, 117, 133, 152, 153, 154, 175, 185, 193, 210, 211, 268
  of marriage, 106, 107
  of movement, 103, 335
  of religion, 33, 98, 118, 175, 185, 194, 202, 205, 217, 268, 323, 324, 364, 367, 371, 373, 375
  of speech, 7, 29, 46, 103, 117, 144, 154, 195, 204, 205, 210, 268, 371, 372
  of the person, 70
  of the press, 7, 103, 141, 154, 326
  of thought, 28, 99, 100, 133, 146, 154
  positive, 232

Germany
  Abortion Reform Act, 48
  Basic Law, 2, 47, 48, 50, 62, 77, 80, 90, 92, 93, 100, 220, 221, 230
  German Academic Exchange Service (DAAD), 92
Goh Chok Tong, 197
Griffin, James, 232

Habermas, Jürgen
  constitutional patriotism, 196
hate speech, 185
Hatta, Mohammad, 310, 314, 316, 322
Hinduism, 5, 286, 292, 301, 305
Holocaust, 2, 335
homosexuality
  decriminalization of, 32, 37
Hong Kong
  Basic Law, 4, 6, 15, 160, 167, 169, 170, 172, 173, 177, 186
  Bill of Rights Ordinance (BOR), 15, 160, 168, 169, 170, 171, 173, 179, 180, 181, 182, 183
  One Country, Two Systems, 7, 15, 160, 167, 169, 186
honor, 44, 45, 46, 54, 113, 115, 121, 145, 159, 189, 191, 192, 196, 198, 201, 211, 212, 213, 214, 228, 248, 250, 253, 254, 256, 257, 297
human dignity. *see* dignity
human flourishing, 25, 188, 219, 377
human nature, 10, 16, 219, 223, 228, 238, 244, 245, 246, 249, 253, 254, 255, 257, 263, 264, 265, 356, 359
human rights
  European Court of Human Rights, 171, 179, 182, 183
  human rights law, 2, 91, 137, 143, 144, 145, 146, 147, 162, 163, 165, 166, 168, 173, 174, 181, 185, 187, 188, 209, 231
  international, 1, 2, 90, 165, 174, 335
human trafficking, 3, 182, 183, 377

humanity, 18, 42, 50, 89, 128, 147, 164, 179, 180, 191, 203, 205, 214, 216, 225, 228, 243, 282, 285, 287, 289, 291, 296, 297, 298, 300, 301, 302, 306, 309, 316, 320, 321, 324, 325, 330, 335, 336, 356, 358, 359, 375, 377
Hume, David, 194

ICCPR (International Covenant on Civil and Political Rights), 4, 6, 15, 80, 91, 123, 144, 145, 147, 154, 160, 163, 164, 168, 169, 170, 171, 172, 173, 179, 180, 182, 183, 231
 Second Optional Protocol, 350
ICESCR (International Covenant on Economic, Social and Cultural Rights), 80, 91, 144, 160, 163, 164, 168, 169, 170, 172, 231
identity
 gender, 32, 134, 178, 181
 group, 14, 125, 133, 136, 188, 300
 personal, 44, 47
 religious or cultural, 182
 sexual, 179
imago dei, 17, 122, 189, 275, 279, 332, 333, 334, 337, 342, 343, 347
India
 AADHAAR (Targeted Delivery of Financial and Other Subsidies, Benefits and services act, 2016), 29, 31, 32, 33, 37
 civil code, 26
 Constitution of, 12, 33, 34, 209
 Directive Principles of State Policy (Constitution), 12, 23, 24, 26, 27, 28
 Fundamental Duties (Constitution), 12, 23, 24
 Preamble (Constitution), 12, 23, 24, 26, 209
individualism, 37, 40, 42, 46, 47, 49, 50, 51, 55, 56, 60, 202, 272, 273, 281
 expressive, 3, 11
 liberal, 74, 188, 243
Indonesia
 Anti-Terrorism Law, 149
 Bali bombing, 148, 149, 150, 151
 Constitution (1945), 15, 139, 140, 142, 146, 151, 153, 154, 158, 159, 308, 309, 316, 317, 322, 324, 330, 331
 constitutional amendment (1999–2002), 6, 15, 139, 140, 141, 144, 145, 159
 Criminal Code, 152, 153, 154
 Cultural Islam, *Pancasila* Islam, or Islamic formalism, 323, 324
 Declaration of Independence (1945), 308, 309
 Electoral Commission, 141
 Indonesian Communist Party, 144
 Indonesian Communist Party (Partai Komunis Indonesia, PKI), 318, 319
 Information and Electronic Transactions (ITE), 153
 New Order, 18, 19, 308, 309, 316, 317, 318, 319, 320, 322, 323, 324, 326, 328, 329
 People Consultative Assembly (Majlis Permusyawaratan Rakyat, MPR), 140, 142, 319, 321
 People's Representative Assembly, 141
 post-Suharto era, 141, 308
 Press Law, 152, 153
 Social Security, 143, 145, 146, 155, 156, 157, 158
 Third Amendment, 142
Inglehart, Ronald, 9, 11
Islam, 5, 18, 19, 208, 308, 309, 310, 316, 320, 322, 323, 324, 325, 326, 327, 328, 329, 330, 356

Japan
 Attorney Act (1949), 55
 Civil Code, 44, 56, 57, 58, 59
 Constitution of, 7, 13, 40, 41, 42, 43, 46, 47, 49, 50, 51, 52, 54, 55, 57, 58, 59, 60, 87, 90
 Diet, 44, 45, 46, 56, 58, 59
 Edo era (1603-1867), 45
 emperor, 13, 41, 42, 293
 Family Register Act, 45, 58
 feudal system, 41, 42, 43
 Kokutai, 13, 42
 landlord-tenant system, 42
 Meiji Constitution, 41, 42, 47
 Meiji reform, 92
 State Redress Act (1947), 58
Jehovah's Witness, 52, 98
Jemaah Islamiah, 149
John Paul II, Pope, 122, 337, 347, 349
 Evangelium Vitae (1995), 337
 Sollicitudo Rei Socialis (1987), 337
John XXIII, Pope, 335, 374
 Pacem in Terris (1963), 335
juristocracy, 191
justice
 social, 15, 18, 36, 114, 115, 117, 118, 119, 122, 125, 131, 134, 136, 139, 309, 315, 316, 322, 329, 330, 374, 375
 social and economic, 14, 26, 28, 97, 114, 184

Kant, Immanuel, 37, 48, 189, 224, 225, 226, 243, 247, 285, 300
 autonomy, 225, 275, 300
 intrinsic worth, 21, 22
 Kingdom of Ends, 243
 view of dignity, 28, 38, 48
Kaplan, Seth D., 9
Kateb, George, 243
Keown, Damien, 272, 273, 274, 275, 278

Kim, In Soo, 361
Korea, Democratic People's Republic of, 358, 364, 365, 367
Korea, Republic of
  Civil Code, 74, 75
  Constitution of, 62, 63, 64, 66, 67, 68, 69, 72, 76, 77, 78, 87
  Criminal Code, 73, 76, 78
  Human Rights Committee, 371, 373, 374, 375, 376
  Human Rights Declaration, 371, 372
  Japanese colonial occupation, 19, 81, 357, 363
  Jeju 4.3 incident, 20, 366, 367, 368
  National Council of Churches of Korea (NCCK), 369, 371, 372, 373, 374, 375, 376
  Seobuk Young Men's Association, 367
Korean War, 19, 20, 91, 357, 366, 369

Lama, Dalai, 272
Lee Hsien Loong, 197, 212, 213
Lee Kuan Yew, 5, 193, 197
Lee, Teng-Hui, 89, 95
legal moralism, 3
legal transplant, 10
legitimate/illegitimate child, 13, 45, 57, 58, 61
Leo XIII, Pope, 334
  Rerum Novarum (1891), 334, 335
Leonen, Marvic, 127, 128, 131, 134, 136
liberalism, 140, 158, 189, 194, 334
liberalization, 90, 97, 234, 340
  economic, 197
  political, 197
liberty. *see* freedom
life imprisonment, 48, 56, 147, 349

MacArthur, Douglas, 42
Mahathir, Mohammed, 5
Malaysian Federation, 192
Marcos, Ferdinand, 14, 113, 119, 120, 121, 122, 126, 127, 333, 342
marriage
  betrothals, 44
  interracial, 133
  same-sex, 1, 7, 14, 47, 107, 109, 133, 134
  transgender, 161, 178, 179
May, James R, 3
McCrudden, Christopher, 2, 23, 72, 131, 136, 137, 166, 270, 280
Mencius, 16, 244, 245, 246, 247, 248, 249, 250, 252, 253, 254, 256, 257, 265, 266
military sexual slavery, 120
  comfort women, 81, 82
modernization, 8, 11, 356, 357, 358, 359, 360, 361, 377, 378

Modi, Narendra, 6
Moyn, Samuel, 9

national self-determination, 8, 322
Nishitani Keiji, 17, 269, 276, 277, 279

one person one vote principle (OPOV), 259

parliamentarism, 190
paternalism, 196
  anti-paternalism, 202
  state, 190
patriarchy, 73, 331
  ethos, 195
  family structure, 13, 58, 75
Paul VI, Pope, 335
  Octogesima Adveniens, 335, 336
Peng Zhen, 228
Peng, Feng-Chi, 92, 100
PERPU (Peraturan Pemerintah Pengganti Undang-Undang), 149, 150
personhood, 30, 48, 51, 184, 189, 218, 224, 225, 232, 237, 244, 245, 315
Philippines, Republic of
  Catholic Bishops' Conference of the Philippines (CBCP), 19, 122, 333, 341, 342, 343, 344, 345, 346, 347, 348, 349, 350, 351, 352, 353, 354
  Conciliar Document (1991), 344
  Constitution (1935), 111, 112, 114, 115, 116, 119
  Constitution (1973), 113, 117, 128, 131
  Constitution (1987), 111, 112, 113, 118, 120, 121, 125, 129, 131, 134, 137
  People Power Revolution (1986), 5, 14, 19, 120, 342, 343
  Spanish-American War, 14, 112, 338
Pius XII, Pope, 335
populism, 6, 9
preferential option, 332, 336, 337
privacy, 3, 4, 30, 31, 32, 34, 41, 42, 44, 48, 49, 51, 52, 55, 60, 68, 69, 125, 130, 173, 181, 235, 240, 241
  decisional, 14, 130, 131, 132, 137
  informational, 14, 102, 103, 130, 132
  marital, 133
  spousal, 134
proportionality review, 100, 101, 104, 105, 106, 108
Prussia, the Kingdom of, 47, 92
  Constitution of, 47
public discourse, 4, 5, 18, 19, 187, 192, 198, 199, 212, 306
public humiliation, 30
Public Interest Litigation (PIL), 29
public order, 146, 155, 194, 203, 238

rationality, 18, 48, 121, 189, 195, 205, 226, 228, 247, 277, 282, 333, 334
Rawls, John
  overlapping consensus, 3, 22, 23, 64
relationism, 192, 208
relativism
  cultural, 5
  moral, 337
religious diversity, 5, 192, 203, 320, 326, 356, 358, 359
respect
  moral, 251, 254, 273
  of individuals, 40, 42, 44, 46, 50, 97, 281
  social, 273, 274
right
  absolute, 35, 77, 78, 149, 173, 231
  copyright, 54
  defensive, 48, 53, 55
  enumerated/unenumerated, 14, 21, 25, 67, 68, 69, 70, 71, 85, 87, 93, 101, 102, 103, 105, 108, 131, 169, 335
  ESC (economic, social and cultural rights), 15, 143, 144, 145, 146, 155, 156, 157, 158, 159, 161, 162, 163, 164, 169, 185, 232
  individual, 11, 12, 32, 33, 36, 37, 42, 46, 53, 54, 62, 63, 69, 70, 72, 73, 74, 75, 78, 99, 117, 122, 126, 140, 146, 147, 152, 154, 155, 158, 159, 171, 218, 271, 272, 309, 315, 320, 335
  natural, 34, 35, 36, 77, 79, 243, 258
  nonderogable, 146, 148, 149, 152
  of personality, 14, 53, 68, 69, 70, 71, 75, 78, 79, 80, 83, 104, 105, 220, 224, 226, 228, 231, 236, 237, 238, 239
  of religion, 33, 146, 202, 204, 316, 320, 323, 330, 336, 372
  of workers, 26, 335, 345, 375
  parental, 68, 123
  socioeconomic, 25, 27, 29, 35, 36, 134, 139, 140, 155, 156, 159, 164, 169, 170, 173, 175, 176, 184, 185, 199, 209, 218
  to assembly, 185, 232, 316, 317, 372
  to be free from cruel punishment, 15, 120, 144, 145, 148, 161, 171, 173, 174, 179, 180
  to be free from torture, 15, 36, 144, 145, 146, 148, 149, 175, 179, 232
  to dignity, 26, 32, 35, 72, 153, 154, 155
  to education, 27, 28, 29, 98, 144, 156, 232, 312, 316, 317, 329
  to equal concern and respect, 50
  to equality, 15, 26, 144, 170, 173, 174, 176, 178, 185, 317
  to fair trial, 144, 175, 199
  to food, 25, 27, 209, 215, 232, 335
  to health, 144, 175, 232, 237, 238, 239, 329
  to honor, 54, 69, 145, 153, 154, 155, 220, 224, 237, 238, 239
  to inheritance, 13, 43, 44, 57, 58
  to life, 4, 12, 15, 25, 26, 27, 28, 29, 30, 32, 33, 35, 36, 37, 77, 78, 79, 136, 143, 144, 146, 147, 148, 162, 170, 175, 183, 184, 209, 223, 232, 237, 238, 239, 335, 372
  to marital autonomy, 237, 238
  to marriage, 14, 43, 44, 133, 178, 179, 335
  to name, 220, 223, 237, 238, 239
  to participate in economic advancement, 316
  to physical integrity, 238, 239
  to privacy, 13, 14, 21, 29, 30, 31, 32, 37, 73, 102, 103, 105, 130, 131, 180, 181, 210, 211, 220, 224, 237, 238, 239, 240
  to property, 43, 44, 96, 97, 105, 117, 135, 136, 145, 213, 231, 237, 238
  to reputation, 14, 54, 69, 83, 103, 104, 105, 108, 211, 220, 224, 229, 237, 238, 239
  to residence, 26, 232
  to self-determination, 13, 30, 32, 48, 49, 52, 53, 68, 70, 72, 73, 74, 78, 79, 218, 240, 321
  to shelter, 209, 335
  to social security, 140, 143, 144, 146, 156, 157, 176, 232
  to social welfare, 15, 85, 173, 175, 176, 177, 316
  to work, 26, 144, 156, 163, 172, 173, 232, 335
  to worship, 232, 335
  women's, 78, 115, 241, 312, 336, 348, 376
Roman law, 113
Rosen, Michael, 37, 69, 72
Rubin, Edward, 9
rule of law, 4, 151, 154, 165, 185, 191, 203, 209, 221, 233, 234, 239, 243, 335

same-sex civil partnership, 177
sanctity, 31, 74, 131, 304, 332, 337, 352
separation of powers, 139, 141, 191, 209, 260, 261
Singapore
  Advanced Medical Directive Act (AMDA), 201
  Dignity Kitchen, 200
  foreign female domestic workers (FDWs), 214
  Maintenance of Religious Harmony Act (MRHA), 205
  Maintenance of Religious Harmony white paper (1989), 194, 205
  Mental Capacity Act (MCA), 201
  paternal democracy, 192, 196
  Penal Code, 206, 215
  Presidential Council for Religious Harmony (PCRH), 205
  Prevention of Human Trafficking Act (PHTA), 201
  Protection from Harassment Act (POHA), 200

shared values white paper (1991), 191, 193
    Vulnerable Adults Act (VAA), 201
Sino-British Joint Declaration (1984), 160
social engineering, 191, 209
social hierarchy, 197, 210, 244, 289, 290, 306, 359, 360
social welfare, 26, 85, 114, 137, 143, 175, 199, 329
solidarity, 117, 190, 191, 192, 203, 217, 219, 332, 336, 337, 342, 343, 344, 345, 355, 371, 375
    Christian, 337
    family, 44, 45, 56, 60
South Africa, Republic of
    South African Constitutional Court, 96, 148, 176, 178, 184
South Asia, 285, 288, 289, 321
statism, 190, 203
Sueki Fumihiko, 270, 277, 282
    trans-ethics (chō rinri 超倫理), 270, 282
suffrage, 14, 114, 115, 116, 170
Suharto, Haji Mohammad, 6, 18, 19, 317, 318, 319, 320, 322, 328
    Broad Guidelines of State Policy (Garis-Garis Besar Haluan Negara, GBHN), 318
Sukarno, Ir., 309, 310, 314, 315, 316, 318
Sunstein, Cass
    incompletely theorized agreements, 23

Taiwan
    Act Governing the Relations between People of the Taiwan Area and the Mainland Area, 106
    Additional Articles of the Constitution, 88, 89, 90, 97
    Administrative Execution Act, 100
    Assembly and Parade Act, 97
    Civil Code, 90, 103, 106
    Conscription Act, 98
    Constitution of the Republic of China, 87, 88, 93, 94, 115, 223
    Criminal Code, 97
    Disciplinary Measures for the Prevention of Repeat Offenses by Communist Espionage Criminals during the Period of National Mobilization for the Suppression of the Communist Rebellion, 99
    Drug Control Act during the Period for Suppression of the Communist Rebellion, 94
    Household Registration Act, 102
    Judicial Yuan, 88
    Juvenile Proceedings Act, 104
    Legislative Yuan, 97
    Martial Law, 88, 94, 95, 99
    Social Order Maintenance Act, 103
    Supreme Court, 90, 96
    Temporary Provisions Effective during the Period of National Mobilization for Suppression of the Communist Rebellion, 88
Tanabe Hajime, 17, 269, 276, 279, 280
    metanoetics, 279
    repent (zange 懺悔), 17, 279, 280, 282, 283
terrorism, 148, 149, 150, 326
    anti-terrorism, 6, 15, 149, 150, 151
theology
    liberation, 336
totalitarianism, 49, 50, 284, 365

UDHR (Universal Declaration of Human Rights), 1, 2, 8, 9, 33, 66, 80, 87, 90, 91, 116, 123, 143, 144, 145, 154, 163, 182, 190, 222, 223, 231, 308, 335, 372, 373, 375
United Nations
    Charter, 1, 2, 66, 87, 116, 120, 123, 223, 231
    Human Rights Committee, 170, 179, 183, 184, 185

virtue ethics, 16, 244, 245, 246, 248, 249, 250, 251, 252, 255, 256, 257, 258, 259, 262, 267

Waldron, Jeremy, 3, 18, 37, 111, 115, 165, 243, 244, 287, 288, 302
Watson, Alan, 10
Watsuji Tetsurō, 17, 269, 281, 284
    relationality (aidagara), 273, 281
Westen, Peter, 198
Widodo, Joko, 6
World War II, 2, 5, 8, 14, 41, 42, 58, 91, 93, 116, 119, 184, 335

Xunzi, 16, 245, 246, 252, 254, 255, 256, 257, 258, 259, 262, 263, 264, 265, 266, 267, 268

Yusril Ihza Mahendra, Minister, 151

Milton Keynes UK
Ingram Content Group UK Ltd.
UKHW020612291023
431526UK00015B/72